SISTERS AND REBELS

Also by
Jacquelyn Dowd Hall

LIKE A FAMILY:

THE MAKING OF A SOUTHERN

COTTON MILL WORLD *(coauthor)*

REVOLT AGAINST CHIVALRY:

JESSIE DANIEL AMES AND

THE WOMEN'S CAMPAIGN AGAINST LYNCHING

SISTERS

and

REBELS

A

STRUGGLE FOR

THE SOUL OF

AMERICA

—

JACQUELYN
DOWD HALL

W. W. NORTON & COMPANY

Independent Publishers Since 1923

NEW YORK • LONDON

Portions of Chapter One first appeared in "Open Secrets: Memory, Imagination, and the Refashioning of Southern Identity" by Jacquelyn Dowd Hall. Copyright © The American Studies Association. This article was first published in *American Quarterly* 50, no. 1 (1998): 109–124. Reprinted with permission by Johns Hopkins University Press.

Portions of Chapter Three: "'Lest We Forget'" first appeared in "'You Must Remember This': Autobiography as a Social Critique" by Jacquelyn Dowd Hall. Copyright © Jacquelyn Dowd Hall. This article was first published in *The Journal of American History* 85, no. 2 (1998): 439–465.

Portions of Chapter Four: "'Contrary Streams of Influence'" first appeared in "'To Widen the Reach of Our Love': Autobiography, History, and Desire" by Jacquelyn Dowd Hall. Copyright © Jacquelyn Dowd Hall. This article was first published in *Feminist Studies* 26, no. 1 (Spring 2000): 230–47. Reprinted with permission.

Portions of Chapter Nine: "Writing and New York" first appeared in "Women Writers, the 'Southern Front,' and the Dialectical Imagination" by Jacquelyn Dowd Hall. Copyright © The Southern Historical Association. This article was first published in *The Journal of Southern History* LXIX, no. 1 (Feb. 2003), pp. 3–38. Reprinted with permission by The Southern Historical Association.

Portions of Chapter Eleven: "'The Heart of the Struggle'" first appeared in *Like a Family: The Making of a Southern Cotton Mill World* by Jacquelyn Hall, Robert Korstad, Mary Murphy, James Leloudis, Lu Ann Jones, and Christopher B. Daly. Copyright © 1987 by the University of North Carolina Press. Foreword and afterword © 2000 by the University of North Carolina Press. Used by permission of the publisher. www.uncpress.org.

For information about permission to reproduce selections from this book, write to Permissions, W. W. Norton & Company, Inc., 500 Fifth Avenue, New York, NY 10110

For information about special discounts for bulk purchases, please contact W. W. Norton Special Sales at specialsales@wwnorton.com or 800-233-4830

Manufacturing by LSC Communications, Harrisonburg
Book design by Barbara M. Bachman
Production manager: Anna Oler

LIBRARY OF CONGRESS CATALOGING-IN-PUBLICATION DATA

Names: Hall, Jacquelyn Dowd, author.
Title: Sisters and rebels : a struggle for the soul of America / Jacquelyn Dowd Hall.
Description: First edition. | New York : W. W. Norton & Company, [2019] | Includes bibliographical references and index.
Identifiers: LCCN 2018057931 | ISBN 9780393047998 (hardcover)
Subjects: LCSH: Lumpkin, Katharine Du Pre, 1897–1988. | Lumpkin, Grace, 1891–1980. | Glenn, Elizabeth Elliott Lumpkin, 1880 or 1881–1963. | Sisters—Georgia—Biography. | Women, White—Georgia—Biography. | Women authors, American—Biography. | Women political activists—United States—Biography. | Group identity—Southern States—History—20th century. | Southern States—Race relations—History—20th century. | United States—Intellectual life—20th century.
Classification: LCC F291.L89 H35 2019 | DDC 305.800975/0904—dc23
LC record available at https://lccn.loc.gov/2018057931

W. W. Norton & Company, Inc., 500 Fifth Avenue, New York, N.Y. 10110
www.wwnorton.com
W. W. Norton & Company Ltd., 15 Carlisle Street, London W1D 3BS

1 2 3 4 5 6 7 8 9 0

To my husband, Bob Korstad, whose faith sustained me,
and to the students
who contributed so much to this book

CONTENTS

PART FOUR: WRITING A WAY HOME

Katharine Du Pre Lumpkin on campus of Brenau College
(now University), Gainesville, Georgia, 1900.

INTRODUCTION

———

WHEN KATHARINE DU PRE LUMPKIN'S AUTOBIOGRAPHY, *The Making of a Southerner* (1946), appeared in paperback, she chose for the cover a turn-of-the-century image of herself as a child. The girl in the photograph seems incandescent, from her cloud of blond hair to her long, lacy dress. Weeds brush the child's feet; her hand rests on the edge of a huge wooden barrel half-filled with dead leaves. Swaddled in whiteness yet confined by a dark, spiky fence, she is a daughter of the Old South, but there is no remnant here of a treasured plantation past, not a jasmine or a magnolia in sight. She glances to her right, with a doubtful, questioning expression. She is poised to step out of the frame.[1]

I first stumbled upon *The Making of a Southerner* in the early 1970s while writing a dissertation about a white southern women's anti-lynching crusade. I saw Katharine as a figure who had inherited that crusade's antiracist banner and carried it forward, passing it on to the student activists of my generation.[2] Taking her stand with scholars such as W. E. B. Du Bois and C. Vann Woodward, she had chipped away at the myths of southern history. But unlike the revisionists—indeed, unlike most historians to the present day—she placed a woman at the center of southern past. Taking herself as her subject, she sought to show how both sexism and racism are grounded in the socialization of the child.

To me Katharine's book was like summer lightning. Subdued but evocative, it backlit another world. I admired the honesty with which she probed the effects of privilege, crediting its gifts, testing the tensile strength of the web it spun, acknowledging its obfuscations, and exploring the conditions and contradictions of self-transformation. I was drawn to her gentle irony and quiet, persuasive style. Plainness, I thought, has its advantages, especially in a literature of regional self-discovery so given to mournful apologia and Gothic excess. But I was puzzled by her book's silences. It breaks off abruptly in the mid-1920s, at the point when, as Katharine explained it, she had rejected "as untenable on any grounds whatsoever . . . the Southern system of white supremacy and all its works." It then leaps ahead to the 1940s to comment on the South's progress over the intervening twenty years. Who and where was the author by the time she turned to autobiography as social critique?[3]

Born into a former slaveholding family in 1897, Katharine was, as she tells us, "dipped deep" in the cult of the Lost Cause as a child. Emerging full force in the wake of the late nineteenth-century white supremacy campaigns, that self-serving memory of the southern past romanticized slavery and reconfigured the Civil War as a struggle, not to preserve human bondage, but to uphold states' rights. It also demonized Reconstruction as a "tragic era" of "Negro rule" that justified disfranchisement and segregation. "No lesson of our history was taught us earlier," Katharine remembered, "and none with greater urgency than the either-or terms in which this was couched": Soldiers might perish, slavery might end, mansions might crumble, but as long as whites retained their dominance over blacks the South's cause "had not been lost."[4]

Katharine's effort to free herself from that legacy began in earnest when she encountered liberal Christianity and the social sciences at a small but vibrant women's college in her native region. She left the South briefly to study at Columbia University, returning in 1920 to spearhead the YWCA's campaign to build an interracial student movement in the face of Jim Crow. She left again five years later, eventually settling with her partner, the radical Smith College economist Dorothy Wolff Douglas, in Northampton, Massachusetts. Braving the job market in the late 1920s, just as professionalization and discrimination combined to stamp the social sciences as a masculine preserve, she experienced at first hand the dashed hopes of academic women, whose numbers declined steadily over the next forty years.[5]

For Katharine, as for so many of her generation, the Great Depression had a galvanizing effect. Faced with mass poverty and inspired by mass mobilization, she abandoned the impersonal voice of scholarly writing—the price of admission to an academic position—in favor of activism and advocacy in behalf of a robust labor movement, a strong social security system, and other far-reaching New Deal legislation. At the same time, she returned to the South, not as a literal, geographic place but as a site of political commitment and moral passion, a landscape of the heart. Coming out as a white Southerner, she wrote *The South in Progress* (1940). In 1946 she published her autobiography, her breakthrough work. *The Making of a Southerner* spoke to its own historical moment: a decade of hope when southern civil rights advocates, labor unionists, radicals, and liberals joined forces to put race, region, and, to a lesser extent, gender at the center of the New Deal's predominantly economic agenda. It also served as the inaugural work in a still-vigorous tradition of personal narratives by white Southerners grappling with their complicity in America's original sin.[6]

The South has long elicited from its writers a "rage to explain." Whether they looked back in pride, anger, or sorrow, most white Southerners who committed themselves to print shared a belief in the region's fundamental difference from the rest of the country, a conviction that, as W. J. Cash put it, the South is "not quite a nation within a nation,

Katharine Du Pre Lumpkin and Grace Lumpkin in winter dress,
late 1920s–early 1930s.

but the next thing to it." Katharine grew up in a family in which southern exceptionalism was an article of faith, and she understood all too
well that idea's invidious uses. Armed with that knowledge, she challenged the Janus-faced image of the region as either the not-modern—a
Lost Cause, a lotus land of memory, a touchstone of yearning and loss—
or the nation's collective unconscious, the repository of racial nightmares
that white Americans refused to face. Against these dream states, she
deployed what she called the "plain facts" of a history of regional dissent,
the national dimensions of racism, and the essential Americanness of a
diverse and ever-changing region.[7]

KATHARINE, IT TURNED OUT, was neither the only activist in her family, nor the only writer who deployed the Lumpkin family history to
political ends. Her older sister Elizabeth was a celebrated orator for the
Lost Cause who aspired to an acting career and taught before marriage
at a southern women's college. As Katharine labored over *The Making of
a Southerner*, Elizabeth drafted a nostalgic plantation romance. Another
sister, Grace, decamped for New York City in search of love and a writing career. By the early 1930s she had married a Jewish fur and leather
worker from eastern Europe, become what she called a "warm fellow
traveler" of the Communist Party, and entered into a gravity-warping
friendship with Whittaker Chambers, who, in a dramatic about-face,
went on to become one of the McCarthy era's most influential anticommunist informers and writers.[8]

In 1932 Grace published a novel that helped to transform an obscure
labor conflict in Gastonia, North Carolina, into a national and international *cause célèbre*. Hailed by left-wing critics as one of "the first truly
revolutionary novels to be written in the United States" and broadly
embraced as a counter to the "reactionary and regressive regionalism" associated with the Nashville Agrarians, *To Make My Bread* has
a notable symmetry at its beating heart. Both Grace and the women
she wrote about—most notably Ella May Wiggins, the strike's martyred
balladeer—were wrestling with "the conflicts and connections between
the old culture and the new" at a time when modernity was sweeping
through the South with shibboleth-toppling force.[9]

Grace's star rose and fell more precipitously than Katharine's. Following the success of *To Make My Bread*, she published a steady stream

of fiction and feminist labor reportage. Summing up her stature in 1942, *Twentieth Century Authors* described her as "one of the most promising members of the younger members of the 'new' Southern school." The 1954 supplement commented only that she had "published no books in recent years." By then critics were summarily dismissing her and other radical writers. As a leading southern literary scholar put it: "The fullness of time has not ratified their literary importance. As novelists they are forgotten." That judgment began to change only after her death, when *To Make My Bread* was rediscovered by a new generation of feminist readers.[10]

Once I linked these fascinating sisters, I found myself obsessed with origins and influences. What produced them? How did they coproduce themselves? And what were the dynamics and undercurrents among them as, embedded in separate but overlapping circles of allies, lovers, and friends, they vied with one another to speak for their family and their region? Elizabeth, the eternal loyalist; Grace, the mercurial novelist; Katharine, the steady, engaged scholar—together they captured my imagination, as writers striving to shape memory and history, as sisters competing for cultural authority, as improbable voices from the deepest South, and, not least, as women whose work had been buried and then partially resurrected.

Moving to Chapel Hill to launch an oral history program at the University of North Carolina in 1973, I seized the opportunity to seek the sisters out. Elizabeth had died a decade earlier, but I found Katharine and Grace in Virginia, to which each had retired. Our conversations were as disconcerting as they were mesmerizing. Grace had totally reversed course in the late 1940s, denouncing her former allies as "self-made psychopaths" and joining in the orgy of confession by which ex-Communists purged themselves of their radical pasts. By the time I met her, she had almost nothing to say about her struggle to carve out a place as a white southern woman in a male-dominated, New York–centric literary and political movement. She described her younger self as an innocent abroad, led astray by the engaging young Communists she met in New York and by her sister Katharine—who was, she said, always the radical one. Over and over, she had cut herself off from the past: when she left home in the 1920s, broke with the Communist Party in the 1940s, turned to the far right in the 1950s, and returned to the South in the early 1960s. Each reinvention deepened her isolation; each required new layers of secrecy and rationalization. Although I was grateful to have met her, I saw the impossibility, even treachery, of basing my vision of her life on this encounter in her later years. I grapple in this book with the internal and external forces that propelled her conservative conversion. At the same time, I try to save her from herself by documenting the convictions and creativity of her earlier years.[11]

Katharine, nearing her eightieth birthday, willingly and vividly recalled her early life. She was also eager to talk about her latest book: an effort to rescue the pioneering feminist abolitionist Angelina Grimké from obscurity and restore her to her rightful place in the great social movements of her day. But when I shifted to questions about her relationship to her family and her political and personal life after she left the South, she resisted, politely but firmly, with a fixed and practiced resolve. Her reticence went further: she purged wide swaths of her adult life from her papers, destroying much of the private correspondence that had not already been relegated to the "ash heap" when Dorothy Douglas died.[12]

This burning of papers—a scourge of historians seeking to make visible the same-sex partnerships of the past—erased Dorothy from the narrative of Katharine's life. Gone also were the years when Katharine was cut off from her family, who felt betrayed by her autobiographical revelations and refused to acknowledge her book. Gone was what Lillian Hellman called "Scoundrel Time": the early 1950s, when McCarthyism turned the left-wing political ideas and associations of the 1930s and 1940s into ominous "un-American activities" and equated homosexuality with treason.[13] Silently omitted was the startling fact that Grace had named names, implicating Katharine and colluding in the storm of red-baiting that shattered the life she and her partner had so carefully built.

Generation, sexuality, and politics—all contributed to Katharine's reserve. She grew up in a family in which reputation was everything and an era when telling secrets to strangers was not the pastime it has become today. When she left the safe confines of a women's college, she found that the romantic friendships she had formed so unselfconsciously were being cast by sexologists in a morbid new light. She lived her adult life in committed partnerships with women, over a period in which such relationships were pathologized, sexualized, and finally celebrated—none of which was commensurate with how she saw herself. For her, as with Grace, though for different reasons, the anticommunism and homophobia of the 1950s had dropped a curtain between then and now.

Although I never lost interest in the Lumpkin sisters, I found myself caught in the eddies of what seemed to be irreconcilable desires. I wanted to write about Katharine, but I also wanted to befriend her. In the end, I was not courageous—or bloody-minded—enough to write this book while the sisters were alive. And even now my memory of our conversations confronts me with what is so tantalizing and poignant about biography: the feelings of loyalty and responsibility it generates, the tension it produces between respect for privacy and lust for knowledge, the way it can position even the most respectful author as an intruder, a thief in the houses of the living and the dead.[14]

As Katharine wrote, she could hear the hurt, disapproving voices of people she loved humming in her ears. For her, those voices personified the resistance that keeps a writer from writing and contests one's authority to interpret the past. As for me, I never sat down to work on this book without remembering something that Katharine said during our first interview so many years ago. Carried away by my own preoccupations, I kept asking about her relationship with Grace beyond the point at which it became clear that this was not a subject Katharine wanted to pursue. Suddenly, she shifted to a different voice. "My young friend," she said, changing the balance of power with a phrase. "Don't try too hard in your work to account for things by these interpersonal relationships in the family—important as they are. Look not only for the likenesses and the interinfluences but look for the differences."[15]

I came to see the sisters as the most intimate of strangers: estranged and yet forever entangled by their mutual obsession with a region they imagined and reclaimed in utterly different ways. Those entanglements and obsessions lie at the core of the story I tell. But, heeding Katharine's admonition, I put each sister in her separate milieu. At the same time, I tack back and forth between a fine-grained portrait of these ordinary yet extraordinary women and the maelstrom of historical events and processes in which they were involved.

In doing so, I began to see their times in a surprising new light. I was struck by the power of a forgotten tradition of socially conscious religious faith. I watched the 1920s emerge as a decade that, despite being stereotyped as a carnival of frivolity and reaction, had in fact fed a buried stream of "left feminism" that links women's liberation to racial and economic justice. Other aspects of modern American history rearranged themselves as well: The troubled but generative relations between the black and white women who worked together during that period and in later years. The conditions of literary and intellectual accomplishment—the institutions, networks, and private settings that have enabled, sabotaged, and marginalized women's thought. The political opportunities found and lost during the 1930s and the early 1940s. The role of women and African Americans as the "visionary conscience" of a capacious Popular Front.[16] Embedded within this personal yet epic narrative are two metaphorical strands. First, the expatriate's search for an emotional and intellectual home. Second, the pressure of personal, family, and collective memory on efforts at self- and regional reinvention.

THROUGHOUT THIS BOOK I treat *The Making of a Southerner* as an artful act of self-making and political intervention, but I also look to it for the myths and experiences of the Lumpkin clan. I do so confidently because Katharine so carefully distinguishes what she remembers—what imprinted itself on her mind—from what she can only surmise. Her book, moreover, is a bricolage in which she layers her own memories into other traces of the past: her parents' stories, her older sisters' writings and memories, original documents and newspaper accounts, the historical and sociological studies she read. I, in turn, add my own layers of research and reflection. One discovery proved especially revealing: her father's bitter, murderous memoir in which he detailed his complicity in the atrocities committed by the Reconstruction era Ku Klux Klan. Never openly acknowledged, their father's acts hovered in the background of all the sisters' writings, especially in Katharine's oblique but powerful account of the violence hidden in the heart of family life and her meditations on slavery, abolitionism, and Reconstruction.

To fill the silences of the 1950s, I spent years filing Freedom of Information Act requests with the FBI, then sued the Department of Justice. The process was maddening, but I treasure the memory of my lawyer declaring in a meeting with high-ranking officials, "The American people have a right to know their own history!" Striking a small blow against governmental secrecy, we finally won a court ruling that gave me access to a trove of evidence about the impact of a culture of surveillance and suppression on activist intellectual lives. These sources, along with letters and diaries written by the sisters in their old age, which were providentially given to me by their nephews, drew me forward into the "Great American Inquisition," Grace's betrayal of her sister, and the two women's separate returns to the South after the fall of Jim Crow. I end with the story of how they faced mortality at a time when they were more directly connected with each other—often painfully so—than they had been since they left their native region.[17]

My goal is not to canonize Grace and Katharine's writings or to hold up their politics for imitation. As the literary scholar Cary Nelson puts it, "We recover what we are culturally and psychologically prepared to recover and what we 'recover' we necessarily rewrite, giving it meanings that are inescapably contemporary, giving it a new discursive life in the present, a life it cannot have had before."[18] In that spirit, I offer this rendition of the sisters' lives, their major works, and the left feminist politics in which they were immersed. I do so in the confidence that these women made enduring contributions to an unfinished political project: the reconfiguration of race, gender, and class within the South's spatial and ideological borders.

Since the Lumpkin sisters' day, the American South has changed dramatically. Yet popular understandings of the South remain largely focused on racism, white male demagoguery, ugly electoral politics, and violent vigilante injustice. This view of the South and its history has allowed us to externalize and attempt to expunge conditions that were national in scope without forfeiting our belief in America as a land of innocence, equality, and progress. That strategy, however, has grown tattered and self-defeating. We cannot muster the political will to address our failings by projecting them onto a distinctive and supposedly un-American region. We need what Katharine tried to provide: a history of imagination, of possibility, of people—women and men, black and white—who never quit believing they could remake the South even when compelled to leave it behind. Southern history can still be written as tragedy, but not by implicit comparison to an American romance.

Katharine Du Pre and Grace Lumpkin, in their very different ways, followed a seldom noticed but common pattern: the southern expatriate's circuit of return. I cannot write about them and their journeys without saying more than they wanted said. But I do it Katharine's way, focusing on the self-in-society, considering the undertow of the psyche but stressing politics and ideas. Her quest is my warrant. For despite the dangers and her own deep reticence, she never quit sounding the past's open secrets. And she never quit trying to remake the South into a place to call home.

PART ONE

—

HOME

"Me and you, we got more yesterdays
than anybody.
We need some kind of tomorrow."

—TONI MORRISON, *BELOVED*

"SOUTHERNERS OF MY PEOPLE'S KIND"

———

THE LUMPKINS OF GEORGIA WERE ALWAYS SPOKEN OF IN THE plural, so numerous and tangled were their lines. Joseph Henry Lumpkin, the first chief justice of the Georgia Supreme Court, and his brother Wilson Lumpkin, the governor who banished the Cherokee to Oklahoma on the Trail of Tears, were the best-known figures, but the state is pocked with streets, towns, and buildings named for prominent members of the Lumpkin clan. The Lumpkin sisters' father, William Wallace Lumpkin, descended not from these grandees but from more modest stock: slave owners whose influence was confined to the plantation, the county courthouse, and the Baptist church.[1] But the distinction hardly mattered. Long after the slave owners' descendants had abandoned the plantations and thrown in their lot with the New South's railroads, towns, and textile mills, lineage still counted—more so than we can easily imagine. So much so that when William died, his obituary ended with a litany of long-gone "relatives and ancestors." So much so that, at the height of her fame as a proletarian writer, Grace Lumpkin would base her authority in part on her identity as a "descendent of a Southern family which helped make the laws of Georgia and build up the economic and political power of the Southern upper class." So much so that, for all its candor, Katharine's autobiography strained against her fear of bringing "disgrace on the family name."[2]

This "cult of family" rested on legends that stretched back to Jacob Lumpkin, an obstreperous militia captain and planter who migrated to Virginia in the seventeenth century.[3] The Lumpkins' claim to this colonial ancestor was tenuous at best. In all likelihood, William Lumpkin descended from a less colorful Virginia settler, but his great-grandfather, Joseph, did move from Virginia to Georgia in the late eighteenth century, drawn by the offer of virtually free land. Both Grace and Katharine imagined him traveling in an impressive caravan: "a coach and four white horses, two large wagons with five mules," and a retinue of slaves. Arriving just before Eli Whitney patented the cotton gin and launched the antebellum cotton boom, Joseph settled in Oglethorpe County, twelve miles from Lexington, the county seat. There he found rich loam for growing short staple cotton, rolling uplands ideal for corn, and virgin forests for firewood and lumber. The broad Savannah River carried his cotton to Augusta, which soon became the distribution center for the farms and plantations that stretched along the South Carolina–Georgia line. His son, the first William Lumpkin, married twice, sired twenty-one children, and acquired over 1,000 acres of land and upward of thirty-seven slaves. William's second wife outlived him, and when she died in 1852, the family homestead went to Adoniram Judson Lumpkin and his wife, Nancy Pittard. There, Katharine wrote, "my father, an only child, was born and spent his first years until the war came and altered everything."[4]

The "big house" where William grew up was imprinted on his daughters' imaginations as if they themselves had caught the breezes sweeping through its central hall or watched as horses and carriages carried aunts, uncles, and cousins up the tree-lined avenue at Christmastime. Conflating their father's memories with images from the plantation romances they loved to read, they pictured a "mansion of stately pillars, immaculate whiteness, ostentatious lines." The Lumpkins *were* among the largest landowners in the area but, like the great majority of planters in the cotton belt, they lived in a "strictly utilitarian" farmhouse, unpainted and unadorned, though "solidly built, with great chimneys at either end and square rooms running alongside a hall upstairs and down."[5]

In "An Old Time Georgia Christmas," published in his local newspaper in 1906, William Lumpkin wrote down his well-honed, turn-of-the-century version of his favorite antebellum tales. This domestic idyll is set firmly out of sight of the cotton fields, where the backbreaking labor of slaves produced the abundance William so enticingly evokes. The locus of William's remembrance is the "old family home" with its separate kitchen, connected to the main house by a pathway of split oak logs. As in many slaveholders' reminiscences of childhood, the action centers on Christmas day, with its crush of relatives and its cornucopia of mouth-watering food: for breakfast "the crispist, hottest, bestest waf-

The Lumpkin family home in Oglethorpe County, near Lexington, Georgia, built ca. 1790, after the family migrated from King and Queen Courthouse, Virginia, in 1784.

fles in the whole world," and for dinner turkeys, chickens, hams, brandy peaches, every kind of cake and pie, "all homemade, all home-raised."[6]

In these treasured memories, certain slaves loomed larger than life. To William they belonged to a lost utopia, a vanished childhood that represented an ordered, harmonious interracial world. To his daughters the slaves were storybook figures; repeatedly cropping up in their writings, these figments of their father's imagination were immortalized in print even as their moral valences changed. "Uncle Jerry," the black foreman, was "a fabled giant," six feet eight inches tall, and "every pound of him was muscle and bone." He was illiterate (or so his master and mistress thought), but every Sunday William's mother read to him from the Bible, after which he preached to his slave congregation, reciting from memory, chapter and verse. "Runaway" Dennis was a shy, quarrelsome loner. He too was taken under the wing of his mistress, who always intervened to make sure he got nothing more than a "stern reprimand" when he returned. "Aunt Winnie," Uncle Jerry's wife, cared for young William and "in all things having to do with the women and children of the slave quarters was her mistress's deputy."[7] "Aunt Sarah," the cook, presided over the magical kitchen. Pete, William's body servant, marched into battle with his master when the Civil War broke out. "I gave him a home as long as he lived," William claimed, "and—though I was a man and he was black and I was white—I cried when old Pete died."[8]

ADONIRAM AND NANCY LUMPKIN, reinforced by the church, the law, and the worldview they and their neighbors shared, planted in their son the unshakable belief that "the slaves deserved and needed their slavery," that "chattel should render the master unquestioning obedience," and that a good master should rule firmly but justly, looking after the spiritual needs and physical well-being of the men, women, and children in his care. They also taught William that he was a gentleman by inheritance; the rights and obligations of his station were and would remain his, no matter his material fortunes. Yet gentlemanliness was the most contingent of patrimonies. It required a rigid code of behavior that turned on honor and duty, paternalism toward loyal dependents and, especially, chivalry toward white women. "Young Will" took to heart those demands and expectations. He had no reason to doubt that when he reached adulthood he would inherit not only the Lumpkin name but "all the appurtenances in land and slaves." When he turned ten on Valentine's Day 1859, the whole plantation "family" gathered in symbolic recognition of what his future would bring. "Uncle Jerry," as William told it, "bowed his great head in solemn dignity, and tiny Aunt Winnie curtsied to this, her child, whose 'mammy' she had been and still was."[9]

As it turned out, William had only a few years to live as a "young master" among his family's slaves, and many of these years were spent during a civil war that "patently threatened his heritage." Yet until the end, as Katharine's autobiography described it, he went on "expecting to be even as his father had been."

> Above all, he would know his slaves, each by name, and each for his good points and his foibles. . . . He would expect constantly to guide and discipline and keep them contented by skillful handling. First and last, he would know that every plan, every decision, every quandary nagging his mind, save those of marketing his cotton and purchasing supplies from the outside, resolved itself into a human problem, if it could be so called: the problem of managing his black dependents. He would know he was master in all things on his plantation, everything, nothing excepted, including the life of his slaves.

The assumption of rulership stamped the character of the planters, Katharine wrote. "But more particularly . . . it stamped their sons," who saw it taken away.[10]

William Lumpkin was twelve years old when the South seceded from the Union. His father suffered from epilepsy and was thereby spared from battle (his affliction, considered shameful at the time, found no place in family stories), but William watched his cousins and uncles march off, one by one, to join the fight. In the fall of 1864, with General William Tecumseh Sherman already occupying Atlanta, fifteen-year-old Will begged for permission to join the army. On November 14, Sherman torched the city and prepared to launch an unprecedented attack on the home front designed to destroy civilian morale. He was determined "to make Georgia howl." According to family legend, William joined "Fighting Joe" Wheeler's ragtag cavalry and spent the final months of the war as a courier to a captain who was harassing Sherman's troops as they abandoned their supply line to the north and cut a gash from Atlanta to the sea.[11]

The war was "wildly active and exciting for Father," Katharine remembered. That may be so, but a search of Civil War records yields nothing about his service, and one wonders whether he saw much action at all.[12] If he was in "Wheeler's cavalry," which is itself a catchall term, much that happened did not make its way into the war stories the Lumpkin children heard. William spoke often of the "mad carnival of destruction" perpetrated by Sherman's troops: "burned depots, stark scorched sticks where water-towers had stood . . . rails turned and twisted in grotesque shapes around trees," silver and jewels taken, houses and barns wrecked, "insults to helpless women and old men."[13] For him, as for other white Southerners, the heroism, gallantry, and law-abiding nature of the Confederate soldier became an article of faith. Lost to memory was the degeneration of Wheeler's cavalry into what a later historian called a "plundering band of horse stealing ruffians"; in William's home county, they were "dreaded fully as much, if not more than the yankees."[14] Nor did William speak of whatever brutalities he committed or of the human slaughter he observed.

Straggling home in the spring of 1865 with his body servant, "black Pete," by his side, William found the world of his childhood melting away. Even before the war, his parents had watched their lush fields turn to red clay ruts as they planted and replanted cotton, a soil-leaching crop. Like other Georgia planters, they talked of moving west. By 1860 they had boarded up their home, rented out their slaves, and moved to Union Point, a small railroad depot town in Greene County, some thirty miles away. Five years later the Lumpkins still owned their plantation in Oglethorpe County, and by 1870 they had also managed to buy a 300-acre farm near Union Point. But emancipation had cost them their slaves.[15]

Stripped of their captive labor force, the Lumpkins looked to their son to make a crop. "The negroes had been told they were free, and a number of my father's slaves had left the plantation," William remembered. The rest, he said, were "utterly demoralized," a stock phrase that obscured what he could not bring himself to say: the slaves he idealized in memory, the slaves who, he told his children, were "known for their warm devotion and willing obedience," had immediately struck out for freedom, searching for lost loved ones and hoping to become small farmers endowed with the dignity and independence that in the rural South only landowning could provide. Even those who stayed refused to return to gang labor in the fields.[16] "The only crop we could make was what I could make," William Lumpkin remembered, "and though I was only a boy . . . I made some corn, and one bale of cotton . . . and to make this corn and cotton, I ploughed barefooted and ate Irish Potatoes for bread for about six weeks." Such was the meaning of defeat for William Lumpkin: the South invaded, its landscape ravaged, its economy completely destroyed, his own plantation falling into ruin, his slaves gone, the ignominy of backbreaking labor. But for him the worst was yet to come. Like most white Southerners, he accepted the reunification of the country and the end of slavery; those questions had been decided on the battlefield. What he could not accept was Radical Reconstruction, which ushered in "a shocking change in the relation of white to black."[17]

If Abraham Lincoln had lived, William Lumpkin always said, "the South never would have been made to suffer during Reconstruction." As Lumpkin saw it, the bullet that killed Lincoln allowed a vengeful faction known as the "Radical Republicans" to capture Congress. Even Sherman's villainy paled in comparison to that of "the Godless Three"— Charles Sumner, Thaddeus Stevens, and Benjamin Wade. In Lumpkin's view, these former abolitionists scorned Lincoln's policy of sectional reconciliation and set out "to bring the South to her knees, to take the land from [her] people and divide it among the freed slaves."[18] Many Radical Republicans *were* determined to exact retribution, enforce black people's rights, and ensure their party's ascendancy. But Congress rejected out of hand the idea of confiscating the largest estates and redistributing the land to former slaves and to whites who had remained loyal to the Union. Moreover, it was neither Lincoln's assassination nor the vindictiveness of Republican leaders that provoked Radical Reconstruction in 1866. It was the intransigence of a militant minority of conservatives like William Lumpkin, who were determined to impose slavery-like forms of subordination on the freedpeople. In response, Congress temporarily disfranchised antebellum officials who had renounced the United States and supported the Confederacy, and put much of the South under military occupation. More reluctantly and controversially, it also enfranchised black men.[19]

The result, as the northern journalist James S. Pike put it, was "a society suddenly turned bottomside up." Across the South, state governments fell into the hands of a coalition of African Americans, white

Northerners who went south for principle or profit, supposedly with no more belongings than a carpetbag would hold, and white Southerners who, for a wide variety of reasons, were willing to tie their political fortunes to those of the ex-slaves. State legislatures ratified the Fourteenth and Fifteenth Amendments, with the goal of guaranteeing blacks' civil and voting rights. They raised taxes, created the South's first public schools, extended social welfare provisions, and expanded the railway system—sometimes lining their own pockets, as corrupt politicians throughout the country were wont to do, but also benefiting both blacks and whites.[20]

Reconstruction allowed African Americans "to negotiate the terms of freedom from new circumstances of strength." Seizing the moment, the freedmen and women of Greene County embarked on what a local grand jury called "a mighty revolution the consequences of which cannot even be imagined." They formed an all-black community called Canaan. They went on strike against abusive labor contracts, virtually halting agricultural production. They built schools and churches. They organized a militia and prepared for armed self-defense. And they formed one of the most successful branches of the Georgia Equal Rights Association, an organization devoted to securing political rights. "Negroes held every office in the County," William Lumpkin remembered. "We had negro members of the Legislature, and negro militia." Lumpkin exaggerated: white Democrats held on to critical bases of power; their entrenched wealth and manipulation of the legal system made blacks vulnerable to economic pressures and denied them the protection of the law. But the freedpeople and their white allies *did* build a Republican party in Greene County, which trounced the Democrats in local and statewide elections from 1867 to 1869.[21]

To William Lumpkin, Reconstruction was indeed a mighty revolution. "Unthinkable even as it happened," it loomed in his imagination as a moment of nightmarish possibilities, a dream from which he never really awoke. "Our property was all gone except the land," he remembered, "and bills were presented in Congress to confiscate our land. The majority of us expected to be banished from the South."[22] Driven by this phantom apocalypse and enraged by the freedpeople's bid for autonomy and political participation, he devoted himself to a guerrilla movement led by loose congeries of secret, paramilitary groups known as the Ku Klux Klan. By day, he worked as a laborer on his father's farm and read for the bar with Alexander Stephens, former vice-president of the Confederacy. Under cover of darkness, he joined his neighbors in a campaign of terror aimed at destroying black schools and political associations, intimidating Republican leaders and voters, and ending majority rule.[23]

IN 2002, I STUMBLED ACROSS a copy of an extraordinary memoir buried among Civil War odds and ends in the North Carolina state archives. Entitled "Where and why I was a Kuklux," it places William Lumpkin at the center of the local Klan's crimes. This brief reminiscence had been given to the United Daughters of the Confederacy by Elizabeth Lumpkin in 1913, three years after her father died. It burns with a murderous rage that stands in stark contrast to "An Old Time Georgia Christmas," the paean to slavery William published in 1906. These two documents, written within a year of one another, are filled with wild exaggerations, misrememberings, fossilized lies, and real experiences distorted beyond recognition. Yet, taken together, they could hardly be more revealing. One is a fond homage to the slaves who cared for him as a boy, the other a vicious attack on the freedpeople; one is written for public consumption, the other labored over in secret.[24] These documents capture the mix of entitlement, racism, and humiliation that allowed men who saw themselves as paternalistic Christian gentlemen to justify turning themselves into "cowardly midnight prowlers and assassins" after the war.[25]

"Where and why I was a Kuklux" is invaluable for other reasons as well. Insider descriptions of what was often called the "Invisible Empire" are few and far between. Indeed, when the first thorough study of the Klan appeared in 1971, the author found only two significant contemporaneous accounts by Klan members, along with a few substantive reminiscences written after 1905, when Klansmen like Lumpkin began to talk more publicly about what they had done.[26] Moreover, unlike other Klan memoirs, "Where and why I was a Kuklux" names people and places, detailing William Lumpkin's participation in specific and well-known atrocities. Even its description of the behavior that supposedly drove him to such measures is illuminating, for it reveals the "mighty revolution" wrought by black agency and self-defense.

William Lumpkin committed his memories to paper in the shadow of Thomas Dixon Jr.'s twisted melodramas, *The Leopard's Spots* and *The Clansman*. A stew of autobiography, political commentary, and sexual obsession, these national bestsellers, which appeared in 1902 and 1905, became staples of reading for children in the Lumpkin home. Claiming to write from memory, Dixon portrayed Reconstruction as a "tragic era" in which a cabal of "renegade Negroes," carpetbaggers, and scalawags inflicted "an orgy of misrule" on the "beaten and prostrate" South.[27] "Some people have said that Dixon's Clansman overdraws," William wrote. "The Clansman does not tell the one thousandth part of what we went through." Reconstruction stripped away the prerogatives of white manhood, beginning with a highly symbolic gesture: Union soldiers allegedly forcing returning Confederates to cover or cut off the buttons on their tattered uniforms. "Mine were cut off by a Negro," William claimed. Then "Hell broke loose in Georgia." The "white people were insulted every day, and in every way." Spat on and slapped by a black soldier, William "could do nothing but stand and grit my teeth and cry." Nor could he protect white women from a fate that in his eyes was literally worse than death. "I have seen a rosy cheeked bright eyed Southern girl stagger into her father's home, her teeth knocked out, her lips bruised, her eyes blackened, her hair matted and torn, and heard her pray to die," he wrote, "and I stood and prayed that she might die—and she *did die thank God*."[28]

"You may ask why we submitted to all this," Lumpkin concluded. "We had surrendered. . . . We were helpless, and utterly hopeless." He then went on to place himself squarely at the scene of the Georgia Klan's most notorious crime: the brutal beating of Abram Colby, Greene County's most consequential black leader, a man whom he described as "a big yellow negro[,] a member of the Legislature. He was the meanest negro we had."[29]

Born and raised in Greene County, Abram Colby had managed, despite his enslavement, to acquire a range of skills and resources well suited to the demands of building "not just a new political citizenry but a new political culture."[30] He was the son of a white man, John Colby, one of the richest planters in the county, and a teenaged slave named Mary. When John Colby died in 1850, he deeded Mary and their seven children to a friend who promised to ensure that they could live as free people, although technically still enslaved. The friend kept his promise, and Abram Colby considered himself a free man. Working as a barber and a laborer as well as a minister, Colby gained both standing among blacks and a keen understanding of whites. By the time Reconstruction began, he owned his own land and lived with his wife, their four children, and his mother in a house "given to us by my father, who was our master and a white man." Abram Colby possessed a powerful physique, unshakable self-confidence, and staggering courage. Taken together, these qualities made him a charismatic leader.[31] They also made him a chief target of the Klan's effort to eradicate the wellsprings of black solidarity and self-assertion.

Pursuing the "distant shadow of right or equal justice," Colby represented the freedpeople of Greene County at the first Freedmen's Convention in January 1866. He then built a tightly organized branch of the Georgia Equal Rights Association. In 1868, he was elected to the state house of representatives by a margin of two to one. When he and other black representatives were betrayed by their white Republican allies and expelled from the legislature, Colby campaigned for federal help in regaining his seat and continued to mobilize Greene County's black voters. Unable to defeat Colby politically, conservative Democrats tried to buy him off for $5,000, a princely bribe. "I will not go back on my people for all [the wealth] in Greene County," Colby replied.[32]

Two nights later, William Lumpkin, along with dozens of other masked Klansmen, broke down Colby's door, terrorized his family, and dragged him into the woods. His crime? He had, they said, "influence with the negroes in other counties and had carried the negroes against them." When Colby refused to renounce his political allegiances, the men stripped him, beat him for hours, and left him for dead. With his back cut to shreds and his spine so badly damaged that he lost the use of his left hand, Colby dragged himself to a nearby cabin. When asked two years later how long it took him to recover, he replied, "I have never got over it yet. They broke something inside of me." What hurt him most was that his "little daughter" had died within the year: the Klan had "actually frightened her to death."[33]

Unlike many victims of Klan violence, Colby could and did name his attackers—"I knew the voices of those men . . . as well as I know my own," he said.[34] He did not mention William Lumpkin, but his memoir puts him at the scene of this and other crimes. "I have given you only a few instances of the punishments we used," Lumpkin wrote. "There were many others before we gained *supreme control.*" Did he feel any guilt, ambivalence, or regret? Quite the contrary. "When we met we always had a prayer," he insisted, "and we committed no act that could not be approved by any Christian man or woman on earth."[35]

Throughout the state, the Klan assassinated or terrorized grassroots Republican leaders and destroyed the infrastructures of political life.[36] In 1871, the Republican Party collapsed, making Georgia the first state to be "redeemed" by conservative Democrats. Across the South, the battle raged until 1876, when paramilitary forces overthrew Reconstruction in South Carolina. The North's will to remake the South evaporated, and the federal government left the ex-slaves to their fate.

"Where and why I was a Kuklux" ends with a cry of triumph. As long as white supremacy lasted, William Lumpkin believed, the South had lost the battle but not the war. "The white race must rule and though we surrendered at Appomattox, and had the negroes put over us as our masters, *we* were the Masters. . . . Though there were troops . . . and in fact all the powers of the Federal Government to keep us oppressed, we ordained things to be done, not begged for them, commanded and did not serve. We dictated and did not cringe." In the end, what one historian has aptly called "martial manhood" was rewarded. "A new Sun arose for the South—the glory of the Anglo Saxon shown in every man's face."[37]

"THE SOUTH MIGHT be 'restored,'" Katharine said of the end of Reconstruction, "but not the old life for Father."[38] The South's commanding presence in the federal government had all but vanished, and blacks continued to vote, albeit in sharply reduced numbers. Many of the "Redeemers" turned out to be as eager as the Carpetbaggers they vilified to profit from the rise of cities, factories, and railroads. Their vaunted paternalism notwithstanding, the planters among them proved relentless in their efforts to reduce the white yeomanry to sharecropping and transform their former slaves into a rural proletariat. The future belonged to such agrarian chameleons, but it belonged even more to Georgia's merchants and lawyers, especially to those who could combine the skills of oratory, so prized in the Old South, with the ability to grease the wheels of the New South's commercial revolution.[39]

At first it seemed that William would rise quickly in the new order. Oratory was his strong point. None of Alexander Stephens's students was wittier or more eloquent; none seemed better suited to the law. He was well connected: a string of eminent guests dined at the family's hand-hewn black cherry dining table, which was supposedly handed down to each generation's first-born son and stands now in the Joseph Henry Lumpkin House in Athens, Georgia. When William turned twenty-three in 1873, he hung out his shingle. Just as important, he married well, choosing Annette Caroline Morris, a beautiful, accomplished girl from Meriwether County, near the Alabama line.[40]

Annette's mother, Elizabeth (Eliza) Patillo, descended from two lines of French Huguenots, the Patillos and the Du Pres, dissenting Protestants who fled France to avoid religious persecution. The Du Pres sailed first to Virginia, then moved on to Tennessee and Kentucky, and finally settled in Meriwether County on land that the Creek Indians had been forced to cede to Georgia not long before. When the war came and Annette's father, John Morris, joined the Confederate Intelligence Service, Eliza took her children and went to live with her parents, Henry Patillo and Nancy Du Pre.[41] There five-year-old Annette spent her childhood "in happy oblivion of the bitter war . . . wrapped in a warm sense of close, protecting family."[42]

Like William, Annette wrote a brief memoir of a childhood Eden that lingered, as his did, on a plantation's delicious tastes, sights, and sounds.[43] "The hum of bees," Katharine wrote, "sang through all Mother's memories." It was especially the hum of domestic life that Annette recalled, and white women stood at the center of that lost world. Grandmother Patillo was the towering figure in Annette's youth. It was *her* dairy that Annette treasured, *her* old-fashioned flowers, *her* well-swept yard. Present only in their marked absence were the slaves over whom Grandmother Patillo presumably presided. The fat blue plums, the yellow roses, the red apples that filled Annette's reveries—all shimmered against a background of white: white bowls holding sweet, pure cream; a "white roadway" winding up to a carriage house, a "white, beautifully kept yard." Unlike William, when Annette pictured herself scampering along the boardwalk that led from the big house to the kitchen, she made no mention of the "Aunt Sarahs" laboring at the other end.[44]

That absence puzzled me. It was not unusual for former slave owners to banish the ghosts of their slaves. Often they simply stopped using the word, referring to their human property as "servants" instead. Annette was only eight when her rural childhood came to an end, so perhaps the slaves had simply not imprinted themselves on her memory. Still, I wondered why her stories seemed at once so vividly detailed and so insubstantial. Why did Katharine know and tell so much about her father's family history and so little about her mother's, despite the fact that she treasured her mother's influence and dissenting Huguenot ancestry? At first, I attributed this disparity to William's force of will. He filled his children's heads with slaveholding stories; perhaps Annette added only supporting details—delicate, domestic filigrees.

But there was more to Annette's embellishments than that. Her memoir to the contrary, there was in fact no plantation in her past, no "big house" in the usual sense of the word. Her grandfather Patillo was a carpenter and a farmer on someone else's land. He owned farm implements, a horse, a mule, and other livestock. But according to the census he did not own slaves. If Annette frolicked in the orchards and arbors of a grand plantation, it belonged to her grandparents' landlord, not to them. Inadvertently reflecting on how the plantation legend could turn all sorts of dross to gold, Annette ended her memoirs with the comment, "These poor memories grow sweeter as I write."[45]

Annette may have dreamed her grandparents' plantation into life, but her nostalgia for the countryside was real enough, and it was made all the more poignant by the war, which brought her rural idyll to an abrupt and wrenching end. Her father went missing almost as soon as the war began. He never returned, and the family never knew his fate. Her grandfather, her mother, and her oldest sister died of typhoid fever two years later, leaving Grandmother Patillo to raise five grandchildren on her own. "Those combined blows were enough to have crushed any one, but the present duty to the orphaned children demanded thought and action."[46] "Through that sad summer and fall [Grandmother Patillo] bravely held her own," gathering the crops, caring for the little children. Finally, unable "to face another farm season with such a heavy load," she put Annette on a train—the first the child had ever seen—and sent her to live with friends and relatives in Augusta, where she "slept alone in a great four-post bed."[47]

Annette never saw her grandmother again. She also never saw a penny of her mother's estate, which—according to family legend—was squandered by an uncle who sold the property for Confederate currency that crumbled to dust when the South surrendered.[48] In fact, there was never much of an estate to squander. Yet such stories of lost property contained a larger truth. They evoked the disappointment of a generation of women who had traded obedience for protection, only to find that their men could not fulfill the bargain between the sexes on which antebellum southern society relied. They also allowed striving daughters to maintain the glamour of "old family" even as they found themselves thrown back on their own resources in ways that they had never expected to be.

For white women in the antebellum South, marriage was destiny. The Civil War threatened to thwart those expectations by killing and maiming so many of the region's white men. Women like Grandmother Patillo had to manage alone; in the chaotic aftermath of surrender, orphans like Annette had no choice but to take charge of their own lives. Mourning the loss of the world they had known, making their way to towns and cities, teaching in the region's small academies and in-home schools, working as seamstresses, or finding other ways to make do, white women oscillated between fear, depression, and anger—against the North, against fate, against the failures of men—and the satisfactions of self-possession.[49]

Augusta, which had a large free black population, was a key manufacturing center for the Confederacy. It was also a haven for white refugees after the fall of Atlanta to Sherman's troops. By the end of the war, many of its citizens had descended into poverty, but some merchants and manufacturers prospered. Among them were the friends and relatives with whom Annette went to live, first Charles and Caroline Elliott and then her aunt Adeline Allen. Born in Ireland, Charles Elliot started out as a machinist and became a moderately prosperous merchant during the war. Adeline Allen belonged to Augusta's crème de la crème. A spinster, she lived in the household of her brother, Joseph V. H. Allen, a commission merchant who branched out into life and fire insurance and, in 1870, became mayor of the city. The Allens lived in Augusta's Second Ward, home to the rich and powerful. Together, the Elliotts and the Allens offered Annette every advantage, including a "splendid education," better by far than she could have hoped for on the farm. She attended Miss Nebbutt's School for Girls, but mostly she was tutored at home by the Rev. John Heely, who had graduated from St. John's College in Dublin and ran the Augusta High School, to which only white boys were admitted. When she turned eighteen, she got a teaching job.[50]

Not long afterward, she went to Union Point to visit one of her sisters, traveling alone in a railway car. There, in that oddly intimate yet public space, she met William Lumpkin. For him it was love at first sight. "She is my wife, if she will marry me," he thought. But "he had to do some courting," for Annette was "handsome and had beaux." She was also a "strict Episcopalian" who "took her religion seriously and personally," an avid reader who would pass on her love of learning to her children, and a woman who combined seriousness with gaiety and loyalty to the past with a rare openness to what the future might bring. She held out for a while, but suitors who had prospects and who had come through the war unscathed were few and far between. This suitor, moreover, was the scion of a notable family, albeit fallen on hard times, whereas she had acquired the accoutrements of ladyhood, not on an antebellum plantation but in a bustling city. She was self-made in the crucible of war. When the good looking, able-bodied young lawyer proposed, Annette accepted. They were married in Augusta in 1875. She was nineteen and he was twenty-six.[51]

ANNETTE GAVE BIRTH to three daughters in quick succession, Caroline, Valentine, and Genevieve. All died of diphtheria in a single terrible week. A fourth girl, Sarah Pope, also died in childhood.[52] Elizabeth Elliott, born in 1881, was the first of the Lumpkins' children to survive. Three sons followed, Hope Henry in 1882 (named, according to family legend, because they "hoped he'd live"), Alva Moore in 1886, and Morris Carmichael in 1888. Grace arrived in 1891, followed two years later by Bryan Hopkins. Katharine, the baby of the family, was born in Macon on December 22, 1897.

At first William and "Annie," as she was often called, lived with his parents, but within a few years they leapt—according to the Greene County tax digests—from owning nothing to claiming watches, horses, tools, and silver plate.[53] William also leapt from the Baptist church of his ancestors, the choice of common folk and the South's largest denomination, to his wife's more rarified Episcopalian faith, with its genteel congregations, stately liturgies, and Church of England roots. Still, in a region in ruins, there were "many lawyers and few clients with money," and, despite his promise and social connections, it quickly became obvious that William could not make a living at the law. Soon Annette was writing to her sister that she was unable even to come for a visit because of "hard times."[54]

William might rail against men on the make who, he believed, had turned "our South into a place of naked, shameless greed."[55] But he could not escape the bitter reality: scrambling to support a large and growing family, he became an agent of the transformation that he deplored. Fearful that he might "have to go to plowing" as he had after the war, he sought an appointment as the Register in Bankruptcy for the Northern District of Georgia, appealing for help to an old family friend, General John B. Gordon. A war hero and railroad speculator who had been the Grand Dragon of the Ku Klux Klan in Georgia, Gordon had become one of the most powerful men in the state. William got the job and combined it with lawyering. Within a few years, he too was trying his hand at railroad speculation, the chief avenue to quick wealth in the postbellum South. Moving his family to Milledgeville, he went to work for the Georgia Railroad, borrowed money from a building and loan association, and briefly set himself up as president of the Old Capital Railway Company, a tiny line that ran between Athens and Milledgeville.[56]

Soon bad luck caught up with him. He was injured in a railroad accident and, before he could recover, a trusted employee made off with his life savings, or at least so Elizabeth would later claim: "Such agony and pain my dear parents lived through; suffering with every breath they drew."[57] William fell back on a dreaded "salaried position," a serious comedown for a "young master" raised to equate independence with manhood. He became a soliciting or commercial agent charged with drumming up shipping orders for the Georgia Railroad. In essence, he was a traveling salesman, forced to ingratiate himself with customers and away from home "more than half the time." Soon Annette and the children were also on the move, following William as he was transferred to Gainesville, Macon, and other depot towns.[58]

William went to his grave identifying himself as a "lawyer for the Georgia railroad." In reality, he spent the rest of his working life as an obscure lieutenant in the army of salesmen, dispatchers, and ticket sellers that sped the South's new transportation system along its ever-multiplying tracks. He also, as Elizabeth succinctly put it, continued to have "bad luck with money."[59] He might be a gentleman by inheritance, but "'old family,'" Katharine observed, "still meant the good things of this world—land, houses, servants, everything on a luxurious scale"—a

"LEST WE FORGET"

———

ALTHOUGH SHE WAS LESS THAN A YEAR OLD IN 1898 when the Lumpkins left Georgia for South Carolina, the move etched itself onto Katharine's imagination, so often was the story told and retold. It stood in contrast with another storied journey: her ancestors' original march from Virginia to Georgia, with their human property in tow. "With not a single Negro, not a horse or mule, or carriage, or head of cattle, not the smallest suggestion of a 'cavalcade,' did the William Lumpkins of . . . Georgia, in hot, grimy day coaches of the Southern Railroad, cross over into South Carolina as the old century turned. The Lumpkin drop-leaf dining table from Father's old home, the Du Pre piano . . . two fragile gold lockets loved by all for the soft gray locks in them of our grandparents' hair; and the great family Bible on whose pages, stained and faded with age, was entered the solemn record of births and deaths. These few things, lost to all eyes but ours among our nondescript necessary furnishings, alone of our material possessions could have told the world of our 'old days.'"[1]

The Lumpkins may have seen themselves as lonely exiles, but they were enacting a series of classic moves. The exodus that historians call the Great Migration and portray mainly as the flight of blacks to the urban North after World War I actually began in the 1880s as rural Southerners, white and black alike, beat a path to the villages, towns, and cities that were springing up across the South. Scions of antebellum planting families gave up the dream of plantation life and abandoned decaying ancestral homes, while poor black and white farmers piled their own "nondescript necessary furnishings" onto wagons or second-class railroad cars and took to the road, sometimes searching for a decent landlord, sometimes retreating from debt, eviction, or persecution. Workers, clerks, salesmen, and small businessmen wandered from town to town along the railroad lines. Propelled both by large-scale social transformations and by personal needs and ambitions, the Lumpkins were among scores of families crisscrossing the region in restless, converging streams.

Such dislocations felt contingent, unexpected, accidental. But taken together they formed patterns, as the effects of bad luck and brave choices were magnified by the transportation and communications revolution that was transforming Georgia, South Carolina, and the entire Southeast. By 1898, railroads and telegraph lines reached into most southern counties; cotton mills harnessed the water power supplied by fast-falling streams; and political and economic power was shifting rapidly from the Low Country of cotton and cavaliers to the Piedmont, a band of rolling hills stretching from the southern Appalachian Mountains to the coastal plain and dominated by small farms and merchants on the make.[2]

Columbia was the capital of South Carolina. Located in the Midlands, it looked Janus-faced toward the Piedmont's boom and the Low Country's aristocratic pretensions. Torched in the riot that met Sherman's arrival at the end of the Civil War, Columbia had been "redeemed" by a paramilitary force called the Red Shirts. At its head stood Wade Hampton III, a wealthy planter, the state's most venerated Confederate warrior and, in the wake of the Red Shirts' campaign of terror, the first Democrat elected to the governorship of South Carolina since the Civil War.

By the time the Lumpkins arrived, as Grace later observed, Columbia had begun "to wake from a long slumber in which it had rested since the march of Sherman to the sea." Welcoming "the magic kiss of business" was a new generation of urban entrepreneurs who, in the same breath, rehearsed the story of the city's suffering during the war and Reconstruction, celebrated what the newspaper called its present "energy, ambition and enthusiasm," and made "fantastic claims and rosy predictions of things to come." The city that once lay "prostrate under the conqueror's heel," these boosters regularly reminded the populace, was now "alive and growing. . . . Its lovely residence streets are lined with the houses of enterprising citizens; . . . its depots are crowded with passengers and freight; its stores and its warehouses are packed with goods, and its cotton factories are models for the world to copy." The city's population doubled between 1890 and 1920, increasing to 37,524 souls.[3]

William Lumpkin's job as a railroad shipping agent put him at the very hub of the city's hustle and bustle. Union Station was a crossroads where farmers and textile mill workers, blacks and whites, rich and poor jostled for psychic and physical space. Standing on the granite steps of the green-domed State House, which anchored the neighborhoods in which they lived, the Lumpkins could survey the landscape of the urban South, a landscape that was just assuming its modern shape.

Two blocks away lay South Carolina College, rechartered in 1906 as the University of South Carolina, where the state's elite men matriculated (including all of the Lumpkin sons). To the north and south stretched Main Street, on which stood the pride of Columbia: a seven-story skyscraper that gave the city what passed for metropolitan glitter. Across the railroad tracks and farther to the southwest stretched identical mill workers' houses, clustered in company-owned mill villages just beyond the city limits. The factories, Grace wrote, were "near enough so that early in the morning, at midday, and at evening the sound of the factory whistles mingled with the sounds that came from the engines in the yard of the station."[4]

Mill workers made up a third of the city's white residents. Feared and despised by the townspeople, they, in turn, resented "the silk hat boys," even as they fought fiercely to distance themselves from African Americans, whom they saw as their chief competitors and as constant reminders of the depths to which they too could fall. Preying on the hardships and resentments of the mill workers and of their impoverished rural cousins, South Carolina's notorious demagogues, Benjamin Tillman and his protégé Coleman ("Coley") Livingston Blease, mounted a challenge both to the old-school aristocracy epitomized by Wade Hampton and to the New South urban elite.[5]

Elsewhere in the South, rural dissidents broke with conservative southern Democrats to form the Populist movement, a massive grassroots uprising that struck fear in the hearts of men like William Lumpkin by appealing to black farmers to make common cause with whites. Tillman and Blease ignored the substance but used the language of Populism and rode to power by exploiting racial divisions among the poor. Launching a white supremacy campaign just four years before the Lumpkins arrived, they rewrote the state constitution, accomplishing what national scrutiny had kept William Lumpkin's Redeemer generation from doing. They evaded the Fifteenth Amendment, driving blacks out of politics altogether through nominally legal measures such as literacy tests, poll taxes, and all-white Democratic primaries. The laws, Katharine observed, "were like a series of sieves through which men could be successively sifted. If one failed to catch all the Negro voters and hold them away from the polls, there was another that would hold back more, and still another and another until hardly a trickle could get through." In 1904 the South Carolina legislature pushed through another innovation: systematic de jure segregation designed to separate blacks from whites in public places such as railroads, streetcars, restaurants, and hotels. "Jim Crow" laws, as they were called (the term, which was derived from black minstrelsy, came to stand for the whole post-1890 racial order), spread throughout the South, reasserting white supremacy in New South cities where mobility and anonymity threatened to undermine the Old South's face-to-face forms of domination.[6]

Although relegated to separate and unequal public accommodations and excluded from most work in the mills, African Americans at the turn of the century continued to live scattered about the city as they had always done. In the Lumpkins' neighborhoods, black laundresses, cooks, and laborers could be found living in dank alleys or clustered on nearby blocks. Increasingly, however, they were crowded into segregated enclaves or relegated, along with the poorest whites, to a dismal section near the river, where unpaved streets threaded between rows of weather-beaten shotgun houses consisting of two or three rooms strung along one side of a narrow hall. Out of view to the east, a small but vibrant black middle class gathered around Allen University and Benedict College, educational institutions founded after the war. Electric streetcars, the first in the state, wove the city together while at the same time exerting a centrifugal force. Over time "streetcar suburbs" drew middle-class whites away from the town center, creating a more and more segregated—and in that sense also more modern—urban way of life.[7] These New South townspeople might deplore the excesses of Tillman and Blease, but they shared the demagogues' commitment to white supremacy, and they embraced the new order ushered in by disfranchisement and segregation. To them the "whites only" signs in the city's new railroad station, along with the class-segregated mill villages on the wrong side of the tracks, appeared to be as much a sign of peaceful, rationally managed social relations, and thus of the city's progress and modernity, as its skyscraper, its Opera House, its electric streetcars, and the garland of suburbs strung along the outskirts of town.

THE LUMPKINS HAD COME "to the Palmetto State as strangers," Katharine wrote. "To be a Georgian in South Carolina was not to feel immediately at home. We were torn loose . . . from our past and from all its material symbols of superiority and comfort; we were set down among the clans of Carolina for whom name was paramount, and to whom our Georgia name . . . was unknown." South Carolina prided itself on having been the "cradle of the Confederacy," and it rivaled Virginia in the pretensions of its Low Country aristocracy, as signified by the saying that North Carolina, flanked by these neighbors, was a "valley of humility between two mountains of conceit." Even Columbia, dominated as it was by nouveau riche mill owners and brawling politicians, revered its "old families" and tracked social status along the lines not only of wealth but also of breeding. In Georgia, the Lumpkins' reduced circumstances had not trumped their genealogy. They had but to say their name and they were understood to belong to an illustrious planter family that "lost everything in the War."[8] In "Old Columbia" such recognition shimmered just beyond their reach.

Notwithstanding William's modest position as a railway soliciting agent living from paycheck to paycheck, the Lumpkins at once sought entry to Old Columbia's tightly guarded social world. Pursuing the will-o-the-wisp of the perfect setting, a cheap house on a tree-lined avenue where the doorjambs boasted "old stock" family names, they moved eight times during their first fifteen years in the city. They started out on Elmwood Avenue, not far from the Confederate cemetery and within a stone's throw of the State House, the governor's mansion, and other elegant homes. At one point they were apparently reduced to living in the commercial building on Main Street that housed the office of the Georgia Railroad. But usually they resided in solid but modest neighborhoods of story-and-a-half frame cottages near the university, where their neighbors—whatever their lineage—were a mix of white-collar workers and professionals, ranging from cashiers, salesmen, and real estate agents to store owners, ministers, lawyers, doctors, and professors.[9]

When I tried to retrace their wanderings, I found that parking lots and student apartments had wiped out most of their former abodes, each of which, Katharine wrote, had been "blood brother" to the last: "situated on a 'good' street, in a 'good' neighborhood, with a small yard, few flowers and shrubs, as many rooms as could be secured for the rental, size being primary for a family of nine." No sooner had the family settled into a new place than the rent would go up or a more promising house down the street would beckon. "The humor was not a little wry," Katharine wrote, when a house they occupied for all of two years "was dubbed by the older children 'Nomads' Rest.' Being very young, I thought they were saying 'No Man's,' which all but confirmed my worst fears."[10]

In each neighborhood, it fell to Annette to conduct the delicate negotiations that access to society required. "South Carolinians had pride of family position?" Katharine remembered. "Well, so did we. The delicate contours of my mother's face, the fine texture of her smooth skin, the slender beauty of her expressive hands, meant in my childhood a secure sense of 'background.'" Annette might long for "dear old Georgia" and chafe at living among strangers who were "so loyal . . . and jealous of anything said against their State." But when the ladies of the neighborhood came to conduct their covert inspections aimed at identifying the Lumpkins' "forebears and standing in the place from whence they had come," she could deploy the plantation legend to maximum effect, deftly mentioning the ancestors on both sides who had come to Virginia before the Revolutionary War, the Lumpkins in high office, the French Huguenots who might be middling carpenters and farmers in Georgia but had plenty of cachet in South Carolina where, in the Low Country, they stood at the pinnacle of the social hierarchy.[11]

Luckily for the Lumpkins, Annette also turned her face toward the future even as she helped to secure her family's acceptance by embellishing its plantation roots. Hers was a modern project: the creation of a bourgeois, urban household centered on the nurture, education, and upward mobility of children and the intense cultivation of private family life. To be sure, that household relied on the domestic work of black women, much as antebellum households had done. "In a land where a separate servant class existed and help came exceedingly cheap," Katharine observed, even the genteel poor could afford domestic help. For the

Lumpkins that meant a "Negro cook, paid something around two and a half dollars weekly, with a new face in the kitchen every few months." Annette very likely sent out the laundry as well: most white women who could afford to do so relegated that onerous task to the black laundresses in town.[12] At one point the Lumpkins were able to hire a live-in servant: Mary Haynes, age twenty-two, a black woman who could neither read nor write. But the ever-changing stream of faces yielded no beloved "Aunt Winnie" or "Aunt Sarah." If the children knew these women's names, they "at once forgot them." They gave Annette their undivided affection; they took tremendous pride in the "tradition of mother's beauty and popularity"; and they credited her, not the servants, with fulfilling their wants and needs.[13]

Annette *was* a resourceful household manager. Like "Marmie" in *Little Women*, she sewed dresses for her three daughters and everything except suits for her four sons. She darned socks and made over hand-me-downs (Grace, who inherited even Elizabeth's underwear, feared she was "never going to have anything else new"). Annette loved "flowers, animals and birds," and she filled their drab parlors with music, for she had a lovely contralto voice and could play the Du Pre piano. William could not carry a tune, but the boys sang so exquisitely that "in the evenings people came and stood about the fence to hear them." Indeed, when Morris was contemplating a run for political office in the wake of World War I, his backers saw his "really excellent baritone singing voice" as one of his major assets on the campaign trail.[14]

Above all, Annette made sure that Sunday morning found the Lumpkins at Columbia's posh Trinity Church, no matter where they happened to be living at the time. The first major Episcopalian outpost in the Midlands, Trinity had come through the burning of Columbia relatively unscathed, except for the proverbial loss of the communion silver and the destruction of the parsonage and the Sunday school building. Rising in Gothic splendor opposite the State House and adjacent to the university, the church's cruciform-shaped sanctuary glowed with the patina of old money and the aura of the antebellum past. Wade Hampton III had been among its founding members, and when he died in 1902 he was buried in the crowded church cemetery, along with much of the Midlands gentry. Adopting South Carolina's "peerless chieftain" as their own, after Sunday services the Lumpkins "would troop in reverent pilgrimage to his always flower-strewn grave."[15]

C.5.—WADE HAMPTON MONUMENT AND GLIMPSE OF TRINITY EPISCOPAL CHURCH.

COLUMBIA, S. C.

Wade Hampton Monument on South Carolina State House grounds
steps away from Trinity Episcopal Church (now Cathedral),
where Hampton is buried.

"As prime a necessity as bread was payment on the family pew,"
Katharine remembered. And no wonder, for parishioners who could not
scrape together the money were consigned to the ignominy of the "Free
Pews." Only pew-holders, moreover, could vote in church affairs. The
Lumpkin family might skimp on clothes, eat simple meals, and forgo
luxuries. But a stranger "could hardly have guessed we did not come
out of our lost mansions when Sunday came, and one old family after
another would tread with infinite pride and dignity old Trinity's deep-
carpeted aisle."[16]

"THEIR MOTHER TEACHES THEM their prayers; I teach them to love
the Lost Cause," William Lumpkin liked to say. This equation of private religious instruction with Civil War commemoration captures the
fervor with which, as Katharine remembered it, William went about
"impregnating our lives with some of his sense of strong mission." It
also suggests that his quest for a place in South Carolina society came
to rest on two props: on his family, where he was, as Katharine put it,
"head and dominant figure, leader, exemplar, final authority," and on the

William Wallace Lumpkin (left), Confederate Veteran, *1906,*
and Annette Caroline Morris Lumpkin (right).

effort to assert a distinctive understanding of what the Lumpkins called
"our Southern disaster (we would never concede the word 'defeat')."[17]
In an autobiographical novel she wrote in the late 1930s, Grace caught
perfectly the emotional atmosphere William's twin obsessions created in
the Lumpkin home. When "Robert Middleton," the name she gave the
character modeled on her father, left his native Georgia,

> he became one of that large group of Southerners who had many
> traditions behind them, but no promise for the future. . . . Though
> he tried to reconcile himself he was never actually reconciled to
> the loss of past glory. He always promised himself and his wife
> that he would go back to practicing law and even kept his license
> framed on the wall of his small office. But in his heart he knew
> that this would never happen. From the day he began to work as
> a salaried employee of a railroad Robert began to project his lost
> ambitions and tireless energy into the lives of his children.[18]

In practice William's hopes for his children and his obsession with
past glory were inseparable. His role in the movement to commemorate

the Confederacy gave him stature in his children's eyes; their involvement demonstrated his success as a firm but loving father. The ideas and iconography of the Lost Cause and the emotional bonds of the family reinforced one another, cultivating race, class, and regional loyalties where they could grow most virulently: in the hearts of susceptible and idealistic children. Yet like all great mythologies, the Lost Cause had unintended consequences and protean political uses.[19] It endowed the Lumpkin sisters with a sense of the southern past as both a burden and an opportunity, entangling them in self-deceptions, yet teaching them the power of stories not only to describe, but also to act on the social world. Each, in her own way, would search out new patterns in the tangled threads of memory and history; each would weave a new story from what she found.

The effort to honor the memory of those who died in battle and assist the survivors had begun almost as soon as the Confederacy surrendered. As federal officials moved through the South, finding, identifying, and burying Union soldiers in national cemeteries, southern Ladies' Memorial Societies took up the work of burying and memorializing the Confederate dead. In the years that followed, white Southerners produced a flood of novels, biographies, reminiscences, and formal histories aimed at understanding the tragedy that had befallen them and justifying themselves to what they saw as a hostile world.[20]

William Lumpkin had enlisted in "the party of remembrance" early on. He had attended one of the first regimental veterans' reunions, a gathering of the Third Georgia Regiment in Union Point, Georgia, that took place in 1874, shortly after he completed his apprenticeship with Alexander Stephens and launched his ill-fated legal career.[21] By the time he moved his family to South Carolina, ad hoc local memorial groups had come together to form the United Confederate Veterans (UCV), and veterans' "camps" (as local organizations were called) honeycombed all of the former Confederate states, each, Katharine wrote, "bearing the name of some hero living or dead." Camp meetings were important social occasions in rural areas, and cities competed for the bonanza of hosting huge UCV parades, pageants, and reunions. For William, the timing of this development was a godsend. He might be a lowly station agent in a state where the Lumpkin name did not immediately open doors, but he did have his service in the Confederate army, brief though it was, and he could cloak himself in the aura of the plantation, which still carried tremendous cultural weight. Inhabiting the iconic persona of the Confederate veteran who "had had lost so much and regained so little," he made the Lost Cause his avocation. The more worldly success eluded him, the more important his participation in the war for public memory became.[22]

Elaborated in print, etched in what the French historian Pierre Nora has called *lieux de mémoire*—sites for anchoring memories even as they threaten to slip away—and performed in the speeches, pageants, and parades that accompanied veterans' reunions, the Lost Cause narrative Lumpkin and his compatriots promoted was nothing if not paradoxical. It served to rehabilitate aging Confederates and romanticize the antebellum past while, at the same time, promoting sectional reconciliation and creating an illusion of continuity by wrapping a mantle of Old South legitimacy around a modern racial order and a new, business-oriented elite.[23] It was this use of the past as a resource for the present that made the Lost Cause a myth of such "incalculable potentialities." Within its narrative frame, the plantation became a benevolent "school of civilization" for blacks. Slavery was not the nation's original sin; it was the white man's burden. It was "well-ended, although by altogether wrong means."[24] The Confederacy had fought not to preserve human bondage but to uphold the Constitutional principle of states' rights. The North had prevailed through brute force alone: the sheer weight of its manpower and industry had overwhelmed the Confederacy's brilliant and heroic military defense. Might, however, did not make right: white Southerners were still God's chosen people, tested by defeat but vindicated in their principles. Stripped of its horrors, the war served as a testing ground in another way as well: it was an arena in which soldiers on both sides had acquitted themselves with honor.

In this telling, Reconstruction was a testing ground as well. It had exposed blacks' incapacity for citizenship and the evils of federal intervention. The South's white leaders, who had plunged the country into a fratricidal war, now reemerged as patriotic Redeemers who succeeded in purging the demons let loose by Reconstruction and paving the way for reconciliation on the white South's terms. Populism and its aftermath, the white supremacy campaigns, which had helped to spark the Lost Cause movement, were reframed as well. By joining forces with black voters, dissident white farmers had, unfortunately, created a rift in "the white South's solid front." But a new generation of business-minded leaders had risen to the challenge. Finishing the work of the Redeemers, they paved the way to racial peace and economic prosperity through disfranchisement and segregation.[25]

White women played a central role in the mobilization of memory, first as prodigious writers and members of local memorial societies and then through the United Daughters of the Confederacy (UDC). Indeed, at its peak, the UDC far surpassed its male counterpart, the United Confederate Veterans, in efficiency, energy, and fund-raising acumen. It used those formidable skills to assert women's cultural authority over virtually every representation of the region's past: lobbying for state archives and museums, raising money for historic sites, interviewing former soldiers, writing history texts, pressuring local school boards to replace "Yankee school books" with works by southern writers, and ensuring that statues of Confederate soldiers stood in front of practically every courthouse in the region.[26]

The understanding of history the women propagated was reinforced by a cohort of white historians trained in a new archive-based, seminar-driven "scientific" history developed in Germany. These university-based scholars—men, one and all—rejected the local sources, oral histories, and personal memoirs that constituted the UDC's stock-in-trade and based their authority on their expert use of official documents. Yet, blinded by their own prejudices, they took the perceptions and self-justifications of white Southerners at face value while ignoring the reams of evidence reflecting blacks' experiences and points of view. This misuse of science produced a distorted version of the nation's past, a tale remarkably similar to the myths about the benevolence of slavery and the evils of Reconstruction the UDC and the UCV promoted. Ironically, the impersonal voice the scholars affected, an innovation as critical to historical writing as the discovery of perspective was to painting, helped to propel the Lost Cause narrative into the modern world. Organized women had taken the lead in creating the South's landscape of memory and prodding southern state legislatures to assume responsibility for the archives on which scholars relied. But it was the new history, cleansed of association with what the professionals saw as meddling, dilettantish women, that stamped that narrative with the unearned authority of scientific truth.[27]

Brought to the screen in D. W. Griffith's blockbuster 1915 film, *Birth of a Nation*, the Lost Cause epic insinuated itself into American—not just southern—public culture, driving to the margins the counter-memory of the Civil War as a struggle for liberty and democracy. Indeed, the cult of the Lost Cause offered "ironic evidence that the South marched in step with the rest of the country."[28] As migrants from eastern and southern Europe transformed northern cities, industrialization sparked violent class conflict, and a virulent form of scientific racism ricocheted through the Western world, nativist northern elites commissioned sculptures of American heroes and revived colonial and classical architectural styles, projecting an image of a stable, homogeneous Anglo-Saxon social order onto the face of an increasingly polyglot nation. In the North as in the South, this commemorative project sought to banish racial and ethnic minorities from public memory just as they were excluded from public power.[29] Buttressed by professional historians, amplified by new technologies of mass communication and entertainment, and incorporated into both northern and southern civic culture, the Lost Cause version of history endured for generations. Indeed, it lingers to this day, undergirding the failure of white Americans to reckon with the legacies of slavery, segregation, and exploitation that are woven so tightly into their country's past.

FOR THE LUMPKINS, the cult of the Lost Cause was a family affair. Annette became a member of the United Daughters of the Confederacy. Grace and Katharine joined the UDC's chapter of the Children of the Confederacy, attending monthly meetings where they were "trained to love and honor the Confederate Cause" through essays, recitations, and patriotic music. All four of the Lumpkin boys joined the Sons of Confederate Veterans, an offshoot of the UCV, and all made speeches in behalf of the Lost Cause.[30] But it was Elizabeth, the eldest, who was her father's favorite, Elizabeth who inherited his gift for oratory, and Elizabeth who most fully embraced and was embraced by the subculture of the Lost Cause. As she remembered it,

> When I was small, about seven years old, I think, Father was trying to teach my brother Hope, a little younger than I, a "speech." Nobody in those days thought a *girl* could make a *speech*. . . .

Elizabeth Elliott Lumpkin (left) and Grace Lumpkin (right)
as Lost Cause orators, Confederate Veteran, *1905.*

Hope . . . did not want to speak at that age . . . but *I* did. I clasped
my hand dramatically . . . and said, "O, Papa, *please* let me learn
it!" And I did [and] he was delighted and so was my Mother.
They found I had a voice for speeches and natural gestures and
apparently unlimited capacity for learning speeches and dramatic
recitations.[31]

Elizabeth was seventeen when the Lumpkins arrived in Columbia, and William at once presented her to his UCV camp. The program
consisted of a rousing story about his war service as "a lad of 15 years"
followed by his "beautiful daughter" reciting "the thrilling words of a
Confederate poem."[32] When Columbia's town fathers broke custom by
inviting Georgia veterans to South Carolina's reunion in 1901, they chose
Elizabeth, "a Georgia girl now living here [to] welcome the visitors to
her adopted home." Appearing before a rapt crowd two thousand strong,
she put forth what the local paper described as "one of the most remarkable efforts ever made by a woman in this city."[33] Two years later she
starred alongside her father at a region-wide reunion in Columbia that
involved the whole family and that Katharine would never forget.

Katharine had just turned six, the decisive moment when a young child's uninhibited receptiveness to a bombardment of sensation and information usually gives way to a different state of being: that of a self-conscious individual, an "I" capable of autobiographical memory, the narrative of self on which adult identity rests.[34] "I may have been drinking in [the Lost Cause] since the time of my babyhood," Katharine observed, "but all before that is indistinct, cloudy." Now, in the three event-packed days during which Columbia hosted the 1903 veterans' reunion, she was "dipped deep in the fiery experience of Southern patriotism." She was dipped as well into "the sense of our complete belonging" that such an initiation into public memory can afford.[35]

"The grand reunion," Katharine remembered, was held in the month of May. . . . Earlier would not do, lest we have April showers; later would not have been good, after the summer's heat had set in, and a torrid, sultry spell might mow the old men down like grain under the sickle." The whole town was caught up in the "bustle and business of preparation. What child would not love it when everywhere was unbounded enthusiasm and her own family in the thick of everything? Twenty thousand veterans and visitors coming—almost more people than the city itself." William took charge of welcoming the aging veterans, especially the Georgia contingent, as they poured into Union Station and bivouacked in a huge tent on the State House lawn. Annette assisted in the veterans' free lunchrooms downtown. Twelve-year-old Grace sang in the children's chorus. At twenty-two, Elizabeth was among the "bevy of the State's most beautiful young ladies" who organized balls and receptions, served as sponsors and maids of honor, and waved to the crowd from atop flower-bedecked floats. Morris, age fifteen, made a speech to the veterans, and a UCV general "pinned the badge of 'honorary member, U.C.V.' upon the child's patriotic breast."[36]

Too young to participate directly, Katharine watched from the sidelines, swept up in the excitement of the crowd. Red and white bunting festooned every building, and incandescent lights turned Main Street into a child's "dream of fairyland." Thousands leaned from windows and lined the streets. "Men doffing their hats so long as the old men were passing, women fluttering their handkerchiefs. School children ahead of them, spreading the streets with a carpet of flowers, lavishly, excitedly." Bands played march tunes until, Katharine remembered, "it seemed one's spine could not stand any more tingles." Then came a moment that a child "would never forget." "Roll of drums; blare of trumpets; then the first high, clear notes of *Dixie!*" after which Elizabeth stepped forward to address the crowd. All the other speakers were veterans or sons of veterans. But it was Elizabeth who stirred the hearts of the old soldiers as they had never been stirred before, or so the local newspaper claimed.[37]

Her "ringing, carrying voice" struck all the right notes: white supremacy; the importance of "racial purity"; the urgency of securing books for the public schools that do "full and complete justice to the Confederate soldier."[38] Most of all, Elizabeth assured the elderly soldiers that, "old and gray and wrinkled" though they might be, they could still enjoy the love of a young girl, if only vicariously. "I love you," was her signature line. "You grand old men who guarded with your lives the virgin whiteness of our Georgia." We daughters can only envy the "honor our lovely mothers gloried in. . . . they could love and marry Confederate soldiers. . . . We can [only work for them] with tireless fingers . . . run with tireless feet."[39]

On the closing day, William Lumpkin had his moment on the stage. "Lights were extinguished," Katharine remembered. "We waited while the curtain descended and rose again. Gleaming through the darkness was a bright camp fire with a kettle hanging from a tripod. Around the fire one could see men in bedraggled uniforms. One soldier lounged up to the fire—'Quaint reminder of long ago as he stood in the half light, pipe in mouth, pants tucked into his socks, coatless and collarless.' He began to tell a tale of war. More men slipped out and settled down by the fire. . . . A hushed house as the tale proceeded . . . lights gradually brightened . . . the speaker was recognized . . . Col. W.W. Lumpkin, a soldier of the Confederacy again."[40]

Over the next few years, Elizabeth was inundated with invitations to speak at veterans' events and letters of praise for her performances. Her father served as her manager and coach, suggesting ideas for her speeches, instructing her on which invitations to accept, trying to ensure that her appearances were covered by the press, and traveling with her throughout South Carolina, Georgia, Virginia, and Tennessee.[41] Elizabeth, reported one observer, was "grand, glorious, gifted . . . transcendingly superior to any man or woman I have ever seen in any role on any stage." At the end of her perorations, "strong old men threw their arms around each other and wept."[42] Only Jefferson Davis's daughter Varina

Anne, known as "Winnie," had ever enjoyed such adulation. Until her death in 1898, Davis was the chief avatar of the movement. She was also the means by which her father, the former president of the Confederacy, redeemed himself as a symbol of the Lost Cause. Rumor had it that he was trying to escape in women's clothes when Union troops captured him at the end of the war, and Winnie's birth, which offered visible evidence of Davis's virility, helped to override the image of Davis fleeing in bonnet and skirts. Although Winnie Davis was well educated and independent, a substantial woman in her own right, she was known best as "the daughter of the Confederacy . . . the war baby of our old chieftain." She never spoke in public; simply by appearing on the stage she attracted adoring crowds.[43] "Nobody but Winnie could be the 'Daughter of the Confederacy,'" Elizabeth remembered. But at their South-wide reunion in Louisville in 1904, the veterans named Elizabeth the "Daughter of the United Confederate Veterans," "the nearest similar honor that it was possible to pay."[44]

It is easy to see women like Winnie Davis and Elizabeth Lumpkin as bodies onto which men old enough to be their fathers or grandfathers could project fantasies of eternal vigor, sometimes even bodies that could be literally embraced. At a reunion in Georgia, it took a phalanx of guards to protect Elizabeth "from the ardor of the enthusiastic and admiring veterans." When fifteen-year-old Grace appeared on the veterans' reunion stage, her youth seemed to excite the soldiers even more. Told that a woman was going to speak, the veterans sighed in resignation. A speech by a woman "in any assemblage where men are present is generally regarded with a half sinister indulgence," the newspaper admitted. "But there came a surprise. It was not a woman at all, but a . . . . child-woman. She appeared under the influence of an occult power, and as she spoke the soldiers stood upon their feet and cheered wildly." Then they rushed the stage, grabbed Grace's hands and kissed her, congratulating her father, who stood at her side.[45]

Re-remembering her own experiences in her first novel, *To Make My Bread* (1932), Grace made a Confederate reunion a key moment in her protagonist's political education, lingering not only on the messages about class and race embedded in such events but also on how they surrounded women's bodies with a strange brew of lust and etherealization. "Through the great hall, people sat forward and listened, and there was not a murmur," except for the voice of a girl "here to speak for the women of the

South" and the "heavy breathing of the old men. They leaned forward toward her, and seemed to swallow what she said with their open mouths, and at times when she spoke more fervently tears rolled down their cheeks." Climbing onto the stage, a veteran kissed the girl; others followed until she, like Grace as a girl, was surrounded by the throng. Finally, someone called for the rebel yell, "a long weird sound [that] hung over them ugly and shrill and threatening, then up it went into a terrible shriek."[46]

Walter Hines Page, a southern expatriate who became one of the region's sharpest early critics, underscored the dynamic Grace conveyed in her fictionalized account. By placing their daughters on the reunion stage, he argued, the "wonderful military relics" of the UCV duped them into shoring up their fathers' waning power.[47] The Lost Cause was a patriarchal as well as a white supremacist project, and young women like Elizabeth and Grace Lumpkin inevitably absorbed its message. And yet—like the rise of a New South business class and the spread of segregation—their presence on the Lost Cause stage signaled not only the pull of the past but also the swirl of change.

In late nineteenth-century southern politics, public speech remained a prized form of communication in contrast to what Columbia's daily newspaper called "the chilling process of press reproduction."[48] It also remained largely the province of men, who monopolized not only the hustings but also the pulpit and Confederate reunions. At the same time, a popular oratorical movement sprang up that proved enormously attractive to women. Female graduates of schools of expression secured positions in southern women's colleges, most of which were founded between 1880 and 1900. There they developed a form of oratory as "a performative fine art closely allied with drama and dance" rather than with political debate. Emboldened by the experience of presenting themselves on a public stage, most students went on to hone their skills in women's clubs and missionary societies.[49] Elizabeth did what few southern women could dream of: she turned her theatrical gifts into a professional career.

Shortly after the Lumpkins arrived in South Carolina, she began studying at the Georgia Normal and Industrial College, a recently chartered institution in Milledgeville, Georgia, that emphasized teacher training and business skills.[50] In 1899, she transferred to Georgia Female Seminary (renamed Brenau College the following year), located in Gainesville, a small town in the mountains of north Georgia where the Lumpkins had once lived. Brenau could not claim a place among the most highly ranked of the southern women's colleges.[51] Still, at a time when a minuscule number of American women attended college, it offered a comparatively rigorous education in classical studies, English, mathematics, science, and modern languages modeled on that deemed appropriate to men. Unusually for a private liberal arts school, it also sought to prepare women to support themselves through teaching and office work. Its independent, degree-granting conservatory of music, art, oratory, and kindred subjects was a special source of pride: it boasted the school's most admired teachers and was among the largest and best in the state, if not in the region, as its officials liked to claim.[52]

Elizabeth enrolled in the conservatory, where she studied with Florence M. Overton, a graduate of Emerson College in Boston, a private institution devoted to communication and the arts, and one of Brenau's most revered teachers.[53] After two years, she received a "Bachelors of Oratory," then went on to seek further training. She attended the Curry School of Expression in Boston (now Curry College), which, along with Emerson, was the most influential school of expression in the country, and spent a month at an obscure institution in New York City called the Empire School of Expression. She took courses at South Carolina College, which had nominally admitted women since 1894, but made no provisions for them and treated them with such hostility that only an intrepid few dared to attend.[54] Attempting not only to support herself but also to send money to her impecunious father, she took in private students and taught at the Mt. Carmel Graded School in Abbeville, South Carolina. In 1903 she parlayed her efforts into a position as a professor of speech and head of the Department of Reading and Expression at Winthrop Normal and Industrial College in Rock Hill, South Carolina.[55] Founded at the behest of the faux-populist governor Coleman Blease, Winthrop aimed to train white women to become teachers, secretaries, and farmers' wives.[56]

Elizabeth's perfect gestures, her "carrying voice," and her ability to move strong men to tears were portrayed by the press as spontaneous expressions of filial loyalty and southern patriotism. In fact, whatever her natural gifts, they were the polished products of education and practice. Using those tools, she bested men at a man's game and, at the same time, carved out a space of financial independence and cultural authority in a women's institution. After introducing Elizabeth at a reunion in

Virginia, Congressman John Lamb observed, "No speaker I have ever heard was listened to with such rapt attention." Asked how he felt when the address ended, Lamb replied, I "feel as if I never wanted to make another speech during this mortal life." If she had been a man, Elizabeth sometimes mused, she would have "charged with Pickett at Gettysburg when every hope was lost" and been on the front lines of every battle. "Her figure was alive with passionate feeling," noted one observer, "and you could put a flag in her hands and conquer the world."[57]

When addressing the men and women of her own generation, Elizabeth did not hesitate to admonish as well as praise, blurring the line between feminine forms of expression and male-coded political oration. The boosters who promoted sectional reconciliation as a lure for northern capital and a goad to economic progress, she complained, had "learned to count profit and loss where honor is concerned." She hinted darkly about contemporary threats to "the purity of our race," thinking most likely of white men who flagrantly engaged in sex across the color line. Home should be a place "where the man is what he demands the woman shall be," she pointedly declared, critiquing the double standard that sanctioned sexual license for men while ostracizing women who strayed even slightly from the rules of sexual decorum.[58]

CONFEDERATE REUNIONS OFFERED the most impressive stage for the Lumpkins' pedagogical efforts. But William and Annette also seized the most quotidian moments of family life to forward their children's moral and political education. Katharine remembered especially a family ritual called the "Saturday Night Debating Club" modeled on the techniques of William's mentor, Alexander Stephens, who had summoned his students to stand before him and debate the controversial issues of the day. All week the children prepared their arguments on southern history and social problems. "We would hurry through Saturday-night supper and dishes. A table would be placed in the parlor, Father seating himself behind it, presiding," with chairs for the debaters on either side. "And what a game! . . . And how the plaster walls of our parlor rang with tales of the South's sufferings, exhortations to uphold her honor, recitals of her humanitarian slave regime, denunciations of those who dared to doubt the black man's inferiority, and, ever, and always, persuasive logic for her position of 'States Rights.'"[59] At school, Katharine used that training to triumph in lopsided debates on the question "Are Negroes Equal to White People?" More than thirty years later she could recall her own fervor and the burst of applause when she finished her argument: "and the Bible says that they shall be hewers of wood and drawers of water forever!"[60]

The confidence with which Katharine entered such debates, and the pleasure she felt in her own eloquence and erudition, underscore the double-edged impact of her Lost Cause education. The hate-filled rhetoric of South Carolina's racial extremists seldom surfaced at veterans' reunions, but to Katharine there was no doubt that race lay at their core, as it lay at the core of her father's teachings. "There was the glamorous, distant past of our heritage," she remembered.

> Besides this, there was the living, pulsing present. . . . Let some changes come if they must; our fathers had seen them come to pass: they might grieve, yet could be reconciled. It was inconceivable, however, that any change could be allowed that altered the very present fact of the relation of superior white to inferior Negro. This we came to understand remained for us as it had been for our fathers, the very cornerstone of the South.[61]

The situation, Katharine said, was anomalous. Certainly, William believed in men's authority and women's "secondary and supplementary" role. Women were to "sit silent when men were speaking; not to pit our opinions against the more knowing males." A woman was a "creature of intuition" who needed "the firm, solid frame of a male protector and guide." Yet even as such precepts were sifting into their consciousness "as softly . . . as snow floats down on a still winter night," Katharine and her sisters were learning contrary lessons—from their mother especially, but also from their father. Chief among them was a love for "things of the mind" and the belief that "those who have brains are meant to use them," girls and boys alike.[62]

Annette Lumpkin's learning reinforced that belief. It was, Katharine reflected, a "proud family possession," especially among her daughters. Perhaps "we took peculiar pleasure in it, feeling our own prestige advance, who were but females in a world of male superiority." All three loved the story of their mother's Irish tutor, who encouraged her to read the New Testament in Greek when she was eight years old and then, when she was ten, put her to work studying Locke's *Human Under-*

standing. Each afternoon, under their mother's tutelage, the Lumpkin children spent an hour reading aloud: the Bible (they memorized the New Testament, a few verses at a time) and *Pilgrim's Progress*; the works of Alfred, Lord Tennyson; Thomas Dixon's trilogy on Reconstruction, Thomas Nelson Page on Robert E. Lee; Dickens, Tolstoy, Zola, and Balzac, the great nineteenth-century realists whose heroes were caught up in history's great narrative sweep and whom Grace later saw as the precursors of her generation of proletarian writers.[63]

ON DECEMBER 21, 1905, Elizabeth married Eugene Byron Glenn after what seems to have been a tumultuous, doubt-filled courtship. (Had Elizabeth been too forward in revealing her feelings? Was her suitor losing interest after winning her heart? Did his attractive qualities outweigh his faults?)[64] Glenn was a doctor from the mountains of western North Carolina, a stronghold of small farmers who had little use for Deep South pretensions. He boasted no ancestors such as those the Lumpkins claimed: no governors or supreme court justices. But he came from a line of Confederate sympathizers, and he had what William Lumpkin so painfully lacked: the resources and the know-how to prosper in the urbanizing, industrializing South. His great-grandfather had acquired 1,000 acres of land in Buncombe County early in the nineteenth century, and his parents, whom Grace would later portray as a "stern old man with a white beard" and a "plump, rosy-cheeked mountain girl," were among the largest landowners in Avery Creek Township. As the nearby city of Asheville mushroomed into a prosperous tourist center, the Glenns invested in talc mines and manufacturing and speculated in real estate. By the time Eugene met Elizabeth at one of her Lost Cause presentations, his brother had been elected to the North Carolina legislature, and Eugene had worked his way through medical school in Philadelphia, fought in the Spanish-American War, and become chief of the surgical staff at a hospital established by George W. Vanderbilt near his palatial Asheville estate.[65]

But it was not Glenn's prosperity and prospects that caught the South Carolina press's attention. It was the "Confederate wedding" staged by the Lumpkins at Trinity Episcopal Church. This event may not have "attracted the intense interest . . . of the entire South," as local newspapers proclaimed, but it certainly represented the pinnacle of William's

Elizabeth and Eugene Glenn's "Confederate Wedding," Confederate Veteran,
*1906. Elizabeth and Eugene Glenn are in the center. Annette Lumpkin stands
behind the couple; William Lumpkin is standing behind Elizabeth. Katharine
is in the left bottom corner, leaning in, with Grace to Elizabeth's right.*

quest to secure his standing in his adopted city by virtue of his wife's
charm, his children's talents, and his own claim to military service and
plantation roots. It was also an example of the lengths to which William would go to ignore reality in favor of "a dream of what [he] wished
things to be." Weddings in the antebellum South were, in fact, simple
affairs, held at home with a few relatives present, and most were sim-
pler still during the Civil War, when even a bolt of factory-made cloth
was hard to obtain. Walking a fine line between the impressive and the
pretentious, William plunged deeply into debt and commandeered Elizabeth's savings, all in the name of staging an elaborate, and quite fantas-
tical, simulacrum of a wedding among the plantation elite.[66]

The church was "draped in Southern smilax and festoons of gray
moss—so characteristically Southern, and so sentimentally associated—
probably on account of its color, with the Confederacy," the local paper
observed. Grace was "first bridesmaid." At her father's urging, Elizabeth
had chosen the rest in part to consolidate his ties to influential families

across the state. All were dressed as "typical Southern girls of before the war."[67] Next came the scene-stealers, an honor guard of Confederate veterans in full uniform—all, like William Lumpkin, generals and colonels, if not in reality, at least by virtue of their leadership in the UCV. For no other young woman would "the old soldiers in gray rally from all parts of the Southland to act as escort of honor in the nuptial march." The Rev. Ellison Capers, a Confederate general cum rector of Trinity Church and Bishop of the Diocese of South Carolina, presided, and, along with the traditional words of the wedding ceremony, he recited the treacly poems of Father Abram Ryan, the so-called poet-priest of the Confederacy.[68]

At the center of all of this pomp and circumstances stood Elizabeth Lumpkin and Eugene Glenn, by all accounts a study in contrasts. "Dainty and fragile with olive skin, a pointed face, brown wavy hair and brilliant dark eyes," the bride wore "a beautiful gown of white crepe in princess style, the deep yoke studded with medallions and finished with a bertha of rose-point lace." "Exceedingly masculine," with large bones, burly arms, broad shoulders, and a "heavy-jowled face," the bridegroom gamely put up with all the "fol-de-rol," although, as Grace remembered it, he wished "two people could get married without all of this damned fuss."[69] After the ceremony, the crowd attended a reception at the Lumpkins' dilapidated but lavishly decorated home. "The most attractive feature of the whole affair," according to the official organ of the UCV, was the "manner of the bride," who "sent a message to the Veterans that, however truly she loved her husband, she would ever love us all the more."[70]

As Elizabeth stepped away from the Lost Cause stage, her "first bridesmaid" filled her shoes. Grace joined her mother as a member of the Wade Hampton Chapter of the United Daughters of the Confederacy. Both women represented the local at the UDC's national meeting, and Grace served as "directress" of its children's chapter. Encouraged by her father, despite his conviction that she would "never equal [Elizabeth] in oratory," she held forth to crowds of thousands about the virtues of the Confederacy, "the whitest nation that ever came to birth," and about the heroism of wives and daughters who "fought none the less because they carried no guns."[71]

As late as 1911, when she was twenty years old, Grace continued to carry on the family tradition. In fact, in that year, she assumed a new commemorative role: she starred in the annual reunion of South Carolina's Red Shirts, the terrorist organization led by Wade Hampton, which had taken up arms against Reconstruction in 1876. Sharing a podium with Governor Blease, the bête noir of old-liners like her father and New South leaders alike, she was introduced by the mayor, welcomed the Red Shirts to the city, and then rode as a "maid of honor" in a parade that featured a "Ku Klux band" and "four Negroes who voted the Democratic ticket in 1876."[72]

By contrast, when Katharine grew old enough to contribute to the cause directly, she found the experience dispiriting. Taken by her father to recite at a veterans' camp on the outskirts of town, she encountered a sad collection of lost and bewildered elderly men rather than the glamor she expected. "After the first time I went as a duty," she reflected, "but it held no lure for me." When the grateful veterans gave her a portrait of herself, an enlarged photograph tinted and set in an ornate gilt frame, she recoiled at the sight of her garish double. That eerily touched-up image was not who she wanted to be. Even her parents were embarrassed, and they never hung the picture on the wall.[73]

THIS UNEASE WAS TELLING, for as Grace remained on the commemorative stage, Katharine began, little by little, to lose faith in the tenets of her Lost Cause education. What saved her, she believed, were the contingencies and contradictions to which she was exposed. There was, in the first instance, the anxiety that lay just beneath the surface of her parents' beliefs. Her turn-of-the-century childhood was bathed in her father's reminiscences; bittersweet, self-serving, and beguiling, they surrounded human bondage with a noxious golden glow. But memories are stories of experience, not experience itself, and his were shot through with the disquiet caused by Reconstruction, Populism, and the white supremacy campaigns. If ever there was a man who saw the South as uniquely united by timeless ideals, it was William Lumpkin. Yet he himself was a product not of consensus and continuity but of dissension and rupture, dizzying displacements and rapid moves. It took effort to reconcile the racial violence and class conflict of the late nineteenth century with a "dream replica" of a paternalistic past.[74] Those rifts and tensions created an atmosphere in which doubts could grow. Then too there were the anomalies of Katharine's upbringing in a household where girls were expected both to excel and to defer and her position as the youngest child, the one who watched from the sidelines, thrilled by the spectacle but not quite taken in.

Looking back from the vantage point of the 1940s, when she wrote her autobiography, she stressed three moments in particular as the pivots on which her refashioning turned. The first shocked her into color-consciousness and planted seeds of doubt about her father. The second altered her understanding of his place in the larger world. The third confronted her with the injuries of class. Each in the end taught what C. Wright Mills called a terrible and magnificent lesson: to locate herself in history by questioning the common sense of her place and time.[75]

The first of these ruptures occurred shortly after the 1903 Confederate reunion, while the Lumpkins were still basking in that event's afterglow. The family had settled temporarily into what could almost pass for the house of their dreams. Called the "Century House" and located in Ridgeway, a depot town almost twenty-five miles from Columbia, it had high-ceilinged rooms, a wide central hall, and a deep, shady lawn. Playing in the yard one summer morning, Katharine was startled by a terrible noise:

> Of a sudden in the house there was bedlam—sounds to make my heart pound and my hair prickle at the roots. Calls and screams were interspersed with blow upon blow. Soon enough I knew someone was getting a fearful beating. . . . I edged over so that I could gaze in through the kitchen window. . . . Our little black cook, a woman small of stature though full grown, was receiving a severe thrashing. I could see her writhing under the blows of a descending stick wielded by the white master of the house. I could see her face distorted with fear and agony and his with stern rage. I could see her twisting and turning as she tried to free herself from his firm grasp.[76]

That "white master," whom Katharine leaves unnamed, was her father. Terrified and trembling, she covered her ears and crept away. The beating was an open secret, omnipresent but never spoken of by the family or the neighbors, who surely could not help but hear. There were no repercussions from the outside world.

In the wake of this shocking event, Katharine struggled to parse right from wrong. "To my hesitant question, 'What had the cook done?' I was told simply that she had been very 'impudent' to her mistress, she had 'answered her back.' . . . Small child though I was, . . . I knew 'impudence' was intolerable." Confronted with such a provocation, what else could a "white master" do? Katharine knew that not so many years before it had been right "for Southern white gentlemen to thrash their cooks." She knew as well that her father had ridden with the Klan on its midnight raids against the former slaves. But these were stories "removed from all sight and sound." The violence she had seen in Ridgeway was visceral and ugly: a tiny woman, an enraged man, the thud of a stick on flesh and bone. To a girl who was subject to the disciplinary power of a man who was "head and dominant figure . . . final authority, beyond which was no higher court in family matters," the beating may have been so disturbing in part because of the dangerous possibilities it represented. What she remembered was this: her desperate wish to distance herself from a woman to whom such things could be done.[77]

"Thereafter, I began to be self-conscious about the . . . signs and symbols of my race position," signs and symbols that drew her into a magic circle of privilege and safety by policing the line between black and white.[78] That line was never etched in stone. For even as segregation hardened, the two races continued to pursue "separate lives lived together," parallel and relational, each conditioned, however unequally, by the other. Whites might walk at their ease through the scenes of official segregation, oblivious to the people of color all around them, free to enjoy the fruits of white supremacy with little thought of how they were achieved. Yet they depended, at every turn, on blacks' physical and psychic labor. Blacks, for their part, might create a separate world relatively free from white pressure or surveillance. But, except for the most independent members of the black middle class, none could escape the "felt menace of possible violence" or forgo working in white homes and businesses and shopping in white-owned stores. Almost no one, white or black, could avoid the "haunting sense of proximity," the "distanced nearness" that pervaded southern life.[79] The modern system of segregation was built person by person, encounter by encounter. And those encounters ranged across the whole spectrum of human possibility: desire, pleasure, or mutual respect could crop up in the most unlikely places, yet each interaction also created a mine-

field where laughter could turn to menace, love to loathing, camaraderie to insult and rejection. Weighing the past, anticipating the future,
reading the body and between the lines, black and white Southerners
created a hybrid, hierarchical culture with its own rituals, secrets, and
half-hidden meanings: a culture of Jim Crow.

"As soon as I could read," Katharine remembered, "I would carefully
spell out the notices in public places. I wished to be certain that we were
where we ought to be." It was easy for a white child to find the line sep-
arating "White" and "Colored" in some places, more difficult in others.
Streetcars were especially troublesome, as no wall or rail provided a tangible dividing line. If whites were standing in front, the conductor might
order blacks to give up their seats and move to the back, perhaps with
a tap on the shoulder, perhaps in a "loud rough voice so all could hear."
What should "a little white girl" do in such a situation? Stand quietly
in front? Or take some bone-weary woman's seat, glimpsing as she did
so "the still dark faces in the rear of the car, which seemed to stare so
expressionlessly into space"? The streets too could be hazardous. They
belonged to Katharine and her kind, yet they were also public space.
Sometimes a black child might hesitate for a moment before she stepped
aside. Should Katharine push and shove or should she give ground, avoid
a scene, let the moment pass?[80]

Longing, as all children do, to feel at one with her surroundings, she
clung more anxiously than ever to the bulwark of her parents' certainties
and protection. She tried to forget the dissonant image of violence in
the kitchen, at the center of her family's life. But never again could she
enfold herself quite so securely in their assumptions about the benevolence of patriarchy and the righteous superiority of their race. Never
again could home be so simply a safe, sheltering place. Her confidence
had been fissured as if by an earthquake, leaving on one side innocence
and trust and on the other mixed feelings and, faintly at first, the hair-
line cracks of doubt.[81]

KATHARINE'S FAITH IN her father eroded further when he ran for the
United States Senate in the Democratic primary of 1908. Wherever he
looked, William saw dangerous tendencies: demagogues like Ben Tillman and Coleman Blease, who railed against Negro domination in one

breath and "the old aristocracy" in the next, business-minded politicians who identified themselves with the Lost Cause but really cared only for "getting ahead." What these men had in common, William believed, was that, unlike the planter-statesmen of old, they pushed special interests instead of the good of the white South as a whole.[82]

Lumpkin had first stepped into the political maelstrom two years earlier when he challenged Tillman in the senatorial primary of 1906, an effort that drew a bit of welcome attention from William's home state. After a long list of the prominent men to whom William was distantly related, the author of a pamphlet on "famous Georgians" noted that "across the Savannah river W. W. Lumpkin, of South Carolina, is illustrating the family name in the Palmetto State, and the political seers have already assigned him in prophecy the senatorial toga."[83] Alas, that was not be: William withdrew from the race when confronted by Tillman's overwhelming popularity. In 1908 he stayed the course, traveling in tandem with eight candidates on a grueling barnstorming tour that took them to twenty-five towns in sixty-four days.[84]

This plunge into politics proved to be both quixotic and humiliating. William's candidacy, which had no discernible backing, testified, on the one hand, to his location at the peculiar intersection between New South enterprise and Old South gentility and, on the other, to the chaos of the South's one-party, post-disfranchisement political system. In the absence of any organized opposition, the Democratic Party became a morass of shifting factions with no regular means of recruiting candidates and little accountability to voters. The result was a free-for-all among Democratic politicians that generated spectacularly vituperative stump speeches but no real redress for the poor. Rhetoric was everything, and all but the most resolute business-oriented candidates tried to co-opt the language of Populism by portraying themselves as "horny-handed sons of toil."[85] Lumpkin infused that theme with his heartfelt, if incoherent, concerns. He vowed to represent the farmer, for "I was born and raised on a farm and hope to end my days on a farm," as well as the railroad workers and "commercial travelers," for he himself was a railroad worker and a "traveling man." Like all the other candidates, he spoke against trusts and tariffs, which benefited the North at the expense of the agricultural South. But the gallantry of Confederate veterans and the nobility of white southern womanhood remained his chief preoccupations. To that he added one point on which he stood alone: prohibition, an issue identified primarily with preachers and with women, who could not vote.[86]

On the hustings, the qualities that had always inspired his children's awe and admiration turned William into a holdover from another era, a "teller of tales" in a "Prince Albert coat, stiff-fronted shirt with studs, wing collar, black tie; a clean-shaven man, his thick gray hair worn *en pompadour* . . . long and swept back.[87] The Columbia newspaper, which had supported his short-lived candidacy in 1906, now damned him with faint praise. Reporters spoke of his oratorical skills; he was, they said "poetical, humorous and impressive." He was the "handsomest man in the race." But beyond that they could add only that he "made his usual patriotic speech."[88] E. D. Smith, later known as "Cotton Ed," a racist demagogue in the mold of Tillman and Blease with a long political career ahead of him, won hands down, while Coleman Blease steamed to victory in the gubernatorial race. Transfixed on the sidelines, the Lumpkin children could not miss "the eloquent fact" that their father came in next to last in a field of eight.[89]

Katharine was almost eleven when her father embarked on this mortifying campaign. A year later, William finally got his chance to recapture the chimera of his plantation past. In 1909, he scraped up the money for a down payment on a 200-acre farm near the tiny depot town of Killian in the Sand Hills, an area notorious for the barrenness of its soil and the destitution of its people. The Lumpkins' simple farmhouse was by far the most imposing for miles around. Their nearest neighbors, scattered along dirt roads in tiny shacks, were the poorest of the black and white rural poor: wage laborers, tenants renting other people's land, and sharecroppers who scraped by with "nothing, not even a mule or plow," working for landlords for a share of the crop.[90]

Like William's campaign for the Senate, this move could not have been less practical. William was sixty years old, and his children were venturing out on their own. His oldest son, Hope, was long gone. He had graduated from college and taken a divinity degree at a shrine to the Lost Cause: the Episcopal seminary at the University of the South (popularly known as Sewanee), where William's status as a descendent of an elite Georgia family and a "colonel" in the UCV earned him a place as a trustee.[91] Now he was married, serving as an assistant rector in

Charleston, and teaching at a military academy.[92] Alva, impatient with his father's pretensions and impracticality, had left home as soon as he could get away; he had just finished law school at the University of South Carolina and was working as an agent for the Georgia Railroad. He was about to join a law firm in the city and launch a lucrative law practice and successful political career. Morris was living with Alva at a boarding house and working for the Georgia Railroad as well.[93]

In 1908 Grace had enrolled at the College for Women, a small private school in Columbia. Located in a mansion that had once served as Wade Hampton's home and then as a convent for the Ursuline Nuns, the college had been founded as "The South Carolina Presbyterian Institute for Young Ladies" in 1890. By the time Grace arrived, the school had only a vestigial connection to the church, and it had the distinction of being led by a gifted woman. A native of Newberry, South Carolina, and the daughter of a Reformed Presbyterian minister, Euphemia McClintock had graduated from the Woman's College of Baltimore, renamed Goucher College in 1910. Always strapped for money, McClintock nevertheless managed to upgrade the school's dilapidated historic buildings; more important, she recruited the best teachers she could find.[94] Grace stayed for two years. An indifferent student, she was caught up in the sports that had taken women's colleges by storm. But she also published romantic short stories in the student magazine, a gratifying experience that suggested where her talents and ambitions might lie. At the end of two years, Alva scraped together enough money to allow her to transfer to Brenau, the better-appointed Georgia college Elizabeth had attended a decade before.[95]

That left Annette, Katharine, and seventeen-year-old Bryan to help William manage the farm. William bought a horse (Old Nelly, who, luckily, knew how to plow) and, with a black hired hand, prepared the fields for the cotton, corn, and sweet potatoes he planned to grow. He bought cows, chickens, and pigs. Soon, in Katharine's words, he would be "master in all things," as his father had been. He would ride "over his own acres, knowing every field, stream, hill, and pasture, as he knew the palm of his hand." Instead he died of throat cancer. He did not live to harvest a single crop.[96]

———

WITH WILLIAM GONE, Annette and her city-bred children faced the challenge of scratching out a living on a barren farm. At peak seasons, black laborers—men, women, and children alike—would do the most grueling labor. But Bryan would have to plow, plant the crops, and milk the cows. Katharine sometimes helped, dropping corn in the furrows behind the plow or crawling along between the rows to plant and water sweet potatoes by hand. Once she even tried to pick cotton, a task she thought would be easy enough since she had so often seen black children far younger than herself dragging their cotton sacks through her family's fields. She was shocked by how exhausting it was to bend and pick, bend and pick in the broiling sun.

Most of all she was shocked by the yawning gap between herself and the children she met at the local one-room, four-month school. South Carolina had one of the lowest literacy rates in the country; its leaders shunned compulsory education, required no certification for teachers, and provided no state-supported secondary education. Under those conditions, even city schools were inadequate; in much of the countryside they were dismal to nonexistent. Katharine's gingham dresses and black stockings, nothing special in Columbia, stood out against her classmates' faded calicos and hand-me-down overalls. She wore neat hightopped shoes; they came to school barefooted in summer and in winter wore ill-fitting brogans. Raggedy and reticent, they watched her warily. She, in turn, did her best to hide her learning, sensing, as she later put it, that she had a "pre-arranged advantage in a race which made me always win."[97]

Discomfiting as they were, Katharine's years in the Sand Hills offered a strange and wonderful freedom, an escape from the sheltering, constricting atmosphere in which she and her sisters had been reared. "Rather than have no companions . . . accustomed social distinctions were allowed to melt away," Katharine remembered. Bowing to necessity and lacking William's firm hand, Annette allowed Katharine to make friends with poor children and to come and go more freely than ever before.[98]

On Sundays, Annette and the children sometimes hitched up Old Nelly and drove twelve miles to the Church of the Good Shepherd, which had begun as a mission outpost of Trinity in northeast Columbia. There they joined a congregation made up of "worthy people of limited means," mostly mechanics, machinists, and other employees of the Charlotte, Columbia, and Augusta Railroad. But twelve miles was a long journey, so sometimes the family worshipped with their white rural neighbors at an unadorned little Baptist church so poor that it could afford only an itinerant preacher who came once a month. In truth, these were the Sundays that Katharine preferred. She wanted to meet the children whom she otherwise saw only at school, and she was fascinated by the severity and ardor of evangelicalism, with its focus on the sensational details of sin and public expressions of repentance and conversion, so different from the reserved formality of her upper-class Episcopalian faith.[99]

At the Church of the Good Shepherd all was familiar. In the country, Katharine found herself listening to long, fiery sermons aimed at igniting the defining passion of evangelicalism: the moment of emotional crisis and conversion when sinners came to Christ, accepting Jesus as their Lord and Savior and receiving assurance that they were among those destined not to burn in hell but to enjoy eternal life. In August, when the crops were laid by, came a week-long revival, the great event of the year. A classmate invited Katharine to sing in the choir. For weeks in advance, rumors about the coming drama swirled; even a child could "smell and taste the backwash of talk." There were men in the church who drank and threw dice. But these were "almost open sins, freely admitted when men and boys came up to be saved. For those 'living in sin' it was different. . . . Not the men involved, but the women, were outcast, and their children with them, if they were wrongly come by." Suspense focused especially on two of the area's most notorious sinners. The first was a "burly, drinking farmer" who had fathered a brood of illegitimate children whom he refused to support. Every summer, like clockwork, he repented when "the devil and hell and the fiery pit became too much for him." In sharp contrast stood "Miss Sarah," who had been "living in sin" for years but who refused to be shamed or saved. She stayed away from church throughout the year, but she came to revivals, walking proudly and asserting her claim to membership in the community of faith. Would these two repent and change their ways? Would they increase the harvest of the saved?[100]

Even Katharine found herself caught up in the atmosphere of suppressed excitement, curiosity, and fear. "Each night would come the invitation, climax of everything. The choir would begin its singing, at first softly. . . . The preacher would cry, 'Will you come?'" Katharine would watch anxiously. "Would they come? I never knew whether I wanted them to come or to resist this luring voice pushing against them:

Jesus is merciful,

Jesus will save. . . ."

Miss Sarah resisted. She would neither come forward nor bow her head in shame. "And after all was over, she left the church directly and alone, with dignity—it must be said, almost with condescension." Not so the red-faced farmer, "he of the brood of unclaimed children." Once again he came forward to be saved.[101]

"When the week was spent and all who could be brought to Christ had been, then remained only the baptism. On Saturday water was hauled in barrels to be poured by sweating men into the tomblike pool hidden beneath the pulpit. . . . The preacher descended into the water, and while we sang, took his quivering converts one after another, to dip them bodily in the rite of immersion, calling down the blessing of God on each one." If Katharine had been stirred by the long evenings of singing and praying and anxious waiting, she was not stirred now. "It was broad daylight of a hot August noonday; flies were buzzing around my face, yellow jackets zooming, my clothes were sticking to me uncomfortably with the oppressive heat."[102] When the service ended, she could hardly wait to climb into the buggy with Bryan and Annette and drive away home.

Still, for Katharine, as for all the participants, the revival served as a community-making event. No longer a stranger, she had a new circle of friends. And that circle expanded when Annette decided to send her to a better school, where one of the two teachers was rumored to have a high school diploma. It turned out, however, that the woman "knew no more Latin than we did, and studied it less." Worse, she was tyrannical and sycophantic by turns, currying favor with the children of the better-off farmers "even as she showed her true colors against the poorer children." Katharine and her friends, those better off-children, were determined to protect and avenge. "It took but a few occasions of her stinging ruler striking the cringing hands of helpless little boys and girls to launch us, who apparently had nothing to fear from her, on a year of joyous insubordination. . . . Nor were we long content with our own misdeeds . . . ; we found ways of leading our fellows astray while enabling them to escape retribution. If at long recess we should lead them all down to a stream so far away none of us could hear the bell and keep them there until she must come and get us, what could she do? Could we not plead plaintive innocence, and if this failed, how could she punish a whole school?"[103]

Intoxicated by her own daring and at her success in breaking through the "encrusted reticence" of the country children, Katharine embarked on bolder adventures. She persuaded Annette to let her go with Bryan to parties at neighboring farmers' homes. Soon she and her friends had decided to do the unthinkable: they would defy the church directly by organizing round dances at the Woodmen of the World's hall in town.[104]

"The rumble of the coming storm" began soon after the first dance. "When the preacher came for his monthly round, this was what he preached about. . . . Our companions became the butt of constant chiding, reproaches, outright demands to cease and desist for their very souls' sake." All year the children danced and all year the church leaders fulminated against them. By the time the yearly August revival began, these fulminations had taken their toll. Katharine got her first taste of ostracism when no one invited her to sing in the choir. Then she watched as her little band of rebels began to give in. "The very first night, the preacher, aflame at our arrogant wickedness, began his denunciation of our stiff-necked ways, our straying on the downward path, our risking our precious souls to eternal damnation. Each night it was the same. . . . Then it began. First one, then the other of our erstwhile companions . . . began to go down that fated aisle, tearful and contrite." After that, the Woodmen of the World's hall ceased to ring with the laughter of dancing children. Worse, even at school all the camaraderie was gone. When the penitents saw Katharine, they ducked their heads and spoke shyly, if at all. She found herself in the "ignominious isolation" she had feared.[105]

IN DECEMBER 1911, Katharine turned fifteen. Grace had returned from Brenau College the spring before and, with a "B.D." ("Bachelor's of Domesticity") degree in the new field of home economics, had found a job teaching at a newly opened grammar school in Columbia. With Alva's help, Annette was trying desperately to sell the family's heavily mortgaged farm. Restless and lonely, Katharine wanted to follow her sisters to school in the Georgia mountains. Again Annette looked to Alva, and together they signed a note enabling the youngest Lumpkin child to borrow the money she needed. Leaving for Brenau in January

1912, Katharine put the Sand Hills behind her, eager to embrace "the wide and expanding life toward which I could now turn my eyes."[106]

Yet something had begun in that desolate place: an uneasiness that would percolate to consciousness in the light of what she would later learn. Freed of her father's influence just as she reached adolescence, Katharine had seen things around her that she might not otherwise have seen. She watched the black field hands come and go as strangers, a far cry from the cheerful, devoted slaves whom her father's nostalgic stories had conjured up.[107] She was used to black poverty, but in the Sand Hills her white playmates were hobbled by a destitution that the logic of racial thinking could not excuse or explain.

Katharine had learned the meaning of whiteness—as a metaphor of family, a mark of privilege, and a boundary between herself and others that must, at all costs, be maintained—when she saw her father beat the cook. Now, to that secret glimpse of racial violence, she added a perception of grinding class inequity—a perception that would, in retrospect, lead her to see black poverty in a new light. For if white skin was no defense against immiseration, then racial inferiority could not explain the even deeper destitution of blacks.

"The Sand Hill religion," in particular, made Katharine "conscious of herself as a self": a separate being, an individual with her own angle of vision, her own contrarian judgments and ideas. She had grown up among church folk who saw card playing and dancing as civilized pleasures and looked with bemusement on commoners who took them to be threats to the immortal soul. For them, Sunday services did not entail endless sermons and extemporaneous prayers; they were a time for soaring, stately hymns and communal voices repeating the poetry of the Book of Common Prayer, followed perhaps by a spot of golf. As children came of age, they were confirmed in a solemn laying on of hands, not converted in a public release of longing and fear. All of this Katharine had simply accepted. Like white supremacy, religious complacency and class privilege were the air she breathed. But in the Sand Hills, "Beliefs suddenly loomed before my mind. I saw and heard what purported to be the same religion I believed in, but it seemed very changed."[108]

Katharine would never throw off the mantle of Episcopalian reserve. But she would also never again rest easy in the church's assumed superiority, its too comfortable routines. In similar fashion, the unstable authority of an ill-educated, hard-pressed teacher cracked the façade of adult infallibility and made Katharine aware of her own powers. Faced with injustice perpetrated by a cruel but cowardly adult, she could have reacted in any number of ways. As it happened, she learned the possibility of rebellion and the pleasure of using her class and educational advantages in others' behalf. The result was an inkling of the activist teacher and writer she would become.

By the time she left for Brenau College, Katharine later claimed, "I was by no means entirely at home with my old heritage. Enough had gone on in the time-and-place limits of my short lifetime to disturb this seeming rapport. It could have come to nothing, of course—a passing flurry of doubts, and then forgetfulness. Perhaps it would have come to very little if I had chanced to be a student in less dynamic years."[109]

"CONTRARY STREAMS
OF INFLUENCE"

Aᴛᴛᴇɴᴅɪɴɢ ʙʀᴇɴᴀᴜ ᴄᴏʟʟᴇɢᴇ ꜰᴏʀ ᴛᴡᴏ ʏᴇᴀʀꜱ ᴀᴛ ᴛʜᴇ
cusp of the twentieth century, Elizabeth Lumpkin had taken advantage
of a women's oratorical movement and parlayed her studies into a brief
college teaching career. Eleven years later, in 1910, Grace opted for a
self-consciously modern domestic science curriculum, also designed for
women, and she squeezed the whole program into two semesters. Neither
Elizabeth nor Grace recorded her memories of the school, and Elizabeth
left virtually no trace in the college's few surviving early records. In contrast, Katharine spent close to "six crucial years in mental development"
at the college and wrote evocatively about that experience in her autobiography.[1] Arriving in the spring of 1912, she took preparatory courses to
make up for the deficiencies of South Carolina's abysmal public schools,
then opted for a liberal arts curriculum aimed at a "systematic, rational and scholarly course of study" covering all branches of knowledge
and leading to a bachelor of arts degree. She gravitated especially to
the new social sciences, which assumed that education should encourage
innovation and critical thinking rather than the perpetuation of received
knowledge. She stayed on after graduation, serving as the first secretary
(or salaried director) of Brenau's chapter of the Young Women's Christian Association (YWCA).[2]

For her Brenau was a delight and a revelation, although at first her pleasure rested on the dangerous seductions of home. After all, she was not only following her sisters; she was also returning to Georgia, where reminders of her illustrious ancestors were thick on the ground. Her own family had lived briefly in Gainesville, where Brenau was located, when William was assigned to work at the railroad depot in town. She could "feel a sense of history here—our own family history. . . . The townspeople were like my people in speech and manner and thought and action," Katharine remembered. "Their ways had all the warm familiarity of the ways of my upbringing. Their likes and antagonisms were the old likes and antagonisms which were then my own." The streets, with their canopies of oaks and elms, and the "easy, slow-moving give-and-take" of the business section—where textile workers mingled with farmers, Brenau students flirted with gray-uniformed Riverside Military Academy men, horse-drawn carriages vied with a scattering of automobiles, and "time waited on the human amenities"—reminded Katharine that she was among her "own kind."[3]

In this snug surround, the disquiet that Katharine had brought from the Sand Hills could have receded in memory, buried beneath what she called "the thick overlay of the old-ways-are-right in which we Southern students were encased." Instead, it was re-remembered, and with that re-remembering her identity was redefined. "All beginnings contain an element of recollection," writes the anthropologist Paul Connerton. Looking back in *The Making of a Southerner*, Katharine would tell a story both of remembering and of awakening: the slow, conscious and unconscious turning of a young girl toward a woman's abiding desires, commitments, and aspirations.[4]

BRENAU HAD BEEN FOUNDED in 1878, at the start of a second wave of southern educational reform.[5] After freedom, African Americans, who had been denied the right to read and write, put their faith in education, along with land ownership and the right to vote, as a route to full participation in American life. As members of Reconstruction legislatures, they fought to establish public schools for whites and blacks alike. They also clamored for admission to and helped to establish the region's first colleges for African Americans, most of which were sponsored by northern missionaries after the war. Redemption curtailed this black-led crusade, stunting opportunities for blacks and poor whites and ensuring that by the time Brenau opened its doors the South was suffering under a far higher illiteracy rate than any other region.[6]

Those conditions inspired southern reformers and northern philanthropists to band together in behalf of a new wave of educational reform centered on preparing white children to make their way in a mobile, print-oriented world. To forward such learning, they built schoolhouses, lengthened school terms, enforced compulsory education, and inaugurated new forms of pedagogy that replaced rote memorization with child-centered learning. Male leaders looked to women both as allies and as teachers whose cheap labor could underwrite these educational innovations. To produce those well-prepared teachers, they argued, the South had to provide higher education, not just for the elite but also for the daughters of poor and middling folk. To that end, educators raised the academic standards of the region's older women's colleges, founded new same-sex liberal arts institutions, and created a system of normal schools aimed specifically at preparing women for paid work.[7]

This broadening of white women's educational opportunities was promoted by town leaders who saw both private and public women's colleges as good investments, markers of civic progress, and a means of advertising their daughters' accomplishments and solidifying their class position. Perched advantageously at the base of the Blue Ridge Mountains, Gainesville served as the seat of Hall County, the primary destination for market-bound farmers throughout northeast Georgia, and the educational and industrial hub of the region. To a wide swath of the community, Brenau's campus was a badge of urbanity, just like the hydroelectric plant and the recently paved streets.[8]

Women sought access to education for their own reasons. Annette Lumpkin's generation had been the first in the South to turn to teaching, not just as a last resort, but as a means of postponing marriage and clinging to the world of books and ideas they had discovered in their youth. The next generation feminized the teaching profession, rapidly replicating a change that had occurred in the Northeast and Midwest from the 1820s to the 1850s. Before the Civil War women comprised less than 25 percent of the South's teachers. The 1880s saw a dramatic shift. By 1900, when Elizabeth arrived at Brenau, 60 percent of teachers were women, closing the gap between the North and South.[9] Also during this period, women pressed—mostly in vain—for admission to the South's all-male state colleges and universities.[10] And in small but growing numbers, aspiring girls like the Lumpkin sisters began to dream of intellectual vocations and professional careers.

Brenau drew the bulk of its students from relatively well-off and well-educated families. Most students' fathers were businessmen, professionals, or farmers, and, at least by the early 1930s when the first surveys were undertaken, half of these men had attended college, as had half of students' mothers. Yet the school had initially been committed to keeping costs low. That began to change in 1900, when the college was purchased by Dr. Haywood Jefferson Pearce, who was among the small cadre of American educators holding doctorates from German institutions. By the 1910s, when Grace and Katharine matriculated, President Pearce was explaining to the parents of prospective students why Brenau's amenities, including the "elegance of the dormitories and the excellent character of the cuisine," justified rising costs, which averaged $200 a year. Still, in comparison to other schools Brenau continued to be relatively affordable. And the wall between town and gown remained extremely permeable, at least as far as the white middle class was concerned. Contributions from local supporters sustained the college, examinations and recitations were open to the public, commencement was a major community affair, and summer Chautauquas—the wildly popular educational summer camps that dotted the countryside at the turn of the century—took place on Brenau's grounds.[11]

Still, accessibility went only so far. The daughters of the poorer farmers and the burgeoning population of textile workers went to work, not to college. Nor, it went without saying, did Brenau open its doors to black women, whatever their means. Even the Eastern women's colleges (except for Wellesley) discriminated against black students in admittance or housing. But Brenau proved to be especially recalcitrant. It did not admit its first black student until 1973, over a half century after Katharine graduated and after most other southern institutions had been desegregated.[12] As a student, Katharine saw this absence as perfectly natural. Indeed, she had been raised to view even segregated black colleges with suspicion: they made blacks ambitious and impudent, the opposite of the "good darkey" of whom the Lumpkins approved. Growing up in Columbia, she had seen the Allen University students who marched past her family in their Sunday best as a threat. These young black men's fine clothes and dignified bearing, she remembered, spelled "aspirations not encompassed in our beliefs about their 'rightful place.'"[13]

Gainesville boasted no such educational institutions; it had only one public school for blacks, where children were crammed three or four to a desk and expenditures per pupil averaged half of those for whites. As they did across the South, African Americans responded by building their own schoolhouses, doing their heroic best to make up for such glaring disparities with their own limited resources. By the 1910s, they had created two private institutions, one of which was founded by an extraordinary young black woman named Beulah Rucker. A child of former slaves, Rucker had put herself through high school by milking cows and cleaning houses. With little but her diploma to rely on, she had then thrown her belongings in a wagon and headed for Gainesville to fulfill her dream of lighting what she called "a torch of instruction for my race." There she became a leading figure in one of the largest black communities in the Georgia upcountry, a region where, in rural areas, whites outnumbered blacks by more than four to one.[14]

Known as a relatively safe haven from the violence that hounded blacks in the region, Gainesville saw its black population mushroom during the fall of Katharine's freshman year, when whites enraged by an alleged rape drove African Americans out of the surrounding country-side. The vast majority of these refugees worked as cooks, laundresses, and day laborers. But Gainesville's black community also sustained a small middle class of teachers, ministers, and businessmen as well as its own theater, restaurants, churches, fraternal orders, barbershops, and stores. Huddled on the southeast edge of town, as far as possible from the posh white neighborhood anchored by Brenau, this black world remained even more distant from Katharine's consciousness than it had been at home.[15]

Not long after Katharine made her way to Brenau, Juliette Derri-cotte, the most charismatic of the small band of southern black activ-ists Katharine was destined to encounter, sped from Athens, Georgia, toward Alabama's Talladega College in a "dirty Jim Crow car." Like Katharine, Derricotte was born in 1897. Her father was a cobbler; her mother, who was apparently white, drove what Juliette later saw as a hard bargain with life, trading resignation to her own narrow lot for opportunities for "Jule," who, like her mother as a girl, longed to "go far and far into that fascinating world of books, that always-beyond land of learning." Juliette wanted to attend Athens's Lucy Cobb Institute, a private girls' school run by Mildred Rutherford, the Historian General of the UDC, whose green lawns and red brick buildings she passed every day on her way to elementary school. She learned "the bitterness of color" when her white mother had to tell her tall, sandy-skinned daughter that she could not go to Lucy Cobb because she was black. When it came time for college, however, Juliette's mother made a way out of no way; the whole family pitched in, stretching pennies "until they made a road to a college door."[16]

Talladega, a coeducational institution founded by local blacks and the American Missionary Association after the Civil War, was directed by white New Englanders who believed in the intellectual capacities of the ex-slaves. W. E. B. Du Bois summed up the enormous accomplishments of such institutions: "In a single generation they put thirty thousand black teachers in the south," a large proportion of whom were women, helping to "[wipe] out the illiteracy of the majority of the black people of the land."[17] At the close of the nineteenth century, black colleges faced new and often overwhelming challenges. Donations to the missionary societies' work in the South began to dry up, and northern philanthropists, in league with southern educational reformers, increasingly tied their support to vocational training. Talledega survived to become a first-rate liberal arts college, and Derricotte, who was one of the first women on the debate team, president of the YWCA, and the valedictorian of her class, was the school's "most important girl."[18]

KATHARINE PLAYED A strikingly similar role at Brenau, although she could not have imagined such a parallel. Rummaging through the jumble of documents that constituted the school's archives when I first arrived on the scene, I found Katharine everywhere.[19] Indeed, those compendiums of photographs, mementos of student life, glimpses of pecking orders, nicknames and pranks (so predictable, so touching) showed almost too much of Katharine's future development in embryo. I had to resist the feeling that the tender beginnings of everything that happened later in her life could be seen here. I had to remind myself—as, in *The Making of a Southerner*, Katharine would always remind her readers—that the twig is never finally and surely bent, that her life could have unfolded very differently after she left Brenau.

Following her tracks, I quickly understood why she so valued her intellectual and sentimental undergraduate education. As she would later discover to her consternation, even Brenau's most demanding course of study did not count for much in the eyes of the Southern Association of College Women, an accrediting agency that took the New England women's colleges as its gold standard: it considered a bachelor's degree from Brenau to be the equivalent of just one year of college work in those four-year institutions.[20] Assuming the inferiority of southern women's schools, historians of education have long followed suit, writing brilliantly about women's private liberal arts colleges in the Northeast, but providing relatively few of the fine-grained studies that would allow us to understand how successive generations of black and white southern women have changed themselves and their region by seizing the opportunities that higher education provided. Brenau has rated barely a mention even in the relatively sparse literature on southern women's education.[21] Yet by viewing it at close range and in its own context, rather than comparing it to the nation's oldest, most expensive, and most richly documented women's colleges, I came to see this small, obscure school in the mountains less as a pale imitation of a New England model than as an incubator of intellectual open-mindedness and aspiration, at least for Katharine and an intrepid minority of her peers.

That was so in part because Brenau was a more cosmopolitan institution than its size and location might suggest. Although Georgia provided the vast majority of its 370 students, the school drew young women not only from across the South but also from across the country. A smattering even came from abroad. Thomas Jackson Simmons, co-president of the college from 1910 to 1913, and his wife, Lessie Southgate Simmons, an opera singer who headed the voice department, traveled around the world, and they brought back many of the artifacts that decorated the school's parlors and filled its museum. Like other orientalists, they were collecting exotic specimens as spectacles for Western consumption. But the Simmonses, along with other faculty members, were also genuinely committed to fostering "a deeper sense of international citizenship" and "an intelligent interest in all the countries of the world."[22]

The word "Brenau," according to the Brenau Creed, meant "refined gold," and school officials were quick to assert that "refinement means fundamental culture and not merely that which comes from reading."[23] To that end they exposed the students to a dizzying array of cultural events, including elaborate plays, concerts by the New York Symphony Orchestra in which Brenau music students participated, and speakers of many stripes. Those whom Katharine must have heard ranged from Southerners like the UDC's Mildred Rutherford, decked out as a matron of the 1850s and speaking on "The South of Yesteryear," to nationally known figures such as Robert La Follette, Wisconsin's Progressive governor, and Helen Keller, famous for her triumph over disability and also a fervent socialist and advocate of birth control.[24]

Once a year, Brenau students took the train en mass to Atlanta's new auditorium-armory to attend a performance of the Metropolitan Opera, one of the city's two major cultural events, each of which catered to different aspects of the white urban South's musical tastes. The opera, which chose Atlanta as its only out-of-town venue and played for a full week every year to sold-out crowds, was supported by the city's vigorous women's clubs, which were responsible for the classical music scene. The city's second major event, which most definitely did not appear on Brenau's social calendar, was the Georgia Old Time Fiddlers' Convention, a boisterous, male-dominated gathering that attracted farmers and mill workers as well as members of the city's elite, many of whom saw "old time music"—which was in fact a product of commercialization and urbanization—as a link to a distinctively southern but vanishing rural past.[25]

Reveling in these cultural riches, Katharine fell in at once with a serious crowd, not the debutantes "of family" but students who meant to "do something" after college. She gravitated to the social science curriculum, which was stirring excitement on college campuses as it gradually displaced the combination of classical studies, modern languages, history, literature, music, and the arts that had prevailed from the antebellum period through Elizabeth's day.[26] Her group's mentor was Samuel Gayle Riley, a shy, overworked professor who arrived at Brenau in 1899 and taught there off and on until 1920. He was in charge of all the history courses and, by the time Katharine matriculated, had introduced courses in political science, sociology, and economics as well. Riley was a preacher's son and a devout Baptist who had attended Georgetown College in Kentucky, then gone on to Princeton, where he received bachelor's and master's degrees. After studying law at the University of Michigan, he settled into a career of teaching at various small colleges in the South. He belonged to a new generation of southern intellectuals, often educated in the North and occasionally abroad, who were bringing a critical cast of mind and a familiarity with modern intellectual trends to colleges and universities across the region. These young men (very few southern women could secure jobs in higher education) shared a commitment to racial moderation, sectional reconciliation, and progress through education.[27]

"So far as I was concerned," Katharine wrote, "this one man was my education."[28] Brenau students christened Mr. Riley the school's "hardest," "most profound," and "most exacting" teacher and quaked at his examinations, which demanded that they think in a "historical, connected and general manner." He introduced courses on "Woman in Modern Society" and the "Social Aspect of Child Life," took students to visit settlement houses and factories, and directed their attention to "such practical questions as charities, factory legislation, the labor movement, woman's work and wages, [and] child labor." He favored Progressive historians such as James Harvey Robinson and Charles Beard, who emphasized economic conflict and looked to the emerging social sciences to provide new tools for historians.[29] He also assigned the works of the philosopher John Dewey, who cast aside his predecessors' stress on deterministic natural laws and a priori truths in favor of experience and reflection.

To William and Annette Lumpkin's generation, history was the story of the heroic accomplishments of individual leaders, and God's will or the laws of nature—which amounted to the same thing—could be discerned in the fortunes of individuals and nations. Turn-of-the-century scientific historians put their faith in facts rather than laws, but they too assumed that great men drove history on its forward course. Mr. Riley had written his master's thesis not on one of the political or institutional topics favored by the scientific historians but on the Cherokees of Georgia. In his hands, society ceased to be a congeries of individual atoms, and history became an evolutionary process determined by social and economic dynamics whose causal relationships a smart young woman could decipher. Like Annette Lumpkin's legendary tutor, who had made her "feel the worth of her mind," he demanded that Katharine and her friends "use our minds, go to the sources, have no truck with undocumented hearsay, keep our eyes always on the vast play of forces."[30]

The contradictions at the heart of women's education encouraged that critical stance. The originators of women's colleges broke with tradition by basing institutions of higher education on the premise that women's minds were equal to men's. But they also scrambled to reassure nervous parents that education would not endanger their daughters' virtue or diminish their femininity. Brenau's President Pearce exemplified this tension. His homilies to the students encouraged the rejection of confining roles. "I am glad," he announced,

> that a new day for woman is already dawning—a day in which woman is to be a co-partner with man in the great business of life. Under this new order of things, with unshackled mind and unfettered spirit she will contribute her share toward the solution of the great problems of life and civilization. . . . I am not one of those who believe that woman's only place is a keeper of the home and her only function that of mother. . . . Under this new order, woman will be . . . independent of man.

At the same time, Pearce included in the "Brenau Creed" the assertion that "a woman's mind and soul are just as feminine as her body and that her mental habiliment should be adapted to her feminine nature."[31] Through its curriculum, its elaborate rules, and its homelike atmosphere, Brenau aimed to ensure that adaptation.

The domestic science program that Grace Lumpkin had followed exemplified this effort to reconcile higher education with tradition. During the first decade of the twentieth century, home economics courses sprang up at colleges across the country, reflecting the aims of reformers who wanted to reorganize the home along scientific lines and professionalize women's traditional work. They believed that refashioning housekeeping as a scientific enterprise would cure poverty and other social ills, and they saw the haphazard lower-class housekeeper as the chief impediment to their goals. The select women's colleges, North and South, resisted this innovation; they had fought too hard to establish women's right to a strenuous academic curriculum. Brenau touted its embrace of domestic science as a sign of practicality and progress, attacking "self-satisfied but nevertheless uninformed housekeepers" in language that mirrored that of the new American Home Economics Association. It designed its program both for students who wanted to carve out new careers and for those who were preparing "for the life which is distinctly womanly." In deference to a clientele of middle- and

"Oriental Parlor," Brenau College, Brenau Bulletin, *April 1913.*

upper-class white Southerners who still depended on black women to perform laborious household tasks, the school emphasized that the new curriculum aimed "to train the head of the home—not cooks, but those who are to direct cooks, and who should know more about cooking than any cook knows."[32]

BRENAU'S BUILT ENVIRONMENT signaled its desire to open new possibilities to women while ensuring that they would not venture too far. Viewed from the outside, Yonah, Bailey, and Pearce Halls could be taken for prisons or asylums. Inside, they mimicked grand homes, with theme-decorated Italian, Egyptian, and Oriental parlors separated by staircases from the classrooms and private "sleeping apartments" above. Pearce Auditorium, modeled on a European opera house, offered the school's most impressive interior: an elaborately carved staircase, red plush seats, gilt railings, a pipe organ, stained glass windows, and a huge ceiling fresco of Aeneas at the court of Dido. Next door stood Simmons Memorial Hall, built during Katharine's day to house the library and the YWCA. With its fluted Ionic columns, symmetrical design, and interior of marble and tile, Simmons perfectly embodied the neoclassical revival that altered the nation's town- and cityscapes at the turn of the century in tandem with the South's commemoration of the Lost Cause. The fourth major building was Overton Hall, which housed the conservatory of music, art, and oratory. Each night, dressed for six o'clock dinner, students promenaded two-by-two with their special female friends around Yonah Hall's recreation room arcade. Students and faculty then gathered in the adjacent dining room, where a teacher sat at the head of each table, a small orchestra played in the background, and black waiters in uniforms glided quietly to and fro. Across the street from the entrance to the college stood Grace Episcopal Church, which each of the three Lumpkin sisters dutifully attended in accordance with the school's strict rules mandating daily chapel on campus and Sunday worship at a church in town.[33]

By the 1910s, the forces of modernity were competing with these traditions, positioning students on the brink of a new moral, sexual, and aesthetic independence. Dress had always been a bone of contention. The founders had been determined to "avoid occasion of mortification and envy" by requiring both rich and poor students to wear uniforms of "Shepherd's plaid calico" with gingham sunbonnets. On Sundays students donned black alpaca suits and hats, and for concerts and graduation they wore inexpensive white muslin. Over time uniforms disappeared, but the administration continued to condemn "expensive dressing."[34] Grace, Katharine, and their peers delighted in annoying their teachers by embracing simplicity with a vengeance, often showing up for breakfast in crumpled middies and dirty tennis shoes. Dubbing themselves the "Early Risers," Grace and her group posed for the 1911 yearbook with irreverent yawns and half-closed eyes.[35]

Brenau officials encouraged "literary and dramatic interpretation" on the grounds that they forwarded an intimate understanding of great literature. For many students, however, the chief attraction of Brenau's constant round of plays, pageants, and impersonations was the opportunity to appropriate and perform an array of female types. Inundated by new technologies of image production, a rage for classification, and a belief that physical characteristics offered clues to inner character, turn-of-the-century Americans were fascinated by such ideal types, especially permutations on the "American girl." Versions of this icon varied enormously, ranging from the female figure as a symbol of the Republic to the politicized New Woman. To be seen at all, women had to represent themselves in conventional guises; the challenge lay in how to use images promulgated by others as avenues to self-definition.[36]

Isabel Archer in Henry James's *Portrait of a Lady* posed the question succinctly: "Am I what I wear? . . . Am I what I appear to society or am I my own unique self?"[37] The bride, the suffragette, the nurse, the actress, the artist, the automobile girl, the athletic girl, the school teacher, the old maid—these were just a few of the images Brenau students tried on for size. The brightly colored illustrations in the yearbooks became more daring in the 1910s: depicting women dressed in long loops of pearls and off-the-shoulder, spaghetti-strap evening gowns, they suggest how far Katharine's generation had come from the calico and gingham required of students twenty years before.[38] One thing, however, held steady: the ideal American girl was white and native born.

The challenge for the college lay in how to simultaneously foster and monitor such experimentation. By 1899, when Elizabeth was studying at Brenau, the administration had already replaced its "old system of espionage," in which faculty members spent their time ferreting out misbehavior, with what it called a "system of self-governance." After all, administrators reasoned, depriving a girl of the opportunity to take responsibility for her own behavior had "a tendency to dwarf her character" and leave her unfit for "the near future which she must meet, ofttimes unsupported and alone." Students deemed immature and irresponsible continued to be hedged about by intricate rules. The rest, classed as "self-governing" or "privileged girls," could leave the campus without a faculty chaperone until six in the evening and entertain gentlemen callers in the parlors for one hour, one night a week. Enforced by student honor councils that reported to a discipline committee of the faculty, this system sought to give the administration insight into the attitudes of the students and require them to watch over one another. This they did, dutifully judging and punishing their peers' infractions. But they also created a student culture that had its own values and standards.[39]

The result was an ongoing tug-of-war in which the faculty meted out punishments and negotiated with the student government over expanding pockets of freedom, while individual students stretched the rules as they lost their privileges and then won them back again. In a 1901 cartoon in the campus yearbook, "Miss New Girl" says, "Pray tell me what is the good of being on the self-governed list?" "Miss Old Girl" replies, "Why, you see, it gives the Faculty the satisfaction of thinking that you won't break the rules."[40] And break the rules the students did. By the 1910s, transgressions abounded, ranging from turning up late for breakfast to skipping classes, weekday chapel, or Sunday church, to cheating on exams and lingering at ice cream parlors to flirt with Riverside Academy cadets. Even Katharine lost her privileges due to unexcused absences during her second year.[41]

Grace had engaged in similar skirmishes. The administration had always promoted ladylike exercise, but it viewed intercollegiate team sports with trepidation. Like their peers everywhere during the 1910s, Brenau students—dressed in their ubiquitous middies—played roughly, cheered passionately, and competed keenly. Field Day, with its races and contests, was a major event on the social calendar, as were tennis tournaments and hockey, basketball, and baseball games. As she had at Columbia's College for Women, Grace made the basketball squad. Not content with these intramural campus events, Grace's class petitioned the administration to allow them to compete with teams from other schools. The administration resisted, but within a few years had to give in.[42]

The offense that brought the harshest punishment was clandestine joyriding with a man. At the end of her junior year, Katharine, speaking up for the underdog, made an unusual appearance before the faculty, which seldom included students in its deliberations. Three of her friends, it seemed, had sneaked away from campus for an automobile ride. They had pleaded guilty, promised "to be blameless in the future," and thrown "themselves on the mercy of the faculty." Katharine repeated the student honor council's recommendation for leniency, citing extenuating circumstances. The faculty expelled one of the students but placed the others on probation and took away their privileges. As part of their punishment, the president announced the girls' fate from the rostrum at chapel the following week.[43]

By the time Katharine was a senior, the matrons and chaperones who had supervised the dormitories and sororities earlier in the century had given way to young, unmarried counselors, and the faculty began to suggest that erring students might need not only punishment but also psychological evaluation. Senior privileges expanded in 1914, and by 1916 they included attending movies in town, albeit only on Friday nights and with the proviso that the faculty had to approve of the "character of the pictures to be shown." In the 1920s, the faculty would give up its attempt to prevent unchaperoned strolls and ice cream parlor gatherings and concentrate on holding the line against such grave improprieties as drinking, necking, and spending the night in private houses in town.[44]

Within this sequestered environment, the chief purpose of which was to keep young women away from men, students created an intricate, inward-looking social world composed of special friendships and confidences shared only among themselves. The demands of the classroom competed with an all-absorbing array of clubs, rituals, teas, midnight feasts, and all-female dances. Sororities maintained their own houses, staged informal entertainments, and governed themselves through a Panhellenic association. "The life," as students called it, sharpened genteel social skills, but it also taught unintended lessons: how to exercise leadership, compete openly, and act collectively—how, in short, to exercise the very competences and prerogatives most tenaciously associated with men.[45]

When the 1914 yearbook editors divided the sophomore class into diligent "brass tacks" and lackadaisical "rusty nails," they placed Katharine among the brass tacks. She was a girl who would do

All her own work and another girl's too,
Fill in the vacancy made by some fraud,
Shoulder the task which none will applaud,
Get up a program or write a new song. . . .

Vigorous, ready to work, eager to take the lead—those qualities, which had left her isolated in the Sand Hills, now won her the admiration of her teachers and peers.[46]

In *The Making of a Southerner*, Katharine remarks in passing that she was among the "student leaders" but gives no details that would distinguish her from the common run of her peers. The Brenau yearbooks, on the other hand, suggest that, like Juliette Derricotte at Talladega, she was indeed one of Brenau's "most important" girls. She was elected president of the freshman and sophomore classes, the literary society, and the athletic association. She led the tennis team. She was chosen by the faculty for membership in Phi Beta Sigma, a national honorary sorority, and immediately tapped by the Brenau chapter of Phi Mu, a sorority of which Grace had been a founding member and in which she remained active after she left the school.[47] In her senior year—the jewel in her crown—she was elected by the student body to serve as president of the YWCA.

Such campus leaders set the rhythm of student life, which turned on local loyalties and national identifications, home and away. The spring "States Day Pageant" was one of the big events of the year, surpassed in pomp and circumstance only by commencement. As president of the South Carolina Club (as Grace had been before her), Katharine helped to organize the festivities. With most students in clubs affiliated with their home state and the rest gathered into a "Northern Club," the whole student body spent days creating elaborate floats, songs, and banners, then paraded through the campus and out into the surrounding residential streets with a band playing both "Dixie" and "Yankee Doodle Dandy." In a grand finale, everyone sang "The Star-Spangled Banner" beneath a placard emblazoned "Reunited." Celebrating the diversity of the student body even as they represented the nation as a federation of almost-sovereign states, Katharine and her friends embraced both states' rights and national reconciliation.[48]

In all these ways, campus life raised Katharine's sights above the boundaries of Georgia and South Carolina, underscoring her membership in an imagined national community without directly challenging her regional loyalties. But it would take something stronger than secular student activities, and even more forceful than the new ways of thinking that Katharine was learning in class, to infuse student culture with what proved to be its deepest and most far-reaching spiritual and political meanings. For Katharine and other students like her, that something was a new faith: the social gospel, which was brought to Brenau by the traveling professional secretaries of the YWCA, emissaries of a women's movement that reached around the globe. To Katharine, the Y offered a religious message that would have "eruptive consequences." It also provided models of independent womanhood and pathways for engagement with the wider world.[49]

BEGINNING IN THE mid-nineteenth century, middle-class women in the United States and Britain began forming local Young Women's Christian Associations. Their goal was to save the souls, strengthen the bodies, and preserve the sexual virtue of young, native-born women fleeing the farms and flocking to the cities in search of wage-earning work. Spurred by worries about vulnerable "women adrift" and by a belief in the unique moral responsibilities of women like themselves, YWCA members stationed themselves at ports and train depots to prevent newcomers from falling into the hands of scheming men. They opened inexpensive boarding houses modeled on middle-class homes; provided residents with meals, employment referrals, libraries, and gymnasiums; and organized Bible study groups and religious services.[50]

By the 1870s, a separate organization had emerged on college campuses, mainly at church-related schools in the Midwest. These student Ys focused more single-mindedly than the city locals on converting individuals and encouraging them to bear witness to their faith. Participating alongside the Young Men's Christian Association (YMCA) in the Student Volunteer Movement for Foreign Missions and the World Student Christian Federation, an umbrella group for national student associations, the student YWCA sent hundreds of emissaries abroad, where they taught in mission schools run by church boards and served with missionaries in hospitals and relief agencies.[51]

These separate city and college strands united in 1906 under the leadership of Grace Dodge, a visionary philanthropist and social reformer. The new organization, the YWCA of the U.S.A., developed a weblike structure in which a national board headquartered in New York guided but could not dictate the activities of local affiliates. The board was made up of professional secretaries and volunteers elected at national conventions. The association was organized into interest groups and geographical fields.[52]

After the turn of the century, city Ys began spreading slowly in the South. Following the path of industrialization and urbanization, they provided settlement house–like services in a region with few welfare programs and no robust settlement house tradition. Student chapters proliferated at both black institutions and white women's colleges. Along with their YMCA counterparts, these nonsectarian, student-led groups held a near monopoly on campus religious life. They also provided many of the student services that would later be assumed by colleges themselves.[53]

As on many college campuses, until 1906 the Brenau YWCA was a strictly local affair. Once it affiliated with the unified organization, however, its leaders began to see themselves as part of a national and even international movement. It sponsored a Japanese student, who came to Brenau to prepare for missionary work in her own country. It held freshman receptions, vesper services, and Bible and mission study classes, all of which inducted "new girls" into campus life and bound students to each other and to the institution.[54] Student life revolved around elaborate hierarchies and cliques, which were promoted not only by sororities, but also by the fact that dormitory rooms mirrored class status. "The wealthier classes of the South," explained the administration, "demand for their daughters the conveniences of life to which they have been accustomed at home."[55] At the top of the pecking order were the stylish debutantes; then came the "all-around" girls like Katharine, who ran the student organizations; and finally the poor scholarship girls and the "grinds" who clung in obscurity to the bottom rungs.[56] In contrast, the YWCA embraced practically all of Brenau's predominantly Protestant student body and may have included Catholic and Jewish students as well, especially during the years around World War I, when the association became increasingly identified with its secular activities rather than with its Christian roots. Certainly, the Y fostered an ecumenical spirit, a "broader and higher vision" that took young women beyond state boundaries, small-town class distinctions, sorority cliques, and sectarian squabbles, emphasizing instead broadly Christian and democratic values.[57]

In her first published work, an essay in the student yearbook, Katharine recounted her introduction to the group. She had been an "obscure little Freshman" when she stepped from the train. There to greet her at the Gainesville depot were the friendly members of the YWCA. Soon these older girls were encouraging her to join "important committees"; then younger girls began coming to *her* for advice. Four years later, she was elected president of the YWCA because of her "willing service from the first." "The YWCA," Katharine concluded, "is molding many like this. It 'discovers' girls who would never be known. It gives the opportunity for all to show what is in them. It gives every girl an equal chance. It teaches how to live."[58]

How to live—that was the question. For Katharine, the answer came in what she called "an infinitely attractive guise." She had already been torn loose from her childhood religious moorings. Now, guided by the national YWCA secretaries who visited the college, she and her friends began to incorporate into their study groups the foundational writers of liberal Christianity, especially Walter Rauschenbusch, whose *Christianity and the Social Crisis* (1907) was one of the most influential books of its time, and Harry Emerson Fosdick, the popular theologian "who," Katharine remembered, "was then the flaming 'modernist' in most southern religious minds." In this covert curriculum's transforming light, students found themselves doubting the literal interpretations of the Bible on which they had been raised. They glimpsed the idea that the Bible was a historical document, a record of the religious and social development of a people. Trying to reconcile religion with Darwinian science, they drew parallels between the evolution of species and the evolutionary emergence of a just society.[59]

Caught up in soul-searching conversations, enthralled by books, listening to YWCA secretaries who were less interested in individual conversion than in social transformation, young women arrived at a new understanding of what Brenau students called "Everyday Christianity." At its center stood a God not of judgment but of love, an immanent being whose kingdom of universal brotherhood could be realized on earth.[60] Seekers after this "new heaven," Katharine remembered, did not preach "a call to repentance such as revivalists might sound. There was no 'wrath of Jehovah' here, or 'sins of the fathers visited unto the third and fourth generation,' no hint of a vengeful Deity." But neither did they issue a call to "staid duty." Infusing old words with new meanings, they portrayed God as a loving father and Jesus as a gentle teacher who refused to recognize social distinctions and whose example could be followed in this world. The infinite, God-given worth of each person; the Kingdom of God as a new social order; the injunction to act with "Christian consistency" by harmonizing values and action, means and ends—these were the principles and precepts that galvanized Katharine and her friends. "Let this religion spread," she believed, "and it could be potent to transform the world by changing the men who made it. To some of us these were little short of John-on-Patmos voices—'And I saw a new heaven and a new earth: for the first heaven and the first earth were passed away.'" Likening herself to Jesus's disciple after his mountaintop revelation, Katharine was, she remembered, drawn into the company of believers there and then.[61]

She would have been surprised to learn that most later observers assumed that the social gospel found little purchase in the poor, rural, evangelical, race-obsessed American South and that many scholars would come to view it as a naïve effort to apply moralistic nostrums to modern ills. For to her and many of the South's most ardent dissidents both before and after World War I, liberal Christianity was, quite simply, indispensable. To the God-haunted South, it supplied perhaps the only rationale for activism with broad appeal. To women who were torn by conflicting ideals—urged, in the words of Brenau's President Pearce, to pursue the "development of all of the powers of body, mind and soul" but also expected to subordinate the self to others' needs—it suggested that responsibility to others *required* the flowering of all of one's talents and abilities.[62]

The social gospel, moreover, was more protean and persistent than scholars have acknowledged. In the 1920s it would provide the common ground on which antiracist Southerners could stand. Leavened in the 1930s by the Christian realism of Reinhold Niebuhr, which stressed the limits of moral suasion in the face of entrenched evil, it metamorphosed into a radical form of Christian activism based on the use of economic, political, and moral leverage to overcome structures of oppression. This long social gospel tradition was overshadowed by more conservative forms of Christianity after World War II, but it continued to evolve. Melding with the prophetic theology of the black church, on the one hand, and with existentialism on the other, it reemerged full force in the late 1950s and 1960s, inspiring civil rights and antiwar advocates to seek both to change laws and to achieve what Martin Luther King Jr. called "a revolution of values" through civil disobedience and nonviolent direct action.[63] Equally significant was how individuals inspired by this tradition helped to imbue society with liberal ideas even as they left behind their religious faith.[64]

WRITING ABOUT HER formative years, Katharine stressed the importance of 1914, when the social gospel burst upon her. What she does not say is that 1914 was also Brenau's year of romantic friendships, and that no one was more intensely involved than she. "Crushing" was the term used for the romances that swept through the nation's women's colleges around the turn of the nineteenth century. At Brenau, those relationships went by the name "love casing," and they ran the gamut from mutual attractions through courtships of younger, more "obscure" girls by campus celebrities, to unrequited infatuation with idealized, remote figures—a student leader or a young teacher, an "infinitely lovely, infinitely distant star."[65] During Katharine's years at Brenau, the whole campus became a stage for these dramas of desire. The "Italian garden"; the paths of Brenau Park; the pavilion on Lake Lanier; the large wooden platform called the "Crow's Nest," which served as the seniors' exclusive retreat; the little shingled bungalow into which Katharine's sorority moved in her junior year; the dormitory rooms where students entertained one another with secrets and sweets; even Gainesville itself and the Blue Ridge mountains beyond, which offered sites for buggy rides and automobile excursions—Eros invested them all with magic and meaning.[66]

But love casing, with its playful rivalries, secret-sharing, and dramatically broken hearts, did more than suffuse the spaces and rituals of campus life with heightened significance. The pleasure of touch, the appreciation of beauty, and the eroticism of intimate talk solidified students' ties to one another and gave them the heady experience of performing courtship in all its guises: loving and leaving, pursuing and being pursued, flirting and idolizing from afar. Katharine was not only a student leader, devoted especially to the ecumenical, egalitarian, inclusive ideals of the YWCA; she was also, according to the yearbooks, the school's "champion love caser," exuberantly and unselfconsciously wooing, winning, and deserting a changing cast of girls.[67]

We know—or think we know—what the young women at Brenau did not even suspect: that this was the last moment in which such powerful emotions could seem to have nothing to do with sexual desire; the last moment in which women could move unselfconsciously along the spectrum from heterosexual to homosexual love. Unbeknownst to Katharine and her friends (indeed, to most Americans), by the 1910s medical researchers were busy cataloguing what they saw as a growing epidemic of "sexual inversion," a term that referred not so much to sexual orientation as to any behavior that seemed to mimic that of men or encourage intimate friendships between women. After World War I, these sexologists' studies, amplified by the ideas of Sigmund Freud, would seep through popular culture, gradually toppling the assumption that women were innocent of sexual desire, inadvertently laying the groundwork for the emergence of modern lesbian subcultures and identities, and furthering one of the signature ideals of the 1920s: "companionate marriage," which devalued female friendships by valorizing sexual and psychological intimacy between husbands and wives even as they remained within separate and unequal spheres.[68]

Or so the story goes. But that now-familiar chronicle of the fate of romantic friendship underestimates continuity and says too little about

Annual sophomore/senior Valentine's dance at Brenau College,
organized by Katharine Du Pre Lumpkin as president of the sophomore class.
Photograph is from the 1915 student yearbook, Bubbles.

the infinite variety and malleability of desire. Some women-loving
women, embracing lesbian identities, would pursue lives of passion darkened by secrecy and fear. But many others, especially within the enclaves
of upper-class life, continued to enact their same-sex relationships
according to the model of romantic friendship, supported by a dense web
of supporting players that included friends and family members who
may or may not have been aware of the erotic dimension of their unions
but who would, in any case, never dream of publicly characterizing those
unions in sexual terms.[69]

Even so, Brenau in the years before the Great War still seems bathed
in a fragile innocence. Faculty members who objected to "crush manias"
did so only because they associated them with bobbed hair, dirty middies, and other frivolities and distractions.[70] Never again would students
like Katharine be able to devote themselves to "love casing" with quite
so little fear of criticism, so little thought that they might be doing anything abnormal or wrong.

The sophomore-senior dance was a case in point. Katharine, whom her classmates called "K.D." or, in this case, "Captain Coquette," was president of the sophomore class, and the dance was an innovation. Students filled the Brenau social calendar with pageants and plays in which girls took male parts and with dances in which the seniors dressed as men and entertained the juniors. Katharine proposed something new: a reversal in which the younger girls would perform male roles and take on male prerogatives. On Valentine's Day, K.D. and her lieutenants decorated the gymnasium with hearts, smilax (the tender twining plant that had decorated the sanctuary at Elizabeth's "Confederate wedding"), and red and white paper streamers. Dressed in white middies with red ties, the sophomores acted as "gents," escorting the seniors in a grand march, filling out dance cards, and leading their partners in the two-step to the sounds of a local band. It was, the sophomores reported, "the best time we had ever had," and they penned a tribute to Katharine in the yearbook of 1914:

Our leader herself we all hailed as K.D.
Such carriage, such ease, and such grace,
Such ability, too, one could very well see
The moment one looked in her face.[71]

That same spring found "Miss K. Dee" commenting on her picture in the yearbook—"it looks as tho' I were a flirt"—and writing a humorous column of advice to the lovelorn that simultaneously parodied heterosexual romance and suggested the pleasure young women derived from playing *all* the romantic roles. "Knowing that you have had many opportunities to observe girls' troubled affairs of the heart and that you are capable of giving that advice which results from experience," wrote one interlocutor, "I appeal to you to suggest a means by which I can regain my lost happiness." The source of that lost happiness was apparently Dorothy ("Dude") McKeown, a tall, big-boned girl from Ohio who rivaled Katharine as Brenau's chief "love-caser." "I would suggest," wrote Miss K. Dee, "that you make a few dates with [McKeown] while the moon has such a charm; this, together with whispered words of love, will regain for you your place in her affection. Take courage, be brave. Dude McKeown's *heart* is big."[72]

The following year Katharine placed an ad entitled "Professional Crushing" in the *Brenaurial Review*: "I will tell you how to utilize the

Dancehall, Susceptibility, Moonlight and Stars, Gentle Breezes and Mellow Lights for the purpose of Popularity, Sorority Rushing or General Friendship." By then, Katharine was so well known for her flamboyant courtships that other girls gained fame by romantic association: Laura Brown, for instance, was singled out by the yearbook editors because she was "very much sought after by two of Brenau's celebrities," the president of the student union and Katharine, who was then president of the YWCA. According to Brown, "I am very much attached to both of them, and am especially proud on Saturday and Sunday nights, when I see my lovers presiding over their various organizations."[73]

This association between Katharine's leadership of the YWCA and her devotion to affairs of the heart—that is, between religion and romantic friendship—has a long history. Throughout the nineteenth century, the notion of women's moral superiority undergirded the assumption that women were innately free from lust and naturally drawn to one another. At the same time, evangelical Protestantism encouraged women who had no language in which to express sexual feelings for one another to conceive of their relationships as spiritual unions. In the twentieth century, secularization, in combination with the stigmatization of same-sex attractions, undermined those assumptions.[74] But the YWCA's social gospel–based belief in love as a transformative spiritual force, its stress on female friendship and solidarity, and its character as one of the rare nineteenth-century organizations that, to this day, has steadfastly remained a separate women's institution, continued to nourish women's ardent, expressive relationships with one another.

In an allegory entitled "The Game of 'Make Believe," written in 1917, Katharine simultaneously looked back on her college experience and dreamed of a future in which she would continue to usher younger women into the YWCA fold. First to appear in her reverie is the "Small-Girl," anxiously striving to "learn what was in those heavy books, because then only could she 'teach school.'" Soon the small girl is earning her own living by bringing the YWCA's message to girls "who had not been able to go away to college—girls whose eyes were tired because of much drudgery of cleaning up and milking cows and working in fields." Next came the "Ambitious-Girl," who "wanted honors and got them; who wanted high grades and got them; who wanted popularity and got it." Invited to YWCA summer conferences where the "key-note was 'give' and not 'get,'" the ambitious girl found herself in the company of young women whose strivings were harnessed to a cause larger than themselves.[75] A world where solidarity replaced conflict and competition and where the clash between Eros and Agape, the individual and society, personal fulfillment and public service, disappeared—this was the ideal that swirled through Katharine's reverie.

Most college women experienced student crushes as brief episodes in lives devoted to marriage, motherhood, and the civic activities that had become an acceptable aspect of women's proper roles. They thought nothing of flirting with women while also carrying on elaborate courtships with men. For others, college marked the beginning of a lifetime spent in women's institutions and in partnership with women. In either case, romantic friendships, which combined sense and sensibility, personal attraction and loyalty to the group, beckoned students toward an ethic of self-fulfillment through service to a larger cause, sometimes starting and stopping with loyalty to the school but sometimes extending to society as a whole. Desire, in that sense, was central to the remolding of identities that took place within college walls.

Those walls, however, provided only a temporary and provisional place of grace. All around pressed the demands of family, the strictures of society, the limits on the opportunities open to educated women in the early twentieth-century South. What would happen after graduation? How, in the adult world, could young women caught up in the romance of learning, the eroticism of friendship, and the aspirations of the social gospel weave all their desires and ambitions into a seamless web?

A year after she left Brenau, Grace contributed a short story to the college yearbook that crystallized these concerns. Like the stories she had written at the College for Women, this one revolved around heterosexual romance, but it differed from those earlier boy-meets-girl tales in its tone and scope. Her heroine, a college graduate, wonders what "these four years of work, yes, hard work [will] mean to her in afterlife?" "Should her mind, soul and body be merged into another's personality to be lost sight of?" Should she marry her beau, "let his wishes be her wishes, his home the magnet which should attract and hold all her thoughts?" Or should she use her God-given education to further "His kingdom on earth"? The girl goes to the city, where she ministers to the poor. There, miraculously, she is rescued from trampling horses by the man she left behind, now a successful surgeon. Her vulnerability as a single woman and his promise that "the fulfillment of our love for each other will strengthen our love for mankind" overcome her scruples. As the story fades to an end, we are given to understand that the couple will marry, and "the Little Girl," as she is called throughout, will have it all: romantic love, the ongoing pursuit of knowledge, and the chance to use her talents to further "His kingdom on earth."[76]

Like Grace's short story, Katharine's college records contain a hint of unease, a suggestion that she, too, sensed how difficult it would be to create a life in which love and work, self-development and social service, remained harmoniously linked and mutually reinforcing. Your personality, read the "Class History and Prophecy" during Katharine's senior year, has "already made itself felt tho' you are yet but a girl. . . . You will make your way in the world, your goal will be high, but you will reach it! Your name will be remembered for many generations. You are very lovable and you attract many people to yourself, but beware of too intimate friendships—the lines in your palm record more than one 'love case' in college. Remember that it is your love of humanity, not individuals, that attracts the 'crowd' to you."[77]

In what sense, and in whose eyes, were Katharine's friendships "too intimate"? Did some of her friends see her as veering dangerously between sexual and spiritual love, exclusivity and communion, unruly desire and serene self-giving? Caught up in the fever of romance, was she already tripping on the boundaries between same-sex love and compulsory heterosexuality that would harden after the war?[78]

Each time she attended chapel, a concert, or a major convocation, she would have found herself looking up at Brenau's most striking visual image, the fresco drawn from Virgil's *Aeneid* that stretched across the ceiling of Pearce Auditorium. It is hard to imagine a richer metaphor for the liminality of young women at a same-sex college just before the war. A product of the vogue for Classical Greece and Rome that swept across the United States at the turn of the nineteenth century, the painting signaled the affinity between the Roman paterfamilias and the belief in hierarchy, destiny, and paternalism associated with the plantation past. But Dido, the Queen of Carthage, is a powerful woman, and her story, which is in part about the eros of storytelling, could be read in a multitude of ways.

When the painting's narrative opens, Dido has vowed never to marry again, but Venus is determined to make her fall in love with Aeneas, a Roman soldier who has been blown ashore during his wanderings after the Trojan War. The painting pictures Aeneas telling his story to Dido.

By the time he finishes, Cupid will have worked his magic: Dido will be hopelessly, fatally in love. In the end, duty, piety, and patriotism tear Aeneas away. The god Mercury warns him to flee ("An ever uncertain and inconstant thing is woman"). Dido feels betrayed ("May an avenger rise up from my bones"). She curses him and kills herself, dying in her sister Anna's arms.

Anna is the third character in the painting, although in *The Aeneid* others are listening to Aeneas's story as well. The choice is suggestive: two sisters, with the man who will separate them. And the message seems mixed. Dido is beautiful, intelligent, powerful, and independent, but she forfeits everything for the love of a man. Is the lesson "avoid marriage if you want to reach your full potential"? Or is it "you are fated to give up your independence for a man"? And what of the sister? Is Anna Dido's true friend? Or is she somehow complicit in her sister's fate?

After college most of the young women in the auditorium would weave their identities from the joys, obligations, and dependencies of family life. As Katharine observed, for her generation "the conception prevailed" that you could not have both marriage and a career; pursuing "the one meant giving up the other."[79] That would have been even truer in her sister Elizabeth's case. Once married—at the relatively late age of twenty-four—she had almost no choice but to put aside both her teaching and her peripatetic speaking career. Hungering for love *and* independence, service and achievement, Grace and Katharine would go on searching for ways, however provisional or unconventional, to fulfill all of their desires. So would Elizabeth within her more traditional sphere.

PART TWO

—

"A NEW HEAVEN AND A NEW EARTH"

*"The incongruities of the old life . . .
produced the struggle against it."*

—KATHARINE DU PRE LUMPKIN,
THE MAKING OF A SOUTHERNER (1946)

"THE INNER MOTION
OF CHANGE"

———

K ATHARINE GRADUATED FROM BRENAU IN THE SPRING OF 1915, with a week of ceremonies that mixed a performance of Molière's satirical play, "The Learned Ladies," with an address delivered by the female president of a women's college in Virginia. These events were followed by a baccalaureate sermon; a farewell vesper service by the YWCA; the Crow's Nest ritual, in which the seniors surrendered their retreat to the juniors; and an alumnae banquet, which Elizabeth (and possibly Grace) attended.[1] It was a grand send-off, but Katharine, who was not yet eighteen, had decided to stay on, clinging to the intimacy and pursuing the opportunities she had found at Brenau.

A terse letter from Eva Pearce, a professor of English, the president's sister, and one of the school's most zealous disciplinarians, suggests that she stayed for another reason as well: she had to support herself and repay her loans from the college. "We have decided to have you return and give you credit on your account, amounting to fifteen dollars a month," Pearce wrote. "I am expecting to get service from you, so you may prepare for a very busy semester." As it turned out, Katharine stayed at the college for two critical years, working as a classroom assistant, a dormitory chaperone, and secretary of the YWCA.[2]

By 1917, when she finally left Brenau behind, "contrary streams of influence" were carrying her far from the narrow round of "service" that

Eva Pearce had in mind. In 1912, Woodrow Wilson, the first Southerner
to win the presidency since the Civil War, had been swept into office
by the momentum of the Progressive movement and the white North's
acquiescence in Jim Crow. Two years later Europe plunged into war,
giving Katharine an unforgettable lesson in economics as foreign mar-
kets closed, cotton prices tumbled, and some of her friends had to pay
their tuition in warehouse receipts for cotton instead of cash. All this, as
she put it, created "tugs at the fringes of our pleasant horizon. . . . Large
forces had begun to shake our world, even our remote piece of it closed
in snugly there in the foothills of north Georgia." By the time she left
Brenau in 1917, the United States had entered the conflagration.[3]

When Wilson ran for reelection in 1916, Katharine stepped forward
as president of the Wilson Club, stumping for the incumbent on the slogan, "he kept us out of war." The club's members could not vote; it would
be four more years before the nineteenth amendment would give women
that fundamental right. But their activities made news: they installed
telegraph equipment in the school's auditorium, insuring that Brenau
would be the only place where Gainesville citizens could instantaneously
hear the election results.[4] Less than a year later, the president led the
nation to war. The conflict transformed Europe into a charnel house and
the United States into a world power, ignited the Russian Revolution,
and whipped up a spirit of nationalism that engulfed everything in its
path. The South sent a million men to fight, bringing black and white
soldiers into volatile contact with one another. After an initial devastating drop in cotton prices, the region's economy boomed, creating a vora-
cious demand for labor, pulling people off the farm, and, in combination
with new federal protections, giving white southern workers a leverage
they had never had before. "If the war didn't happen to kill you," a character in one of George Orwell's novels observed, "it was bound to set you
thinking." For the first time, many Southerners found themselves with
money in their pockets, jobs in industry, or plans to set sail for distant
shores. The Lumpkin family was among them: in one way or another,
all of its members were on the move. Coming to adulthood during these
world-changing years, Katharine and Grace joined a postwar generation
of women who found new routes to self-making in the opportunities
opened by the war.[5]

MANY YOUNG WOMEN in the orbit of the YWCA had been opposed to America's involvement in the European conflict. Dorothy Page Gary (later Markey), a YWCA activist who, under the pen name Myra Page, would become a proletarian novelist and one of Katharine's and Grace's lifelong friends, remembered both their generation's diffuse but heartfelt pacifism and how it was overcome. As a student at Westhampton College in Virginia, Markey published an antiwar poem entitled "The Deserter," in which a German soldier crawled across "no man's land" trying to make a separate peace. When Wilson declared war she initially held on to her pacifist convictions. But her teachers peppered her with stories "about all the atrocities that the German army was committing on the Belgians, cutting off hands, slashing women's breasts, making the Iron Cross and burning it into old men." In the end, she took Wilson at his word: this would be a "war to end all war." It would be over quickly. It would "save the world for democracy." When Markey returned home to the port city of Norfolk that summer, she and her friends signed up to work at Red Cross canteens, serving coffee and rations to sailors on the piers, going home to sleep for a few hours, and then returning to dance at the Officers' and Servicemen's Club. "We were serving our country," she remembered. "We had a function, and we were having an exciting time."[6]

Katharine followed suit. As secretary of the Brenau student Y, she helped to redirect students toward doing "our bit" for the soldiers "over there" in pace with the nation's unprecedented mobilization of resources, achieved in part through the blunt exercise of federal power and in part through an intense propaganda campaign. Inspired, as the Brenau yearbook put it, by the demand that they adopt a broader, "sympathetic, sacrificial" stance, students observed meatless and wheatless days and swore off tearooms and ice cream parlors, using the money they saved to purchase a $1,000 liberty bond, raise a $2,100 students' war fund, and support French orphans. They joined Red Cross auxiliaries, filled soldiers' kits, knitted garments, wound bandages, and made surgical dressings. They augmented student rituals with daily flag-raising ceremonies; dressed up as soldiers, sailors, and Uncle Sam; and staged a "Pageant of the Allied Nations." Ninety-nine percent of the student body attended self-organized "world democracy classes," which aimed to "train women for citizenship during and after the war." Soon they were characterizing themselves not just as "we girls of Brenau" but also as "citizens of this great nation of ours. . . . A new world-order was being established," explained the Brenau yearbook, "and as we awakened to this fact we began to prepare ourselves for service."[7]

Back in South Carolina, Grace and Annette, too, were caught up in the melding of Progressivism with home front mobilization. In 1915, a reform-minded politician named Richard I. Manning won election to the governorship. He and his followers were responding to a confluence of events: the cresting of the women's suffrage movement, army intelligence tests that revealed appalling rates of ill-health and illiteracy among southern conscripts, reformers' anxieties about the unlettered mill workers in their midst, and worries about the single women who were converging on cities in pursuit of excitement and wartime jobs. Their Progressivism was for whites only; it was a modernizing project that focused especially on white women and children and on uplifting poor whites through education. Still, in a state dominated by racial demagoguery, their efforts to strengthen the social safety net created openings for interracial cooperation that black leaders could exploit.[8]

The Lumpkins' own Trinity Church became a site for these uplift and interracial efforts. Katharine remembered the Episcopalianism of her childhood as a staid and status-seeking affair that stood in sharp contrast both to Sand Hills evangelicalism and to the social gospel she encountered at Brenau. But by the time Grace returned home from college in 1911, Trinity was in the hands of an unusually forward-looking young priest, the Rev. Kirkman Finlay, and his civic-minded wife, Isabelle Cain. Characterized by his admirers as a "Christian Democrat," Finlay took it upon himself to abolish the system of "pew-rents," which the Lumpkins had struggled so hard to pay, and extended voting on church affairs to all adult members of the congregation rather than limiting it to pew-holding men. In alliance with Trinity's Women's Auxiliary, he channeled the church's resources into social service, establishing missions not only among the skilled workers at the Church of the Good Shepherd, which the Lumpkins had attended during their Sand Hills years, but also in the Olympia and Palmetto mill villages, where Trinity sponsored some of Columbia's first kindergartens, playgrounds, and other programs for the poor.[9]

When the United States entered the war, Finlay went to France, where he ministered to soldiers under the aegis of the YMCA. By the

1920s he had become bishop of the newly created Diocese of Upper South Carolina. In that position, he emerged as one of the state's leading advocates of interracial cooperation. Unlike the Methodists and the Baptists, the South's largest denominations, the Episcopal Church had not broken apart over the issue of slavery. Only the Civil War had briefly split the denomination. Quickly reuniting, the church witnessed a mass exodus of its black members, who had made up almost half of its antebellum communicants but who now fled to newly formed, autonomous institutions. Those who remained were relegated to separate parishes, denied representation in diocesan governing bodies, and prevented from forming their own governing associations. Working closely with black religious leaders and black women's clubs, Finlay helped to strengthen black churches, promote black schools, and establish a home for delinquent black girls. He also tried in vain to convince his diocese to give black parishes the right to representation in its governing convention.[10]

As parishioners and members of the Women's Auxiliary, Annette and Grace were exposed to Finlay's efforts. But the main vehicle for Annette's plunge into civic life was an extension of the commemorative movement to which she had long been devoted. Unlike most patriotic societies, the United Daughters of the Confederacy had always had a social mission: at a time when war pensions, the nation's first major social welfare program, were reserved for Union soldiers and their families, it tried to care for Confederate veterans and their descendants and thus to "honor the dead by helping the living." In the years before World War I, some UDC members widened that mission. Wearing various hats, they organized garden and literary clubs, advocated temperance, opposed child labor, pressed for the expansion of the public school system, and promoted educational opportunities for white women. Like their Progressive era counterparts throughout the country, they sought to parlay their cultural authority—which in their case was based on their role as keepers of the Confederate flame as well as on their more general claim to female moral superiority and responsibility for children—into efforts to bring women's influence to bear on the issues of the day.[11]

Such ambitions faced extraordinary obstacles in a society shadowed by slavery and committed to an elitist, antidemocratic New South development strategy that relied on low taxes, small government, minimal social services, and the exploitation of both natural resources and the black and white poor.[12] By idealizing the Old South as a society based not on materialism but on noblesse oblige, organized women sought to promote a more expansive sense of community responsibility. By documenting a heritage of women's strength and achievement, they hoped to inspire contemporaries to action and silence critics of women's expanding public role. It is telling, and typical, that when Annette Lumpkin wrote a brief reminiscence about the Civil War, she evoked a long procession of soldiers' funerals but then closed with a tribute to the home front: "Truly, those were days not only to try men's souls, but to put to the test all that was greatest in the souls of the women!"[13]

Annette recorded her memories at the behest of the Lost Cause group in which she was most active and invested: the Girls of the Sixties, an organization that exemplified the outlook of women who saw no contradiction between regional pride and national patriotism, paeans to Confederate manhood and faith in modern "woman power," reverence toward the past and the creation of a new social order. Formed in 1917, the Girls of the Sixties aimed "to collect and preserve personal reminiscences and unpublished data of . . . scenes and events of the War Between the States." But it also functioned as a local unit of the National Woman's League for Service, whose goal was to mobilize "the woman power of the nation" for service during World War I, with a special emphasis on supporting and protecting the women who were surging into the workforce in unprecedented numbers, serving not only as nurses or telephone operators but also as ambulance and motor car drivers and in other novel positions.[14]

Trained "by the best of teachers—experience," tempered by "war service and mother service," and full "of the old fighting spirit," the Girls, as they called themselves, began "knitting night and day." At the same time, they eagerly adopted "modern methods" to meet "the altered conditions" of the times. Ranging in age from fifty to seventy (Annette Lumpkin was sixty-one in 1917), they spent countless hours at Camp Jackson, the vast army training facility on the outskirts of Columbia, where they sewed for the soldiers, chaperoned dances, helped to create a community club for enlisted men, and equipped a canteen. They also worked for the Red Cross, sold liberty bonds, adopted two French orphans, and in other ways threw themselves into service to the nation.[15]

When the hostilities ended, the Girls of the Sixties went back to reading aloud from their memoirs, enjoying musical programs, and ending their "brilliant afternoon affairs" with both "Dixie" and "The Star Spangled Banner." Still, they did not "rest on their laurels," nor did they care to dwell "unduly in the past." On the contrary, these women prided themselves on "being alive to the importance of modern issues and the greatest problems of the immediate hour" and welcoming "modern progress in all its lines." Aligning themselves with the Progressive administration of Governor Manning and his wife Malvina, a local leader of the National Woman's League for Service, the Girls of the Sixties supported an improved road system and municipal beautification; applauded "all expenditures for city advancement," even if that meant increasing the public debt; and recommended that Columbia build "a fine city park, a new opera house, and a public market."[16]

AS A YOUNG WIFE and mother in Asheville, Elizabeth also blazed new paths of civic activism while continuing to carry the Confederate flame. Marriage had quickly ended her speaking career: the veterans might grow frailer and frailer as the years went by, but the UCV's female "sponsors" were forever young and virginal—or at least so they were always portrayed. Trading in her sponsor's position for a more matronly role, Elizabeth served as president of the local chapter of the United Daughters of the Confederacy, entertained veterans at annual luncheons in her home, and helped "them in every way possible" until the late 1920s, when the last of the Civil War generation was passing away.[17]

Yet even as she carried the project of commemoration forward, Elizabeth's last speech to a large gathering hinted at interests that went beyond shoring up men's egos and preserving the memory of their valorous past. Addressing the Monteagle Sunday School Assembly, a mixed-sex, interdenominational gathering place for religious studies and other educational and cultural pursuits, she urged the "brainy, helpful women of the South" to take a hard look at what they proudly called "the 'South of Progress.'" If they "realized how the other half really live," she was sure "their souls would grow 'hot with the thing called shame.'" "You have heard complaints against the mill system. Have you ever been in the great mills of the South?" Many of the poor women who work there

Elizabeth and Eugene Glenn, with their children, from left,
Marion, William, Ann, and Eugene Glenn Jr., with Annette Lumpkin,
Asheville, North Carolina, ca. 1916.

"are ambitious," she assured her audience. They or at least their children could accomplish something; "but they need help!" Come to this "center of high thought and culture . . . not for pleasure alone," she urged. Rather, come with "a single purpose in view, the practical upbuilding of [the] South. . . . What a woman cannot do for the uplift of a world cannot be done."[18]

Confederate veterans meeting at Elizabeth Lumpkin Glenn's home in the Montford neighborhood, Asheville, North Carolina, ca. 1915–1926.

Elizabeth gave birth to her first child in 1907, only four months after delivering this final address. Eugene Byron Glenn Jr. was followed immediately by another son, whom she named William Wallace Lumpkin in honor of her father, but he died within a year. This baby was remembered ever after as "Little Lumpkin," and the whole family was shaken by his loss. A few months later, Elizabeth gave birth to Marion Sevier. Her only daughter, Ann Dudley Lumpkin, arrived in 1912. Her youngest son, also named William Lumpkin, was born two years after that.[19]

Besides raising four children born in quick succession, Elizabeth spent the early years of her marriage absorbed in the housekeeping, socializing, and volunteer work that came with her role as the wife of a doctor whose wealth and prominence escalated as Asheville's economy boomed. Beginning in 1880 with the arrival of the Western North Carolina Railroad, tourists from across the nation streamed into the city, attracted by the beauty of the mountains and the much-advertised healthy climate. Many stayed, joining local boosters in a building spree that accelerated through the 1920s, producing the upper-middle-class

Montford neighborhood where the Glenns lived as well as a series of lavish hotels and resorts, dozens of tuberculosis sanitariums, and the city's first skyscraper, erected in 1924.[20]

Already well established when he and Elizabeth married, Eugene Glenn went on to reorganize Meriwether Hospital when its founder died and to serve as its surgical chief of staff and then its president and chief stockholder. Both he and Elizabeth became fixtures of the city's development-minded professional and business class. He served as director of the Asheville and Buncombe County Good Roads Association, one of the first such bodies in the South, and as president of the county medical society. He was also an active member of numerous fraternal and civic associations. Elizabeth added to her leadership of the UDC the vice-presidency of the Asheville Women's Club and the presidencies of the Woman's Interdenominational Missionary group and the women's auxiliary of the Episcopal Church, which she attended while her husband maintained his more modest Methodist faith.[21]

At the same time, she plunged into the eugenics movement, an aspect of social welfare reform that was becoming one of the chief preoccupations of North Carolina's organized women. First introduced by medical doctors and social welfare professionals in touch with national and international trends, eugenics rested on the pseudoscientific notion that "the bettering and strengthening of the human race" depended on preventing the "feeble-minded" from procreating and thus passing along their supposedly heritable defects—and with them their proclivities for pauperism, promiscuity, and criminality—to future generations. This effort, which in the two decades after World War I focused primarily on institutionalizing poor white girls, had particular resonance in western North Carolina, a region notorious for its population of supposedly backward, inbred mountaineers.[22] Seeking to master eugenic theories and disseminate them to the public, the Asheville Women's Club turned to Elizabeth to help lead that campaign. She responded by drawing on national experts on "the work of social hygienists," whose goal was to stamp out venereal disease and prostitution and promote sex education, to help write papers, distribute articles, and argue in the affirmative in a public debate over whether eugenics should become "a subject in the curriculum of the public schools."[23]

Two years later, she jumped at the chance to return to her first love, the dramatic arts, as chair of a Shakespeare tercentenary celebration promoted by a women's club–based group called the Drama League of America. A local version of a "veritable Shakespeare frenzy" that erupted in towns and cities across the country, this series of events culminated in an elaborate pageant, which Elizabeth directed and in which young Thomas Wolfe, who would go on to become North Carolina's—and, in the 1930s, one of the South's—most famous writers, played Prince Hal. Held at the Manor, an English-themed resort built on land acquired by a railway tycoon, the pageant included white students from all the schools in the city.[24] Like so much else that happened in his hometown, this women-led event became fodder for Wolfe's fiction. Elizabeth surely counted herself lucky when she escaped appearing as a character in *Look Homeward, Angel,* which included a comical send-up of what to her and many others was a serious and successful effort to bring local citizens together in a celebration of Anglo-Saxon "high thought and culture," of which the vogue for Shakespeare was a prime example.[25]

When World War I broke out, Elizabeth took advantage of new opportunities to extend her voluntary activities, following in her mother's footsteps but also going well beyond her. She used her influence to expand the UDC's purview beyond Confederate memorialization into support for the Red Cross's war preparedness work. Under her watch, the UDC also participated in the efforts of the Woman's Committee of the Council of National Defense, whose North Carolina affiliate broke with the conventions of Jim Crow by encouraging black women's participation and refusing to segregate county councils by race.[26]

Joining the board of the Asheville Library Association in 1918, Elizabeth became a driving force behind the transformation of a book collection maintained by volunteers and available only to those who could afford paid subscriptions into a free library "where the children of the rich and the poor" had access to "books that will uplift and enlighten." She also stepped into regional leadership of the North Carolina Library Association and in 1920 was appointed by the governor to serve as the state representative to the American Library Association's annual meeting.[27] As one of a small group of commissioners selected by the city after it took over responsibility for Pack Memorial Library, she worked for years to increase the facility's holdings, keep it open at night for the use of "working men and women," and raise money for an impressive building designed in a Renaissance Revival style.[28]

When, in 1918, Elizabeth and the other two members of the subscription library board had transferred the Asheville Library Association's property to the city, they did so on condition that it "maintain and operate a free public library for white residents." Over the years that followed, this facility sporadically reserved one room for the city's black citizens.[29] As black women sought to take advantage of women's suffrage, black soldiers returned after the war, and black laborers were drawn to Asheville by a construction spree, racial tensions escalated, as did efforts at amelioration such as the creation of a Colored Betterment League and an interracial commission dedicated to "foster a better spirit of understanding between the two races."[30] In this context, civic leaders such as Elizabeth came to see that including blacks in their effort to "uplift and enlighten" was both "an act of simple justice to the sable citizens of this community" and beneficial to the city as a whole.[31]

Yet the benefits they anticipated could be blithely self-interested and condescending. As one supporter explained it, providing such amenities was good for business: it would reassure northern tourists that Asheville was "a progressive city" determined to do right by "its colored wards." It would also keep young blacks from "reading filthy publications," joining gangs, and becoming "parasitical impedimenta."[32] Whatever their mix of reasons, the city fathers did finally allocate the funds to hire a black librarian and establish what was popularly called "The Colored People's Library" in the Young Men's Institute, the hub of business, civic, and social activities in Asheville's segregated black community. Elizabeth was credited with being "one of the most active civic leaders in promoting" this free public library for blacks, although that accolade needs qualification: she was among the most vocal of the library's handful of *white* supporters. At the opening of the one-room, one-thousand book facility in 1927—a pale imitation of the services available to whites—she and another white library commission stalwart were present to address the crowd.[33] She went on in the 1930s to champion the creation of playgrounds for both black and white children for similar reasons: such segregated, supervised public spaces, she believed, would reduce crime by uplifting the poor.[34]

Annette Lumpkin's civic efforts, like those of her male counterparts, were premised on segregation. The canteens and service clubs the Girls of the Sixties helped to create and run were for whites only, as were those formed by the National Woman's League and most other World War I groups. Elizabeth's leadership in establishing a library for blacks suggests that she belonged to a less fearful generation. At a time when the alterative to segregation was exclusion, not integration, she never considered making Asheville's much superior Pack Memorial Library fully available to all residents of the city. Yet the Progressive movement of which Annette and Elizabeth were a part did open a space in which blacks could advocate for themselves and white women's understanding of responsible citizenship and public welfare could grow. Grace, Katharine, and their cohort would vastly expand that understanding.

FOR GRACE THAT EFFORT began in 1911 when, upon her return to Columbia from her year at Brenau, she became a foot soldier in the struggle of reformers to wrest appropriations for the public schools from a parsimonious legislature, eradicate adult illiteracy, and expand women's civic, educational, and professional opportunities. Moving in with her mother, she took a job at a grammar school housed in a brand-new building that put the dilapidated, one-room schoolhouses attended by the vast majority of the state's children to shame.[35] There she found herself with a ringside seat to a battle for gender equity in which her brother Alva, who been elected to the South Carolina House of Representatives three years before, played a leading role.

Columbia's College for Women, where Grace had begun her higher education, was led by the intrepid Euphemia McClintock. Partly because she wanted to give young women access to the quality of instruction available to men and partly because the school had always struggled financially, in 1913 McClintock launched a campaign to transform the school into a coordinate college of the all-male University of South Carolina.[36] The boards of both institutions, along with the university alumni association and most of the faculty, endorsed the merger. On the floor of the state legislature on January 14, 1914, Alva Lumpkin introduced a resolution authorizing the trustees of the university to proceed with the plan.[37]

"The feminist movement . . . has reached South Carolina and the women are to have a new, active part in the affairs of the state, a part which calls for a broader and more liberal training than is offered by any institution within our borders," the resolution's supporters proclaimed. Keenly aware that antipathy to coeducation ran deep, they were careful to emphasize that "the social life of the College will be entirely distinct from the University"; women would be taught by USC professors and have access to the library and laboratories, "but otherwise there will be no commingling of students."[38]

Despite strong support from his colleagues in the legislature, Lumpkin's resolution was torpedoed at the last minute by leaders of the Presbyterian Church, which had founded but provided no financial support for the college.[39] They were determined to merge the school with the church-controlled Chicora College for Young Ladies in Greenville. A College for Women freshman named Lois MacDonald, who would go on to work closely with Katharine in the YWCA, vividly remembered what happened next. She and her classmates viewed Chicora as beneath them "academically and socially and [in] every way." When they read about the merger in the local paper, they "nearly tore the place to pieces. Nobody went to class that day, and there was a howl like nobody's business." McClintock resigned immediately and left Columbia and her native state. MacDonald refused to return to the College for Women the following year, along with what she remembered as ninety percent of her peers.[40]

At approximately the same time, Grace left Columbia as well, taking a job at a two-room schoolhouse in Latta, a rural village that stirred to life only in tobacco season and when cotton farmers drove their wagons into town, but which was now trying to upgrade its abysmal school system. She also worked for the YWCA, organizing recreational programs for industrial workers and for members of a division called the Girl Reserves, which was created in 1918.[41] Like Progressive era reformers everywhere, she and her coworkers saw no contradiction between expanding their own opportunities and offering others a chance for self-transformation. Summing up their ideals, one South Carolina activist explained: We "work with the people, and not for them. [Our] purpose is to . . . draw [the workers] into the full current of life."[42] Such sentiments meshed seamlessly with the ideal of service Grace had encountered at Brenau. Putting them into practice also had the merit of giving her a means of supporting herself while she waited for the next stage of her life to unfold.

That unfolding came from what might seem an unlikely direction:

the sorority she and Katharine had joined at Brenau. It was not unusual for either black or white sorority members to remain active after graduation, and when Grace returned to South Carolina she assumed a regional leadership role. First, she helped to establish a state alumnae association. Then, rising rapidly though the association's ranks, she won election as president of her province—the first elected office she had occupied, unlike Katharine, who took the leadership in virtually every organization she joined. That position involved planting and guiding Phi Mu chapters in women's colleges across the South, including Georgia, where she regularly visited Katharine at Brenau.[43]

Together the sisters helped to lead Phi Mu to a new commitment to social service. They traveled to Niagara Falls for the sorority's national convention, the first to be held outside the South—Katharine as Brenau's delegate to the convention and Grace as toastmistress of the affair. The "Bond of Phi Mu," Grace told the gathering, is "making us better prepared to take our places in the line of life's 'dreamers and builders and workers.'"[44] Katharine's response to Grace's toast reportedly moved the audience to tears. "In a yesterday," she announced, "we knew a north and a south—on that yesterday we could not have met in such an assemblage as this; although all American-born, we recognized a Mason and Dixon line, and to my mind the Greek letter world has been a leading agency in effacing that line." Phi Muism, she concluded, means "the creation of the true American girl."[45]

The sisters were on hand again in 1916, when the sorority's national convention adopted a creed composed by the Brenau chapter. Written by Katharine, Grace, or the two of them together, the creed began with the motto, "To lend to those less fortunate a helping hand" and urged members "to esteem the inner man above culture, wealth, or pedigree." To implement those ideals, the delegates voted to create a National Philanthropic Board with responsibility for launching a program of public service, in part by channeling money and energy into the YWCA, with which Phi Mu shared many members. The convention then chose Grace Lumpkin to serve as the board's first director.[46]

Returning to Columbia to take up her duties, Grace looked to Walter Rauschenbusch, the founding father of the social gospel, for inspiration. Citing him, she urged her sorority sisters to focus on "refashioning this present world" rather than keeping "our eyes fixed on another world." As a first step in that direction, she recommended that local chapters begin with the defining gesture of Progressivism: a social survey that would yield "knowledge of conditions" in their own communities. Beyond that her proposals were vague but intriguing: in good Progressive fashion, they stressed ameliorative goals and the subjective benefits of social service, but they also foreshadowed a later political sensibility, one that emphasized not the reformer's helping hand but the organized power of the working class. Phi Mu, Grace suggested, should foreswear the goal of "any definite, palpable straightening out of things." Instead, it should work with the right spirit and give the disadvantaged "a chance to grow, a chance for freedom, . . . a chance to right the wrongs that have been put upon them." In response, local chapters pursued projects that ranged from war relief to visiting prisons, orphanages, and nursing homes to working at settlement houses, usually in cooperation with the YWCA.[47]

In her capacity as secretary of the college YWCA, Katharine mobilized this effort at Brenau, beckoning students toward an ideal of public service and broadening her own engagement with the wider world. At Brenau, as at most schools North and South, idealistic sorority sisters and YWCA members might venture across the railroad tracks to teach cooking, sewing, and Sunday School lessons to the white children who worked in Gainesville's textile mills. But they would not consider extending fact-finding and service projects into black neighborhoods. Neither Grace nor Katharine questioned this stance, nor did they raise objections to Phi Mu's membership requirements, which included "white race and 'Christian birth and faith.'"[48] Yet quietly, at the level of consciousness if not of action, the deep currents of liberal Christianity, the influence of the women's movement, and the spirit of Progressivism were drawing both sisters toward an awareness not only of class-based but of racial wrongs.

THE CHIEF CONDUIT for that new sensitivity was the YWCA. Almost as soon as the YWCA of the U.S.A. coalesced in 1906, its National Board called an all-white conference to formulate guidelines for including black women in the association. The group met in Asheville, North Carolina, in 1907, just as the white supremacy campaigns had reached a climax, leaving the South in segregation's iron grip. In that context, the participants attempted the impossible: to reconcile the Y's religiously inspired belief in what the white southern reformer Lily Hardy Hammond termed a "bond of common womanhood deeper than all racial separateness" with its assumption of white superiority and conviction that segregation was perfectly compatible with—even intrinsic to—Christianity and sisterly cooperation.[49]

The white Southerners present declared themselves "quite anxious and willing to help." But helping was one thing, fraught as even that might be; collaborating with black women in their local communities and deliberating with them in national conventions was quite another. In the end, the southern delegates to the Asheville meeting found themselves paralyzed by the clash between their fears and phobias and their good intentions. "On account of the prejudice they did not think it best" actively to further the establishment of black city Ys in the South. Black student associations, which were proliferating rapidly in the region's historically black colleges, could continue to organize and seek affiliation directly with the National Board.[50]

The National Board did not resist these ambiguous conclusions. It did, however, hire its first consultant on "colored work," Addie Waites Hunton, an educator who had helped to found the National Association of Colored Women (NACW) in 1896. Only a year before, in 1906, Hunton and her husband William, the first black staff member of the national YMCA, had fled Atlanta in the wake of a murderous riot. Like many expatriates, she felt personally implicated in the travails of her native region. In 1908 Hunton was joined on the national staff by Elizabeth Ross (Haynes), a Fisk University–trained sociologist who served as a "special worker for colored students." Both were inspired choices. Headquartered in New York, they traveled across the South, deciding which self-initiated community and student groups would be allowed to call themselves YWCAs, encouraging black women's efforts, and pressing the National Board to clarify its policy on how work among them should proceed.[51]

In 1915, just as Katharine was graduating from college, Eva del Vakia Bowles, the YWCA's first permanent, full-time staff member in charge of "colored work," organized a conference in Louisville, Kentucky, which claimed the distinction of being the first interracial gathering of women in the South. By then, a large proportion of the female students at black colleges were participating in the Y. Official black city Ys were also emerging in southern cities, affiliating directly with the

National Board when they lacked the approval or cooperation of local white associations.[52]

The Louisville gathering, which brought together white and black women leaders along with representatives from the National Board, hammered out an agreement that had two main provisions. First, an interracial committee would be selected to represent the southern region, a step forward because black women had no official representation on the National Board and thus no voice in the governance of the association. Second, the Y would adopt a policy that assumed that new city Ys would function as "branches" of white "central" associations. That arrangement implicitly ratified segregation, not just in the South but throughout the country, and it gave local whites, who held the purse strings and sat on the governing committees of the black branches, a galling amount of control over "colored work." Eva Bowles and other black national staff members despised segregation, but they defended the branch relationship as a pragmatic means of uniting black and white women in a common endeavor based on shared religious ideals and a commitment to the advancement of women and girls. The branch solution had another significant advantage. It offered black women, most of whom were recruits from the student Ys, one of their few prospects for professional employment and allowed them to serve their own communities, opportunities they zealously guarded and fought to enlarge.[53]

A few months after the Louisville conference, Katharine found herself singled out for a venture in "interracial understanding" which, only a few years earlier, would have made her "shudder with apprehension and shock." Along with a carefully selected group of student leaders and Y secretaries from other white women's colleges in the South, she was invited by a national staff member to attend a meeting in Charlotte, North Carolina. There she experienced for the first time the face-to-face encounters through which the Y was seeking to overcome racial barriers in the Jim Crow South.[54]

Two days into the Charlotte meeting, the YWCA secretaries placed a proposal before the group. The staff member in charge, Katharine remembered,

> was a Southern woman. She spoke to us as such. She assured us that she had been reared even as had we. She said that she could understand our first impulsive misgivings. Once she had stood at

the crossroads we now confronted. She urged us to consider the matter. Take until morning. We could accept or reject.

The proposal was this: There was a Negro woman leader in the city then: a woman of education, a professional woman, herself belonging to the YWCA staff. It was suggested that she speak to us on Christianity and the race problem.[55]

This woman, moreover, was no "Jane" or "Mary"; she was Miss Adela F. Ruffin, an adult staff member whom the students must treat as they would a white woman of their own class or not meet at all. Should they shake her hand? Must they refer to her as "Miss," an honorific that white Southerners deigned to use in regard to blacks only in a "darkey joke" and ridiculed when blacks insisted on using it among themselves? White supremacy did not require literal, physical separation. Many times Katharine had seen white adults "shake the hand of a 'darkey' in a genuinely kindly way." She knew that white Southerners like her parents prided themselves not on how little contact they had with blacks but on how well they knew them—as opposed to outsiders who supposedly understood neither the foibles of blacks nor the nuances of master-servant relationships. What white supremacy did require, in the form it had assumed by the early twentieth century, was an intricate code of conduct that signified and enforced relationships of power. Central to that code was the myth of innate or ingrained racial inferiority, which "a woman of education, a professional woman" flatly contradicted.[56]

The prospect of treating Ruffin as an equal, indeed, as a superior, threw Katharine and her friends into a double bind. To accept the YWCA's challenge was to break the unwritten law that African Americans—especially the educated few, who liked to "imitate white people" and thus to blur the imaginary line between white and black—must be kept "in their place." This was not just a matter of individual choice; all around them, Katharine and her friends could sense the presence of a "cloud of hostile witnesses." What if people knew? What would they say? And yet to refuse this engagement was to fail the test of "Christian consistency." Were not all souls equal in the sight of God? Had the students not dedicated themselves to the universalist imperatives of the "brotherhood of man"? Intensifying their dilemma was their reluctance to disappoint the YWCA secretaries they so admired.[57]

"We were like a little company of Eves," Katharine remembered, guiltily plucking the apple of knowledge from the tree of life. But these were Eves of a special sort, for they "had been taught it was wrong to eat this apple," and yet, "as it was put before us we felt guilty not to." To eat from the tree of knowledge, to acknowledge the full humanity of a black woman who was their equal in every way, was to open their eyes to "what was good and evil" and thus to risk having their world turned upside down. In the end, Christian consistency won out. Miss Ruffin stood before them, and they listened respectfully to what she had to say.[58]

Looking back at this moment, Katharine could not recall Ruffin's words, but she could remember her low voice, speaking in the cadence and timbre not of a "colored woman" but of an "educated woman," the ideal to which Katharine aspired. Most of all, she could remember her own relief. She had half expected to be punished for her transgression, so sharply did the fear of sinning against white supremacy vie with the YWCA's admonition that "love thy neighbor" meant treating a black woman respectfully, if not as a sister under the skin. "I had touched . . . this tabernacle of our sacred racial beliefs," Katharine wrote, and "when it was over, I found the heavens had not fallen, nor the earth parted asunder to swallow us up."[59]

Safely back at Brenau, she could "breathe freely again, eat heartily, even laugh again." She could also try to put the incident out of her mind. "But still I would now and then find something stirring up an inde-finable sense of discomfort—and then remember."[60] As she turned this moment over in her mind, wearing it smooth, confusion changed into pleasure: the pleasure of membership in a new, dissident community and of discovering and acting on a new best self—both of which propelled her into a future in which she might choose, act, and feel differently than she had before.

Soon, in her capacity as secretary of the YWCA, Katharine was leading delegations of Brenau students to gatherings at the Blue Ridge Assembly grounds in the North Carolina mountains, where white YMCA and YWCA members met for separate summer conferences. Created in 1912 by Willis D. Weatherford, the YMCA's student secre-tary for the South and Southwest, Blue Ridge aimed to foster "Christian manhood" and "to help bring Jesus' religion to bear on modern life."[61] Along with other welfare and religious groups, the Young Women's Christian Association paid a fee for the use of the grounds (which, along

Students from across the South gathered at the
YMCA's Blue Ridge Assembly, 1920.

with gifts from the Rockefeller Foundation and other philanthropies, helped to support the assembly) and organized its own separate gatherings. Blue Ridge could rightly claim to be one of the few places where large numbers of white Southerners could gather to discuss racial and economic issues. Even more unusual was its policy of welcoming black speakers such as Adela Ruffin and Eva Bowles.[62]

In *The Making of a Southerner*, Katharine characterized these early experiences as "meager beginnings," signs of a "feebly breathing, hardly existing South" whose "puny influence" made only the faintest of marks on student life. In Brenau publications, the news from Blue Ridge was not about social issues and black speakers at all; it was about the tennis tournament, with Katharine on the championship team. In contrast, during the two postgraduate years she spent working at the college, questions about race pressed ever more insistently against Katharine's mind. But away from YWCA gatherings, away from the "warm company of fellow-dissidents," she found herself "not yet ready to trust my budding heresies to any but those who I knew would not be scandalized."[63] Going home from a Blue Ridge convention, Katharine's friend Dorothy Page Gary felt similarly constrained: "Up there in the beautiful rarified air," she remembered, "so many things seemed possible. When you get back into the routine of everyday life, it isn't so easy to carry through." As Katharine put it, "we went on living in our surroundings, following all the prescribed racial rules and regulations," and finding what comfort they could in the fact that inwardly they were changing, even if outwardly they continued to conform.[64]

For her, this "inner motion of change" took the form, as it had in the Sand Hills, of seeing things that had always surrounded her, hidden in plain sight.[65] Brenau relied on black washerwomen, maids, cooks, waiters, and gardeners—a whole retinue of figures whose cheap labor was essential but who could not send their own children to the school. Katharine had always taken this black presence for granted. If she had heard wartime rumors about black women who were refusing to work as servants and forming an organization with the motto "a white woman in every kitchen," she would have shared her elders' chagrin.[66] Now "certain old mental habits began to slip away." She quit referring to the African Americans around her in the insulting terms she had once so readily used. And she found herself questioning "the indefinable assumption that we whites were to be served, not as a job performed for which we paid certain specific individuals, but as a duty owed to us by Negroes as a race."[67]

Yet none of this protected her from the seductions of D. W. Griffith's extravaganza, *The Birth of a Nation*, when it arrived in town. She had read Thomas Dixon's books as a child. "Now they came alive in this famous spectacle," which brought together not only Dixon and Griffith but also Woodrow Wilson—three Southerners who had moved north at the end of the nineteenth century. Griffith drew on Wilson's *History of the American People*, as well as on Dixon's novels, and Wilson was rumored to have helped to quell criticism of the movie by endorsing it from the White House. "It is like writing history with lightning," he was supposed to have said, "and my only regret is that it is all so terribly true."[68]

Katharine saw the movie beneath the fresco of Dido and Aeneas in Pearce Auditorium, where she had attended so many edifying events during her college years. Hoping to reform the cinema by promoting uplifting films, Brenau administrators had purchased their own equipment and begun screening what they saw as Hollywood's best productions. *Birth of a Nation* qualified, notwithstanding its obsession with rape and miscegenation and its justification of the murder and suppression of blacks. Sponsored by the alumnae association, it was trumpeted in the press for a month before its May 1916 showing and attracted viewers from across the county.[69]

"We poured out to the picture," Katharine remembered, "everyone, students, townsfolk. The hall was packed. Several showings were held so that all could come. I went," she confessed, "in truth, went more than once." Local editorialists concentrated first on the film's verisimilitude (every historical detail was "carefully counterfeited") and then on its portrayal of Lincoln as a gentle man who went to war reluctantly and wanted to welcome Southerners back to the union "as if they had never been away."[70] The ads, however, featured the "Horrors of Carpetbag Rule" and the "Wild Rides of White-Robed Knights."[71] These were the scenes that Katharine remembered, for they put a chain of associations in motion in which Griffith's images meshed with and revised the stories her father had told. Here, stamped in celluloid, reexerting their crippling pull, were the figures of the carpetbagger bent on putting "the white South under the heel of the black South," the white virgin fleeing a fate worse than death, and the Ku Klux Klan dashing to the rescue like ghosts in the night.[72]

"All around me people sighed and shivered, and now and then shouted or wept, in their intensity," Katharine remembered. What had those outbursts of emotion meant, she wondered? Were they merely a response to "a spectacle, with new techniques?" Or did they suggest the resonance of Griffith's racial and sexual obsessions? "I did not know, not at the time," Katharine wrote, "except that I felt old sentiments stir, and a haunting nostalgia, which told me that much that I thought had been left behind must still be ahead."[73]

WHEN KATHARINE GRADUATED from Brenau in 1915, the class prophet had offered this prediction: "You will enter into sociological work, for the lines in your hand indicate that you have the making in you, of another Jane Addams!"[74] Leaving the school three years later, she spent what she called "a little intervening period" on the staff of the Norfolk, Virginia, YWCA, but she "was aiming all the time at a national" Y position. Her sights were set on New York City, home to Columbia University—

*Katharine Du Pre
Lumpkin at
twenty-one.*

"the only place any women [she] knew in South Carolina had gone for their graduate work"—and, just as important, on Columbia's Teachers College and the YWCA's National Training School, which were also beacons for ambitious southern women, black and white. She wanted to study sociology and become a national Y secretary, a position that, in her eyes, epitomized the combination of "professional life" and social service she craved.[75]

By then, most of her siblings were also on the move. Morris, following in Alva's footsteps, had been elected to the state House of Representatives, but resigned to join the army. By the time Katharine started classes at Columbia, he was slogging through the French countryside in the nightmarish Meuse-Argonne offensive, where American doughboys died by the thousands during the final campaign of the war. Alva had gone from state representative to state senator and, by 1918, was acting attorney general of South Carolina. Hope Henry Lumpkin, the oldest brother, had embarked on his own foreign adventure. After completing his divinity degree, he volunteered for foreign mission work in Fairbanks, Alaska. Grace too was planning to set forth on a surprising journey. Phi Mu had decided to undertake war work of a special sort: providing recreational and other morale-boosting services not for soldiers, but for French women workers and American women serving abroad. Canceling its annual meeting, the sorority donated the money to the YWCA to send a Phi Mu war worker to France. Chosen for that honor, Grace was waiting for the approval of the Y's recruiters, who "were forced to fend off a flood of volunteers."[76]

"FAR-THINKING ...
PROFESSIONAL-MINDED"
WOMEN

AT COLUMBIA UNIVERSITY KATHARINE FOUND AN "ACROP-olis on the Hudson" that seemed a galaxy away from Brenau, the cozy, bucolic campus she had left behind. It is not hard to imagine how imposing the university must have appeared to her in 1918: those blazing skyscrapers; that first subway ride; the colonnaded gateway through Columbia's cliff of granite walls. As a newcomer in the city of promise, she was repeating a defining moment in countless American lives. "All over the country, the ambitious and the eager, the want-to-be wealthy and the would-be smart," the editors of the *Nation* observed, "have their eyes on Manhattan Island—the Mecca and the model for the continent." That was never more true than in the decades after World War I.[1]

Perched on a hill in Morningside Heights, the university consisted of a compact superblock of architecturally integrated, classical revival buildings laid out in a series of small, closed courtyards centered around a bronze sculpture representing Alma Mater and Low Library's great dome. To the north lay Harlem, once a rural retreat, by 1920 a haven for eastern European Jews, and on its way to becoming a vibrant black city within a city. Around the university and to the south sprawled the Upper West Side, a hodgepodge of classes, races, and ways of life.[2]

Before the war, Columbia may well have offered the best graduate education in the country; certainly, it was unsurpassed in the social sciences that Katharine wanted to pursue. Charles Beard and James Harvey Robinson in history, John Dewey in education, R. A. Seligman in economics, and Franz Boaz in anthropology were among a score of scholars who were pioneering new modes of knowledge. Dramatically expanding the range and methods of social research and casting aside the search for absolutes, they came to understand the individual and society as interdependent, and the world, in Dewey's phrase, as "something still in the making." For them, ideas produced in the university had to be tested through application.[3]

The Great War dimmed this brilliant scholarly community. President Nicholas Murray Butler, who presided over Columbia from 1902 to 1945, threw academic freedom to the winds and dismissed faculty members who opposed US entry into the war. Beard resigned in protest; Dewey capitulated, although he defended antiwar protests and later realized that his prowar stance had been a mistake. Butler's actions put the purposes of intellectual inquiry to a revealing test. Could faculty members function as critical intellectuals, or did "service to society," to which Katharine was dedicated and which both Butler and his opponents advocated, imply strict obedience to the state? However individuals answered that question, the war made Columbia a less open and intellectually venturesome place. For some women and other outsiders, "cold and reactionary" was not too harsh a term.[4]

"IT WAS AS A self-conscious Southerner that I arrived in New York," Katharine remembered. She had been taught to believe that she "belonged to a people of a special mold," a people knit together "by harsh conflicts gallantly weathered. . . . a courteous, kindly people, swift to sympathy, hospitable, gay, affectionate, withal proud, and of noble spirit and high ideals." The North, by contrast, loomed in the distance, cold, mercenary, and inhospitable. At Brenau she had met women from all over the country, and those friendships reconfigured "the North" as a "far friendlier territory," if still a categorically different land. An admixture of other influences—Mr. Riley's evolutionary approach to history, which replaced the fixity of tradition with the inevitability of change; the YWCA, which introduced her to "the great wide world"; the social gospel; the war itself—had leavened regional loyalties with patriotic Americanism, countered residual beliefs with cosmopolitan ideas, and given the mantra of white supremacy an increasingly hollow ring. By the time she left Brenau, Katharine's Southernness was laced with unease: her very self-consciousness was the product of clashing values, an effect of change. Already in flux, that ambivalent regional identity would be consolidated—even crystallized—rather than eroded by her expedition to "the Northern side."[5]

At Columbia, she found herself marked as a Southerner in unanticipated ways. Her accent, inflected by the distinctive cadences of the Deep South, instantly set her apart. That she expected. She was also well prepared to face hostile questions about "our Southern ways." What surprised her was the confusing position in which she found herself. When she tried to register for classes, she learned that Brenau was not on Columbia's list of accredited colleges; in order to earn a master's degree, she would be required to study for two years instead of the usual one.[6] Yet along with this badge of intellectual inferiority came an unexpected cachet: the perverse glamour of the outsider who speaks for an exotic place.

Katharine had grown up assuming that all Northerners fancied themselves "the self-ordained champions of Negro slave and Negro freedman." Instead, she found that her professors and fellow students, however eager they might be to make invidious comparisons between the slow, backward South and the dynamic, sophisticated North, were not inclined to criticize the region's treatment of its black population. On the contrary, they seemed perfectly satisfied with the notion that white Southerners "alone understood Negroes and should be left alone to deal with them." As Katharine had expected, no signs in New York blared "For Colored," "For White." But neither did the city offer the "natural give and take, coming and going" between the races that she had half-hoped to find. The lines that excluded blacks from white clubs, hotels, and neighborhoods did not have to be spelled out to be strictly enforced.[7]

What Katharine was experiencing was both a resurgence of scientific racism and a rapprochement between North and South, which the narrative of the Lost Cause, by playing down slavery, demonizing Reconstruction, and praising the valor of soldiers on both sides, helped to bring about. Woodrow Wilson's 1912 election had signaled the triumph of reconciliation (the "birth of a nation," in D. W. Griffith's terms). As segregation spread through the federal government and hardened in northern cities, the conflict between North and South gave way to a clear line between black and white.[8] The war further eroded sectional ardors, without by any means obliterating deep regional identifications. It also unleashed a paroxysm of hatred aimed at immigrants, Bolsheviks, and anarchists as well as the rural African Americans who were pouring into northern cities.

In 1917, the federal government began whipping up xenophobia by repressing antiwar protests and deporting immigrants whom it suspected of planting the seeds of Soviet-style revolution on American soil. During the "Red Summer" of 1919, US Attorney General A. Mitchell Palmer orchestrated a nationwide dragnet against aliens and dissenters, while white mobs across the country attacked blacks, who fought back with what struck white observers as an alarming new spirit of militancy.[9] The Great Migration would eventually give African Americans a political beachhead from which to influence national politics. But in the years surrounding World War I, even multicultural Manhattan was a tense, segregated, and corrosively racist place.

Disillusioned, although also, as she admitted in hindsight, secretly relieved to find that "the proud North [shared] our guilt," Katharine looked to the classroom for the stimulus she desired. "I expected to find myself in a place where fresh, free air circulated," she remembered. "I was going as a student to a very hub of learning. I sought there . . . something to quicken my thoughts and supply them with rich, nourishing materials. I sought companionship in learning, a sense of others striving to unravel the mysteries of why men behaved as they did and perhaps what could make them behave differently." In short, she expected what Mr. Riley had exemplified, "except in magnified terms, since here would be notable scholars, great minds, liberal learning on every side." For the most part, she was disappointed by what she found. At Brenau learning had seemed alive. In the sociology department at Columbia, scholarship did not move and breathe; it was "a corpse on which men of learning performed a continuing autopsy."[10] She had, she wrote, been "handed a stone when I had come here for bread."[11]

Franklin H. Giddings, one of sociology's founding fathers, ran the department as a one-man show. A staunch conservative, he rejected the new field's reformist roots, advocating instead a strictly empirical approach modeled on the natural sciences. "We need men . . . who will get busy with the adding machine and the logarithms," he wrote. He also inflicted on his students a version of social Darwinism built around the concept of "consciousness of kind."[12]

Drawing on Charles Darwin's notion that species advanced toward higher forms of life through a process of natural selection, Herbert Spencer and William Graham Sumner claimed that human beings progressed through competition and adaptation: left to their own devices, the fit would inexorably triumph over the unfit. Humankind advanced from primitivism to civilization as superior races conquered or absorbed inferior ones. This way of thinking justified racism, imperialism, and laissez-faire capitalism. It assured the privileged that they owed their advantages not to their inherited wealth and control over the state but to the inexorable and divinely sanctioned laws of evolution.[13]

Yet evolutionism also encouraged cautious forms of uplift and reform. So-called primitive peoples—from the ex-slaves and slum dwellers to the native inhabitants of colonized countries—could develop the traits of civilization, such as diligence and self-control, and pass those traits on to their progeny. Evolution thus served as a means of assimilating new groups while at the same time buttressing the faith that white, Protestant culture would prevail. Feminist versions of evolutionism, moreover, helped to power the women's movement by suggesting that mothers played a special role in passing on acquired characteristics and by giving white women new authority as protectors and civilizers of backward peoples at home and abroad.[14]

Katharine had already absorbed evolutionary thinking—first through the subtext of the Lost Cause, which assumed that slavery had been a civilizing institution, and then, in its progressive form, through the social gospel and Mr. Riley's interpretation of history, both of which saw uplifting the weak as the key to social and spiritual progress. These popular forms of evolutionism had been like the air she breathed: they shaped her values and perceptions without registering as a set of formal ideas. By contrast, in Giddings's classroom, she found herself confronting social Darwinism in an explicit and profoundly conservative form.

To be sure, Giddings had made his reputation by softening the ideas of Spencer and Sumner. Departing from his mentors, he argued that in advanced societies competition would give way to cooperation based on fellow feeling or "consciousness of kind." But when it came to African Americans, he stressed evolution's glacial pace. Blacks, he maintained, were currently inferior, although capable of improvement over time. As long as they remained in a lower stage of development, signaled by their inability to control their animal instincts, they must be cordoned off from the superior race. White racism, moreover, flowed naturally from the tribalism inherent in Giddings's ideas: in the foreseeable future, no amount of preaching or meddling could persuade whites to include blacks in the "community of fellow feeling" to which other groups might be gradually admitted. To make matters worse, World War I had pushed Giddings farther to the right. In the throes of a nervous breakdown, he lashed out against Bolsheviks, modern women, and other leveling influences.[15]

From Giddings's classroom Katharine took "the very lesson I could best have done without." Reading William Sumner's *Folkways* (1906) in particular set her mind agog. She was, as she remembered it, "raw, fresh from the South. . . . Everything that I was seeing, learning, hearing, was mediated through this kind of veil of southern experience."[16] That exquisite sensitivity to racial matters made her susceptible to the terrible fatalism of social Darwinist thought. Sumner's dictum that "in the folkways, whatever is, is right," was, as Katharine put it, "a blow at one's weakest spot." When it came to race, everything around her, even the tentative interracialism of the YWCA, "had fostered a disposition against too much change too rapidly." "Now," she remembered, "I must go away with a heavy sense . . . that scientific minds surmised that the 'mores' were so imbedded in men's social habits as to make it nearly impossible to alter them—at best taking generations of time, at worst centuries."[17]

Katharine was neither the first nor the last modern intellectual to take such ideas to heart. Well into the 1940s, long after anthropologists such as Franz Boaz and Margaret Mead had discredited biological explanations of human difference in favor of a thoroughgoing environmentalism, hereditarian ideas lived on in the eugenics movement and in popular racism, and white liberals continued to argue that race relations had to evolve slowly and naturally. Even Gunnar Myrdal felt compelled to devote an entire chapter in *An American Dilemma* (1944) to repudiating the Sumnerian notion that changes in racial attitudes had to precede state action.[18] In the 1950s and 1960s, as civil rights protests and judicial decisions began to dismantle segregation, white Americans still clung to the belief that "you can't legislate morality." Such assumptions undercut the optimistic faith that inspired both social Christianity and the civil rights movement—the belief that the combined force of religious ideals, courageous examples, and governmental intervention could change behavior and transform hearts and minds.

LUCKILY FOR HER, Katharine did not read Sumner in a vacuum, nor was Giddings her only teacher. She sought out a circle of women who had no trouble reconciling the belief that mores matter with the conviction that they could and should be changed. She was drawn in particular to Teachers College, which had been founded and financed largely through the efforts of Grace Dodge, the first president of the YWCA's National Board. The vast majority of the school's students were women, including hundreds from southern black colleges. Its leading light was William H. Kilpatrick, John Dewey's chief interpreter, a major figure in the progressive education movement and the foremost teacher of teachers in the nation.[19]

Katharine also took courses at the YWCA's National Training School, which was the hub of the network of "far-thinking . . . professional-minded" women Katharine had encountered at Brenau.[20] Founded in 1908, the school had started out in a grand old house on Gramercy Park, then moved to the YWCA's new eleven-story headquarters building at 610 Lexington Avenue when it opened in 1912. But it retained the homey trappings of a women's college: its dormitories and parlors, chapel services and student ceremonies contrasted sharply both with the monumental, masculinist atmosphere of Columbia and with the jostling modernity of the urban surround. Combining nineteenth-century notions of women's religiously inspired benevolence with the culture of professionalism that was transforming American middle-class life, the school's purpose was to provide the specialized religious training that would convince women "who could study in the best universities in the world" that serving as a YWCA secretary was "a profession worthy of their powers." After the war, the school moved in an increasingly reformist direction. It encouraged its students to study the social sciences and social work at Columbia; introduced new courses on "Women in Industry"; and sponsored lectures by Florence Kelley, Lillian Wald, Mary van Kleeck, and other luminaries of Progressive era reform. Here too Katharine found herself in the orbit of John Dewey, whose ideas had a profound impact not only on the YWCA but also on a broader circle of female activists and intellectuals.[21]

Like most turn-of-the-century intellectuals, Dewey had been profoundly influenced by Darwinian theory. But where social Darwinists believed that society was moving along a predicable path, driven by an unfettered struggle for existence that must be allowed to take its course, Dewey viewed the world around him as an unstable site of agency and accident. Human nature was not fixed; in fact, it demonstrated an extraordinary plasticity, whereas social institutions and practices were more resistant to change.[22]

This stress on contingency and choice undergirded Dewey's advocacy of participatory democracy and radical political action. It also promoted an ideal of self-realization that resonated with Katharine's college experience and spoke to the conflicts between her aspirations and her upbringing, which stressed female self-sacrifice and loyalty to kith and kin. Individuals, Dewey believed, reached their full potential through generous, creative, intelligent participation in social life. The "mutual adjustment" of individual and society, a key Deweyan term, did not require conformity to current norms. Indeed, it might well entail a reconstruction of society.

Inspired originally by the social gospel, Dewey came to see the school rather than the church as "the key institution in the saving of souls for democracy."[23] Children learned best not by being force-fed subject matter, but through active, experiential inquiry. Such learning would yield citizens capable of the cooperation and collective decision making that democracy requires. Schools should not reproduce the existing social order. Rather, they should prefigure a more profound, not-yet-realized American democracy, a society that would nurture the full powers of all its citizens and foster the public good.

The YWCA expanded and elevated the female educator's role. Embracing Dewey's vision, it passed on to young women like Katharine the notion that they could serve as the mediators and communicators who would make education for democracy the means for saving the world. That idea had feminist implications, which became more explicit over time. At the outset, the YWCA had couched its mission in the ostensibly gender-neutral language of Christian service, despite its axiomatic belief in women's special responsibilities and vulnerabilities. But as the suffrage movement crested, it identified itself more and more with the struggle for women's rights. In 1918, it changed the name of its publishing house from the Association Press, a title it shared with the YMCA, to the Woman's Press, a bow to its role as "an integral part of the greater woman movement of this day."[24]

After 1920, when other women's organizations gave way to mixed-sex groups that promised more resources and political clout, the YWCA clung to its identity as a worldwide organization of "women working for women." This was in part an oppositional stance that crystallized in the postwar period as the YWCA found itself threatened with absorption by its larger and richer male counterpart. While the city division of the YMCA increasingly avoided controversial issues and marketed itself as a payment-based provider of lodging and recreation, the YWCA took stands on peace, labor, immigration, and, eventually, racial issues. In accordance with its commitment to local autonomy, it also maintained a nonhierarchical management style and a diffuse, weblike structure based on "group work"—the formation of self-governing affinity groups that set their own goals and believed that process was as important as results.[25] Carried throughout the country by the professionals who studied at the Y's National Training School, this vision of a diverse and democratic "fellowship of women and girls for the . . . freeing of personality and the release of power" gave the YWCA both its adamantine idealism and its institutional shape.[26]

Courses at Union Seminary and in the history department reinforced what Katharine learned at these women's institutions. At Union she took courses from Harry Emerson Fosdick, the liberal theologian whose early books she had read avidly at Brenau. She also studied with James Harvey Robinson, the leading exponent of the "New History," an iconoclastic approach to the study of the past.[27] She had encountered Robinson's textbooks in college. But nothing in those tomes had prepared her for Robinson's famous "History of the Intellectual Classes of Europe," a graduate course that attracted over two hundred students a year, many of them female teachers from the provinces. In what may have been his last course before he left Columbia to help found the New School for Social Research, Katharine found the living, breathing approach to scholarship she had glimpsed at Brenau.[28]

The New History that Robinson espoused stressed the social and economic conflicts that underlay political and military events. He believed that the study of history should be democratic in substance and in method. Borrowing from the social sciences, it should focus not just on great men but on the "seemingly homely, common, and inconspicuous things" that shape ordinary lives.[29] By uncovering the origins of contemporary beliefs and practices, the New History would free people's minds from what Karl Marx called the "dead hand of the past," enabling them to respond creatively to the challenges of the present day. Robinson had no truck with "monumental history" or ancestor worship; virtually all the thinkers he paraded before his students had feet of clay.[30] His essential message, as one student explained it, was that human beings could, by deploying their own intelligence, make the world "less a shambles and an idiocy than it had so often been." Wil Lou Gray, who went on to become South Carolina's leading educational reformer, remembered what she took from Robinson's classes: "a big view of history and a plea that we recognize we were a part of the world and that change was inevitable."[31]

The histories that Katharine had absorbed as a child had also linked past to present, but they did so covertly, through a chronicle of heroes whose noble self-sacrifice underwrote the current regime. At Brenau, Mr. Riley had prepared his students to see history not as a matter of larger-than-life ancestors but as what the Columbia philosopher Irwin Edman termed "an experience lived and a problem that had to be faced."[32] Robinson and his cohort of New Historians drove that lesson home by showing how a new story of the past—a story that acknowledged conflict, concerned itself with the masses, and looked for the hidden economic springs of political events—could yield a new understanding of the present and pave the way to a more enlightened and egalitarian future.

These ideas worked their way into Katharine's imagination, planting the seeds of an approach to history and economics she would cultivate in later years. But even progressives such as Dewey, Kilpatrick, Fosdick, and Robinson had little to say about her chief preoccupation: the mysterious and often toxic interlocking of race, gender, and region. Indeed, Kilpatrick, a fellow Georgian who lived until 1965, was "able to advance his opinions on race beyond his native prejudices," yet could never bring himself to speak out against segregation.[33]

In a seminar at Columbia's Summer School, a spinoff from Teachers College, Katharine finally got a taste of the "natural give and take" between the races that she had expected New York to provide. Here she met Juliette Derricotte, a fellow Georgian who had just graduated from historically black Talladega College in Alabama and had come north to study at the National Training School in preparation for a career with the YWCA.[34] Derricotte minced no words when the discussion turned to their native state. She punctured the comfort Katharine had taken in the shortcomings of the North, making crystal clear the difference between a system of white supremacy that was "of the bone and sinew of society, and ways, however prevalent, that are yet non-institutionalized." She talked in plain language about the realities of segregation and about what "Southern Negroes wished for in education, citizenship, job opportunities, equality before the law, and what in fact they had."[35]

In Derricotte's presence, Katharine glimpsed something she could not have imagined before: a world in which white people like herself did not occupy center stage, but loomed on the margins, armed with menacing customs and laws. She had grown accustomed to the notion that, as a member of a privileged race, she should be careful not to offend black sensibilities. Now it was she who found herself "sensitive to being white, and Southern white at that." She had experienced Southernness as an identity that aroused both condescension and curiosity. Suddenly she also saw whiteness in a new light—as a stifling armor that cut her off from the knowledge she craved. She was already ambivalent about Northerners' assumptions that, "whoever we were and whatever our knowledge," white Southerners alone could speak with authority on the South. Derricotte shattered the remnants of that pleasant fiction. For all her love of history, for all her immersion in the past, Katharine now realized, she had never "studied the South." All she knew was "what had been handed on to me as my heritage and what had come in my limited experience." She had never done what Mr. Riley prescribed: "'gone to the sources,' 'checked facts against hearsay,' sorted out 'unbiased from biased history.'"[36] Brenau had offered a bracing, critical rendition of the European and American past. But it was this exposure to the "devastating potency of facts," marshaled by a black student speaking both from study and experience, that made Katharine realize how little she knew about the history unfolding in her own backyard.[37]

At the close of the term, the professor invited the whole class home for tea. This was "eating with Negroes"—a grievous breach of racial etiquette to the rest of the Lumpkin clan. Black women might nurse white babies and prepare white families' food. A treasured servant might chat with her mistress or her charges in the kitchen, a feminized private space. But sharing a meal in the dining room or tea in the parlor was strictly taboo. Not long before, doing so would have struck Katharine herself as "a momentous thing."[38]

The fact that she did not view this moment as a personal crisis, a test of a new-found faith, suggests how much she had changed. Confronted at a YWCA conference with the suggestion that she listen to Adela Ruffin speak on "Christianity and the race problem," she had agonized over the state of her own soul. Invited to tea in New York, she suffered from no such scruples. "I thoroughly enjoyed having Negroes in my classes," she remembered, "eating with them, and listening to them, and feeling 'oh, my, this is very exciting.' I was just throwing overboard all these stupid things."[39] How quickly, under the pressure of new circumstances, one could shake off aspects of supposedly unshakable "racial mores"! And if an individual could do so, Katharine increasingly found herself thinking, in good Deweyan fashion, then why not white Southerners as a group?

WHEN IT CAME TIME to write a master's thesis, Katharine chose a topic that must have struck her advisor as rather odd. The "Social Interests of the Southern Woman" required no logarithms or adding machines. It had nothing to do with "consciousness of kind." It did not "come out of my classes at Columbia, I assure you," Katharine told me. "I drew it "from the atmosphere," from "the energies and the impetus that came out of the woman's suffrage movement [and from the] rising movement of women . . . into occupations which they had hitherto not known."[40]

This study was a novice's effort. Yet for all its awkwardness, it provides both a contrast to and a remarkable foreshadowing of Katharine's later preoccupations. In it, we glimpse a young woman emerging into critical consciousness, as she tries to "tell about the South" in the ostensibly scientific, objective voice of the social sciences while at the same time searching for subjective meaning, a new way of understanding where she came from and who she might become.[41]

Her goal in this first foray into scholarship was to compare southern women's access to education, their entry into the professions, and their involvement in voluntary associations with opportunities enjoyed by their counterparts in the North. Focusing on women who were preparing themselves for "some form of leadership," she ignored both the

South's entire "colored population" and the immigrant women of the North on the grounds that only native-born white women would be likely to have made a public mark.[42] That assumption reflected how little she knew about the prominence of southern black women in the public life of their own communities and in national black women's organizations, as well as the fact that the sources she relied on made no mention of the Adela Ruffins and Eva Bowleses of the world. Using the *Woman's Who's Who of America*, the Directory of Women's Clubs, the findings of college accrediting agencies, and the occupational census, she also ignored her own education for leadership at Brenau in favor of what her experience in the North had encouraged her to assume: that southern women's colleges were institutions that fit women to be either a "home-getter" or a "home-keeper," and that, in part because of their inferior education, southern women had "progressed much more slowly into fields of public endeavor" than had women in the North.[43]

For an explanation of why this was so, Katharine turned to Sumner and then to history, switching from the flat, passive voice with which she recited the South's deficiencies to an animated account of how a plantation society "entirely unlike that of other parts of the country" was dragged into modernity with its "ancient customs" intact. Rich soil and an "enervating climate," she argued, had necessitated slave labor and set the South on a collision course with the more energetic North. The "terrific force of the Civil War" tore that whole social fabric into shreds. For Sumner, Reconstruction served as a prime example of the axiom that "legislation cannot make mores."[44] Following him, but modifying his evolutionary fatalism ever so slightly, Katharine observed that the victorious North had tried to force a "ruined and prostrate" region to change its "mores" overnight.[45] No doubt, she continued, "this violent method may have been the only one that could bring the South out of its . . . stationary state of existence." But it failed to achieve a "gentle evolutionary weaving into the life of the people" of forward-looking ideas. Instead it required a "dazed adaptation" to new conditions that resulted in "forty years of economic, social and political discord."[46]

Under such circumstances, Katharine implied, Southerners clung desperately to traditional attitudes, especially in regard to "woman and woman's 'sphere.'" Applying to gender a key concept of interwar social science—the notion of "cultural lag"—she underscored the persistent culture of deference, dependence, and chivalry that surrounded women with a "body guard of customs," denying them the freedom "to think and to speak." While "the North was moving forward . . . the South was standing still." "Social Interests of the Southern Woman" ended with a burst of optimism based not on received wisdom but on experience too personal to find its way into *Who's Who*. In the few short years since she had entered college, Katharine concluded, independent, socially minded women had become "one of the distinct features of the new South." "The current is running deeply toward change."[47]

WHILE KATHARINE WAS balancing Sumner against Dewey, the pessimism of Darwinist sociology against the idealism of the YWCA, and a growing sensitivity to the South's deficiencies against intimations of change, Grace was preparing to represent the Y in war-torn France, a topsy-turvy world where the conventions of southern white womanhood might not apply. The sisters' mother and grandmothers had been caught up in a ghastly conflict fought on home ground, and the United Daughters of the Confederacy had etched the heroism of women into the collective memory of the Civil War. Both Grace and Katharine had channeled their expanding notion of service into "doing our bit" when World War I began. Even Elizabeth, the true believer who venerated Confederate veterans until the day she died, had stepped forward to lead Asheville's Red Cross, moving effortlessly from loyalty to the Confederacy to patriotic service to the nation. But none of this home front service challenged the dichotomy between male soldier and female civilian that made fighting for one's country a defining feature of citizenship.[48]

Women's overseas service in World War I threatened that time-honored equation. Two developments made women's labor vital to modern warfare in a way it had never been before: technological innovations, which transformed battle into a clash of impersonal, industrial killing machines, and the feminization of the new white-collar occupations that made large-scale organizations and mass communication possible. In a nation initially divided over the wisdom of American intervention, moreover, women played a critical ideological role. Their presence at the front as nurses, clerks, telephone operators, and canteen workers reassured an uneasy public by domesticating the war. Yet admitting women to the battle front had potentially disruptive consequences. It held out the promise, as the Brenau College yearbook put it, that in a "new era in world history" women might become full "citizens of this great nation of ours."[49]

The YWCA had entered war work full bore in 1917, when the War Department appointed Raymond Fosdick, brother of the famous preacher Harry Emerson Fosdick, head of its new Commission on Training Camp Activities. To Fosdick, women represented both the army's greatest problem and that problem's solution: as prostitutes, they were carriers of venereal disease; as moral guardians, they could protect soldiers from temptation. The commission moved quickly to stamp out prostitution by persecuting sex workers and creating "sanitary zones" around military training camps throughout the nation. But Fosdick aimed to uplift as well as to protect the soldiers: like other Progressives, he believed in the power of organized recreation and a homelike atmosphere to mold character, and he viewed the training camps as laboratories for making upstanding citizens out of a motley array of young men plucked from every class and ethnic group and transported far from home.[50]

Sharing his concerns but focused less on the morals and morale of the soldiers than on the war's impact on women, the YWCA approached Fosdick with a plan to open "hostess houses" where friends and families could visit soldiers under carefully supervised conditions. Over the objections of military officials who recoiled at the idea of women trespassing on men's space, Fosdick accepted the Y's offer and helped to secure a million-dollar budget for the work. This unprecedented influx of funds allowed the Y to create a War Work Council that not only ran hostess houses near training camps across the country but also provided employment bureaus, emergency housing, and other aid to the women who poured into war-related industries and took jobs vacated by men.[51]

Like all the Y's efforts, this outreach to factory workers proceeded along segregated lines. From its inception in 1908, the industrial program had been a haven for staff members as interested in economic equality as in religious conversion. ("Just go right ahead being a Socialist . . . there is not the least difficulty in combining your secretarial work and Socialism," the department's founder Florence Simms had assured a potential recruit.) But like the nation's settlement houses, which turned a blind eye to black migrants to northern cities, the program initially served only white workers.[52]

That changed when African American women seized the moment

created by wartime labor shortages to leave domestic service for the factory floor. Appointed in 1917, the Y's first National Industrial Secretary for Colored Work operated not under the auspices of the industrial program but under the direction of Eva Bowles, who, since 1913, had been secretary of a subcommittee on colored work and who now took charge of this field for the War Work Council. With the support of sympathetic white industrial program secretaries, African American activists created a parallel program for black working-class women. They also made claims for justice based on those women's patriotic economic contributions.[53] At the same time, Bowles and her colleagues established dozens of hostess houses and other services for black soldiers and their relatives.

When the American Expeditionary Force (AEF) agreed to extend Fosdick's welfare program overseas, the YWCA's spectacular success at home helped to open the way for the large-scale employment of women at the front. Most of the 16,500 women who volunteered for military service did so as nurses, telephone operators, and other civilian employees of the military or of the Red Cross, the YMCA, and other male-run agencies, and their official charge was to serve "our boys over there." The YWCA

YWCA World War I poster.

had a different mission. Unique in its administration by an all-female professional staff and its unshakable commitment to "women working together," it took responsibility for providing women war workers with their own morale-boosting services, their own women-only recreational spaces, and their own "homelike and restful" housing.[54] At the invitation of the Union Chrétienne des Jeunes Filles (the French counterpart of the Y), it also established a network of Foyer des Alliées ("Hearth of the Allies") for the French women who loaded the munitions trains and worked in other industrial occupations. In addition to these services, the YWCA taught English to war brides and staffed cemetery huts for the families of American soldiers who died in battle.[55]

Most of those who applied for overseas service were single white-collar and professional women. This was especially so in the case of the YWCA, which hired almost one-fifth of its war workers from within its own ranks and whose 260 recruits included a large portion of teachers. On the strength of Grace Lumpkin's sponsorship by Phi Mu, her leadership of the sorority's public service arm, and her Y and teaching experience, the Y chose her to join that small band.[56] But by the time she had been vetted and trained, the war was over, much to her consternation.

Like many women war workers, whom the military tried to confine behind the lines and to position as moral guardians of men, Grace craved the proximity to battle that allowed women, as the journalist Margaret Deland put it, "to stand up beside the boys and say, 'Here! Look at me! I'm just as good a soldier in my way as you are in yours!'"[57] "The idea of taking chances just as our boys had on being submarined was very wonderful," Grace wrote. "When Peace came—there was a let down. No more danger of submarines—no more guns roaring at the front as a thrilling and inspiring background to whatever work there was to be done."[58]

As it turned out, Grace had not missed her chance, for it took almost two years for the American Expeditionary Force to bring all of the country's soldiers home, and the number of women war workers sent to the front actually peaked during demobilization. Moreover, the YWCA believed that, with so many men dead and their country in shambles, French women had "gone into industry to stay." To serve them, the Y resolved to maintain the Foyer des Alliées. Beyond that was the whole project of postwar reconstruction: the creation of the democratic world order that idealists believed would rise from the ashes of battle. Putting aside her dreams of working at the front, Grace quickly reconceived her mission. She would be a messenger bringing hope from "American girlhood and womanhood to French girlhood and womanhood" and helping women to rebuild a war-torn world.[59]

Grace sailed in January 1919 and, if her reports to Phi Mu are any indication, she seems to have found the storybook adventure she desired. "After all we had heard about January storms," she reported, "it was especially fine to have 'sunshine, moonshine, stars and winds a'blowing' the whole way over." On the tenth day, as she and other YWCA emissaries disembarked on the chaotic pier at Liverpool, the wind turned icy. British YWCA representatives greeted them with buns and strong tea, and the next night they were treated to "hot soup and wonderful hospitality." Traveling by boat, train, and army truck, they met larger-than-life women who had baled hay for the British Land Army and nurses who had lived in tents at the front, racing motor cars and ambulances along foreign roads and confronting the dreadful realities of modern war.[60] To Grace, such figures represented new models of womanhood—courageous, free-wheeling, and worldly-wise.

Arriving in the heart of Paris, Grace found herself ensconced in the YWCA's 250-room Hotel Petrograd. After a week spent mingling with men and women from all the allied countries, listening to ragtime in the hotel salon, and visiting foyers for French munitions workers, she departed for her first assignment: providing services for nurses at an American army base in Bazoilles-sur-Meuse, which the Americans stationed there had christened "Bazoilles-submerged." Reaching the base in the middle of the night, she could not put down her suitcases for fear they would sink into the muddy, melting snow.[61]

Along with her luggage, Grace dragged her trusty Corona typewriter, pecking out reports for the Phi Mu magazine at a time when women journalists were barred from the front. Her sketches of France, like those of many American soldiers, mixed wonderment with horror. Writing from the Meuse Valley, she practiced her budding literary skills on portraits of the Roman ruins, the beautiful walled towns, the snow-covered hills "with their fir trees, a lacy mixture of white and green," and the gently winding roads, which she likened to "awkward girls with many angles growing into soft, curving full blown womanhood." At the same time, she described a landscape transformed by the vast bureaucracy of war. "That gets one," she wrote, "the bigness and quickness of this thing that has been done. Building after building put up, organization after organization [ensuring that thousands were] housed and clothed and fed."[62]

As soon as she had settled in Bazoilles, she hitchhiked two miles to fetch refreshments for a base-wide dance in her honor, an errand that epitomized the complex position of women war workers, who were expected to provide not only skilled labor and moral guardianship but also entertainment for soldiers hungry for the company of American girls. Welfare organizations had initially opposed dancing on military bases, but soon gave in, and the "dance problem" became the problem of how to provide enough attractive but well-behaved partners for dance-crazy American men.[63]

Accustomed to living at home under her mother's eye or in a dormitory under the close watch of college officials, Grace relished this erotically charged camaraderie. One of the short stories she wrote at the College for Women, "A Musical Courtship," suggests the associations between work, sex, and popular culture that had occupied her girlish imagination but only now could find real-life expression. In that story, a poor little piano teacher strikes up a musical flirtation with the handsome piano-playing bachelor in the apartment upstairs. The girl's "proper soul" will not allow her to do more than greet him politely when they meet on the stairs, but when she hears him playing "Dearie," "Some One Thinks of Some One," and other romantic songs in quick succession, she goes to her piano and answers back. Suddenly, the door behind her opens and he is at her side. "The rest," seventeen-year-old Grace had written, "was not music." In France, Grace's dance programs were filled out mostly by a fellow named "Wallace" with whom she danced to numbers like "Kiss Me Quick," "Nurses' Favorite," "Jazz Baby," and the "Y.M.C.A. Fox Trot." Those programs were among the handful of mementoes she held on to for the rest of her life.[64]

Still, the fact that it was her job to slog through the mud fetching refreshments for a dance party is telling. As much as war workers enjoyed the openness of France, they also sensed, and sometimes resented, the drudgery of what amounted to glorified housework and the degree to which women's labor was conflated with men's entertainment. "Dancing is generally conceded to be a pleasure," wrote one canteen worker, "but when one has, in the space of a few months, danced 78,571 miles—or three times the distance around the earth—it ceases to

be such." Like women in brothels or commercial dance halls, war workers were expected to put their bodies at the service of men.[65]

Grace's reports home and the cache of wartime letters and photographs she saved suggest that she enjoyed the pleasures of female companionship at least as much as the opportunity to mingle with men,
as did the many war workers who used the Y's woman-only spaces to
re-create the patterns of sociability they had experienced in women's
colleges, voluntary organizations, and circles of intimate friends. From
Bazoilles Grace moved on to the nurses' embarkation center at Savenay
and then to her biggest adventure: a summer camp for French women
workers at Quiberon, a fishing village on the craggy coast of Brittany.[66]
Americans tended to see French women as dangerous temptresses. Yet
at Quiberon, Grace took responsibility for women who epitomized the
danger the military and most welfare organizations wanted to avoid:
dancers from the Grand Opera of Paris and actresses from the Théâtre
de la Gaîté. Far from scorning them as morally dubious entertainers,
Grace saw them as hard-pressed workers. They, in turn, adored her and
cherished the relief the Y's camp offered from their "confining and hum-
drum jobs."[67]

SETTING UP LIVING QUARTERS in a house and a tent, Grace entertained her charges with gymnastics and long walks. But she specialized
in weekly pageants and tableaux vivant, like those that had captured the
imagination of students when she was in college. In France, she could
experiment with even less restraint. Producing "The Dreams of a Young
Bachelor," she dressed her French charges in elaborate costumes "by the
house of Lumpkin" and had them play at being sailors with cigarettes
dangling from their lips, perform mock marriages, create tableaux based
on fairy tales, Greek myths, and Renaissance plays, and sing and dance
to her own intricate choreography.[68]

The most memorable of the dancers was sixteen-year-old Jacqueline
Lewis, who went on to attain the rank of "grand sujet" in the Grand
Opera in 1923. Friendships virtually never bloomed between American women and the French women they sought to help. Yet Lewis sent
"a thousand and a thousand very tender kisses" to her "great friend"
after Grace returned to the states. Calling herself "Your little 'Jackie,'
girlfriend who loved you so much," Lewis remembered their days at

Grace Lumpkin, while serving as a war worker for the YWCA, with Jacqueline Lewis, a dancer from the Grand Opera of Paris in Quiberon, France, 1919.

Quiberon as the happiest of idylls, marred only by the fear "of a happiness that 'doesn't last.'"[69]

Traveling alone, thrown back on her own resources as she improvised services and programs with little supervision, Grace seems to have taken on each new challenge with aplomb. Her final assignment sent her to Chateau Thierry, where the travel-writing rhapsodies of her early reports gave way to more somber observations. Here, she wrote, was truly "devastated France," where the once breathtaking countryside had been trampled into muddy ruts by the armies of the world. Her job was to supervise a house near the Belleau Woods and Fere en Tardennois cemeteries, where grieving American families came to search for the graves of young men who had made a "terrible sacrifice for the liberty of the world." Outside her window, she could hear the "scrape, scrape" of the boots of the gravediggers as they went about their melancholy task. She could also see huts on once prosperous farms occupied by women who had lost everything and "come back to the ruins to die."[70]

The gravediggers Grace mentions were German prisoners of war. But they could as easily have been African Americans, who were often confined to the grisly labor of burying and reburying the dead, tenderly handling the bodies of comrades who might well have shunned or tormented them in life. At home and abroad, Katharine wrote, the "races were kept meticulously apart; white boys in this part of camp; Negro boys in that part; white boys in these trenches; Negro boys in others."[71] Uncertain about how to train and deploy troops in a segregated army, the military had delayed for months before drafting black men and then drafted them out of proportion to their numbers. In France, only one out of five African American soldiers saw combat; most worked as stevedores and manual laborers. The US military issued a document, called "Secret Information concerning Black American troops," warning French officials not to "spoil the Negro" by offering even black officers the most common of courtesies: a shared meal, a shake of the hand, a word of praise. Above all, French civilians must not fraternize with black soldiers, which might lead to sex between white women and African American men.[72]

African American women struggled in vain to get to Europe, drawn, like their white counterparts, by the ideal of a war for democracy and driven by a burning desire to champion the honor, heal the bodies, and lift the morale of maligned black soldiers. Although the YWCA sent no African American emissaries abroad, Addie Waites Hunton, the pioneering consultant on "colored work" who helped to carry the association into the South a decade earlier, did manage to sail for France under the auspices of the YMCA. There, Hunton remembered, she and two other African American women aid workers fed, entertained, and comforted black soldiers in the face both of the "awful toll of death and suffering" and of blind prejudice, "that biting and stinging thing which is ever shadowing us in our own country."[73]

The YWCA paid little attention to this small handful of black women at the front, "notwithstanding the fact that they were women, and Americans, just like the others." Isolated, overworked, and often snubbed by white officers and YMCA war workers, Hunton and her comrades nevertheless found service in France exhilarating, in part because African American soldiers embraced them so warmly, in part because of their solidarity with the black troops from French colonies who were recruited to fight in the war, and in part because French civilians often ignored US propaganda against interracial fraternization. This experience abroad, wrote Hunton, "furnished . . . the first full breath of freedom" many African Americans had ever known, and she went on to become a central figure in the interracial women's peace movement and a dedicated pan-Africanist who championed the cause of colonial peoples struggling for independence around the world.[74]

GRACE LEFT FRANCE in the summer of 1920, returning to her hometown in South Carolina and plunging back into the social welfare efforts she had pursued before the war. She worked on and off as an industrial secretary for the YWCA and traveled the South speaking to women's groups about her wartime experiences and the challenges of postwar reconstruction. As an area director for the Student Fellowship Fund, a position she secured with Katharine's help, she raised money for students in central and eastern Europe who, as she told a Florida audience, were "staying at their studies in the face of indescribable difficulties."[75] At the same time, she drew on her training in home economics to secure a home demonstration position with the Agricultural Extension Service. Designed initially for farmers but expanded to industrial workers during World War I, the service's initiatives ranged from teaching farm women to can tomatoes and market eggs, to instructing textile workers on how to cook, sew, and economize and encouraging promising young women to attend the adult education "opportunity schools" run by Wil Lou Gray.[76]

In 1923 Grace plunged into what would prove to be a formative adventure. She found a room in a hotel owned and operated by a lumber company in a remote western North Carolina mountain community in Swain County and spent three months traveling through the Hazel Creek watershed, meeting the local people and soaking up the local culture. The area's most famous resident, Horace Kephart, had enshrined Hazel Creek in the popular imagination. He had moved there in 1904 in search of a "Back of Beyond" in which to experience the healing power of nature, but it was his observations of his neighbors, captured in *Our Southern Highlanders* (1913), that provided generations of readers with a picture of Appalachia as a "strange land" populated by castaways living much as their British ancestors had lived. What Grace saw, however, was not an isolated remnant of the past but a community that, once the Southern Railroad arrived in the early twentieth century, had been caught up in the booms and busts of a modern industrial economy.[77]

All of these experiences augmented Grace's earlier exposure to the travails of working women and strengthened her ties to the network of women she had met through her involvement in the Y and in the phil-anthropic work of her college sorority. But like many other women who served in France, she had come home wanting more from life than before: more romance, more adventure, a bigger place in a larger world. Unmar-ried, twenty-nine years old, and, once she moved back to Columbia, still living under the wings of her mother and brothers, Grace enrolled as a "special student" in literature at the University of South Carolina. Cul-tivating her talents as a writer, she began summoning the audacity for what would turn out to be a project of radical self-reinvention.

In postwar South Carolina, she found unexpected encouragement, even incitement, for that project. That incitement came initially from a critical bombshell: the publication in 1920 of H. L. Mencken's essay, "The Sahara of the Bozart," a caustic attack on southern literary cul-ture. Mencken's indictment of the "ugly dry-rot of sentimentalism and ancestor worship" that pervaded the region brought forth a howl from traditionalists. But to aspiring writers already chaffing against the moonlight-and-magnolias school of plantation novels, Mencken's was a voice of liberation.[78]

In Charleston, the Poetry Society took upon itself the task of leading a "literary revival that would sweep the state and spread over the whole South like a forest fire." The society's estimation of its own potential was too high by far, but it did launch a *Yearbook* that became one of the best small literary magazines of the era and a model for those that followed.[79] It also sponsored prize contests that recognized budding authors such as Olive Tilford Dargen, another writer who lived in and took her inspira-tion from Hazel Creek. Inspired by this ferment, emerging women writ-ers elsewhere in the South took as their subject the hardships of white rural life. Upending the plantation romance, they painted unsparing portraits of farm women struggling for transcendence or redemption.[80]

Meanwhile, in the women's clubs and UDC chapters to which Annette and Elizabeth were devoted, the cultural project conceived at the turn of the century chugged serenely along. In 1921, Columbia's Cur-rent Literature Club hosted an appearance by a doddering Thomas Nel-son Page, the doyen of plantation novelists and a favorite of the Lumpkin family. But now Page's effusions did not go unchallenged. Not only did the budding white literati find them downright embarrassing, but black women's clubs quietly promoted their own, alternative visions by study-ing and promoting the work of black writers. In this parallel world, the honored guest was W. E. B. Du Bois, whose research constituted a sustained attack on what he would later call "The Propaganda of History," as perpetrated both by professional historians and by the UDC.[81] What iconoclastic white writers and black club women had in common was a refusal to turn a blind eye to the South's underside and a resolute focus on new southern subjects: the ex-slaves, toiling white farmers, and embattled mill workers of their own times.

Within the Lumpkin family, William's quixotic move back to the land had had an ironic effect: it had thrown Katharine and, to a lesser extent Grace, who was already at the local College for Women at the time, into intimate contact with an unknown world, a world of poverty otherwise hidden behind the protective wall of not-knowing that allowed most genteel Southerners to go about the business of boosterish money-making in an Old South haze. Elizabeth's marriage to Eugene Glenn had also been revealing: the Lumpkins had always vacationed in the mountains, but Grace's summer visits with the Glenn family, and especially her sojourn on Hazel Creek, brought her into contact with the hardscrabble lives of mountain farmers, miners, and timber workers in the coves and hollows beyond the beaten tourist track. From 1912, when she got her first teaching job, through her sojourn in France and her YWCA and home demonstration work in the early 1920s, Grace played lady bountiful to poor women at home and abroad. Unlike Katharine, she did not ground herself deeply in the insights of the social sciences. But she was an astute observer: nothing was lost on her, least of all the broken bodies of working-class women, thrown away by a political economy of exploitation and a culture of neglect.

"We lived on a farm part of my childhood and I played with children of white tenant farmers, and the Negro children who worked in the cotton fields," Grace explained. "I have lived in mill villages and in the mountains . . . I saw a great many things that made me realize that the 'Sunny South' hides brutality and darkness behind the gracious face it tries to show to the world." That brutality and darkness would become the subject of her fiction, but what would set her work apart was her attention to the domestic, "the non-epic everyday": the music sparked by the gathering of rural folk in the mills; a child finding pleasure in rhymes and games; a mother calling out in a howling mountain storm.[82] Whether Grace was preparing French women to rebuild Europe, gossiping with young mill workers who shared her yearning for knowledge, romance, and adventure, helping their mothers learn to read in opportunity schools whose lesson plans endorsed trade unions and social legislation, or perambulating around the mountains, she was honing both her political and her writerly imagination. In that sense, the farm women, mill mothers, and working girls who came faithfully to adult education classes, home demonstration clubs, and YWCAs after long days of hard labor shaped these sites of learning even as they were shaped by them, and they taught as much as they learned.

The reform impulse of the Progressive era in which Grace and Katharine came of age entailed the sober practicalities of changing both the behavior of the poor and the policies of the state, but it also required the solidarity that flows from seeing strangers in new ways. "The Social Gulf is always an affair of the imagination," Jane Addams observed. For that reason, reformers used the tools of representation—photography, reportage, and fiction—to stir readers' consciences by bringing the poor sharply into view.[83] They also relied on the authority of experience, pitting their own testimony—"I was there. I saw this with my own eyes"— against the habits of denial. Well before she broke into print beyond student and sorority publications, Grace was caught up in this representational project. Consciously and unconsciously, she was gathering the stories and images on which her radical fiction would rely.

"A CLEAR
SHOW-DOWN"

———

A S GRACE MADE HER WAY HOME FROM THE FRONT, KATH-
arine, now twenty-three, set off on her own journey of return. None of her
professors at Columbia had noticed or encouraged her. But at the YWCA's
National Training School, which she attended after finishing her master's
degree in sociology in the fall of 1919, her presence registered.[1] Finding
college-educated women for staff positions was a constant challenge. "The
strongest are needed," as one report put it, women of "marked personality
who to tenderness add force and grasp, who show capacity for friendship,
and who to a fine character unite an intense moral and spiritual enthusiasm."[2] Katharine, the Y's National Board concluded, exemplified those
qualities. She was also a Southerner, and locals in the South were begging
both for what the Nashville YWCA termed a "trained experienced person" and "a southerner" and for "young women who will . . . work things
out along modern lines." Katharine "fell in love" with the YWCA in college. In the spring of 1920, she found herself called by the association to
become the national student secretary for the southern region.[3]

"NINETEEN-TWENTY BROUGHT me home," Katharine wrote, "but not
to a South of happy promise. . . . One sensed that a prolonged struggle
had begun."[4] The Great War had upset the balance of southern race,

class, and gender relations as surely as it redrew national boundaries in
Europe. Having gone to battle eager to earn first-class citizenship through
exemplary service, African American soldiers returned to face a wave of
violence. Black women who had taken advantage of wartime opportunities to escape domestic service became objects of wrath as well. Adding to
the tension was a crackdown by employers on the union locals organized
by white textile workers during the brief period in which they had enjoyed
a whirring economy and federal protection.[5] Spurred on by the Russian
Revolution, a postwar Red Scare simultaneously demonized radicals and
immigrants and tarred social justice advocacy as a Bolshevik plot. Most
unsettling to Katharine was the second coming of the Ku Klux Klan.
Founded in Atlanta in 1915, the KKK soon spread its "baleful wings" over
the Midwest and West, assailing a grab bag of enemies: not just African
Americans, but also immigrants and Bolsheviks, promiscuous women and
philandering men, Catholics and Jews.[6]

And yet, as Katharine emphasized, the 1920s were marked by "prolonged struggle" rather than by the wholesale triumph of reaction. In
the prevailing narrative of American history, US involvement in the
Great War, understood by many as a senseless catastrophe brought on
by the pursuit of naïve, misguided ideals, ushered in an era of political conservatism and frenetic materialism. But that view narrows the
scope and masks the vitality of the progressive impulses unleashed by
the conflict. African American veterans took the lead in struggles to
make good on the war's democratic promise. Socialists and Communists emerged from the Red Scare to create new forms of left-wing
politics.[7] Alarmed by white violence and black militancy, a small group
of white southern moderates reached out to black leaders to form the
Commission on Interracial Cooperation (CIC) and then, under the
leadership of a suffragist named Jessie Daniel Ames, launched a white
women's antilynching crusade, advancing efforts at racial equity within
the limits of segregation. Closest to home for Katharine was the ferment generated by the students and industrial workers who stepped
forward as a "vibrant, buoyant, insistent" force for change within the
YWCA and as members of a Christian student movement aimed at
confronting the human costs of industrialization and the iniquities of
imperialism and segregation.[8] Taking up her duties in the fall of 1920,
Katharine Lumpkin put herself at the heart of the students' and workers' endeavor.

THE INTERRACIAL MOVEMENT is usually identified with the cautious CIC, and most of what we know about the YWCA focuses on its city division, whose locals built and supervised the residential and recreational facilities for young working women with which the organization is most often identified.[9] That emphasis, however, has obscured the vanguard efforts of the Y's student and industrial programs. In the spring of 1920, just as Katharine was preparing to leave New York, these Y-affiliated groups claimed a right to self-governance and a strong voice in the association. Stepping forward at an historic national convention in Cleveland, Ohio, the student program campaigned to end the requirement that members belong to an evangelical Protestant church. To the alarm of those who feared "the trend in our time toward radical socialism," the industrial program's thirty thousand working-class members presented resolutions that put the Y on record as endorsing the social creed of the Federal Council of the Churches of Christ in America. That creed recognized the necessity of collective bargaining and called for establishing minimum wages and maximum hours as well as ending child labor. The conferees also pledged to go beyond moral suasion by mobilizing newly enfranchised women to push for progressive legislation.[10]

Less successful was an appeal by southern black women for control over the affairs of segregated city branches and representation in the governance of the national organization. The Cleveland convention failed to act on their demands, setting the stage for decades of struggle over the gap between the Y's practice and its lofty self-image as a multiracial organization dedicated to the interests of girls and women "of every race, every creed, every occupation."[11] But the gathering did take a step that would have far-reaching implications. It urged the student division to design an "interracial education" program capable of bringing to "the Negro question" the same attention the Y was giving to issues of labor.[12]

Katharine's commitment to implementing the interracial program brought her into collaboration with a trio of remarkable young African American women—Juliette Derricotte, Juanita Jane Saddler, and Frances Harriet Williams—who insisted on equity and authority as matters of practice as well as principle. She also worked closely with a network of industrial secretaries and workers' education advocates, most of whom were socialists or social democrats, as they cultivated "the emerging leadership and class-consciousness of industrial girls."[13]

Like Katharine, these black and white activists belonged to a coterie of women who were born just before the turn of the century, joined the first wave of southern women to attend college in significant numbers, and came to political consciousness in the years surrounding the war.[14] Most hailed from middle-class families, but some grew up in quite humble circumstances; in the case of the black Southerners, virtually all were born to parents who were one generation removed from slavery. These young women had discovered the YWCA as students in the South's black coeducational institutions or white women's colleges or, in a few cases, in the elite women's colleges of the North. Many had gone on to pursue graduate study in New York City. Trained in religious education and the social sciences, they embarked on careers at a moment when the leadership of churches was monopolized by men, the barriers that excluded white women from the academy were just beginning to be breached, and even superbly educated black women were barred from most of the professions save teaching. Some of these women married, but most remained single, in part because of the difficulties and taboos faced by those who wanted to combine marriage and motherhood with demanding careers, and in part because the Y's organizational culture bound them together in a common political and spiritual purpose that allowed strong friendship networks and intimate partnerships to grow in tandem with professional careers.[15]

The historian George Chauncey has suggested that by the 1920s, when modern homosexual communities emerged in urban areas, the Young Men's Christian Association's residential hotels had become centers of gay sex and social life. Although never directly acknowledged, this development led YMCA leaders to fear that its stress on Christian brotherhood might discredit the organization by encouraging a dangerous intimacy among men. These anxieties helped to motivate the YMCA's attempts to coopt the YWCA: by merging the two groups' activities, male leaders hoped to transform the women's association into a female auxiliary in which young men could mingle with respectable young women.[16]

Same-sex relationships within the YWCA were relatively immune to such concerns, as they had been in the nineteenth century. Florence

Simms, a Christian socialist, the revered founder of the Y's industrial program, and a key figure in ushering working women into a central role in Y affairs, lived in an openly avowed partnership with another woman. The widely admired student secretary Winnifred Wygal, a founding member with Reinhold Niebuhr of the Fellowship of Socialist Christians, was passionately involved with two different women at different times and cultivated intimate friendships with many others as well. Juliette Derricotte agonized over her prospects for marriage, but she was deeply attached to Juanita Saddler. (Anticipating a reunion with Saddler after crossing the Atlantic, Derricotte exclaimed, "I think I shall jump overboard when I get a glimpse of thee.")[17] Married women staff members also sustained passionate friendships with female colleagues, both before and after their marriages.[18] Yet even these ardent romantics could not escape the self-consciousness produced by the post–World War I spread of Freudian ideas and popular anxieties about the expression of same-sex desire. No wonder they resisted labels, destroyed their letters, pursued their relationships with discretion, and kept to themselves and their trusted friends the pleasures and heartaches expressed so freely by Katharine and her classmates during their prewar college years.[19]

Like the affective relationships it fostered, the Y's identification with the women's movement endured into the 1920s while changing in response to new pressures and circumstances.[20] The members of Katharine's cohort were more likely than their predecessors to work through mixed-sex organizations, both from their base in the Y and in their later careers. And they distanced themselves from the brand of feminism that, in the 1920s, came to be associated with the National Woman's Party, an elitist, single-issue organization that campaigned for an equal rights amendment to the Constitution and opposed protective legislation for women workers. Indeed, so thoroughly did the Woman's Party monopolize the "feminist" label that Katharine's generation seldom used the term. Instead, they "took it as a given that women should enjoy the same political rights and educational and professional opportunities as men" and focused on drawing young women into the leadership of the Christian student movement, which was otherwise dominated by YMCA men.[21] Key to their efforts was the younger generation of college students and industrial workers whom they nurtured and from whom they learned.

Together, these two groups of black and white southern women— the student and industrial secretaries who took up their duties at the start of the decade and the students and workers they recruited—set in motion an intergenerational chain of learning that encouraged successive cohorts of young women to develop the passion and self-confidence to forge activist identities and professional careers. In the 1930s, women influenced by the industrial program bolstered the southern labor movement. During the era of conservative retrenchment sparked by the Cold War, the student division, along with the black leaders of the city Ys, led the Y in sustaining its critique of racism and of women's place in the social order. Throughout the twentieth century, black women's struggles for racial justice and women's rights were grounded in large part in the association's brand of ecumenical liberal Christianity.[22] And practically every white southern student who stood with the civil rights movement of the 1960s seems to have been mentored by the YWCA or another social gospel–based youth organization.[23]

During the half decade Katharine devoted to the association, exhilaration alternated with angst and confusion. In her struggle to articulate the ideas and implement the strategies that underlay her work, we can see what institutional studies almost never reveal: how activists test their assumptions in practice and are liberated by their forays across social fissures or stymied by social constraints. By the time she left the Y in 1925, Katharine's involvement with the southern industrial secretaries had riveted her attention on "the economic influences which play upon . . . actions and attitudes."[24] Through her relationship with the African American student secretaries, she had arrived at a way of seeing the "Negro problem" that was rooted in the Y's moral imagination but embraced structural solutions. In combination, these two separate but overlapping experiences—collaborating with the white industrial secretaries to empower working women and create cross-class alliances and with the black student secretaries to change racial attitudes and practices—shaped the political consciousness she carried forward in the years to come.

KATHARINE SPENT MOST of her time as southern student secretary in Atlanta, where she often shared an apartment with her widowed mother, but initially she was based in Richmond, Virginia. In both cases, she was constantly on the road, traveling by train over a vast territory, with regular trips to the Y's New York headquarters. She was responsible for perhaps two hundred college associations, each of which had its own character and concerns, and much of her time was spent teaching young women the mechanics of running an organization. On some campuses, she found associations that were making "splendid progress" but still needed a tremendous amount of help in understanding the Y's social ideals. At others she "was kept very busy 'being nice,' but . . . after days full of people and walks and events and some meetings . . . felt that nothing really had been done."[25] Such frustrations came with the territory, but they also reflected the fact that at first she had no model for going beyond the routine work of a YWCA secretary to take up what she saw as her main challenge: reaching across chasms of social distance to build a student interracial movement in the segregated South.

That began to change while she and Louise Leonard (McLaren), the Y's industrial secretary for the southern region, were sharing a bare-bones apartment in Richmond. The two women became "great friends," and that friendship helped to inflect Katharine's interest in race relations with class concerns and gave her a model for bridging racial divides. Leonard had grown up in a well-to-do Pennsylvania family, graduated from Vassar, and attended the Y's National Training School, where she came under the influence of Florence Simms. Named the first national industrial secretary for the South in 1920, she was in charge of nurturing the city Ys' industrial clubs, but she was especially interested in bringing students and workers together. Soon the two groups were exchanging delegates at their separate summer conferences and organizing regional industrial commissions and local study groups focused on social problems.[26]

At these gatherings, the student and industrial secretaries worked to discourage an attitude of "doing for the industrial girls" and to create an atmosphere in which students and workers could learn from each other by bringing their distinct experiences to bear. Wage-earning women contributed their firsthand knowledge of the economic system "at the point where its pressure on human lives is hardest"; students brought the perspectives of the social sciences. Pooling these resources, the participants sought to understand the economic and social forces that bore down on all of their lives. These insights, the secretaries believed, would provide workers and students alike with a "greater capacity of social action, for working with other people, for taking into account various viewpoints . . . in other words, a capacity to act as citizens in a commonwealth as well as members of a special group."[27]

In the summer of 1922, Louise Leonard and Katharine Lumpkin decided to launch a more daring boundary crossing venture. Together, they organized a students-in-industry project in Atlanta, where Katharine now resided. Their goal was to enable young Y secretaries and "college women who have missed much of life's drudgery [to] know in their own bodies and minds what it means to be a part of the present industrial system." Pursuing that goal through a combination of study and lived experience, they began by asking the students they recruited to read the works on economics, sociology, and social Christianity that were influencing their own thinking.[28] The recruits then plunged into an "exploration of an unknown field," walking the streets in search of unskilled jobs, working long hours under terrible conditions, living in rooming houses, and subsisting on what they earned. They met each Sunday to discuss their experiences and listen to lectures. They also documented the practices of exploitative employment agencies and watched "the capitalists" testify at a legislative hearing on a bill limiting women's work to ten hours a day. As one student reported, the men "told of the wonderful life a woman in a cotton mill leads. . . . And there was not a soul there to speak on the other side, somebody who could say: 'Those things are not true—I've been there and I know.'"[29]

Reflecting on their six weeks of labor, the participants resolved to enlist others "in such study and action as will ultimately change the industrial order." At least two of them did so, devoting their lives to the ideals they absorbed from this "wonderful experiment" and from their ongoing involvement in the YWCA.[30] Alice Norwood (Spearman Wright) went on to Columbia University in search of "a much broader perspective" on what she had learned. After working as an industrial secretary, she became an administrator in a New Deal work relief program and one of South Carolina's most prominent white advocates of civil rights.[31] Lois MacDonald, a poor farm girl from South Carolina who was serving as secretary of a student Y, came away from working the night shift at the Fulton Bag and Cotton Mill determined to pursue a career in industrial reform. After studying at the London School of Economics and earning a PhD at New York University, she joined the NYU faculty, despite the skepticism of a dean who "said women could not teach economics." She also joined Louise Leonard in codirecting one of the country's premier workers' education institutions, the Southern Summer School for Women Workers, which held its first session in 1927.[32]

———

THE SUCCESS OF THE students-in-industry project reinforced Katharine's belief in the life-altering impact of bringing students into contact with people unlike themselves. By the time it ended, she also had an administrative blueprint for restructuring the southern student division so as to ensure that the interracial program she envisioned would spark "a real movement of women for democracy" shaped equally by blacks and whites.[33] At the Y's 1922 convention, the National Student Assembly voted to create a new governing body for the southern division: an interracial southern student council made up of students, alumnae, and professional secretaries. Council members would be elected at the YWCA's all-important summer conferences: whites at the YMCA-affiliated Blue Ridge Assembly in the mountains of North Carolina, blacks at their own separate conferences at Talladega College in Alabama. An interracial committee with black and white co-chairs was charged with helping the secretaries carry out a program of interracial education.[34]

Bowing to the exigencies of segregation while at the same time guarding their autonomy, Frances Williams, Juliette Derricotte, and Juanita Saddler would retain responsibility for the Ys in the South's black colleges, which comprised approximately half of the country's one hundred black student associations, while also ministering to the besieged minority of black women in the overwhelmingly white institutions of higher education in the Midwest. Lumpkin would continue to oversee white southern Ys. But she would no longer serve as the sole head of the southern division. Instead, she and Williams would share that leadership role.[35]

At a time when white "central" city Ys sought both to distance themselves from and to control the affairs of black branches, and white Southerners within the Commission on Interracial Cooperation assumed that they, not their black colleagues, would set the pace for the interracial movement, the southern students' new structure represented a bold departure. It was also convoluted and unwieldy. Complicating yet enriching the situation further was the fact that each of the four student secretaries brought to this experiment in mixing autonomy with shared authority her own race- and class-inflected background, temperament, and concerns.

Looking back from the vantage point of the mid-1930s, Frances

Williams said that Katharine was "the first southern white girl whom I really liked." But she remembered tensions as well. Interviewed in the mid-1970s, Katharine put it this way: "We were trying to be such good collaborators. [We] both wanted to do well by each other. And I don't think [Williams] trusted me, and I was probably a little scared of her ... because she was a very outspoken woman."[36] Indeed she was, in ways that set her apart from Juliette Derricotte and Juanita Saddler, who worked so smoothly with Katharine that the three women constituted "a perfect working machine," according to Ethel M. Caution, a Harlem Renaissance poet, Y activist, and dean of women at Talladega College.[37]

The differences between Williams and her colleagues were subtle but significant. Each of these young women rejected the badge of inferiority and fought to protect herself from the soul-scarring wounds racism inflected. Writing to Saddler, Derricotte acknowledged that an "act of discrimination produces a destructive hatred inside of me." Still, she was a master of what was for Katharine a deeply familiar and comforting form of politesse. In both her work with black college Ys and her interra-

Juliette Derricotte, a YWCA student secretary in the 1920s, traveled the world on behalf of the World Christian Association and served as dean of women at Fisk University. At thirty-four, she died in a car accident in Dalton, Georgia, due in part to the fact that she and her fellow passengers were not taken to the nearby whites-only hospital, sparking an outcry that helped to push the YWCA toward an increasingly forthright stand against segregation.

cial activities, she used the insults she endured as object lessons to shame white students and present young black women with a model of fearless and dignified Christian womanhood to which they could aspire.[38]

Juanita Saddler, too, was sustained by an abiding Christian faith. Characterized by her friends as a "brooding beauty," Saddler was "part-Cherokee, and often spoke proudly of her double heritage." She was born in Oklahoma Territory in 1892, where both her parents were classified by the census as "mulattos" and her father was a lawyer and a judge. After graduating from Fisk University in 1915, she served as a YWCA branch secretary in Winston-Salem, North Carolina, then moved to New York to work for the student Y and was immediately taken under Derricotte's wing.[39]

For Derricotte and Saddler, joining the student staff had been like "stepping into this little world of youth and belief and glorious golden dreams." In that world they had found "for the first time sincerity in a white person's profession of friendship."[40] Frances Williams, by contrast, remembered her years with the YWCA as an "unhappy period," in part because of the way she was treated by the white New York staff, but also because the Y offered too little scope for her talents and ambitions. Born in slavery, Williams's grandmothers on both sides had passed on their passion for education to her parents, who graduated from Berea College in Kentucky, a school founded by abolitionists as the South's first inter-racial and coeducational college. Her father earned a master's degree at the University of Cincinnati and went on to become the only black prin-cipal of a high school in St. Louis, Missouri. Her mother served on the Y's first colored work committee under Eva Bowles. Frances graduated as valedictorian of her high school class in 1919, attended the University of Cincinnati for a year, and then transferred to Mount Holyoke, despite the school's efforts to dissuade her from coming when the deans discov-ered that she was black. Majoring in sociology, she was elected to Phi Beta Kappa and awarded a fellowship to the New York School of Social Work, a storied institution now affiliated with Columbia University, at a time when few such schools were admitting African American women.[41]

Immediately after Williams finished her graduate work, Eva Bowles offered her a position with the student Y. Williams had no particular interest in working for a Christian women's organization. But she was in dire need of money, and she was well aware that for her, as for other members of the small group of black women who earned degrees from elite northern colleges in the late nineteenth and early twentieth centuries, professional opportunities were vanishingly small. Asked by an interviewer why she had accepted Bowles's invitation, Williams replied: "I had no alternatives. It was a way to earn my bread and butter, darling. This was stern necessity."[42]

Juliette Derricotte and Juanita Saddler were bound by ties of affection and admiration to the white members of the National Student Council staff, especially to the council head, Leslie Blanchard, and to Winnifred Wygal, whose "knowledge of far places" came from her involvement in the World Student Christian Federation.[43] Frances Williams, on the other hand, found herself at odds with the national staff from the start. Interviewed in the 1970s and 1980s, she recounted an early, emblematic incident with undimmed fury. She was living at the African American YWCA in Brooklyn while taking preparatory courses at the National Training School when a white administrator insisted that she move into the Training School's otherwise all-white dormitory "so the other girls would see how to live with a colored girl."[44] Williams complied but smoldered at this preview of one of the maddening aspects of a black secretary's job: she was expected to venture out of supportive, autonomous black institutions in order to model small acts of integration in an oblivious or hostile white world.

Williams's continuing problems with the white Y staff were manifested, as she saw it, mainly in their gossip about her perceived arrogance and their tendency to play favorites among the black secretaries on the basis not of excellence but of geniality.[45] She saw herself as a cut above Juanita Saddler and Juliette Derricotte (both of whom were products of the small-town South and black colleges) because of her urban upbringing, her parents' status, and her excellent education. She especially resented being bypassed in favor of Derricotte when it came to representing the Y at international conferences.[46] But Frances Williams's straight-talking self-confidence was more hard-won than most of those around her—including Katharine—imagined. As she later told her close friend and confidant NAACP head Walter White, she could be "terrifically shy & backward" in social situations. "My over-aggressiveness at times is the result."[47]

In this context, the wonder is not that Williams's and Lumpkin's effort to forge what Katharine called a true "corelationship" sometimes foundered but that they managed to work together so effectively and, in the end, to build such mutual respect. Writing to a white national student staff member, Katharine tried to work out her understanding of what sharing authority with a black colleague would entail. She and Williams would be identically positioned in relationship to the southern student council as well as to the national staff. If students or staff had a problem or question, they could go to either secretary, although there would be a "natural division of labor" in which Katharine would advise on white schools and Williams on those for blacks. In the end, however, she had to admit that her thoughts were "clear as mud." This new way of working "must be wrought out in experience . . . beginning with the determination to recognize oneself as only one-half of a proposition." The problem was that, over the previous two years, all involved had grown accustomed to viewing Katharine as the head of the southern division. Now she and Williams must come to grips with "the fact that we are two instead of one—and yet we must work as nearly as possible as a unit." She was, she concluded, "terribly glad we are to try this way of working—it's the closest yet to a fair and right scheme that I have seen."[48]

Williams was less sanguine. Writing to "Jule" (Juliette Derricotte) and "Jane" (Juanita Jane Saddler), she recounted a fraught discussion with

Frances Harriet Williams, a YWCA student secretary in the 1920s and 1930s who shared leadership responsibilities with Katharine in the southern region. She went on to work closely with Walter White of the NAACP and to serve as race relations advisor to the head of the Office of Price Administration during the New Deal.

Katharine. She had begun by spelling out *her* view of their division of labor: she would have the right to make all decisions regarding the black schools in her charge, consulting with Katharine as needed but without being bound by her suggestions. When Lumpkin wanted her "to do a special piece of work" such as visiting a white campus or speaking at a whites-only summer conference, she (Williams) would "take orders . . . and report back."[49] Williams was especially concerned that certain black and white staffers would view Lumpkin as her senior in the southern field and would "be ever so eager to go over my head to her." To prevent that possibility, she suggested that Derricotte and Saddler consult with her about any issues that arose concerning the black members of the student council rather than talking to Katharine about them directly.[50]

A few weeks after this loaded conversation, Katharine responded to Williams in writing. She made no objection to Williams's suggestion that she stop consulting directly with Derricotte and Saddler, although she hinted at her regret at the change. But she did stress her different "way of thinking": "I guess I am always rebellious at 'taking orders' from anyone and equally so at giving them—so the idea is not congenial to me; my conception is that of a cooperative evolving of what is done."[51]

Katharine could not have been more well-meaning, and she could not have reflected more clearly the Y's foundational commitment to a collaborative, democratic decision-making process summed up in the oft-repeated phrase "thinking it through together."[52] But she underestimated the weight of the unequal power relationships between blacks and whites that created a yawning gap between the Y's racial practices and its heart-felt ideals. She could assume, as Williams could not, that she would have the support of the white headquarters staff and that all involved would treat her with respect. She could afford to rely on "a cooperative evolving of what is done." Frances Williams, by contrast, knew what she was up against. She had been asked to hammer out a highly unusual relationship with a white Southerner and to work in tandem with two black colleagues whom she saw as favored by the white staff despite being less qualified than she. She wanted the terms of engagement spelled out.

Such tensions could put "great strain on [the secretaries'] will to fellowship," Katharine reflected, but both she and Williams were careful not to let them "interfere with the work." Determined to get "as much money for the South as possible," they presented a united front at national staff meetings where, as Williams remembered it, they "would aid and abet one another . . . in a remarkable fashion."[53] Nor did the two women's differences preclude moments of authentic human connection. After bluntly spelling out her ground rules for collaboration, Frances Williams had gone on to say that she was borrowing two books from Katharine's desk to read on her travels: Kahlil Gibran's *The Prophet* (1923) and *Towards Democracy* (1883) by the British Socialist and early gay activist Edward Carpenter, a gesture that suggests the eclectic intellectual life these young women shared and the measure of social ease that they managed to achieve.[54]

DESPITE THESE COMPLICATIONS, the southern student secretaries forged ahead, united by their shared understanding of themselves as leaders of a Christian youth movement that was aligned with the struggle for women's rights and their determination to make racial equity central to the agendas of both. Three assumptions shaped how they planned to achieve their goals. The first was that the Y could and should provide black and white students with an extracurricular education within their separate colleges and in interracial settings. Through the study of liberal Christianity, the social sciences, and black history and literature, young Southerners would learn to frame race relations both as a moral problem and as a man-made system that could be comprehended and transformed. From that understanding would flow a passion for justice tempered by analysis. Their second assumption was that fundamental change had to come from the bottom up: the Y secretaries could expose students to new ideas and experiences, but their aim was a democratically run "student movement project," driven by young people rather than by themselves. The third was that the best way to overcome invidious racist stereotypes and nurture "respect for personality" across the color line was to bring white students into contact with their black peers, as well as with the African American secretaries themselves.[55]

Guided by these ideas, the secretaries hammered out a program of interracial education. They began by drawing up bibliographies to distribute to student groups and creating a circulating "Library on Race" to which colleges could subscribe.[56] Even this seemingly innocuous endeavor felt significant, given how little white students knew about the subject and the degree to which social Darwinism and other forms of scientific racism still pervaded most published works. Only a few years earlier, the national Committee on Colored Work had feared that encouraging white southern students to study race might be "a dangerous thing" because there was "very little appropriate literature" on the subject. Determined to avoid pernicious fare and to expose themselves and their student constituency to contemporary currents in African American thought, Katharine and her colleagues solicited advice on readings from the black leaders on the committee and passed new material back and forth among themselves.[57]

In 1923, Katharine Lumpkin and Frances Williams launched the second phase of their educational project: establishing interracial groups dedicated to the study of local conditions. In a region where spaces for meeting on a basis of equality were almost nonexistent and white students were schooled in bigotry and condescension and black students in dissemblance and distrust, holding such seemingly anodyne gatherings required herculean effort. Traveling to Nashville, Lumpkin consulted with the general secretary of the city's white central YWCA, who helped to identify white participants from Scarritt College for Christian Workers and Peabody Teachers College, both of which promoted liberal Christianity and the advancement of women. On her trips to the city, Frances Williams had to overcome the skepticism of the autocratic white president of Fisk University, one of the South's premier black institutions, in order to recruit an equal number of African Americans, all of whom were, she reported, "girls of good brain power, sane balance and loveliness of spirit."[58]

Separately, Lumpkin and Williams worked to prepare students for these unprecedented encounters. For Williams and the other black secretaries, that meant giving black students a sense of "real kinship with our student movement" by convincing them that behind the seemingly solid façade of white supremacy stood a saving remnant of white allies and friends. For Lumpkin it meant ensuring that white students would engage with their black peers on a basis of equality and respect. In both cases, the goal was to create respites from the etiquette of what Richard Wright termed "living Jim Crow," challenge deeply ingrained assumptions of white privilege and black subjugation, and establish an atmosphere of "natural . . . give and take."[59]

Reporting on the Nashville group's progress, Frances Williams was ecstatic. By the spring of 1923, the students had elected black and white co-chairs and undertaken surveys of local conditions in areas such as housing and education. They had not found "new problems or stagger-ing facts," but they had formed "new friendships which would be walls of steel protecting them from future on-rushes of prejudice storms and keen edge instruments which would help them clear up the under-brush of inter-racial problems which life might bring them."[60] A year later, Katharine reported that, although they had failed to form a similar group in Atlanta because of the refusal of the president of Agnes Scott, a prestigious white women's college, to allow the school's students to attend, the Nashville gatherings had expanded to include young men from the YMCA, and students were forming similar groups on other campuses entirely on their own initiative. By 1925, she was predicting the emergence of "an organized student interracial movement in the South within the next five years."[61]

That optimism rested not only on these student-led gatherings but also on the response of white students to the African American secretar-ies who appeared with Katharine on carefully chosen white campuses. The most encouraging of these visits took place at Hollins College in Virginia and North Carolina College for Women in Greensboro. Adela F. Ruffin, the black city Y secretary whom Katharine had so memora-bly encountered as a naïve college girl five years before, had spoken at both institutions. But Katharine Lumpkin and Juliette Derricotte had more intensive and challenging events in mind. In addition to an eve-ning address open to both the campus and the community, Derricotte would meet with small groups of students over the course of two days, leading them in what she characterized as "free and frank" discussions that would encourage them to confront their own "prejudices and igno-rances" and to see "segregation, discrimination, and denial of rights" as what they were: tools for maintaining white supremacy.[62]

Katharine made advance visits to each school, talking with admin-istrators, faculty members, student leaders, and local residents to make sure that they understood who the speaker was and what would be dis-cussed. Her aim was to stave off controversy and minimize the degree to which her African American colleague would feel the sting of disre-spect. "We would back and fill," she remembered, trying "to search out some new *modus vivendi* which fitted into our shifting canons of what the Southern traffic would bear, and into our colleagues' canons of how far they could go in flouting principles of common decency." At even the most enlightened of white institutions, "we whites would be entertained

in the college guest room, have our meals with the students, move without restraint about the campus. Where would our Negro colleague stay,
where eat, and what do, during those hours while she waited to speak
before the students?"[63] At North Carolina College for Women, "a thoroughly democratic school" where the groundwork had been laid by Lois
MacDonald (the Atlanta students-in-industry project alumna who was
serving as student secretary for the college), it did not occur to anyone to
invite Derricotte to dinner on campus after her talk, much less arrange
for her to stay on campus. Instead, MacDonald found Derricotte a place
to board in the black community. When the dinner bell rang to summon
white students and faculty to the dining room, MacDonald dined in
town with Derricotte and an African American friend.[64]

  After these trips, Katharine filed a glowing report. Juliette Derricotte
was "splendid and wise and fearless. . . . There was no question about the
challenge" she laid down. In the discussions at Hollins, "there was no
'putting the lid on': no caution or fear as to what could be said or left
unsaid." The students asked about "equality between the races, what it
really means and whether it can and should exist." They considered "the
conception of 'white supremacy' and what it is doing to race relations
today." They also brought up all "the usual ideas" about the "'mental
inferiority' and . . . morality of the negro" and the threat of amalgamation, but in the spirit of asking whether there was any truth in their
"cherished conceptions" and "laying bare what needed to be discarded."[65]
According to Derricotte's separate account, once the students had concluded "that there was no logical basis" for theories of black inferiority
and immorality and understood that "white people were more concerned
[about] and were the greatest offenders in regard to amalgamation," they
were left with the conclusion that "the *fear of equality* had crowded out all
thought of *justice*." Derricotte's visit, the president of the campus Y concluded, "stirred Hollins more deeply than I have ever seen it stirred."[66]

  A guide to interracial education drawn up by an unnamed student
staff member in 1925 suggests how far the secretaries were—and were
not—willing to go in encouraging students to confront taboo topics and
the anxieties that such discussions could arouse. Couched as a series
of rhetorical questions implicitly addressed to white students, it began
by asking whether World War I had been caused by "the competition
between different groups of the white race in their selfish scramble to
expand into these parts of the world occupied by the darker races and

to dominate them." It then posed a series of other questions: "What do we mean by race?" What have anthropologists to say on the differences in capacity between races? Is the idea of race superiority a tradition such as the divine right of kings, or the superiority of male over female, or is it a scientific fact? Is "race aversion" a reflection of the desire of one race to dominate another? The final question probed interracialism's ultimate goal. Did "full racial justice" require an end to segregation, in custom and at law? Would the end of segregation entail "amalgamation"? Would amalgamation spell the end of "race"? Reinscribing the racial essentialism it called into question, the discussion guide ended by asking whether, in order to achieve a just society, white women would have to marry black men: "Must we be prepared to sacrifice our racial inheritance—perhaps the most precious thing we have—in order to contribute the most to the universal good?"[67]

Given the national hysteria over "race mixing" and the fact that interracial marriage was a felony in North Carolina and illegal in most southern states, it is no wonder that, as Katharine observed, even adults who were sympathetic to the brand of interracialism practiced by the CIC sometimes feared that the student Y was "going too fast." Those fears, Katharine believed, reflected their recognition that "'youth' is apt to be rather ruthlessly consistent as to conclusions, if forced to face facts vividly." Interracial contacts, along with "new understandings and resulting convictions," might "lead youth (at some not far distant day), to 'extreme ideas' about race relations." To Katharine this possibility was what made the project of interracial education so important, although she had no doubt that, as it proceeded, "we shall be questioned more, and blocked often."[68]

CRITICISM OF THE STUDENT Y was indeed plentiful, and it came from a variety of quarters. The white leaders of city Ys were among those who feared the departure from the strictures of segregation and were anxious about where the honest conversational community the student secretaries were trying to promote might lead. They worried especially that, because the relative autonomy of the Y's various divisions was lost on the public, the students' interracial activities might sully their own reputation.[69]

College administrators could be an even bigger problem. Schools such as Brenau, Hollins, and North Carolina College for Women offered an intellectual and political environment that was more lively than most studies of southern women's education would lead us to expect. But in an era when universities throughout the country dismissed iconoclastic students and professors with impunity, the presidents of the region's small denominational colleges, which most white women students attended, exercised autocratic power. They, in turn, were beholden to church-appointed trustees dedicated not only to preserving the racial status quo but also to perpetuating what Katharine called a "conservative and 'orthodox' making" religion, or, at best, what Frances Williams described as "the easy going brand of Christianity which was 'This is the right way, but we must be practical.'"[70] Administrators of public institutions had the "legislature to deal with." At the South's few white coeducational institutions, women students constituted a small, closely watched minority, confined to a single dormitory or dispersed among respectable families in town. They were, as Katharine observed, "held accountable for every act" in ways that men were not.[71]

The experience of Thelma Stevens, who went on to lead the women's wing of the national Methodist Church in struggles for peace, racial justice, and women's rights, was a case in point. At Hattiesburg State Teachers College in Mississippi, she teamed up with her roommate, the president of the college YWCA, to invite an African American teacher to a series of Wednesday night discussions about black education. After the woman's second visit, the president called the two girls to his office. As Stevens remembered it, he exclaimed: "'I didn't start this college to train a bunch of Yankee schoolteachers!' 'Don't you ever let another black person' (he called them 'niggers') 'come on this campus to meet with the student body. . . . If you do I will have to *ship* you both.'" Stevens could not afford to be expelled. Going to college in the first place had been "a miracle." She was the orphaned daughter of small farmers and had grown up working in the fields, barely attended school four months a year, and then taught for three years before a college scholarship unexpectedly "landed in my lap."[72] So the two Y leaders contacted the teacher, who arranged for the students to continue meeting with her in a black church.

The student secretaries, too, had to work around the limits that college administrators imposed. As she traveled to white colleges, Katharine encountered presidents who outlawed student governments altogether and deans of women who practically ran college Ys. Both were alarmed by the Y's emphasis on student self-government and quick to complain when students who "used to receive great . . . spiritual blessing" from the Y instead got the idea that they should "have far more liberty" and fewer "rules and regulations."[73]

The South's black institutions, most of which were coeducational, varied widely but could be just as problematic. Atlanta University in Georgia and Talladega College in Alabama stood at one end of the spectrum of the college environments the African American secretaries encountered. Grace Towns (Hamilton), a member of the southern student council who, in 1926, was elected vice-president of the National Student Assembly, the first black woman to be chosen for such a high post, grew up on the Atlanta University campus, where she was encouraged by her teachers to channel her talents into the YWCA. After marrying an Atlanta University professor, she worked closely with Frances Williams on the Y's professional staff, then became the first woman to serve as executive director of the Atlanta Urban League, a position that put her on the frontlines of the civil rights battles of the 1940s and 1950s. Marshaling a steely will, rare political acumen, and a strikingly elegant demeanor, she seized the opening created by the 1965 Voting Rights Act to become the first African American woman to win election to the Georgia legislature.[74]

Dean of Women Ethel Caution made Talladega College available for black students' summer conferences and welcomed the Y's interracial committee meetings to the campus as well. Caution was proud to offer the rarest of gifts: an opportunity for "seclusion and a chance for an intimate group fellowship" at "a place where we have colored and white faculty demonstrating how possible it is for the two groups to work together in peace and harmony."[75] As a student at Talladega, Juliette Derricotte had been president of the campus YWCA. Dean Caution and her colleagues viewed Derricotte as one of the school's most distinguished graduates, and they embraced her warmly when she came to town.

At the other end of the spectrum were institutions that placed insuperable obstacles in the path of the black secretaries. When Frances Williams reported on a visit to Le Moyne Institute in Memphis, which had been founded by abolitionists in the American Missionary Association, she could hardly contain her indignation. The white president had fired most of the well-trained black teachers and replaced them with whites "of a very mediocre grade." Controlling "her faculty so that one feels they would even ask her if it was proper for them to breath[e]," the president prevented Williams from bringing up the "race question" by canceling her meeting with the faculty and carefully monitoring her encounters with students.[76]

Adding immeasurably to the demands on the black secretaries was the fact that they were expected to work with students not only in the South but throughout the Midwest at a time when restrictive housing covenants were solidifying segregation in the cities and the second incarnation of the Ku Klux Klan was seizing political power. Juliette Derricotte remembered her first year with the Y, which she spent visiting Midwestern campuses where black students were often excluded from college associations, as the loneliest and most miserable of her life.[77] Frances Williams observed that by the 1920s even Oberlin, her parents' alma mater and one of the first integrated colleges in the country, was no longer a place of "absolute freedom." "Unwritten laws have grown up prohibiting colored students from taking . . . part in [school] functions." The Midwest, Williams believed, was becoming the new "danger point of the country in race relationships."[78]

Also transregional in scope were denunciations of the student Y by businessmen, politicians, and religious leaders. In 1920 the *Manufacturers Record*, a Baltimore-based southern trade magazine, labeled a summer conference focused on the social gospel "a scheme for teaching socialism."[79] A year later, Vice President Calvin Coolidge published a series of scurrilous articles in a women's fashion magazine called *The Delineator*. Entitled "Enemies of the Republic," they were illustrated with a flock of lambs being instructed by a wolf in mortarboard and sheep's clothing. Posing the question, "Are the 'Reds' stalking our college women?" Coolidge sounded the alarm against the postwar youth movement, socialist professors, and YWCA conferences that promoted Bolshevism and racial amalgamation.[80]

CRITICISM OF THE Y escalated after December 1923, when Katharine and Frances Williams traveled to Indianapolis to attend the International Convention of the Student Volunteer Movement for Foreign Missions (SVM), a group that brought together the YMCA and the YWCA, but whose leadership was dominated by men. Dedicated to "the evangelization of the world in this generation" when it was founded at the turn of the century, the SVM initially appealed to students who, in the imperialist spirit of the day, "felt a divine call to go from our own favored 'Christian' nation" to reform "the backward peoples of the world." By the early 1920s, however, students were pushing the organization toward an influential, but now largely forgotten, Christian internationalism that promoted a robust blend of anti-imperialism, antimilitarism, and antiracism.[81]

Frances Williams had successfully negotiated with the hotel and the Student Volunteer Movement to ensure that the gathering would be fully integrated. Seated according to their states of origin, young men and women from the South found themselves "actually facing students of other races and talking over their common problems."[82] When they broke up into small groups and selected their own topics for debate, the vast majority of the students chose to focus on race, with war a close second. Speakers drew direct connections between militarism, Western exploitation of colonial societies, and lynching. They also announced that "anyone in this audience who refuses to eat with a colored person" is stoking the flames of mob violence. As Williams saw it, "Indianapolis set a precedent below which no Christian convention can afford to go."[83] "Rejoicing" to see students "coming forward on the issue[s] that for some of us meant so much," Williams and Lumpkin left with high hopes for "a new national youth movement" in "revolt against racial discrimination, economic injustice and international strife."[84]

Williams and Lumpkin returned to the South determined to build a network of students "with an Indianapolis background" who would report back to their classmates on what they had learned. Instead, they encountered "antagonism and controversy." Worse, they found that the students who had been "aroused" by Indianapolis often found themselves being "squelched promptly" by their schools.[85]

A 1925 attack claiming that participants in the YWCA's summer conferences at the Blue Ridge Assembly were advocating "the marriage of the whites to Negroes . . . as the Christian thing to do" caused similar consternation.[86] An irate southern businessman, who (as often happened) failed to distinguish between the YWCA and its male counterpart, complained to the YMCA's general secretary in New York. The secretary assured him that this "explosion of foolishness" was either the work of a single "insane" or "neurotic" girl or an example of the irrational thinking in which "a group conference of women" was prone to engage.[87] The YWCA's national leaders disavowed official responsibility but characterized the individuals who raised the issue not as "abnormal" but as sincere young women trying to discern "the implications of the Christian Way of Life in race relationships."[88]

At one point, Katharine had to put out a fire in her own backyard. A Baptist minister in Columbia who was convinced that the Y was advocating "intermarriage between the races" threatened to see "that the Y.W.C.A. was taken out of the University of South Carolina and that not a college in South Carolina would send delegates to the Blue Ridge next summer." It would, Katharine commented, be a "rather simple matter for him to accomplish this. . . . Needless to say, it would not confine itself to the State of South Carolina." She rushed to the scene with a carefully measured response. No, the YWCA had not advocated intermarriage. It had, however, sponsored discussions of race relations, and in such discussions intermarriage was bound to come up. She skirted more difficult questions, making no promises about what the YWCA might or might not advocate at some future date. The threat blew over, but such incidents were bound to occur again. "We can do no other than move quietly on where conviction leads us," Katharine concluded. "And we must not be governed by fear at any point."[89]

AS THESE ATTACKS SUGGEST, YWCA summer conferences were a lightning rod, and for good reason. Important as study groups and campus visits were, these gatherings at the Blue Ridge Assembly were the key sites of both industrial and interracial education. Ensconced on the conference center's 1,570-acre grounds in the mountains of western North Carolina, far removed from the influence of their families and less socially conscious peers, young white women were at their most receptive to the message YWCA leaders wanted them to hear. As Lois MacDonald remembered it, exposure to the social sciences and the South's racial and industrial problems at Blue Ridge "clicked something in my temperament," combining with her participation in the students-in-industry project to send her on the path to an activist intellectual career.[90] Thelma Stevens recalled that the Y's stance on race "just hit me right in the eye." Alice Norwood, who had also found the students-in-industry project transformative, looked back on those summer conferences as "the cutting edge, relative to the backgrounds from which all of us southern girls had come."[91]

Katharine Lumpkin, front, with unidentified YWCA
friends at the Blue Ridge Assembly in the mountains
of North Carolina, ca. spring 1924.

For young women like these, the southern student Y's annual gatherings functioned as what the critical theorist Nancy Fraser calls counterpublics: spaces in which a select group of young women, many of whom had been singled out as potential leaders by the YWCA secretaries and all of whom had been elected as delegates by their schools, could withdraw and regroup in preparation for activism directed toward wider publics, including their home colleges and communities.[92] For that reason, the presence of the black secretaries was crucial. They could speak with authority about "what the Negro wants"—"equality and opportunity and justice," as Eva Bowles put it.[93] They could also model a kind of relationship students might otherwise never see: that of self-assured black women leaders interacting on a basis of equality with their white peers.

That, however, was the rub. The Blue Ridge Assembly was controlled not by the YWCA but by its founder and president, Willis D. Weatherford of the YMCA. Weatherford was the author of a widely used college textbook entitled *Negro Life in the South* (1910) that decried "promiscuous mingling" of the races and painted a dire portrait of the sexual immorality, criminality, and ignorance, which he urged white Southerners to help blacks overcome.[94] As president of Blue Ridge, he was dedicated to fostering "sound and constructive" discussions of racial issues, and by World War I, both the YWCA and the YMCA were inviting black speakers to address their respective gatherings.[95] They were also welcoming "fraternal" delegates from the sex-segregated black summer meetings at Talladega and King's Mountain. But these black guests arranged their own lodging in nearby Asheville or were relegated to the "Booker T. Washington Cottage," where Blue Ridge's black employees sometimes boarded as well. They were not allowed in the dining room of magisterial Robert E. Lee Hall. In contrast, as Juliette Derricotte pointedly put it, whites were "given the freedom and privileges of the grounds."[96]

As a student, Katharine had traveled to Blue Ridge and listened in rapt attention to women such as Adela Ruffin speak. It had never occurred to her to wonder how these token "representatives of the race" occupied themselves in their free time. The first summer conference she attended as a Y student secretary for the South changed all that. As she remembered it, Ruffin and Juanita Saddler, the guest speakers, were housed in the Booker T. Washington Cottage, whose "face modestly turned to front the mountainside." At mealtime, someone brought them their trays. When Lumpkin arrived to conduct them to their first meeting, she "knocked at the door [and] heard dishes rattle." Ruffin had steeled herself against such slights. She had spoken at Blue Ridge before, and she ran an underfunded black branch of the Y in Richmond, Virginia, where she was barred from using the central's lavish facilities. Saddler, on the other hand, "had not known that these would be the conditions of her entertainment." Lumpkin could imagine Ruffin "ticking off excuses for this thing we had done." But Saddler's "composed aloofness spoke an unmistakable message. . . . One knew with utmost sureness [that she] rejected these symbols of inferiority which had been thrust upon her in this Christian conference. She considered them unwarranted, then or at any other time, either for her in her person or for her race."[97]

From the outset, black women's participation in the Y's organizational life had been stymied by the exclusion of African Americans from hotels across the country. At the insistence of black leaders, the association ceased to hold its national conventions in the South after 1922.[98] But as longtime YWCA secretary and civil rights activist Anna Arnold

Hedgeman explained: "In the South the weapon [we faced] was a meat axe; in the North, a stiletto. Both are lethal weapons."[99] Until 1934, when the National Board accepted the colored work committee's repeated recommendation that it hold national conventions only in fully integrated facilities, the committee in general, and Frances Williams in particular, spent untold hours negotiating with northern hotels over their racially exclusionary policies and scrambling to respond when they reneged on their promises or found excuses for myriad forms of discrimination during ostensibly integrated conferences.[100]

Travel too was a minefield, littered with reminders of white privilege and the stigma of Jim Crow. As a child, Katharine had searched out the "white" and "colored" signs to make sure she was in her proper place. Now those anxieties rearranged themselves; the signs and symbols that had once been so reassuring became ominous and disorienting. One incident in particular seared itself in memory. Changing trains in Danville, Virginia, on their way to a conference, Katharine and Juliette Derricotte entered the station, as Katharine remembered it, "by different doors: hers, 'For Colored,' mine, 'For White.'" A wooden rail separated the two women in the waiting room. Then came the train, with the "colored" coach up next to the sooty, smoking engine. Katharine knew "the sign to be found there, and the signs in our several comfortable coaches. . . . One sign was meant to stigmatize, the other to assert superiority." "Never," she recalled, "had I seen so plainly as on this day how deadly serious the white South was in its signs and separations, or understood in clearer focus its single-mindedness of aim."[101]

Under those circumstances, the policies of the Blue Ridge Assembly, which had been created explicitly to host Christian student conferences, were especially galling. Summers spent in this enticingly beautiful place stirred the consciences and spurred the aspirations of a long line of white southern girls. For the black secretaries who were supposed to bear the brunt of white students' interracial education, in contrast, these gatherings became sites of racial injury, all the more so because the ostracism they encountered occurred in a setting where they had every reason to expect inclusion and respect.[102]

In the spring of 1923, a little more than a year into the southern division's experiment in interracial education, Josephine Pinyon Holmes, one of the Y's first "special workers for colored students," set a direct confrontation with these issues in motion. In an obliquely worded but challenging resolution submitted to the executive committee of the National Student Council, she asked for an end to separate housing and dining facilities for black students attending the nominally integrated regional summer conferences in the North and implied that black students in the South should also be allowed to attend conferences with and on the same terms as whites. In a second set of resolutions, she proposed that African American secretaries be eligible to attend conferences of their choice and that they not be asked to devote too much of their time to interracial duties, a protest against the tendency to channel black professional women into narrow "race relations" roles. The executive committee, in keeping with the Y's commitment to local autonomy and democratic self-governance, asked for reactions from the regional divisions, each of which interpreted the resolutions in its own way.[103]

Katharine Lumpkin led the interracial southern student council's discussion of the Holmes proposals, which, she observed, was especially substantial because "we were facing things that were . . . more fundamental" than the usual fare.[104] Frances Williams and probably Juanita Saddler participated as well. The students assumed that Holmes's reference to integrated regional conferences simply did not apply to the Jim Crow South, and they ignored her cri de coeur regarding the burden of interracial education. Nor did the secretaries push them to consider these proposals. Instead Katharine "rather ruthlessly flung them" into confronting a different question: whether the southern student council could and should invite black secretaries to Blue Ridge and "have them entertained exactly as any other secretary—as to living and eating." The council said yes; such a practice would be "reasonable, profitable, and consistently Christian."[105]

Yet when the secretaries insisted that they stop to consider the consequences of that decision, the white students "hit the block of 'what our communities and families' will say." Instead of endorsing what everyone agreed was the Christian course of action, they circled around quandaries that would stymie white interracialists for another two decades or more. Personally, the council members declared themselves "willing and eager" for change. But they worried that, as elected representatives, they did not have "the right to commit their fellow students to a line of action in a matter like race relations, when it is clear that only a few . . . might be in sympathy."[106] A minority believed that "as followers of Jesus we should strive to make our attitudes and practices as consistent as possible with His way of life and not be bound and inhibited by fear of ultimate consequences." Yet in the end, even those who had grown into "a Christian conviction on the matter" were unwilling to face what they assumed those consequences would be: censure for themselves, the alienation of their peers, and the refusal of parents and college administrators to allow white students to attend summer conferences.[107] That backlash, they feared, would halt the progress of the student movement in the South by depriving white students of the social teachings and interracial experiences that only Blue Ridge could provide.

IN DECEMBER 1923, twenty-six-year-old Katharine wrote a searching letter to Leslie Blanchard, the head of the National Student Council, which was also a conversation with herself. Marked "CONFIDENTIAL—VERY," it explained why she had directed the southern student council's attention so intensely toward the treatment of her black colleagues. It also suggested that she was struggling to formulate the ideas that would permanently shape her understanding of self and region. "It seems to me," she began, that "we are at a point where some clear show-down must come."[108] Juliette Derricotte, Frances Williams, and Juanita Saddler had made it clear that, as Katharine observed of Saddler, they were no longer willing to tolerate the "symbols of inferiority" that were "thrust upon them" each time they climbed the rhododendron-lined road to the Blue Ridge conference grounds.[109] Worse still, from Katharine's perspective, they might decide not only to boycott summer conferences, but also refuse to participate in other aspects of interracial education that entailed compliance with Jim Crow, including speaking at white colleges. Katharine was "entirely sympathetic with their attitude; all my personal feelings run that way." Beyond that, she admitted, lay "utter confusion."[110]

She still believed that only interracial communication—a multiplying of the free, frank, even transgressive conversation that she and her colleagues encouraged—could accomplish the change of consciousness she sought. But she could no longer convince herself that the goal of exposing white students to "comradeship with a person like Juliette" justified "putting our colored [secretaries] and students thru this humiliating process, and ourselves as well." She also believed that democratic self-governance was critical to the "Christian student movement" she envisioned.[111] It was her job to advise autonomous college associations, not to dictate to them. Yet she could not do what the leaders of the city Ys and the National Board had long done: bow to or hide behind the will of the white majority and thus fail the test of "Christian consistency" where her own behavior and the student division's practices were concerned. What then was to be done? Should the secretaries put aside their principles, submerge their personal feelings, and devote themselves to an incremental process that might "carry the many along"? Or should they stand with a "prophetic minority" of students and commit themselves to a course of action that might undermine the organization's ability to reach the minority's more cautious and conservative peers?[112]

Underlying these conundrums was the racially biased evolutionary thinking Katharine had absorbed as a child and then encountered in graduate school as scientific fact. Now she was facing the implications of that thinking on the ground. If, as she had learned, the South's racial mores were so deeply entrenched that they were virtually impervious to change, then "to buck such ingrained custom . . . is to break your whole cause on it." Yet it was precisely because she believed so firmly in the power of "mores" that she could not in the end concede the point that W. D. Weatherford and many others in his generation maintained: that the good done by Blue Ridge outweighed the relatively trivial discomforts of the forms of segregation it imposed. On the contrary, Katharine took with utmost seriousness the "breaking of bread." "I am not one of those," she said, "who take the position that . . . eating together is . . . non-essential." Just as Jesus was the outward and visible sign of God's love for humankind, sharing food was "one of the most fundamental 'outward and visible signs' of that inward attitude of recognition of the worth of persons." That was why its prohibition was such a potent symbol. Looking back to her own childhood, Katharine concluded her letter to Leslie Blanchard with an extraordinary burst of insight into what made racialist ideologies both so contingent and so deeply and tragically ingrained. White supremacy, she explained, is "ground into our social inheritance . . . handed on from one generation to another, it becomes a habit of mind and thought; it is put there by that most vicious process of indoctrination that begins . . . with the Southern child, before she is conscious of herself as a self."[113]

Within days after Katharine's anguished letter, the executive committee of the National Student Council accepted the Holmes resolutions, which the southern division leaders took as an endorsement of the black student secretaries' refusal to observe the rituals of segregation on the Blue Ridge conference grounds. Accordingly, they asked Weatherford to suspend the rules that confined black guests to separate eating arrangements and "a particular cottage" so that Juliette Derricotte would consent to attend the summer conference in 1924.[114] Weatherford refused the request. He doubted that "a group of college students [was] in a position to know quite clearly all the ramifications of this intricate and difficult problem." There were bound to be some girls "who would object," and "even if this was not the case we have the whole wall of prejudice that is to be faced in the South."[115]

In 1926, a white student council member wrote to Weatherford again: it was outrageous for "Blue Ridge, of all places," to maintain such invidious racial distinctions. In reply, Weatherford offered a compromise: the Y's African American speakers could take their meals with a select group of whites in a separate dining alcove in Robert E. Lee Hall and sleep in the regular dormitories or cottages as long as they occupied rooms with private baths, thus observing a taboo against shared restrooms that was enshrined in North Carolina law and fiercely defended by segregationists.[116]

Both sides in this tug-of-war had good reason to fear "the wall of prejudice" they faced.[117] Both were torn between Christian principles and institutional survival. But two things set the southern student council apart. First, African American students and staff had a voice in the council's governance and decisions. Second, the student YWCA saw itself as a youth movement increasingly committed not just to trying to "carry the many along" but also to playing what its leaders called a "spearhead" role both in the Y and in society as a whole.[118]

Influenced by this self-conception, southern student activists and secretaries spent the next two decades trying to find ways around the roadblocks that Weatherford and his allies imposed. Their opposition to segregation was intensified by the tragic death of Juliette Derricotte in 1931. Gravely injured in an automobile accident in rural Georgia, she was taken to a private residence and treated by white physicians who never considered taking her to a local hospital, setting off waves of shock and outrage within the student Y. In the years that followed, the southern student council began holding integrated gatherings at various locations while continuing to sponsor whites-only conferences at Blue Ridge for students who, out of conviction or under pressure from their families and schools, were unwilling to cross the color line. Finally, in 1945, the students withdrew their support from Blue Ridge altogether and stopped sponsoring segregated summer conferences.[119]

Leasing a private campground in 1946, the students found themselves threatened by the third coming of the Ku Klux Klan. Jean Fairfax, who was then serving as Tuskegee's dean of women and would go on to become "one of the unsung heroines of civil rights movement," remembered that the women appealed in vain for police protection and then "sat up all night, singing and praying, waiting for the assault. . . . It was a terrifying experience." A hundred hooded Klansmen carrying guns and torches did swoop down on the camp, but they arrived after the participants had left.[120] In that same year, the national YWCA convention adopted an "Interracial Charter," based on an earlier document written by Juanita Saddler, pledging itself to full integration of its own organization and the rest of society. The groundwork laid by the southern student division bore fruit when, despite the opposition of some city Ys, the vast majority of southern delegates joined in this historic vote.[121]

INVITED BY THE national staff to renew her contract as student secretary in the spring of 1924, Katharine hesitated. "I see the coming year as a time demanding everything that we are and can become," she wrote. Before she took up the challenge, she wanted to "build into my experience elements which it has lacked, and which served to handicap me seriously."[122] Taking an unpaid leave of absence, she spent seven weeks on the assembly line of a shoe factory as part of a students-in-industry project in Philadelphia, deliberately avoiding a venue closer to home so that her mother could more easily turn a blind eye to her unorthodox daughter's endeavors. What Katharine took away from that immersion in the world of blue-collar labor suggests how her thinking had evolved. "I realized more strongly than before how unrelated is . . . our kind of a job, to the normal life led by the mass of humanity," she reported. "We cannot entirely off-set this difficulty; but my experience this summer convinces me that we must work" not only to change racial attitudes but also to confront the "vast over-all mechanism" of a capitalist economy that structured the lives of both blacks and whites.[123]

For Katharine, this way of thinking threw the limits of interracialism into sharp relief even as it helped to free her from the last vestiges of racialist thinking. The Y's approach to race relations rested in part on the belief that bringing whites into contact with blacks who shared their intelligence and sophistication would transform their racial views and sensitize them to the injustices and cruelties of segregation. This strategy of tilting the color line could have "eruptive consequences," as it had for Katharine, first as a student at Brenau and then as she worked side-by-side with the black student secretaries. But it had serious weaknesses as well. Among them was the fact that what amounted to "vertical segregation" was compatible with prevailing assumptions about the cultural, though not the biological, inferiority of blacks as a race.[124] For racist ideology had always admitted exceptions. Indeed, this exceptionalism was, in Katharine's words, the white South's "ace-in-the-hole. . . . 'Of course,'" the argument ran, "*some* Negroes have ability; *some* can 'take' an education; *some* can achieve." The masses, however, were destined to be the "hewers of wood and drawers of water" that they had always been.[125]

Gradually, however, Katharine had come to see that white workers had their "place" almost as surely as did their black counterparts and that the powers-that-be were as fiercely opposed to prolabor measures as they were to attacks on the racial status quo. "If such were the case, then surely wage-earning whites and Negroes were, functionally speaking, not so unlike after all. By so much, the proof of group incapacity, because of poverty or the lowly work men did, lost its persuasiveness."[126] What passed for the signs of racial or cultural inferiority were in fact the injuries of class. At the end of the day, tilting the color line might change white attitudes and ease the plight of the black middle class. But it left a profoundly undemocratic system of discrimination and exploitation in place.

Katharine would always cherish the "great solidarity" she had experienced during her years with "that famous So. Division" of the YWCA.[127] But in the months after her Philadelphia experience, she began to think of moving on. Her friend Winnifred Wygal, a member of the National Student Council staff, countered with "a wild idea which came to me in the middle of the night": Boston needed a "remarkable" person to serve as metropolitan general secretary; Katharine could apply for the job and study part-time at the Harvard Graduate School of Education, which in 1921 became the first entity to award Harvard degrees to women.[128]

Katharine had been "fascinated . . . and . . . completely caught up

in" the Y's southern industrial and interracial efforts, but she had found
watching over the routines of local associations "very dull."[129] City Ys, in
particular, held no attraction for her. More important, she had begun to
see even her and her colleagues' proudest accomplishments—the egalitarian relationships they forged, their success in arranging "momentary
respite" from the strictures of segregation, whether by creating their own
free spaces or by ignoring "the ban of . . . public places against the Negro
people"—as too "superficial an attack upon a deeply rooted disease."[130]
Now she wanted time to explore the implications of a new way of thinking. She wanted, as she put it, "to . . . refill my own reservoir." Turning down Wygal's offer, she decided to devote herself wholeheartedly to
what she had failed to find at Columbia University: the kind of "moving
and breathing" scholarship that would teach her how to get "the world's
work done."[131]

"GETTING THE WORLD'S WORK DONE"

W HEN KATHARINE DECIDED TO PICK UP THE DROPPED
threads of her education, she set her sights on Madison, Wisconsin, a
state capital and university town that relished its reputation as an intellectual arcadia between the coasts. In the years before World War I,
the state's insurgent governor, Robert M. "Fighting Bob" La Follette,
drew on the University of Wisconsin faculty for the nation's first "brains
trust," which helped him challenge the power of Wisconsin's railway and
timber barons, strengthen the rights of labor, and extend social services.
Out of this intellectual and political ferment emerged the "Wisconsin
Idea," which committed the university to "getting the world's work done"
by, as Katharine put it, "serving . . . the people of the state."[1]

The economics department (which included sociology, social work,
and a workers' education program) was at the forefront of this effort.
Founded by Richard T. Ely, a leading advocate of the social gospel, the
department included such Progressive era luminaries as Edward (E. A.)
Ross, famous for his muckraking attacks on capitalist greed, and John R.
Commons, who virtually created the field of labor history. Together, they
stood proudly apart from the neoclassical economists who would ultimately dominate the field. Eschewing the neoclassicists' worship of the
free market and reliance on statistics and mathematical techniques, they
stressed the study of history and advocated governmental regulation.[2]

Hope Lumpkin,
the sisters' oldest brother,
rector of Grace Episcopal
Church, Madison,
Wisconsin.

As Katharine remembered it, a desire to learn more about labor "and especially to seek more scientific fact on race" was "the main object of my migration."[3] Madison was unrivaled for the study of labor, but in other ways she would have been better served by returning to Columbia University, where Franz Boaz and his associates in anthropology were revolutionizing attitudes toward race and she would have enjoyed a ready-made circle of friends. The problem was money: fellowships were hard to come by, especially for women, and Katharine had to make her own way, relying mainly on the minuscule savings from her small YWCA salary to put herself through school. An offer of help from her oldest brother Hope sealed her decision to head not to New York but to the upper Midwest.[4]

Hope Henry Lumpkin served as rector of Grace Episcopal Church, located on Madison's Capitol Square. A strikingly handsome man with an athlete's tall, broad-shouldered physique, he was Katharine's "special favorite."[5] After graduating from the University of South Carolina and preparing for the ministry at Sewanee, Hope had taken a position as assistant rector and priest-in-charge of city missions at a venerable

Anglo-Episcopal church in Charleston. He had also taught at Porter Military Academy, a school founded after the Civil War to educate former soldiers and orphaned or destitute boys. Then in 1914, he shocked everyone by decamping with his wife Mary and their young sons for the Episcopal mission in Fairbanks, Alaska. When the day of departure arrived, he was escorted to the Columbia, South Carolina, train station by an assembly of relatives and half the city's Episcopalians. There the bishop proffered an inscribed copy of the Book of Common Prayer, enjoining Hope to convert the heathens who "in their blindness still bowed down to wood and stone." In fact, the lives of the Tanana Athabascan peoples had been ripped apart by the Klondike gold rush, and most had already adopted Christianity, which they combined with indigenous religious practices. In Fairbanks, Hope served as rector of St. Matthews Episcopal Church, traveling by boat and sled to minister both to the Indians and to Alaska's scattered miners (the most raucous parishioners imaginable). Enjoying the adventure of a lifetime, he and his family broadened their horizons without by any means abandoning the assumptions of Western, Protestant superiority that sent them to the mission field.[6]

HOPE WAS CALLED to Madison's Grace Church in 1920. A year later he entered the graduate program in sociology at the University of Wisconsin and began working part-time toward a PhD. His dissertation focused on Hugh Latimer, a sixteenth-century bishop who preached against the pomp of the Catholic Church, advocated mercy for the poor, and was executed for heresy during England's Protestant Revolution. Hope approached contemporary issues through the scrim of cautious social gospel ideals. Invited to speak at Sewanee in 1925, for instance, he delivered a series of lectures on the dangers of dance halls, moving pictures, and spooning in parked cars; the "lack of flexibility and plasticity in the ruling classes"; the vulnerability of "women and children in industry"; and the importance of service to society, including, he cryptically suggested, "service in regard to some races."[7]

As soon as Hope heard that Katharine was considering Madison as a place to return to her studies, he invited her to live with his family. This arrangement did more than ease her financial worries. It afforded her a unique entree to the university community. Grace Church was the congregation of choice for many legislators and faculty members, and Hope served for a time as honorary chaplain of the university. In his multiple roles as rector, chaplain, and graduate student, he developed close friendships with many of the school's leading lights. The Madison Literary Club, which brought the town fathers together with university faculty and administrators, often met for drinks and discussion at the rectory. The revered professor Richard Ely, founder of the economics department, was a frequent guest in the Lumpkins' home and became godfather to their youngest child. When Governor La Follette's mother died, it was Hope who presided at the graveside service. All in all, Katharine recalled, Hope's offer "was irresistible," and she "made a beeline" to Madison in the fall of 1925.[8]

She was resuming her graduate career at a time when white women's academic prospects looked particularly bright. Female students had surged into the academy in the 1910s, and by 1920 the proportion of women among the faculty of colleges and universities, including the women's schools where most were employed, had reached almost 30 percent. Nearly 15 percent of Wisconsin's faculty was female, a figure much lower than the national average but far higher than that at Ivy League institutions, which proved especially impervious to change. To be sure, Katharine did not imagine that she would find a perfectly level playing field. There was only one female professor in her department: Helen Clarke, who had been hired in 1921 to teach the principles of social service and case work methods, topics that were clearly marked as women's concerns. Knowing that she would be at a disadvantage on the job market without formal classroom experience, Katharine applied at once for a teaching assistantship. But teaching at Wisconsin turned out to be "reserved for the men." Katharine was disappointed, but only mildly so. She shared her generation's optimism. Women were just beginning to enter the professions; once they proved their mettle, such remnants of discrimination would surely pass away. As Katharine remembered it, she enjoyed a "wonderful relationship" with the faculty and her male peers. "They were friends and . . . colleagues," she said, and she never felt "unaccepted" because of her sex.[9]

From the outside, her personal life seemed equally happy and secure. She reveled in the beauty of a city renowned for its parks and lakes. Hope and Mary entertained often, and Katharine joined the company of distinguished guests. Mary played the piano and, as in Hope's and

Katharine's childhood, everyone gathered round to sing. Katharine took her nephews to vaudeville shows; she played tennis in the summer and skated on Lake Mendota when the water froze. Every August she trooped with the whole family to a cottage on Lake Ballard to spend the month deep in Wisconsin's vast, evergreen North Woods.[10]

John Henderson Lumpkin Sr., the third of Hope and Mary's four sons, remembered that Katharine had an easy way with children. "I used to think Aunt Kay was the most beautiful woman I'd ever seen in my life," he recalled. "I thought she was one of the most sophisticated women—and didn't even know what that word meant. . . . She dressed beautifully, she had lovely skin. . . . I stayed in her room constantly. . . . She'd have to run me out of her bedroom if she wanted to undress and go to bed. . . . I was in love with her," he concluded, "no question about it."[11]

John's and Katharine's photograph albums contain almost identical images: a glinting birch grove, a rustic cabin, Katharine with bobbed hair, dressed for the out-of-doors in knickers and wool socks and a tie. These are vacation pictures, meant to make memories and reinforce family ties. Yet Katharine seems very much alone. She gazes not at the camera but into the distance, pensively. The bright light of youth has given way to chiaroscuro; her features have sharpened into the handsomeness that later friends would remember; her eyes, always melancholy, recede in shadow.[12]

Seven years had made a big difference. At twenty-eight, Katharine was no longer the exquisitely self-conscious Southerner who had tiptoed into New York in 1918. "I was raw then as far as my knowledge of the world was concerned," she recalled.[13] She had arrived in New York wearing the ankle-length dresses of the Gibson Girl, fluffed with petticoats and pulled tight at the waist; in the photographs from that period, she is always surrounded by women. Now, back in the bosom of her family, she had adopted a style that would come fully into fashion in the 1930s: that of the man-tailored sophisticate, a hallmark of the era's great film stars and of the newly visible and self-conscious lesbian subculture that, in the 1920s, emerged in bohemian enclaves across the country.

Were Katharine's choice of Wisconsin and her decision to live with Hope's family as straightforward and practical as they seem? A colleague, interviewed half a century later, said that at some point during this period Katharine had been overwhelmed by a terrible depression and that at first the disciplinary rigors of Wisconsin were "torture, sheer

Katharine on vacation with her brother Hope Lumpkin's family in northern Wisconsin, summer 1925.

torture." Dorothy Gary Markey, Katharine's friend from the YWCA, suggested a disquieting possibility. In the early twenties, Katharine had told her about a "too-close relationship with an older brother, about which she felt guilty. It happened quite a few times." That brother had become a minister, Markey remembered.[14] There is nothing else in the record to suggest that Katharine suffered from such abuse, nothing to tell us whether anger or guilt vied with gratitude and admiration for a larger-than-life brother—nothing except this secondhand testimony and photographs of a woman with melancholy eyes.

In the end, Katharine thrived in Madison's tolerant, stimulating atmosphere. In contrast to her experience at Columbia, her mentors at Wisconsin praised and rewarded her accomplishments. By her second year she had won a fellowship—at a time when few of the university's fellowships went to women. She did "splendidly" on a stiff preliminary examination. Never, according to her advisor E. A. Ross, had "any candidate for the doctor's degree in sociology here obtained such uniformly high rating." By the end of 1927, she had launched her field research, supported by a Harriet Remington Laird Fellowship. Designated especially for women, the award carried with it—in true Wisconsin Idea fashion—the expectation that the recipient's research would be useful to the people of the state. Her older brother Alva, who had helped both her and Grace through college and was a staunch supporter of women's education, was delighted. "You are a great child," he wrote, "and we are proud of you."[15]

Majoring in sociology and minoring in world politics and labor economics, Katharine acquired the tools with which to build the larger frame of reference she craved. She took courses on "Capitalism and Socialism" with John R. Commons and "American Labor History" with his star student, Selig Perlman. She attended the famous "Friday Nights" where students and professors in the social sciences met to talk about labor issues at the Commonses' home. She excelled in seminars on urban problems, the American family, poor relief, criminology, and economic theory, mainly with E. A. Ross but also with William H. Kiekhofer, chairman of the economics department, and John Gillin, an authority on criminology and poor relief and a tireless advocate for strengthening social services provided by the state. Putting theory into practice, she joined other students to picket in behalf of striking workers.[16]

Yet, invigorating as it was, Wisconsin—like Columbia—fell short of Katharine's expectations, and much that she learned she would later have to unlearn. She had been raised to see the North as an overbearing and self-righteous bully, rife with "unwarranted holier-than-thou attitudes" and blind to its own shortcomings. By the time she arrived in Wisconsin, she had swept aside—or at least thought she had swept aside—such assumptions. But there was a whiff of smugness about Madison, with its virtually all-white, native-born population and its capital-of-Progressivism self-image, that sometimes set her teeth on edge. It was "interesting and healthy, and sometimes very amusing," she recalled. But the truth was that she sometimes found herself "reacting with the same feelings of resentment and defensiveness which I had always known so well."[17]

Living with her own family had the paradoxical effect of giving Katharine's privileged access to Madison's inner circles and keeping her sense of regional difference alive. Her nephew John remembers the mortification of being marked as a Southerner on Memorial Day. Each year, the Lumpkins and a small group of southern expatriates—so few, as

John remembered it, that you could count them on one hand—would march with the big parade through town, then peel off at a tiny cemetery where Hope would lead a service for the Confederate dead. While his friends trekked on to the main ceremony, John took comfort in his aunt's presence, stilling his embarrassment by holding her hand.[18]

More problematic for Katharine was E. A. Ross, who proved an ambiguous mentor. Earlier in his career, he had risked his job by speaking out on controversial issues. He continued to believe that the sociologist had a "solemn duty to raise hell," but in the xenophobic 1920s he put his energies into nativist programs of immigration restriction. Initially concerned about how to maintain the vitality of American individualism while regulating it for the common good, he ended up arguing that the innately "energetic, self-assertive, and individualistic" Aryan race could preserve its vigor under such external constraints only as long as immigration restriction prevented mixture with inferior and conformist immigrant groups.[19]

Katharine had struggled to free herself from the dead weight of social Darwinism, which suggested that mores were profoundly resistant to change. Yet here, promulgated by a leading opponent of laissez-faire capitalism, were the very assumptions of racial superiority that she had been working so hard to overcome. "I probed about to find what I had come for," she recalled. "In despair of finding it anywhere, I undertook my own self-education . . . while continuing to carry out the necessary requirements for my doctorate."[20]

Those "necessary requirements" proved to be more constricting than she had imagined. Like other women attracted to the social sciences, Katharine sought knowledge in the service of social change. But during the postwar years a new concept of the role of scholars in a democracy began to shift the meaning of the Wisconsin Idea. Social scientists, the advocates of professionalization increasingly claimed, should not speak as critical outsiders. They should not bring a moral vision to bear. Rather, their role was to act as expert advisors to politicians whose top-down public policies would periodically be ratified at the polls. John R. Commons was a case in point. He had once believed that labor economists should align themselves with the working class. Now he argued that they should moderate class conflict. His disciple, Selig Perlman, went even further: scholars should produce scientific knowledge; they had no place in the labor movement at all.[21]

This rupture between idealism and scholarship, combined with the relentless march toward specialization, was especially problematic for mission-driven academic women, who found it harder and harder to reconcile activism with scholarly careers. The great expectations of the 1920s evaporated as economics, sociology, political science, and history modeled themselves on the "hard sciences," thereby stamping themselves as masculine domains. This process was gradual, uneven, and contested. Its impact at Wisconsin was blunted by the economics department's habit of hiring its own students, which served to keep elements of the Wisconsin Idea alive.[22] But it was also powerful. Eventually mavericks and radicals of both sexes would find themselves shut out of the academy as its leaders cut the tie between scholarship and dissent.

Along with these changes came an intensification of the founding ideology of professionalism: the notions that practitioners could and should be judged according to objective criteria and that success depended entirely on individual merit. For women, this idea cut two ways. On the one hand, it gave them a foothold in arenas from which they had been excluded on the a priori, customary grounds of sexual inferiority. On the other hand, the myth that academia was a meritocracy made it virtually impossible for women to defend themselves as an unfairly disadvantaged group. Instead, they sought to prove themselves as individuals, confident that their professionalism would "outshine their sex." Those who did manage to find a place in the academy confronted the classic dilemma of the outsider: to win acceptance they took on the attitudes and behaviors of insiders. "Social science," as one observer put it, "captured women, not women social science."[23]

Katharine responded to these circumstances—the shrinking purview of the professorate, the tendency to equate objectivity with masculinity, and the academy's marginalization of radicals and of women as a group—by adapting and resisting at the same time. Seeking a career in teaching and research, she set out to master the rhetoric of her discipline. In the process, she absorbed its assumptions and struck its objectivist pose. For the moment, the religious language that had given her work for the YWCA its moral urgency fell away. Her early writing bears the marks of an exercise undertaken less out of passion than of expediency: an outsider's attempt to get past the gatekeepers and win professional acceptance in a highly exclusive club. Yet even as she ran the gauntlet of graduate school, she smuggled her identification with women and her preoccupation with region into whatever she wrote. The melding of class with race and knowledge with action to which the YWCA had attuned her continued to shape her choices and concerns.

For her dissertation, she settled on a study of "girl delinquency." Looking back, she explained this as a practical choice. At Columbia, she had written about the social interests of southern women, a topic close to her heart but of no interest whatsoever to professional sociologists. At Wisconsin, she chose a subject that had the twin advantages of interesting her professors and carrying the policy implications that both her fellowship and the "Wisconsin Idea" required. At first glance, the result appears surprisingly dutiful and desiccated. But between the lines of this excursion into a forbidden, rebellious, female world lay personal associations and complicated meanings.

Katharine, it turned out, was less interested in the causes of delinquency than in the question of why some girls were *labeled* as delinquents while others were not. Consulting case files of 252 young women who had been committed to the Wisconsin Industrial School for Girls, she analyzed the social situations that promoted their delinquent "careers." She discovered that an extraordinary proportion of young women locked up for delinquency had not committed crimes but status offenses: they had engaged in—or seemed likely to engage in—what their families, social workers, or law enforcement officials defined as immoral sexual behavior.[24]

In the end, she drew fairly conventional conclusions. Delinquency often resulted, she observed, when girls with low IQs found themselves unable to cope with the challenges of growing up in "defective" families. She did not comment on the biases of IQ tests, which purported to measure innate mental ability, but in fact reflected environmental conditions. Nor did she challenge experts' emphasis on shoring up families by reinforcing patriarchal structures rather than on combating poverty or protecting women's and children's rights. Still, along with a vanguard of female social scientists whose ideas had a powerful influence on criminology as a whole, she rejected the notion of the wayward girl as a physiologically determined "abnormal type," as well as the eugenics theories that her sister Elizabeth espoused. Recent researchers have confirmed what she observed in her understated way: from its inception in the late nineteenth century, the juvenile justice system has systematically discriminated against the poor and (insofar as it had served them at all) racial minorities. Girls suspected of sexual activity have been labeled first as fallen women, later as mental defectives or delinquents, and then as products of a "culture of poverty." Whatever the rubric, they have been punished for their sexuality in ways that boys have not.[25]

Pursuing a topic seemingly distant from the South and its "racial ways," Katharine drew an implicit analogy between the efforts of society to force girls to adhere to their society's standards and mores and the "vicious process of indoctrination" imposed on white children in the Jim Crow South. Individuals who deviated from sexual or racial norms could expect harsh punishment: imprisonment for the delinquent girl; ostracism and exile for the young white woman who refused to abide by the racial rules. More subtly, the same went for entry to the academy: it came at the price of self-censorship and, in Katharine's case, the repression of the voice of region, the voice of home. It was, for the moment, a price she was willing to pay.[26]

IN THE SPRING OF 1928, as Katharine was racing to finish her dissertation, two job offers arrived, both at women's colleges. One was for a permanent position at the state college for women in Denton, Texas. The other was from Amy Hewes, head of the Department of Economics and Sociology at Mount Holyoke, the oldest of the "Seven Sisters" women's colleges. A distinguished activist scholar, Hewes was one of a small group of intellectuals who followed their interest in Progressive reform into research on the Soviet Union, which they used as a case study from which to draw lessons for strengthening trade unions and social welfare provisions in the United States. Katharine had been recommended to Hewes by a Wisconsin graduate teaching at Mount Holyoke. On the strength of that endorsement and warm letters from Katharine's advisors, Hewes offered her a one-year replacement position, waiving the usual interview. She also held out the promise that she might ultimately take over the major courses in her field. Katharine opted for the riskier but more prestigious opportunity. After receiving her PhD in the summer, she departed for South Hadley in western Massachusetts, eager to follow what seemed to be the rising arc of an academic career.[27]

Established in 1837, Mount Holyoke served as a model for the women's colleges that proliferated after the Civil War. The women attracted to its faculty eschewed marriage and dedicated themselves to demanding regimens of teaching and research. They, in turn, looked to younger women such as Katharine to replenish their ranks and carry on their tradition. Most of these recruits also abjured marriage. But that did not mean that they lived alone. The emotionally and sometimes erotically charged female friendships that were common among their predecessors continued to flourish in this protected atmosphere.[28]

Katharine had lived much of her adult life in such female social worlds. At Brenau she had woven the love of learning, the pleasures of intimacy, and the aspirations of the social gospel into a seamless web. In the YWCA she found an extension of that connection between same-sex relationships and progressive ideals. By the time she became a student secretary, however, discretion had replaced artlessness, and she left behind nothing to suggest whether the friendships she forged in her twenties contained an element of requited or unrequited romance.

Still, it seems clear from her life's trajectory that the "crushes" she had experienced in college had a different meaning for her than for most of her classmates. For them, those attachments were fleeting ardors preceding adult lives devoted to marriage, motherhood, and civic activities. For Katharine, they were experiments in self-discovery, rehearsals for what at some point she would come to understand as her heart's desire: an enduring relationship with a woman in which intimacy, politics, and intellectual endeavor were mutually reinforcing. She found that relationship—apparently for the first time—at Mount Holyoke almost as soon as she arrived.

Dorothy Wolff Douglas held a tenuous part-time position at nearby Smith College, where she had been teaching off and on since 1924. She had recently separated from her husband, Paul Howard Douglas, a renowned economist who soon became a United States senator. As classes began in 1928, she was dividing her time between Smith and Mount Holyoke, where, like Katharine, she had secured a temporary, replacement position in the economics and sociology department. When the two women met, Katharine was about to turn thirty-one; Dorothy was thirty-eight. For Katharine the encounter was life-changing, a turn of the kaleidoscope that would reveal the future's design. Writing at their desks in Williston Memorial Library on a lightless winter day, hiking through the Holyoke Mountains that ringed the town, or strolling across the greensward in the glory of an early fall, she and Dorothy began fashioning a relationship that offered both companionship and largeness of purpose, a refuge within which Katharine would experience exciting and terrible times.[29]

In many ways, the two women could not have been more different; in others, it is easy to see how their paths could converge. While Katharine was growing up in genteel poverty, nourished on stories of the old South's ruling class, Dorothy Sybil Wolff was coming of age in the heart of a new plutocracy, a Jewish elite whose fortunes came from speculation and international finance. Dorothy's mother Clara Frances (Seligman) Cohen belonged to the first American-born generation of what has been called "the leading Jewish family in America." Her eight uncles had emigrated from Germany before the Civil War. Starting out as itinerant peddlers, they rose to found the Wall Street investment banking firm, J. W. Seligman & Company, in 1864.[30] Dorothy's father, Lewis Samuel Wolff, came from an equally successful if less legendary family. Also from Germany, his father Samuel and his uncle Abraham were naturalized citizens who became partners in Kuhn, Loeb & Company, an investment bank founded in 1867. Second only to the Yankee titan J. P. Morgan & Company, and second to none in railroad financing, Kuhn, Loeb played a central role in the capitalist transformation that took place after the Civil War. In the 1890s the company stewarded the wave of corporate mergers that made Wall Street the center of the nation's economy and the United States the financial capital of the world.[31]

Like all the great Wall Street houses, Kuhn, Loeb was a family affair. For many decades, all the partners were related by blood or marriage, and in due course Lewis Wolff followed his father and uncle into the firm. In 1884 he made partner. In that same year he married Clara Cohen and took her to live with his widowed mother Dorothea in an imposing residence on East 70th Street. There they raised their two children: Stanley, born in 1885, and Dorothy, born on May 1, 1890. Snubbed and excluded by the city's Anglo-Dutch grandees as Jews and outsiders whose rise spelled the doom of "Old New York" and excoriated by the Populists and Progressives as "malefactors of great wealth," the Seligmans, the Wolffs, and their counterparts carved out their own elaborate and tightly knit social world.[32]

Dividing their time between New York and a country seat in Shrewsbury, New Jersey, the Wolffs followed the decorous routines of the high-minded, unostentatious wing of the *haute bourgeoisie*. Grandmother

Dorothea, after whom Dorothy named her youngest child, had been born in the ancient city of Worms, Germany, and she brought the aura of the Old World into a family that, as one friend put it, desired "to be American in attachment, thought and action." Unlike her mother-in-law, Clara Wolff ventured well beyond the home, channeling her talent and energy into the array of voluntary organizations through which women built a "female dominion" within the larger empire of Progressive era reform.[33]

Although she extended her reach to the New York branch of the Charity Organization Society, a national, nonsectarian organization that sought to impose order on the chaos of private giving, Clara devoted herself primarily to Jewish women's groups, especially to the Emanuel Sisterhood and other efforts associated with Temple Emanu-El, the epicenter of Reform Judaism in the United States and a prime venue for the mixture of worship, philanthropy, and social display memorably captured in Stephen Birmingham's *"Our Crowd": The Great Jewish Families of New York*. Lunches and kindergartens for children, music and religion classes, vocational training and employment bureaus, a self-support fund backed primarily by Kuhn, Loeb—these were only a few of the services through which the Emanuel Sisterhood sought to assimilate and uplift the impoverished eastern European Jews who began to pour into Manhattan's Lower East Side in the 1880s. Focused on the welfare of women and children, the one territory over which women could assume unchallenged authority, groups such as the Emanuel Sisterhood allowed uptown Jewish women to join their Protestant sisters in extending their influence from the home into the public sphere. "I have given without stint during my lifetime," Clara Wolff said in her will, explaining why she made no bequests to charity and left all her money to her two children instead.[34]

As for Dorothy's father, he seems to have been a dutiful son, an indifferent banker, and—if his last will and testament is any measure—a controlling parent, at least where Dorothy was concerned. Content to let others guide the firm, Lewis Wolff spent much of his time traveling abroad with his family, usually with a servant or two in tow. He retired in 1891, when Dorothy was only a year old, and in 1892 the Wolffs sailed to Europe for a fifteen-month tour. (Katharine, by contrast, had never been outside the country when she and Dorothy met.) Twelve years later, when Dorothy was fourteen, her father composed a long, complicated will, spelling

out exactly how his money should be divided and invested if he predeceased his wife. In providing for his children, he made a sharp distinction
between Dorothy and her brother. Stanley, he stipulated, would receive his
inheritance in increments upon turning twenty-one, while Dorothy would
get nothing until she married and then would inherit only with her mother's written approval. Did Lewis hope that his daughter would follow the
pattern of her mother's generation, leaving home only when she made a
suitable marriage and then confining herself to homemaking, charity, and
travel? Did he fear that she might marry outside the faith—a choice that
many in her generation did in fact make, although, at least until the 1920s,
at the risk of scandal, disinheritance, and worse?[35]

Whatever Lewis Wolff's intentions and desires, there was not much
he could do about the changes that swept through the German Jewish
community in the years before and after World War I. Even within the
Wolffs' immediate circle, there were abundant examples of new, increasingly cosmopolitan choices and styles. The daughter of Lewis Wolff's
uncle Abraham, for instance, married the peripatetic Otto Kahn, a bon
vivant who moved effortlessly between the hushed, high-ceilinged offices
of Kuhn, Loeb and the jazz clubs of Harlem. The country's most influential patron of the arts, Kahn played financial angel to cultural institutions ranging from the Metropolitan Opera to Paramount Pictures and
consorted with millionaires, bohemians, and starlets at his mansion on
Fifth Avenue, "the most opulent street in the world." Such men were
secularists—Kahn never attended synagogue—and they were at ease in
or out of *"Our Crowd."*[36]

As it turned out, neither of the Wolff children followed in their parents' footsteps. Like many young men of his generation, Stanley had no
interest in investment banking. Instead, he went to Amherst and then
to law school at Columbia. In 1911, he married a society girl whose family hailed from the upper reaches of New York's Protestant elite. Dorothy took advantage of the new educational opportunities that opened
to women in the early decades of the twentieth century. She attended
Finch School for Girls, a fashionable institution run by a socialist feminist who believed in an education for girls that "develops individuality,
cultivates the human interests and sympathies, and is abreast of modern
thought."[37] She then went to Bryn Mawr College, a Seven Sisters institution known both for promoting innovative scholarship and for recruiting the daughters of the Northeast's Protestant upper crust.

Founded by conservative Quakers and located in an affluent sub-urb of Haverford, Pennsylvania, Bryn Mawr could not have been an altogether welcoming place. To be sure, the trustees no longer enforced a religious test for faculty members; since the late nineteenth century, the college had admitted a smattering of Roman Catholics and Jews. But anti-Semitism still permeated the Seven Sisters, from the cliquish hierarchies among students to the assumptions of Carey Thomas, Bryn Mawr's illustrious, autocratic president, who openly embraced the notion of "Nordic" racial superiority, with its denigration of African Americans, Jews, and eastern European immigrants.[38]

Dorothy, however, was buffered by wealth, and she had gone to high school with the daughters of the Protestant elite. If she felt like an out-sider at Bryn Mawr, she did not let it show. A lithe 5' 4", with blue eyes, dark wavy hair, olive skin, and delicate features, she was a splendid ath-lete. She was also clever and irreverent, a thoroughly modern girl who was known for her "sangfroid" and "éclat" as well as for her serious-ness of purpose and social concerns. She loved literature and published elegant essays and short stories in the student literary magazine, but it was reform that seized her imagination.[39] She concentrated on politics, sociology, and history and devoted herself to one of the Progressive era's leading women's organizations, the National Consumers League.

The choice was telling, for the National Consumers League took female reform in a new and ultimately quite radical direction. Led by the New York feminist and socialist Florence Kelley, the League aimed not to reform or uplift the poor, but to use women's power as consumers to protect workers from exploitation. During the Progressive era, the League coordinated the drive to curb child labor and pass protective leg-islation mandating minimum wages and maximum hours for working women. In the 1930s it used such laws as an entering wedge for broaden-ing the government's obligation to all workers. Pushing the New Deal to the left, the league fought for labor laws and welfare provisions tailored to the needs of blacks and women and tried to bring working conditions in the South into line with those in the rest of the nation.[40]

Graduating from Bryn Mawr in 1912, Dorothy headed straight to Columbia University, determined to use sociology and economics to remold "our social arrangements and social ideals." When Katharine arrived four years later, she would step tentatively into the Upper West Side. Dorothy, by contrast, strode confidently onto home ground. At

*Dorothy Sybil Wolff
(Douglas),
ca. 1912.*

Columbia as at Bryn Mawr, she was, according to her future husband, a
"brilliant . . . student." Paul Douglas had grown up in the backwoods of
Maine, raised by his stepmother after she left his hard-drinking father,
a traveling salesman who contributed nothing to Paul's support. Home
schooled until high school, Paul had worked his way through Bowdoin,
a small liberal arts college for men. He was dazzled by Dorothy and the
city. The young couple divided their time between lectures and seminars on Morningside Heights and exhilarating trips to Greenwich Village, the country's premier destination for aspiring writers, bohemians,
and assorted young rebels. They reveled in modern art, heard Margaret
Sanger lecture on birth control, took in the iconoclastic plays of George
Bernard Shaw, and sought out the classes of Charles Beard and John
Dewey. These were, Paul Douglas remembered, "happy and slightly
pagan days." He and Dorothy exemplified the "new intellectuals" of the
pre–World War American left: college-educated men and women who
cast aside particularistic religious, ethnic, and regional identities, found

their way into the avant-garde enclaves of American cities, and were swept up in the intersecting currents of sexual egalitarianism and socialist revolution.[41]

Dorothy finished her master's degree in the spring of 1915, and that summer she married Paul Douglas at Raquette Lake, New York, where the Wolffs sometimes summered among the wealthiest of the wealthy in palatial Adirondack "camps." Her father had died three years earlier, leaving intact the will that gave her mother the power to determine whether her daughter's choice of a poor, if promising, Protestant suitor would stand in the way of the trust fund she was now eligible to receive. Clara welcomed Paul into the family, and Dorothy inherited a sizable fortune. Imagining a life dedicated to "high academic endeavor and social crusading," the newlyweds planned to live on Paul's salary while Dorothy—who was, Paul remembered, "the most generous and altruistic person I had ever met"—used her income to support "worthy causes and individuals."[42]

After their wedding, Dorothy followed Paul to Harvard. There he pursued an additional year of graduate study spent locked in debate with F. W. Taussig, the country's most powerful conservative economist, a man whom Dorothy came to think of as an exemplar of all that was wrong with the field. Harvard did not admit women to its graduate schools. So Dorothy studied philosophy at Radcliffe, a coordinate institution that granted degrees to women who studied at the university.[43]

When the United States declared war in 1917, the Douglases—like many of their peers—were torn between their antiwar principles and the lure of democratic ideals. Paul registered for the draft as a pacifist, then wavered. Caught up in the promise of "making the world safe for democracy" and impressed by such bold wartime experiments as government operation of the railroads and safeguards for labor, he tried to enlist, but was rejected because of poor eyesight. Instead, he settled labor disputes for the federal government in Philadelphia while Dorothy worked for the US Bureau of Labor Statistics and undertook research for the National Consumers League. Arguing in behalf of minimum wages for women, she underscored the principle of equal pay for equal work and anticipated later debates over the gender pay gap produced by workforce sex segregation.[44] At the same time, she pursued her lifelong practice of "endowing" individuals and organizations who shared her political beliefs, with the ultimate goal of creating a society in which the state would provide for the welfare of all rather than one in which the poor depended on the benevolence of people like herself. In so doing, she furthered a little noticed tradition of female philanthropy based on "small but timely gifts" rather than on large bequests and foundation funding.[45] When the war ended, the Douglases renounced their support for a conflict that many in their circle came to see as driven by anti-German propaganda, imperialist rivalries, and war profiteering. Taking to heart the Quaker injunctions that have inspired so many American reformers—to oppose violence, speak truth to power, and act in obedience to one's inner light—they joined the pacifist Society of Friends.[46]

Over the next three years, Dorothy and Paul moved from place to place as he tried to find a permanent academic position. Finally, in 1920, he landed a plum job at the University of Chicago, and they settled in Hyde Park. Chicago was both the fastest growing and, arguably, the most corrupt city in the nation. "Both the criminal syndicate of the underworld and the upperworld of industry and finance," Paul remembered, "were aided and protected by the political 'system,' which they in turn supported." Soon Paul was cultivating close ties to Jane Addams and other Hyde Park reformers, tangling with the unholy alliance of the mob and the machine, and honing the skills that would eventually drive his political career.[47]

Paul thrived in the gritty, hard-driving city. At the same time, he churned out a book "nearly every other year," building a national reputation as an advocate of institutionalism, the study of social and economic institutions and other nonmarket forces; a practitioner of econometrics, the use of mathematical models to test economic theories; and an expert on wage theory and social security. He also spent sixty to seventy hours a week on his classes, in which—like his old antagonist, Taussig—he ruled by fear.[48]

Dorothy, in the meantime, gave birth to three children, Helen Schaeffer, John Woolman, and Dorothea. Barred from teaching at the University of Chicago by nepotism rules, she used whatever time she could steal from domestic duties to serve as a research assistant in the Department of Industrial Relations and collaborate with Paul on books and articles. In fact, she was not only his inspiration but also his coauthor on a study of how altruism and philanthropy affect economic behavior, for which they received the E. A. Karelsen Prize from the American Economic Association.[49] She loved the children and they her, but it was one thing to combine motherhood with independent scholarship and philanthropy, and quite another to fade into the background while her increasingly distant and preoccupied husband became a rising star. Paul's métier was the podium, not the minutia of family life: "I can see him now," Paul Samuelson, a prized student at Chicago, remembered, "stretched out in Roman fashion on the Cobb hall classroom desk, puffing furiously on his cigarette, his seersucker suit wrinkled and his shirt collars pointing up convexly toward the heavens."[50] As their family grew, moreover, it became harder and harder to live on Paul's salary, so he spent more time on the road, funding his research through speakers' fees, while Dorothy's income increasingly went not to worthy causes but to support the family and her husband's career.

Swept forward by the confidence that she and Paul could transform marriage into a partnership based on shared intellectual and political labor, Dorothy—like so many feminists of her generation—found herself trapped in tenacious patterns of sexual inequality that no amount of idealism could will away. Nothing in her experience, or in the repertoire of early twentieth-century feminism, gave her the tools with which to revamp, or even to question, the fundamental inequalities of domestic life. But that did not dampen her desire for paid work, which for her and her generation of white, middle- and upper-class women was the sine qua non of emancipation. In 1924, she saw an opportunity both to fulfill that desire and to salvage her marriage. When Amherst College in Massachusetts tried to recruit Paul to its faculty, she persuaded him to accept a visiting assignment so that she could take a temporary position at neighboring Smith College, the largest and perhaps the most politically progressive of the New England women's schools.[51]

In Amherst, both Paul and Dorothy seemed to flourish. They held Quaker meetings for worship in their home, creating the nucleus of what would become the Connecticut Valley Quarterly Meeting of Friends. Paul threw himself into research, making the discoveries that led to *The Theory of Wages* (1934), the book on which his standing as an economist would rest. He traveled to Haiti with an interracial delegation from the Women's International League for Peace and Freedom, which issued a report that opposed America's "drift towards imperialism" and helped to end its military occupation of the country. He also visited Russia in 1927, the most promising postrevolutionary year, a trip that would come back to haunt him later in his career. Traveling as an advisor to a trade-union delegation, Douglas studied collective farms and factories, interviewed—and was interviewed by—Trotsky and Stalin, and returned intrigued by what he learned.[52]

Douglas told Devere Allen, editor of the pacifist magazine *The World Tomorrow*, that the trip had "strengthened my faith in Socialism" by demonstrating how a people inspired by a "national ideal and moral unity" could bring rapid modernization and economic democracy to a backward, autocratic land. He argued for recognition of the Soviet Union and wrote essays on Soviet trade unions, social welfare provisions, and wage practices, drawing parallels with American institutions and policies and praising the "new Russia's" economic accomplishments while ruing its curtailment of political rights. Convinced that social scientists and reformers had much to learn from the Soviet experiment, he reached out to American scholars and senior Soviet officials, seeking their cooperation in a long-term study of Soviet life. In the end the project faltered, but the enthusiasm of the scholars Paul contacted suggests that for many American intellectuals at the time, whether pro-Soviet or not, the Russian Revolution and its aftermath offered an exhilarating intellectual challenge. "An experiment of such massive scale has never before been carried out," Paul observed, "and this experience calls for research for the good of the rest of the world."[53]

Dorothy stayed at home, starting at Smith as a lowly reader assisting professors in the Department of Economics and Sociology. Then in a burst of effort, she completed her Columbia University dissertation in economics, a study of how the Belgian sociologist and syndicalist Guillaume de Greef fused social science with reform. In the fall of 1926, she gave birth to Paul Wolff Douglas, her fourth child. A year later she won promotion from reader to part-time temporary instructor.[54]

A PHOTOGRAPH OF the Douglas family taken in Amherst just a few months after the birth of their last child seems all too painfully posed. It is Christmas day, and Paul and Dorothy face one another, smiling over the heads of their children, including the latest addition to the family cradled in Dorothy's arms. Behind them a wreath and stockings decorate a holiday mantel. Meant not just to document but to *create* the happy family within its frame, the photograph, at least in retrospect, seems so brittle it is about to crack. Paul's heart, he said, "belonged to Chicago and so, I believed, did my future." It may also have belonged to the daughter of a renowned sculptor and prominent University of Chicago professor, a glamorous younger woman named Emily Taft, fresh from a brief career on the stage. In the fall of 1927, Paul moved back to the Midwest, taking Dorothy and the children with him. The next summer, the family sailed together to Europe, but if the trip was meant as a journey of reconciliation, it turned out to be a farewell instead. The Douglases separated when the ship returned in September.[55] Dorothy resumed her part-time position at Smith. She also picked up a few courses in the Department of Economics and Sociology at nearby Mount Holyoke, assuming her duties just as Katharine arrived.

Seventy-five years later, the first full-fledged biography of Paul Douglas appeared. The Douglases' marriage suffered, it tells us, "from widening political differences between a wife whose radicalism was becoming more doctrinaire and a husband whose progressivism was tempered by his Quaker beliefs." In fact, what is striking is how much Paul and Dorothy had in common. They were socialists, attuned to international influences, but very much in the pragmatic American grain. In the years immediately following their breakup, Paul became more deeply involved in left-wing politics than ever before. He took the lead in forming the League for Independent Political Action, which tried to rally workers, farmers, and consumers around a third party aimed at replacing capitalism with a "cooperative commonwealth," the group's term of choice because it saw socialism—its real goal—as too loaded a label. In 1932 Paul laid out the group's vision in a passionate treatise arguing that both major parties were "dominated by capitalistic interests and unscrupulous politicians who will countenance no tampering with the economic order. They are committed to an outworn individualistic philosophy which cannot cope with modern industrial problems."[56]

Dorothy could not have agreed more. She also shared with Paul the belief that "a disembodied idea is generally as unhappy as a disembodied spirit!" Like him, she sought always to ally herself with people who were using "their energies [to] tangible effect," rather than "frittering away their political idealism in . . . hopeless 'crabbing.'" Revolutionary ideas and policy-oriented actions, utopian dreams and reformist changes—to Dorothy these were never either/or propositions. They were the essence of engagement with the possibilities of the times.[57]

In short, there is nothing to suggest that political differences pushed the Douglases apart or that at the time of their breakup (or later, for that matter) Dorothy's views were "doctrinaire." Both Paul and Dorothy were dedicated to social transformation. Dorothy and Katharine would take this effort in new directions, combining critiques of capitalism with a vision of advocacy expansive enough to redress not only class inequities but also those based on sex, race, and region.

IN THE SPRING of 1929, Dorothy once more returned to Paul in Chicago. Katharine won a fellowship from the Social Science Research Council to expand her graduate research on delinquent girls. Taking an apartment with three southern women who were pursuing graduate study in New York City, she set out to mine the records generated by the city's venerable Charity Organization. A little more than a year later, Dorothy sued her husband for divorce. Paul had treated her with "extreme cruelty," she claimed, shoehorning the tangled details of their estrangement into one of the few formulas the divorce laws allowed. His conduct caused her "great mental and physical suffering" and further "cohabitation would result in the permanent impairment of her health." By then Dorothy had finally won a more secure position at Smith—as a full-time assistant professor on a two-year appointment—and her long, romantic partnership with Katharine had begun. In the fall of 1930, the two women took up residence in Northampton along with Dorothy's children, eleven-year-old Helen, John, nine, Dorothea, seven, and Paul, now four years old. Dorothy had been granted custody. She did not ask for alimony or child support. Soon afterward Paul married Emily Taft. When, with Emily's help, Paul published his memoirs in 1971, he barely mentioned Dorothy, noting briefly that she had a "very stimulating . . . mind." Emily, on the other hand, was a "perfect companion, counselor, and wife."[58]

WRITING AND
NEW YORK

———

WHILE KATHARINE WAS SEEKING TO DEEPEN HER UNDER-standing of workers' lives by working on a Philadelphia assembly line and contemplating her departure from the YWCA, Grace was making up her mind to leave home. It was the summer of 1924, and she had recently returned from her stay on Hazel Creek. She had fifty dollars in her pocketbook and a plan: She would move to New York and stay for two years, working during the day, taking courses at Columbia University at night, and honing her writing skills. So armed, she would return to the South and become a new kind of southern writer, a modern woman attuned to modern forms of sexual and literary self-expression.[1]

Together, the magnetic pull of Columbia University for the women in her YWCA circle and the lure of Greenwich Village fed her conviction, which was shared by countless other Southerners, that only Manhattan could give her the cultural wherewithal (the skills, the self-confidence, the fund of experience) to transform herself into the person she wanted to be. She had lived through books since spending blissful Sunday afternoons listening to her mother read aloud. She had tried her hand at short stories in her teens. "I knew I loved to write," she remembered, and, although she had not excelled in school (Katharine, she would always say, was "the brilliant" one), the stories she had published in college magazines had won her teachers' praise. Carting her typewriter overseas, she had made her first attempts at reportage. Returning home in 1920, she had honed both her reform and her literary imagination as a Y industrial secretary, a home demonstration agent, and a "special student" in literature at the University of South Carolina. It was in this period, as Katharine later observed, that writing became for her "a real conceivable goal."[2]

That goal was nurtured by "the South itself," for the immediate postwar years were marked not only by the reincarnation of the Ku Klux Klan and the intensification of women's reform efforts, but also by the first flush of the Southern Literary Renaissance, whose beginnings Grace had glimpsed in South Carolina. Grace would later claim that she arrived in New York as a blank slate, a southern naïf influenced first by Katharine, her younger but purportedly more sophisticated sister, and then by the brilliant young radicals she happened upon in the city. In truth, the leap from expanding the imaginations of South Carolina mill workers and creating pageants for French working girls to writing novels was not as vast as it might seem. Both were premised on the belief that art could transform society and on the central idea of the social gospel: that human beings could remake themselves and their world.[3]

Grace was, she claimed, twenty-five years old when she packed her bags, said goodbye to her family, and boarded a train to New York. In fact, she was thirty-three.[4] That act of revision was indicative both of her penchant for self-reinvention and of the youth-worshipping culture in which she meant to make her way. No budding writer without a serious publication to her name wanted to admit that she had already passed her thirtieth birthday, the "dead-end of youth." Men felt that pressure as well, but youth and beauty were women's stock in trade. To take one notorious example: Louise Bryant, "the Queen of Bohemia," escaped the tedium of Portland by running away with John Reed. At twenty she had lightheartedly changed her age to eighteen, then moved her birth date backward as she aged. Grace in particular had every reason to shed seven years. Writing and New York, which, as Katharine put it, "went together," may have been her goal, but she also sought love and political adventure. Her imagination was filled with the version of the romance plots she had rehearsed in her student writings: she dreamed of being swept off her feet by an exciting stranger while also making her own mark on the world.[5]

It was a lot to ask. Grace had always been seen as the plain member of the family. It was her mother who was a legendary beauty, and Katharine too was considered a "very lovely woman." More daunting was the fact that she was a white southern woman seeking entry to a male-dominated literary world in which the South still figured, at best, as exotic and, at worst, as a benighted, backward land. She would need every advantage she could muster: ersatz youthfulness, nerve, and a talent for shaping the material of Southernness into a persona of romantic and cultural interest. "All that happened was continually edifying me and astonishing me," Grace remembered.[6] Indeed, her first years in the city offered more political, intellectual, and erotic adventure than even her fertile imagination could have anticipated.

ON THE ADVICE of Katharine and her own and her sister's YWCA friends, Grace immediately contacted *The World Tomorrow*, a magazine perched on the border between the Village and the Lower East Side. Founded in 1918 by the Fellowship of Reconciliation, a loose coalition of Christian socialists and pacifists, *The World Tomorrow* provided a rare forum for isolated and persecuted antiwar activists during World War I. Like other left-wing journals, it ran afoul of the postal service, which tried to bar it from the mail under the 1917 Espionage Act. But it survived to become one of the most vigorous of the little magazines of the 1920s and early 1930s and the leading voice of the Christian internationalism that blossomed in the decade after the war. The Socialist Party leader Norman Thomas had been *The World Tomorrow*'s founding editor. At the helm in the mid-1920s were Anna Rochester, who, with her partner, Grace Hutchins, took Grace under their wing; Devere Allen, who had been a fiery student activist during the war; and Kirby Page, who had rallied students to his anti-imperialist, antimilitarist, antiracist perspective at the 1923 Student Volunteer Movement convention that Katharine and Frances Williams had so memorably attended.[7]

The World Tomorrow offered Grace a perfect way station. Subtitled *A Journal Looking toward a Christian World*, it sought to apply an ethic based on the social gospel to a broad range of issues and to use the techniques of progressive education to generate public support for its ideals. The men and women in the magazine's orbit opposed violence, whether it took the form of the "impersonal mechanical destruction of men at long range" that characterized modern warfare, of lynching as a mode of terror and control, or of a capitalist system that squelched the creative spirit. They also held that, because competition and acquisitiveness nourished the seeds of war, peace depended not only on democratizing institutions and guaranteeing rights but also on creating a just society that fostered rich personal lives for all. A key term in *The World Tomorrow* lexicon was "the beloved community." Coined by the theologian-philosopher Josiah Royce, founder of the Fellowship of Reconciliation, and defined by the prewar bohemian writer Randolph Bourne as a fellowship of equals bound in friendship and committed to democratic change, the ideal of a beloved community would be popularized by Martin Luther King Jr. as the embodiment of the combination of reconciliation, peace, and justice that was the civil rights movement's goal.[8]

The World Tomorrow's staff tried to enact these ideals not just in their public actions but also in the way they ran they ran the office. The magazine, Grace remembered, "had, as a matter of principle all sorts of girls of various nationalities and political views working in that outer office. There were two Negro Girls, two Spanish Anarchists, a Communist, a Jewish socialist, and a 'peacenik' who was myself." Granted, all were lowly clerical workers, as were so many aspiring women. But the editors saw the magazine more as a beloved community of like-minded intellectual workers than as a business, blurring the line between the editors and the staff.[9]

Taking charge of the circulation department and carrying out her tedious job with efficiency and care, Grace proved to be adept at office politics as well. As a result, she found that her skills were valued and her opinions mattered. So much so that, within two years, she and the other young women in the "outer office" were maneuvering their way into an essentially self-governing arrangement.

Their opening came when the magazine's business secretary, Alice Beal Parsons, resigned because she wanted more say in editorial matters. Grace Hutchins, who was serving as the unpaid secretary of the Fellowship of Reconciliation, considered applying for Parsons's job but hesitated because such a move might smack of favoritism, given her intimate relationship with Anna Rochester. She was also concerned about how the women in the outer office would respond to the change because of their "genuine devotion and admiration for Alice." Above all, she feared that elevating herself over the rest of the staff would upset the office's delicate balance of power, especially in light of "the girls' . . . desire for more cooperation and less bossing." In 1925, however, she assumed the position and, in league with the rest of the female staff, reorganized the office along ultra-egalitarian lines. In a manifesto to *The World Tomorrow* readers issued in 1926, Grace Lumpkin and her colleagues announced their refusal "to accept office conventions peculiar to the present social order." Instead, they created a cooperative, in which they chose a manager from among themselves, set their own wages and holidays, and met twice a month to discuss both editorial and business matters. The goal was to "put into practice now, as far as possible, the principles for which *The World Tomorrow* stood" and to signal that the various kinds of work that went toward publishing the magazine were neither "superior nor inferior one to the other."[10]

The women also proudly informed the magazine's supporters that "here have been mingled Negro and white on an equal basis." What they did not tell the public was how they pressured the editors to maintain that atmosphere. Long committed to racial equality, *The World Tomorrow*'s editors forged close ties with civil rights organizations and published black authors. They also hired a young black woman named Wilhelmina White and refused to tolerate white staffers who "wouldn't hear to working with colored people!" At one point, they moved to new quarters because White "was being subjected to indignities and pressure was being brought on the World Tomorrow because of her presence." White, however, occupied the bottom rung of the office staff; the editors were trying to keep a shoestring operation afloat and, in the interests of what they saw as efficiency, at moments they considered letting her go. They kept her on—and she blossomed—because of influence that Grace and the other white office workers brought to bear.[11]

Grace's chief ally in these efforts, and her most treasured friend, was Esther Shemitz, the magazine's advertising manager and the "Jewish socialist" on its staff. Born in New York City in 1900, Esther was the daughter of intensely religious Russian immigrants who moved to New Haven, Connecticut, when she was ten years old. On graduating from high school, Esther won a scholarship from the New Haven Socialist Party to attend the Rand School of Social Science, a socialist institution in New York. Before taking a job at *The World Tomorrow*, she had worked as a bookkeeper for the International Ladies Garment Workers' Union, a hub of Jewish working-class radicalism. But like many US-born children of Jewish immigrants, she left her parents' Old World religiosity behind.[12]

By all accounts, Esther was a "whole-hearted person, single-minded, who threw herself into whatever she was doing with great devotion." Thanks to the city's smorgasbord of working-class cultural institutions, she threw herself especially into "ART." She began by taking courses at the Leonardo Da Vinci Art School, which opened in 1923 on the Lower East Side, a densely packed maze known for its eastern European Jewish population, but home to a mix of immigrants from around the world. To skeptics, the Lower East Side seemed an unlikely source of artistic genius, but the school persisted in admitting "poor art students of all nationalities and creeds." Its student body included factory workers, truck drivers, and businessmen; its Saturday night lectures drew lively, equally heterogeneous crowds. Esther, Grace remembered, "paid only a dollar every Monday for instruction from the finest Italian sculptors and painters in the city, who gave their time."[13]

Securing a "lunch room scholarship," in which she traded labor for instruction, Esther also studied at the Art Students League, which grew from its bohemian beginnings in 1875 into a major force for transforming New York into the art capital of the world. In the League's imposing home on West 57th Street, she took classes modeled on the ateliers of Paris and Munich, where students worked on their own, with an instructor coming in twice a week for critique, and studied with the likes of Thomas Hart Benton, an early member of the avant-garde who was among the founders of a new regionalist school of American painting.[14]

Esther and Grace made a striking pair. They were a study in contrasts: Grace's fair skin and blond hair, cut short at the time but later wound around her head in a coronet braid; Esther's angular features, brown eyes, and black bob. Grace's exotic Southernness (friends from that era describe her as "a real Southern lady," "an innocent . . . a southern child"); Esther's eastern European Jewishness, with its connotations of plebian energy and Old World suffering and sophistication. Grace's mix of romanticism and writerly ambition; Esther's "radiant selflessness," her serious, unadorned style.[15]

The two women quickly became inseparable. They found an apartment together: the narrow top floor of an old brick row house owned by Alice Parsons at 71 Bedford Street. It had high ceilings, a fireplace—all the accoutrements that made the Village so alluring. And, wonder of wonders, they turned out to be living but two houses down from Edna

St. Vincent Millay, the most famous denizen of Greenwich Village and the avatar of the sexual revolution.[16]

Suitably ensconced, Grace enrolled in Columbia University's pioneering extension division, which had been started by Teacher's College at the turn of the century. Among her instructors was Lillian B. Gilkes, a left-wing writer who was impressed with Grace's talent and who, almost half a century later, would try to rescue her former student's work from critical neglect. Gilkes's courses supplemented Grace's Village contacts with access to a lively Upper West Side writers' scene, including a Writers Club, to which Grace would one day return as an honored speaker, and a variety of student-oriented literary journals, including *MS.: A Magazine for Writers*, published by the English department.[17]

"I was just in heaven because it was using all of my mind, and all of my heart, and all of my energies," Grace remembered. Hurrying from work to classes, she and Esther ate on the fly. They devoted every spare minute to writing and painting, spent their money on books, and took in "all the shows on 57th Street and as many concerts at Carnegie Hall as we could afford." Among their most exciting discoveries were the black artists and performers who were beginning to make their mark. They heard the singer Roland Hayes at Carnegie Hall and read the poetry of Jean Toomer and Langston Hughes. They were entranced by Alain Locke's *The New Negro* (1925), an anthology of works by young authors who claimed both the European literary tradition and African American forms of cultural expression as their own.[18]

Grace devoured the products of the Southern Renaissance as well. As defined by the Nashville Agrarians—a group of poets and writers who would go on to play an outsize role in determining how the story of southern literature was told—this literary awakening had been inspired by a "crossing of the ways." "With the war of 1914–1918," according to Allen Tate's often repeated formulation, "the South reentered the world—but gave a backward glance as it stepped over the border: that backward glance gave us the Southern Renaissance, a literature conscious of the past in the present." At the core of this literary enterprise was an exploration of "the white South's cast of mind," which was, as the Agrarians defined it, characterized by a tragic sense of life, a deep-rooted pessimism, and an obsession with history and place.[19]

As lived by Grace and her compatriots, however, this awakening was much more capacious than that. It was not confined to the Agrarians' concerns. Instead, it was fed by multiple currents, including black writing and radical literature, which, in turn, were more interwoven than critics have allowed. This cultural ferment brought together people from vastly different backgrounds and perspectives, fostering fierce debates, unexpected webs of relations, and surprising intellectual convergences, all of which created new ways of thinking, seeing, and feeling. Whether they hailed from the South, Harlem, or the Lower East Side, and however sharply they differed among themselves, these writers shared a critical aesthetic and political orientation, a desire to register the pressure of the present moment and to bring to visibility both the southern diaspora in northern cities and the world of the southern hinterlands and the highlands, the poor farmers and mill workers in all their quotidian and explosively political struggles.[20]

ALMOST AS SOON as Grace and Esther had settled in together, Grace's mother came for an extended visit, bringing news of "torturing anxiety" and "terrible days." The previous March, Elizabeth had undergone surgery in Richmond, Virginia, and, according to the *Asheville Times*, her fifty-four-year-old husband had collapsed from "nervous exhaustion" upon returning from visiting his wife. In fact, Eugene Byron Glenn had long been drinking himself to death. He had been hospitalized for a similar breakdown in 1922. Now he was suffering from chronic interstitial nephritis. He died of kidney failure on March 30, 1924.[21]

Intimations of a hidden story behind Elizabeth's mysterious illness and her husband's unraveling are scattered throughout the fiction of Thomas Wolfe. Asheville's most famous native son, Wolfe filled his writings with characters based on what most literary scholars agree were imaginatively filtered but barely disguised portraits of people he knew. The Glenns lived within easy walking distance of the boarding house run by his mother, and at one time or another Dr. Glenn treated each of the Wolfe family's members, including young Thomas. Beginning with *Look Homeward, Angel*, which appeared in 1929, five years after Eugene Glenn's death but while Elizabeth Lumpkin Glenn was very much alive, Wolfe turned the "burly, brusque, drunken" family doctor into what the southern literary scholar Floyd C. Watkins characterizes as "one of the most human and unique figures in American fiction." Initially called Dr. Hugh Glynn and then Hugh McGuire, that character was readily identifiable by local readers—including Elizabeth's youngest son—as Eugene Byron Glenn because of his gargantuan taste for liquor, "inebriated kindheartedness," and surgical skills.[22]

In his published fiction, Wolfe sometimes associated the doctor's death with heartbreak over the faithlessness of a woman with whom he had had an extramarital affair. But in an unpublished novella-like manuscript entitled "The Death of Stoneman Grant," Wolfe fashioned a portrait of the doctor's wife as the faithless one. That portrait was surely inspired by Wolfe's animus toward his estranged mistress, but it was built around details from Elizabeth's life, including her hospitalization. Described as a "city-girl from Richmond," the wife complains that she "could have been a great artist, the greatest actress of this generation." Unhinged by menopause, which Wolfe describes as "that period of bestial dementia which is the crowning degradation of the sex," she is reduced to producing the sets for amateur productions of Shakespeare, a nod to the Shakespearean tercentenary celebration which Elizabeth led and in which Wolfe participated. She sees her husband as "an inspired butcher . . . who, in spite of his immense competence in his profession, has remained just what he was when I married him—a mountain peasant whose only interest in life, outside of alcohol, is in the various tumours, cancers, kidneys and appendices on which he tries his skill." As for the doctor: "He had known his wife well; he had known that she was vain, idle, and sometimes stupid, he knew how cheap were many of her pretensions, how false her delusions; and he loved her better than he loved his life."[23]

It is impossible to know what grain of truth may lie in Wolfe's misogynistic portrait. But his writings make clear that the Glenns' travails were subjects of gossip and speculation in a tight-knit town, and the fact that Elizabeth did not return from Richmond for her husband's funeral suggests that the crises that befell the Glenns in 1924 had emotional as well as medical roots. So does a small, privately held cache of Annette's letters to one of her sisters.

They tell us that while Elizabeth recovered from whatever had beset her in what seems to have been a discreet Richmond psychiatric clinic that catered to doctors and their families, sixty-eight-year-old Annette took over the care of her home and her four children, then aged seventeen, fifteen, twelve, and ten. It was an overwhelming task, which she would not have undertaken except under the direst of conditions. "I have been *rebellious* that duty pointed so straight," she reflected. "I must plunge in though so poorly prepared by age and, I may say, training for all that is involved." A month later, Annette reported that Elizabeth was still in Richmond. She had begun to recover physically, but was still too emotionally fragile to come home. When Elizabeth did finally return to Asheville more than two months after her husband's death, it was to a sanatorium four miles outside of town. While there, she decided to sell her house. It would not be good for her to live "in the surroundings of 20 years, in her weak state every stick and stone gives one a pang," Annette explained.[24]

Elizabeth followed through on that decision, finding ways to cope with the aftershock of her ordeal and taking charge of her life as a widow with four children to support. Eugene had died intestate, and his property was divided between his wife and children. That property included a life insurance policy, real estate holdings, and investments in his family's talc business, as well as a controlling interest in Meriwether Hospital. Managing these resources, Elizabeth moved to an even larger house in the same upper-middle-class neighborhood in which she and her husband had always lived. She also kept her youngest son, William, at Sewanee Military Academy, a prep school that was part of the University of the South, the bastion of Confederate values to which the Lumpkins were devoted, and then sent him on to the University of South Carolina and then to medical school. At the same time, she returned to her voluntary activities, seeing the new Pack Memorial Library building through to completion and championing the provision of a modest facility for blacks.[25]

By 1927, she had assumed the position of treasurer and business manager of Meriwether Hospital, taking the place of Eugene's brother. In that same year, she was singled out for listing in *Who's Who in the South* and invited to join the local Chamber of Commerce, one of the city's most powerful—and virtually all-male—organizations, distinctions she enjoyed by virtue of her position as an executive of Meriwether Hospital and her appointment as a member of the city's library board. She also starred in Asheville little theater productions. The following year she enrolled in the Asheville Law School. At fifty-two, she became the seventy-third woman to pass the North Carolina bar and be admitted to practice. Hanging out her shingle at an office on Pack Square and specializing in legal issues pertaining to women and children, she maintained a small practice for at least fourteen years.[26]

ANNETTE COULD NOT have been more relieved by Elizabeth's recovery, which freed her from a burden of responsibility "so heavy no words are adequate." And she was thrilled to be visiting Grace and touring New York City. She stayed for a week at her daughter's "dear little apartment," where, she said, Grace and Esther were "like little girls fixing their doll house," then moved to a cheap hotel on the Upper West Side where Katharine had once boarded. She mined the genealogical records at the grand New York Public Library, looking for tidbits to add to her precious store of information on the Du Pre clan. She lunched with Grace at Wanamaker's, which was shockingly expensive but "such a charming place of wonderful color." She adored Esther, who was "so cultured, an artist and musical." Grace and Esther were busy with their day jobs and evening classes, she reported to her sister. And they lived in the most interesting neighborhood. "Next door but one is a young poet Edna St. Vincent Millay who won the Pulitzer Prize for best short poem, 'The Harp Weaver.' She has four books at least on the market, and they are selling!"[27]

Annette came by her enthusiasm naturally, for she was no stranger to artistic longings and romantic self-invention. In fact, it would be hard to say who took the bigger leap—Annette, from a carpenter's cottage in the backwoods South to a bustling port city's upper crust, or Grace, from South Carolina to New York. Grace might alter her age and reinvent herself as she went along, but it was Annette who had created a plantation legacy out of whole cloth. "One would love to be young and in this big swirl," she wrote, suggesting how much her own unspoken desires may have influenced her unorthodox daughters as she wistfully gave her blessings to their adventures.[28]

In the months that followed, Annette kept up a warm correspondence with "you darlingnest girls." She was especially proud of Grace's work on *The World Tomorrow* and shared the magazine with her sisters. She longed for another "pleasure jaunt" to New York. Still, she was worried. She feared that "the girls" were so busy with their jobs and lessons that they didn't take time to rest or eat. "Feed your bodies," she advised, "else they will not support all you want to do. . . . Spend for good substantial food." Poor though she was, she managed to send Grace a little money, a "nest egg . . . an emergency fund."[29]

Annette gave Grace another gift as well: fearing that her sons would sense "wild disaster in the air," she kept to herself much of what she knew about Grace's polyglot "swirl." During the previous summer, Annette had also obscured the fact that Katharine was working in a shoe factory in Philadelphia. And she very likely told no one everything she knew about Elizabeth's ordeals, except perhaps the sister in whom she had confided during the difficult early years of her own marriage. Hewing to the pattern of strategic concealments that marked so much of Lumpkin family life, Grace and Katharine, in turn, protected their mother and staved off their brothers' interference by, as Katharine put it, managing to "slur over" much of what they thought and did.[30]

Six months after her trip to New York, Annette died without warning while visiting her sister in Florida. She left each of her children $26.24. She had nurtured her daughters' love of language and given them her steady support. She had also surrounded them with a precious zone of privacy, the space to form their own values and dream their own dreams apart from the authority of the Lumpkin men, albeit at the cost of a family culture built on half-truths and silences rather than a respect for differences honestly confronted.[31]

A year after her mother's death, Grace made her first serious foray into print. Coauthored with Esther, it appeared in an issue of *The World Tomorrow* devoted to "Social Equality—The Crux of Negro-White Relations," a subject that would certainly have scandalized the Lumpkins of South Carolina. Entitled "The Artist in a Hostile Environment," their article went straight to the heart of issues that would prove to be central to the concerns that Grace shared with her generation of artists and writers: the relationship between aesthetics and politics, engaged art and propaganda.[32]

Faced with the intensification of racism at the end of World War I and, at the same time, invigorated by the vast expansion of the publishing industry in the 1920s and the influx of black Southerners to the northern cities, black intellectuals had responded with a burst of creativity rooted in the hope that "each book, play, poem or canvas by an Afro-American would become a weapon against the old racial stereotypes." But their faith in the politics of culture went far beyond that. By writing freely and well, the New Negro aimed not just to assert a common African American identity that transcended old divisions between South and North, rural and urban, the masses and the elite, but also to expand the boundaries of citizenship, build a pluralistic polity, and revise what "we the people" might mean. By using art in the battle for social inclusion, black intellectuals aimed both to accrue cultural capital and to reshape American culture at its core.[33]

Members of the older black elite, represented especially by W. E. B. Du Bois, editor of the NAACP's magazine, *The Crisis*, had begun calling for a new black literature in 1923, and they promoted and published the Harlem Renaissance's young writers and endorsed many of the impulses behind those writers' work. Foremost among these was a determination to portray African Americans as "complete, complex, *undiminished* human beings" and an interest in the southern roots of a black working-class culture long denigrated by whites and middle-class blacks. But they also remained committed to a politics of uplift and respectability, and they could not stomach the portrayals of uninhibited sexuality and urban lowlife that increasingly animated their protégés' work—representations that, to their minds, reinforced white stereotypes and undermined black progress. Because of those tensions, a variety of approaches to politics and literature mingled in the pages of black magazines. These periodicals, along with other cultural institutions, took up residence in Harlem, which black migrants had transformed into the nation's largest, most exciting African American community seemingly overnight. Less noticed were the downtown venues that also nurtured this black literary awakening: little magazines such as *The World Tomorrow*, which were dominated by whites, but were also among the few integrated cultural institutions in the nation.[34]

Inspired by these controversies and interactions, "The Artist in a Hostile Environment" addressed three fundamental questions. The first was whether there was or should be such a thing as "Negro art." The second was where that art should look for its inspiration and subject matter. And the third was whether it should serve bluntly political goals. To answer these questions, Grace and Esther took as their point of departure Alain Locke's observation that protest literature had, for too long, made the Negro "more of a formula than a human being—a something to be argued about, condemned or defended, to be 'kept down,' or 'in his place,' or 'helped up,' to be worried with or worried over, harassed or patronized, a social bogey or a social problem." The artist, they believed, should express a personal vision rather than react to the external "snarl of life with one of the fifty-seven varieties of remedies." The Negro, moreover, should not be confined in any way—why shouldn't the great actor Paul Robeson, who had starred in Eugene O'Neill's *Emperor Jones* and *All God's Chillun Got Wings*, "lighten his skin and play Hamlet" just as white actors had traditionally darkened theirs to play Othello? "Surely the art of make-up is not at fault here."[35]

At the same time, the authors parted ways both with white critics who condemned black protest writing as propaganda and with black intellectuals such as Locke who imagined, in the heady optimism of the moment, that race was becoming a mere "idiom of experience, a sort of added enriching adventure and discipline, giving subtler overtones to life, making it more beautiful and interesting, even if more poignantly so." However much Grace and Esther might applaud Locke's position, they understood that the particularities of the black experience—the hard facts of violence and poverty, the curse of a caste system—could not be so easily transformed into cosmopolitan universals or transcended through art. For the vast majority of blacks, whether they remained in the South or joined the Great Migration, such dispassion was impossible. Given the reality, not of "race" per se, but of social violence based on racial ideologies, it was only to be expected that the black artist would and should use "every ounce of energy within him" to counteract the brutality that assailed his people from every side. How could the Negro artist "throw off the overwhelming burdens of the sufferings of his oppressed fellows and of his own tortured person?" the women asked. How, in the face of insults, humiliations, and atrocities, could "he ever forget his body and his lacerated mind, his color, his race, sufficiently to let his soul soar out into the clear atmosphere of creation where all are one?"[36]

As for subject matter, if art is self-expression, why shouldn't the Negro artist represent the complex lives of African Americans hidden beneath the "minstrel, mammy and uncle types" that contaminated white writing? Praising both the iconoclastic blues-based poetry of Langston Hughes and the spirituals treasured by the older black elite, Grace and Esther embraced the whole range of African American vernacular forms. They ended their essay with a clear-eyed analysis of the political economy of art and the dangers of white patronage. Their concern, however, lay not with the bête noir of the Harlem Renaissance: the individual white benefactor who supposedly steered black writers toward "the primitive and exotic." Instead they targeted the material realities that shaped the larger, white-dominated literary establishment, which included consumers as well as publishers, editors, and grant makers. In a country where blacks were still relegated to the field and the kitchen, where even "educated colored men and women, our artist included, must fall back on the most menial and poorly paid jobs such as porter, bus boy, kitchen help, elevator operator," black artists had to overcome crushing odds. First, the barrier of class- and race-based poverty, which cut them off from early training in the arts. And second, the necessity of winning over an antagonistic white public. "White America," Grace and Esther concluded, "because of its majority in numbers and influence, its potential book buyers with power to sway the pendulum of sales in either direction, is indeed . . . the patron tenderly treasuring limitations in regard to what the Negro may or may not dare."[37]

WITHIN MONTHS OF publishing this article, Grace and Esther were delighted to find themselves engaged with the "Negro artist" not just on the stage and the page but also in the person of Wallace Thurman, one of the most brilliant, volatile, and uncompromising of Harlem's rising stars. Arriving in New York from Utah by way of California in 1925, Thurman took over as editor of *The Messenger*, a socialist magazine founded by A. Philip Randolph, and then, in the fall of 1926, joined Grace, Esther, and the otherwise all-woman office staff of *The World Tomorrow*, relieving Grace of her duties as circulation manager. A more-or-less closeted homosexual with a deep, resonant voice, an infectious laugh, very dark skin, and a keen awareness of color prejudice among blacks, Thurman seemed to know everybody and to have read everything. The women staffers took to him at once.[38]

The World Tomorrow editors Devere Allen and Kirby Page were impressed by Thurman's personality and talent, but otherwise he drove them to distraction. He might work for the magazine, but his "thoughts were elsewhere most of the time." The ambitious young writer was at war with the black establishment and obsessed with launching *Fire!! A Quarterly Devoted to the Younger Negro Artists*. The situation only got worse when *Fire!!* hit the streets in November 1926. Deemed by later critics a folk masterpiece, it succeeded so well in shocking the older generation that it quickly expired. Thurman had put every penny he earned at his day job into the project. When his overcoat was stolen, Allen and Page bought him a new one; everyone loaned him money, including the women on the office staff. The editors made allowances, held endless conferences, came up with new systems and plans.[39]

In the end, they fired him, the staff's "office cooperative" plan notwithstanding, much to Grace and Esther's chagrin. "Pretty critical of how things have been going," Grace wrote, contacting Anna Rochester and Grace Hutchins, who were in Germany studying Russian in preparation for a trip to the Soviet Union. The two women wrote to the editors in Thurman's defense. Perhaps they had given the "young colored man" too many different jobs when circulation needed his full attention. And besides, Hutchins argued, "the race question" was involved. "There are so very few positions in the white world that are open to educated Negroes that it is a very real tragedy when one fails." Patronizing as Hutchins's remarks sounded (Thurman wanted to write the great American novel, not succeed at office work), they spoke to the issues that "The Artist in a Hostile Environment" had raised. Struggling to fulfill his own vaulting artistic ambitions, Thurman could not escape the constant scramble for money that often kept even the most talented black writers from pursuing their craft.[40]

A few months after he left *The World Tomorrow*, Thurman, along with Langston Hughes and George Schuyler, the self-styled "black H. L. Mencken" who had become the main force behind *The Messenger*, published a series of articles that raised the stakes of artistic debate. Whereas Grace and Esther had tried to explain Negro artists to and defend them against an implicitly white audience, these three men forced into the open the conflicts *within* the black intelligentsia. The first volley came from Schuyler, who argued that since "the Aframerican is merely a lampblacked Anglo-Saxon," the idea that art should express the peculiar psychology of the Negro simply reinforced racist stereotypes. In response, Hughes fired off "The Negro Artist and the Racial Mountain," often considered the finest essay of his life. Blasting the "Nordicized Negro intelligentsia," he defended his vision of an art that took its inspiration and materials from "low-down folks."[41]

Thurman weighed in with stinging articles in the *New Republic* and the Marxist *Independent*. Like Hughes, Zora Neale Hurston, and others, he scorned the old guard, who, he believed, were consumed by the canker of race consciousness, evidenced by their investment in their roles as spokesmen for and uplifters of the race and in their belief—as he saw it—that black artists should confine themselves to exposing injustices and showcasing black accomplishments. He defended *Fire!!* for going "to the proletariat rather than to the bourgeoisie for characters and materials." He attacked NAACP head Walter White, whose antilynching novel *Fire in the Flint* "recounted all the ills Negroes suffer in the inimical South and made all Negroes seem magnanimous, mistreated martyrs, all southern whites evil transgressors of human rights." He argued brilliantly *against* essentialist notions of race and *for* the aesthetic value of the culture of the black common folk.[42]

Thurman's aim was both to express and to transcend a racial identity that white Americans were not about to let him forget. In his case, that quest was doomed—for the very reasons that Grace and Esther had so vividly enumerated. Thurman could not live up to his own standards, which demanded that black writers overcome the barriers of poverty and discrimination through sheer genius. He died from compulsive drinking in 1934, at the age of thirty-two.[43] But the interracial literary exchange he believed in was not just an impossible dream: it took place in Harlem and in venues like *The World Tomorrow* as well as imaginatively, as black and white writers read one another's work. It remained, throughout the interwar period, a source of inspiration for many of the era's most creative artists and intellectuals on both sides of the color line.

Grace brought her own preoccupations to that conversation. She and Esther had called their article "The Artist in a Hostile Environment," not "The *Negro* Artist in a Hostile Environment." Behind the figure they called "our artist" was not only an African American but also a woman, struggling, in her own way, to reconcile art and politics and to "wrench or cajole" recognition from an "antagonistic public." And behind that were the fresh memories of a white Southerner whose own people were responsible for "lacerated" black bodies and minds. By identifying herself for *The World Tomorrow* readers as "a student of interracial problems both in the North and the South," Grace asserted her authority as a voice from the South—a place whose cultural meaning writers like herself would do much to redefine—and as a commentator on race both in her region of origin and in the city, newcomer though she might be. She wrote—as she had acted in the racial politics that played themselves out on *The World Tomorrow* stage—from an angle of vision that reflected not only her own brush with the South's interracial movement but Katharine's deeper involvement as well. At its best that movement revolved around an appeal for honesty and understanding between the races and a concomitant demand that whites *see* the evils of discrimination, which were embedded in daily practices, hidden in plain sight.[44]

AS GRACE AND ESTHER wrestled with the complex relationships among race, politics, and art, a conflict was brewing that plunged them directly into the political fray. That conflict introduced them to a group of young Communists who would have an incalculable impact on both their lives. It also drew Grace into a circle of women who were carving out a special role in journalism, long the province of men, by developing a distinctive brand of feminist labor reportage. Pursuing a democratic vision of character and plot, these women foregrounded the poor, amplified new voices, reassessed which characters could drive the action, and, not incidentally, made a bid for the authority of writers who, like themselves, came from previously marginalized groups.[45]

On January 25, 1926, eight thousand workers walked off their jobs in Passaic, New Jersey, only half an hour from downtown Manhattan by rail. The owners of the woolen mills in and around Passaic had feasted on huge returns during the boom years of the war. When the postwar recession sent profits plummeting, they responded with wage cuts that bit deeply into the livelihoods of a mostly foreign-born workforce already subsisting on meager earnings and crowded into fetid slums. The United Textile Workers of America (UTW), which was an affiliate of the American Federation of Labor (AFL), an umbrella organization dominated by skilled craftsmen, had nothing but disdain for the millhands of Passaic, not only because they were considered unskilled greenhorns but also because half of them were women, and it refused to aid the strike.[46]

Into this vacuum stepped a small group of young Communists. Tarred as a collection of bomb-throwing Bolsheviks in the wake of the Russian Revolution, Communists had been forced underground during World War I, then resurfaced to form the Workers Party of America in 1922 (later the Communist Party, USA). Led by Albert Weisbord, a slight, bespectacled twenty-five-year-old Harvard Law School graduate who turned out to be a brilliant organizer and vigorous public speaker, the activists in Passaic formed a United Front Committee that attracted broad support, especially among leftists and liberals in New York.[47] Using new forms of publicity, such as moving picture cameras, and aligning themselves with new organizations, such as the American Civil Liberties Union (ACLU), they set out to create sympathy for labor, no small feat after a decade of relentless probusiness, antilabor legislation and propaganda. Central to their effort was an ardent commitment to defending and expanding the rights of free speech and assembly, which had been swept aside during World War I and, in the early 1920s, were still routinely curtailed by authorities at every level.

Their opportunity to defend those rights came when Passaic officials banned mass picketing and two thousand strikers circumvented the order, claiming that they were simply passing by the mill gates, two by two, on their way home from a union meeting. The next day, policemen blocked the street and mounted officers charged into the crowd. When the strikers refused to disperse, the police chief set off tear-gas bombs. What horses, clubs, and tear gas could not do, high-pressure fire hoses accomplished. When the picketing resumed, the police not only brutalized strikers and bystanders but also turned on reporters and photographers, beating them bloody and stomping their cameras to smithereens. This was a public relations disaster for the police and the mills. Even editors who had been hostile or lukewarm toward the strikers were furious: their own had been attacked and they broadcast news of the conflict to the nation.[48]

With the blessings of *The World Tomorrow* editors, Esther and Grace traveled back and forth to join the picket lines and report on the strike. On one occasion Esther was trapped with a group of workers in a union hall as the police massed outside to keep the doors shut and prevent them from marching. Now and then, the strikers would push the doors ajar, and the police would slam them shut again. At last the weight of the crowd forced the doors wide open. As it did so, according to a young reporter at the scene, a "slender girl in a brown beret rushed out before the police could stop her. The demonstration surged after her. 'Get that bitch in the brown beret,' an officer shouted," and the police closed in, swinging their clubs. The "slender girl" was Esther, and she wore her bruises proudly. The young reporter turned out to be Whittaker Chambers, who would one day become the "hottest literary Bolshevik" in New

York. Chambers was smitten, and he managed to sit beside Esther on the train back to the city.[49]

In the weeks that followed, Grace and Esther returned to Passaic again and again. At one point they started out from the union soup kitchen with four New York friends and eight strikers to picket at one of the city's major mills. Two policemen and a plainclothesman attacked the group, clubbing them back toward the kitchen. One woman "was struck so viciously on the spine that she collapsed." The police chief stood on the corner, watching the violence but refusing to intervene.[50]

Grace was also on hand when the police burst into strike headquarters and arrested Weisbord and twenty-four members of the United Front Committee. Then the mill owners secured an injunction against demonstrations of any sort. Despite the injunction and with many of their leaders in jail, thousands of strikers and supporters turned out to picket the mill. Joining the picket line, Grace transformed what she observed into a "snapshot" for *The New Masses*, her first work of labor reportage.[51]

Like *The World Tomorrow*, *The New Masses* was a little magazine whose advent offered proof that the left was regrouping in the wake of postwar reaction. Heir to *The Masses*, the chief vehicle for prewar literary radicalism, *The New Masses* offered irreverent cartoons, ingenious illustrations, and a fresh, vivid combination of fiction and radical reportage. Free of any party label, it aimed to speak for the "new creative forces" at work in the country and to offer "a haven for young artists and intellectuals." Saluting the public-spirited "New York liberals and radicals, who . . . went out to Passaic to show their solidarity with the workers," the second issue of the magazine featured a symposium on the strike.[52] Among the writers invited to participate were John Dos Passos, whose most recent novel, *Manhattan Transfer*, made him one of the country's leading literary lights, and Norman Thomas, the chief voice of socialism in America. Also in the lineup were a number of lesser knowns, including Grace, whose article was entitled "God Save the State!"

Placing herself at the scene, marching behind a young boy but just to the side of the action, she rendered the clash of forces not as a confrontation between brawny male laborers and capitalist oppressors (as, in the 1930s, it would so often be represented) but as a drama in which women and children took center stage. As she described it, a policeman asked the boy, "What are you doing here?" "Picketing," the child answered. "Go away or you can choose trouble!" the officer said. As the boy turned around, Grace caught his eyes. "They had fear way back in them, but he had whipped his lips into a twisted smile." The boy went down the line, speaking to the strikers, then returned to the front, looked at the officer and said, "We'll picket." As the line stepped forward, policemen with clubs and guns barred the way. Suddenly the county sheriff appeared and pulled from his pocket a copy of New Jersey's riot act. Passed in 1864, it outlawed "tumultuous assemblies," which the authorities construed to include both picket lines and meetings by strikers or their support-ers. Red-faced with rage, the sheriff recited the archaic words, ending with "God save the state." Then he screamed, "Sweep 'em out, boys!" As the police rushed in "the air became thick with . . . the sound of clubs striking against human bodies. A woman and a child lying silent on the ground, a policeman standing over them, his club raised. Another woman screaming as a bluecoat struck her down. . . . A law of 1864 for workers of 1926. A law enforced by great blue arms swinging clubs against human, quivering flesh. God save the state, and to hell with human beings."[53]

Brief but vivid, this article located Grace in a network of women composed both of prewar radicals and of younger, postwar recruits who not only covered the strike for left-wing magazines but also helped to engineer the United Front Committee's brilliant publicity campaign. The best known of these was Elizabeth Gurley Flynn. Immortalized as labor's "Rebel Girl" by Joe Hill, songster for the legendary Wobblies, Flynn spent the postwar years in tireless efforts to defend the victims of political repression, and she brought to the Passaic conflict both her fund-raising abilities and her incomparable oratorical skills. Flynn, in turn, recruited her longtime friend Mary Heaton Vorse to serve as pub-licity director for the United Front Committee. Vorse, who had virtually invented labor journalism during the Lawrence, Massachusetts, strike of 1912 and served as its chief exemplar through the 1940s, brought in Margaret Larkin, a talented twenty-seven-year-old who had just arrived in the city and was looking for work.[54]

Growing up in New Mexico, Larkin had developed a keen interest in folk culture, from the art of Navaho weavers to the songs of cowboys, and she and Grace would soon cross paths again as chroniclers of the Gasto-nia, North Carolina, strike of 1929. Working day and night, Larkin put her talents and passions to use in Passaic, organizing concerts, bringing in motion picture crews, and, with Vorse, editing a weekly *Textile Strike*

Bulletin unlike anything the labor movement had produced before. The bulletin featured workers' writings, a women's column, children's poems, and songs, which, as Vorse put it, "in the manner of folk songs everywhere . . . are added to by all who sing them." Vorse "always dreaded the arrival of the Communist Party's *Daily Worker*," for "it hits you in the eyes how little it is adapted to the workers and how uninteresting the most interesting material can be made to be." By contrast, the bulletin created by the two women fairly breathed with life. Often quoted by the mainstream press, it served as a conduit into popular culture for class-based images and themes. Like Grace, Vorse and Larkin were groping toward a form of aesthetic and political expression that would permeate the culture in the years to come, first in reality-based "proletarian literature" and then, more broadly, in the documentaries of the 1930s and the "proletarian regionalism" that would seek to fuse the two.[55]

For these left feminists, women's voices resonated most strongly, and they augmented them at every turn. Vorse's passionate history of the conflict, published by the strikers' relief committee, made those affinities clear. Women, in her account, were key to the strike's success. Whether workers or working men's wives, they were not at home "scabbing in their hearts." Instead, they were running the soup kitchens, leading the picket lines, organizing women's meetings, and, in all these ways, giving the lie to the myth that "you cannot organize the women." Indeed, their strength was rooted in their experiences *as* women.[56]

The contributions of John Dos Passos and Norman Thomas to *The New Masses* symposium underscored just how gendered radical writing could be. A pathbreaking modernist and an intimate of Ernest Hemingway and F. Scott Fitzgerald, Dos Passos shared the scorn of many alienated "Lost Generation" writers for earnest do-gooders and high-minded ideals. Passaic represented a tentative first step toward the activism that would soon consume him and would later reshape the aesthetic and political alignments of his peers. Where Vorse, Larkin, and Lumpkin positioned themselves as fighting side-by-side with articulate, brave, intelligent workers, Dos Passos portrayed the workers as distant figures, square, silent, and gray. Norman Thomas distanced himself as well by explicitly rejecting the women's intimate reportorial style. In "Lessons of Passaic," he explained the evils of high tariffs, from which the German owners of the Passaic factories benefited. Such economic facts, he concluded, "may have greater educational value than the more colorful incidents of the strike which I have omitted."[57]

For Margaret Larkin and Grace Lumpkin, both newcomers from the hinterlands, Passaic taught lessons of a visceral sort. Larkin was "stunned and appalled by what she saw and lived, and it was an education in the facts of life. She never felt the same after that about anything." "These things are unforgettable," Grace wrote, and they propelled her into a vortex of sharpened perceptions and novel alliances.[58]

The strike finally ended in December 1927, almost two years after it began. The mill owners steadfastly refused to meet with the strikers, claiming communist involvement as their reason. The UTW-AFL denounced the United Front Committee as dangerous and unnecessary. In response, Weisbord reluctantly promised to step down if the mill owners would negotiate with the UTW. The mills agreed to do so, secure in the knowledge that the union was too poor, too cautious, and too out of touch with the workers to be a formidable foe.

For the workers the result was far from a resounding victory, but neither was it a devastating defeat. A number of mills rescinded the wage cuts that set off the conflict; union locals took root for the first time. Large sectors of the public were confronted with the dismal conditions of working-class life. The Passaic strike benefited the communist movement as well: although the AFL and the mill owners succeeded in pushing the party aside, the conflict gave a small, faction-ridden group of radicals based mainly in New York and Chicago new credibility, both in the international communist movement and among liberals, social democrats, and independent radicals.

For many on the left, Passaic seemed to betoken the reawakening of a spirit of resistance that had been squelched by wartime repression. For Grace, to whom the war had opened horizons rather than dampened ideals, the strike offered a headlong dive into issues and affiliations that would shape her life and work in the years to come. Like her job at *The World Tomorrow*, Passaic registered so powerfully in part because it resonated with themes from the past and in part because it carried the shock of the new. She had read Progressive era exposés. She had seen children pulled from school and put to work in the cotton mills; known women who were forced to labor at home all day and then stand at their looms through the night; confronted poverty that ravaged bodies and minds. But never had she seen such seemingly powerless people risk so much for so long in such a dramatic, inventive, and unified fight. At home in South Carolina she could not have imagined herself on a picket line dodging "great blue arms swinging clubs against human, quivering flesh." What she could imagine was herself as a writer, and she began immediately to shape the experience of Passaic around a new persona, that of the activist writer who amplifies the voices of the dispossessed.

"KOK-I HOUSE"

———

As the passaic strike wound to an end, grace plunged into a more famous cause célèbre: the Boston trial of the Italian anarchists Nicola Sacco and Bartolomeo Vanzetti. The International Labor Defense (ILD) was leading an ongoing series of marches against the threatened execution of the two men. Dusting off a World War I–era ordinance against "sauntering and loitering," authorities were threatening mass arrests.[1] Sacco's and Vanzetti's core supporters—Italians and eastern European Jews—could be counted on to take the risk, but their arrests meant nothing to the Boston establishment, which had led the postwar fight for immigration restriction and viewed them as members of the inferior races. Looking for names that carried weight, the defense committee summoned the "leaders of American letters, science, art, education and social reform." "Come by train and boat, come on foot or in your car! Come to Boston! Let all the roads of the Nation converge on Beacon Hill." Answering the call, Grace was one of "100 Sympathizers" who boarded a steamship headed to Boston from New York on August 20, 1927.[2]

Although fixed in the political iconography of the left as "the good shoemaker and the poor fish peddler," Sacco and Vanzetti were in fact well-versed anarchists working to end all forms of state power and bring forth a society based on free speech and communal ownership of property. They endorsed the principle of meeting repression with retaliatory violence, but in practice the two men and their comrades spent their time participating in strikes and demonstrations, distributing anarchist literature, and building an alternative culture.[3] That distinction was lost on the public and government officials, making the proverbial "bomb-throwing anarchist" a particular object of terror.

In 1917, Sacco and Vanzetti had traveled from the United States to Mexico en route to Europe, where they hoped to fight in the revolution that had burst out in Russia and promised to spread across the continent. They never made it to Russia, but the trip brought them to the attention of an ambitious young Department of Justice official, J. Edgar Hoover, who spearheaded the department's "alien radical" division and used the wartime Red Scare to launch his long career. At the height of Hoover's campaign against immigrants and activists, Sacco and Vanzetti fell into a police trap in South Braintree, Massachusetts, an industrial town south of Boston, and were charged with robbing a payroll truck and murdering the paymaster and his guard. Convinced that innocent men were being persecuted for their ideas, a small band of dissidents representing both the prewar bohemian left and the postwar communist movement came to their defense.[4]

For four years, their efforts were sustained mainly by the contributions of Italian Americans, "twenty-five and fifty cents at a time." Then in 1925 the newly formed ILD took up the anarchists' case. Affiliated with the Communist Party but made up of radicals and liberals of various political persuasions, the ILD adopted a novel strategy of relentless publicity, demonstrations, and aggressive legal action. Its aim was not only to mobilize the general public in behalf of the accused but also to put "the capitalist persecutors . . . on trial before the working class." This approach helped to spark massive protests in behalf of Sacco and Vanzetti throughout the United States and in every major European city.[5] The American Federation of Labor, with its base among skilled, native-born workers, was conspicuously silent, but union locals across the country organized walkouts and demonstrations.[6]

The outcry reached a crescendo in the spring and summer of 1927. The eminent Harvard law professor Felix Frankfurter (whom Franklin Roosevelt later appointed to the US Supreme Court) published a damning review of the legal proceedings, charging that state and federal authorities had colluded to deny Sacco and Vanzetti a fair trial. A few weeks later, the defendants lost their last appeal and were sentenced to die in the electric chair.[7] In response, the ILD's Sacco and Vanzetti Defense Committee began staging mass marches in front of the gold-domed State House on Beacon Hill. Forty minutes before the appointed hour of execution on August 10, Governor Alvan T. Fuller granted Sacco and Vanzetti a twelve-day stay of execution. Hoping that he would commute the death sentence to life imprisonment, the defense committee renewed its efforts. On August 20, with the governor still undecided and Sacco and Vanzetti facing death on August 22, Grace Lumpkin and other supporters from New York arrived in Boston to join the demonstrations.

Among them was Katherine Anne Porter, who was just beginning to publish the short stories that would make her one of the most celebrated of her generation of southern writers. She left a record of the experiences she and Grace shared: the placards they carried in the "blazing August sun"; the weary Irish cops who allowed the picketers to circle in front of the State House once or twice and then closed in to arrest them; the "stale air" in the Joy Street jail. Packed into a cell with Grace and a crowd singing "Solidarity Forever" and waiting to be bailed out, Porter remembered longing to smoke and "wishing for something to read."[8]

Once out on bail, Lumpkin and Porter spent their time not at the left-wing defense committee's dingy rooms on Hanover Street, but at the Bellevue Hotel near the State House, headquarters of a newly formed Citizens National Committee for Sacco and Vanzetti, headed by leading liberals such as John Dewey, Jane Addams, and John R. Commons, which tried to rally mainstream opinion and bring legal expertise to bear. Parlor D in the Bellevue swarmed with volunteers working around the clock. As Porter remembered it, she, Grace, and the other women addressed envelopes, answered telephones, copied Sacco and Vanzetti's letters to their friends, and served as "kitchen police"— doing all the "dull, dusty little jobs" the male luminaries avoided.[9] In fact, Grace did more. Wiring the New York headquarters of the ILD, she enlisted Esther in using *The World Tomorrow*'s mailing list to urge the magazine's subscribers to write to President Calvin Coolidge and the US attorney general demanding that the Department of Justice open its files. Those files, the committee believed, would reveal what later proved to be true: that Justice Department agents had engaged in a conspiracy to convict Sacco and Vanzetti that began well before and continued throughout the trial.[10]

On the day before the execution, Grace again joined the picket line. Italian immigrants marched side-by-side with descendants of Boston Brahmins, prominent or soon-to-be prominent Communists, Greenwich Village bohemians, and a number of the country's brightest literary lights. Among the best known of these figures were John Dos Passos, who had been an ironic observer of the Passaic strike but devoted himself entirely to this cause, and Edna St. Vincent Millay, who, in an uncharacteristic political gesture, arrived with her wealthy husband to bail out protesters and hand out copies of her poem, "Justice Denied in Massachusetts."[11]

At 11:00 p.m. on August 22, Governor Fuller announced that he would not prevent the execution. Grace and the others made their way to Charlestown Prison where Sacco and Vanzetti were being held. The surrounding slums had been cordoned off for a distance of a half mile. Supplied with gas masks, tear gas, and machine guns, eight hundred policemen lined the prison's granite walls. Firemen stood by with high-pressure hoses. The play of floodlights turned night into eerie day, as officers on horseback "galloped about, bearing down upon anybody who ventured out beyond the edge of the crowd."[12] The protestors waited silently, in witness against a "terrible wrong"—a wrong, as Katherine Anne Porter put it, not just against "the two men about to die, but against all of us, against our common humanity." "For an endless dreary time," the protestors stood "massed in a measureless darkness, waiting, watching the light in the tower of the prison." Just after midnight on August 23, the light blinked off and on, off and on again, seemingly signaling the jolt of the electric chair.[13]

Returning to the Hotel Bellevue, Lumpkin huddled with Porter and others, "keeping a vigil with the dead." The memory of Sacco and Vanzetti, Porter wrote, "was already turning to stone in my mind. In my whole life I have never felt such a weight of pure bitterness, helpless anger in utter defeat, outraged love and hope, as hung over us all in that room." Tried in court the following day, the demonstrators paid their fines and straggled home.[14]

"What I wish more than all in this last hour of agony is that our case and our fate may be understood in their real being and serve as a tremendous lesson to the forces of freedom—so that our suffering and death will not have been in vain." So wrote Bartolomeo Vanzetti a few hours before his death. In the years that followed, countless artists and writers took up that challenge. "Prosecutors, judges, and the hostile public majority have not in twenty years found a single literary defender of their position," the first full-fledged history of the case concluded. Inspired by Vanzetti's "exalted sense of language as an incantation," the American literati memorialized the case in poems, plays, novels, histories, and reportage.[15]

For many writers and intellectuals, the stock market crash that occurred two years later was "like a rending of the earth in preparation for the Day of Judgment."[16] But for others, the persecution of Sacco and Vanzetti—in Katherine Anne Porter's memorable phrase, this "never-ending wrong"—made all the difference. It drove home the conviction that injustice lay deeply rooted in ostensibly democratic processes and institutions. It "revealed the whole anatomy of American life, with all its classes, professions, and points of view and all their relations, and it raised almost every fundamental question of our political and social system."[17]

ON LEAVE FROM *The World Tomorrow*, Grace Hutchins and Anna Rochester had been visiting Russia when the mass protests in the United States began. In a letter-pamphlet, they shared their impressions with Grace, Esther, and other friends. They believed that Russia was embarked on an inspiring experiment and that world revolution was just a matter of time. The Sacco-Vanzetti case and the worldwide outcry it inspired reinforced their convictions, and they joined the defense effort as soon as they returned to New York.[18] Within a year after the execution, they joined the Communist Party. With Robert W. Dunn, a leader of the ILD, they founded the Labor Research Association (LRA), which from then on served as their institutional home. A Marxist think tank for the labor movement, the LRA sponsored widely used reference works, pamphlets on industrial conditions, and books such as Hutchins's 1929 volume, *Labor and Silk* (for which Esther provided line drawings) and her *Women Who Work* (1934), one of the most important analyses of the "woman question" produced by the communist movement.[19]

Esther Shemitz also quit her job at *The World Tomorrow*, working first for the Amtorg Trading Company, an import-export business established by the Soviet Union (which was later suspected of harboring industrial spies), and then as advertising manager for *The New Masses*.

Grace soon followed, eking out a living as a clerical worker, sometimes at Amtorg and sometimes at *The New Masses*, where contributors received no payment and editorial staff members, almost all of whom were men, were lucky to make $5 a week. "Thinking it would give me more time for writing," Grace even worked as a chambermaid with "50 beds to make and rooms and bathrooms to clean."[20] For her, the effort to write would always involve a struggle, and often a losing one, for the barest minimum of self-support. "Writing is a pain. It is also the most satisfying joy," she reflected at one point. "And besides," she said at another, "I need . . . to make some money."[21]

In September 1927, Grace published her first short story in *The New Masses*, a contrived but charged tale of race and sex mediated through the vexed relations of black and white women. "White Man—A Story" took its inspiration from the great Mississippi flood of 1927, which displaced almost a million people and turned into a national scandal involving former US senator LeRoy Percy, the most powerful man in the Mississippi Delta. Percy had earned praise from around the country for his opposition to the Ku Klux Klan and his paternalism toward the thousands of black workers who toiled on his vast plantation. As the rising tide broke through the levees, reclaiming the Delta's loamy cotton-growing bottom lands, it revealed the self-interest at the heart of Percy's regime. If he evacuated the black refugees who clung to the levees or crowded into Red Cross camps, he risked dispersing the labor force on which his family's fortune depended. He chose instead to save white residents and risk black lives by forcing them to fight the flood, setting off a firestorm of criticism in the black press. When, a quarter of a century later, Percy's son, William Alexander Percy, published his acclaimed memoir, *Lanterns on the Levee*, he devoted a full chapter to the disaster, deflecting blame from his father and concluding that "out of the 1927 flood our people learned mutual helpfulness."[22]

In "White Man—A Story," Grace did not take on the Percys directly, but she did link the flood metaphorically to a regime of sexual and economic exploitation, portraying a world in which black laborers and sharecroppers were trapped by the plantation system as well as by the muddy, roiling waters. Her unnamed narrator is a déclassé planter's daughter very much like herself. Now working as a teacher, the young white woman sets the action in motion, struggles with her own motives and emotions, and then watches helplessly as tragedy results. The action, however, centers on Alma Lee, a beautiful, enigmatic biracial woman whose mother is the narrator's father's illegitimate daughter. He has abandoned his secret family, and his white daughter feels responsible for their fate. She visits Alma Lee and her mother, fretting over whether to give them money when she earns so little herself. The two African American women are polite and deferential. But behind that mask the narrator senses something else: "antagonism or maybe contempt," or perhaps simply an unwillingness to accept "half-way measures"—an insight reminiscent of Katharine's as she confronted the limits of interracial cooperation.[23]

Finally, the narrator conceives a plan. She arranges for Alma Lee to work as a servant for friends who promise to send her to school. But soon history compulsively repeats itself. Alma's white employer seduces her. They have sex in the willows as the water slowly begins to rise. The moment of truth comes one evening as Alma Lee is sitting on the porch steps hidden by wisteria vines. She is awakened from a reverie by the sound of her lover's voice, telling guests that "he had just read about a white girl marrying a Jew." Someone says, "Well, Jews are human beings." He replies, "Yes, and so are niggers, but you don't marry them."[24]

The man's wife, the iconic asexual white lady, discovers the affair and banishes Alma Lee from the house. The girl is pregnant, and when the narrator sees her next, she is engulfed in a strange passivity, a cosmic despair. It is as if her lovely face and taut neck have been severed from her body's "motive will, its active desire."[25] When the Mississippi River overwhelms the levee, the girl's family flees to a Red Cross camp. Alma Lee stays behind and dies as the river sweeps away everything in its path.

As Grace portrays it, the flood does not inspire "mutual helpfulness," and water is not a symbol of transcendence or rebirth. It is a site "for recycling sadness." Like an extraordinary number of such characters in southern white women's interwar novels, Alma Lee has been overworked, neglected, and thrown away. Disappearing into the landscape without proper burial, her body becomes part of a perverse political economy—a "melancholic detritus" in a traumatized land.[26]

In Grace's college essay, "The White Road," whiteness symbolized a "straight, clean, sheltered" life. In "White Man—A Story," by contrast, white is "the color of danger." It signals the sexual violation of black women, the analogue of their economic exploitation. Alma Lee is marked by her own biracial beauty. It advertises her origins. It renders her vulnerable. It relegates her to the realm where "dirt and desire" combine in a deadly mix.[27]

At a time when white novelists routinely peopled their novels with black caricatures, this story's black characters were not even remotely what Grace and Esther had termed "minstrel, mammy and uncle types."[28] Nor was Alma Lee a typical "tragic mulatto" passing for white or a wanton "Jezebel," the main alternatives to the asexual mammy found in most literature at the time. She did, however, fit another stereotype: she is paralyzed by conflicting loyalties, a cipher rendered helpless and speechless against the racial order of the times.[29] She was, in short, just what Grace and Esther had deplored in "The Artist in a Hostile Environment": "more of a formula than a human being."[30]

In "White Man—A Story," Grace took up the subjects to which she would return: the ambivalence and estrangement of the white daughter who is complicit in a system geared to her oppression; the declining plantation aristocracy; and the lives of southern women, black and white, middling and poor, which were shaped and damaged by the sexual economies in which they circulated as well as by the terms of their labor.[31] In other ways as well, "White Man—A Story" foreshadows Grace's future work, particularly in the opaqueness of its black characters. The narrator understands, as precious few white Southerners did, that there are masks behind the masks along the color line. Yet however much she might strive for empathy, Grace, like the well-meaning white teacher in her story, would always be stymied by the "stripe of segregation": the barriers to imagination thrown up by centuries of slavery and decades of Jim Crow.[32] Also emblematic was the story's melancholy ending, its atmosphere of struggle against forces that were, like the river and like the nameless, faceless "White Man," too powerful to overcome.

TWO YEARS AFTER this story appeared, Grace and Esther moved from their apartment on Bedford Street into an even more enchanting abode. Greenwich Village was falling victim to its own success as an influx of newcomers combined with a booming economy to drive up rents. Joining an exodus of artists and writers who had no money to speak of and an attraction to working-class milieus, the two women looked for a cheaper place. They found a dream home that was the envy of all their friends: a "darling little brick house" at 639 East 11th Street, in a working-class

Grace Lumpkin in front of the fireplace in Kok-I House, a rear courtyard building in the East Village, where she lived with her friend Esther Shemitz and later with husband Michael Intrator, late 1920s through the 1930s.

neighborhood in the East Village near Tompkins Square. They called it "Kok-I House" because it was "really cock-eyed, slanting this way and that."[33]

Such rear courtyard buildings were notorious tuberculosis traps. But Grace and Esther were "clever with their hands," and they transformed the interior into what struck their friends as "a cozy farmhouse in the heart of the slum."[34] Grace had a small study, a room of her own where she could spend hours in front of the typewriter she had carried to Europe, clung to in South Carolina, and brought north on the train. In the living room, the women scraped the exposed beams and the hardwood floor, hung soft rose curtains, and spread a scavenged oval rug. Wooden shelves held Grace's knickknacks and mementos. Esther hung reproductions of impressionist paintings and abstract water colors of New York. In the evening, they cozied up to a brick fireplace. A rough round dining table and "country chairs" completed the magical effect.[35]

In their spare time, the two women began dropping by the Communist Party's bookstore and perambulating around "a dilapidated little park that acquired a reputation as New York's Red Square," site of the city's major demonstrations and home to the party's headquarters, its newspaper, the *Daily Worker*, and its Workers School.[36] As they did so, they found themselves crossing paths with the vibrant young Communists they had met during the Passaic strike and the Sacco and Vanzetti marches. "I had gotten curious after picketing with them," Grace remembered. "Doing all the work and inspiring everybody to do it," they demonstrated how "full of energy and enthusiasm" revolutionaries could be.[37]

Among this group was Whittaker Chambers, the reporter who had been so taken with Esther during the Passaic melee. He helped hang her paintings at an exhibition at the United Workers' Cooperative Apartments in the Bronx and ran into her and Grace at meetings of the John Reed Club, the party's literary arm. Soon he was spending evenings at Kok-I House, bringing with him a circle of friends.[38] Sender Garlin was a native-born radical from Glens Falls, a lumber town in upstate New York. Jacob Burck, a Polish bricklayer's son, was a talented cartoonist and muralist who would go on to win a 1941 Pulitzer Prize as editorial cartoonist for the *Chicago Sun-Times* and later be threatened with deportation because of his political beliefs. Then there was Kevin O'Malley, dubbed the "Romeo of the Tenements" because of his movie-star looks and his habit of making the rounds at parties looking for pretty girls willing to put him up for the night.[39] The final member of the group was Michael Intrator, whom Chambers described as an acutely intelligent "child of the slums."[40]

O'Malley played the zither. Jacob Burck impressed with his art. According to Chambers, Intrator represented "the working class at its most intelligent and militant. . . . He had a mind largely untrained and unschooled, but direct, forceful and supple, with an unerring ability to drive to the heart of any discussion or problem. He also had an endless intellectual curiosity. . . . He was, besides, simple, human, humorous." At Kok-I House, Chambers dazzled with his erudition. Intrator often sat back quietly, observing the goings-on, but when he did speak up, he swept aside "anything that was incidental, distracting and not germane."[41]

In Grace Lumpkin's favorite photograph from those years, she is dressed in a peasant blouse (a nod to the bohemian preference for the folkish and the handmade). On the back of the picture, she carefully noted her monthly rent: $14, plus extra for heat and water. At Kok-I House the fire never went out; the tea kettle was always boiling; and Grace and Esther, however pinched for cash, could be counted on for an appreciative audience and a free meal.[42] Yet they were as absorbed as the men by ideas and politics and dreams of artistic careers. They were radical artists in the making and, at the same time, experts at creating a home away from home, a home without fathers or mothers where supposedly equal comrades could find an erotically charged domesticity, a half-familiar, yet wholly modern setting for intimate, amusing talk.[43] No wonder that Kok-I House lingered forever in Grace's memory, carrying with it the densest of imaginative freight. And no wonder that, as time went by, the two women, who were saddled with all the usual emotional and domestic labor, would find that old patterns of male privilege persisted beneath the lofty rhetoric of sexual egalitarianism and socialist revolution.[44]

THE RADICAL INTELLIGENTSIA, both before and after the war, valued mingling with workers, whom they invested with all that the middle class lacked: vitality, authenticity, revolutionary potential. But romanticization was one thing, romance another. When it came to sex and marriage, neither the Greenwich Village bohemians nor their communist successors tended to cross class and ethnic lines. Grace Lumpkin was an exception. In 1925, she was still listed as a member of the United Daughters of the Confederacy and being addressed by her mother as "Dearest Little Child." By 1927, she had joined picket lines, gone to jail, and published articles about strikes, race, and sex. Two years after that, she fell in love with Michael Intrator. A Jew, a Communist, and a working-class member of the most militant, most violent, and most successful left-wing labor union in New York, he personified the "wild disaster" her mother had sensed in the air.[45]

Michael Intrator had "the nicest eyes I had ever seen on a man," Grace remembered. He also had a mop of dark hair. His amused tolerance for human foibles, his way of puncturing pomposity with a wry remark, and his matter-of-fact enjoyment of life's pleasures all made him irresistible. To intellectuals who looked to the proletariat for the spark missing from bourgeois life, he was the real thing.[46] To Grace he was the love of a lifetime—despite heartbreak, the rare person against whom she would not utter a single, surviving bitter word.

Born in 1903, Intrator was twelve years Grace's junior. He had arrived in the United States with his parents, Nathan and Anna, in 1905, at the height of the Jewish flight from eastern Europe. In Blazowa, Galicia (now part of Poland, then a part of the Austro-Hungarian Empire), his ancestors had served as merchants and middlemen. In the United States, Nathan worked as a cloak presser, and Anna ran a candy store. The family bounced back and forth between the Lower East Side and Brownsville in eastern Brooklyn, an area of waste dumps and stone quarries that was rapidly becoming a dense neighborhood of tenements and garment factories populated by the largest concentration of Jews in the country, many of whom were recent immigrants from Russia.[47] Scorned by the gentiles who seemed to own the city, "Brunzvil," as its Yiddish-speaking residents called it, was also "the dust of the earth to all Jews with money." To Michael's parents' generation, Brownsville was both a mecca and a ghetto. The terrors of the Old World's pogroms darkened their memories, and their lives turned on endless labor.[48]

Brownsville had no public high school but was rich in sites for self-education. Crowded into a tiny railroad flat, Michael and his four brothers spent their time on the street corners; in the hushed reading room of the Children's Library on Stone Street, with its Gothic façade, storybook tiles, and carved wooden benches; or at the Labor Lyceum, where children attended Socialist Sunday Schools, union activists planned strikes, lecturers spoke on "the Negro problem," and music and theater thrived. Heirs to a European socialist tradition, ignored by the city's politicians, gouged by landlords, and exploited by sweatshops, Brownsville's residents flocked to the Socialist Party, which regularly sent representatives to the state assembly and the city's board of aldermen. They joined labor organizations, staged rent strikes, and argued their causes on street corners and in kitchens, taverns, and barbershops. Employers and politicians fought back, using gangs to bust up unions, targeting pacifists and socialists during World War I, and gerrymandering the area in order to cripple the Socialist Party.

Michael Intrator cut an impressive figure, both on the streets and in the Young People's Socialist League. His brothers looked up to him, depended on him, and tried to follow his example. When their mother died young and their father married a woman whom the boys disliked (and who eventually absconded with his savings), all five left home, making their way by dint of their native intelligence and their fierce loyalty to one another. Michael joined the International Fur Workers Union–AFL and learned a lucrative, albeit seasonal craft: he was a cutter, one of the most highly skilled and deeply prized jobs in the needle trades. When young Communists on fire with the possibility of world revolution began appearing on soapboxes, Michael and his brother Charlie joined the Communist Party.[49]

At work Intrator supported the legendary labor leader Ben Gold, who, with other communist insurgents, was transforming the Fur Workers into the most militant left-led union in New York. Starting in the early 1920s, these left-wing furriers had fought tooth and nail against corrupt union bureaucrats. Mauled by gangsters hired by the union, they formed self-defense units and "developed . . . the psychology of shock troops, . . . handy with knives, belts, pipes."[50] Men on both sides of the conflict ended up crippled or killed. Intrator himself was stabbed in one of these altercations, although, according to Whittaker Chambers, "he paid no attention to the wound until he collapsed from it."[51] By 1925, the Communists had won the support of the majority of the Jewish rank and file. In 1926, Ben Gold and his allies called for a general strike of the New York fur market. The outcome was a spectacular victory for the labor left. The fur workers won a forty-hour, five-day work week and other benefits, unheard-of luxuries in the garment industry.[52]

Intrator's affiliation with the tough and triumphant left-wing furriers gave him plenty of political cachet, but it was his aspirations as a writer that gave him access to Grace Lumpkin's downtown artistic circle. At night he took courses at the Communist-sponsored Workers School. During the Passaic strike and the Sacco–Vanzetti case, the school's offerings grew from five or six courses to fifty, enrolling more than a thousand students a year. This smorgasbord included "Problems of Working Class Women" taught by Arthur W. Calhoun, who would go on to write a classic study of the American family, and a "Proletarian Writers Workshop" led by *The New Masses* editor Mike Gold. John Dos Passos could be found discussing his work. Hubert Harrison, known as "the father of Harlem radicalism," covered "the Negro Problem, . . . including the tabooed topic of sex and the bugaboo of 'Social Equality.'" In "Voices of Revolt," students were introduced to Tom Paine and other plebian heroes of the American Revolution. Courses on "Civics and Citizenship" and American history complemented those on Marxism and the Russian Revolution.[53]

Intrator enrolled in a course on Marxist philosophy taught by Bertram D. Wolfe, the school's director and one of the Communist Party's leading intellectuals, and Wolfe quickly singled him out as one of the most articulate students in the class. One day Michael sauntered into Wolfe's office with his friend Sender Garlin. The two young men were seeking advice about "the art of writing." "We want to do work for the party," Michael said, "and we want to become good writers with a clear and decent style. Have you any suggestions?" Wolfe told them to try the *Daily Worker* if they could "stand working under a pompous fool," by whom he meant Robert Minor, who had just taken over as editor.[54]

A tall Texan with "extraordinarily bushy eyebrows, a long cocky stride, and a booming voice," Minor had abandoned a career as a cartoonist to work full-time for the party. Bertram Wolfe could be a snob, but Robert Minor *was* notorious for his egotism and cant. He was also notorious for sweeping the radical labor journalist Mary Heaton Vorse off her feet and then abandoning her for a former lover—an episode that more than one male writer used to symbolize the foolish love of a do-good woman for a no-good Communist man, much to Vorse's chagrin.[55] Problematic as he may have been, Minor was smart enough to know that the paper needed freshening, so he hired Intrator to cover the needle trades and other labor news. It was here that Intrator and Whittaker Chambers met and became friends. Soon, in addition to their jobs at the *Daily Worker*, they were coediting a newspaper published by the National Textile Workers Union of America, the newly formed, left-led "dual union" that would go on to lead the legendary Gastonia, North Carolina, strike of 1929.[56]

Dual unions were the result of a schism that, by the time he met Grace Lumpkin, was propelling Michael Intrator in a political direction that vastly complicated his position in the New York left and had fatal consequences for his nascent writing career. As Stalin maneuvered his way to power in the Soviet Union, the 1928 World Congress of the Communist International, or Comintern (the Soviet-dominated organization that coordinated the international communist movement), proclaimed that capitalism was in crisis and the world was entering a revolutionary "Third Period" in which American Communists should abandon the strategy of "boring from within" the AFL, as Ben Gold and the radical fur workers had done, and organize independent left-wing unions instead. Jay Lovestone, the head of the Communist Party, who had long been an advocate of the doctrine of "American exceptionalism"— the notion that, given the strength of US capitalism, the Communists had to work within the trade union establishment—made the mistake of resisting this mandate and, in June 1929, was expelled from the Communist Party.[57]

Intrator had not initially opposed independent unions, as witnessed by his brief coeditorship of the National Textile Workers Union of America rag. But he was first and foremost "a labor union man," and ultimately he was convinced that the interests of the workers were best served by a unified labor movement, not by separate left-wing unions. He may also have foreseen that the decision to adopt a strident revolutionary rhetoric and forgo alliances with socialists and other non-communist union organizers would alienate potential sympathizers. In any case, when Jay Lovestone formed his own tiny opposition party in the fall of 1929 (calling itself, grandiloquently, the Communist Party–Majority Group), Intrator joined the organization and won election to its National Council. Fired for apostasy by the editors of the *Daily Worker*, he returned to work in the fur industry, where he opposed the decision of his old comrade-in-arms Ben Gold to create a dual union. Joining a Lovestone-backed faction within the AFL-affiliated fur workers union, he fought in pitched battles not only against the bosses and the AFL old guard but also against the new Communist Party–backed union.[58]

WHITTAKER CHAMBERS HAD NOT taken sides in these internecine conflicts, but he too left the *Daily Worker* and found himself on the outs with the Communist Party.[59] Although Chambers, unlike Intrator, would soon work himself back into the party's good graces, their shared alienation during this particularly combative period in the communist movement helped to seal a lifelong friendship between what would have otherwise been an unlikely pair. An odd looking, gnomic figure, Chambers struck some people as charismatic, others as repellant, and still others as a disconcerting mixture of the two. He dressed like a derelict, had rotten stumps for teeth, and cultivated an air of grandiosity that Grace at first found off-putting.[60] He had grown up in a spectacularly unhappy family in Lynbrook, a suburb on Long Island's South Shore, run away after high school, worked as a railroad laborer, and made his way to the New Orleans demimonde. Those adventures turned him from an unhappy suburbanite into a veteran of the road with riveting stories to tell. When he entered Columbia University in 1920, that persona played well among his fellow students, especially the ambitious sons of Jewish immigrants who made up an ever-increasing proportion of the student body despite the efforts of Columbia's administrators to keep them out. To these "prodigies of erudition," Chambers was an anomaly—the first really clever WASP they had ever known—and they introduced him to bolshevism and high-toned intellectual discussion.[61]

Drifting away from college in 1923, Chambers sailed to Europe, where he found himself more attracted to the Communists furtively selling their outlawed newspapers on the streets of Berlin than to the Lost Generation writers in Paris. Converted by Lenin's bracing vision of a vanguard party of professional revolutionaries and his attacks on the decaying middle class, Chambers joined the party on February 17, 1925. At first he supported himself by clerking half-heartedly at the New York Public Library and in a Greenwich Village bookstore while writing for various publications. Then in 1927, he took a job at the *Daily Worker*.[62]

By the time he and Michael Intrator left the newspaper two years later, Chambers was embroiled in two simultaneous, chaotic love affairs. First he took up with the estranged wife of a friend and invited a young man named Frank Bang, to whom he was sexually attracted, into their tiny quarters. When this *ménage-à-trois* unraveled, Chambers turned to a Communist comrade named Ida Dailes. A red-haired divorcée, Dailes worked as a stenographer and taught "The Fundamentals of Communism" at the Workers School. In the fall of 1929, Chambers's father died suddenly, and Chambers and Dailes installed themselves in his mother's house in Lynbrook. For the next year, Chambers lived off a small inheritance from his father and entertained a string of city friends. Intrator was among them, and the group often escaped to Atlantic Beach, on the western tip of Long Beach Island, where they camped and cooked out in the dunes. By chance, Grace and Esther were camping there as well, taking the Long Island Railroad out of the sweltering city. The women mostly kept to themselves, but they may have shared clam suppers with the Lynbrook group and lingered to drink and talk into the night.[63]

In the fall of 1929, a few months after Grace and Esther moved into Kok-I House, workers in Gastonia, North Carolina, walked off their jobs at one of the South's largest and harshest textile mills and joined the Communist-led National Textile Workers Union of America, whose newspaper Intrator and Chambers were editing. Within a year, Grace was publishing the strikers' ballads in *The New Masses* and working intensely on a coming-to-political-consciousness novel in which women played a leading role.[64] Over the course of that same feverish season, she surprised her friends and shocked the Lumpkin family by taking Michael Intrator as her live-in lover.

Grace and Mike seem to have begun sleeping together while Esther was hitchhiking through the South in search of material for political drawings such as those she had contributed to Grace Hutchins's *Labor and Silk*.[65] When she returned from her adventures, she found Mike ensconced at Kok-I House. She also found herself insistently wooed by Whittaker Chambers. At first she resisted, but soon she was embroiled in what seemed to some of her friends to be a dubious romance.

Chambers later claimed that Grace Hutchins and Anna Rochester disapproved of his critical stance toward the Communist Party and for that reason urged Esther to keep him at arms' length. It is much more likely, however, that Esther hesitated for her own reasons. She saw herself as a revolutionist; he saw her as a "woman-child who yearned, beneath her . . . independent façade, for a powerful man to take control of her life" and tried to persuade her to abandon her political art. Besides, Chambers was still living with Ida Dailes; in fact, in the spring of 1930, the census recorded them as husband and wife.[66] At the same time, he was swearing to Esther that the affair was over; he was just trying to find a way to leave Dailes "without hurting her feelings too much." In the midst of this turmoil, Dailes announced that she was pregnant. Chambers pressured her into having an abortion. She "submitted," and then he abruptly left her. When Esther finally gave in to his importunings, he shoehorned himself into Kok-I House with her, Grace, and Mike.[67]

For a few months the two couples shared the tiny flat, escaping when they could to a rented college at Oceanside, Long Island, or to camp on the beach. On April 15, 1931, Whittaker and Esther married, summoning Grace Hutchins and Anna Rochester as witnesses at a spur-of-the-moment civil ceremony in City Hall. The couple then moved into the building that adjoined Kok-I House, and the two men cut a door through the wall so the newlyweds would have access to a bathroom, which their apartment lacked. "We were so close," Grace remembered. "We were like family."[68] To others, these living arrangements had different connotations. "You are all living in a sea of shit," Jacob Burck reportedly told Chambers, echoing the sentiments of friends who believed that Chambers was bisexual or gay, that he and Mike Intrator were lovers,

and that "the girls appeared to be Lesbians," as signaled by the usual projections: "Esther," claimed one Kok-I House habitué, "was masculine in
appearance and in her voice. Grace was the softer, more feminine type."[69]

It is difficult to know what to make of such gossip. Bohemian New
York thrived on sexual speculations. "Who was flirting with whom?
Who was sleeping with whom?" Talk about sex knit downtown writers
together, and literary and sexual experimentalism went hand in hand.[70]
In that atmosphere, Whittaker Chambers's checkered past and the sexual possibilities inherent in the foursome's living arrangements guaranteed that rumors would fly. Such rumors fixed on homosexuality, in
part because, despite their sexual heterodoxy and the presence of many
gay men and lesbians on the left, most radicals saw homosexuality as
a perversion and treated it with an uneasy combination of fascination,
revulsion, and denial. That attitude prevailed even as the wave of gen-
trification that transformed Greenwich Village into a tourist destination in the 1920s remade the area into the country's premier gay and
lesbian enclave.[71]

As for what actually happened in Kok-I House and at the shore:
Whittaker Chambers *did* have a long history of erotically charged relationships with men, and he admitted to engaging in casual, clandestine same-sex affairs throughout the early years of his marriage. Before
Intrator entered her life, Grace sometimes spoke of Esther as her "partner" rather than as her roommate or friend.[72] Decades later, she said
that "Chambers probably had been a homosexual in his early years" and
that she sometimes thought he "had more influence over" Michael Intrator than she did. But all four friends denied any homosexual involve-
ments with one another, and nothing in the extant record contradicts
that claim.[73]

Chambers fended off the rumors by maintaining that Grace and
Esther "were widely known in the Communist movement for their invi-
olable 'prudery'" and that Mike was a "womanizer."[74] Unlike allegations of homosexual or bisexual behavior, calling Intrator a womanizer
only enhanced his stature as a proletarian hero, a manly "child of the
slums."[75] Emphasizing the women's sexual reticence made the men who
wooed and won them all the more virile in their own and their male
friends' eyes.

When asked about Intrator by interviewers in the 1970s and 1980s,
Grace said nothing to confirm Chambers's characterization, but there

is plenty in her fictional writings to suggest that she was profoundly ambivalent about the promises and contradictions of modern heterosexual love. A story told as comedy by her nephew John and as feminist dystopia by Grace illustrates the point. Shortly after Mike moved into Kok-I House, Grace's brother Hope, his wife, and their son John paid a visit to New York. According to John, who was eleven or twelve at the time, the Lumpkin brothers had heard that "Grace was living with some man." Alva, who had helped to put Grace and Katharine through college, had come through town regularly, attending conventions in his role as a director of various insurance corporations, joining the New York Southern Society, and giving the Flag Day speech as Supreme Chancellor of the Knights of Pythias, one of the secret fraternal orders to which his father had also been devoted. But whenever Alva visited, Grace found some excuse to keep him and her lover apart. Hope, the revered oldest brother, was not so easily deflected. Dressed in his clerical garb, or so the family story goes, he took John and made his way down to the Lower East Side. They located Kok-I House, marched up the narrow staircase to the landing, and knocked on the door. When it opened, they found themselves face to face with a man who, as John remembered it, had "a big bushy beard and a big bushy mustache. Looked like he might have a bomb in his hand."[76] (In fact, Intrator seems to have been clean-shaven.)

"Who in the hell are you?" Hope asked.

"Who in the hell are *you*?" Mike Intrator replied.

"I'm Grace Lumpkin's brother—does she live here?

"Yes."

"Well then, I repeat, who in the hell are you?"[77]

In an unpublished play entitled "Remember Now" written almost twenty years after this event, Grace conjures the same scene. In her version, the woman tries frantically to prepare for her brother's visit by throwing her lover's clothes in a suitcase and begging him to stay somewhere else for the night.

> "Are you ashamed?" he asks?
>
> "Of course I'm not ashamed. But I can't, I just can't hurt them, or shock them. He's my eldest brother, and a clergyman."
>
> "If you aren't ashamed, tell him. Stand up for what you believe. Where's your courage? I told my mother all about us. She knew."
>
> "You are a man."

"That's exactly the point. We believe men and women should have the same freedom to live as we choose."[78]

The man in "Remember Now" is raffish and ironical. He scoffs at his lover's panic and refuses to leave. He may believe that women should have the same freedom that men have, but in this lightly fictionalized portrait he clearly has the upper hand. She cooks for him, makes him coffee. He teases and romances and patronizes her. "I've enlarged your horizons, my girl," he says at one point. "In more ways than one," she answers, "but I am a writer, too, you know."[79]

What was a memorable adventure for her nephew John was for Grace an invitation to self-doubt and self-justification. She felt, as one friend put it, that she and Mike got "a rotten deal" from her family regarding their relationship. As a result, she was "hair-trigger in his defence."[80] Defending not only Mike but also her own sexual and political choices, she would go on to dot her fiction with colloquies between middle-class daughters seeking emancipation and families that condemn them and hold them back. These stories suggest the anxiety that underlay her struggle to assert her political and artistic independence and organize her sexual life and intimate relationships in emancipatory ways without, at the same time, cutting herself off from her "own people" completely.[81]

Two potboilers, which Grace published in 1933 under the pseudonym Ann Du Pre, are especially suggestive in this regard. In *Timid Woman*, a dutiful, sheltered spinster gradually becomes aware of how stifling southern gender conventions could be. Forced to become a governess after her father's death, she falls in love with her employer, an older man whose wife is in a sanatorium. Throwing caution to the wind, she runs away with him and his modern, sexually liberated daughter, trading the death-in-life of respectable southern womanhood for adventure in the wider world and true love with a married man.[82]

In *Some Take a Lover* (1933), Grace relocated the daughter-heroine to New York, where "Natalie" scandalizes her rich and dissipated Long Island relatives by living with her working-class lover, whom she likens to Daumier, the nineteenth-century artist whose lithographs and paintings caricatured the powerful and compassionately portrayed the lower classes. The time is the end of the 1920s, as the stock market crash is about to overtake a selfish, greedy, and self-obsessed nation. The aptly named "Singletons" are gathered in the grandmother's house waiting for her to die. Natalie, the "least good-looking of the handsome Singletons," is the only one who really cares about the old woman and the only truly decent character.[83] Over the course of a weekend lulled by highballs and cigarettes and punctuated by sexual revelations, Natalie engages in a long argument with her family over how she has chosen to live her life. The grandmother wants to know what Natalie calls herself: a mistress, a concubine, a paramour? Is she expecting "to have any bastards" with her live-in working-class lover? To make matters worse, the old woman fumes, "This artist is a foreigner. We can't have foreigners in the family." A drawling cousin from the South accuses Natalie of joining "the lower classes."[84]

In this novel, three models of modern womanhood clash. Natalie's sister tolerates her husband's infidelities in order not to lose her meal ticket and her man. She sees Natalie as an "innocent naïve child" who doesn't understand that women must take refuge in marriage and resign themselves to their husbands' affairs. After all, "men have the power. They can love—and go away, without a thought. They use women—and leave them." Another character represents the vamp who uses men as men have always used women. Natalie, by contrast, is the truly liberated woman. She supports herself by writing, rejects the double standard, and believes not in promiscuity but in open, honest relationships between comrade-lovers free from the strictures of church and state.[85]

The women's movement, with its "tide of so-called freedom for women has receded now, Natalie, except for driftwood like you," one character remarks.[86] Yet it is Natalie who receives the grandmother's blessing. The others, the old woman finally realizes, are knaves or fools. As the novel ends, Natalie returns to the city, to bohemian poverty, and to her lover, with whom she shares both her interests and her intimate thoughts. She "thinks of telling [him] all that had happened. They would laugh over it . . . but be sober too, . . . thinking . . . of the ugliness and pain" of life among the hypocritical, materialistic middle classes.[87]

The fact that Grace never claimed authorship of this portrait of a woman living the unorthodox life she herself had chosen speaks volumes about how much her choices cost her, how deeply she cared about her family's approval, how aware she was of the dangers and contradictions of women's sexual emancipation, and how difficult it was for her to take responsibility for her own choices. This novel also suggests that, for all her protestations, Grace was divided against herself even when her romance with Intrator was at its height. If she was "hair-trigger in his defence," it was partly because the taboos and prejudices she attributed to her relatives were also lodged deeply in herself. When, in her earlier short story, the "White Man" of the title equates marrying Jews with marrying "niggers," she was drawing on her own experience of a time when some saw Jews as a separate, atavistic race.[88] Moreover, she had been brought up to associate unsanctioned sex with African Americans. In an unpublished tale of sex, abandonment, and retribution written in the early 1930s, she makes the unease provoked by that association especially clear. When the white daughter in this story gets pregnant, her father compares her to an "ignorant bestial black woman." In the end, the daughter is excommunicated from the church, her family abandons her, and she leaves town in disgrace.[89]

Grace's dialogue with her family was also a dialogue with herself. She was a woman "making love on the edge of a cliff," as one character in *Some Take a Lover* puts it, trying to forge an ethic that reconciled virtue with emancipation, fidelity with free love, female agency and autonomy with heterosexual romance.[90] She was also trying to forge a politics that rejected the privileges of race and sex, even as they bound her both from within and from without.

These obscure writings register the texture of an entire sexual culture in transition. At the heart of prewar radicalism lay a feminist demand for both love and work; a rejection of separate spheres in the name of intimacy between the sexes and shared participation in the public world; and a critique of marriage as an institution that, under capitalism, stifles love, turns men into tyrants, and reduces women to dependents who are incapacitated for life's struggle and function as items of exchange.[91] Suffragists and other progressives joined communists and socialists in calling attention to Soviet efforts to reform the family and emancipate women. They pointed especially to attempts to increase access to sex education, abortion, and divorce; create cooperative laundries and nurseries; and encourage relationships based on mutual attraction rather than religious and legal compulsion or economic necessity.[92]

Anti-suffragists, in turn, claimed that the Bolsheviks were promoting free love and had "nationalized women" by making them "the property of the state and freely available to men." In the wake of the post–World War I Red Scare, which tarred the left with immorality and sexual perversion, many feminists backed away from their earlier calls for radical reform and their "enthusiasm for the Russian revolutionary project." At the same time, the men who dominated the Communist Party ceased to see sexual politics as a subject for experimental thought and public discussion.[93] Stripped of its association with feminism and socialism, sexual liberation could become, as it was for most of *Some Take a Lover*'s characters, just another form of narcissism, exploitation, and bad faith. As middle-class women sought refuge in an ideal of "companionate marriage" that excluded alternative sexualities, they found themselves imprisoned by a renewed cult of domesticity, all the more so when hostility toward wage-earning women escalated under pressure from the Great Depression.[94] Women who continued to move precariously on the "tide of so-called freedom for women" did so amid crosscurrents that threatened at any moment to toss them into the sea.

The publisher's marketing strategy for *Some Take a Lover* and the critical responses to the novel make the sex-obsessed yet increasingly sexually conservative spirit of the moment clear. Macaulay Company, which would also publish Grace Lumpkin's explicitly political novels, packaged *Some Take a Lover* in a gaudy cover studded with drawings of women in gowns so diaphanous they left little to the imagination. Most reviewers focused on the novel's "flighty sensualists" rather than on the idealistic, liberated heroine who gets both the money and the artistic, working-class lover. Whether they panned the book for relying on the "stalest clichés of cheap fiction" or praised it for its realism, all saw the evils of "equal, undisputed sexual freedom" as the moral of the tale.[95]

Unlike Natalie and her working-class lover, Grace Lumpkin and Michael Intrator *did* marry—on May 4, 1932, a year after the wedding of Esther Shemitz and Whittaker Chambers. Michael was twenty-eight. Grace, who had been lying about her age ever since she arrived in New York, claimed on their marriage certificate that she was thirty-four. In fact, she was forty-one. In the years that followed, she remained in touch with Katharine and sporadically visited her sister Elizabeth in Asheville. But she almost never returned to South Carolina and saw her brothers less and less.[96]

That growing estrangement intensified the importance of her ties to Whittaker and Esther Chambers. Indeed, the two couples may well have been drawn closer because Esther experienced an even sharper rift. From the day of her wedding she was "not welcome in her mother's home, so hostile was her religious mother to a non-Jew." Her parents

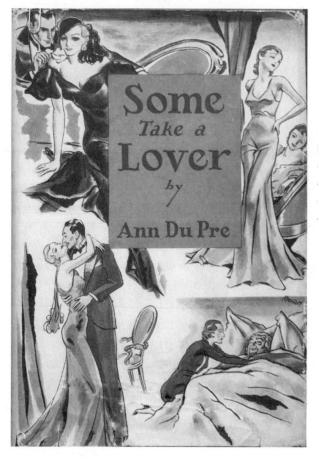

Cover of Some Take a Lover, *a novel that Grace Lump-kin published under the pseudonym Ann Du Pre in 1933.*

refused to meet her two children: Ellen, born in 1932, and John, in 1936. Esther did not attend her mother's funeral. When her sister died, she went to the service but sat and grieved alone.[97] In Grace's case, alienation was paired with obsession. As her family receded from her life, they colonized her fiction. Figures from her childhood loomed ever larger in her stories and novels as time went by.

—

PART THREE

A CHOSEN EXILE

*"The sacred watchwords were
not love-and-marriage
but love-and-revolution."*

—JOSEPHINE HERBST

"THE HEART OF
THE STRUGGLE"

———

A NEW FIGURE EMERGED FROM THE GASTONIA, NORTH Carolina, textile strike of 1929: a poor white Southerner capable of class-conscious action and solidarity across the color line. By transforming an obscure conflict into a symbol of "the passionate emotions and conflicting philosophies" of the times, a circle of women writers, activists, and labor educators helped to write that figure into history. In so doing, they made their own dissident voices heard.[1] They also helped to forward a reimagining of the South, not as a romanticized or feared backwater, but as a place where, as the Lumpkin sisters' longtime friend Louise Leonard put it, "history has been in the making" and women were "in the heart of the struggle."[2]

Throughout the 1920s, critics aligned with the communist movement had been calling for "proletarian fiction," defined as works written by or from the perspective of working-class people and expressing the realities of working-class life or, more broadly, as literature in sympathy with socialist values. Mike Gold, the guiding spirit of *The New Masses* and a leading proponent of this new genre, predicted that the proletarian writer would be "a wild youth," a brawny blue-collar worker who "writes in jets."[3] No one expected the call for radical fiction to be answered by women inspired by an uprising of workers in the American South.

Yet three white southern women grasped the literary possibilities of the drama: Grace Lumpkin, laboring at her typewriter in Kok-I House; the poet Olive Dargen, writing under the pseudonym Fielding Burke in the mountains of western North Carolina; and Dorothy Markey, aka Myra Page, the soft-spoken Virginian who had known the Lumpkin sisters since their days in the southern student YWCA.[4] The left-wing literary critic E. A. Schachner proclaimed this burst of writing by "Southern nonproletarian women" "one of the most significant storms in the development of the American novel." Seeing "a promise of their own emancipation in the Southern working class's fight for freedom" and drawing on an intimate knowledge of the region, Grace and her compatriots produced what he saw as the first realistic portraits of the South and "the first truly revolutionary novels to be written in the United States."[5]

GASTON COUNTY WAS AMONG the South's and the nation's leading textile centers, and Gastonia's mammoth Loray Mill, where the strike began, exemplified the South's rise to dominance of the American textile industry in the 1920s and the dispossession, suffering, and strife that rise entailed. The South's industrial revolution had been gathering force for a half century, and textile manufacturing formed the revolution's leading edge. Concentrated in the Piedmont, the mills drew their labor force from once self-sufficient white farm families who were driven into tenancy by the system of merchant-dominated agriculture that replaced plantation slavery after the war. In the mountains, timber and mining companies stripped away natural resources, forcing farmers up onto barren ridges or down to join their piedmont counterparts in the mills. Barred from most textile jobs, blacks scratched out a living as tenants or wage laborers on the land or were pulled into the timber mills, coal mines, tobacco factories, domestic service, and menial jobs in towns. Whether they were piedmont sharecroppers or small farmers fleeing the denuded mountainsides, Gastonia's textile workers found themselves in a world defined by company-owned mill villages, low wages, child labor, the virtual absence of labor regulations, and their employers' ready access to the police power of the state.[6]

Cultural marginalization went hand in hand with exploitation, as mill workers became easy targets for the class- and region-based condescension that pervaded American life. That disdain produced contradictory and shifting caricatures of the white southern poor. One image of rural Southerners coalesced at the turn of the century when Appalachia was discovered—or, rather, invented—by folklorists, missionaries, and local color writers. These observers saw mountain Southerners as isolated, unspoiled Anglo-Saxons, "yesterday's people" in a static land, and sought to preserve their quaint culture from commercialization. Like the contemporaneous romance of the Lost Cause, the idea of the "'purest of the pure' Anglo-Saxons" hidden away in the southern highlands helped to ease the fear that eastern European immigration was turning Anglo-Saxon America into a polyglot nation.[7] When the immigration restriction acts of the 1920s ended that perceived threat and vast numbers of white and black Southerners joined the Great Migration to the North, this sentimental view of mountain folk merged with an older stereotype of rural Southerners as slothful, ignorant "rednecks" who, as one reviewer of Grace's novel put it, contribute "nothing to American life except crop surpluses and interesting mental and physical diseases."[8] Out of this fusion of the "poor white" with the mountaineer came the hillbilly made famous in the 1930s by Al Capp's "Li'l Abner," the most popular comic strip of all time. Joining the black southern rube in the city represented by the wildly popular radio program, *Amos 'n' Andy*, Lil' Abner, Daisy Mae, Mammy Yokum, and their ilk became omnipresent figures of comedy and ridicule. On one of the Lumpkin family's regular summer vacations in western North Carolina, Annette Lumpkin's sister summed up the prevailing view: "This is the home of the mountaineers who are said to be very ignorant people, have no desire to better their conditions in any way."[9]

Southern mill owners put this multivalent image to use. They asserted the racial-ethnic superiority of their cheap and docile "Anglo-Saxon" labor force over the "foreigners" on whom their northern competitors relied. Ignoring the contradiction, they also represented themselves as the rescuers and civilizers of backward poor whites. This strategy helped to stave off local criticism of the mill owners and discourage northern trade unions from trying to organize in the South.

Neither outsiders' scorn nor employers' power kept southern farmers-turned-mill-workers from joining the upsurge of unionization after World War I. When their budding locals were crushed by the mill owners in league with the state, they voted with their feet, maintaining a modicum of autonomy and creating labor shortages by moving from mill to mill or back and forth between mill and farm. By the late 1920s, however, the New England textile industry had been decimated by competition with the low-wage and antiunion South. Taking advantage of their increased leverage, southern mill owners imposed scientific management schemes that required workers to tend more and more machines at once, weaving and spinning at a killing pace. What workers called the "stretch-out" sparked a strike wave that began in the mountains of East Tennessee, then spread to Gastonia and other piedmont towns.[10]

The Gastonia strike was not the largest, the most violent, or the most successful of these confrontations. But three elements set it apart. The first was a woman named Ella May Wiggins, the strike's chief balladeer and the white strikers' key emissary to the black community. The second was the arrival of communist organizers and the hysterical response their presence provoked. The third was the involvement of the women writers and reformers who were drawn to Gastonia by the prominence of women in the struggle.

Ella May in particular compelled these women's attention because she so perfectly embodied two of their central concerns: the gendered plight of working-class women, which was the chief focus of feminists who were determined to put "the woman question" on the left's political agenda, and the possibility of working-class interracialism, which was essential to the success of labor organizing in the South. Born to an itinerant logging family in the mountains in 1900, Ella May had married a charming ne'er-do-well named John Wiggins and followed a labor recruiter to Gastonia in the 1920s. By 1929, when the strike began, she had given birth to nine children, four of whom had died, the youngest of pellagra, the quintessential disease of poverty and malnutrition. Her husband had deserted her. She had taken back her maiden name and taken a lover, with whom she had her last child. Living in a black neighborhood, she was supporting her children by working in one of Gaston county's harshest mills. In speeches and songs, Ella May drew on her own experience, appealing to women as mothers or potential mothers and attacking the mill for depriving them of the means to nurture human life.[11]

At rallies throughout Gaston County and beyond, workers called especially for "A Mill Mother's Song" (later renamed "The Mill Mother's Lament"), her most powerful and best-loved ballad.

We leave our home in the morning,
We kiss our children goodbye,
While we slave for the bosses
Our children scream and cry.

And when we draw our money
Our grocery bills to pay,
Not a cent to spend for clothing,
Not a cent to lay away.

And on that very evening,
Our little son will say:
"I need some shoes, dear mother,
And so does sister May."

How it grieves the heart of a mother,
You every one must know.
But we can't buy for our children,
Our wages are too low.

It is for our little children
That seems to us so dear,
But for us nor them, dear workers,
The bosses do not care.

But understand, all workers,
Our union they do fear,
Let's stand together workers,
And have a union here.[12]

By expressing the exploitation of labor by capital as a violation of mothers' rights, May touched a chord of sentiment that was widely held and deeply felt. Yet May's mill mother was a far cry from the dominant culture's domestic ideal. She was a single mother and a wage earner: it was she who must buy for her children; it was her wages that were too low. Like the women writers who were drawn to her story, May saw in the strike a chance to use her talents and change the world. Able to write and figure with ease, she served as secretary for the local union and joined a delegation that went to Washington to lobby for the workers' cause. In her music as in her life, women were not simply victims; they were political actors who put traditional roles and local culture to subversive uses.

THE COMMUNIST PARTY's decision to target Gastonia was the result of a dramatic about-face. The party had long seen the region as a peculiar "reservoir of reaction" populated by ignorant and individualistic poor whites and by victimized and dependent Negro peasants, neither of whom were candidates for collective action.[13] A small group of black communists, however, pushed back against this view, and in 1928 the World Congress of the Communist International combined its injunction to form dual unions with a directive to the Communist Party, USA (CP) to "organize the black agrarian population to struggle for control of the land and against . . . lynching, Jim Crowism, and segregation." Alongside this commitment to "self-determination in the black belt" (the plantation areas of the South that contained almost half of the country's black population) came a call to "stamp out all forms of antagonism, or even indifference among our white comrades toward the Negro work" and to attack "white chauvinism"—that is, racism—wherever it was found.[14]

Acting on this call, the National Textile Workers Union of America resolved to encourage a rolling wave of strikes among southern textile workers. It aimed to take advantage of what the Socialist Party leader Norman Thomas termed the "criminal sluggishness" of its rival, the American Federation of Labor, which made little attempt to organize the South even as its stronghold in New England collapsed.[15] It also hoped to make those strikes a test case for the party's robust stance on racial equality, despite the fact that 99 percent of the region's textile workers were white. That meant changing the hearts and minds of white workers, creating interracial unions, and destroying "the dangerous weapon of race hostility so carefully cultivated and so effectively used by the bosses."[16]

Fred Beal, a stocky, ruddy-faced, blue-eyed former textile worker, stepped forward to carry this outsized burden. Speeding south on a motorcycle in the early days of 1929, he made his way to Gastonia, where workers at the Loray Mill had been protesting against the stretch-out for close to a year. Almost as soon as he arrived, five workers were fired for attending a union meeting, the local voted to strike, and 1,800 Loray Mill workers walked out. One day after the union presented its demands, including the abolition of the stretch-out and the granting of higher wages, shorter hours, decent housing, and union recognition, the governor sent in the National Guard, and the local newspapers began churning out antiunion propaganda.[17] Dismissing the workers' grievances, they portrayed labor organizers as nothing more than an entering wedge for atheism, communism, free love, and social equality—indeed, as a threat to "the very way of life . . . of the citizens of Gaston County."[18]

In fact, local women, not outside organizers, turned out to be the backbone of the strike. Among the most steadfast was Ella May. By transforming the hymns she was raised on into union songs, she mesmerized both her fellow workers and the parade of writers and organizers who passed through town. She also did what to most observers would have seemed virtually unthinkable: she joined a black organizer and leader of the Party's Negro Division in recruiting black workers, many of whom were her neighbors in Bessemer City, home to a number of mills that employed a highly unusual proportion of blacks. "If Gastonia has never realized that militant women were within its bounds," a writer for the *Charlotte* (North Carolina) *Observer* commented, "it certainly knows it now."[19]

The presence on the picket lines of so many women—and their children—did nothing to prevent a violent response. A "Committee of One Hundred" hacked the union's headquarters to pieces and destroyed the relief supplies that dribbled in from New York. Soon the company began evicting striking families, piling their belongings helter-skelter in the mill village's dusty streets and yards. Within two months after the walkout, the mills were running at full capacity, staffed by new recruits and by strikers who were compelled to work in order to eat.

As the holdouts huddled in a "tent city," Gastonia's townspeople turned their attention to other things, especially to the 39th annual Confederate veterans' reunion held in nearby Charlotte in early June.[20] While thousands cheered the veterans marching along Charlotte Street, the strikers staged their own march to the mill gates to call workers out on strike. The police beat them back, and Orville Aderholt, Gastonia's police chief, raided the union's headquarters without a warrant. Shoot-

Ella May's orphaned children. Left to right: Albert, 3; Myrtle, 11; Chalady, 13 months; Clyde, 8; Millie, 6.

ing broke out, and five people were injured. Among them was Aderholt. When he died of his wounds, the police charged Fred Beal and other unionists with murder. In response, the CP–affiliated International Labor Defense (ILD) and the American Civil Liberties Union, the chief leftist champions of civil liberties and labor rights, retained the services of a nearby minister-turned-lawyer and, for the first time, brought the combined force of international publicity, mass demonstrations, and legal defense to bear on the South's notoriously unjust economic and criminal justice systems.[21]

The tragic climax came on September 14, 1929. As Ella May and other strikers were returning from a union meeting, a pack of cars gave chase to their truck. Careening along at high speed with its passengers clinging to the sides of the open bed, the truck was almost home when it was forced off the road. Scattering under a hail of bullets, many of the unionists saw one of their pursuers shoot Ella May at point blank range, piercing her heart. Pregnant with her tenth child, she fell to the truck's floor and died on the spot. "Oh Lord, he's shot me," she is said to have cried.[22] Despite eyewitness testimony, May's killers went free, while Beal and six other unionists were convicted of the police chief's murder.

The strike and ensuing court cases wound to an end in the spring of 1930. In a retrial of the men accused of Ella May's murder, the defense attorneys held Ella May up "as a vile wretched woman" who ran with a crowd "seeking to overthrow the government." The jury found the accused not guilty. When the North Carolina Supreme Court refused to overturn the verdict in the Aderholt case, Fred Beal and others fled to Russia.[23]

THE STRIKE WAVE of 1929 was "an unrivaled eye-opener" for many white Southerners, as the historian C. Vann Woodward later observed, and Grace was in an ideal position to perceive the significance of the conflicts in her native region.[24] Her Lower East Side circle of radical trade unionists, Communists, and fellow travelers—including Michael Intrator, who had briefly edited the National Textile Workers Union's journal—avidly followed the union's southern campaign. She was also in touch with the women she had worked with in the YWCA. These included the New York University economics professor, Lois MacDonald; the former head of industrial work in the southern region, Louise Leonard, who was now directing the Southern Summer School for Women Workers; and Myra Page, who had written a PhD dissertation on *Southern Cotton Mills and Labor*, funded by the industrial division of the YWCA, and was at work on her own Gastonia-based novel.[25]

Determined to make the Southern Summer School "the classroom of the southern labor movement," Louise Leonard and her colleagues recruited students from among the strikers in Gastonia and other sites of labor struggle.[26] Eleanor Copenhaver (Anderson), who succeeded Leonard as head of the Y's industrial work in the South, made her sympathies—and her growing radicalism—clear. She saw in "the upheavals of 1929 a mass movement" similar in its potential "to the Reformation or the Renaissance." Urging her constituents to take seriously "the philosophic meaning of communism," she deplored the antilabor use of the "bugaboo of race" and praised the Communist-backed National Textile Workers Union for "urging full brotherhood for the black brother." She believed that the industrial division of the YWCA was better prepared than any other women's organization to respond to the situation but agonized over a basic tension between the association's determination to encourage the self-determined leadership of increasingly class-conscious working women and the control exercised over local city Ys "by the wives of the men who are their industrial overlords." Differing from the Communist Party's analysis of events more in rhetoric than in substance, Copenhaver, Leonard, and Lois MacDonald stressed the class and racial dimensions of the 1929 conflict and "the magnitude and subtlety of this revolution."[27]

The central goal of these labor educators was to release "the powers of southern women workers," but they also used their contacts and credentials to break through the wall of middle-class hostility that surrounded the Gastonia strike.[28] They were joined in this effort by Betty Webb, a Brenau College graduate who succeeded Katharine as the Y's southern student secretary and whose friendship and accomplishments were a special point of pride for both Katharine and her cosecretary Frances Williams.[29] Webb had stepped onto the national Y stage when she spoke on "Interracial Cooperation and Understanding" at the association's 1924 national convention, describing her upbringing as a white Southerner with "race prejudice . . . [as] a part of my social heritage" and then testifying to the transformative impact of collaborating with black women.[30] Marrying a fellow activist but pointedly keeping her maiden name, Webb was just finishing a graduate program at the Brookings Graduate School of Economics and Government undertaken in the same spirit in which Katharine had pursued hers: to acquire "the best intellectual equipment" with which to promote "a fundamental reorganization of society, political, economic, and social."[31] After receiving her PhD, she was hired by the American Civil Liberties Union to return home to North Carolina to organize a "Fair Play for the Gastonia Workers" committee. Because her father was a prominent judge and state legislator, no one, her friends observed, had "so many connections of political importance." Moreover, no one was more "radical and unafraid."[32]

During the last act of the prolonged drama, Grace Lumpkin made her own pilgrimage to North Carolina, visiting Elizabeth in Asheville, then traveling to Gastonia and on to Charlotte, where she encountered the music of Ella May. "We were sitting in the National Textile Workers Union Hall . . . waiting for the meeting to begin," she remembered. "It was a cold night. Somebody started Solidarity and then we sang Ella May's 'ballets.'" In the group was Daisy McDonald, one of the strike's other balladeers. At the end, McDonald asked her husband to lead the gathering in "A Southern Cotton Mill Rhyme," which was destined to become one of the most famous of the traditional songs that Ella May had put to political uses. Alert to the significance and power of this music, in the spring of 1930 Grace sent a brief but resonant dispatch to *The New Masses* about what she had heard. In October 1931, she secured a 300-dollar advance from the Macaulay Company for a novel she initially called "Swan Crossing," after Swain County, the western North Carolina community where she spent the summer of 1923. *To Make My Bread*, the title she ultimately chose, appeared in September 1932.[33] Taken together, these two publications helped ensure that Ella May would not be forgotten and that, during the Depression decade, the Gastonia case would become a legend and a battle cry.[34]

GRACE'S DISPATCH TO *The New Masses* signaled what would turn out to be one her novel's great strengths: its suggestion that a people under assault can find in their vernacular expressive culture the inner wherewithal not to survive as "our contemporary ancestors" but to transform themselves through acts of political reinvention.[35] She began by carefully transcribing the lyrics of Ella May's "A Southern Cotton Mill Rhyme," preserving for later generations a song of the mills that, she observed, had "never appeared in print before." In an endnote and a later letter to the editor, she then explained the song's provenance and evolution, staking out an approach to traditional music that rested on what Margaret Larkin, another female labor journalist who took Ella May's ballads to New York, termed the "curious mingling of old and new."[36]

Daisy McDonald's husband, Grace explained, "had worked at the loom next to a man in a mill in Buffalo, South Carolina. . . . This weaver had spoken out the words of the Rhyme under the noise of the looms, making them up as he worked. And the song has gone from one worker to another and now it is known to hundreds of cotton mill hands."[37] Having traced one of Ella May's signature songs from its creation by a particular weaver to its transmission through the networks of mobility and person-to-person communication that bound one mill village to another, Grace then turned to the music's political uses. The last stanza, she said, usually went like this:

Just let them wear their watches fine
And rings and golden chains
But when the Day of Judgment comes
They'll have to shed those things.

During the Gastonia strike, the workers changed "when the Day of Judgment comes" to "when the great Revolution comes." "Folk songs," Grace concluded, "are made and changed from the knowledge and needs of the people who sing them."[38]

Indeed, there is evidence that "A Southern Cotton Mill Rhyme" had "changed from the knowledge and needs of the people" even before the Gastonia strike.[39] When the folklorist Archie Green set out to follow "the bread crumbs in the forest, strings in the labyrinth" in order to locate the ballad's origins, he found a version of the song in a chapbook published in 1900. In that iteration, the composer wanted "no animosity between my employer and me" and stressed the scorn the "ignorant factory set" endured.[40] Following that same thread, I came across another clue. The Monroe, North Carolina, *Journal* printed the "Rhyme" in a column of "Favorite Poems" in 1916, with lyrics indicating that well before they encountered radical organizers from the North, southern mill workers had revised the chapbook version into the group-conscious song that Lumpkin heard and collected.

Workers' cultural creativity had another layer as well, which Grace Lumpkin's description of "A Southern Cotton Mill Rhyme" made clear. When she first heard the song, she explained to *The New Masses* readers, it was sung to an original tune, "perhaps the blending of some old ballads. . . . But I know," she continued, "that the Rhyme, with a little adaptation, has been sung to the tune of 'John Hardy,' a mountain ballad that is on Columbia Record No. 167-D, sung by Eva Davis who lives in the Great Smoky Mountains near Proctor, North Carolina." Eva Davis, a white banjo player, was one of the first women to make a commercial recording when the record industry began to market "hillbilly" music in the early 1920s.[41] "John Hardy," like "John Henry," with whom he was sometimes confused, was a legendary black worker in the tunnels of West Virginia. He was supposed to have composed the song on the gallows before being hung for murdering a man in a barroom brawl. When Ella May and other mill village balladeers adapted what folklorists took to be archaic English tunes, they were as likely to be borrowing from the radio, the phonograph, and African American musicians as from what they had learned at their grandparents' knees.

By attending so closely to folk music's political implications, to the creative interchanges between commercial and traditional music, and to the roles of women as organizers, artists, and cultural transmitters,

Grace evoked the many ways in which the South's working people fused music and social struggle.[42] In so doing, she stood not only against the early folklorists who scoured the mountains in search of ballads that had traveled unchanged from the British Isles but also against left-wing condescension.

Most of New York's communist cultural critics viewed the provinces as insular and sordid. For them European modernism and, increasingly, Soviet-style socialist realism were the fonts of worthy culture. Even as they prescribed a new kind of literature, written by and for working-class audiences, they continued to see American folksong, especially the vernacular idioms of the white South, as "defeatist, melancholy . . . and trivial."[43] Commercial "hillbilly" music was beneath contempt. Accordingly, when the Communist Composers League sought to use "music as a weapon in the class struggle," it "produced difficult, technically advanced works of jarring harmonic dissonance and acute rhythmic complexity" which failed utterly to capture a popular audience.[44]

When the party's metropolitan cultural apparatus did attend to vernacular music, the results were less than encouraging. The *Red Song Book*, a compilation of *Music for the Masses* published by the Workers Music League in 1932 just as *To Make My Bread* appeared, passed over Ella May's "A Southern Cotton Mill Rhyme" in favor of her "I.L.D. Song," a forgettable paean to the Communist-affiliated International Labor Defense. Adding insult to injury, Communist critics panned the "immaturity" and "arrested development" of the southern music the *Red Song Book* did contain. A lone voice defended these indigenous creations. Writing for *The New Masses* in 1933, Margaret Larkin praised them as "a direct and vigorous expression of large numbers of American workers."[45]

The Communist Party's response to African American culture offered a partial exception to its disdain for the music of the South. Under the editorship of Mike Gold, *The New Masses* opened its pages to "Negro songs of protest." The magazine published the pathbreaking work of Lawrence Gellert, a now-obscure white radical based in the Appalachian resort town of Tryon, North Carolina, who began collecting "work songs, chain gang songs, hollers, and blues" as early as the mid-1920s.[46] It also served as a major outlet for Langston Hughes, who championed the blues "as both an urban folk music and a proletarian art form rich in political implications."[47]

By amplifying the voices of people such as Ella May, Grace Lumpkin, Margaret Larkin, Lawrence Gellert, Langston Hughes, and other forward-looking emissaries of leftist culture helped to ensure that folk music would become the soundtrack of insurgency during the Great Depression. To be sure, in the North that music served less an as organic form of group expression than as a type of entertainment to be performed in concerts or tacked on to the end of union meetings. But in the South union meetings routinely wandered back and forth between songs and speeches, the secular and the religious, call and response.[48] At a time when, in Germany and other countries, the idealization of "the volk" fed reactionary and exclusionary forms of nationalism, this efflorescence of working-class expressive culture demonstrated that folk traditions could encourage a spirit of pluralism and democracy as well.

In the 1950s, almost a quarter century after Grace discovered "A Southern Cotton Mill Rhyme," Pete Seeger recorded the song. Neither Seeger nor anyone else remembered that it was Grace Lumpkin who made this powerful expression of mill workers' consciousness available to later generations. Nonetheless, her approach to music and other aspects of folkways as a "living process of oral tradition" reemerged in the folk revival and civil rights movements of the 1950s and 1960s, claimed a central place in the academy in the 1980s, and reverberated in social movements around the world.[49]

LIKE GRACE'S *New Masses* article, *To Make My Bread* does not dwell on the details of the Gastonia conflict. It turns instead on how gender, intertwined with race and class, shapes working-class men's and women's lives. Also like that article, it reveals a sensitive understanding of the social history of the mountains and mills and of the changes in consciousness that accompanied the transition from rural culture to a southern cotton mill world. John Steinbeck's *The Grapes of Wrath*, which captured the displacement of farm families by the Dust Bowl and their migration to California, would become a central narrative of the 1930s.[50] *To Make My Bread* takes up an equally wrenching but earlier and much less noticed exodus: the flight of southern farmers from the land to the factory floor.

To tell that story, more than half the novel takes place takes place not in the mill village but in the mountains of western North Carolina, an area that Grace knew well, first from childhood holidays and then from the three months she had spent in Hazel Creek before she moved to New York. She may have been attracted to the area by Horace Kephart's classic portrait of Appalachia as a place "where time stood still," but, as *To Make My Bread* demonstrates, she had come away with a much more realistic understanding of the world she had seen. Kephart entirely ignored timber workers and miners, and mentioned migrants to the mills only in passing, focusing instead on moonshiners and other exotic figures. Grace, by contrast, took the impact of the industrial revolution on the mountains as her theme.[51]

Following the McClure family from 1900 to 1929, her novel takes the form of a bildungsroman, the coming-of-age story favored by the nineteenth-century authors whose books the Lumpkin children, under their mother's tutelage, loved to read aloud. But *To Make My Bread* is a bildungsroman with a difference. In its classic form, such stories were geared to the aspirations of an emerging middle class and premised on a male-coded ideology of individualism. Whether the hero accommodated himself to the social order or rebelled against it, he was figured as an autonomous individual wrestling with the external world. Coming-of-age narratives for female protagonists typically involved a "voyage in," a journey toward the spiritual realm or self-abnegation through marriage.[52]

To Make My Bread, by contrast, revolves around dual heroes, Bonnie McClure, whose prototype is Ella May, and her younger brother John, and it traces the process by which both come to political consciousness and act on what they learn. Their intertwined development, moreover, cannot be separated from that of their widowed mother and their grandfather, who also confront the tensions of rural life and the shattered promises of industrialization. Drawing intricate contrasts and connections between the siblings and the models of manhood and womanhood their elders represent, the novel asks not how the solitary individual learns life's lessons, but how interdependent men and women, configured as gendered selves-in-society, change in relation to each other and in response to moral contradictions and material alterations.

These transformations depend as much on the characters' stances toward the past as on their visions of the future. Indeed, as the literary scholar Richard Gray puts it, *To Make My Bread* is "fired into life" by its portrait of how each member of the McClure family wrestles with "the conflicts and connections between the old culture and the new."[53] Although published during the Great Depression, it reflected the agony of the South in the 1920s, as rural people confronted not only the shock of factory labor but also the contradictions between rural solidarities and market pressures, the fatalism of the church and the liberatory uses of the gospel, patriarchal values and women's changing roles—contradictions that prepared a rising generation to seek out new ways of understanding the world.

In this sense, "there was a telling link between what [Grace Lumpkin] was doing and what she was dramatizing."[54] Sometimes empowered, sometimes crippled by inherited practices and values, both the author and her protagonists struggled "to make sense of old loyalties and obligations in the light of dramatically changing circumstances."[55] Fifteen years after Grace Lumpkin's novel appeared, Katharine Du Pre Lumpkin's autobiography, *The Making of a Southerner,* would offer its own meditation on the burden of southern history and the dynamics of social change. Writing in different contexts, in distinct genres, and in conscious or unconscious dialogue with one another, each of the Lumpkin sisters enacted a hope and a promise: dissident Southerners of different classes could fashion new selves and a new society from the materials of the old.

THE NOVEL OPENS with a sweeping view of the valley where the McClure family lives. As the mountaintops disappear in the swirl of a spring snowstorm, the panorama dissolves into a telling mise-en-scène in which a group of men gather around the stove at the crossroads store owned by a man she calls Hal Swain. Like such businesses throughout the South, Swain's store is a point of contact between the local community and the outside world, a space where political allegiances are consolidated and economic deals are done. In the men's terse exchanges, their steady gazes or cunning or downcast glances, you sense at once the differences of character and of access to education, credit, and land that shape their reactions to the forces poised to transform a harsh and beautiful land.

In sharp contrast to the myth that mountain people were untouched by modernity until the coal companies and textile mills arrived, Lumpkin neither romanticizes her characters nor paints them as premodern victims of outside exploitation. Proletarian writers, she argued a few years after *To Make My Bread* appeared, do not make "villains of those who represent the views we do not like and angels of those who represent views we like." We "are interested in life and character." We know that "all men have more than one side to their natures, depending somewhat, also, upon the viewpoint of the onlooker."[56]

The viewpoint of the onlooker in *To Make My Bread* is that of the omniscient narrator, a trustworthy guide who sees "the social, economic, and cultural fault lines that crisscrossed the mountains." Hal Swain is a case in point. The store owner is fair in his dealings, generous to his neighbors. And yet—like the family into which Elizabeth Lumpkin married—he is an agent of the capitalist juggernaut to come.[57] He becomes the local go-between for the logging company, which destroys the virgin forest. He then sells vast acres for a rich man's game preserve, facilitating a trajectory quite like that of Asheville, which was already tying its fortunes to tourism when Grace began to spend summers there as a child.

As the men leave the store to hurry home ahead of the gathering storm, the scene shifts to a different, equally gendered space: an isolated cabin where the recently widowed Emma McClure is about to give birth to her deceased husband's child. Cut off from other women by the "blank whiteness" of the sudden spring snow, she must rely on her father, John Kirkland, who has joined her household after a logging company cheated him out of his land.[58] "Granpap" carries his Civil War battle scars proudly but faces the mortal rites of childbirth with fear and dread. Emma has already buried three of her first six children. A daughter, Bonnie, is still in her crib. Two older sons watch fearfully from a corner of the room. Emma's screams, the bloody birth, a later moment when the starving children suck the marrow from leftover bones on the cabin floor—these images take us straight into an economy of scarcity where women bear the brunt of suffering and men are often dead, absent, or undone by their own folly or by economic disasters that strip them of their independence and ability to provide.

Enticed by a labor recruiter, Emma McClure agonizes over whether her family should join the South's internal migrant stream. "She knew that if Emma McClure was given the opportunity she could learn how to work the machines." Both in fiction and in history, poor women's identities rested on their ability "to make my bread" by contributing to the family economy, whether that meant feeding and nurturing children, wresting a living from the land, or learning to tie a weaver's knot.[59]

Daughters like Bonnie McClure watched and learned from their mothers, absorbing not only their childrearing and domestic skills but also their frustrated aspirations and their ethic of care.[60]

Once the McClures arrive in the mill village, Emma confronts the realities of "machine civilization" as well as the lack of freedom that living in a company town entailed.[61] At first, the deafening noise of the looms seems "like the throb of a big heart beating for the good of those who worked under the roof." But soon Emma's "mind had to whip her muscles to make them keep up" during the dreadful last hour of the night shift, while the shameless section boss sat near the toilets, yelling at women who were "staying too long . . . to hurry up in there." As the time-clock discipline of the factory replaces the rhythms of the seasons, she begins to see herself and her neighbors as "hands," interchangeable tenders of the machine they serve. At that point, "to make my bread" takes on a sinister meaning. The mill becomes an all-powerful, irresistible monster, murmuring, like the ogre in the fairy tale, "I'll grind your bones to make my bread," a metaphor that vividly personifies Marx's concept of alienated labor.[62] Emma McClure was right: she could and did learn how to work the machines. But she could not control the pace or reap the fruits of her labor.

Emma's education in injustice takes place within the family and community as well as on the factory floor. Venturing into town with her sister-in-law Ora, Emma confronts the vast material gulf between rich and poor, unmediated, as it was in the countryside, by neighborhood and kinship ties. The two women stare from a distance at the mill owner's mansion, complete with black servants coddling a white baby who has everything their children are denied. Anticipating a rare treat—ice cream sodas that cost a nickel apiece—Emma and Ora slip nervously into a drugstore, a new, modern space of consumption where the sexes mingle but the classes, like the races, do not. The waiter looks right through them, and the town folk whisper, "They're mill hands," as the two women slink from the store.[63] Worst of all, Emma comes to feel that she has failed as a mother. No matter how hard she tries, in an industry built on low wages and child labor she cannot fulfill one of the dreams that drew her to the mill. She cannot keep Bonnie and John in school.

Nor, despite valiant effort, can she overcome the grief and stave off the misfortunes brought on by the failure or fecklessness of the McClure men. Her husband had died before the novel begins. Her older sons either abandon the family or get themselves killed. All Emma has left is Granpap, whom she loves, cajoles, and tries to protect. "He was a good man and what man didn't want to be head of the house he was in? This was only right," Emma thinks to herself when Granpap moves in. Yet she circumvents his authority, fighting him directly when the stakes are high. He, in turn, is steadily diminished by the market forces that push him off the land. Once in the mill village, he becomes a "cotton mill drone," the epithet applied to men who could not or would not make the transition to waged work. Like William Lumpkin, he clings to the past. Turned away by a man at the mill office who says, "you're too old t' work in the mill," he walks fifty miles to a Confederate reunion to salve his wounded pride, losing Emma's precious quilt along the way.[64] He invests what little money the family has in a nearby farm (shades of the Lumpkin's ill-fated move to a Sand Hills farm), and Emma subsidizes the venture by traveling back and forth from the farm to work in the mill, a common arrangement in the early twentieth-century South. When the farm fails, Granpap heads for the hills, leaving his daughter and her children to struggle on alone.

As hope wanes, Emma glimpses the meaning of class through the lens of gender. It is a relationship between haves and have-nots that undermines working-class manliness, injures women both as workers and as mothers, and creates a gnawing sense of helplessness and deprivation. Still, she sees through a glass darkly, apprehending her circumstances through two powerful cultural scripts: the prevailing notion of technological inevitability, and the otherworldliness of the evangelical church. She cannot imagine that workers might act collectively to harness the power of the ogre-like machine, and she looks for comfort to the church's teaching that the poor who accept their lot on earth will reap their reward in heaven. Pulled between fatalism and aspiration, ambivalence and determination, residual beliefs and new forms of understanding, she registers the hope, pain, and confusion of the first generation of white Southerners swept up in the industrial revolution.[65]

It is left to the second generation, Bonnie and John, who come of age in the mills, to go beyond fatalism by trying to tame capitalism through collective action. But their praxis—the fusion of activism with critical thinking—flows not from jettisoning the ideas of the past in favor of off-the-rack Marxism, but from an ongoing interchange between "the old culture and the new."[66] In this sense, they carry on what their mother began.

For Bonnie McClure that interchange is steady and unconflicted. From childhood on, she works and learns at her mother's side. When she marries and has children, she, like her mother, places her hopes in them. But when misfortune piles upon misfortune, she does not blame herself or think, "What is there to do, except wait and hope for heaven?"[67] Instead, she moves steadily toward politicized motherhood and new forms of social knowledge: she begins to apprehend the world around her as a social system that can be changed.

Her journey begins, like Ella May's, with the conviction that the mill, far from bringing "better things" for their children, is depriving women of the ability to nurture human life. Bonnie's roving husband leaves her, and she asks for permission to go home to nurse her newborn child. "If I let you," the supervisor says, "I'd have to let every other woman who's got a young baby do the same. And there are plenty of babies in this village, Bonnie." "And plenty of them dies," Bonnie replies. Standing at her looms and wondering how to replace her children's raggedy clothes, she puzzles out an everyday theory of what Marxists call surplus value: the difference between the fifty cents she earns for weaving sixty yards of cloth and the six dollars that same cloth costs at the store. "Somewhere in between," she figures, "somebody makes five dollars and fifty cents."[68]

It takes no vanguard party to explain exploitation, no didactic message from the novel's Fred Beal–like communist organizer, who is, as one Marxist critic complained, "a complete blur," to persuade Bonnie to join the union.[69] Once she does, she is as willing to confront working-class sexism as she is to make demands on the mill owners. "There'll be some who'll say women should stay at home, and not mix in men's affairs," her audacious aunt Ora cautions. "But they don't say hit when we go out t' work, and I can't see why they should say hit now." "Yes," replies Bonnie, "if we work out, we've got a right to speak." And speak she does. Drawing on her gifts as a singer, honed in the church, she transforms the music she was raised on into songs that allowed the union "t' reach people's hearts as well as their stomachs."[70] For Bonnie, as for Ella May, artistic expression is a means of self-invention and of political action that draws on and reconfigures indigenous cultural forms.

Also like Ella May, Bonnie becomes the union's most effective emissary to the black community. As the literary scholar Suzanne Sowinska argues, Lumpkin and her southern compatriots were the first proletarian novelists to delineate the links between the "Woman Question" and the "Negro Question" and to imagine a road to class justice built on interracial alliances among working-class women grounded in black and white women's similar experiences of caregiving and waged work.[71] Bonnie is not immune to the forces that kept black and white workers apart: the competition for jobs, coupled with the racist stereotypes that assured white workers that, however degraded they might be, they were still not the lowest of the low. But when the union confronts the question of whether to recruit black workers, Bonnie comes down on the side of self-interest and "common sense." Parrying the boogeyman of intermarriage raised by another worker, she says, "I'm not a-talking about marrying."

> I'm a-talking about working together and fighting together. The marrying can take care of itself. We are all working people and I can see without looking very far that what [the union organizer] says is true. That if we don't work with them, then the owners can use them against us. Where would we be if they went over to Stumptown and got them in our places? It's plain common sense that we've got to work together.[72]

When Bonnie volunteers to serve as a go-between in black communities, a woman named Mary Allen paves her way, ensuring the failure of the company's effort to use black scabs to break the strike. In *To Make My Bread*, as in the Gastonia strike, interracial organizing is "women's work." Bonnie's efforts reflect both traditional customs of caregiving and new roles for women in the public sphere.[73]

IN COMPARISON TO the path taken by his paragon of a sister, John's road to political consciousness is rocky and fraught. His grandfather and older brothers offer only flawed models for manhood; like William Lumpkin, they teach lessons he must later unlearn. Compelled to separate himself from his mother and to assert the independence that manliness requires, he learns to feel "contemptuous of women and of any kind of womanish ways in a man."[74] His remaking begins in earnest when his mother dies of pellagra and he finds a mentor in John Stevens, an itinerant weaver. Stevens has seen the world. He brings back news of Sacco and Vanzetti and other working-class struggles and gradually helps John understand how mill owners could be, at one and the same time, good men and agents of a system that is the root cause of workers' poverty and even of his mother's death. In the end, John too becomes a union leader, but unlike Bonnie he has been divided against himself throughout most of the book.

A set piece in which Granpap takes John to a Confederate reunion captures the process of miseducation and reeducation that lies at the heart of John's bildungsroman and at the heart of the Lumpkin sisters' lives and works. Just as Katharine's later autobiographical writings would linger on her childhood memories of the Confederate reunion of 1903, so Grace draws directly on her own and her sister's experiences, but she narrates this episode from John's point of view. He is bedazzled by the tall buildings, the red and white streamers, the young women in their white gowns, the former generals resplendent in gray uniforms with gold braid, the doors that open to the poor privates who stream into town. Seated with the veterans in the great hall, he listens eagerly to a "Pitch-fork" Ben Tillman–style politician who offers paeans to white suprem-acy and describes the mill owners as saviors of "the free white." The speaker praises the aging veterans before him not for their courage in battle but for saving "the South during Reconstruction." Now they can reap their reward: jobs in the mills from which blacks are excluded. The rally ends with a speech by the perfect unifying symbol: an Elizabeth Lumpkin–like daughter of the Confederacy whose unquestioning love secures the power of patriarchs, whether they preside over the humblest cottage or the grandest old plantation home.[75]

Yet the manufactured unity of the audience dissolves as soon as she leaves the stage. The dignitaries go off to a "ball for the higher-ups," while the poor veterans gather around campfires on the street, getting drunk and swapping the very same stories about the KKK that William Lumpkin liked to tell.[76] For John, the whole experience is disappoint-ing and dispiriting, not at all the grand, manly adventure he expected it to be. Gradually, over the course of the novel, he frees himself from the myths such spectacles were meant to promote. What Grace can-not imagine, and so leaves unexplored, is how he might also reject the prerogatives manhood confers. Instead, she makes Bonnie the one who most fully and explicitly rejects the blend of patriarchy and racism that shored up the power of the white elite.

Like Ella May, Bonnie dies in the end. Killed for her interracial organizing and the power of her songs, she passes on the baton of leadership to her brother. For critics, then and later, that plot twist raised questions. Who is the novel's hero? What message does the author send about the place of women in class struggle?

When *To Make My Bread* was published in 1932, male readers tended to answer one way, females another. To the editors of *Working Woman*, a Communist Party–sponsored magazine devoted to the "woman question," *To Make My Bread* offered "The Story of Ella May Wiggins in a Novel." Accordingly, the magazine reprinted excerpts about Bonnie's death and funeral.[77] Two years later, when Michael Gold, Granville Hicks, and other leading left-wing critics edited an anthology summing up the proletarian literary movement's achievements, they made a different choice: they included a section entitled "John Stevens" focused on John McClure's political mentor, the itinerant weaver.[78] That choice reflected the "anxious masculinism" that pervaded many left-wing cultural productions and organizations and dictated the iconography Grace Lumpkin's publisher chose for the cover of her book.[79] Featuring a sturdy working-class man with his wife and children by his side, it obscures the fact that *To Make My Bread*'s male characters are anything but upstanding protectors and breadwinners and that the female heroines are, for the most part, making their way alone.

The feminist scholars who, in the 1980s and 1990s, recovered the work of Grace's generation of radical writers appreciated *To Make My Bread*'s treatment of the complex relations between gender and class and its attention to women's solidarity across the color line. But they too sometimes mistook John as the novel's central protagonist. To them, Bonnie's death suggested the limits of Grace Lumpkin's ability to imagine a female hero.[80] Few critics in either era noted the significance of Grace's decision to make John and Bonnie dual heroes from the start, signaling her departure from the individualist assumptions of the bildungsroman and setting up a contrast between the differently gendered apprenticeships that made Bonnie the wiser, more self-directed, and, presumably to her killers, the more radical leader.

Such misapprehensions aside, the key fact for Grace was this: she could not have hoped for a more positive reception. *To Make My Bread* won the Maxim Gorky award from the Revolutionary Writers Union, as well as praise from critics who generally loathed proletarian realism.[81] Writing for a New York literary magazine, the suffragist and civil rights advocate Martha Gruening echoed the sentiments of a wide range of readers: *To Make My Bread* is "deeply felt and honestly told. . . . Grace Lumpkin has recreated the rough, poverty-stricken and yet dignified life of these mountain people. . . . She makes us see them as she sees them . . . with understanding and tenderness." Reviewers for both *The New Masses* and the *New York Times* concurred: "Grace Lumpkin knows the life she writes about. . . . That is her greatest asset, that and her scrupulous honesty, simplicity, and lack of pretense." She presents her characters with "a craftsman's and a psychologist's respect."[82]

Reviewing *To Make My Bread* for the *Daily Worker*, V. J. Jerome departed from this glowing assessment, faulting Lumpkin for failing to wear her politics on her sleeve and attending too faithfully to rural Southerners' points of view. He granted that *To Make My Bread* bore some of the hallmarks of an ideal proletarian novel and, in that sense, served as "a guide for those still to come." But he detected in Grace's approach "a certain fetishism of local color, a fetishism having its root, perhaps, in autobiographical unfoldment, but which may be politically interpreted as a nostalgia, a home-sickness for the rural mountain scene."[83] A few other critics took the opposite tack: rather than feminizing *To Make My Bread* as nostalgic "local color," they pigeonholed it as a formulaic "strike novel." Such naysayers, however, did nothing to detract from the novel's reputation, which shone even brighter as the decade progressed. It was dramatized on Broadway and in trade union halls around the country and cited by those who, in the late 1930s, saw it as exemplifying a new "proletarian regionalism" that embraced regional and cultural diversity and challenged the assumption that "southern" and "radical" were contradictions in terms. *To Make My Bread* made Grace Lumpkin a left-wing literary star.[84]

CULTURE AND
THE CRISIS

W HEN GRACE LUMPKIN TOOK UP THE CAUSE OF THE GAS-
tonia strikers in the spring of 1929, an orgy of stock market and real estate
speculation was spinning out of control, and the South was already in
the grip of a punishing agricultural depression. By the time *To Make My
Bread* reached the bookstores in September 1932, the whole country had
plunged into an economic abyss. At first Grace and Michael were luckier
than most. He could get work as a highly skilled fur cutter. She received
decent advances for *To Make My Bread* as well as for *Timid Woman*, the
first of her two pseudonymous romance novels.[1] She also got help from
Grace Hutchins, who continued to take an interest in her and Esther
Shemitz long after all three had left *The World Tomorrow* and aligned
themselves with the communist movement.[2]

In 1933, Grace received a coveted invitation to Yaddo, a legendary artists' retreat in upstate New York. She cherished this godsend: Breakfast
in bed or in the mansion's beautiful dining room. The sacrosanct hours
from 9:00 to 4:30 when guests were required to remain in their studies
devoting themselves to "creative work," free from distraction save for
the delivery of a box lunch. The elaborate Italian gardens. After-dinner
gatherings in an era when, as one guest remembered, "it was not dangerous . . . to be interested in communism" and the conversation, while usually devoted to literary gossip, sometimes turned to "proletarian themes."

All that, plus the chance to become part of a supportive network of artists from a wide range of backgrounds she would otherwise have been
unlikely to meet. Icing on the cake: Yaddo's all-powerful director, Elizabeth Ames, extended Grace's one-month residency to three, a favor
avidly sought by penurious writers trying to stay afloat during the Great
Depression.[3]

Still, seasonal fluctuations and layoffs in the fur industry and retrenchment in the book and magazine trade soon hit Grace and Michael hard.
Michael found himself working only ten weeks out of a year. They were
so poor they had no heat. My "last five dollars," Grace wrote, "is repos-
ing in the top drawer of my desk, and I don't know when I will get
another one."[4]

By 1933, when Grace wrote these words, the country was sliding into
the cruelest winter of the Depression, and massive demonstrations of
the unemployed were roiling American cities. Nowhere were conditions
bleaker than in the South. Grace seized the moment, throwing herself
into a whirl of activism and reportage aimed at parlaying literary attention into political weight. As she did so, she pursued a project that she,
Katharine, and Dorothy shared: the effort of radical women intellectuals
and professionals to redefine their positions as white-collar "brain workers" so as to align themselves with working-class struggles.[5]

That effort, and the left turn of American intellectuals of which it
was a part, was driven by four events. The first was the spectacular failure of capitalism, long predicted by Marxist thinkers. The second was
international fascism, which swept through Europe, threatening socialist experiments and capitalist democracies alike. The third was the accelerated pace of social and economic transformation in the Soviet Union,
as the world's first socialist nation transformed itself under the Five-Year
Plan and, at the same time, stood as the chief bulwark against Hitler. Finally came a series of uprisings among American workers that
heightened both the mood of crisis and hopes for transformation. These
clashes with authority in the South raised the possibility that revolutionary impulses could grow in what many had seen as the most barren of
native soils. Foreshadowed by the 1929 Gastonia strike, these upheavals
included the 1931 mine wars in Harlan County, Kentucky, and the 1934
general strike in the textile industry, the largest such strike in American history.

Taken together, these events suggested that capitalism was crumbling, and a fundamentally new society was struggling to be born. Many Americans were simply stunned by misery. Instead of questioning the economic system, they blamed themselves. For them the Depression would leave an "invisible scar," a longing for security, a determination to hold on to what they had. For others—including those who were already primed for radical solutions by their experiences in the 1920s—the cataclysm had a galvanizing effect. In their eyes, the question became not simply how to bring the economy back to health, but how to create a just and humane social order—perhaps a higher stage of capitalism, perhaps a society beyond capitalism, be it a social democratic or a communist state.[6]

"America was on the move," Dorothy Douglas remembered, and a generation of artists, intellectuals, and professionals threw themselves into the movement wholeheartedly.[7] Some joined the Communist Party, but most swelled the ranks of the civil rights advocates, socialists, social democrats, and left-leaning New Dealers who, at mid-decade, became the heart and soul of a black-labor-left-liberal coalition known as the Popular Front. The Popular Front is usually understood as beginning in 1935, when the Soviet-dominated Communist International abandoned its attacks on socialists and liberals in order to build an alliance against fascism, and ending in 1939 when Russia staved off a German attack by signing a nonaggression pact with Hitler. But as Grace, Katharine, and their circles experienced it, it was much less narrow and Soviet-driven than that. Rooted in the ferment of the late 1920s, it peaked with the mass movements of the 1930s and endured until the Red Scare of the 1950s. Led by the labor movement and marked by a blend of conflict and cooperation, suspicion and respect, it can best be seen as a political formation predicated on a move toward a common agenda: a robust critique of capitalism and a desire to give voice to the dispossessed, combined in some quarters with a commitment to racial equality and women's liberation.[8]

AMONG THE FIRST SIGNS of the intellectuals' left turn was a petition that appeared in the spring of 1930 protesting against police crackdowns on Communist-led demonstrations of the unemployed and federal efforts to outlaw the CP and jail or deport its leaders. The more than one hundred writers, educators, and artists who joined this protest ranged from unknowns like Grace Lumpkin, whose first novel would not appear until 1932, to such prominent figures as H. L. Mencken and Franz Boaz. Less than a year later, Edmund Wilson, editor of the *New Republic* and the doyen of American liberalism, published an electrifying call to American progressives to assert "emphatically that their ultimate goal is the ownership of the means of production by the government."[9]

The presidential election of 1932 intensified the atmosphere of dissent. Herbert Hoover, the unpopular Republican incumbent, responded to the crisis by clinging to a balanced budget, bolstering major banks and businesses, and looking to private charities and local governments to provide a modicum of relief. The Democrats fielded Franklin Delano Roosevelt, a genial patrician from New York who promised a "new deal for the American people" while offering little evidence that he differed significantly from his opponent or that he could rise to the enormous challenges a new president would face. William Z. Foster headed the Communist Party ticket; his running mate was James Ford, a black postal worker from Alabama, an unprecedented nomination for any political party. Norman Thomas, the Socialist Party's perennial nominee, charged that the Democrats and Republicans were "merely glass bottles with different labels, and both of them empty of any medicine for the sickness of our times."[10]

By the fall, Roosevelt was poised to win in a landslide, and Thomas was attracting impressive support. But to a growing number of intellectuals, even the Socialist Party was, as John Dos Passos put it, "near beer."[11] Some began inching toward membership in the CP, the only organized force whose ideas and actions seemed to them to be commensurate with the crisis at hand. Many more began to think of themselves as "small c" communists, or "fellow travelers," a term coined in literary circles to describe men and women "who are not members of the Communist Party but who sympathize with the revolution and assist in their capacity as artists and writers."[12]

The emergence of such alliances was enabled by changes in the party itself. From its founding, the CP was geared toward the industrial working class. Accordingly, its leaders made a habit of distancing themselves from "parasitic" intellectuals. They also drew a bright line between the class-based fight against the exploitation of black and white working-class women and the bid for "emancipation" by bourgeois feminists who could aspire to "high-salaried" positions.[13] Scorning socialists and social democrats as well as middle-class reformers, the party was as devoted to maligning potential allies as to fighting common enemies on the right. That predilection, in combination with the virulent antiradicalism encouraged by the post–World War I Red Scare, ensured that the party could not reach much beyond its Northeastern immigrant base.

Beginning with the Passaic strike and the defense of Sacco and Vanzetti in the late 1920s, however, rank-and-file party members had moved slowly toward a more expansive, collaborative stance. That process accelerated in the early 1930s as Hitler rose to power and racial equality became increasingly central to the radical agenda, directing the New York–centric party's attention toward the terra incognita of the American South.[14] Simultaneously, the Depression's brutal impact on women, families, and communities tempered Communists' obsession with male workers in heavy industry. Responding to hunger and evictions, the party reached out to the unemployed at the neighborhood level, not only mobilizing massive protests but also sending local organizers "door-to-door, kitchen-table-to-kitchen-table" and "taking on the meanest task."[15] As women and African Americans joined the communist movement in larger numbers, they became what the literary scholar Barbara Foley calls "the visionary conscience" of the left. They drove home the point that the "better world" the left envisioned required not only control over the means of production but also profound changes in the relations between women and men, blacks and whites.[16]

IN "WHY I AS A White Southern Woman Will Vote Communist," published first in the Baltimore *Afro-American* and then in the *Daily Worker*, Grace Lumpkin became one of the first in the long line of radical artists and writers who endorsed the Communist Party ticket during the 1932 presidential campaign. Speaking as "a white southerner . . . and a descendant of an old southern family who settled in 1670 in the heart of the south," she located herself in the scenes of her youth: the move from Georgia to South Carolina; the cotton mills on the outskirts of her new home town; the hardscrabble farms of the Sand Hills where tenants' children barely learn to read and write. She then turned to an explanation of post–Civil War history notable for its departure from southern apologias and its prefiguration of late twentieth-century scholarly themes.[17]

For white farmers, she suggested, land ownership signaled independence, which implied racial superiority because it set them apart from people who were landless and enslaved. Why, then, did this conviction of superiority persist when sharecropping and "wage slavery" engulfed black and white alike? The answer, she suggested, lay in what modern scholars might call sexualized racism: white conservatives' deliberate use of "the cry of 'rape' . . . to scare black workers and keep white and black workers apart." Only the Communist Party "gives us any hope," she concluded, for it is the only party "that stands completely for equal rights for Negroes and whites."[18] On the eve of the election, she wrote "Where I Come From, It Is Bitter and Harsh: Why We Should Vote Communist," excoriating her native region in an even more strongly worded appeal. Issued as a press release by the Ford-Foster Committee for Equal Negro Rights, a CP-sponsored group, it was part of an unprecedented effort to win African American support for the party's presidential candidates. Unlike tepid reformers, the CP "*demands . . .* political, economic, and social equality for Negroes," she concluded.[19]

In the same month in which these endorsements of the CP appeared, Grace joined the League of Professional Groups for Foster and Ford, an independent organization led primarily by socialists and social democrats and open to all "leftward moving intellectuals . . . committed to the revolutionary movement in terms of the class struggle."[20] Although relatively short-lived, the league produced one of the era's most resonant manifestoes, *Culture and the Crisis: An Open Letter to the Writers, Artists, Teachers, Physicians, Engineers, Scientists and Other Professional Workers of America*. Like the *Port Huron Statement*, the declaration of principles issued by Students for a Democratic Society in 1962, *Culture and the Crisis* captured the ideals and ambitions of a generation. By redefining the social position of those "who share the task of crystallizing, disseminating and perpetuating American culture," it sought to theorize a new relationship between mental and manual labor and persuade "brain workers" to throw in their lot with the working class.[21]

Culture and the Crisis had been gestating throughout the summer of 1932 among members of the independent left. "Why should intellectual workers be loyal to the ruling class which frustrates them, stultifies them, patronizes them, . . . and now starves them?" it asked.[22] "There are teachers on the bread lines. . . . Department stores have their pick of PhD's at $12.00 a week. . . . Artists find no market for their wares.

Writers find no publishers." Even in the best of times, "the independent intellectual or professional worker suffers . . . spiritual degradation . . . when false money standards are applied to his creative craft."[23]

Against this dark reality, *Culture and the Crisis* offered a utopian vision: a fundamental reorganization of society in which "the professional workers, whom capitalism either exploits or forces to become exploiters, are liberated to perform freely and creatively their particular craft." In such a world, an economist would "purposively plan the . . . social objectives of industry." An architect would "express his finest aspirations in buildings of social utility and beauty." Doctors would pursue "preventive medicine." And teachers, writers, and artists would "fashion the creative ideology of a new world and a new culture."[24]

Most of the fifty-two individuals who signed this document belonged to the tight-knit circle of men who dominated left-leaning literary magazines and organizations in New York. But progressive women did not see the "brain worker" as gendered male. Indeed, teachers, social workers, and other members of predominantly female professions took the lead in the broader effort to reassess the significance of modern mental labor and forge a new role for professionals in working-class struggles. Early in the 1930s, radical social workers formed a rank-and-file movement aimed at organizing unions rather than elevating their professional status. Instead of deploying casework methods to adjust individuals to their social situations, they joined their clients in efforts at reform.[25] Similarly, activist educators sought to transform the American Federation of Teachers from a professional organization into a militant union.

Grace had compelling personal and political reasons for aligning herself with a vision that made the class struggle *her* struggle, not a cause she supported but one in which she too was implicated. On the one hand, she was married to a militant industrial worker. On the other, she was "a descendent of an old southern family" writing proletarian novels at a time when Marxist critics were still arguing over whether anyone but manly blue-collar workers could write authentically about the working class. "The Communist Party tells us to become class-conscious," she explained. "This is a fine word, and has a fine meaning. . . . To know where I belong, not with those who have brought the world to its present state of chaos and misery, but with those who are working for a world in which each will have a share of the good things of life."[26] Political identities, she suggested, do not simply reflect one's "relationship to the means of production." They involve self-fashioning, commitment, the search for a spiritual home.

THE TILT OF intellectuals to the left, combined with Communist organizers' embrace of African Americans and the South, set the tone for the left-liberal alliances and ideological convergences that propelled Grace into the signature legal and political struggles of the early 1930s. The first of these was the Scottsboro case, which raised issues of both sexism and racism, and inspired Katharine and Grace to join other white southern women reformers in a feminist antiracist response. In 1931, Alabama officials arrested and summarily convicted nine young black men for allegedly raping two white female mill workers hoboing through the state on a train. When the International Labor Defense (ILD) rushed to defend the "Scottsboro boys" against a "legal lynching," a routine example of southern injustice became a cause célèbre. Wresting the case away from the NAACP and mobilizing outrage across the world, the communist movement drove home the centrality of race and the South to the politics of the era, just as Sacco and Vanzetti symbolized the xenophobia of the 1920s.

In contrast to the Sacco and Vanzetti case and the Passaic strike, the Scottsboro defendants were not radicals or striking workers who could tap into urban communities for support. They were unknown, mostly illiterate African Americans on trial in the Deep South, where the Communist Party drew its rank-and-file membership from a black population that had been stripped of the most elemental resources and rights. Yet in this overwhelmingly hostile environment, ILD lawyers succeeded in taking the case to the US Supreme Court and securing a new trial. Almost as remarkable was the fact that Ruby Bates, one of the alleged rape victims, recanted and testified for the defense.

Grace Lumpkin joined the campaign through the Scottsboro Unity Defense Committee, a "broad inter-racial and non-partisan" effort led by a talented group of Harlem Communists. Formed in 1932, this committee represented a breakthrough in black organizers' efforts to increase the party's influence among African Americans.[27] The presence of "famous writers" furthered the committee's goals, as did the unexpected involvement of white Southerners such as Grace Lumpkin, which the organizers underscored as a sign of the ILD's broad appeal.[28] Speaking to the press about the Scottsboro Unity Defense Committee's founding meeting, Viola Carter, a prominent Harlem club woman, observed: "My conscience suffered a terrific jolt as I sat and listened to white men from Alabama and Tennessee talk about justice for black boys, and saw white women from South Carolina, Texas and Virginia, who have been in the forefront of this struggle."[29]

Both Grace and Katharine played a role in another ILD effort to mobilize "the finest, most advanced men and women" behind the Scottsboro defense campaign: a petition signed by one hundred "prominent Southern women," all of whom were white and many of whom were YWCA activists moving steadily to the left. Grace, described as the "author of the recent novel 'To Make My Bread,'" was among the lead signatories, as were Eleanor Copenhaver (Anderson) and Lois Mac-Donald, leaders of the Y's industrial program and the Southern Summer School for Women Workers. Identified only as a native of South Carolina, Katharine signed the petition as well, along with an impressive cross-section of other southern activists, including a host of rank-and-file workers who had attended the Southern Summer School for Women Workers and participated in the 1929 strikes.[30]

Jessie Daniel Ames, director of the Atlanta-based Association of Southern Women for the Prevention of Lynching (ASWPL), was deeply opposed to ILD involvement in both the Scottsboro case and the antilynching campaign. She and her loyal lieutenants, most of whom belonged to an older generation of suffragists and reformers, believed that only strategic appeals to fair-minded white Alabamians and to the governor and state supreme court had a prayer of saving the accused. But a number of ASWPL members, especially those associated with the YWCA and the Methodist church, broke ranks and signed the petition. "As Southern women, and as adult citizens of 20th century America," they proclaimed, "we refuse to hide any longer behind the protecting wall of prejudice and violence. We protest against the 'ideal' of 'Southern chivalry' that supposes the honor of Southern womanhood can best be preserved by such savage and unjust actions as the trial, conviction, and contemplated electrocution of the seven young Scottsboro Negro boys."[31]

This woman-centered rhetoric contrasted sharply with that of reformers—Communists and liberals alike—who saw lynching as a crime of men against men, with black women as bystanders and white women as entering the story primarily as liars, hysterics, or sluts. Throughout the Scottsboro case, the defense portrayed the alleged rape victims as mill village tramps who thought nothing of "promiscuous intercourse" with black and white men alike. If Ruby Bates and her companion, Victoria Price, were assaulted, they had asked for it.[32] If not, their false cries of rape were symptoms not only of the "cold-blooded ruthlessness" of poor whites but also of an endemic "pathology of women." John Spivak, the radical journalist who covered the Scottsboro trial for the ILD, put it this way: "in the 'depths'" where Ruby Price was "born and lived . . . all feeling was killed. Being raped does not trouble her. She rapes easily and apparently likes it."[33]

Like the signers of the ILD women's antilynching petition, Frances Williams, Betty Webb, and other members of the Lumpkin sisters' YWCA women's network brought their perspectives to black-labor-left-liberal coalitions. Williams had become a friend and trusted advisor of Walter White, the influential head of the NAACP. Through that relationship, she worked to shift the NAACP away from its traditional focus on the civil rights concerns of the "talented tenth" and toward a critique of capitalism and advocacy for black workers. She did so by forging links between the association and the left-led Joint Committee on National Recovery, which sought fair treatment for black workers in the federal relief programs initiated by the Roosevelt administration.[34] At the same time, she and Webb, who was now teaching at Vassar, enlisted the YWCA in the NAACP's campaign for federal antilynching legislation.[35]

Determined "to free or compel" Dixie congressmen to vote for the Costigan-Wagner bill, which mandated federal prosecution of law enforcement officials who colluded in mob rule, Walter White concentrated on shattering the assumption that the white South solidly opposed intervention. To that end, Frances Williams and Betty Webb persuaded southern Ys to pepper their congressmen with pro-legislation letters.[36] At Williams's urging, White invited Betty Webb to testify in a dramatic two-day hearing before the Senate Judiciary Committee held in February 1934. Her regional and family background caught the attention of the senators, as did her claim to be able to speak for the women of her generation because of her leadership of the South's interracial student movement. "They felt she had a keen mind, she was unusually attractive, and was sure of her ground," Frances Williams observed. The hearing was a "tour de force," in part because it included such an impressive display of support from white Southerners, and the bill was readily voted out of committee. In the end, a filibuster by conservative southern congressmen torpedoed the legislation, but the campaign for its passage consolidated the YWCA's determination to pair education with political advocacy. It also strengthened the NAACP's position as a key member of the New Deal coalition and stirred the embers of the ILD-led, mass-based antilynching campaign.[37]

These campaigns against mob violence and legal lynching not only put race on the left and liberal agendas but also stimulated the emergence of a left feminist perspective that united women with a wide spectrum of experiences and affiliations. Left feminists rejected both the sexism that underlay "Southern chivalry" and the racism behind the "savage and unjust" treatment of black men and women by lynch mobs and the courts. Over the course of the 1930s and early 1940s, they would also bring to the crafting of public policies a vision of justice that assumed equality for women even as it prioritized issues of race and class.[38]

GRACE'S INVOLVEMENT IN the Scottsboro case and the campaign for federal antilynching legislation consisted primarily of working with the Scottsboro Unity Defense Committee to mobilize support in New York. But during these same years she was also making forays into the Deep South, traveling the back roads with organizers for the Communist-backed Alabama Sharecroppers Union, venturing into Mississippi and Louisiana on similar missions, and joining Myra Page and other leftist journalists on trips to Birmingham, where unionists were trying to organize the mines and mills.[39] For radical Northerners in the 1930s, such journeys acquired the cachet of later trips to the front during the Spanish Civil War or to Mississippi during the civil rights movement. Grace Lumpkin wrote about these events as an insider. Offering a damning critique of the place that formed her, she asserted a unique voice and identity: that of the rebel daughter of the South who rejects the privileges her race and class afford.

Her most memorable venture took place in the summer of 1933, when antiblack violence erupted in Tuscaloosa, home to the University of Alabama and supposedly an oasis of enlightenment in a deeply reactionary state. The crisis began in June 1933, when three young black men found themselves charged with the murder of a white woman who lived in a black settlement on the outskirts of town. Rumors of rape swirled around the case, and there was every reason to believe that, despite the flimsiness of the evidence against them, the defendants were destined for the electric chair. The ILD immediately dispatched lawyers from Birmingham and New York to Tuscaloosa, but the local judge refused to allow them to defend the men. When the trial opened, an angry mob surrounded the courtroom, the judge called in the National Guard, and the lawyers fled under cover of night. The next day the ILD announced that it would "continue the fight," sending a shudder of hysteria through the white community. Convinced that "Jew lawyers" were bent on turning Tuscaloosa into what Grace called "another Scottsboro case" and that Communist organizers were instigating a black uprising in the countryside, the town fathers created an elaborate espionage system to spy on black gatherings and run strangers out of town.[40]

Soon espionage gave way to intimidation carried out by a middle- and upper-class Citizens Protective League in concert with the anti-black, antiradical third wave of the Ku Klux Klan. Fearing a lynching, the judge ordered the prisoners moved to Birmingham. On the way, deputy sheriffs turned the men over to vigilantes. Riddled with bullets, two of the prisoners died, but one survived to tell the tale. The Tuscaloosa *News* blamed the lynching squarely on "the Communistic organization known as the International Labor Defense." As during Reconstruction, the editors explained, an "outside agency inflamed people to such a point that the community was tense with fear of racial disorders . . . so when a handful of men took the matter into their own hands and put those Negroes to death, a certain relief was undeniably felt by even the most thoughtful and law-abiding of our citizens."[41] Six weeks later, a second lynching occurred: a mob reacting to an accusation of attempted rape murdered a black man who was so disabled that he could barely walk, let alone jump out from behind a bush, tear a woman's dress, and run away, as he was alleged to have done. At this point, town leaders began to deplore the breakdown of law and order and distance themselves from the KKK, but they made no effort to punish the members of the mobs.

The outcry against these atrocities was led by the mainstream white newspapers in Birmingham and fanned by the black and leftist press. Seizing the opportunity to forward its campaign for federal antilynching legislation, the NAACP sent a delegation to persuade Franklin

Roosevelt to intervene. The Commission on Interracial Cooperation (CIC), parent organization of the Association of Southern Women for the Prevention of Lynching, sent Arthur Raper, author of *The Tragedy of Lynching* (1933), a classic study of mob violence, to conduct an investigation.[42]

Meanwhile, the National Committee for the Defense of Political Prisoners, a writer-led group that was especially active in the South and that often worked closely with the Communist Party and the ILD, began inviting sympathetic white Southerners to serve on its own investigating team. It hoped to recruit distinguished liberals, including the historian C. Vann Woodward, but ran up against their deep suspicion of Communist motives and tactics.[43] Grace Lumpkin said yes immediately, as did Hollace Ransdall, a veteran teacher at the Southern Summer School for Women Workers who investigated the Scottsboro case for the American Civil Liberties Union. Howard Kester, a southern YMCA activist turned socialist and pacifist, readily signed on as well.[44] Convinced that an investigation by a northern-based, Communist-affiliated group would "add to the prevalent hysteria in Alabama," the CIC tried to convince the National Committee for the Defense of Political Prisoners to hold its fire until Arthur Raper had published his report. When the defense committee rejected that request, the Interracial Commission rushed a summary of Raper's findings into print.[45]

Undeterred, Grace Lumpkin, Hollace Ransdall, Howard Kester, and seven other men and women continued with their own investigation. Before they could reach Tuscaloosa, the Ku Klux Klan staged a march, presumably as a warning to blacks not to cooperate with the "outside citizens" who were on their way to town. "The strain has been terrific on all of us all," Howard Kester told his wife after the group arrived.

> Being watched and spied upon at every turn has caused us to be quite jerky. . . . Much of our work has been on the surface but a lot has been underground and secret. We've had to be as careful as could be everywhere. Today I got in a jam and in the twinkling of an eye became a book salesman from the Methodist Print[ing] House. . . . Last night was my first night of sleep. We have to see most of our people around midnight in various places. Life is hell, hell, hell! We are afraid there will be an epidemic of deaths among our informants after we get away.[46]

Despite the danger, Kester, Lumpkin, and the other investigators found that black informants talked quite freely. This firsthand testimony left no doubt that public officials had not only connived, but likely participated, in mob murder and that the killers' names were widely known. The investigators also secured interviews with key white figures. The judge, Grace Lumpkin observed, "was a fine old Southern gentleman. I liked him at once; and, yet, underneath, I hated him for the part I knew he had indirectly played in those lynchings." She also met a deputy sheriff who was a notorious "Negro killer," with "about a dozen to his credit already."[47] Waiting for an interview, she watched him with a grandchild in his arms. " 'My wife and me have two grandchildren and we think they are the greatest things in the world.' I have no doubt that was true," Grace observed. "It is true that he is a human being with family affections, but he is also a murderer and a villain."[48]

"We have gotten some 'hot stuff' no one dreams of," Howard Kester told his wife. But the committee never issued its report, in part because Tuscaloosa's town fathers managed to deflect national attention by quietly dropping the trumped-up rape charge against the surviving prisoner and driving him out of town along with most of his family and other black witnesses. It would have been difficult in any case to write an exposé on the Tuscaloosa lynchings more damning—and more redolent of the radical mood—than the one Arthur Raper ultimately published. Raper made official connivance in mob violence abundantly clear and traced lynching directly to its economic roots. "At the very bottom of race relations in the Black Belt, lies the determination of the white man to continue his economic exploitation of the black man," Raper concluded.[49] Raper's hard-hitting pamphlet, like the ILD-sponsored women's petition against lynching, suggests that, for all their rivalries and hostilities, the two sets of southern antilynching activists—one allied with the cautious Commission on Interracial Cooperation, the other with a network of radicals that spanned the Mason-Dixon line—found themselves converging on the class-conscious, antiracist political agenda that would increasingly enable robust left-liberal coalitions.

In an article entitled "Southern Woman Bares Tricks of Higher-Ups to Shunt Lynch Blame" published in the *Daily Worker*, Grace Lumpkin reinforced Raper's charges. "We found every evidence to show that the crime against these boys . . . was done with the knowledge and approval of those higher up." But the most disturbing evidence she offered came directly from her own family history, and it spoke not just to the events of 1933 but to her father's character and her family's complicity in what the ILD called "the lynch-economic system of oppression of Negroes in the South."[50]

She drew directly on her father's memoir of Reconstruction—which Elizabeth had donated to the United Daughters of the Confederacy many years before but Grace had obviously read—to trace a line from her father's generation of KKK vigilantes to the lynchers of Tuscaloosa. In William Lumpkin's day, the local Ku Klux Klan had avoided detection by carrying out its "midnight missions" in neighboring counties, she explained. Similarly, Tuscaloosa officials were careful to turn the defendants over to the lynch mob only after the group crossed the county line, creating jurisdictional confusion and making it all the more unlikely that the killers would pay for their crimes. "This manner of getting rid of prisoners . . . is a new method to us, but it was well known to members of the Ku Klux Klan during Reconstruction. It seems that Alabama is learning from those who took the law into their own hands just after the Civil War." Then and now, Grace concluded, the "best people" are able to hide their crimes: "It must have been men from another county that came in and did it," they say. "The old Ku Klux technique. . . . They can look you in the face with clear eyes, and say, like Pontius Pilate, 'My hands are clean.'"[51]

By equating her father's generation with what her sister Elizabeth would have called "the bastards" of the latter-day Ku Klux Klan, Grace did more than reject a cherished family myth.[52] She also challenged the view of Reconstruction that pervaded both formal histories and popular culture. William A. Dunning, then doyen of Reconstruction studies at Columbia University, portrayed Ku Klux Klansmen as high-minded gentlemen who acted with great restraint in the face of terrible provocation, threw off "Negro rule," restored law and order, and helped to reunite the nation. Two years after Grace's article appeared, W. E. B. Du Bois subjected that myth to a blistering critique, but it continued to be echoed by Dunning's successors and taught in schools until the 1960s, when scholars influenced by the civil rights movement finally exposed its racist underpinnings and effects.[53]

This brief article proved to be the germ of what Grace thought would be her most important project: a sweeping novel that would trace the roots of the South's economic and political system to "the deep and bitter struggles of Reconstruction" and turn "the Southern side" of that story upside down.[54] In the meantime, she secured a literary agent, Maxim Lieber, who represented Katherine Anne Porter, Langston Hughes, John Cheever, and many other prominent writers of the 1930s and 1940s. Lieber helped her acquire a contract with Lee Furman, Inc., a new imprint of the Macaulay Company aimed at publishing "works of permanent value as distinguished from books issued merely for popular consumption" for a less ambitious novel based on her observations of the Alabama Sharecroppers Union.[55]

PUBLISHED IN 1935, *A Sign for Cain* tells two intertwined tales. The first was inspired by the Alabama Sharecroppers Union, whose members were withstanding mass evictions and shootouts in a bid for fair treatment within a grindingly exploitative cotton tenancy system. In this story, two local organizers, one black and one white, work together and in their separate communities to overcome the habits and fears that fostered resignation and kept the black and white rural poor apart. In the second story, which overshadows the first, Grace brings her own ideological and personal preoccupations to bear on what, in the hands of William Faulkner and others, was becoming one of the stocks-in-trade of southern fiction: the disintegration of a planter clan.[56]

At the head of this family is William Lumpkin reincarnated as Colonel Gault, who received his title not for his Civil War service but for his role in "redeeming" the state from Reconstruction. Dressed—to his children's embarrassment—in the old-fashioned "Prince Albert coat" that William Lumpkin always affected, he is "a helpless old man with the dignity and ludicrousness of one whose life is measured by outworn values."[57] Tormented by the conviction that Snopes-like industrialists are turning the South into a "commercial . . . money-mad place," he lives "in a dream of what he wished things to be."[58]

The colonel's children, by contrast, are very much of the moment, so much so that they could be taken as the southern counterparts of the decadent, bickering relatives in *Some Take a Lover*, the pseudonymous novel Grace had published two years before. One son, Jim, is a hard-drinking wastrel. The other escapes into the Episcopal ministry. A country-club-going social climber, he plays golf on Saturday, argues for mild social nostrums, and hopes to become a bishop one day. While the sons stay close to home, Caroline, the daughter, goes to New York "to make her place in the world." Now she is a successful writer who puts "her whole self in her novels," including her open marriages, divorces, and affairs.[59]

The story's central conflicts begin when Denis, the black organizer, leaves his job in a northern steel mill and returns to the Gault plantation where he was born and his family labored. He joins forces with Bill Duncan, a local journalist whose combination of charisma, radicalism, and sexism makes him a dead ringer for Grace's husband. We gather that both are Communists, although virtually no one in the novel mentions the word, and, when they express their hopes and ideals, they do so in language that a broad swath of radicals and reformers could readily embrace.

When Caroline reluctantly returns home, summoned by the news that her father is dying from throat cancer (much as William Lumpkin did), she and Bill Duncan commence a long, drawn-out courtship that combines a duel over ideas with a mostly off-camera affair. He cares about the "millions of women . . . forced to be productive machines, producers of children and producers of goods," but treats Caroline with a whiff of condescension. Railing against "men's superiority, their smug self-conceit," she sees herself as "an unreconstructed rebel, against every rule, everything that limits my freedom, against the domination of men." Yet even as she fumbles her way toward a serious, if problematic, position—the elevation of individual artistic freedom over pursuit of the common good—Caroline exhibits the dependency and manipulativeness of a stereotypical bourgeois woman. "Buffeted by her emotions [and] unable to care for herself," she demands "chivalry and devotion" and is determined to make Bill "give up those activities which did not coincide with hers, or about which she did not approve."[60]

The novel ends in a melodramatic crescendo of violence that seems hasty and tacked on. Jim Gault, the wastrel son, permits Denis, the novel's black hero, to be jailed for a murder that he himself committed, then ends up murdering him in his cell. In the final scenes, Bill rejects Caroline completely when he learns that she has helped to cover up her brother's crime, then looks on in horror as, bizarrely, she drops to her knees and hobbles toward him "like a beggar . . . on the stumps of his legs," pleading for another chance. The black and white sharecroppers meet to plan a funeral procession. We are left with a glimmer of hope that they will regroup to fight another day. "The light from the lantern spread over the men as they passed through the back door. It made them appear larger, of heroic proportions, and their shadows thrown against the white-washed wall of the cabin made it seem that others were walking with them, so that their number was multiplied."[61]

WHEN *A SIGN FOR CAIN* appeared in the fall of 1935, it did not enjoy the heady attention *To Make My Bread* had received three years earlier, but it was respectfully reviewed by the *New York Times*, the *Saturday Review of Literature*, and other mainstream and leftist publications.[62] Isadore William Miles, an African American public school teacher and teachers' union activist who reviewed the 1935–1936 crop of "Negro literature" for the journal of the national association of black college women, underscored the novel's major strength. Miles burned with indignation at the "vicious or shoddy" treatment of black characters in the white fiction of the time, especially the "slave psychology" of Mammy in the runaway bestseller *Gone with the Wind*. Grace Lumpkin's characters, she argued, "are in a class by themselves from the standpoint of personal integrity. . . . Denis is . . . a man with a purpose and strength to carry out that purpose even though the end be death."[63]

Isadore Miles was right: Denis was a paragon, perhaps too much so. Reversing negative stereotypes, Grace created a self-educated intellectual devoid of human frailty and complexity. Yet to her credit, she places him firmly in the context of his family and community, and uses him to illuminate the inner dynamics of both. His interactions with his mother are especially well drawn. Like Emma McClure in *To Make My Bread*, Denis's mother represents the pull of the past, but she is also a survivor with a wily understanding of power dynamics and realistic fears about her son's chosen path. Cultivate white patronage, she urges. Use your learning to become a preacher, not a union leader. Don't risk everything in a dangerous alliance with "po white trash." Denis honors such pulls and concerns, for he understands the people and place he came from in his bones.[64]

As Isadore Miles observed, in Grace's treatment of her black characters "the old and the new are shown side by side with no maudlin sentiment for the old nor magical promises for the new." But, unlike *To Make My Bread*, *A Sign for Cain* is not a novel of development. From the outset, the ideas and values of the main characters, whether black or white, are fully formed. Under Denis's tutelage, other characters do come to see the light, but we do not enter into the process by which they grow and change.[65] The Gault family is even more static. Its members are condemned from the start by their utter failure to do what makes the white working-class heroes of *To Make My Bread* so dynamic: they cannot imagine how to rework the old in the light of the new. The father clings to the past, while his children abandon all claim to the virtues of honor, loyalty, and noblesse oblige that he associates with the vanishing planter elite, adopting instead the worst vices of the rising middle class.

Caroline Gault is a prime example, and the gender politics that inform Grace's treatment of her and her relationship with Bill Duncan make *A Sign for Cain* not only inferior to *To Make My Bread* but also deeply disturbing. "I suppose Miss Lumpkin means to make [her central female character] out a complete fool," observed a reviewer for the *New York Post*. Indeed, Grace could hardly have created a more unsympathetic protagonist. *To Make My Bread* remains accessible in part because late twentieth-century feminism created a context for appreciating a story of development in which working-class women link class emancipation and racial justice to their own liberation and, like the real-life Ella May, use artistic expression as a tool of political action.[66] By contrast, in *A Sign for Cain* Grace offers a caricature of a bourgeois feminist writer as a bundle of contradictions who learns nothing and honors her muddled ideals only in the breach.

In her review of Grace Hutchins's *Women Who Work*, which appeared the year before *A Sign for Cain* came out, Grace put her own spin on a view of the "woman question" that many Communist-affiliated left feminists shared. She acknowledged the oppression of women as women, upheld the ideal of sexual equality, and endorsed access to birth control, which, along with publicly funded day care and maternity leave, had long been part of the Communist Party program and was enshrined in its 1934 "Mother's Bill of Rights." But at the core of her critique, as of Grace Hutchins's left feminist theorizing, was the double burden of "working-class women, who are forced to work like men while receiving less wages, and at the same time" perform unpaid reproductive and household labor, giving "birth to one child after another under the most adverse circumstances." Lumpkin upbraided union organizers for failing to mobilize women's "enormous potential and actual energy in fighting

MISS LUMPKIN AND
MRS. DOUGLAS

K ATHARINE LUMPKIN AND DOROTHY DOUGLAS SPENT THE summer of 1930 in Reno, Nevada, hiking in the Sierras and relishing the austere beauty of the desert. Dorothy loved the outdoors and the American West. She could "outwalk any man" while carrying on a discussion "with all her keen analysis and humor," as one friend observed. But in 1930 she and Katharine were in Reno on a wrenching errand: to establish legal residency so that Dorothy could sue her husband for a divorce. It had been a difficult decision, both because of the children and because, in the era before no-fault divorce, parting was a public, mortifying, and drawn-out affair. In Massachusetts, Dorothy would have had to establish Paul's responsibility for compromising their marriage and testify against him in open court, and even then the process would have taken three years.[1] Reno offered an alternative to that excruciating prospect. Since the turn of the century, the city's lawyers and businessmen had ensured a flow of tourist dollars by allowing unhappy pilgrims to stay for three months and then dissolve their marriages quickly, with few questions asked.

While Dorothy and Katharine waited in Nevada, Paul avoided the embarrassment of facing his colleagues at the University of Chicago by accepting an invitation to spend six months at Swarthmore studying the causes of and cures for unemployment. That assignment, as he put it, "permitted me to lick my wounds in private." It also launched him as an expert on one of the key policy issues of the New Deal: the creation of a comprehensive system of social security.[2]

As soon as the divorce was finalized, Katharine and Dorothy moved to Northampton, where Dorothy had been teaching off and on since 1924. She had chafed at her position as a lowly part-time, temporary instructor and was gratified to be promoted to assistant professor, if only on a two-year appointment.[3] With Dorothy at last settled in a more satisfying position, the two women took up residence with Dorothy's four children on Prospect Street, an elm-lined avenue of parks, campus buildings, and lovely homes.

On the day after Thanksgiving, a Mount Holyoke graduate named Adaline S. Pates (Potter) joined the family. Desperate to avoid a "Captaincy in the Army of the Unemployed," Pates had been trying in vain to find paid employment of any sort, and she jumped at Dorothy's offer of a job caring for the children. Tactful, good humored, and generous to a fault, Pates proved to be both an indispensable caregiver and a lifelong friend. "The position is almost perfect," she wrote. "The family is . . . delightful, and I am only afraid that I don't do enough."[4] As the whirl of children's games and studies calmed down "to a mild cyclone" in Pates's capable hands, Katharine and Dorothy began speaking of their plans in the first-person plural. From the confluence of very different histories and personalities, a new family and a cascade of research and advocacy began to unfold.

"This is such a moving age!" Dorothy exclaimed.[5] Each woman had yearned to combine the pursuit of knowledge with political commitment. But Dorothy's aspirations had been eclipsed by her marriage to an ambitious, preoccupied, and apparently unfaithful man. Katharine had come to see interracialism as a nostrum that fluttered "on the surface of things," and her studies at Columbia and Wisconsin had failed to give her the tools for action she craved. Now, as the force field of American politics shifted to the left, Dorothy's socialism and Katharine's social gospel–inflected antiracist feminism found a new valence. In this context and in partnership with one another, they spoke more and more forcefully to the issues of the day.

The turmoil in the working-class communities that surrounded them and the stirrings of radicalism on the Smith campus encouraged that effort, and Dorothy threw herself into the local fray. Seeking to carve out a place for herself in an intellectual community in which her partner was already ensconced, Katharine set out on a project of institution building and collaborative scholarship. Anticipating the insight of the "new labor historians" of the 1960s and 1970s, she and the students she recruited placed "workers in the context of family and community networks" and learned to see those networks as "shaping as they were shaped by" economic change.[6]

FOUNDED IN THE seventeenth century as an outpost on the Massachusetts frontier, Northampton became one in a string of trading centers for the fertile Connecticut River Valley. The river formed the town's eastern border, and as Northampton grew, its broad avenues, forking off Main Street like branches on a tree, ran quickly into tobacco and onion fields. To the west sat Smith College. Above rose the Holyoke Mountain Range, shrouded in the iron-cold winter, but emerging in vibrant emerald when spring finally came.[7]

To students and faculty, Northampton offered all the amenities of a lively, self-contained college town. Beyond a cluster of bookshops and tearooms buzzing with college gossip and high-toned debates, however, lay a county seat whose burghers often looked askance at the 119-acre "island of youthful excitement grafted onto Northampton's rolling western edge." The juggernaut of industry had transformed Northampton into one of the valley's chief manufacturing centers after the Civil War. Italian, Irish, French Canadian, and Polish immigrants flocked to the town's silk, casket, and cutlery factories, replacing the Yankee farmers' daughters who were the first to toil in New England's mills. Working-class families crowded into boarding houses and modest duplexes along the railroad tracks and beside the Mill River, which generated the energy that ran the early factories. By 1930, first- or second-generation immigrants made up 60 percent of Northampton's population of 25,000, while a tightly knit network of conservative Yankee bankers, merchants, and lawyers profited from their labor and gripped the reins of power in the town.[8]

Calvin Coolidge was the town's favorite son. As mayor, flinty, phlegmatic "Silent Cal" had applied pinchpenny Republicanism to local affairs. Elected governor of Massachusetts in the wake of the "Red Summer" of 1919, he grabbed national headlines by suppressing a Boston police strike and whipping up the hysteria that culminated in the execution of Sacco and Vanzetti. As vice president under Warren Harding, Coolidge put himself at the forefront of the right-wing critics who singled out the YWCA as a font of socialist propaganda.[9] Harding's death made Coolidge president in 1923. In 1924 he rode to the White House on a pro-business, red scare platform, aided by his handler, Bruce Barton, the chief popularizer of "muscular Christianity," which pitted itself against the supposedly feminized social gospel embraced by the YWCA.[10] During Dorothy's first fall semester on campus, the Smith student body snake-danced to Greene Hall to hear the election returns, the first to be announced on the radio, and erupted with "whistles, kazoos, rattles, cowbells, and waves of song" when Coolidge won with the largest plurality in the nation's history.[11] In 1928 Herbert Hoover ascended the presidency, ensuring four more years of Republican rule, and Coolidge returned to Northampton, his popularity seemingly undimmed. Eight months later the stock market crashed, setting off a decade of tumult in which much of what Coolidge and Hoover stood for would be repudiated.

FOUNDED IN 1875, Smith aimed to foster "intelligent Christian womanhood." Like other women's colleges, it served from the outset as a haven for aspiring female scholars. But the administration also made a special effort to recruit men to the faculty, and it treated them differently than it did their female peers. Male faculty members were usually married, whereas women, who were almost always single, were hedged about by special rules and expected to live cloistered lives. By the 1920s they had thrown off those tethers. Demanding autonomy and professional respect, women faculty moved off campus and into their own homes and apartments, often in pairs. Some were romantic partners; others were staunch friends. In either case, they created new spaces in which professional women could combine "ladylike standards" with independence, companionship, and "an authentic current of intellectual life."[12]

An ethos of silence and forbearance surrounded these same-sex unions. The aggressively marriage-minded students of the 1920s and 1930s might scoff at what they regarded as plain-Jane spinsters, and sophisticates among the younger faculty might wink knowingly at so-called Boston marriages. Yet a tradition of discreet but devoted, supportive, and loving female partnerships continued to flourish at Smith and other women's colleges as well as in religious and reform networks, North and South.[13]

Katharine and Dorothy shared what one student described as "a kind of Edwardian refinement" that located them squarely within this protective female tradition. Dorothy's highly unusual position as a divorcée and the mother of four children served as another shield. Her contemporaries would not think to question her partnership with Katharine because they could not imagine that sexuality might be fluid, ambiguous, and mutable rather than fixed for all time. Known to all but their close friends as "Miss Lumpkin" and "Mrs. Douglas," Katharine and Dorothy discouraged speculation by evoking while not quite replicating the unions of well-to-do single women of an earlier, less sexually self-conscious time.[14]

Even so, the mantle of reticence went only so far. Love affairs and committed partnerships among professional women abounded, as did same-sex relationships among men, but charges of lesbianism or homosexuality could ruin a career. Except for a small group of sexual radicals, even the most tolerant of intellectuals and leftists saw same-sex desire as a psychological disease, while anticommunists combined innuendos of sexual deviancy with charges of sedition. Those damning assumptions intensified over time. In the mid-1930s, for example, Dorothy and Katharine joined a losing battle to repeal a teachers' loyalty oath imposed by a red-baiting legislature determined to weed out what one politician called "these long-haired men and short-haired women [who] are a menace to the country." In 1960, Smith professor Newton Arvin, a gay man and National Book Award–winning literary scholar who had moved in leftist circles during the 1930s, was persecuted by the police and forced into retirement by the college for "lewd and lascivious" behavior. Over the unanimous protest of the faculty, the trustees also fired two untenured professors who were among Arvin's friends and sexual partners and who found themselves swept up in the scandal.[15]

In the decades after this harrowing episode, a remarkable transformation occurred. By the 1990s openly gay men and women held high office in local government, and the tabloids took to speaking of Northampton as the lesbian capital of the Northeast. In this atmosphere, some former friends and colleagues were willing to acknowledge that Katharine and Dorothy might have been lovers. But even then, they did so sotto voce. Most would go no further than Adaline Pates, who, having lived with the family for years, still doubted that the two women had a sexual relationship. They were more like sisters, she speculated. They were "always together. . . . They were not physical, but they were very, very close."[16] In important ways, Pates had it right: Katharine and Dorothy were always together. Intellectually, politically, emotionally, and financially, their lives were utterly entwined.

The climate of discretion and relative tolerance that surrounded women's partnerships suited Katharine and Dorothy perfectly. Just as important was the leadership that helped to make Smith an unusually open and politically engaged place. William Allan Neilson served as president of the college from 1917 until 1934. A neat little man with a trim Vandyke beard and bright blue eyes, Neilson sported a puckish sense of humor, a Scottish burr, an "air of absolute imperturbability," and an uncanny ability to charm students, faculty, and alumnae alike. He was the first non-minister to lead the college. Although Smith still described itself as a Christian institution in which every course was taught "in the spirit of evangelical piety," Neilson opposed the quotas that excluded most Jewish students and professors from elite colleges and universities. He also broke custom by refusing to deliver sermons at chapel services in John M. Greene Hall, turning these occasions into forums for his legendary blend of fatherly cajoling and stirring orations on world affairs. One day he might scold the students for behaving like the "spoiled brats of Park Avenue," the next he might speak on Sacco and Vanzetti.[17]

He tried to do away with the "gold coast" where society girls lived in lavish private homes by housing all two thousand of Smith's students on campus in two quadrangles of new dormitories. Yet scholarship students continued to earn their keep by waiting table for their better-off peers. Local working-class girls made their way onto the campus almost exclusively as dormitory maids. The number of black students was minuscule and limited to the light-skinned daughters of men such as NAACP head Walter White.[18]

Throughout the xenophobic 1920s, Neilson was seen by many on the faculty as "the one college executive in the country who has seriously tried to preserve academic freedom" and take courageous stands on the issues of the day. Encouraged by the atmosphere he helped to generate, left-leaning faculty members sought to create links between "knowledge workers" at Smith and progressive activists and labor organizers from near and far. An array of student organizations was involved in this effort. These groups included the "Capital WHY Club," formed in 1928 to consider the "whys and wherefores of social problems," and a student–faculty Socialist Club that backed Norman Thomas in the presidential election of 1932 along with two Smith College professors who ran for Congress on the Socialist Party ticket.[19] In the 1930s, Smith students formed chapters of the American Student Union and the American Youth Congress, Popular Front organizations made up of socialists, communists, and independent radicals that had a profound impact on campuses across the country. Further to the left, the Victory Club, a chapter of the Young Communist League, promoted "civil liberties for all" and declared its solidarity with "youth of all lands who fight for peace and freedom against fascism, oppression, and tyranny."[20]

These groups brought in a steady stream of radical speakers who riveted attention on the issues and attitudes that animated Katharine's and Grace's overlapping circles. Norman Thomas and others lectured on the "Gastonia tragedy" and "Industrial Conflict in the South." Myles Horton, head of Highlander Folk School, an experiment in workers' education, trekked north from the mountains of East Tennessee to describe an effort at "teaching, or rather causing the students to conclude, that the entire economic and social system will have to be changed."[21] Mike Gold, the "young, sincere" editor of *The New Masses*, came up from New York to talk about "The Artist in the Communist Society" and "Proletarian Literature." He touted the superiority of "New Russia," where colleges were not "country clubs" and "women are barred from no activity they wish to undertake."[22] Franz Daniel, a "fiery socialist" who became a key figure in the mobilization of southern textile workers, summed up the revolutionary mood. Comparing John D. Rockefeller to the mobster Al Capone, he explained how the wealth produced by the "labor, skill, and thought" of workers was appropriated by the owning class. "There will be a storm roused by those who have everything to gain, and nothing to lose," he concluded.[23]

AS SOON AS THEY settled in Northampton in the fall of 1930, Katharine and Dorothy joined the debate over how to stop the economy's terrifying downward spiral. First, they began planning a book about President Hoover's failure to meet the economic crisis "aimed at the lay reader who has done some thinking and is dissatisfied." Casting about for a title that "would arrest attention and not be positively stuffy," they fixed on "America Unemployed!" Before they could find a publisher, however, Hoover had lost to FDR, and editors were interested in looking ahead to what the new president might do.[24]

Revising their plans in the midst of Roosevelt's "First Hundred Days," Katharine and Dorothy proposed a "collaborative tome" on the question, "How much economic security can reformism, of the characteristically American variety, bring to the working class?"[25] They enlisted two other radical economists in the effort, both of whom became lifelong allies. The first was Colston Warne, a former student of Dorothy's ex-husband. Warne was a leading figure in the prolabor wing of the Depression era consumer movement and president of Consumers Union, which would survive a steady drumbeat of anticommunist attacks to become the world's largest consumer protection organization.[26] Their second coauthor was a Southerner: Broadus Mitchell, a socialist on the faculty at Johns Hopkins who had written pioneering studies of the southern textile industry. Despite this intellectual firepower, the response from potential publishers was discouraging. Stimulating as it had seemed "in the heat of discussion," even to Katharine and Dorothy the project began to sound "dull on paper" as they watched the unemployment rate rise to an astronomical 25 percent and millions of jobless people take to the streets.[27] Failing to find a publisher, they abandoned the project but not their effort to influence federal policy.

In that endeavor, Dorothy played the more public role. She was, one friend said, "an activist who combined heart and head." Her abiding sympathy for "the great common people"—especially women workers—went hand in hand with faith in the potency of ideas. As an elected member of the board of trustees of Northampton's Central Labor Union, a frequent speaker at meetings of the town's Socialist Party local, and chair of the Committee on Women in Industry of the national League of Women Voters, she advocated for workers' rights at the local, state, and national levels.[28] She also used these platforms to publicize her and Katharine's shared understanding of the roots of the Depression and to put forward their evolving ideas about how the government should respond.

Because workers during the 1920s had so little bargaining power, they believed, businessmen were free to invest their windfall profits in plant expansion and stock market speculation rather than in higher wages.

As a result, the "common man" could not "buy the necessary goods to keep the wheel of American industry going." Faced by overproduction and underconsumption, businesses laid off workers, idled factories, and defaulted on loans, sending the economy into freefall. Roosevelt responded initially with business-friendly nostrums. Paying farmers not to grow crops and suspending antitrust laws to allow trade associations to set prices and production quotas, he tried to stabilize the economy by restricting production. The benefits were supposed to "trickle down" to workers. Katharine and Dorothy offered a different solution. Anticipating John Maynard Keynes's stress on *demand* as the key to economic stability but turning it in a democratic socialist direction, they urged the federal government to meet the immediate crisis with large-scale public works programs funded by progressive taxes on income and inheritances. They also argued for addressing the endemic insecurity of workers in a capitalist economy with a far-reaching program of unemployment insurance. Their goal was to increase mass purchasing power and create a floor beneath which living standards could not fall.[29]

Unlike most liberal economists and policy makers, their concerns did not begin and end with the "common man"—the iconic figure around which New Deal rhetoric adhered. "The weight of unemployment," Dorothy stressed in one local speech, "falls upon the industrial woman doubly, as a worker and as the member of the family." Not only was she "last hired, first fired," but she had to stretch the family's shrinking budget when other members were out of work.[30] Among the initial remedies Dorothy advocated was a federal-state employment service, with a woman serving as assistant director. For "unless there are women among the personnel who are in a position to give them study and understanding," Dorothy warned, women workers "will not receive adequate consideration."[31]

This focus on women workers dated back to Katharine's experience in the YWCA and Dorothy's participation in the National Consumers League in college and during the early years of her marriage, but it was intensified by contemporary events. "The industrial situation here is rotten," Dorothy wrote early in 1934, reporting to the director of the Massachusetts branch of the National Consumers League on working conditions at a local weaving mill. Investigating the outrageous treatment of the largely female workforce, she pleaded with the textile workers union to send in better organizers and castigated the company in the local newspapers.[32]

Dorothy poured as much energy into the classroom as she did into the political arena, and she quickly won a reputation as an inspiring teacher who saw economics as "something other than mathematical model building." She introduced students to the problems of workers, farmers, African Americans, and consumers.[33] After the galvanizing election of 1932, she wrote for the new journals created by radical teachers and social workers.[34] Near the end of her life, she observed ruefully that "I still kick myself for not producing more. I'm still full to the eyelids with stuff waiting to be written." In fact, her record of scholarship compared well to that of others in the economics department. She had a firm foothold in the college, and at least some of her colleagues valued her role as a public intellectual who brought expert knowledge to bear on the burning issues of the day. Still, having started out as a married woman uncertain of her future plans and willing to fill in on a part-time, temporary basis, she rose slowly through the ranks. Finally becoming a tenured full professor in the mid-1940s, she served briefly as chair of the economics department in 1946.[35]

Katharine faced an even steeper climb. Still beholden to her graduate school professors, she spent the early years of the Depression trying to find a voice of her own, a place in the academy, and a means of combining her passion for "southern history and problems" with a career as a sociologist addressing contemporary policy concerns. She began by publishing two articles on delinquent girls in the *American Journal of Sociology*. She went on to coauthor an article with Dorothy on the history of "communistic settlements" in the United States, the subject of Dorothy's doctoral dissertation and first book. With Katharine as the lead author, the two women then sought funding that would allow them to combine research on the issue of mass unemployment with their concern for the special vulnerabilities of women and children. Writing to Mary van Kleeck, director of industrial research for the Russell Sage Foundation, they proposed an "intensive investigation" of the pressures that sent mothers and children to work as well as the values they "attach to work life after they have undertaken it." They planned to focus especially on the effect of men's unemployment on these decisions, on gender differences between boys and girls, and on differences among women in different occupations.[36] Katharine applied to the Social Science Research Council for funds for the child labor aspect of their study, adding to her proposal the idea of comparing conditions in the United States and the Soviet Union. When both of these grant applications were rejected, Katharine turned to Bryn Mawr's Graduate Department of Social Economy and Social Research, where she teamed up with two fieldworkers to collect information on child labor in Alabama and Massachusetts.[37]

Meanwhile, she finished the book for which she had received a Social Science Research Council fellowship in 1929. *The Family: A Study of Member Rôles* (1933) had begun with her graduate work on "problem children" and their "social situations." In the face of the Depression, that project had evolved into an investigation of the effects of economic catastrophe on Italian American families straining to adjust to "an industrial and urban civilization and its complex demands."[38] Completing the manuscript in the summer of 1931, she hoped to publish it in a series edited by her mentor at Wisconsin, E. A. Ross, but he steered her to the University of North Carolina Press. Although reviewers responded positively, the press was convinced that the book would not pay for itself and agreed to publish it only if Katharine bore some of the cost. She (or more likely Dorothy) did so, providing $500, a hefty sum at the time.[39]

Announced by its publisher with what Katharine complained was a "colorless" advertisement, the book appeared in the winter of 1933, shortly after Grace Lumpkin's *To Make My Bread* won the Maxim Gorky award. When W. T. Couch, the press's director, realized that the two women were sisters, he wrote to Katharine with his first and only words of praise: "I read . . . To Make My Bread . . . and I regard it as an unusually fine piece of work." To Couch, as to most readers, Katharine's first book seems to occupy a universe quite distant from Grace's attention-getting novel. Yet the two books revolve around similar themes: the interplay between class and gender, "the dynamic influence upon family life of profound changes in economic relations," and the impact of women's wage-earning on what Katharine called "the patriarchal regime."[40] Those themes mark *The Family* as belonging to a buried stream of left feminist sociological thought, just as *To Make My Bread* represented the feminist currents within the regional and the radical literary traditions.[41]

Drawing on social workers' case records of forty-six New York City families, Katharine considered what happened when husbands were thrown out of work and wives were forced into wage labor. Some families were overwhelmed by the tensions that resulted from a sudden role reversal amidst economic insecurity and despair. Others maintained a fragile equilibrium by clinging to old attitudes in the face of new economic relations: unemployed husbands with working wives went on ruling—or trying to rule—their families with an iron hand; women claimed to be working only out of necessity even when, in fact, they enjoyed their newfound independence and sociability. The families that coped best were not wedded to rigid roles: fathers retained the respect of their wives and children despite their inability to provide; mothers went to work out of necessity but without apology; children asserted their autonomy yet retained their family loyalties. This process of adjustment led to a balance between individualism and solidarity, producing "a higher form of the family" made up of self-reliant personalities united by what Katharine termed "esprit de corps." Even in the most flexible and egalitarian of families, Katharine observed, working women "ordinarily continued to carry at the same time major responsibility for home duties." Men might "help" with the housework, but women bore the burden of the double day.[42] Still, new experiences begat new attitudes. "Thus a genuine redefinition of rôles takes place which is gradually incorporated into family tradition and which the children are therefore brought up to revere."[43]

To underscore her argument that, while what later would be called "gender roles" might be deeply rooted in both men and women, they "*do* undergo change," Katharine turned to the long durée of women's history. "We must remember that man's status as head for centuries gathered about it the most powerful sanctions the mores afforded. . . . To encroach upon it was contrary almost to the existing concept of human nature. For a woman to fail to give due submission and reverence outraged the laws of God and man."[44]

She relied on the work of two British historians: Alice Clark, a pioneering student of women's labor in the transition to capitalism; and, especially, Ivy Pinchbeck, whose study of women in the industrial revolution had just appeared. Both would be rediscovered by feminist historians in the 1970s, when they helped to ground a new wave of scholarship on the family and women's work. "The introduction of machinery with its demand for cheap labor," Katharine explained, propelled poor women and children into factories while confining middle-class women to "conspicuous leisure" in the home. However much working-class women might "individually have resisted the disruption this entailed, their rights as persons were enlarged because as potential wage earners they were no longer entirely dependent legally and literally on a father-head of the family."[45]

This was the thrust of Ivy Pinchbeck's book. Five years later, Katharine pointed out that it was also the "brilliant lesson . . . taught by Engels in his *Origins of the Family*, and by Marx in *Capital*." According to Marx's formulation: "However terrible, however repulsive, the break-up of the old family system within the organism of capitalist society may seem; none the less, large-scale industry, by assigning to women and to young persons and children of both sexes a decisive rôle in the socially organized process of production, and a rôle which has to be fulfilled outside the home, is building the new economic foundation for a higher form of the family and of the relation between the sexes."[46]

Katharine ended her book with the concern that drove her collaborations with Dorothy throughout the 1930s: the need to address the roots of economic security and alleviate the special burdens of wage-earning women. To "breathe the breath of life," Katharine argued, any study of the family must first look outward to the "changing social economic scene," for much of the marital discord her research revealed was caused by the pervasive uncertainties of working-class life. No safety net except private charities and mutual aid associations cushioned working-class families from the myriad disasters that could strike at any time. Always teetering on the brink of poverty, they lacked the material and psychological resources that changes in gender roles required. "Sooner or later," Katharine concluded, "our capitalist society" must be transformed and the government must guarantee the economic security that would allow families to evolve into more egalitarian forms.[47]

WHILE PROBING THE meaning of wage-earning in working-class women's lives, Katharine was struggling to find a means of supporting herself. Even at the halcyon moment in which she started her graduate training, men monopolized most opportunities at research universities, and elite institutions such as Harvard and Yale offered women no regular appointments at all. By the time she and Dorothy settled in Northampton, men desperate for jobs had begun to edge women out of their customary niche in women's colleges as well. This was so even at Smith, where President Neilson, like his peers, seized the opportunity to bolster the college's standing by hiring bright young men who, under better circumstances, would have gone straight to the Ivy League. Citing market forces, Neilson promoted these newcomers more rapidly than he did women, who had no bargaining power because they had nowhere else to go.[48]

Katharine knew that the professions were a male preserve, yet like most academic women of her generation, she did not perceive herself as a victim of discrimination or think of her prospects as determined by her sex. She may also have underestimated the other challenges she faced. She had begun work on her PhD at twenty-six; in 1930 she was thirty-three years old. "Get them young; get the best ten or fifteen years of their teaching and research; then let them go reluctantly," was how President Neilson described his hiring strategy. Similarly, the leaders of the Social Science Research Council saw the ideal fellowship candidate as a young man in his late twenties or early thirties and did not support scholars who were over thirty-five. "Older men," one wrote, "seldom have as much capacity for intellectual growth."[49] In that climate, older women could hardly hope for a second glance.

Then too there was the penumbra of Southernness, an unstable identity that was half chosen and half imposed. Educated in an obscure women's college in the South and a public, albeit distinguished university in the Midwest, Katharine could not tap into the Smith College alumnae network, nor could she rely on connections to the New England elite. To some, coming from "a fine southern family" was a mark of distinction. William H. Kiekhofer, the longtime chairman of the Wisconsin economics department and a friend of Katharine's brother Hope, certainly thought so and took pains to mention Katharine's pedigree in his letters of recommendation. Whether that helped or hurt her is another question. At best, her accent and manners might seem exotic and charming; at worst, these markers of regional origin might call her intelligence and progressive attitudes into question. The North and the South "still have a lot to learn about one another," she told an audience many years later. New Englanders who "were so fortunate as to come of the grand old Abolitionist tradition," in particular, "have been taught to see us Southerners with horns and forked tails." Aspiring intellectuals such as Katharine sometimes felt themselves to be permanent outsiders, all the more so because New Englanders, cocooned in their fading but still considerable economic power and cultural cachet, viewed themselves not as region-bound at all, but as the standard bearers of American literature and learning.[50]

Counterbalancing these disadvantages was Katharine's sterling academic record. She had won a prestigious Social Science Research Council fellowship, which had gone to only four women in its first five years, and had moved quickly toward her first book.[51] When called upon, her mentors wrote warmly and enthusiastically (albeit a touch condescendingly) in her behalf.[52] Kimball Young encouraged her to pursue her work on delinquency, although he was interested mainly in how her "little study" would contribute to the "comprehensive analysis of delinquency and criminality in Wisconsin" that he and John Gillin planned to write. E. A. Ross took to addressing her as "Kitty" and signing himself her "loving friend." When Katharine sent him a first draft of *The Family*, he praised it extravagantly—for all the wrong reasons. Ignoring her critique of patriarchy and her stress on how families might evolve to a "higher form," he saw only "how resistant are member roles to change." Her "picture of the 'provider' pattern and the 'homemaker' pattern" was "unforgettable" and would, he hoped, "counteract the airy speculations of certain radical theorists" and counter the tendency of young people to be "carried away by the apologists for free love."[53] Yet for all their proffers of interest, there is no evidence that her teachers bothered to take the initiative on her behalf. That lack was critical, for until the 1970s, when a flood of women and minorities into the universities forced major reforms, faculty appointments depended almost entirely on personal connections and recommendations.[54]

Marginalized though they were, women too forged such networks and used them to help one another. In Katharine's case, virtually all of the job possibilities that did present themselves came from that direction. She had sailed into her job at Mount Holyoke on women's recommendations, and, before she had been there a year, Jean Davis, a student of John R. Commons whom she had met in Atlanta during her YWCA days, wrote from Wells College in upstate New York to say that the school might need a sociologist, "some one who can push the girls along, and get them interested in the outside world, and give them a sense of responsibility—inspire them." While Katharine and Dorothy were in Reno, another potential opening had appeared at Wheaton College, a second-tier women's college near Boston. Before publishing her Gastonia novel under the pen name Myra Page, Dorothy Markey had completed her PhD and secured a job at the college. When she and her husband, John Markey, who was teaching there too, left suddenly in 1930, bound for Manhattan and its more congenial radical milieu, they suggested Katharine to replace them.[55]

Nothing came of these possibilities for reasons that remain unclear. But in the spring of 1932, Katharine wrote with excitement to her professors at Wisconsin that "a research position in industrial studies has opened up at Smith College . . . for which I am being recommended."[56] In fact, that opportunity had not simply "opened up." It was Katharine's and Dorothy's brainchild, produced by their own ingenuity and resources.

Their plan was to build an alternative intellectual home: a Council of Industrial Studies to provide support for female graduate students and, at the same time, create an "authentic and first-hand" portrait of the Connecticut River Valley, a world of immigrant workers, stark class divisions, and economic suffering that lay just beyond the college's bucolic campus. In its commitment to providing opportunities for women aspiring to academic careers, the council drew on the example of Bryn Mawr's Graduate Department of Social Economy and Social Research, with which Katharine was collaborating on her study of child labor. In its distinct focus on place, it was influenced by the regionalist impulse in sociology, as represented especially by historically black Fisk University in Nashville, where Charles S. Johnson was applying his training in the Chicago school of urban ecology to the study of tenant farming and race relations, and the all-white University of North Carolina, where Howard W. Odum was nurturing the first cadre of influential social scientists to be trained in the South, rather than going to the North to study as Katharine had done.[57]

As Katharine and Dorothy conceived it, the Council of Industrial Studies would provide fellowships to graduate students at research universities, thereby forwarding their work while giving Smith faculty an opportunity to work with doctoral candidates. Each of the students' dissertations would build on the others, constructing a mosaic on which scholars could base an integrated understanding of industrial change in an area that, like the South, formed a distinctive region. Katharine would serve as the council's half-time research director. Providing a level of coordination highly unusual in the social sciences, she would recruit the students, guide the selection of their topics, direct their fieldwork,

and see manuscripts through to publication in the Smith College Studies in History series.[58] Most of the funding would come from Dorothy,
but, in line with her long-standing practice of anonymous support for
"worthy causes and individuals," she sought a route that would "keep
me out of it altogether."[59] Each year she would send President Neilson
$3,500 (an amount that certainly exceeded her salary); he, in turn, would
write personal checks to the college. Of this amount, $1,500 was divided
between two research fellows; the rest covered Katharine's salary and the
council's expenses.

Such "creative financing" by women and for women was critical
throughout the first half of the twentieth century, when women lacked
access to the foundation resources that underwrote the careers of their
male counterparts, and when the colleges at which most were employed
provided little or no funding for research. These self-help endeavors
made interdisciplinary work possible. And, by giving women the rare
opportunity to shape their own research questions and methods and
pursue the fieldwork projects that were the sine qua non of contributions
to the social science, it enabled them to influence scholarship in ways
that they could otherwise never have done.[60]

IN THE FALL OF 1932, Katharine asked President Neilson for office
space for this project. A "small room" with "two small desks" would be
adequate, she wrote, as long as it was "strategically located . . . on the
campus and within easy reach of the Libraries." A larger space "out of
the way of things . . . would not be good at all."[61] Modest sounding as it
was, in the midst of the Depression this was a bold request. Katharine
wanted a room of her own: not a garret to write in but a foothold in
the heart of the college. Neilson consulted with Esther Lowenthal, the
chair of the economics department, and agreed to provide the Council
of Industrial Studies with an institutional niche. Such sponsorship was
invaluable; without it the council would have remained a dream. But
when all was said and done, a niche it was, not a secure academic home.

The council consisted of five faculty members appointed by Neilson.
The history department was represented by Harold U. Faulkner, who ran
for the Massachusetts state senate on the Socialist Party ticket in 1932,
and Merle E. Curti, who was about to revolutionize the field of intellectual history by exploring the social context of ideas. Both men would

come under attack for their leftist politics after World War II. From the economics department came two older and more conventional scholars: William A. Orter, who had little interest in the regional economic history the council meant to pursue; and Esther Lowenthal, perennial departmental chair and later dean of the faculty, who was known less for her scholarship than for her sharp tongue and administrative clout.[62] Dorothy Douglas, the council's fifth and most junior member, had both the strongest commitment to the enterprise and the least institutional power.

Under Lowenthal's leadership, these scholars discussed research strategies, approved candidates for fellowships, and supervised Katharine's work. Katharine, however, "labored under the impression that they trusted my judgment and did not wish me to come to them on matters of detail," and she shaped the council's agenda more or less as she saw fit.[63] Dorothy told Neilson that there was "nothing I should hate more than to find myself in the position of having to interpret or mediate in any way between the other members of the Council and the Research Director," but if friction arose she could hardly avoid the appearance of doing just that. Complicating the situation was the sometimes strained relationship between Dorothy and Esther Lowenthal, whom Neilson consulted on all matters pertaining to the council. As chair of Dorothy's department, Lowenthal ruled on her candidacy for tenure and promotion. Lowenthal had opposed the department's decision to promote Dorothy from an instructor to an assistant professor when she returned to Smith in the fall of 1930, faulting her for her teaching, because (as Dorothy complained to Neilson at the time) she could not very well fault her research.[64]

Muddying the waters further was the open secret of the council's behind-the-scenes financial backing. Officially, it was funded by an "unknown donor" or, as Katharine described it, "a special grant to the college," but at least one research fellow speculated that Dorothy "put up the money to make a place for Katharine." Some members of the faculty must have seen the situation in that light as well. Although the academy at the time was rife with patronage, and it was not unusual for women philanthropists to give through their personal networks and form relationships with the recipients, Dorothy's funding underscored Katharine's lowly and possibly suspect place in the strict hierarchy of the college.[65]

Then there were the college's trustees to consider. How would these wealthy bankers, lawyers, and businessmen, some of whom made their fortunes in the Connecticut River Valley, view the local economic histories the council would produce? More immediately, would they endorse a project aimed at supporting the research of women students who were not necessarily Smith graduates and unlikely to be what one dean called the "sleek daughters of old families, 'the race horse types' . . . in the Smith College tradition"? For the moment, the trustees followed Neilson's lead, as they usually did. With his encouragement, they began appropriating additional funds for the Council of Industrial Studies in 1936. "It is splendid that they have taken hold this way," Dorothy wrote. Yet the whole structure remained rickety since the trustees funded the council only on a year-to-year, hand-to-mouth basis and only at Neilson's behest. Even if Neilson proved willing and able to protect the council, its ambitions could easily outstrip its meager finances, setting it up for failure no matter how hard or creatively Katharine and the research fellows might work. Still, the council was up and running, giving Katharine a good deal of autonomy and an unusual opportunity to pursue innovative research on a potentially large scale.[66] Once the experiment proved itself, she hoped, stable funding and a more secure position would follow.

Katharine launched the project with "a survey of the economic development of the Valley so that future studies might be planned in the light of facts about the region" and then plunged into a search for untapped primary sources. This was her first immersion in the pleasures of local historical research. As a child, she had been saturated in public memory through the rites and rituals of the Lost Cause. In college and graduate school, she had glimpsed a more critical way of understanding the past. Yet like many reform-minded women, she had gravitated not to history—which she had always loved—but to the policy-oriented social sciences, both because they were more welcoming to women and because they promised an understanding of social structures that would help her to get "the world's work done."[67]

Now she found herself relishing a new kind of intellectual adventure. She rejoiced at finding early railroad records stashed in company basements and stumbling across the "Olive Leaf and Factory Girls' Repository," written by the Yankee farmers' daughters who were the region's first textile workers. She unearthed a hitherto unpublished letter from John Brown, the radical abolitionist whose daring attempt to foment a slave insurrection in Northern Virginia hastened the coming of the Civil War. Captivated by these tokens of past lives, she also pursued sources that reflected the voices of ordinary people: oral histories and first-person narratives, which had long been the stock-in-trade of amateur historians, especially of the many women who served as custodians of the local past but whom professional scholars usually ignored or disparaged. Aspiring to what was then belittled as "popular history" but would later be celebrated as "public history," she planned to enlist the valley's inhabitants in the preservation not only of business papers, town records, newspapers, diaries, and letters, but also of the recollections of older residents who had their own invaluable stories to tell.[68]

At the same time, Katharine searched for the outstanding female graduate students on whom the success of the council depended. Much as she had in the YWCA, she intended to raise up a cohort of younger women who could carry on her innovative approach. While there was no dearth of eager and qualified candidates, she had to scramble to find promising women who were ready, willing, and able to launch dissertations focused on the industries and workers of the Connecticut Valley, each of which would yield a publishable book and, at the same time, contribute to the larger whole. Hurriedly arrived at, her first two appointments proved disappointing. In one case, Katharine had to completely reorganize and revise the student's manuscript before it could be published. In the other, the student went the way of increasing numbers of college graduates in the 1930s: she completed her fieldwork and then married, abandoning both the project and her plans for a professional career. To avoid any hint of failure, Katharine stepped in and wrote the book herself.[69]

Shutdowns in the Connecticut Valley: A Study of Worker Displacement in the Small Industrial Community (1934) revolved around the same phenomenon with which Grace had grappled in *To Make My Bread* two years before: the wrenching transformation of the textile industry as New England manufacturers fled southward, in part because northern workers enjoyed a modicum of trade union protection and commanded marginally higher wages than the desperate, displaced, and unorganized farmers of the South.[70] Between 1923 and 1933, 40 percent of New England's textile factories closed, half of the region's 190,000 workers lost their jobs, and their fragile unions were crushed. "The expansion of the textile industry in the South left New England behind completely,"

Katharine observed.[71] As northern communities crumbled around empty mills, southern workers endured the merciless speedups that sparked the Gastonia strike.

By pinpointing the reasons behind the shutdowns of specific western Massachusetts mills, Katharine hoped to explore the links between the world she had left behind and the one in which she was now trying to make her way. In the end, however, *Shutdowns in the Connecticut Valley* was a rushed and narrow effort. It could not explain why particular businesses abandoned New England, in part because executives refused requests for interviews and were careful to leave no paper trail.[72] Katharine's book, however, did raise the critical point that plant closings in the midst of the Great Depression posed "problems of unemployment and general welfare which no municipalities can be expected to solve in and of themselves." And she took the opportunity to argue that the country's localistic relief system, based as it was on an ideal of rugged individualism that blamed the poor for their plight, was inadequate to a "modern, industrial urban civilization" and had broken down completely under the weight of large-scale unemployment. The solution, she believed, was a comprehensive federal safety net that would provide a "maximum of economic security for all."[73] But she did no more than gesture toward that solution. Mostly she simply documented the devastation, burying her political passions under cumbersome scholarly prose, even as a more engaged, critical voice kept trying to break through.

A more penetrating study was not long in coming, and it became a classic in its field. Its author was the council's third research fellow, Vera Shlakman, who stayed from 1933 until 1937, helping Katharine with plans and reports, teaching part-time in the economics department, and going for long walks with Dorothy in the snow. The task Katharine set for Shlakman was a study of Chicopee, a factory town that was especially hard hit by runaway textile mills. Shlakman faced the same company secrecy that had stymied *Shutdowns*, but she proved to be unusually intrepid and resourceful. She mined a rich vein of business papers newly available at the Harvard School of Business's Baker Library. Then, having completed six chapters of her manuscript, she encountered what might have been an insuperable barrier—the sudden decision of the Dwight Manufacturing Company to bar her from using its papers. Banging on the door of the mill owner's elegant house on Boston's Beacon Hill, Shlakman convinced him to relent, providing that she disguise the exact provenance of her data. From him, she also got an eye-opening, impromptu interview about the uses of religion in maintaining a docile labor force. He recommended the Book of Job as instructive reading for workers and stressed that millhands should have "empty heads and full stomachs," the problem being that one "can't always keep their stomachs full."[74]

Published in 1935, *Economic History of a Factory Town* was a landmark in the turn toward new forms of social and cultural history in the interwar years. It advanced scholarship in three key ways, each of which was inflected by the class consciousness of the Depression era and foreshadowed the community-oriented labor history of the 1960s and 1970s. First, like the council itself, it used what later came to be called "micro-histories" to illuminate large-scale developments. Second, it offered a penetrating critique of capitalism. Third, it put working women at the center of American history, as wage-earners, family members, and participants in protest movements.[75]

In all of these ways, Shlakman demolished a cherished view of New England history in which native-born mill girls happily wove and spun under the watchful eye of benevolent owners who were models of Yankee ingenuity and efficiency. In place of this myth of a golden age, she suggested that, both early and late, the logic of capitalism drove labor policies. Faced with independent farm families reluctant to send their daughters to the mills, the founding generation of mill owners promised to safeguard manners and morals and to drive workers only so hard. Once the mills could draw on an endless supply of immigrant labor, they were freed from such constraints. Concerned with the agency of ordinary people as well as the actions of the powerful, Shlakman uncovered voluminous evidence of how both the legendary Yankee mill girls and the immigrant families who took their place struggled for better wages and shorter hours and to establish labor unions in the wake of strikes.[76]

For all her accomplishments, Shlakman never found a firm berth in the historical profession, nor did she publish another book. In 1938 she secured a job at Queens College in New York City, where she taught Herbert Gutman and Alfred Young, two of the founding members of the "new" labor history that emerged in the 1960s and 1970s. Assuming the vice presidency of the New York Teachers Union just as the full force of McCarthyism bore down on the nation's educational institutions, she was called before the first congressional investigating committee devoted entirely to driving alleged Communists out of the schools. When she refused to discuss matters of opinion and association, she was dismissed by the college. Years later, she found her way back into the academy as a professor of social work.[77]

Most of the council's other research fellows produced less distinguished work, but as a community of scholars they offered a model of collaborative interdisciplinary scholarship to which the social and labor historians of the 1960s and 1970s could look for inspiration. They extended the boundaries of labor history far beyond those set by the John R. Commons tradition in which Katharine had been trained. Limiting themselves to institutional studies of unions and industries, Commons and his disciples had ignored women and said little about what the labor historian Herbert Gutman would later call workers' "self-experience." For Commons, the chief theme of labor history was American exceptionalism: the characteristics that supposedly softened class conflict, eliminated the need for a European-style labor party, and made the conservative American Federation of Labor the chief voice of the working man. The working class, in this schema, was figured as the skilled male worker who was concerned mainly with bread-and-butter issues and fiercely dedicated to earning a wage that would allow him to keep his wife at home.[78]

Katharine and the most insightful of the women she mentored took a darker and more comprehensive view. Combining rigorous research with a conviction that history must speak to the writer's own times, they produced a body of scholarship grounded in the same concern for working women and the human costs of unfettered capitalism that inspired their political work. Radical novelists and documentary writers left a strong mark on the history and memory of America between the wars. Less dramatic and less noticed, but no less significant, was the reorientation of knowledge represented by the Council of Industrial Studies and elaborated in Katharine's and Dorothy's later work.

"HEARTBREAKING GAPS"

————

THROUGHOUT THE EARLY 1930S, KATHARINE AND DOROTHY had been preoccupied with the issue of economic security, which they and many others saw as the central problem of their times. Virtually alone among modern industrialized countries, the United States had entered the Depression with no national system for replacing the lost wages of unemployed workers and providing for the elderly, who, in the words of historian David Kennedy, simply "worked until they dropped or were fired, then threw themselves either on the mercy of their families or on the decidedly less tender mercies of a local welfare agency."[1] But as the economy spiraled into freefall, public opinion in favor of federal action soared. When, in the fall of 1934, Franklin Roosevelt and his advisors finally began formulating a Social Security program mandating old-age pensions and unemployment insurance, Katharine and Dorothy joined a national alliance between liberals and radicals, professional and industrial workers, determined to influence the result.

They were driven both by the unprecedented opportunities of the moment and by their conviction that the administration's approach was deeply flawed. Bowing to pressure from southern states-rights advocates and northern business interests, those among the bill's framers who wanted a universal and comprehensive safety net put aside their hopes, scrapped proposals for a national health service, and settled instead for a system that would exclude many of the country's most powerless workers, depend on a regressive tax on workers' wages, allow state legislatures to determine unemployment benefits, and leave Americans to rely on a private, job-based system of health insurance and supplemental pensions.[2]

Writing for *Social Work Today* in the fall of 1934, Katharine Lumpkin offered a radical alternative. Setting aside the minor differences in unemployment insurance plans then being debated by liberal economists and social policy experts—all of whom were white, and the most influential of whom were men—she highlighted the demands that were being "raised passionately in union halls, on the picket lines, and at demonstrations of the unemployed." At stake was a choice between what Dorothy called the "pussyfooting measures" proposed by dueling experts and incorporated in the administration's complicated, omnibus Social Security Act and "a straight workers' measure . . . framed by workers themselves" called the Workers' Unemployment and Social Security Bill.[3]

The outline of this bill had been put forward initially by the Communist-influenced unemployed councils that staged sit-ins at relief agencies, resisted evictions, and organized hunger marches in cities during the early years of the Depression. But it was Mary van Kleeck, a leading member of the left feminist network with which Katharine and Dorothy identified, who wrote the version of the legislation that was introduced in Congress in 1934. Although a decade or so older than Katharine Lumpkin and Dorothy Douglas, van Kleeck epitomized the radical intellectual activism to which they aspired. A Smith College graduate, YWCA leader, and pioneering advocate of minimum wage and maximum hours protections for women workers, van Kleeck served for over forty years as director of industrial research for the Russell Sage Foundation. By the 1930s, this regal elder stateswoman of the Progressive era women's movement had become the preeminent leader of the left wing of American social work and a bold advocate of national and international economic planning, collective ownership of industry, and pan-African liberation struggles. In 1932 she was among the many reformers who traveled to the Soviet Union and was inspired by what she saw.[4] Van Kleeck, Douglas wrote admiringly, was one of those rare leaders who played "a role in an historical process" and, at the same time, could "give a clear picture of the issues at hand." Unlike other reformers "with backgrounds of ease and security," she refused to compromise her principles "when the immediate needs of labor were involved."[5]

When the Workers' Bill campaign began, Dorothy Douglas was working closely with van Kleeck on a controversy that touched on two of her deepest concerns: academic freedom and workers' rights. Ongoing tensions regarding the Summer School for Women Workers at Bryn Mawr College, Douglas's alma mater, had culminated in a conflict over the hiring of Marxist professors and the decision of faculty members and students to serve as observers at a migrant farmworkers' strike at nearby Seabrook Farms, one of the many exploitative, factorylike enterprises that had come to dominate agriculture on the nation's East and West Coasts.[6] The college's trustees voted to oust the workers' school, and its founding president, M. Carey Thomas, supported the decision. The New York alumnae association fought back by asking Douglas and van Kleeck to chair an investigative committee that included Mary Beard, John Dewey, and other luminaries. The committee forcefully defended the summer school against charges that it had abandoned the ideal of objective teaching and accused the trustees of violating the principles of academic freedom. Disseminating its findings to the press, the committee helped to pressure Bryn Mawr into reversing its decision, although ongoing differences soon led the school to sever its ties to the college.[7]

In the midst of this conflict, van Kleeck founded the Interprofessional Association to lobby for the Workers' Bill. Premised on the "mutuality of interest between the industrial, white collar, and professional workers" envisioned by the *Culture and the Crisis* manifesto of 1932, the association rejected two key aspects of middle-class reform: the assumption that women's groups should focus on the special needs of women and children while male experts formulated social security policy and the notion that elites should design social policy *for* the working class. Instead, it promoted "united action" between professional and industrial workers in behalf of social democratic welfare measures.[8]

Headed by van Kleeck, with social workers, teachers, and social researchers as its most active members, the association included men but was led by women. Katharine Lumpkin served on the group's national council. Dorothy Douglas joined its executive committee. Speaking to trade unionists and women's groups in that capacity, she emphasized that hope for the bill's passage lay primarily in the "mass pressure" that blue-collar workers could exert. Yet professionals also faced the perils of economic insecurity, and they were "well placed to add their voice to the demand for such a bill." Drawing on their special expertise and "their contacts with clients themselves," social workers, she argued, could play an especially effective role.[9]

Introduced in the House of Representatives by Ernest Lundeen, a Farmer–Labor Party representative from Minnesota, the Workers' Bill was all of two pages long, but its principles were clear and its implications were profound. Assuming that periodic unemployment was endemic to capitalism, it called, in the name both of justice and of economic stability, for a socially guaranteed floor beneath which workers' incomes were not allowed to fall. To provide that floor, it mandated compensation equal to average local wages for all full- or part-time workers who were unemployed through no fault of their own, whether for structural economic reasons or because of illness, accident, old age, or maternity. The bill included all occupations, specifically barred discrimination on the basis of race or sex, and provided income sufficient to maintain a decent standard of living throughout the entire period of unemployment. It placed administrative control in bodies elected by workers' and farmers' organizations, not in the hands of employers and government officials.[10] Costs would be borne by society as a whole, with funds raised through general taxation supplemented by a progressive tax on inheritance, gifts, and incomes over $5,000. That redistributive funding provision, as Dorothy Douglas emphasized, shifted the burden to people like herself—"the owners of concentrated wealth whom the Federal government alone can effectively reach"—and so had the effect of lessening the gap between rich and poor.[11]

The Communist Party played a catalytic role in the Workers' Bill campaign, which both reflected and forwarded its increasing influence in American life. That influence intensified in 1935, when the Communist International (Comintern) gave its official imprimatur to the direction in which American Communists were already moving by ordering its national affiliates to abandon autonomous revolutionary unions and attacks on socialists and liberals in favor of antifascist coalitions. The Comintern's decision officially freed the party to join forces with liberals, socialists, and independent radicals who embraced New Deal reforms but sought to push beyond them in order to transform capitalism at its core. The party's membership expanded accordingly, transforming a beleaguered sect into a vigorous, although by no means dominant, member of broad black-left-liberal "Popular Front" coalitions.

Grassroots unionists of various political persuasions served as the backbone of the campaign, especially the dissidents who were in the process of forming the militant Congress of Industrial Organizations (CIO) and launching a massive effort to organize the unorganized along industrial rather than craft lines.[12] The bill also won the endorsement of more than seventy municipal governments, a long list of fraternal and veterans' societies, the Socialist Party, and the National Urban League, a black-led interracial organization focused on combating employment discrimination. Petitions bearing over a million signatures flooded Congress. Just as significant were the countless individual pleas that poured into Representative Lundeen's office. Joining what Mary van Kleeck rightly characterized as a "widespread people's movement" were the radical social workers and other professionals represented by the Inter-professional Association, as well as the Midwestern Farmer–Labor Party members represented by Congressman Lundeen. When the *New York Post* conducted a poll in the spring of 1935, it found that 83 percent of its readers preferred the Workers' Bill over any of the other options, with only one in one hundred respondents favoring the administration's plan.[13]

Conspicuous by their absence from this coalition were the female Progressive reformers-turned-policy-makers who now wielded influence in Washington through the US Women's and Children's Bureaus and the Women's Division of the Democratic Party. To be sure, the women who founded and ran the Children's Bureau *did* try to influence the administration's plan: they put forward an ambitious proposal for federally funded pensions for mothers with dependent children, with funding to be equalized between rich and poor states and counties, only to see it pushed aside at the last minute in favor of a public assistance program that provided a bare subsistence, required ongoing proof of poverty, relied on matching funds from the states, and eschewed any effort at equalization. Having lost everything they had fought for, Children's Bureau leaders sought to maintain administrative control over the mother's pension program in the hope that, in their hands, it could be gradually improved. In a losing effort to achieve that goal, they sought to cultivate allies in the administration by endorsing the Social Security Act, warts and all.[14]

Late twentieth-century feminist scholars have called attention to this network of female New Dealers, celebrating its accomplishments and revising the earlier picture of the New Deal as the exclusive province "of bright young men." But they also fault these women for placing so much emphasis on protective legislation for women and focusing so intently on child welfare while men made the critical decisions regarding health care, unemployment insurance, and old-age pensions. They tend to characterize these reformers as maternalists whose strategies were guided by two beliefs: that women's public authority rested on the special moral sensibilities cultivated in the domestic sphere, and that, ideally, working-class men should earn a "family wage" sufficient to support dependent wives and children in the home.[15]

Yet, as the efforts of Katharine, Dorothy, Mary van Kleeck, and their allies suggest, the members of the New Deal women's network did not speak with one voice, and "maternalism" did not encompass their diverse concerns. Indeed, focusing too tightly on these older luminaries obscures a larger world of left feminist action and thought. The National Consumers League, for example, was very much a Progressive era organization, but leaders such as Lucy Randolph Mason, who for the first time focused the organization's efforts on the South, did not see protective labor legislation for women as a buttress to the male breadwinner ideal. They saw it instead both as a necessity in the light of employed women's lack of bargaining power and as an "entering wedge" for the creation of a racially egalitarian, social democratic state.[16]

Departing even further from the stance of older, "maternalist" reformers was a younger cadre of well-educated and underemployed women who flooded into administrative positions as federal programs expanded in the mid-1930s and 1940s. Attuned to questions of racial and gender equity as well as to economic concerns, they sought to push the New Deal in a social democratic direction.[17] Veterans of the student movements of the 1920s and 1930s who were committed to the politics of the Popular Front, these women foregrounded class issues but insisted on racial justice and women's emancipation as well.[18]

Katharine's friend and coworker Frances Williams was one of the few black women who managed to gain one of these sought-after positions and, with it, opportunities commensurate with her talents and ambitions. The southern women's network, combined with her links to the NAACP and the Joint Committee on National Recovery, helped her make that move. Betty Webb in particular played a critical role in paving Williams's way to the nation's capital, and the two women often shared a flat when Webb was in town during these exciting years. As the daughter of a US congressman, Webb had spent much of her youth in Washington, and her name could still open doors in the city. Just as important, during her years as chair of the YWCA's southern student council and then as national student secretary for the South, she had won the respect and friendship of newly influential reform-minded women. Among them was Harriet Elliott, who, as a history professor and dean of women, helped to make the North Carolina College for Women in Greensboro one of the South's most progressive educational institutions. In recognition of Elliott's years of service to the women's division of the National Democratic Committee and other national women's organizations, Franklin Roosevelt appointed her deputy director of the Office of Price Administration (OPA), where she was charged with rationing scarce goods and protecting consumers from runaway prices during and after World War II. "Betty Webb told Elliott, 'You ought to get Frances Williams,'" which she promptly did when she took office in 1940.[19]

In alliance with the pioneering social and cultural historian Caroline Ware in the OPA's Consumer Division, Williams used her position to ensure that blacks comprised 14 percent of OPA's staff at a time when they made up less than 1 percent of employees in other federal agencies. In 1943 Williams became race relations advisor to the new OPA head, Chester Bowles. Building on what the YWCA called the "group approach to modern problems" and the democratic possibilities it entailed, she worked tirelessly and successfully to democratize the agency's administration in local communities and make its local boards accessible to African Americans.[20] She also took it upon herself to remedy her boss's ignorance about the South, summarizing books on the region, hosting dinner parties to introduce him to progressive white southern women as well as to black leaders of both sexes, and stressing a point that had pervaded her thinking and writing for the YWCA: that racial discrimination and segregation were national problems and had to be addressed in every community the OPA served.[21]

Katharine Lumpkin and Dorothy Douglas shared many of the core values both of the older Progressive era women's network and of younger government staffers like Frances Williams who inhabited Washington's "feminist left-liberal scene." Lumpkin's YWCA activism and her research on delinquent girls and working-class families, Douglas's advocacy of minimum wage regulations for women workers, and their fieldwork on child labor—all of these interests linked them firmly to the female reform tradition that put women and children at the center of its concerns. Far from viewing this focus on women and children as a fundamental flaw, they continued to see it as the National Consumers' League did: as a practical necessity and an entering wedge for more inclusive reforms. Unlike the older women's network but like their younger counterparts in government, however, they gravitated toward mixed-sex alliances and strategies, even as they maintained ties to female networks and organizations, advocated for women in leadership positions, and took it as a given that women should enjoy the same rights and opportunities as men.[22]

Where Katharine and Dorothy differed most sharply from these two Washington networks, as well as from male policy makers, was in their position as independent intellectuals, their relative freedom from political constraints, and their faith in the ability of mass movements to influence the New Deal from below. They enjoyed no personal influence within government agencies; they lacked the prestige and access of male economists and policy experts. But they saw themselves as experts nonetheless. Warrant for their authority came not from a claim to female moral superiority but from their hard-won credentials as social scientists, their refusal to draw a sharp line between objectivity and advocacy, and their belief that teachers and social researchers like themselves had the right and responsibility to play a special role in a struggle that united white-collar and blue-collar workers.

To Lumpkin and Douglas in 1935, the chief problem with Washington insiders, male and female, was that they were too willing to bargain away "the rights of the great common people . . . for a little dib-dab." The militancy of farmers and industrial workers and the swell of public sentiment in behalf of federal action had transformed the political landscape, raising the possibility of previously unimaginable coalitions and reforms. Yet most members of the older Progressive era women's network proceeded cautiously. Instead of allying themselves with the forces that would make the 1930s the "age of the CIO," they continued to rely on middle-class women's organizations as a base from which to practice the art of compromise within a male-dominated policy apparatus. Much as they regretted the limitations and exclusions of the Social Security Act, they accepted the measure as what Dorothy Douglas termed "half a loaf." Taking the same stance they adopted toward protective labor legislation for women and children, they hoped that it could be expanded over time.[23]

Invited to testify before a subcommittee of the House Committee on Labor, which took up the Worker's Bill in February 1935, Dorothy Douglas argued adamantly that, unlike protective labor legislation, the Social Security Act was "not half a loaf, but 'stones in place of bread.'" "The whole principle of the thing is one which it seems to me should be shown up for what it is, namely, not a support, not an entering wedge for increased standards of living for labor, but on the contrary what I call a 'dike' to prevent the labor forces from securing that to which they are entitled." In Douglas's view, male insiders, women reformers, and even young leftists in government "continually sacrificed their opportunities by being ready to compromise, which amounted to being ready to be licked before they began to fight."[24]

ON MARCH 8, 1935, a month after Dorothy Douglas testified before Congress, the House Committee on Labor voted unanimously in favor of the Workers' Bill and reported it to the floor. The powerful Rules Committee responded by killing the measure. Congressmen Lundeen then tried to attach it to the Social Security Act, but House leaders refused to open the floor to discussion. Without the benefit of debate, the Workers' Bill garnered only fifty-two votes. The Social Security Act passed both houses of Congress and was signed into law on August 14, 1935, in no small part because conservative opponents saw the Roosevelt administration's proposal as infinitely preferable to the dreaded Workers' Bill and other popular options.[25]

This landmark measure still stands as the foundation of the American welfare state. Yet to those who hoped for a more robust, inclusive safety net, it was, as the historian William E. Leuchtenburg put it, "an astonishingly inept and conservative piece of legislation." The Social Security Act mandated merely that the federal government pressure the states to enact unemployment insurance laws, setting no minimums, preventing benefits from being portable, and allowing those benefits to vary wildly from state to state. Old-age pensions at least had the merit of being federally administered, but, by varying according to how much the worker had earned, they perpetuated inequalities between men and women, whites and blacks, the high-wage North and the low-wage South. Like private insurance, both programs were funded by so-called contributions, but those contributions were in fact regressive taxes on workers' wages, supplemented by payroll taxes on employers, who would inevitably pass the costs on to consumers so that workers paid twice, first at work and then at the store. Eliminated from consideration early on, healthcare coverage remained in the hands of private employers, creating a precedent that would set the United States apart from other industrialized nations and endure into the twenty-first century.[26]

Compounding these flaws was the fact that the Social Security Act denied coverage to the country's most insecure workers. Agriculture and domestic service, which employed more than half of the nation's African American workers and the vast majority of blacks in the South, were categorically excluded, in part because of the choke hold of white southern conservatives in Congress and in part because of habits of mind among liberals that figured blacks and women as subordinates rather than citizens. Also cast to the side were part-time workers and employees of small businesses, public schools, and charitable organizations, shutting out teachers, social workers, and most other wage-earning women.

Almost as an afterthought, the Social Security Act did include one program designed especially for women. Replacing the plan for federally funded pensions for mothers with dependent children, "Aid to Dependent Children" (later "Aid to Families with Dependent Children") was most often simply called "welfare." Modeled on the dole, welfare was miserly and means-tested: recipients had to prove they were poor enough to qualify and submit to surveillance of their private lives.[27]

The result was a hierarchical, two-channel welfare state. Welfare, which came to be seen as a form of dependence on the government, was the inferior channel. Unemployment insurance and old-age pensions, which primarily served white men, belonged to the superior channel. They were regarded as benefits secured by workers' contributions, although these payments were actually taxes in disguise. These "contributory" programs came closest to providing what Douglas aptly described as "definite, regular cash income in lieu of wages, received without questionings and evasions."[28]

This gendered and racialized safety net reinforced four pernicious assumptions. It suggested, first, that most women were and should be dependent wives and mothers; second, that most men could earn enough to keep their wives at home and could be counted on to use any government provisions they received for the benefit of their wives and children; and third, that birth control, child care, and good jobs for women were peripheral to the quest for working-class security. Finally, by tying contributory programs to full-time wage earning, the US system reinforced the belief that motherhood was not socially productive work and so did not entitle women to the same "automatic, businesslike" benefits that wage-earning work entailed.

The Social Security Act represented a historic departure in a nation devoted to rugged individualism, small government, and states' rights. Moreover, the unionists, reformers, and leftist government officials who supported the Act despite its limitations had good reason to believe in its transformative potential, and they pushed hard to expand its provisions. By the 1970s, agricultural and domestic workers had won access to old-age pensions, New Dealer Lyndon B. Johnson's "Great Society" had added Medicare and Medicaid to the modest platform erected in 1935, and many Americans enjoyed a measure of protection "against the hazards and vicissitudes of life" far beyond anything that pre–New Deal generations could have imagined.[29]

Still, the inequities built into America's welfare system had far-reaching consequences. Once established, a fragmented, public-private, contributory model became sacrosanct, enshrining in public sentiment the assumption that a modicum of economic security was not a right but a privilege earned through certain kinds of paid work, deepening the stigmatization of welfare and extending the cumulative impact of what amounted to "affirmative action" for white men.[30] The result, as Lumpkin, Douglas, and their colleagues predicted, is a safety net that falls far short of eliminating poverty, stabilizing the economy, and providing economic security for all.

THROUGHOUT THE SOCIAL security campaign, Katharine Lumpkin and Dorothy Douglas were hard at work on a study of what they viewed as the country's most vulnerable workers: the children who toiled on the South's plantations and in its textile mills, followed the East and West Coast migrant streams, and labored in occupations such as industrial homework and domestic service in the nation's cities. They conceived of *Child Workers in America* as an effort to mobilize public opinion behind ratification of the Child Labor Amendment and then to use this "enabling act" to press for "ultimate solutions": federal measures that would not only prohibit employers from exploiting children but would also help to end the poverty and insecurity that forced parents to send their children to work.[31]

To achieve that goal, Lumpkin and Douglas had to break through a wall of indifference by puncturing the myth that state laws, technological progress, and new attitudes toward childhood had already rendered child labor obsolete. They sought to do so in two complementary ways. Drawing on their training in the social sciences, they marshaled reams of data demonstrating that children were in fact engaged in hard and unrewarding labor "all over the United States today." Taking up the tools of documentary expression—a chief means by which contemporary readers sought to apprehend the cataclysm they were living through and the source of our most indelible images of the Great Depression—they also fashioned portraits of individual children designed to make knowledge touch the heart, thereby moving readers to empathy, anger, and action.[32]

Throughout the book—which was published in 1937 by Robert M. McBride and Company, which specialized in popular history and biography, and reprinted the next year by the International Publishers, a Marxist press—the two women spoke in the first-person plural from a perspective that, because it was unspecified, was seen by readers as northern and white.[33] But it was Lumpkin's experience they meant. *She* had applied to the Social Science Research Council for funding for the project; *she* was listed as lead author; and it was *her* family's ill-fated sojourn in South Carolina's Sand Hills that lay at the emotional heart of the book.[34] Her white playmates from nearby farms, so silent, pale, and still; the black field hands and their children, who "came and went as strangers"; the four-month school session, scheduled around planting and harvest time; her brief taste of how it felt to follow a plow or drag a cotton sack beneath a merciless summer sun—these were the experiences *Child Workers* invoked to counter the pastoral myths and racial blinders that led to the "popular, propaganda-induced impression" that child labor was a thing of the past.[35]

Beginning in the late nineteenth century, women reformers had campaigned for state laws making school attendance compulsory and regulating child labor. Sporadically enforced everywhere and notoriously weak in the South, this patchwork of state laws was clearly ineffective, so child protection advocates turned to federal legislation. Passed in 1916 and 1919, these laws went the way of other attempts to raise Ameri-

can labor standards on the basis of Congress's power to regulate interstate commerce: they were struck down by a Supreme Court devoted
to states' rights and determined to prevent government interference in
the relations between employers and employees. To bypass that obstacle,
reformers proposed a Child Labor Amendment affirming Congress's
power "to limit, regulate, and prohibit the labor of persons under eighteen years of age" whether or not their occupations were involved in
interstate commerce. The amendment sailed through Congress in 1924,
in part because of changing attitudes toward childhood. The concept of
the "useful" child who was expected to contribute to the family economy had gradually given way to that of the child who was "economically
worthless, indeed extremely costly, to its parents, yet considered emotionally priceless."[36] Yet the struggle for ratification languished in the
late 1920s along with the waning of Progressive reform.

Interest in the issue revived with the Depression, spurred on, as Katharine Lumpkin put it, by the "absurdity" of permitting child labor when
millions of adults were out of work. In 1933 FDR endorsed the Child
Labor Amendment, urged on by Eleanor Roosevelt and other prominent
women reformers. Public opinion polls showed that a majority of Americans in both the North and South favored federal regulation.[37]

Drawing on a mountain of previous studies, reports, and exposés,
Lumpkin and Douglas surveyed this history and ranged over every
aspect of the current problem. They sometimes buried their most telling observations in a mass of details, but two things made their long,
dense book compelling. The first was their use of graphic case studies
"drawn directly from life." The second was their determination to depart
from the focus of previous reformers and investigators on urban occupations by riveting public attention on the nation's truly forgotten children: the Mexican migrant laborers who followed the harvests on what
Carey McWilliams would famously call "factory farms" and the African American tenants and sharecroppers of the cotton-growing South.[38]
Denied all but the most rudimentary schooling, coerced by poverty and
by pressure from landowners who required whole families to work in the
fields, and living under unspeakably wretched conditions, these children
constituted a large majority of the country's child workers. Coding the
priceless child as urban and white, reformers rarely gave these children
a thought. At best they relied on the exceedingly weak reed of state-
level compulsory education laws to limit the use of children as migrant

wage laborers on large commercial farms. As for tenants and sharecroppers, their children were not considered to be employees at all. Classified by the census as "unpaid family workers" on "home" farms, they were, as Douglas and Lumpkin put it, "thrown to the wolves by both friend and foe."[39]

"The middle-class public," they argued, had been lulled into embracing a "vague but pretty picture of the agricultural child worker as the big boy or girl helping father and mother on the farm a few hours during the day . . . learning varied skills, developing physical strength and stamina, living and growing in the great out-of-doors." What was wrong with this picture? "Everything," the authors replied.[40] For the *"great mass of children allegedly at work for their parents . . . are not working for their parents at all, but for the planter or other farm owner on whose farm the parent is employed."*[41]

"Meaningless general data for the country at large" masked the enormity of the problem in particular regions and for specific agricultural commodities. The vast majority of the half-million children between ten and fifteen who worked the land were the children of tenants and sharecroppers in the South, nearly all of whom labored seasonally in the fields.[42] Regional disparities were startling. In Mississippi in the early 1930s, 25 percent of all children and 34 percent of black children were at work; in New York State, less than 2 percent.[43] The southern system of land tenure imprisoned blacks and whites alike, but it bore down on blacks disproportionately. The problem of the unpaid child laborer supposedly working on the home farm "is not only a southern problem," Lumpkin and Douglas concluded. "It is a problem of the southern Negro child." "How strange it seems that so . . . important a circumstance has not been shouted from the housetops long ago!"[44]

Lumpkin and Douglas sought to do that shouting through finely drawn vignettes. "Tom is a sharecropper's child, black, in Alabama," they began. His parents and their four children work for the landowner and are collectively in debt to him. He owns the two-room cabin in which they live.

The cabin sits close to the ground, with a single layer of boards for a floor; one window, or rather window hole, in each room (no glass, a wooden shutter instead); a roof that leaks so badly that when the last baby was born, the mother said, her bed had to be moved three times; walls without paper or plaster, of course—indeed—you can see daylight through their cracks; no stove, only an open fireplace; no fence or garden outside (the landlord decrees that the cotton must be grown "up to the doorstep"); no well, because "the creek is so near"; and for an outhouse a hole in the ground with sacking on poles rigged up by the family themselves.

Tom is 12, and has been picking since he was 6 years old. "All the children pick with both hands, and by the end of the first season the lifetime rhythm of pluck, pluck, drop-in-the-bag is long since established."[45]

"What is Tom—and what are all the hundreds of thousands of his fellows in the cotton belt of the South—getting for this investment of his childhood?" Lumpkin and Douglas asked. He is

> not only burying his own childhood in this cotton patch, he is drawing in return not a dollar of pay, from year's end to year's end. The landlord's account simply chalks up so many acres cultivated against the family's debts for the coming year, and if Tom or his brothers did not work, their father would not get his farm for the next season. Tom's and his family's reward is that he continue shoeless and abominably fed, oppressed and half-illiterate from those first months in the fields when he was 6 until he shall be an old man.[46]

The muckrakers and reformers of the Progressive era had used human interest stories and photographs to arouse the sympathy of middle-class readers. But never before the Depression, as the critic Malcolm Cowley observed, had "literary events followed so closely on the flying coattails of social events."[47] By the mid-1930s, the documentary impulse was influencing writers, artists, intellectuals, and reformers across the political spectrum. Dovetailing with social realism in literature, it encouraged Grace Lumpkin and other proletarian novelists to rip their stories from the headlines and to slip freely between fiction and reportage. Other writers abandoned fiction for documentary. The Federal Writers' Project, which funded unemployed writers as part of the New Deal's Work Projects Administration, forwarded that effort. The Farm Security Administration (FSA) employed photographers to build support for its effort to save family farms. The Federal Arts Project and the Treasury Section of Fine Arts built on alternative art schools like those Esther Shemitz had attended in New York, invigorating civic culture through public art, exemplified especially by the murals that enlivened post offices and public buildings in small towns and great cities throughout the country by the end of the 1930s.

Less noticed than the documentary turn in literature and the visual and performing arts was a similar development in the social sciences, where the trend toward value-neutral quantification that marked the discipline was countered by an outpouring of writing based on eyewitness portraits or participant observation.[48] From graduate school onward, Katharine Lumpkin had relied on case studies, the stock-in-trade of female social workers and social researchers, who used them to evaluate the needs and judge the worthiness of the poor or to compile the qualitative studies in which women tended to specialize while men claimed the increasingly prestigious realm of quantitative analysis. But never before had she deployed them as she and Dorothy did now: "to get behind the barricade of statistics and tests and scientific terminology and bring their audience" "into vivid first-hand contact with child labor conditions."[49]

Throughout *Child Workers*, Katharine and Dorothy were torn between conflicting pressures and impulses: the tyranny of the scientific method, a desire to generalize about the "tangled web of economic forces" that perpetuated child labor, and a growing conviction that only particular experience could register the urgencies of the moment.[50] Like them, the scholars, reformers, and photographers associated with the Farm Security Administration focused on the plight of the rural poor, combining social science with portraits of thoughtful, hard-working, resilient farmers. But their goals differed from Katharine's and Dorothy's in significant ways.

Viewing the South's rural poor as potential yeoman farmers, the FSA hoped to restore what it saw as a lost era of small family farms. Influenced by Marxism as well as by Katharine's first-hand knowledge of the hardships of rural life, Katharine and Dorothy instead viewed agricultural laborers as a "great reservoir of underpaid labor" that employers used to impede unionization and depress labor standards nationwide. Extending to rural workers the benefits and protections won by white male industrial workers would advance racial equality, ease the disparities that made the South the poorest region in the country, and empower the whole working class. To that end, the authors argued, "We must almost begin anew" by amending the Social Security Act to bring it into line with the principles of the Workers' Bill, applying minimum wage laws to agriculture, and guaranteeing to farm workers—whose efforts at united action were roiling the country—the mighty weapon seized by industrial workers after passage of the Wagner National Labor Relations Act of 1935: the right to organize and bargain collectively with their employers. They also argued for using federal funds to equalize public education in order to end the chasms between the city and the country, the North and the South, the rich and the poor that condemned so many children to pitifully inadequate schooling and encouraged them to enter the labor force at an early age.[51]

Even then, Lumpkin and Douglas suggested, there were limits to what American-style capitalism could do. Real success in abolishing child labor and advancing child welfare depended on a "socialized economy" that only collective pressure could achieve. "We are frank to say we can see no other solution. . . . It is only as the center of gravity is changed and the great mass of the population whose children are at stake assume control of their own lives, that the simple and obvious necessities of childhood will be met."[52] For Lumpkin and Douglas, abolition was a matter of simple justice. It was also a way of mobilizing support for a vast expansion of workers' rights and protections in a racially and regionally inclusive social democratic state.

IN 1937, AS *Child Workers in America* was appearing on bookstore shelves, Kansas became the twenty-eighth state to ratify the Child Labor Amendment, raising the hopes of the bill's supporters and spurring interest in Lumpkin and Douglas's work.[53] *Child Workers in America* combined a "detailed and definitive study of child labor" with an "intensely interesting human document," the book's cover proclaimed. Readers affirmed that description. "Here is no dispassionate treatment of a sociological topic," commented the *Saturday Review of Literature*. This is no "lifeless academic text," said a writer for the Springfield (Massachusetts) *Republican*, lauding the authors for demonstrating "in the words of the child workers themselves" what going to work at a young age means. Other reviewers noted that the book was the product of "deeply held conviction as well as enormous research."[54]

A year later Congress passed the Fair Labor Standards Act (FLSA), the last major legislative accomplishment of what has been called the "Second New Deal": the turn to an activist government that began with passage of the Social Security and Wagner Acts three years earlier. The FLSA set uniform national wage and hour standards for workers involved in interstate commerce. Bitterly opposed by the National Manufacturers Association and the big growers, North and South, this measure stood as the culmination of the long fight that began with the "entering wedge" of protections for women and child workers. It also represented a triumph for those who were trying to push the New Deal to the left. In putting his weight behind the FLSA, Roosevelt aligned himself with labor and, for the first time, challenged the bloc of conservative southern Democrats in Congress whose support was so important to his legislative agenda. These erstwhile allies were furious and openly cooperated with the Republican minority to defeat the FLSA, which they rightly saw as an attempt to deprive the South of its reservoir of cheap labor. Losing that battle, they resolved not only to block any future expansion of the New Deal but also to reverse what it had achieved.[55]

The FLSA's minimum-wage provisions in themselves discouraged child labor because they applied to children and adults alike, eliminating the incentive to hire children because they were cheap. In addition, the FLSA prohibited child labor in manufacturing and mining, reinforcing public sentiment against the employment of children in industries where mechanization was already making them less and less useful. Moreover, Congress vested administration of the new law in the hands of the female-dominated Children's Bureau, bringing "a sense of relief to all who were concerned to see competent, unbiased enforcement in a spirit of public service," as Katharine Lumpkin pointed out.[56]

For all these reasons, Katharine and Dorothy saw the FLSA as "an enormous gain," and when it came under intense fire from conservatives, they used their status as independent policy intellectuals to "preserve it, at all costs."[57] As always, however, they combined defending the New Deal against the growing strength of the conservative coalition in Congress with "constructive but thoroughgoing criticism" of its limitations. In a major speech to the National Consumers League by Douglas and an article by Lumpkin, a thousand copies of which were purchased and distributed by the Children's Bureau, the two women pointed out that the FLSA suffered from the same "heartbreaking gaps" that marred other New Deal legislation. Because it was restricted to interstate commerce, it left the bulk of child workers in the cities unprotected. Most important, it exempted the "great submerged mass of rural labor," adults and children alike.[58]

Nevertheless, when the FLSA withstood Supreme Court scrutiny in 1941, the campaign to ratify the Child Labor Amendment faded, and child labor disappeared from the reform agenda.[59] Meanwhile, small farmers, sharecroppers, and laborers left the land in droves, pushed off by economic adversity and by federal policies that tried to raise commodity prices by paying large landowners to take land out of production. That displacement accelerated during and after World War II, when military mobilization and new jobs in industry pulled additional young people off the land, and the development of chemical fertilizers and insecticides combined with mechanization to bring agribusiness to the South. Displacement, moreover, was not limited to the farm workers. Factory owners reacted to one of the great successes of the second New Deal—the effort to eliminate the regional and racial disparities that made the South a reservoir of cheap labor—by hiring white men for the jobs that had once been reserved for blacks and women or eliminating those jobs altogether.[60]

The result of all these changes was the Great Migration of African Americans, along with many whites, from the rural South, one of the largest population transfers in American history. The Great Migration brought with it tremendous opportunities. But in the absence of the protections that reformers such as Lumpkin and Douglas advocated, it also created urban ghettos, and in the rural South (as well as the West) it left depleted soil, crippled institutions, and permanent, bone-grinding poverty in its wake.[61]

Like rural deprivation, child labor did not disappear with the sharecroppers' shacks. Driven by poverty and by what Dr. Kenneth B. Clark referred to in 1967 as "criminally inferior" public education systems, poor children continued to leave school early, and they continued to be employed where they remained useful, most notoriously as migrant laborers on corporate farms. The plight of farm workers reentered popular consciousness in the 1960s when CBS News aired an explosive documentary entitled "Harvest of Shame" and the Mexican American activists César Chávez and Dolores Huerta led a massive struggle for unionization and civil rights in California, Texas, and the Midwest. Inspired by the social movements of the 1960s, readers rediscovered the documentary literature of the 1930s, and, one by one, that era's studies of the migrants and sharecroppers reappeared in print.[62] In 1972 Books for Libraries Press reprinted *Child Workers in America*, which had long been forgotten. Two years after that, Congress amended the Fair Labor Standards Act to regulate child labor in agriculture for the first time.[63] As Katharine and Dorothy foresaw, the flaws in the New Deal had lasting consequences, but so too did its expansive potential.

RADICAL DREAMS, FASCIST THREATS

I N JANUARY 1936 KATHARINE AND DOROTHY RECEIVED AN irresistible invitation. The economist and consumer advocate Colston Warne was going to the Soviet Union as a guide for Open Road, a New York agency that specialized in educational travel. It would, he promised, not be "the usual Russian sight-seeing tour." Writing to Anna Rochester and her partner Grace Hutchins, Katharine passed along the exciting news: "DD and I (and she takes her two youngest) are going to S.U. this summer. Isn't that pretty grand? Sailing last of June. . . . We are all full of plans."[1]

Six months later, Katharine and Dorothy, with twelve-year-old Dorothea and nine-year-old Paul in tow, set sail from Quebec down the St. Lawrence seaway on the SS *Empress of Britain*, bound for Cherbourg and Southampton, and then on to the Soviet Union. They were traveling at the peak of American tourism to the USSR, and Colston Warne could hardly have been a more agreeable guide. Dorothy had known him since the early 1920s, when he studied under her former husband at the University of Chicago, and she and Katharine had befriended him when he fled an assault on academic freedom at the University of Pittsburgh and arrived at nearby Amherst in 1930. An independent leftist, he was a sympathetic but not starry-eyed observer of the Soviet experiment. Once they arrived in the country, guides from Intourist, the official state travel agency, were often by their side, doing what they could to monitor what the visitors heard and saw.[2] Yet what impressed Katharine was the sense of freedom and exhilaration that came from exploring a "topsy-turvy land."[3]

"When talking about the USSR, Americans were really talking about their own nation and themselves," the historian Peter Filene has observed. This is certainly true of Katharine and Dorothy who, upon their return, contributed their own observations to the stream of travel accounts that appeared between the collapse of the tsarist autocracy in 1917 and the outbreak of war in Europe in 1939. Like many of the female social workers and social scientists who wrote about the Soviet Union, they avoided discussions of the abstract political philosophies and major political events that preoccupied male journalists, ambassadors, and scholars. Instead, they focused on the implications of the "new Russia's" comprehensive social safety net for America's emerging welfare state. Asked to comment on the twentieth anniversary of the Russian Revolution by *Soviet Russia Today*, a Communist Party–affiliated publication, they drew an implicit contrast between the USSR's success and their own country's failure in abolishing "the evils of child labor even in the midst of a period of unparalleled industrial expansion and with every adult laborer in demand."[4]

Reflecting on her trip in a longer piece in the same journal, Katharine aligned herself with another body of travel writing: the narratives produced by African American men and women who made the "magic pilgrimage" to the USSR and brought back news of Soviet anti-racism, identifying Communism with racial as well as class equality in ways that profoundly shaped the consciousness of the American left.[5] As she struggled to comprehend a disorientingly different society, she found herself speaking for the first time—explicitly and in print—"as a white southerner who had spent the first thirty years of her life a participator in the inflexible and cruel caste system of the bi-racial South, growing more averse to it all the while." She had read and heard about the absence of class and race distinctions in the USSR. Would everyday life bear out that claim? Testifying to her own legacy of privilege, she confessed to having been taken aback to see "an older woman with a kerchief on her head, garbed in a plain cotton dress, unmistakably a Russian worker," check into the hotel in Leningrad where she, Dorothy, and other well-heeled foreign visitors were staying. Waiting for service at a garden dining room in Yalta, she had likewise assumed from the "buzzing attention from the head waiter and his staff" that a large party of tourists was about to arrive, only to discover that the banquet was in honor of a group of "Stakhanovites," industrial workers awarded recognition and special privileges for producing more than was expected. "We hear it said that this is a workers' country," she commented. Observing the "buoyant optimism and . . . secure status" of Russian workers, she "began to believe that it was so."[6]

Still, for her, the litmus test was race. She knew that blacks in the Soviet Union enjoyed "formal equality." But what lay beneath that façade? Veering suddenly from her impressions of Russia in the 1930s to her experiences in the southern student YWCA more than a decade before, she remembered with fresh indignation how she and her black colleagues had escaped the stigmatizing "signs and separations" of the legally segregated South only to confront prejudice, discrimination, and de facto segregation in "the capricious but equally cruel" North. Now she treasured the feeling "that there was no place that we might jointly decide to visit, nor trip we might jointly decide to take, where my Negro colleagues might not go as freely as I." Moreover, "there was a further strangeness" to this strange land. Not only were "Negroes treated not a whit differently from anyone else," but this equality of treatment extended even to "Negro wage-earners . . . because of the preeminently honorable status of the proletarian in the Soviet state." Dreaming of an almost unimaginable future in her own county, Katharine concluded, "Clearly the changed ways are no longer strange ways, but are now an integral part of the people's everyday life."[7]

WHEN KATHARINE AND Dorothy returned from Russia in September 1936, they found their friends riveted on the Spanish Civil War, which many saw as the opening salvo in a worldwide conflict between fascism and democracy. Nationalists led by General Francisco Franco had launched an effort to overthrow the democratically elected Spanish Republic by force of arms. When Germany and Japan sent aircraft to bolster Franco's forces, the United States and most western European democracies not only remained aloof but also imposed an arms embargo that made it impossible for the Spanish Republicans to defend themselves. Only the Soviet Union and Mexico came to the defense of the

Republican forces, with the Soviets supplying military personnel and Mexico offering all the money, food, and moral support it could muster. These acts of solidarity confirmed the conviction of many liberals and leftists that the Soviet Union stood as the chief stay against European fascism and that Mexico served as what Dorothy termed "our outpost of democracy on the American continent."[8]

Hulda Rees McGarvey, a Smith graduate and an instructor in the psychology department who became one of Katharine's and Dorothy's closest friends, would later describe the Spanish Civil War as "our Vietnam": a defining event for her generation, as the Vietnam War was for students in the 1960s. Katharine, Dorothy, and Hulda joined local students, faculty, and townspeople in rallying to the Spanish Republican cause. President Neilson served as honorary chairman of the Northampton Committee to Aid Spanish Democracy. Joining hands with the Smith College chapters of the American Student Union and the American Teachers Federation, the committee entertained the US volunteers who fought in Spain as members of the Abraham Lincoln Brigade and raised funds for the Republican forces.[9]

While Katharine, Dorothy, and their compatriots were engrossed in Spain, a less widely noticed crisis was unfolding in the Soviet Union. Beginning in August 1936, while they were still in the country, and culminating in 1938, Stalin precipitated a wave of trials that engulfed Russia's revolutionary leadership and swept through the ranks of the army, the trade unions, and the general public. Accused of plotting with Western governments to overthrow the socialist regime, Leon Trotsky, who had gone into exile in 1929, was sentenced to death in absentia, while the accused who remained in Russia were forced to confess to most of the charges. Over the next two years, many were executed; countless others disappeared into prison camps. Earlier evidence of the dark side of the Soviet experiment—particularly the famine of 1932–1933, a man-made catastrophe caused by Stalin's policy of confiscating grain to feed the industrial workforce and forcing peasants onto collective farms—had attracted little attention in the United States. In contrast, the conservative and then the mainstream press broadcast the news of the Moscow trials, setting off fierce debates among leftists and liberals alike.[10]

In March 1937, Katharine and Dorothy joined four hundred others in signing an "Open Letter to American Liberals" opposing denunciations of the Soviet government at a moment "when the forces of fascism, led by Hitler, threaten to engulf Europe," and "in Spain an international war, with the Fascists as the aggressors, is being waged." The US ambassador to Russia and other observers had announced that the trials were fair and the guilt of the accused had been established in court. The evidence to the contrary, the four hundred signatories argued, remained inconclusive. In any case, the only country in the world where "a planned socialist society has been established" should be permitted to work out its internal problems without foreign interference. A few months later, a Commission of Inquiry, nominally led by John Dewey, investigated these events. Made up of liberals and left-wing Trotsky supporters, it concluded that the defendants had been framed.[11]

One's stance toward these trials would take on tremendous symbolic significance in the years ahead, becoming a lodestone of political identity for a determined faction of former radicals that came to be known as the non-Communist left (or, more colloquially, as the anti-Stalinist left), many of whom had been supporters of Trotsky. Some of these men and women, while repudiating Soviet communism, maintained a critical view of American society. Others, utterly renouncing their earlier ideals, evolved into the architects of the New Right. Carrying with them the habits of mind and penchant for take-no-prisoners sectarian infighting they had acquired in their radical youth, they rose to positions of immense cultural influence after World War II. Nikita Khrushchev's revelations about Stalin in the mid-1950s, which made clear that the confessions had been extracted by threats and torture and that the trials were part of a reign of terror, reinforced the former Trotskyists' credibility and cast a shadow over those who, in the 1930s, had refused to criticize the USSR.

At the time, however, leftist critics of Russia remained a minority voice. They were seldom heard on the Smith College campus, and they were rendered even less relevant a few years later when the Soviet Union became a US ally during World War II. Throughout this period, Katharine and Dorothy, like a wide range of American observers, saw the USSR's failings as the price of rapid modernization in a despotic and backward agricultural society beleaguered by external threats. Over time, they believed, this developing country would adopt Western-style protections for political rights and civil liberties while the United States would eradicate economic inequality. Political and economic democracy would converge.[12]

TWO YEARS AFTER their Russian adventure, Katharine and Dorothy left for Mexico on a five-month pilgrimage that, like their sojourn in the Soviet Union, amplified their engagement in a global dialogue about how to remake society in the face of political and economic crisis. They arrived in August 1938, not long after President Lázaro Cárdenas had nationalized the petroleum industry, expanded workers' rights and social welfare provisions, and put teeth into the agrarian reforms of the Mexican revolution of 1910 by distributing land to Indian villages according to an *ejido* or communal system of ownership that harked back to pre-colonial times.[13] Homegrown and foreign conservatives charged Cárdenas with "lurching recklessly in the direction of Communism," but his eclectic brand of socialism, which blended popular political mobilization with a strong central state and the expropriation of oil, land, and other key resources and industries controlled in large part by foreign powers, captured the imagination of a broad spectrum of US activists, writers, and policy makers.[14] Among these were southern New Dealers, who saw in Mexico's communal system of land redistribution a model for breaking up the plantation system and addressing the plight of sharecroppers in the South. Quietly charismatic and politically astute, Cárdenas seemed, at one and the same time, to be fulfilling the thwarted promise of the Mexican Revolution and, in Dorothy's words, bringing "a 'New Deal' to Mexico" in line with but more far-reaching than FDR's.[15]

Yet dangers abounded. Would the United States resort to intimidation or military might to maintain international capitalism's access to its poorer neighbor's resources, as it had often done before, or would FDR's "Good Neighbor Policy," with its promise of nonintervention and respect for national sovereignty, prevail? Would Mexico's reactionary forces, which included an openly fascist movement, derail the Cardenistas much as, in the United States, Republicans in league with conservative southern Democrats were trying to bring the New Deal to a halt? Worse, might native and foreign reactionaries collude in overthrowing Mexico's democratic regime, turning the country into "another Spain"?[16]

Eager to see for themselves the forces at work in this fluid and fraught situation, Katharine and Dorothy planned to gather material for a scholarly study, written by Dorothy with Katharine's assistance, which would focus on labor and agrarian movements in a country throwing off "the evil heritage of its 'semi-feudal'" and "semi-colonial" past. They were accompanied by their friend Myra Page, who had recently spent two years with her husband in Russia, where she served as Moscow correspondent for the *Daily Worker* and the *Southern Worker*, the South's only Communist newspaper.[17] Having made a name for herself in radical circles with a novel on the Gastonia strike, in 1935 Page had published one of the few proletarian novels about the Soviet Union: *Moscow Yankee*, a tale of love and work in an era of revolutionary possibility. Now she hoped to follow that up with a book of interviews entitled *Mexico Speaks*.[18]

In Russia, Katharine had reveled in her ability to travel freely with black colleagues and seized every opportunity to observe daily life. Still, she and Dorothy had been "passing travelers": like most such pilgrimages, their visit had been relatively brief and circumscribed by Soviet guides. Their trip to Mexico was different. Instead of traveling in a closely watched group, the three women drove almost 3,000 miles in Dorothy's car, sharing a single room in tourist homes along the way, with Katharine and Myra sleeping on cots while Dorothy, ever committed to plain living, made do with a sleeping bag on the floor.[19]

Like other sympathetic visitors, the three women enjoyed a remarkable degree of access to members of the Cárdenas regime. For Katharine and Dorothy, that entrée came partly through the American Federation of Teachers (AFT), a prime vehicle for their state and local activism in the 1930s, and partly through Mary van Kleeck, who helped to pave the way for them to participate in a series of international conferences as soon as they arrived. The first of these was organized by the International Industrial Relations Institute, a group led by van Kleeck and her partner, Mary Fleddéus, and devoted to promoting economic planning and raising living standards throughout the world.[20] The second gathering was the founding meeting of the General Confederation of Workers of Latin America, spearheaded by Mexico's most prominent labor leader, Vicente Lombardo Toledano, an independent Marxist whom Dorothy described as a "brilliant young intellectual, a school and university teacher, who had a real genius for keeping in touch with the Mexican people." The third was an International Conference against War and Fascism.[21]

As for Myra Page, she came equipped with two letters of introduction that speak volumes about an era when "the left held the high ground on both sides of the Rio Grande" and unabashedly left-wing

Mexico, summer 1938. Myra Page is on the burro. Katharine is to her left.

writers could move with relative freedom between the labor movement, the radical press, and mainstream publishers and magazines.[22] One letter came from Henry Holt, president of the eminent New York publishing house that bears his name, and the other from Vicente Lombardo Toledano. Holt said that Page was well known, not only in the United States but also in England and the Soviet Union, "for her unbiased, accurate and observant articles." For her book "on Mexico and its people," she needed "to talk to leaders of thought and action, as well as to people in various walks of life." Holt was planning to consider the book for publication, he concluded, so please "extend her what courtesies you can."[23] Toledano stressed not Page's objectivity but her leftist credentials. Writing to the Mexican engineers and workers who had stepped in to run the oil industry when foreign experts fled the country, he vouched for Page as a "revolutionary who was recommended to us by our North American comrades."[24]

Within weeks of the women's arrival in Mexico City, Page's connections yielded results: she was invited to the National Palace and granted a two-hour interview with President Cárdenas. Sometimes accompanied by Katharine and Dorothy, she also talked with people whom she rightly saw as some of "the most outstanding figures in Mexican public life," focusing especially on those who were addressing the "predicament of women." They interviewed Anna Maria Hernandez, a high-profile labor leader and factory inspector dedicated to enforcing the rights of working women and children.[25] They also recorded the experiences of Doctor Maria Rodriquez, the chief of Mexico City's juvenile court system, and "other outstanding professional and middle class women," including Katharine Briggs, a YWCA secretary from the United States who helped to plant the organization in Mexico City and to "Mexicanize" it by cultivating indigenous leadership and establishing an atmosphere of international collaboration.[26] Although, like most North Americans in Mexico, Lumpkin, Douglas, and Page were dependent on translators for conversations with ordinary people, they also explored the countryside, "attending fiestas and village meetings, talking with Indian peons and housewives and village teachers, railroad workers and artists, engineers and workmen in the Tampico oil fields," sometimes with the guidance of Pedro Morales, a Zapata guerilla during the violent years that followed the 1910 revolution and then the leader of an agricultural union.[27]

Using their personal observations and interviews, along with press reports and a few early studies, Dorothy published a glowing yet perceptive pamphlet entitled *Mexican Labor: A Bulwark of Democracy*. "'Imperialism' is no academic term to the Mexican people," she observed, tracing many of the country's problems to foreign interests which, in league with local collaborators, treated "Mexico as a sort of colonial territory, the natural resources of which were theirs to exploit." She portrayed the Confederation of Mexican Workers, led by Lombardo Toledano with the support of an "honest, deeply humane" president, as fulfilling US leftists' hopes for what could happen with the simultaneous rise of FDR and the CIO.[28]

After three months in Mexico, Myra Page returned to the United States, but Katharine and Dorothy traveled on to Comarca Lagunera, a vast cotton-growing region in north-central Mexico that, Dorothy observed, at one time resembled "our slave-holding South."[29] There they saw for themselves the plight of the "dark-skinned" farmers whose land and labor had been appropriated by Spanish conquerors and then exploited by local landlords and absentee owners in the United States. The Mexican Communist Party had made serious inroads in the region, successfully pushing for large-scale collectivized cotton production rather than for the smallholder *ejidos* that prevailed in other regions.

Katharine and Dorothy were impressed by "the readiness on the part of the peasants for organization," which called to mind the impulse behind the sharecroppers' unions in the US South.[30]

Most of all, they identified with the unionized teachers, whose efforts reminded them of the workers' education projects they had long supported and whom they saw as an example of the kind of white-collar activism to which they aspired. Stopping at an *ejido* village "with a big school house in view," they met energetic young people, many of whom were women, who had fanned out into the countryside, seeking not only to build schools where none had been before but also to provide a "myriad of social services" and transform the peasantry into the agents of rural socialism. As Dorothy later noted, these efforts aroused the intense hostility of local officials. What she did not say and probably did not fully understand was that this experiment in socialist education also met resistance from the peasants themselves. Some sought to fend it off altogether, while others welcomed it but transformed its teachings in ways that made them more compatible with their own cultural traditions.[31]

Enthusiastic as they were, Dorothy and Katharine were by no means blind to the fragility of the Cardenismo project. Like the efforts of the Farm Security Administration in the United States to remake land tenure in favor of the poor, agrarian reform in Mexico was hated by the landlords and in constant danger of being rolled back. Like the Democratic Party in the United States, Cárdenas's National Revolutionary Party was a "faulty instrument" made up of factions that ran the political gamut, including conservatives who resembled the southern Democrats who "appeared to stomach the New Deal, although all the time they were making common cause with reactionary Republicans."[32]

"Mexico has not had a revolution," Dorothy commented, "not in the Russian sense: the officialdom of the country still comes from the same homes and universities as sheltered their fathers and sheltered them very comfortably, before the peasants and workers took partial power." "Just as with us," a burgeoning reactionary opposition was using "the cry of 'red'" to discredit democratic reforms. "How familiar a ring that has!" she exclaimed. Much depended on the United States, Dorothy and Katharine believed. If New Deal reforms were rolled back, "all the fascist trends within Mexico and across the water would take it as their cue to act with greater boldness."[33] Conversely, Mexico's "successes are a living demonstration . . . of the falsity of Fascism's most cherished lies—from the lie of racial inferiority to the lie of the rottenness and helplessness of democracy. . . . For their sake and for ours, then, the Mexican people . . . need and deserve a strengthening of the Good Neighbor policy" as well as "support and cooperation from all our labor and popular organizations."[34]

Returning to Northampton in early 1939, Katharine fired off an uncharacteristically heated letter to the editor of the *New York Times* reiterating these sentiments and applauding the expulsion from Mexico of the *Times* correspondent Frank Kluckhorn, a scathing critic of the Cárdenas administration. When the *Times* declined to publish her letter, she sent it to Secretary of State Cordell Hull, an advocate of US intervention in Mexico. Describing herself as "a social economist" who has "made it a practice to . . . know something about a question before passing judgment upon it," Katharine assured the Secretary of State that Kluckhorn's dispatches had misrepresented the Mexican situation, creating antagonisms that could lead to the resumption of US coercion and interference in Latin American affairs.[35]

KATHARINE'S UNPUBLISHED LETTER to the *New York Times* survived, as did other traces of these journeys, in the records of the FBI. The bureau's surveillance of Massachusetts intellectuals intensified in the mid-1930s in tandem with a potent, Catholic-led anticommunist campaign, which was fueled by events in Mexico, Russia, and Spain. Papal encyclicals defined Communism as the "mortal enemy of Catholicism," and Catholic leaders condemned the Mexican and Russian Revolutions and the Republican cause in Spain as anticlerical and atheistic. Bolstered by right-wing patriotic groups such as the Daughters of the American Revolution and the American Legion, this campaign helped to prevent the ratification of the child labor amendment in the 1920s by tarring it as a scheme "born and nurtured in Bolshevist Russia" and aimed at undermining the family by "establish[ing] governmental control . . . of . . . youth." From the mid-1930s through the 1950s, anticommunists battled it out with those who cherished the leftist and civil libertarian strains in Massachusetts' political culture.[36]

Katharine and Dorothy had been caught up in one of these clashes since 1935, when they and their Smith College colleagues came face to face with what would prove to be one of the chief mechanisms of

Cold War repression. At issue was a law requiring all public and private school educators—from elementary school teachers to the president of Harvard—to pledge their loyalty to the US and state constitutions, a requirement that singled teachers out for suspicion and opened the way to dismissal for the thought crime of disloyalty as evinced by statements or affiliations with organizations critical of the status quo. Taken up by powerful Irish Catholic Democratic politicians, the loyalty oath campaign sought both to purge radical teachers and to silence resistance to draconian budget cuts in education during the Great Depression.[37]

Despite vociferous objections, the loyalty oath bill passed the state legislature in the summer of 1935. Faced with threats to revoke their charters, Smith, Harvard, and other colleges and universities agreed to comply with the law while leading a campaign to repeal it. At Smith, the effort began in earnest in November, when the local branch of the American Association of University Professors unanimously adopted Dorothy Douglas's prescient resolution arguing that the state legislature's action was "dangerous in principle" and "opens wide the way for worse legislation of a more oppressive character in the future."[38]

A few months later, Dorothy helped to found the Massachusetts Society for Freedom in Teaching to spearhead the fight to repeal what many saw as a bill of the "Heil Hitler type" being "promoted by the Fascist element in America." Twelve hundred public school teachers, college professors, labor leaders, civil libertarians, and members of the League of Women Voters jammed into a legislative hearing in Boston to see Smith College president Neilson defend academic freedom and deflect accusations that he himself was "a red."[39] Deploying his signature combination of humor and reason, he "shook with laughter" when a legislator accused him of being "connected to the University of Moscow." Readily admitting his membership in the American Society for the Advancement of Cultural Relations with Russia, he explained that, while Smith College professors "discuss communism and socialism just as they discuss any other human idea," charges that they "preach communism are ridiculous." Not surprisingly, Neilson earned a place in Elizabeth Dilling's *The Red Network: A "Who's Who" and Handbook of Radicalism for Patriots* published in 1934. Here readers learned that, as his biographer put it, Smith's president "trifled with Russia, blessed sundry organizations standing for civil liberties, and indulged in . . . other 'communistic' deeds." Neilson responded to the publication of *The Red Network* with his usual insouciance: "I feel proud to have been honored with a place."[40]

In 1937 educators and their allies pushed a repeal bill through both houses of the legislature only to have it vetoed by the governor, who immediately created one of the country's first "little HUACs," a year before Congress established the notorious House Committee on Un-American Activities. Led by the right-wing southern Democratic Congressman Martin Dies, HUAC was charged with investigating both fascist and communist activities. But like its state-level counterparts, it focused almost entirely on the red menace, helping to precipitate a "little red scare" that laid the foundation for things to come.[41]

THESE ATTACKS ON academic freedom, coupled with their encounter with Mexican teachers who were on the front lines of rural reform, drew Katharine and Dorothy into a battle for the soul of the American Federation of Teachers that revolved around "united action" with blue-collar workers in a militant and capacious trade union movement. Dorothy had been involved in the AFT since the early 1930s, when it was composed mainly of female elementary school teachers and led by a Southerner after Katharine's own heart: Mary C. Barker, an Atlanta teacher who chaired the board of the Southern Summer School for Women Workers, defended the Scottsboro boys, and championed African American teachers. Under Barker's leadership, the AFT solidified its ties to organized labor and spoke out on the educational and social issues of the day. But it remained torn between defending teachers' prerogatives as professionals and bargaining for their rights as salaried workers.[42]

In the mid-1930s, an influx of young radicals of both sexes turned the union firmly in the direction of what has come to be called "social justice unionism," an expansive effort to promote the interests of teachers as workers while at the same time welcoming the membership of poorly paid substitutes and Work Projects Administration–trained adult educators; building alliances with parent and community groups; and putting the AFT in the forefront of the struggle for academic freedom and racial equality. Along with Mary Barker and other older women, Katharine, Dorothy, and their friend Hulda McGarvey supported these efforts both within their Western Massachusetts local, which grew rapidly in the mid-1930s, and at the national level.[43] Aligned against them were the conservative leaders of the American Federation of Labor, with which the AFT was affiliated, as well as much of the AFT's male old guard, most of whom were socialists and independent leftists who resisted any alliance in which Communists and their allies played influential roles.[44]

Heading the union was Jerome Davis, a YMCA veteran and a socialist whose prolabor stands had cost him his job as the Stark Professor of Practical Philanthropy at Yale Divinity School. As delegates to the AFT's 1939 convention in Buffalo, New York, Dorothy and Hulda sided with Davis in a campaign for reelection that turned in part over whether to revoke the charter of New York's Local 5, the union's largest and most radical affiliate, whose leadership included avowed Communists. On the eve of Davis's opening address, which advocated an international united front against fascism in which the Soviet Union would necessarily play a leading role, the news broke that Stalin was planning to sign a nonaggression pact with Hitler, a bombshell that strengthened the hand of the anticommunist contingent. Davis lost to George Counts, a Columbia Teachers College professor who spent the next year in a secret, single-minded campaign to oust the radicals who remained on the AFT's executive committee. Winning control of the committee at the 1940 convention, he and his allies expelled Local 5 and set the AFT on a course that stressed the ethos of professionalism rather than solidarity with organized labor.[45]

Dismayed by this conservative takeover, Katharine and Dorothy distanced themselves from the national union, but they remained active in their local. The little red scare and its attendant conflicts—the loyalty oath controversy, the struggle for control of the AFT, and the upsurge of anticommunist sentiment caused by Stalin's alliance with Hitler—tempered their hopes but failed to disillusion them or frighten them away from their Popular Front commitments, as happened with some members of the left. Moreover, this red scare subsided quickly when Germany invaded Russia in 1941 and Russia joined the Allied forces, bearing the brunt of the carnage that marked the early years of World War II.[46] Still, the teachers' loyalty oath remained on the books in Massachusetts and in many other states. HUAC and its state-level equivalents continued their investigations. And an ominous bill known as the Smith Act sailed through Congress, sponsored by a Virginia congressman who loathed the New Deal. The Smith Act made it illegal to "teach or advocate" the overthrow of the government or associate with any organization that did, thereby punishing not just violent plans and acts but the expression of political ideas.

LIKE KATHARINE AND DOROTHY, Grace was both invigorated by the political ferment of the late 1930s and caught up in the controversies precipitated by fascist threats. Although *A Sign for Cain* had not made the splash her first novel had enjoyed, it was relatively well received. Any disappointment she might have felt was surely eased when, less than a month later, *Let Freedom Ring*, Albert Bein's play based on *To Make My Bread*, opened at the Broadhurst Theater on Broadway.[47] She must have been taken aback by Bein's decision to eliminate the Bonnie McClure–Ella May character and focus instead on the McClure brothers. But she was elated when her brother Alva brought his family to New York for opening night, and she reveled in sauntering through the theater district seeing her name up in lights. Perhaps above all, given her and her husband's financial straits, she welcomed the royalties she and Bein shared. Looking back, she remembered that, with "a play on Broadway and much attention in the newspapers," those were "wonderful" years.[48] She also remembered a constant struggle to put food on the table and live up to the promise of *To Make My Bread*.

Let Freedom Ring was greeted with rapture by the left and relatively positive reviews from the mainstream press, but it met with "a divided audience" among theatergoers.[49] Closing after three and a half weeks, it was rescued by the radical Theatre Union and reopened downtown at the Civic Repertory Theatre on 14th Street, a showcase for social drama founded by the glamorous Broadway star Eva Le Gallienne and her network of lesbian friends. Margaret Larkin, who, along with Lumpkin, had brought the music of the Gastonia strikers to New York, helped to facilitate the move by persuading the Theater Union to sponsor the play.[50]

After a successful seventy-nine performance run, *Let Freedom Ring* enjoyed an afterlife that testified to how well *To Make My Bread*, which was written in the very different atmosphere of the late 1920s, resonated with the culture of the mid-1930s Popular Front. The AFL's United Textile Workers Union, an implacable enemy of the "dual union" that had sent Communist organizers to Gastonia in 1929, was so taken with the play that it sponsored a tour of New England labor halls and hotspots, including an appearance before thousands of strikers at an RCA plant in Camden, New Jersey, in 1936. A year later, the Federal Theater Project in Detroit enjoyed one of its biggest box office successes with a presentation of the play, attracting enthusiastic audiences of factory workers and university students even as the project came under attack for "subversive activities."[51]

In this fluid political milieu, Grace Lumpkin published steadily, sometimes in official CP outlets such as *The Woman Today* but also in *Social Work Today* and literary journals such as *Partisan Review*, *The Virginia Quarterly Review*, and *The North American Review*.[52] She was elected to the Executive Council of the League of American Writers, the chief conclave of Popular Front intellectuals, at a time when the league was abandoning its earlier insistence on far-left credentials and proletarian roots and assiduously courting established authors. She found herself in demand as a speaker among radical students at Columbia, where she used her appearances as a "famed proletarian writer" to raise money for the Southern Summer School. With no discernible sense of dissonance, she also appeared as guest of honor at a tea sponsored by the New York alumnae of Phi Mu, the sorority that had sent her to France during World War I.[53]

Grace's cachet in this period rested on a growing appreciation of what the renowned folklorist Benjamin A. Botkin hailed as "proletarian regionalism."[54] In the late 1920s and early 1930s, when Botkin, Lumpkin, and others were first developing their dynamic understanding of regional cultures, most left-wing literary critics saw southern writing as a mix of nostalgia and local color, qualities that were doubly suspect because of their association with what Nathaniel Hawthorne famously branded "scribbling women." Confirming the left's suspicions, the Nashville Agrarians endowed an invented, romanticized Anglo-Saxon past with positive meaning, opposing industrialization, the New Deal, and the left by holding up the rural, segregated, supposedly conflict-free South as an ideal. For all these reasons, critics on the left often used the term *regional* as a "stinging word." The Agrarians returned the favor. In an article on southern literature published in 1935, Donald Davidson, the group's most persistently reactionary member, excluded from the canon all books dealing with poor whites and blacks on the grounds that they pandered to "social programs that emanate from the metropolis" rather than reflecting the pessimistic, past-besotted southern cast of mind.[55]

As a wide range of writers and artists found support in federal arts programs and the cultural institutions of the Communist Party and the CIO, however, radical intellectuals increasingly broke free from the oppositions embraced by dogmatists on the left and the right and looked with new respect to collective memory, oral history, and other forms of local knowledge. The cultural historian Constance Rourke took Marxist critics to task for belittling the country's "deeply rooted, widespread folk expression—regional in character, some of it quite explicitly proletarian in sentiment." The strength of Lumpkin's work, especially *To Make My Bread*, Rourke concluded, lay in its "concentration and . . . enlargement" of an impulse that could help make ethnic and regional diversity a hallmark of American democracy, a source of national resiliency, and a seedbed for social change.[56]

In 1937 Benjamin Botkin took this point of view to the second American Writers' Congress. Grace Lumpkin's "proletarian regionalism," he argued, stood in opposition to the "reactionary and regressive regionalism" associated with the Agrarians. By turning a critical eye on power relations *within* regions, the network of southern novelists, folklorists, documentarians, sociologists, historians, and writers to which she belonged rejected mythmaking for a revisionist history of racism, economic oppression, and environmental destruction. In so doing, they refuted the Marxists' charge that regionalists were sentimental antiquarians who failed to grapple with contemporary reality.[57]

Assuming leadership roles in the Federal Writers' and Arts Projects, Rourke, Botkin, and the Harlem Renaissance writer Sterling Brown put the regionalist movement at the center of New Deal cultural policies. They treasured cultural differences not only as a counterweight to the standardization of the "machine age" but also as the basis for a new, pluralistic nationalism in which all could participate. The fruits of their labor—the priceless slave narratives, state guidebooks, and other publications documenting the racial, ethnic, and regional modalities through which ordinary people experienced their lives—all became part of the Popular Front's attempt to "imagine a new culture, a new way of life, a revolution."[58]

EMBOLDENED BY THE embrace of these cultural critics, Grace Lumpkin ventured into one of the period's most notorious literary and political frays: the tug-of-war between the Nashville Agrarians and their black and white critics over who was entitled to speak for the South and how the southern literary canon would be defined. This controversy had begun in 1930 when the poet and novelist Allen Tate and his allies published *I'll Take My Stand: The South and the Agrarian Tradition*, an antimodernist manifesto. As political divisions sharpened in the years that followed, the Agrarians' argument devolved into a jeremiad about the disappearance of the white yeoman farmer, the dangers of Communist influence in the New Deal, and the interference of both the federal government and corporate capitalism in the southern way of life.[59] The Agrarians' best remembered opponents were the regional sociologists at the University of North Carolina, who shone a light on the region's problems and championed planning, industrialization, and other tools of economic progress. But African American writers and white radicals were equally critical. They vigorously contested the Agrarians' nostalgic racism, which sometimes remained offstage but was often quite explicit.[60]

Allen Tate had shown up in New York City in 1924, the same year in which Grace arrived. He was eager to throw off the taint of parochialism and lose himself in the "maelstrom of literary N.Y.," but, like her, he was soon turning to regional themes.[61] In 1936, having made his name with *I'll Take My Stand* and the poem, "Ode to the Confederate Dead," Tate published *Reactionary Essays on Poetry and Ideas*, an attack on leftist writers and, especially, proletarian literature. At the time, he was cementing the Agrarians' involvement with the deep-pocketed, fascist sympathizer Seward Collins, whose magazine, *American Review*, provided the chief outlet for their political opinions. Asked to write about the Agrarians' association with the controversial editor by *FIGHT*, the monthly magazine of the country's largest antifascist organization, Grace asked Collins for an interview. The resulting uproar put her at the center of what has been called 1930s American intellectual conservatism's "most significant cause célèbre."[62]

According to Lumpkin, Collins began the interview by claiming that he and the Agrarians had similar economic aims, which, in his case, involved adherence to the ideas of British ultraconservatives who advocated the restoration of a rooted and stable peasantry. He then went on to declare his opposition to "general education," admit his affinity for Hitler and Mussolini, and suggest that the Agrarians shared those views. Highlighting the association between fascism and racism that made race relations so central to the Popular Front agenda, Lumpkin asked whether Collins supported Hitler's persecution of the Jews. "It is not persecution. The Jews make trouble. It is necessary to segregate them," Collins replied. "And does your group have the same attitude toward Negroes as toward the Jews?" "The same. They must be segregated." The Agrarians might be "sensitive and fine writers," Lumpkin concluded, but by accepting such bedfellows they were creating the "theoretical foundation" of an American fascist movement.[63]

Allen Tate defended his group in an exchange with Lumpkin in the *New Republic* that drew widespread attention to what Collins later termed the "ill-fated interview." He took Lumpkin to task for identifying Collins's views with his own, to which she replied, quite rightly, that it was Collins himself who had made that claim. Adding a mild repudiation of fascism to the Agrarians' usual attacks on communism, Tate argued that industrialization and New Deal–sponsored centralization would inevitably lead the United States toward one of those totalitarian extremes. Lumpkin answered as one Southerner to another. Quoting Tate's declaration that "the Southerner" must use the blunt instrument of politics to "reestablish a private, self-contained and essentially spiritual life," she linked "such a life" to the privileges his grandfather and hers had enjoyed "when slaves worked for them."[64]

Joining the dustup, Collins questioned the accuracy of Lumpkin's account of their conversation, while reasserting the similarities between Agrarianism and the brand of fascism he advocated. But Lumpkin had the last word. The Agrarians, she said to Collins, at least would not "call a lady a liar." Indeed, behind the scenes, Tate admitted that Collins "certainly must [have] said most of the things attributed to him." As to Mr. Tate, Grace concluded, "I leave him with genuine regret and sadness as he goes about with his butterfly net busily recapturing Southern traditions." Thoroughly embarrassed, Tate agonized over whether to break with Collins in order to avoid the taint of fascism, but he continued to send articles to the *American Review*. Within a year, however, the magazine had folded, and the Agrarian crusade had come apart at the seams. Its dissolution arose from rifts among its adherents and other problems but was accelerated by Grace Lumpkin's cheeky intervention.[65]

IN THE LATE 1930s, Grace seemed to be well placed to pursue the proletarian regionalism that Benjamin Botkin and others had recognized as the spark that ignited her socially conscious writing career. Seeking to do just that, she turned to the historical novel on Reconstruction that she had "wanted to write for years." She contacted Robert Cantwell, a well-known novelist and critic with whom she and her husband sometimes socialized, and laid bare both her financial need and her literary ambitions. Could he help her move forward by writing in support of her application for a Guggenheim Fellowship or, if that failed, by recommending her for a secretarial job? Grace had been studying dictation in case it came to that. "I need the money exceedingly," she implored, both "to help pay my way in the world" and in order to "go South" to do research for the novel. Cantwell did try to help. In 1937 he wrote on her behalf for a Guggenheim Fellowship, but to no avail.[66]

A year later, another opportunity presented itself: Louise Leonard McLaren invited Grace to teach at the Southern Summer School for Women Workers. She had taught there at least once before and welcomed the chance to return, all the more so because she could live for free at the Asheville Normal and Teachers College, where the session would be held. She accepted the offer, saved the money she earned, and used it to travel to Duke and the University of North Carolina "where there are all sorts of documents I can look into for my new book."[67]

Returning to New York in the fall of 1938, she again applied for a Guggenheim. An impressive lineup of literary figures endorsed her request, including Pearl S. Buck, John Dos Passos, Sinclair Lewis, and Kenneth Burke. Lois MacDonald also wrote at length, emphasizing Grace's gift for verisimilitude as demonstrated by the reaction of students at the Southern Summer School, who saw their lives reflected so accurately in *To Make My Bread*. Nevertheless, Grace's application was rejected. "She is what is called a 'proletarian writer,'" the selection committee sniffed. "We have skimmed the cream of that particular crop, and she is not of the cream."[68] In reality, little of what Grace had been writing over the previous few years could be classed as proletarian fiction. She had continued to publish scrappy polemics in the left-wing press, but she had not even sketched out her projected historical novel. When she did turn to imaginative fiction, she produced short stories filled with planters' daughters who—like Caroline Gault in *A Sign for Cain*, the most unappealing of the bourgeois feminists she took pains to skewer—see themselves as rebels even as they replicate the gender and racial dynamics they inherit.

A short story entitled "The Bridesmaids Carried Lilies" published in *The North American Review* in 1937, the same year in which Benjamin Botkin held Grace up as a proletarian regionalist, offered a particularly bleak variation on the trope of the flawed prodigal daughter. The main character, Mary Ella, like Caroline Gault, is a pseudo-liberated southern woman who goes to New York and wreaks havoc when she returns home. She sets her sights on a déclassé store clerk but discovers that he is carrying on with a beautiful, passive "nigger girl" who "had been disciplined by the strongest forces society can use . . . to accept whatever happens," especially "prolific birth and casual death with no means of preventing either." Mary Ella's actions precipitate the murder of the black woman's mixed-race child, opening the way to a disturbingly tainted version of a happily-ever-after resolution. The black woman disappears. Mary Ella marries the store clerk. "The bride wore a dress of oyster satin, ordered from New York. The bridesmaids wore white organdy and leghorn hats. They carried lilies," symbols of chastity and death.[69]

As the 1930s drew to a close, Grace put aside the idea of writing a wide-ranging historical novel. Looking to "The Bridesmaids Carried Lilies" as an example of what she would "be able to do in the future," she turned to mining her family history for the story of yet another rebellious middle-class southern daughter: a novel based on the events surrounding Elizabeth Lumpkin Glenn's 1905 "Confederate wedding."[70] Into that seemingly slight work, she poured the ambivalences that had long marked her writing and that now began to complicate her most intimate relationships and threaten the political and literary persona that, since the 1920s, she had struggled so hard to create.

SISTERS AND
STRANGERS

I N GRACE LUMPKIN'S TELLING, THE NOVEL TO WHICH SHE now turned had its genesis in "a keen breath of anguish" she had experienced as a child. On the eve of her eldest sister's wedding, their mother Annette had explained that Elizabeth "would now have another and different life from ours; that she would go away with her husband and belong to him." For Annette that was a wrenching prospect. For years afterward, she continued to "shiver with the ice that was in my heart" on that day. "Without any 'hurrah,' almost like catching a breath," the memory of her mother's reaction presented itself one evening in the late 1930s as Grace stood at the kitchen sink in Kok-I House. "I wiped my hands and went into my workroom, sat down at the typewriter and typed *The Wedding* at the top of the page."[1] But the anguish Grace referred to had as much to do with her current situation—and by extension with the dilemmas faced by many middle-class white women on the left—as it did with the feelings her sister's marriage had stirred in her mother and in her as a child.

While Grace was writing this roman à clef, Katharine and Dorothy were moving into a new home and transforming it into a political hub, think tank, and communal living space all rolled into one. Here, in this lively and protective setting, Katharine took up the challenge of writing about the South as a Southerner for the first time. She did so in the form of regional political analysis, but as she wrote, she found herself swept up in childhood memories and wrestling with questions about her family's past. By the time the sisters' respective books appeared—Grace's novel in 1939 and Katharine's *The South in Progress* the following year—they were becoming increasingly estranged even as they remained bound by the ties of sisterhood, family, and region.[2]

THE WEDDING IS SET in Columbia, South Carolina, the Lumpkin sisters' hometown, as New South businessmen are displacing an impoverished old elite. Poor but pedigreed Jennie Middleton is engaged to Dr. Shelley Gregg, a hard-drinking, practical-minded "country boy who has made good." Like the fiancé in Eudora Welty's celebrated 1946 novel, *Delta Wedding*, he represents "a grafting of new blood onto" a family living by "outmoded values." The plot turns on two questions. Will Jennie Middleton resolve her last-minute doubts and go through with the ceremony? Will her younger sister Susan speak out against the class and racial injustices that Jennie and their parents take for granted? As in *Delta Wedding*, the sisters' dilemmas, acted out on a small domestic stage, reflect the choices facing people on the verge of far-reaching historical change.[3]

Like her prototype, Elizabeth, Jennie has tasted financial independence and public acclaim. Spurred by her success on the veterans' reunion stage, she aspired to an acting career, studied in New York, then returned to the South to teach "dramatic expression." "I had money of my own," she muses. "I could go where I pleased." She dreads the loss of autonomy that marriage entails. As she sees it, the choice of a husband is a perilous gamble, for marriage requires her to submerge her life in her husband's with the hope that, through his success, she can "keep her individual ambitions alive in the world."[4]

The lovers quarrel over seeming trivialities that signify deeper tensions. Like all of the novel's male characters, the doctor identifies men with reason, women with feeling, and he sees Jennie as a willful, emotional child. She views him as arrogant and brutish; she longs to wipe the habitual smirk of bemused pity off his face. Yet in practice, she confirms his assumptions. Maneuvering for advantage in a world dominated by men, she uses tears, coquetry, and other wiles to provoke emotional reactions—whether of love, anger, or desire—in otherwise cool, rational, withholding men.[5]

The resolution of the crisis is never really in doubt; Jennie will capitulate and go through with the marriage. Her insistence on a Confederate-themed ceremony underscores the lure of tradition and the inexorability of wedding preparations, which are designed in every particular to overcome the betrothed couple's apprehensions and ensure that they carry out their promise to enter into this all-important economic and cultural institution.[6] Besides, Jennie can envision no alternative to the prescribed path. In the end, she glides down the aisle on her father's arm, surrounded by a retinue of bridesmaids and Civil War veterans in full Confederate regalia, basking in her own performance and her audience's attention.

Despite *The Wedding*'s seeming conformity to the traditional marriage plot, it offers a portrait of male sexism and female complicity in a context of regional change with no happily-ever-after ending in sight. The Old South is clearly doomed to obsolescence. Jennie's possessive, unreconstructed father has already been bypassed by her husband's New South business and professional class. She seems destined to remain forever "stranded in a middle place," caught between her identity as the "Daughter of the United Confederate Veterans" and her image of herself as a modern woman.[7]

Jennie's sister Susan, who represents Grace and Katharine's generation, listens to the stories of white mill workers and of the black servants whose labor underwrites the Middletons' domestic life and is disturbed by the suffering they reveal. Yet her efforts to intervene on their behalf have no real effect. We last see her at the wedding, aware that some of the guests view the spectacle as slightly absurd but caught up in the pageantry nonetheless.[8] Her childish idealism seems to be free-floating, as likely to attach itself to the romance of marriage or the Lost Cause as to inspire her to defy inherited expectations and conventions.

WHETHER THEY WELCOMED *The Wedding* as a refreshing turn "from propaganda to people" on the part of a "leader of [the] radical literary movement" or faulted its focus on what a writer for *Time Magazine* characterized as one woman's "pathetic, irritating, irrational and commonplace little rebellion," reviewers agreed that Grace Lumpkin's novel was "a slight, simple story" as far removed from *To Make My Bread* "as a picket line is from a pulpit."[9] Even when *The Wedding* resurfaced in the

1980s as a new generation of scholars began reclaiming the radical literature of the 1930s, it did so as "a quiet masterpiece" within the "tradition of romantic comedy." But the feminist literary critics of the 1990s who saw it as an example of women's "radical dystopian fiction" were closer to the mark.[10]

Works in that vein reflected the struggle of middle-class women on the left to make sense of their peculiar combination of sexual oppression and class privilege and to reconcile their artistic and political ambitions with their romantic, sexual, and maternal desires. Those efforts left a trace in their writing, leading them to parcel out their own aspirations and impulses among two or more figures, rather than locating them within one multidimensional female character. In its contrast between the thwarted rebellions of the quasi-feminist Jennie Middleton and her more class- and race-conscious younger sister, *The Wedding* offers a particularly disheartening commentary on the possibilities open to women trying to resolve these dilemmas, which for Grace were at once personal and political. Those dilemmas were rooted in her increasingly fraught attachments to her husband and Whittaker Chambers, two supremely "gravity-warping" men, and her love-hate relationship with the family she had left behind.[11] They also grew out of the ongoing challenge of imagining herself as a class-conscious, antiracist, liberated southern woman in a movement that too often replicated rather than transformed the sexist biases of the society in which it was embedded.

In the 1930s, as in the 1920s, women in the communist orbit confronted a party that was, as both participants and scholars have pointed out, "profoundly masculinist . . . in many of its human relationships, in the orientation of its literature," and in the leadership of its major cultural and political organizations.[12] At the same time, the CP offered a forum for serious discussion of "the woman question" and an increasingly robust vehicle for activism. During Grace Lumpkin's formative years in the movement—the hyper-revolutionary Third Period of the 1920s and early 1930s—the CP had mounted a radical critique of marriage and the family, pointing to the "new Russia" as a model for the liberation of women in both domestic and public life. Party members also celebrated women workers as fighters in the class struggle. In practice, however, they focused their organizing efforts on male workers and filled their publications with a masculinist iconography that juxtaposed big-shouldered male industrial workers with "big-bosomed leisure class women," using exaggerated bodies to signify political essences. The habit of excoriating "bourgeois feminism" as an expression of the selfish individualism of the privileged class easily shaded into scorn for female ambition, a stance that helped to foster relationships between men and women that more often than not fell far short of Communists' egalitarian ideals.[13]

Changing course with the Depression and the rise of the Popular Front, CP leaders began welcoming the intellectuals they had once scorned and collaborating with feminists aligned with the independent left. Local organizers also shifted their attention from the shop floor to the working-class neighborhoods and spoke more directly to women's concerns. As the party's female membership rose from 10 percent in 1933 to 40 percent in 1940, its Women's Commission gained power and funding, subscriptions to *Working Woman* and its glossier successor, *The Woman Today*, increased, and left feminist writers produced a series of searching theoretical critiques. Probing the cultural and ideological as well as the economic aspects of gender oppression, they also produced a steady stream of novels exploring women's everyday experiences and linking women's liberation to racial equality and class emancipation.[14] That stream of writing widened further in the 1940s and 1950s, when African American women developed what has come to be called an "intersectional" understanding of their triple oppression and began publishing powerful works of long-form left feminist fiction.[15] Within the Popular Front more generally, Katharine Lumpkin, Dorothy Douglas, and other professionals sought to transcend what later theorists would call "the unhappy marriage of Marxism and feminism" by infusing feminist consciousness into causes that did not explicitly prioritize gender equality, especially battles for labor and civil rights and for a strong, inclusive social safety net.[16]

Within the Communist Party, however, these promising developments were countered by a rising tide of gender conservatism inspired by the backlash against wage-earning women during the Great Depression and the example of the Soviet Union. Even as the CP became more welcoming to women, it also began muting its critique of marriage and the family, both in order to increase its popular appeal and in response to Stalinist policies criminalizing homosexuality and imposing new restrictions on abortion and divorce. In this unstable atmosphere, some radical women writers did what Katharine did. They combined women's history with classic Marxist texts to parse the class differences in how

women were affected by industrialization and used the Soviet Union as
a touchstone for relating socialism to women's liberation. They also did
what Grace did. They upbraided union organizers for failing to organize women, portrayed the sexual and economic oppression that black
women endured, and wrote passionately about working-class women's
double day. They sometimes created portraits of egalitarian relationships
between lovers and comrades that rested on shared political commitments and cultural labor, and they struggled privately to achieve that
ideal. But, given the assumption among socialists of every stripe that
a humane social order would be achieved in stages, with fundamental
changes in personal relationships occurring only after capitalism was
overthrown, even left feminists usually subordinated their own struggles for equality to the fight against fascism and racism and the necessity of organizing the working class.[17] Neither the left nor the culture at
large gave women a shared language and a public forum for theorizing
their oppression *as women* or for elevating issues of sexism and women's
unpaid reproductive labor to the level occupied by the struggle for control of the means of production.

That vacuum left women like Grace Lumpkin vulnerable both to condescension from their male friends and lovers and to misunderstanding
and dismissal by the men who dominated left-wing artistic and intellectual life. Ella Wolfe, the wife of Michael Intrator's old teacher and
fellow Lovestonite factionalist, Bertram Wolfe, underscored the problem. Women, she observed, "are looked upon and treated as fourth class
citizens, although I consider the native ability of most of them at least
on the same level as the native ability of some of the mediocre peacocks
strutting about 14th Street. . . . The women of our group . . . are given
no opportunity for growth and development. On the contrary, should
they show some special aptitude, they are squashed."[18] Complicating the
situation were ongoing tensions between the CP's middle- and working-
class members, a fault line in which sexism figured in subtle and not so
subtle forms.

In Grace and Michael's case, condescension ran two ways: toward
Grace by people for whom the glamour of an affair with a plebian writer
did not extend to a marriage to a working stiff, and toward Michael for
marrying a writer instead of becoming one himself. Once he left the
Daily Worker, severed his ties with the Communist Party, and returned
to work in the fur industry, Intrator had published only sporadically, and

then only in the Lovestonite journal, *Workers Age*. When Bertram Wolfe summed up his former student's career, he did so with a sneer that perfectly evokes the snarky milieu Ella Wolfe described: Intrator, Wolfe explained, "married Grace Lumpkin, the novelist who took care of the striving to learn how to write, for him."[19] Despite the presence of numerous strong, creative women on the left, many a wife remained either a muse or a nemesis, and a woman who showed "some special aptitude" did not necessarily reflect well on her husband.

Over time, Grace's marriage to Michael Intrator put her in an especially ambiguous and ultimately isolated position. Although Intrator's decision to join the apostate Lovestonites in 1929 did not affect the response of Communist Party critics to Grace's novels or prevent her from serving as a spokesperson for the communist movement, it did insure that she would never be an insider in party circles. As she later told a government investigator, she remained a fellow traveler rather than a party member in part because of Michael's reservations and in part because she "was never completely trusted on [account] of her husband's deviation."[20]

Questions of trust and "deviation" infected Grace's other relationships as well. She had known Myra Page since their YWCA days, and the two women belonged to the same New York literary circle. But Page had never felt that Michael Intrator was "up to Grace's caliber." Once they married, she came to believe that he was an unfaithful husband and to suspect that he may have pressured Grace into having an abortion because they were too poor to raise a child. When he threw in his lot with Jay Lovestone, Page's disapproval turned to dislike. To avoid contact with Michael, she refused to visit Grace at Kok-I House. "This is a big mistake," Grace protested. "It's like the Baptists and the Methodists: both are Christians. You and I both believe in socialism and the working class. We might not agree on everything but we're working for the same thing." Page saw things differently. "Grace cried and I wanted to cry because we were fond of each other, but I didn't," Page remembered. "Grace never forgave me, and I never saw her much again after that."[21]

Grace did maintain her connections to other members of the southern women's network. She relied especially on Louise Leonard McLaren, to whom she looked for job contacts, letters of recommendation, and opportunities to teach at the Southern Summer School for Women Workers. But once she moved in with and then married Michael Intrator, she and the women in that network drifted farther apart, in part because of the cultural gulf that separated them from her husband, however dedicated they were to cross-class solidarities in their political work.

The distance between Grace and Katharine widened as well. Subjectively and symbolically, the sisters remained in constant dialogue with one another. At least through the 1930s, they had mutual friends, returned to similar family memories, were defined by the same regional identities, and were broadly committed to the same leftist causes. Indeed, it is not too much to say that, together, Katharine, Grace, and their southern women's circle were producing what Eleanor Copenhaver Anderson called "a new type of thinking," a shared body of social knowledge about the linkages among class, race, gender, and region and about the place of the South in the nation and the world. Yet not a single shred of evidence has surfaced to shed light on the sisters' face-to-face interactions in these years. When, much later, interviewers pressed her to describe their relationship, Katharine would say only that they were absorbed in their very different literary and scholarly worlds. Underscoring the point, she made the startling claim that she had met Grace's husband only once. Each sister had chosen as a partner a radical Jewish intellectual from New York, and yet chasms separated the world of Dorothy Douglas and Northampton from that of Michael Intrator and the "muscular, bruising" precincts of communist infighting in New York.[22]

Equally complicated and more insidious was the intertwining of politics and emotion in Grace's relationship with Esther and Whittaker Chambers. Like Intrator, Chambers had left the Communist Party in 1929. But he had soon worked his way back into the fold by taking over the editorship of *The New Masses*. Then he abruptly changed course. He had always "had a weakness for the grand gesture, the spontaneous life-altering act, the doomed but courageous stand." In 1932, over his wife's desperate objections, he gave up his burgeoning literary career to accept an invitation to "join the ranks of the true revolutionists" by gathering intelligence for the Soviet Union.[23]

Throughout his years in the Communist underground, Chambers stayed in touch with Grace Lumpkin and Michael Intrator, often turning to them in moments of uncertainty or fear, even though he was supposed to maintain strict secrecy about his clandestine activities and Intrator was persona non grata within the Communist Party. While Esther was in labor with their first child, Ellen, Whittaker tramped up and down in Grace and Mike's living room, or so Grace recalled twenty years later, when, in the margins of her treasured copy of his memoir, she corrected Whittaker's account, which had him tramping the streets and fields instead. Grace was also proud to say that she was on hand to take care of Ellen when John, the Chambers's second child, was born.

In 1938, Chambers experienced a second rebirth. Turning from one pole to its opposite, he "deserted from the Communist Party in a way that could leave no doubt in its mind, or anybody else's, that I was at war with it and everything it stood for." The details of his cloak-and-dagger activities during his previous underground years remain murky and contested, in part because what we know about them comes from ideologically charged retrospective accounts and hard-to-decipher Soviet documents that were released in the 1990s and never mention Chambers by name. And it is not altogether clear why he decided to leave the party. Writing in retrospect about his experience as a twice-born convert—a man who awoke first to the promise of revolution, then reversed course to devote himself to condemning his earlier ideals—he said almost nothing about American politics or about the signature causes with which the CP was associated. Nor did he make much of the Moscow trials or the other developments in the Soviet Union that many ex-Communists cited as the moments when their disillusionment began. Indeed, he claimed to have viewed Stalin as a tyrant long before these events.[24]

As his biographer explains it, Chambers had converted to Communism in the first place because he saw it as a thrillingly cataclysmic force which "for all its faults, possessed the will and the means to destroy the existing world and make possible a new and better one."[25] Now he came to believe that the fundamental struggle of modern times was between Christianity and Communism or, as he put it, between those who believed in "the primacy of God" and those who believed in "primacy of secular Man." Changing sides but not his apocalyptic, Manichean habits of mind, he lumped together liberals, progressives, socialists, and Communists, scorning them all as misguided materialists devoted to false hopes for progress guided by human reason. He cast himself as a tragic hero, fighting what he believed would be a losing war against Communism with the same zeal and the same brilliant outsider's aggrieved self-importance that he had once brought to the cause of revolution.[26]

Taking his family into hiding, Chambers made elaborate arrangements to leave the underground and surface with a new identity and a new means of self-support. Again he remained in touch with Grace and Mike, despite Grace's own continued involvement with the CP. She even lent him her meager savings: "the friend who had least helped most," he recalled. When he finally reemerged, he took a job at *Time Magazine*, where he worked for Henry R. Luce, a press magnate who "worshiped the familiar trinity of Christianity, big business, and the Republican party."[27] In 1940 he was baptized in the Episcopal Church. He also gave up the homosexual affairs he had carried on before and during his marriage.[28] Soon he was serving as an informant for the FBI, making allegations about Communist spies in the Roosevelt administration. Almost a decade later those claims would explode into public accusations of espionage against the prominent New Dealer Alger Hiss, putting the two men at the center of one of the McCarthy era's most consequential causes célèbres. In congressional hearings and conversations with the FBI, Chambers would also inform on Grace's and Esther's longtime benefactor Grace Hutchins, Grace's literary agent Maxim Lieber, and Sender Garlin, one of her early friends in New York. In response, they would make no secret of their scorn for Chambers, whom they painted as a pathological liar, a "homosexual pervert, a psychological case." Grace Lumpkin, by contrast, maintained "complete faith" in Chambers, although she initially resisted his conservative political views.[29]

"HONESTLY, HONESTLY, honey, that Yaddo business is a nightmare," the modernist southern writer Evelyn Scott complained in the first of a series of long letters written in 1940 as Grace was reckoning with the seismic impact of Chambers's about-face. The two women had met at Yaddo, the legendary artists' retreat in upstate New York, to which Grace had been invited on the strength of her first book. For Grace this stay in a heady creative community had been a lifeline. Evelyn Scott, by contrast, had complained about the company, obsessed over what the other guests were saying behind her back to the director, Elizabeth Ames, and become convinced that someone was opening and reading her mail. She came away "with a complete ineradicable contempt for a good-three-quarters of all the people there," all of whom she regarded as fanatical Communists who talked of nothing but "the revolution" and reveled in letting her know that when it came she would be among "the first to be shot."[30]

By the time Evelyn Scott and Grace Lumpkin crossed paths again, Scott's beliefs had hardened into an obsessive, one-woman campaign against Marxists who, in her view, pursued "advances in physical comfort" at any cost, squelched the "individual personality," and were boycotting her work. At Yaddo, Scott had described Grace as "an elderly little girl, straightforward to bluntness and rather engaging," and she remembered her as one of the few decent people there, despite their political differences. Now she sought to enlist her "as a possible healer of the exacerbated wounds left by my Communist enemies."[31]

Grace was flattered by the attention of this well-known literary figure, the descendant of a once-wealthy plantation family who had written daringly of her youthful political and sexual rebellion and, in the 1920s, championed James Joyce, William Faulkner, and other experimental writers. She hoped that Scott would read her work, introduce her to the powerful editor Maxwell Perkins, and advance her career. But she tried to push back against some of Scott's views, especially her division of humanity into spiritually "evolved civilized types" and materialistic "unevolved primitive types," which Grace saw not only as disturbingly similar to Hitler's doctrine of Aryan superiority but also as an implicit slight to her husband. Taking Michael as an example, she argued that a self-educated working man with "noble impulses" could belong in the "company of the great." As for Michael, he was, at best, bemused by his wife's new friend. Scott came away from dinner at their house "slightly sore" at him for doubting her claim of sabotage by her Communist enemies. He "didn't seem to think having acid poured in your typewriter . . . was anything much," she complained.[32]

Grace's defensiveness about her husband masked a painful reality: by 1940 their marriage was faltering, as were her political ideals and her writing career. In the interviews she gave in the 1970s and 1980s, Grace did her best not to talk about Michael Intrator at all, and she saved none of their letters.[33] But in "Remember Now," an unpublished play she wrote in 1951, she offered a portrait of a marriage increasingly troubled by the intertwining of sexual politics with clashing political and religious beliefs, exacerbated by the insistent, disturbing influence of a Whittaker Chambers–like best friend.

The main characters are barely disguised versions of Grace and Michael, with Esther and Whittaker, Grace Hutchins, and Hope Lumpkin in supporting roles. The Grace figure is a Southerner, a "bourgeois intellectual," and a housewife in a movement that makes "a god of the working class." Her husband is a paragon of political rectitude who rejects the sexual double standard and speaks for their shared values. But, as the Grace Hutchins character observes, he is also a philanderer, and his attitude toward his wife is patronizing and belittling. He teases her about being "all right in bed, bourgeois or no bourgeois" and turns "aside too much that is important with a wise-crack." He also charges her with nostalgically "holding on to the past." She counters that she only evokes her family background to lend respectability to the left-wing committees on which she serves. "I cut myself off entirely when I came into the Movement," she claims.[34]

Halfway through, "Remember Now" drops its implicit critique of the gap between the rhetoric of sexual equality and the lived dynamics of a left-wing marriage and shifts to the efforts of the couple's best friend to convince the wife to leave her husband and "go home" to God. The wife calls this Whittaker-based character "a traitor to your friend, a traitor to everything we have believed in" and kicks him out of her apartment. But his entreaties have their effect. As Grace explained it in a retrospective distillation of the real-life events behind the play, she and Michael were "enjoying their fame and their friends and each other. But on any serious subject [he] championed reason, and [her] constant attempts to convince him that there must be a spirit in man, that there must be a God, had a backlash effect that continuously undermined their relationship." Although no longer a CP member, Michael remained a confirmed secularist and "a philosophical Marxist." So, as Grace began to embrace Christianity, they "quarreled, intellectually, and finally emotionally."[35]

In "Remember Now," the husband eventually concludes that, much as he and his wife love one another, they are on "different paths." Soon he is spending less and less time at their flat, "and then came a period when he would go off for days on end and not even be heard from."[36] The wife recounts what happened next in the form of a classic conversion narrative, which Grace would later repeat almost word for word in descriptions of her actual experience:

> It was the time of my deepest despair. I had called on reason. It didn't help. I had called on our philosophy of materialism. It had only left me weak and empty. Then I said out loud "If there is a God, please help me." And instantly, in the most amazing way a

wonderful peace came to me. . . . Loving arms were supporting me, holding me up. There was even joy, as if someone said: "Don't be afraid. I am here." And I went to sleep and slept for hours.[37]

But when she awoke, she was again overcome by the feeling of misery and unworthiness the sinner feels upon recognizing the depths of her fall from grace. "I was homesick" for that experience of God's grace, "but I couldn't get it back again."[38]

She was also homesick for the family she had lost and the region she had left behind. She fled to Asheville to stay with her widowed sister Elizabeth, who was struggling to manage her late husband's businesses and maintain her modest law practice but had succeeded in putting all four of her children through college and returning to her civic and theatrical pursuits. With their youngest brother, Bryan, the two sisters made what Elizabeth called "a little trip, such as the ancient Chinese make, to the tombs of our ancestors in Georgia! Not to worship, but to learn and to see; to obtain facts . . . that we may each use in different ways." Bryan added to his store of genealogical knowledge; Elizabeth interviewed relatives and wrote rapturously about antebellum homes; Grace sought information about her father's legal mentor Alexander Stephens, vice-president of the Confederacy. "It was an interesting and delightful trip," according to Elizabeth; "we like each other better for it!" As Grace remembered it, however, the trip did not go well: Elizabeth "fussed at me all the time. . . . She thought the thing she had to do was to teach me to get out of Communism," a lesson that, for all her confusion and discontent, she was still not fully prepared to accept.[39]

On December 7, 1941, Japan bombed Pearl Harbor, and a day later the United States entered World War II. A few months after that, Michael Intrator finally left Kok-I House for good. By 1942, he had settled in Florida, obtained a divorce, and married a woman he had met in New York. Lost and bereft—more so, by her account, than she had ever been before—Grace left her beloved flat and found lodging at Henry Street Settlement, which by then had devolved from a major bastion of female Progressivism into a service center for the poor. She was "practically penniless," "but the greater hardship consisted in her loneliness and uncertainty about the purpose and direction of her life."[40]

Then, one day, she remembered something her oldest sister had said. Elizabeth was an admirer of the Oxford Group (renamed Moral Re-

Armament in 1938), which she described as "a very wonderful movement for Christianity, that will do more toward combating Communism, which has no religion, than anything I know of." Rooted in a millenarian worldview that "gave cosmic implications to small actions," Moral Re-Armament aimed to perfect the world by changing individuals. Gathered in house parties or small group "cells," its devotees shared intimate stories of sin, shame, and conversion. Ideally they then went on to convert others by bearing witness in the work-a-day world to the experience of surrendering oneself to Christ.[41] Elizabeth had encountered the group in Asheville during its first "city campaign," a cross between its signature house parties and a traditional evangelical rally, which attracted people from all classes and Protestant churches but appealed especially to Moral Re-Armament's target audience: members of the social, business, and professional elite.[42] There she had heard about the movement's chief US strategist and spokesperson, Samuel Moor Shoemaker, the handsome, Princeton-educated rector of New York's Calvary Episcopal Church, which served as Moral Re-Armament's headquarters.[43]

As Grace told it: "My sister had said, if you're ever in need, go to Calvary Episcopal Church on Gramercy Park and you'll get help there. But I had put that behind me. I wasn't going to church. I hadn't been near a church in almost 15 years." Yet go she did, and soon she was sharing her own sin-and-salvation story in Shoemaker's self-help cells and repeating it in various other venues. She found a part-time secretarial position at the Clergy School sponsored by the church. She also moved into a quiet room at Calvary House, an eight-story building next to the church in tony Gramercy Park, which served as a residence for church workers, a training center, and the hub of an evangelizing ministry to the urban poor. Once settled there, she helped to produce and write for the church's magazine, *The Evangel*. Later Shoemaker recommended her for a proofreading position at the Golden Eagle Press, an innovative designer and printer of the work of modernist writers located in Mount Vernon, a city in Westchester County on the border of the Bronx. Until the mid-1950s, she commuted back and forth by subway, working at the press, living at Calvary House, and immersing herself in the affairs of the church.

Sam Shoemaker is remembered today primarily as a founder of Alcoholics Anonymous, the enormously influential self-help group that borrowed its reliance on peer-group confessions and the power of God from

Moral Re-Armament. But in the late 1940s and 1950s, he made his mark as one of the nation's best known preachers by helping to fuel what the historian Jonathan P. Herzog calls "the spiritual-industrial complex": an amalgam of institutions created by corporate leaders and conservative clergymen whose aim was to conflate faith, freedom, and free enterprise and endow American competition with the Soviet Union with religious fervor.[44] Ensconced in strongholds such as the YWCA and the women's division of the Methodist Church, advocates of the social gospel continued to push American society in a different, more pluralistic, internationalist, and social justice–minded direction, and their efforts would bear fruit in the insurgencies of the 1960s.[45] But during these Cold War years they remained an embattled minority. Leading a highly organized and strikingly successful religious revival that filled church pews and turned numerous civic and political events into quasi-religious rituals, Shoemaker and his allies persuaded countless white Protestants to identify communism with godlessness and to see the United States "as a Christian nation in which government must be kept from interfering with God's will in market relations."[46]

Much as the Christian pacifist magazine *The World Tomorrow* had ushered Grace into the New York left, Calvary Episcopal served as a social and ideological way station on the journey that took her from the turmoil and doubts of the late 1930s and early 1940s to certainties more rigid than her version of communism had ever been. Embraced by a new surrogate family at a time when she was profoundly alone, she began to frame herself as a prodigal daughter.[47] Like a reformed alcoholic, she had been saved by rejecting the arrogance of human reason and giving herself up to a higher power.

Grace remained in contact with Shoemaker until his death in 1963 and was forever indebted to the ways of thinking she imbibed at Calvary Episcopal Church. In a few of her later writings, she gave his influence its due. But in most accounts of her divorce and her disillusion with Communism, she collapsed an extended, contingent change of heart into a formulaic story about Whittaker Chambers's central, precipitating role. When I interviewed her in the mid-1970s, she said nothing about her involvement with Shoemaker and his church. Nor did she point to the particular historical events that had shattered some leftists' faith in international communism during the 1930s. Instead she offered this explanation for why she had traded one self-defining set of beliefs and allegiances for another: "Whittaker Chambers came to me and said that he had found God and he said that he wanted me to find God. 'You must return to your family and to God and to your country.' Those three things," for Grace, represented a return to a prelapsarian "home."[48]

Why did Chambers intervene in her life in such a forceful, intimate way? I asked. "Because we were so close," she explained. "We were like a family. It was the only family that I had, Whit and Esther and the children and my husband, at that time. . . . I think that Whit felt a sort of responsibility for me . . . as if I were his sister, and he was trying to get me out of this trouble."[49] Whittaker Chambers certainly had an outsized impact on Grace Lumpkin's life and thought. Still, she formulated this account after his meteoric rise to fame during the early Cold War years, and her stress on his influence was reinforced by repetition. In 1951, when she contacted the drama critic John Gassner for advice about "Remember Now," he advised her to dramatize what was essentially "a struggle of ideas" by playing up the Chambers-based character as the catalyst for action. She promised to do so and, once developed, that fictional narrative stamped itself on her memory each time it was retold.[50] In addition, while Chambers's concern for Grace was real, his paternalism was not necessarily tempered by respect, and there is contemporary evidence that his influence was not immediately so overweening.

Referring to her as "Lumpkinova" in a later letter to his friend William F. Buckley, editor of *National Review*, Chambers scoffed at the "picture of me as a Billy Graham of the Left, slipping in and out of the 11th Street house to save Grace's soul." Yet, he "remembered clearly urging her to go back South where she would be among her own numerous family, with people of her own kind."[51] "I'm shocked to find you back in this Gomorrah," Chambers wrote in the summer of 1941 after Grace returned from her visit to Elizabeth in North Carolina and before she encountered Sam Shoemaker's group. "What in heaven's name are you doing here? . . . The atmosphere here is impregnated with poisons, moral and spiritual. . . . You're being re-born, why try to crawl back into the womb, especially when the womb is corrupt?"[52] Summoning Grace to his office at *Time Magazine*, he tried to persuade her to come for an extended stay on the farm in Maryland to which he and Esther had moved a few years before.

Grace did not go to Maryland; having actually experienced farm life, it held no attraction for her. And she continued to resist a full-scale embrace of Chambers's right-wing views. Indeed, she at first saw no contradiction between Sam Shoemaker's brand of Christian anti-Communism and support for Roosevelt and the New Deal. Concluding his account of their 1941 conversation in his office, Chambers quipped that "in passing, I made some amused remark about Eleanor Roosevelt." Offended by this slight to a woman she admired as the embodiment of a liberalism that she saw as compatible with her current views, "Grace boiled like a geyser and shot off into the night."[53]

In 1945, as World War II was coming to a close, Grace did spend at least four months on the Chambers's farm. A year later she spoke out publicly as "an ex-Communist" for the first time. The occasion was the Paris Peace Conference. The political winds were beginning to shift to the right, and the campaign to make religion a central weapon in the anti-Communist arsenal was intensifying. Always attuned to such shifts, Grace wrote an open letter to James F. Byrnes, who, as Secretary of State, was playing a major role in the conference, imploring him to counter godless Communism by offering up an affirmation of Christian faith that would make clear "the basis upon which our country was founded." Such a statement would be all the more important because intellectuals in the United States were busy passing on Communist "philosophy and propaganda . . . to our everyday citizens." Stressing her bona fides both as someone who had been "with the Communist Party here in America for 10 years" and as the sister of Alva Lumpkin, who had died of a heart attack in 1941 only weeks after being appointed to a seat in the US Senate vacated by Byrnes's resignation, Grace explained why these efforts were so dangerous and, as born-again Christians often do, highlighted her current righteousness by proclaiming the depths of her earlier sins. Once committed to a "philosophy based on materialism and the belief that the end justified the means," Communists lose all sense of conscience, she explained. They become "in a real sense self-made psychopaths."[54] She would repeat this mantra with increasing conviction and shrillness in the years ahead.

A few months before Grace's article appeared, Katharine made the only explicit comment about her own relationship to the Communist Party that has come to light: "I cannot imagine why or how my name could have got on your mailing list," she wrote to Earl Browder, the former General Secretary of the CP. "In any event, it does not belong there, and I wish it removed at once."[55] The fact that Browder had by then been expelled from the party suggests that if Katharine had ever followed the machinations of the national party leadership closely, she was not doing so as the war came to an end. That she would write so adamantly may have had nothing to do with her sister's determination to begin speaking out in behalf of the anti-Communist crusade, but it does suggest a wariness regarding guilt by association that she had not exhibited before. A decade later she seems to have responded to "blunt questions" from her sister Elizabeth about "where she stood in her politics [and] her life," by avowing that she was "not communist in any way."[56]

AS, DURING THE LATE 1930S and early 1940s, Grace's marriage was disintegrating along with the edifice of her previous affiliations and beliefs, Katharine's life was taking its own unexpected turns. Returning to Northampton early in 1939 with plans for writing about revolutionary Mexico, she found herself embroiled instead in a dispiriting and, in the end, futile defense of her job. Her position at Smith had always been precarious. The Council of Industrial Studies had survived through the worst years of the Depression primarily because of President Neilson's protection and Dorothy's anonymous financial support, supplemented after 1936 with small, annual appropriations from the Board of Trustees. Each spring found Katharine on tenterhooks, waiting to see whether she could begin recruiting research fellows for the following year. The fragility of the whole enterprise had become even more apparent in 1937, when Neilson began planning for retirement and told Dorothy that he could make no promises regarding future institutional funding. Another sign of trouble appeared in 1938 as Katharine and Dorothy were preparing to spend Dorothy's sabbatical in Mexico that fall. At their meeting in February, the trustees declined to appropriate funds for the council. Why, they asked, could not the research be done by Smith students and supervised by a regular faculty member? In effect, why employ Katharine at all? Extolling the organization's accomplishments, Katharine asked for and received Neilson's promise to recommend that his successor continue the council in its present form.[57]

With that slim assurance, Katharine and Dorothy left for Mexico, putting aside whatever worries about the future they had. Within a month after returning home in January 1939, however, they learned that the trustees had again declined to provide funds for Katharine's salary or for the research fellows; instead, they appropriated $1,500 "for a survey of materials available for future studies." Katharine responded with a spirited defense of the council and of her own "training and experience." "The Council has proved itself under my direction," she argued. It should not only be "accepted as a going concern" but also be permanently funded and expanded. Research opportunities were vital for female scholars, and providing them was "a unique and important project for a women's college to undertake." Moreover, "the time has long since passed when the Council needs to concentrate upon a survey of materials."[58]

A few weeks later, Katharine swallowed her pride and agreed to conduct the survey, with the proviso that she would hire a research assistant at her own expense for those aspects of the job that were not "of a caliber that was up to my experience." This time the professors on the council, led by Esther Lowenthal, delivered the rebuke. Meeting without Dorothy's knowledge, they decided that Katharine should not be allowed to hire an assistant and that, if she refused to conduct the survey herself, she should be replaced immediately.[59]

The council members may well have chafed at Dorothy's role as the group's behind-the-scenes angel. They certainly objected to Katharine's "attitude." Her letter had been insufficiently deferential; it suggested that she was laboring under the mistaken impression that her professional accomplishments and years of service gave her a claim, if not to a secure position in the college, then at least to a measure of respect. Beyond that, the council members had their own vision of the kind of research that Katharine and the research fellows should pursue. The "survey of materials," as Esther Lowenthal envisioned it, would target business records, a much safer and more conventional endeavor than that of a scholar such as Vera Shlakman, who focused on the dark side of capitalism and on what Dorothy called the "labor point of view."[60]

At this point, Neilson intervened once more. He made clear that Dorothy was a member in good standing of the council and could not be excluded from its meetings. He also convinced the council to withdraw its objections to Katharine's plan to hire a research assistant. Privately, however, Lowenthal was determined that 1939–1940 would be Katharine's "terminal year."[61]

Katharine, in the meantime, hired a talented young scholar, Constance McLaughlin Green, to help with the survey. A Smith graduate and recent Yale PhD, Green had just published *Holyoke, Massachusetts: A Case History of the Industrial Revolution in America*, and was a part-time instructor in the economics department. She was married to a local businessman and trying to piece together a career. A few months later, Katharine wrote to Lowenthal, saying that "my plans for my . . . future have crystallized." Even if she could stay on with the council, she pre-ferred not to. She had enjoyed the "freedom of initiative" her position had afforded, but the council's "year-to-year basis" and "bare subsistence budget" made it impossible to plan ahead and "to carry on effective and creative work." Constance Green could conduct the survey on her own, and, if the council continued, it could do so in her competent hands. Green did stay at Smith, and the council limped along. She resigned in 1948, going on to a career as an independent scholar and a pioneering urban historian, capped in 1963 by the Pulitzer Prize for her two-volume portrait of Washington, D.C.[62]

KATHARINE'S PLANS HAD "crystallized" at a rustic resort in cen-tral New Hampshire where she and Dorothy often spent the sum-mer. Founded as a "haven of simple life" by two New England women who had taught for years at a school for former slaves in the South, the Rockywold-Deephaven Camp was nestled beside Squam Lake on the edge of the White Mountains.[63] Its cabins and common spaces provided exactly what Katharine and Dorothy needed: a place to recover from a bruising semester and decide on a new course of action.

By the time they returned to Northampton in September, Katharine had accepted an invitation from Anna Rochester and Grace Hutchins of the Labor Research Association to write a book on "The South in Progress" to be published by International Publishers, the Marxist press that had reprinted *Child Workers in America* in 1938. Marshaling their creativity and resources, she and Dorothy had also decided to estab-lish a fully independent scholarly base: an Institute for Labor Studies with Katharine serving as part-time research director and Dorothy once more providing the "creative financing" for innovative, interdisciplinary, policy-oriented and collaborative research.[64]

Within a year the institute was up and running, with a slate of trust-ees and an interracial research advisory board drawn mainly from two loose networks, one of left feminist activists and intellectuals and one of southern social scientists. To sustain the venture, Katharine and Dorothy asked their trustees and advisors to make small annual contributions. They also sent circulars to scholars, trade unionists, and government officials who might use and contribute to their research, asking them to pay for a "research membership" on a sliding scale.[65]

Once the United States joined the war, Katharine and Dorothy focused their research on the surge of unionization set in motion by the booming economy and bolstered by a War Labor Board that protected workers' rights in the name of national defense. They had always resisted the pressure to divorce the production of knowledge from the effort to redress the injustices created by industrial capitalism. Now, free from academic restraints and convinced that World War II would prove to be "one of the most important chapters in American Labor history," they decisively closed the gap between the two. Their goal was to supply up-to-the-minute information to labor organizers and policy makers while laying the groundwork for scholarly studies to be written once the conflict was over. Katharine edited a monthly *Information Service Bulletin* drawn from the labor press and a quarterly report entitled "American Labor in the War." She also served as managing editor for two encyclopedia-like books edited by an old friend, the economist and consumer advocate Colston Warne.[66] Concerned with wartime and postwar developments, these books were, as one reviewer put it, examples of "cooperative research and writing at its best."[67]

THE INSTITUTE FOR Labor Studies flourished in a remarkable space: "the Manse," located on Round Hill in the heart of Northampton. Dorothy purchased this beloved but dilapidated structure in 1940, when her mother died, leaving her and her brother $51,000 apiece, about $885,000 in 2017 dollars.[68] She and Katharine wanted to use the house as a private residence, but they also aimed to preserve it as a site for social, intellectual, and political exchange and transform it into a countercultural space designed to bring like-minded women (and a few men) together in ways that were not dictated by the strictures of conventional family life. Not least, they aimed to provide badly needed housing for friends, wayfarers, and refugees whose lives were upended by the war.

The Manse was the ancestral seat of the Stoddard family, a dynasty

The Manse, 54 Prospect Street, Northampton, Mass.

*The Manse, an historic home built ca. 1744 and purchased by
Dorothy Wolff Douglas in 1940. She and Katharine lived and worked there
until the late 1950s, providing rooms and apartments for many
others during the housing shortage following World War II.*

of religious, political, and military leaders that had dominated the Connecticut River Valley during the eighteenth century. In the nineteenth century it became the home of other well-to-do families who turned it into a mixture of Georgian and Victorian architectural design. By World War I the owners could no longer "carry the place financially." They operated it as a faculty residence, opened a tea room serving three meals a day, and then turned it into an inn. In this incarnation the Manse served as a popular gathering spot for town and gown. Dorothy and Katharine had spent many hours there, meeting friends and colleagues and strategizing with their allies in the teachers' union, civil liberties groups, and antifascist organizations. Here they had entertained veterans of the Abraham Lincoln Brigade just back from service in the Spanish Civil War. Here, too, Dorothy had proposed the resolution that kicked off the local battle to repeal the teachers' loyalty oath.[69]

Hiring architects who specialized in historical renovations, Dorothy and Katharine repaired structural defects and brought unity to the Manse's hodgepodge of periods and styles. They turned the tea room into a library and office for the Institute for Labor Studies and used the enclosed porch for political meetings, dances, and other social events. Two bedrooms on the second floor, each with its own fireplace and bath, served as their sleeping quarters. Both women were avid gardeners, and they maintained the lovely cutting garden that curved around the side of the house.[70]

At the same time, they created two apartments on the upper floors, complete with tiny kitchens, one of which was a "Murphy Cabinarette"— a sink, gas stove, and refrigerator all in one fixture. They rented these rooms for a pittance, initially to their friend, Hulda McGarvey, whose husband had just died, and the recently married Adaline Pates, their longtime governess and friend, who moved in with her husband and stayed until the two of them could afford a place of their own. During the acute housing shortage that followed the war, Dorothy and Katharine carved seven more apartments out of the upstairs rooms, which they rented to a succession of impecunious students, foreign scholars, and friends, most of whom were affiliated with Smith College. Three times a week, everyone had dinner together. On other nights they gathered to talk before the fire. Many decades later, the women and men who had lived there still remembered and relished the intellectual and political camaraderie that prevailed.[71]

In 1942 Katharine and Dorothy asked their friend and neighbor, the Marxist art critic and Smith College professor, Oliver Larkin, to add a striking feature: murals in the front hall and stairwell depicting the history of the house and the town. Historical panoramas usually depicted New England as "a place of steadfast tradition" where old-stock Yankees presided over a stable, homey, homogenous pastorale. Such images reinforced the region's claim to being the spiritual heart of the nation but obscured the realities that Katharine and other scholars had documented so meticulously: immigration, industrialization, and then economic decline. But the Manse's murals were not set in some indefinite preindustrial past. They commemorated specific historical events, many of which featured violent conflict and discordant change. In one panel smoke rose from the skeletal remains of a house torched by Indians in 1676 during the conflict known as King Philip's War. Another foreshadowed Shays's Rebellion, an armed uprising of debt-ridden farmers in the wake of the Revolutionary War. Near the end of the entrance hall, Larkin pictured the first train arriving in Northampton, opening the way to New England's transformation into the most urban, industrial, and immigrant-heavy region in the country, even as the myth of "Old New England" captured the popular imagination.[72]

Larkin had arrived at Smith in 1924, the same year that Dorothy began teaching at the college. The crisis of the Depression kindled his social imagination, firing his interest in art that spoke to a society in upheaval. He joined the Communist Party briefly in the early 1930s and, with Dorothy, Katharine, and their friends, played a leading role in Popular Front organizations in Western Massachusetts, especially in anti-fascist groups.[73] Two years after completing the Manse's murals, he sat down to write *Art and Life in America*, which has been hailed as "the major work of art history to come out of the popular front." This scholarly synthesis won the Pulitzer Prize for 1949, and it stood at least until the 1960s as the standard text for the study of American artistic culture. "The modern school of realism," Larkin observed, embraced "the promise and danger of this point in history" by attending to the ways in which ordinary people lived, suffered, rebelled, and endured.[74]

Like Grace Lumpkin and other proletarian regionalists, Oliver Larkin adapted the legacy of the past to present purposes rather than fetishizing tradition as the Lumpkin sisters' Lost Cause relatives had done and as New England's flourishing colonial revivalist movement was wont to do. In her best work, Grace had likewise put her cultural heritage to new literary and political uses. But by the early 1940s, she had begun to reject that project in the name of an imagined return to God and home. Ensconced in "the most interesting homestead in Western Massachusetts" and in the medium of nonfiction, Katharine simultaneously set out on what was, for her, a new kind of writerly journey. She began to turn her memories of home to the purpose of social critique.[75]

PART FOUR

———

WRITING A WAY HOME

"I was not leaving the South in
order to forget the South,
but so that someday I might
understand it, might come to know
what its rigors had done to me,
to its children."

—RICHARD WRIGHT,
BLACK BOY (1945)

"AT THE THRESHOLD
OF GREAT PROMISE"

———

"AS A SOCIAL ECONOMIST AND A SOUTHERNER, I HAVE BEEN a deeply interested student of the South for many years," Katharine declared in the fall of 1939. And so she had. But until the publication of *Child Workers in America*, that interest had found its way into her writing only between the lines, and even that book was framed as a story of "our national disgrace" despite its regional preoccupations. In *The South in Progress* (1940), she came out as a Southerner for the first time. Seven years later, she published *The Making of a Southerner*, the inaugural work in a surge of personal narratives by white Southerners grappling with their own complicity in racism and reflecting on how they escaped from its coils.[1]

Both books were inspired by the possibilities that opened in the late 1930s and expanded during and after World War II, when racial issues moved toward the center of domestic politics without displacing the Popular Front's quintessential class and economic concerns. Reading *The South in Progress* and *The Making of a Southerner* in tandem underscores the impact of this moment on Katharine's views. *The South in Progress* emphasizes her long-held conviction that white supremacy is a "social-economic-psychological complex" whose dismantling requires deep-going structural transformations.[2] Reflecting the opportunities opened by the war, *The Making of a Southerner* combines that conviction with faith that when faced with challenging contradictions and experiences, individuals can liberate themselves from racist phobias and beliefs. Braiding these strands of thought together, Katharine sought over the course of the 1940s to tell about and, by telling, transform the place she had left behind. Together, these two books reveal a self-conscious Southerner in motion, writing her way home.

"One could hardly ask [for] a more vital period of which to write than the one through which we have been passing," *The South in Progress* began.[3] When Katharine left home in the mid-1920s, the South figured in the national imagination chiefly as the culturally barren "Sahara of the Bozart" lampooned by H. L. Mencken and other pundits. By the end of the Depression decade, activists and writers had helped to transform it into an emblem of both suffering and insurgency: America's "exposed nerve," a site of "economic pathos . . . and racist drama" and also a site of possibility, a resonant, authoritative, culturally meaningful location from which to speak.[4]

An explosive confrontation between FDR and the South's ruling oligarchy underscored the region's centrality in the nation's travails. Reelected by a landslide in 1936, Roosevelt signaled a new willingness to take vigorous action in behalf of the "one-third of a nation" that remained "ill-housed, ill-clad, ill-nourished." Standing in his way was what Martin Luther King Jr. would later call "the tragic coalition," a bloc of southern Democrats and northern Republicans in Congress that voted down or filibustered progressive legislation.[5]

In March 1938, the president fought back with an electrifying speech on the courthouse square in Gainesville, Georgia, home to Brenau College, where Katharine had begun her political and intellectual odyssey a quarter of a century before. With fascism looming in Europe, FDR lent his weight to an analogy between the South and Nazi Germany that was beginning to trouble the consciousness of Southerners and non-Southerners alike. Condemning the South's "feudal" economy, which differed little from "the Fascist system," FDR blamed the region's plight on backward-looking politicians and contended that the future depended on replacing them with Democrats who would support an expansion of the New Deal.[6]

The president then carried "the southern question a step further" by authorizing an ad hoc group made up primarily of Washington-based southern liberals to draft a manifesto of its own. Entitled *Report on Economic Conditions in the South* and intended for a popular audience, it described the region as "a belt of sickness, misery, and unnecessary death" and made an implicit but powerful case for a burst of federal aid and regulation designed to restructure its economy. Returning to Georgia to announce the report's publication in the fall, FDR labeled the South "the Nation's No. 1 economic problem" and called on southern voters to repudiate anti–New Deal Democrats who were running for Congress in the upcoming primary elections.[7]

FDR's strike at conservative southern politicians failed in its immediate purpose; most held on to their congressional seats. But a struggle over the South's future had decisively begun. As conservatives redoubled their efforts to blunt the New Deal's most robust measures, left-led CIO unions intensified their campaign to organize the region's farmers and industrial workers. The NAACP led major voter registration and school equalization campaigns. Acting as the "black vanguard of the Popular Front," the National Negro Congress and its youth wing, the Southern Negro Youth Congress, employed boycotts, pickets, and other militant tactics to challenge the underpinnings of Jim Crow.[8] In 1938, more than twelve hundred men and women gathered in Birmingham to form the Southern Conference for Human Welfare. Leveraging the *Report on Economic Conditions in the South* to call for far-reaching reforms, the Southern Conference became the leading voice of the Southern Popular Front, an interracial coalition of labor organizers, civil rights advocates, radicals, and left liberals who saw a robust labor movement, the reenfranchisement of the black and white southern poor, and an activist regulatory and welfare state as the key to reconstructing the South and a reconstructed South as the key to extending the New Deal.[9]

By the end of the 1930s, Katharine observed, the South stood "at the threshold of great promise." Yet it had witnessed a "tremendous . . . consolidation of reactionary forces" as well. "If New Deal reforms . . . were continued and expanded," the region would "forge ahead." If reactionary forces prevailed, "the door of progress will have been slammed shut" and fascism might triumph both at home and abroad.[10] In *The South in Progress*, Katharine aligned herself with the Southern Popular Front, drawing on its key texts, articulating its core insights and values, and sharpening its feminist and antiracist dimensions.

"SOUTHERNERS WHO TRY to know the South as it is have no small task on their hands," she declared. Yet they had one advantage over Northerners ("used here," she explained, "in the broad, old-fashioned sense . . . to mean all in the country who are not Southerners"): confronting the South's dire problems and progressive ferment at first hand, they were "forced by circumstances to go after the truth." Northerners were under no such pressure to revise their views. Despite all the evidence to the contrary, many still saw the South as a "solid, homogeneous entity" and took the conservative southern Democrats in Congress as representative of the region.[11] They overlooked the degree to which these legislators owed their seniority and thus their domination of congressional committees to the disfranchisement and suppression of the black and white poor, who had a dramatic history of rebellion and were ardent supporters of the New Deal. They also failed to notice the emergence of a new breed of southern politicians, which included Ellis Arnall, the young governor of Georgia who, as Katharine Lumpkin proudly put it, was seeking to throw off the bonds of "white supremacy . . . in the form of the white primary" in her native state.[12] Perhaps most important, as Ralph Ellison later observed, Northerners were too quick to accept a "morality-play explanation" of southern conditions "in which the North is given the role of good and the South that of evil," a comforting fiction that, in Katharine's view, ignored the North's complicity in slavery, its abandonment of blacks after Reconstruction, and its collusion with the southern ruling class in exploiting the region's natural resources.[13]

Katharine wrote *The South in Progress* with both northern and southern readers in mind. She wanted to convince "labor and other progressive Northerners" that "their own welfare is tied into the solution of southern problems." She also wanted to encourage the enfranchisement and unionization of the South's working people, creating a constituency for liberal southern Democrats. Her aim was to promote a realignment of the national Democratic Party around its progressive northern and southern wings and build support for what FDR and the *Report on Economic Conditions* had proposed: an unprecedented federal assault on the ills that made the South both a site of intense suffering and a drag on the whole nation.[14]

She began by immersing herself in a flood of studies by Southerners that was, in itself, an indication of the intellectual revolution under way in the region. "The old fund of knowledge to which many of us fell heir as children," she observed, "is very different from the new stock accumulated in more recent years from the researches of scholars and from the experience of men. We must re-examine and reconstruct our ideas on southern history and problems, never an easy thing to do."[15] For that reconstructed knowledge she looked to two buoyant centers of reform-minded scholarship: historically black Fisk University in Nashville, and the University of North Carolina at Chapel Hill, where Howard W. Odum oversaw an academic empire and the university press was disseminating a new scholarship of regional self-discovery. "We are very fortunate to live in a time when such excellent studies of the South are being made," Lumpkin remarked, and she drew on this body of work for her analysis of the "baleful influence" of the "single-crop, plantation economy" and the "blind alley" of the sharecropping system.[16]

Equally important to her thinking were the southern historians who were undermining the shibboleths on which she had been raised. Chief among these was the young C. Vann Woodward, a Southern Popular Front partisan who, surveying the standard literature on the region's past, wondered whether he "had ever encountered . . . volumes so wrongheaded." Into this vacuum he lobbed *Tom Watson: Agrarian Rebel* (1938), his critically acclaimed study of the Populist movement.[17] Watson had eventually turned into a "'rabble rouser' of racial and religious intolerance," as Katharine noted. But in his prime, he had been a "passionately principled mass leader" who promoted a political alliance of black and white farmers, only to be defeated by white supremacists who used "lurid, emotional" rape scares and other racist propaganda "to whip the white vote back in line." These conservative Democrats then turned to poll taxes and similar measures to disfranchise blacks and, not incidentally, to "cut down the votes of the mass of white men who . . . had nearly upset their control."[18]

Radical and liberal writers and organizations mingled freely in the pages of Katharine's book, as they did in her thinking and in the minds of other activist intellectuals at the time.[19] Books on Reconstruction and "the Negro question" by the Communist writer James S. Allen shared billing with studies by Howard Odum and C. Vann Woodward. Myra Page played a particularly important role in Katharine's project; she helped to draft a chapter on labor, relying for information on her own firsthand observations as a left-wing journalist. To bolster her claim that numerous Southerners were "now moving in the full stream of reform," Katharine cited both women's organizations such as the League of Women Voters and the National Consumers League and radical groups such as the Southern Negro Youth Conference.[20]

The South in Progress buttressed, yet went well beyond the ideas that guided the southern white liberals behind the *Report on Economic Conditions in the South*. In doing so, it underscored the striking convergence of a broad swath of black and white Southerners around a common set of assumptions regarding the region's maladies and the need for a far-reaching program of economic reconstruction. At the same time, it illuminated the differences between men such as Howard Odum, whom historians commonly take to be representative of southern liberalism, and left feminists such as Katharine, who also saw themselves as part of the southern liberal tradition but who sought to strengthen the New Deal's redistributionist thrust and infuse race, gender, and regional disparities into its class and economic concerns.[21]

The first of the report's ideas, identified especially with the regional sociologists at Chapel Hill, was that the South's problems could be traced to the waste of its human and natural resources and could be solved through top-down, expert-led planning. The second attributed the South's poverty to its position as an internal colony producing raw materials for the urban, industrial North and, more pointedly, to its domination by Wall Street financiers, who supplied the region with credit, owned much of its industry, and exploited its cheap labor.[22] Katharine looked to labor-based social movements and an activist state, not to expert planners, as the engines of change. But she embraced the notion of the South as an internal colony, all the more so because of her recent travels in Mexico where, as Dorothy Douglas observed, "'imperialism' is no academic term."[23] That experience had alerted her to how, both within the United States and in the relationship between the United States and its poorer neighbor, business interests in the urban-industrial North joined hands with local elites to produce a poverty-stricken plantation economy. By the time the *Report on Economic Conditions in the South* reached publication, its authors had toned down the theme of economic colonialism and eliminated their sweeping attack on finance capital. Katharine, by contrast, used the colonial analogy to argue that only the federal government had the power to "break through the combined strength of northern and southern financial interests which for so long had held back . . . the South."[24]

Her prescription was twofold. First, extend federal measures such as the Wagner Act and the Fair Labor Standards Act to unprotected groups such as domestic and agricultural workers and end "the vicious . . . wage differential" between the North and the South—a chief target of the new industrial unions, which saw the South's cheap labor as their Achilles's heel. Second, pursue a federal program of public aid to education, healthcare, and other social needs targeted especially at the South, home to the vast majority of African Americans and a large population of poor whites, to be funded, as she and Dorothy Douglas always insisted, by taxes on wealthy individuals and corporations. In essence, she wanted redress for a history of exploitation. "What could be more just than steeper taxes on large incomes by the federal government, to help the neediest schools in America, the neediest social services? The South would certainly rate a very large share. Why should not the corporations and individuals who drain out of the region so much of its wealth, be called upon to pay at least some of it back in this highly beneficial form . . .? It would," she concluded, "be only a fair return to the common people" of the region.[25] It would also increase the South's purchasing power, end its role as a drag on the labor movement, and redound to the benefit of the whole country.[26]

Remarkably, at least to those who read it in the wake of the postwar civil rights and feminist revolutions, the *Report on Economic Conditions in the South* said nothing about segregation or racial and gender discrimination. Fearing the worst if white voters saw federal intervention as a threat to Jim Crow, mainstream white liberals put their faith in the belief that prosperity would lift all boats, reducing racial animosity and opening the way to fair treatment of blacks within a system of separation. Even those who strongly opposed segregation steered clear of that radioactive issue.[27]

Katharine shared these liberals' regional and economic concerns but eschewed their attempt to avoid gender and racial issues. She lambasted the "disgraceful" wages of white women in the South and pointed out that black women were paid even less.[28] She attacked racial injustice more extensively and directly. Taking aim at what has come to be called "racial capitalism," she zoomed in on the use of "theories of Anglo-Saxon superiority" to justify the exploitation of low-wage, unorganized, and under-educated black and white labor. "The Negro people," she argued, "are paid lower wages, are shut out from job opportunities, are humiliated by severe social discriminations" in order to keep them imprisoned in a closed labor system not far removed from slavery.[29] An ideology inculcated through conscious and unconscious miseducation, racism divided black and white workers and enabled capitalists, North and South, to exploit the South's workforce and use it as a lethal axe against the labor movement nationwide.

Emphasizing that point, she argued vehemently against the assumption that white workers in the South benefited from this caste and class system. To be sure, every problem that beset the South, from terrible schools to the denial of civil liberties, fell hardest on blacks. "Whether farmer, worker or middle class," Lumpkin wrote, the Negro "is discriminated against in a hundred ways." But by creating a large pool of cheap, unorganized black labor, racial capitalism hurt white workers as well, undercutting their wages and stymying their efforts to unionize. If many, like the former Populists in the wake of the late nineteenth-century white supremacy campaigns, acted against their own interests in response to "old-fashioned, ear-splitting, thoroughly unprincipled" appeals to defend "white supremacy" against the "black menace," she wrote, it is because they "have never had so much as an inkling of education designed to allay their fears, or to counteract the work of vicious agencies and men."[30]

As for the bugaboo of segregation, Katharine did not hesitate to condemn it outright. Separation by law and custom, she declared, "flouts our country's most cherished civil liberties," subjecting black citizens to a "psychological, economic and social environment" that no one, "above all no growing child," should have to endure. Yet, like many others, she also believed that the issue was "so steeped in emotion, so hedged about by feelings of southern tradition and loyalty," that to raise it as an immediate goal was to lose all hope of rallying whites around economic and political reform.[31] By the close of World War II, she would see things differently, distancing herself from liberals who continued to believe that segregation had "no foreseeable end" and arguing instead that "systems of segregation and discrimination built up on" the myth of racial inequality "have no slightest justification, and should go, including the Southern system. It should go."[32] Yet even then, she "had no conception . . . of how it would happen."[33] She could not foresee—indeed, who at the time could foresee?—that a black-led direct action movement would soon topple legal segregation with a series of mighty blows.

Katharine had long been convinced that "so-called racial prejudice was not innate, but a social product; even as alleged racial inferiority was nothing more than a myth. Our established institutions of segregation, subjection, discrimination, against a whole people because of race—in short, our system of white supremacy—all these were nothing more than a man-made arrangement, a historical outgrowth from certain discernible social economic conditions."[34] At the same time, she knew from experience that racism was a violent emotion, communicated in stories and grounded in the body and the deep wells of identification with place and kin. She had seen those feelings acted out in her own family, wrestled with them in herself, and sought to alter them through the face-to-face, person-to-person interracial work of the YWCA. The threat of fascism—understood at the time as an eruption of irrational loyalties and prejudices—brought those memories vividly to mind. Like the "hideous racism of Nazi Germany," she wrote, prejudice burrowed "deep into the . . . emotions of many white children as they grow up."[35]

KATHARINE'S REFLECTIONS on childhood, emotion, and socialization suggested where she was going next. Overtaken by emotionally charged memories and hungering for new ways of blending advocacy and scholarship, she began filling her notebooks not only with the fruits of her research but also with personal "recollections and experiences." By the time *The South in Progress* was published, she had embarked on a more intimate but no less political project.[36] Taking the self-in-society as her subject, she turned to autobiography as social critique.

The velocity of change during the war years encouraged her to move in this new direction. The "Double V" campaign for victory over fascism abroad and racism at home, the Supreme Court's decree that African Americans could not be barred from the Democratic Party's "white primaries" in the South, Roosevelt's historic prohibition of racial discrimination in government and defense industries in the wake of the black-led March on Washington movement, the increasing influence of left feminists in labor unions and government agencies—these and other developments gave demands for an end to segregation and discrimination a hearing that would have been unimaginable during the early days of the

New Deal.[37] Convinced that in this climate, changing the hearts and minds of white Southerners was both necessary and possible, Katharine asserted the value of her dual identity as "a social economist and a Southerner" who could speak with the authority of an insider and, at the same time, use scholarship to demolish myths, mystifications, and illusions. Thinking back over her own life and seized by the belief that a new day in race relations might be at hand, she resolved to use her personal story to show that "no matter how deep were [white supremacy's] roots, and how entangled in our past, nonetheless they could be dug up and cast on the scrap heap as something quite alien to our common human natures." Addressing *The Making of a Southerner* to white Southerners "in transition," she set out "to tell the story of how one Southerner came eventually to learn these plain facts of life."[38]

It is a measure of Katharine's ambitions that when she went looking for a publisher, she bypassed the left-wing and academic presses that had brought out her earlier scholarly work. Instead, she contacted the formidable Alfred A. Knopf, founder and director of a major trade press that had published many of the writers of the Harlem Renaissance and was eagerly looking for new writers from the South. Applying for a Knopf literary fellowship, she argued that three things would make her project unique. The first was her "autobiographical approach." "The Making of a Southerner," she said, will be "written from the standpoint of one who . . . was reared in the tradition she is interpreting, and who, writing as a participant, is able to tell graphically how Southerners of both the old and the new South, and those who . . . were in transition, thought, reacted, and above all, felt."[39] Her second qualification was her training as a sociologist and her interest in history, which would, she wrote, "carry me far beyond my own immediate experience."[40] Finally, by showing how the past stalks the present, yet taking as her "special point of departure . . . the fact of change," she was well placed to avoid the traps into which white southern writers often fell: on the one hand, backward-looking nostalgia, the stock-in-trade of the "school of remembrance" in which she had been raised; on the other, self-deceiving optimism, the bane of those who had been announcing periodically since the turn of the nineteenth century that a "New South" had arrived.[41]

In the spring of 1944, Knopf turned down Katharine Lumpkin's application for a literary fellowship but offered her a contract and a respectable $1,200 advance. By then she was stealing every moment she could spare from her work at the Institute of Labor Studies, slipping away to the desk in her bedroom on the Manse's second floor, and typing the first sections of her autobiography. "Never," she told Knopf, "have I worked at anything so absorbing and altogether enjoyable."[42] She had found the voice in which to write what proved to be her most original and lasting book.

ASKED BY AN EDITOR to explain the need for her autobiography and provide a list of related works, Katharine Lumpkin cited a wide range of history, sociology, anthropology, documentary, and fiction. She also surveyed personal narratives written by other white Southerners, hastening to add that "none of these has attempted to do what I have in mind," for none combined "the method of autobiography . . . with the widest possible research."[43] Yet the autobiographical method posed its own challenges. Although literate women had long written about themselves, relatively few had published formal autobiographies, and until the 1970s the few critics who took this genre seriously identified it with men. More critical in Katharine's eyes, she had no models of white southern memoirists directly confronting the demons of race in their own lives.[44]

A particular "anxiety of self-representation" shaped autobiographical writing by white women in the South. To cast themselves as heroes of their own stories, they had to assert their "claim to membership in the world of words, men, and public spaces" and repress the domestic and bodily experiences that would identify them with the culturally disempowered world of women. At the same time, a female autobiographer who appeared to be too ambitious risked becoming not a hero but a mannish woman. Even the spiritual narrative represented by St. Augustine's *Confessions* was problematic for women, who tended to ground their religious memoirs in relationships with others rather than, like Augustine, presenting the self as a stage for a climactic battle between the spirit and the flesh. To complicate matters further, women writers were often accused of writing *too* autobiographically: they were dismissed as special pleaders who represented a "female condition" rather than a more broadly "southern," "American," or "human" experience. Women were supposed to serve as objects of men's imaginings rather than writing artfully and truthfully about themselves.[45]

Yet white southern women did find ways of constructing autobiographical narratives, often by hiding any trace of anger or ambition and either shoring up patriarchal power or critiquing it only in the most indirect of ways.[46] In the ferment of the 1920s and 1930s, those efforts produced a new form of writing: the modern feminist memoir. Evelyn Scott, one of Grace Lumpkin's closest friends in New York, published *Escapade* in 1923, a thinly disguised "feminist cri di coeur" about her rebellious young womanhood, and followed it in 1936 with her openly autobiographical *Background in Tennessee*, an exploration of her grandparents' lives and the world of her youth. Ellen Glasgow began writing her autobiography, *The Woman Within*, in the 1930s, but her candid account of her coming of age as an artist and her suffering as a woman was not published until 1954, a decade after her death.[47]

For both men and women, the impulse to write about the self and the South drew energy from outsiders' desire to know about the region and Southerners' compulsion to explain. That dynamic was most memorably captured in William Faulkner's *Absalom, Absalom!* (1936) when the Canadian Shreve McCannon demands of his Princeton roommate, the Mississippian Quentin Compson: "Tell about the South. What is it like there. What do they do there. Why do they live there. Why do they live at all." Between the wars, both regional apologists and homegrown critics told about the South, sometimes in fond or defensive remembrance, sometimes in mild, uneasy critique, sometimes in guilt, anguish, and anger, and often in an unsettling mix of all three.[48] Among the best known of these works were W. J. Cash's *The Mind of the South*, a psychologizing critique of his native land, and William Alexander Percy's *Lanterns on the Levee: Recollections of a Planter's Son*, an elegiac defense of a doomed aristocracy. Both appeared in 1941, just as Katharine Lumpkin began imagining her own book.[49]

For all their differences, one remarkable omission tied these writings by white southern men and women together. None took up the challenge of confronting the author's immersion in and complicity with the South's caste system.[50] By contrast, black Southerners who were struggling to assert their humanity and claim their rights in a white supremacist culture could not avoid confronting issues of racism and identity, and from the antebellum period onward, they turned to autobiography as a weapon in that struggle.

Bearing witness to the horrors of slavery and refuting racist stereotypes by seizing the authority of the written word, the slave narratives traced an arc from deprivation to a quest for literacy and a flight north toward freedom and self-possession. This tradition continued after emancipation, but with a new emphasis. The character of African Americans, Booker T. Washington–style "up-from-slavery" narratives asserted, had been "tested and ultimately validated" in the crucible of slavery, and that trial by fire, coupled with the accomplishments of freedpeople, made them worthy of full participation in American society.[51]

Bound to their children, enslaved women could seldom follow the path to freedom traced by the archetypal male hero. But they and their descendants produced a rich vein of autobiography nonetheless. Deploying and, at the same time, transforming the images of the helpless enslaved girl and the suffering enslaved mother popularized by white women's abolitionist texts, black women's narratives often revolved around sexual exploitation, the contradictory meanings of motherhood, and the spiritual search for a place in the "divine scheme of things."[52]

Katharine had been reading the work of black autobiographers, intellectuals, and novelists since her years with the YWCA, and from them and her African American colleagues she had learned to see race as both defining and illusory. By using her own life to "trace to its source the complex development of racial attitudes in a caste society," she sought to do what only black autobiographers had done before: confront the "role of race in making Southerners what they are."[53] She also defied gender conventions, sometimes in straightforward comments about women's "secondary role" but more often as subtext, on the slant.[54]

By composing a self made and remade by race and "by so much else besides," Katharine propelled white southern autobiography in a new direction.[55] Eloquent and analytical, revealing but not confessional, *The Making of a Southerner* became the first of a long procession of autobiographies in which white women and men sought to use their own lives to show how the culture of white supremacy was reproduced and how it could be overcome. These works of passionate self-examination and regional critique evolved with the civil rights and women's liberation movements of the 1960s and 1970s, eclipsing entirely the literature of mourning, remembrance, and defiance on which the Lumpkin sisters and their generation had been raised.[56]

THE MAKING OF A SOUTHERNER is, as one reviewer put it, "a book of hope." By describing her upbringing as a white woman in the plantation South, Katharine sought to identify herself with white southern readers, taking them step by step through her own transformation in order "to deepen and clarify [the] process of aroused thinking" in which they were already engaged.[57] Once she had been the book's protagonist, a malleable, watchful girl at the mercy of good people who create monstrous systems, drilled in a racism that takes "hold of us through our loyalties, affections . . . and ideals." Now, in the 1940s, she was the narrator, a woman who has completely altered her outlook, "rejecting as untenable on any grounds whatsoever . . . the Southern system of white supremacy and all its works." Departing sharply from most male autobiographers, she took pains to stress, not her uniqueness or success, but her commonality with her readers. Like them, she was steeped in memory, yet capable of freedom. Her writing embodied a promise: change can occur from within. What saved her, she stressed, was the "variety of experiences, all southern," to which she was exposed. "To all appearances the South was a highly fixed, stable environment, frozen in its ways. But this same South could and did refashion some of its children. Some of us, although molded in the image of a bygone day . . . yet found the South itself so dynamic, so replete with clashing incongruities, that these could start us down the road toward change."[58]

To describe that "bygone day," with all of its oppressions and contradictions, Katharine devoted almost a third of her book to events that had occurred before she was born. To do so, she relied on what the iconoclastic historian Carl Becker called the "artificial extension of memory," a process that Becker saw as common to "Everyman" and professional historians alike. Some family stories were seared in her memory, not only because she had heard them so often in childhood but also because they were recounted in her parents' written reminiscences, burnished in conversations with her sisters and brothers, and featured in Grace's fiction. Secondhand memories of slavery and Reconstruction in particular came as readily to Katharine's mind as memories of events observed. "We knew it as though we had seen it," she writes of this storied past.[59]

But she also saw memory as Becker saw it and as it is now understood: not as a simple retrieval of the events and feelings of the past, but as an active process of reconstruction or re-remembering shaped by later events. Reading and research, sociology and history were critical to her careful scrutiny of the remembered past. Of necessity, she explained, "I had to let [the book] simmer along during its formative stages, soaking myself meantime in the contemporary literature, the better to recapture my own earlier impressions and experiences, and check them against authentic materials."[60] She was drawn especially to Frederick Law Olmsted's antebellum travel accounts; Fanny Kemble's *Journal of a Residence on a Georgian Plantation*, a dramatic and historically accurate condemnation of slavery; and the Reconstruction era hearings on the Ku Klux Klan.[61] She relied on the work of historians as well, although she found these to be "contradictory and controversial." She looked to the dominant scholars: Ulrich B. Phillips, the reigning authority on slavery, and his mentor, William A. Dunning. But she also consulted Dunning's critics, especially W. E. B. Du Bois and the white Marxist James S. Allen, who saw revising Dunning's narrative of Reconstruction as vital to the social change they sought.[62] In addition, she immersed herself in newspapers, sought out local and family records, consulted her brother Bryan's genealogical research, and beseeched Elizabeth to share the writings their father had entrusted to her care.[63]

Out of this process of research and re-remembering came a depiction of slavery that sought to explain how "the problem of managing . . . black dependents" shaped what the Marxist historians Eugene Genovese and Elizabeth Fox-Genovese would later call the "mind of the master class."[64] The Lumpkin plantation, Katharine argued, was "a community and business rolled into one," in which her grandfather presided over a household that included not only the big house but also the "slave quarters, stables, and springhouse, and the work radiating out into the fields from this hub of activity." Stamped by this assumption of rulership, men like her father could never accept having lost it—or, as they saw it, having it taken away.[65]

Not surprisingly, the Genoveses, writing in the 1980s and 1990s, found much to admire in Lumpkin's work, as did most readers in the 1940s, who saw her treatment of the Old South as "neither romanticized nor derisive."[66] But a handful of critics in both generations viewed the opening sections of *The Making of a Southerner* as an exercise in the very nostalgia and mythmaking that Katharine was dissecting. It is true that she tells many stories of her father's plantation childhood as her father told

404 SISTERS AND REBELS

them, occasionally quoting almost word for word from "An Old Time Georgia Christmas," the fond memoir published in 1906 and reprinted in 1910 when Katharine was thirteen years old. In tones that can seem reminiscent of the southern pastoral, we hear about William Lumpkin's tenth birthday, when, by custom, his father introduced the bowing and curtsying slaves to "your young master," a scene that one reviewer saw as an example of "the paraphernalia that has gone into so many romantic Southern novels."[67] We hear too about Uncle Jerry, the formidable foreman and preacher; Aunt Winnie, "Little Will's mammy"; Runaway Dennis, who always returned; and Pete, William's "body servant," who followed his young master to war and stayed on after freedom. "Indeed, although Pete came and went as a free man," Katharine writes, "in the two decades that followed, he never really left the roof of his none too affluent former master nor broke the peculiar tie which their upbringing had forged."[68]

Yet even in these tales, Katharine is making her moral clear. Finding no evidence to the contrary, she accepts the convenient legend that her slaveholding grandfather was "in no wise a harsh man." But her point is that, regardless of whether a particular master was restrained or cruel, slavery rested on a drive for profits that reduced human beings to things. To demonstrate that reality, she searched family inventories, wills, and deeds, and she opens her account of slavery with the unadorned numbers her research revealed: the dollar values placed on the thirty-seven human beings her ancestors owned. Runaway Dennis was valued at $523 when he was passed on to her grandfather along with horses, cattle, furniture, and tools; Uncle Jerry and Aunt Winnie, no longer "prime," were worth only $400 together.[69] She also draws for perspective on her wide reading. Citing the British socialist R. H. Tawney's insights into the connection between the Protestant ethic and the rise of capitalism, she suggests that if her slaveholding grandfather saw to the slaves' basic material needs, it was because his religion and his economic interests were so closely aligned. Land was cheap and slaves were expensive; it therefore paid to exhaust the land and keep the slaves healthy enough to reproduce themselves.[70]

Eventually she circles back to question her father's stories directly, underscoring the distance between how she once viewed the world and what her later experience and reading revealed. When, as an adult, she read *Narrative of the Life of Frederick Douglass, An American Slave, Writ-*

ten by Himself (1845), she juxtaposed Douglass's quest for literacy and freedom with the tale of "Runaway Dennis" and saw Dennis in a new way: not as the hapless roamer of memory but as one of the "uncounted thousands" of slaves who risked their lives for freedom, fleeing masters both harsh and mild. Douglass's classic autobiography also casts another cherished character in a new light: the fabled foreman and preacher who memorized the Biblical passages his mistress read to him and then repeated them to a slave congregation word for word. Perhaps, Katharine says, Jerry's prodigious feats of memory were an elaborate ruse. Working "a life-long deception on his master and mistress," he had seized the weapon of the written word.[71]

IN HER TREATMENT of Reconstruction, Katharine pursued two related goals. First, "to tell graphically" how that upheaval affected white Southerners of her parents' generation. Second, to show, in vivid, embodied detail, how her father's stories about federal occupation and "Negro rule" permeated her childhood, teaching lessons about states' rights and white supremacy that would dominate white public memory for generations to come. "To my people, as to me in my childhood, who was reared in their history of those fateful months, no 'two sides' to what happened was conceivable," Katharine wrote. "To them there was but one side, made up of true Southerners engaged . . . in a struggle for existence."[72] As for her generation, "it was by no means our business merely to preserve memories. We must keep inviolate a way of life." White supremacy "remained for us as it had been for our fathers, the very cornerstone of the South."[73]

Into this account of how generations of white children "learned race" in the shadow of Reconstruction, Katharine again layers adult research and reflection. Drawing on the thirteen-volume Ku Klux Klan conspiracy hearings of 1871, she marshals first-person accounts of black strivings and white violence, including a description of Abram Colby's political leadership and his beating by the Greene County Klan.[74] What she did *not* find in the Ku Klux Klan hearings was any mention of her father's involvement in these events, nor did she find him in the books and newspapers she consulted. What had he done? What had he seen? She turned to Elizabeth for answers, but her sister, who had been entrusted with "Where and why I was a Kuklux," their father's secret memoir, and had given a copy to the

United Daughters of the Confederacy in 1913, refused to send the original through the mail. Instead Elizabeth wrote to correct "one thing so often misinterpreted in southern history: that is, the Ku Klux Klan." The "crowd of occupation," she insisted, "aided and abetted by bad Southerners . . . urged the negroes on to doing all kinds of lawless acts. There were rapings, murders, burnings, and Father himself was spat upon, and his Mother insulted to his face." The Klansmen in Greene County "never killed a man." They did only what William said they did: they "rode as ghosts of Confederate soldiers," scaring gullible freedmen "into good behavior," or driving them away "if the crime had been very bad."[75]

Katharine could not have seen the violence of Reconstruction more differently. Yet a strained silence lies at the heart of this section of her book. "It is not for me to say what actually happened in middle Georgia," she writes, after describing the "sultry rumors" that swept through the white community, stirring up hysteria and fueling violence. "I only know the story as participants who were fearful antagonists afterward told it. I know what they say happened to them, and, from first-hand accounts heard in my childhood, what one side felt and did about it."[76]

I puzzled for a long time over Katharine's professed agnosticism, which is so clearly belied by the fact that she draws on the Ku Klux Klan hearings to recount "what actually happened" in ways that defied the popular narrative and the Dunning school. What she could not or would not address was her father's role in the violence perpetrated by the Klan. Perhaps, she speculates, he may have been "a rank-and-file young member" who knew little about the group's inner workings or its attacks on public officials. It is possible that she never read "Where and why I was a Kuklux" and so was in fact limited to "accounts heard in my childhood" for an understanding of the "midnight missions" in which he was involved.[77] Yet why would she be kept in the dark while Grace was well aware of their father's memoir—as evidenced by "Southern Woman Bares Tricks of Higher-Ups to Shunt Lynch Blame," the *Daily Worker* article in which she used it to connect her father's stories to the Tuscaloosa, Alabama, lynchings of 1933? One thing is certain: as Katharine approached this fraught subject, she could hear the defensive voice of her beloved oldest sister, surrounded by a chorus of disapproving kin. She could challenge the myth of Reconstruction by amplifying black voices. But she could not draw directly on her father's reminiscences without bringing "disgrace on the family name."[78] In the end, she mounted a detailed brief against the malign myths that reigned virtually unchallenged in her youth, but she did not confront in print the darker truths about her father—truths that, at some level, she must have known all too well.

What she does confront is her own embodied encounter with the anger and cruelty that lurked behind a paternalistic façade. In the most haunting passage in her book, Katharine is eight years old and living with her family in the small town of Ridgeway, South Carolina. Strolling "aimlessly out into the yard before breakfast," she looks through a window and sees a terrible sight. Her father is viciously beating the family's cook. Sounds, sights, and sensations fairly leap off the page. "I could see," "I could hear," she repeats over and over, describing the screaming, writhing woman, the man's face distorted by rage, "the blows of a descending stick."[79]

Katharine does not call this violent man "Father," her name for William Lumpkin throughout the book. Yet she leaves no doubt about the identity of the "white master" who delivers "blow upon blow."[80] She chose those words carefully, evoking the lash of slavery and the terror of Reconstruction and witnessing not only to this one act but also to the countless crimes committed by anonymous white men against anonymous black women. She thus transforms the personal into the political, a disturbing, confusing childhood memory into an allegory of white male impunity and power. To tell the story differently—as the tale of one woman's "Father," infuriated by his lack of money and social standing, terrifying his daughter as he takes out his frustration on the most defenseless person in sight—would have deprived the scene of its iconic power.

Katharine is unsparing about her response to this event, not for the purpose of self-exculpating confession but to suggest the limits of a child's moral sensibility and the conditioning that white children shared. In the moment, she tells us, she is profoundly shaken, whether out of sympathy for the woman's suffering or shock at her father's behavior. Yet she experiences no precocious epiphanies, no awakening to injustice because of what she has seen. Instead, she is jolted into color consciousness; she becomes "fully aware of myself as a white and of Negroes as Negroes." Soon she finds herself anxiously parsing the "signs and symbols" of segregation in order to distance herself from people to whom such things could be done.[81]

Behind this clear-eyed account of racial learning is a trembling figure in the shadows, not just every child, but Katharine at a moment she perhaps had not fully understood until she began to confront memories that at first presented themselves as mere slivers of sensory experience. Leafing through her personal copy of *The Making of a Southerner*, I came upon a note scribbled in her hand. It seems to have escaped her like a cry. "Aftermath of incident in Ridgeway—traumatic for me," she wrote, pointing to the time when, frozen in shock, she witnessed a small woman at the mercy of an enraged man.[82]

In a biography of the feminist abolitionist Angelina Grimké, Katharine's final book, she took as her theme the flight of a woman from the physical and emotional violence hidden at the heart of family life. She opened with Grimké's memories of the cries of slaves and the rages of her beloved brother, so extreme that she feared he would beat a slave to death. When I met Katharine in the mid-1970s, a few months before *The Emancipation of Angelina Grimké* appeared, the memory of her own father's brutality had, if anything, gained in psychic charge. She spoke of the beating in a whisper, explicitly comparing herself to Grimké and implying that in writing about another woman she was writing about herself. Both Lumpkin and Grimké had cringed at the sight of "someone helpless, in the throes of those who rule." Both wrote about the cruelty of men they loved without identifying them by name. And, for both, traumatic memories from childhood provided a source of disturbing knowledge upon which they would later act.[83]

IN THE LAST TWO THIRDS of her book, Katharine weaves a narrative of remaking around a series of carefully chosen turning points, moments of condensed meaning in which she gradually unlearns the lessons she had internalized as a child. At each turn, she captures the ebb and tide of memory. She tries to forget confusing or disturbing experiences, only to have them come into focus later, under the pressure of subsequent events. What at first creates no more than a vague sense of unease becomes cumulatively transforming as contingency and choice combine to call received wisdom into question and suggest alternative views.

Over time, her protagonist becomes fully conscious of "herself as a self": a separate being, an individual with her own angle of vision and growing confidence in her contrarian judgments and original ideas. Men like her father and grandfather, who loom over the first third of the book,

recede from the text as she ceases to hold them in awe. Women gradually emerge from the shadows. The "I" of critical consciousness develops
through affiliation with a new "we," the "little company of Eves" who
encounter the social gospel at Brenau College and the black and white
women with whom she works in the YWCA.[84] Seizing the power of
self-representation, she moves from listening to telling, from absorbing
ideology through story to resisting the moral and recasting the tale.

In her account of her family's sojourn in the Sand Hills, Katharine
captures this process of forgetting and remembering with particular eloquence and grace. Leaving for college at the age of fifteen, she was eager
to forget that "ill-begotten country," but the images of poor people she
had lived among "were photographed indelibly on my mind." Like layers in a palimpsest, those images overwrote the "glamour . . . of the old
plantation" without wholly obliterating it and then were overwritten in
turn. With each revision, each writing, erasing, and rewriting, the faint
impression, or repressed memory, of earlier experiences shone through,
imperceptibly altering more recent memories.[85]

As, in the course of her book, Katharine returns again and again to
this pivotal episode, she explains to herself and her readers, in the register
of felt experience rather than of abstract theory, how the link between
class and race figured in her changing consciousness. "Something, it
seems, was begun out there in the Sand Hills," she writes, eventually
leading her to realize that white poverty was not a sign of "group incapacity." It was produced by a hyper-exploitative form of capitalism based
on slavery, sharecropping, and cheap industrial labor. Having learned to
think of poor whites as "working people" and of the South as "an economy," she moved on to more challenging truths. First, to an understanding of "what it meant to be a party to our Southern ways . . . to have a
hand in imposing their rigors, not alone on persons whom one knew, but
now on the unknown millions whose state one had learned to visualize."[86]
Second, she began to see that what marked the black masses as inferior in
the eyes of whites was in fact the effect of poverty and exploitation.

Even more unusual than this account of how class-conscious thinking exposed racist myths was Katharine's focus on the figure of the black
woman as a colleague, a collaborator, and an agent of change and her
description of how she came to see the South differently by glimpsing it
through black women's eyes. In *The Souls of Black Folk* (1903), W. E. B. Du
Bois articulated the question that was implicit in how even the most

well-meaning white liberals tended to view African Americans: "How does it feel to be a problem?"[87] YWCA women like Katharine initially saw the problem as a matter of treating with "Christian consistency" the exceptional members of a generally inferior race, worrying all the while about where such efforts might ultimately lead. Cooperating with their black colleagues to build an interracial student movement in the Jim Crow South, some came to see the challenge quite differently. In the end, Katharine writes, "it struck me with stunning force that these . . . women were plainly unconcerned with the problem I faced. I might be wrestling with inferiority of race, but not these Negroes. To them it was nonexistent, only a fiction, a myth, which white minds had created for reasons of their own. A vicious myth, to be sure: one with a history, which could and did wreak havoc in the life of their people, but a myth pure and simple just the same."[88] The "Negro problem" was, as Gunnar Myrdal's *An American Dilemma* (1944) put it, a "white man's problem"— and, as Katharine recognized, a white woman's problem as well.[89] It had nothing to do with the nature of black people but arose from a system of discrimination and exploitation imposed on blacks by whites.

Yet even then, Katharine tells us, her reeducation remained incomplete. Haunted by the dogma "that but one way was Southern, and hence there could be but one kind of Southerner," she could not shake the feeling that by renouncing her inherited beliefs she "had turned my hand against my own people." The resolution of that dilemma—and her memoir's final epiphany—entailed the discovery of "how diverse were Southerners, and how different the strains of Southern heritage that had been handed on . . . by the white millions whose forebears had never owned slaves, and also by the Negro millions whose people had been held in slavery." Foremost among these "different strains" was a history of dissent. It was this "fresh reading of our past" that saved her from the ambivalence and anguish that beset white Southerners torn between love and hate of their native land. It was this identification with "the strivings of these various Southerners after a different South" that allowed her to speak in an autobiographical voice that was so strikingly self-assured.[90]

Katharine ended her book in the 1920s, with the conclusion of her five years as head of the southern student YWCA. Her rationale was that, by then, she had learned to think of class and race in new ways, and with that shift in consciousness, her remaking was complete. But she stopped there for strategic reasons as well: the narrator of *The Making of a Southerner* speaks as a native daughter, propelled, as Katharine put it, by the "inner motion of change" and moved by the South's internal contradictions and possibilities.[91] The author, by contrast, had long ago left the region. To write about the 1930s and 1940s, she would have had to adopt the expatriate's voice and point of view. She would also have to draw attention to her leftist politics, her long quest for a professional recognition, and her relationship with Dorothy Douglas, all of which would have distanced her from the white southern readers she hoped to reach. This reticence, which cast a veil over much of her adult life, not only in her autobiography but also in later interviews, could be seen as an effect of the anxiety that led many women either to mute their own voices or to repress intimate experiences in order to claim a place in a male world. Yet it was also integral to her political purposes and to the quiet, persuasive power of her book.[92]

BY THE TIME Katharine's memoir appeared, three of her four brothers were deceased, and Bryan was so horrified that he refused to read the book.[93] Being "very careful not to [say] anything unpleasant," Elizabeth responded graciously. "Love and congratulations," she wrote early in 1947 when *The Making of a Southerner* arrived in the mail. "Thank you so much for the book. I wish I might have written it."[94] Katharine saved that letter, but not a later one in which Elizabeth claimed that *The Making of a Southerner* was "an agony" to their relatives in South Carolina.[95] In the mid-1970s, when I asked Katharine about her family's response, she requested that I turn off the recorder. She had worried especially about whether to expose the secret of her father's beating of the black cook. "This was tough medicine." But it was "my memory and a very vivid one." To use the incident for her own purposes seemed disloyal in the extreme, and "I have not been appreciated for that." But to leave it out would be to omit an experience that "left a lasting impression on me . . . as far as the racial system was concerned."[96]

Counterbalancing her family's reaction were the warm letters that poured in from friends, college classmates, and YWCA colleagues, many of whom she had last seen decades before. A former member of the Y's national staff was amazed by Katharine's "ability to make personal experience serve so universal an end." "Because the major part of the book was about the you I hadn't known and because the you I do know is

Katharine in 1947,
upon the publication
of her autobiography.

so dear to me, I read as if you were talking to me," she continued. "I wish I could see you to catch up more tightly the threads that combine as part of the fabric of me. Thank you for being you. My love ever."[97] Another friend wrote to say that she remembered Katharine's views on race from their heart-to-heart talks in college. She had named her daughter after Katharine and planned to "devour every word" of her book. From even further back in time came a letter from a man Katharine had known when they were children in the Sand Hills. Gazing at her picture on the book's cover, he could "still see some signs . . . of that pixie-like wit, and spirit that you possessed as a lovely girl."[98]

Equally gratifying were the reviews, written mostly by white Southerners, which appeared in newspapers and magazines throughout the country. Reviewers in Macon, Georgia, where she was born, and Columbia, South Carolina, where she grew up, took pride in her local connections and quoted extensively from her "sincere and frank" memoir.[99] *The Making of a Southerner* should be "required reading" for Georgians, said the Rome *News-Tribune*, especially for "many of our present day politicians, who haven't advanced a step in their thinking in the last hundred years." The *Baptist Press* in Nashville pronounced the book "a masterpiece: in knowledge, intelligence, and sheer beauty of expression, it is unexcelled."[100]

In the *New York Times Book Review*, Hodding Carter II, the Pulitzer Prize–winning editor of the Greenville, Mississippi *Delta Democrat-Times* and one of the South's best known liberals, urged everyone who wanted to know why white Southerners "50 or older" were the way they were to read Lumpkin's "crystal clear" examination of a generation "so immersed in the past, so guided by the patriarchal despotism of its war-hallowed elders, so determined that . . . disenfranchisement and separateness of race must be forever maintained" that few could "even now break away . . . from their emotional conditioning."[101] A Memphis State College professor, writing for the *Saturday Review of Literature*, placed Lumpkin in an "ever expanding circle" of Southerners who "are convinced that the old way of life constitutes a flat denial of the ideals of democracy." The publisher of the *Southern Packet*, a monthly review of books that served as a forum for young black and white writers, wrote to thank Knopf for enabling Katharine Du Pre Lumpkin, W. J. Cash, and others "to say things that needed saying. . . . More is going on down here than meets the eye through the press. More men and women are working for justice than this nation realizes. . . . We seem about to embark on a revolution in our interracial pattern."[102]

Beneath this positive response, however, ran an undercurrent of misreading that conflated Katharine's evocation of the beliefs she had inherited with her adult point of view or faulted her for being insufficiently polemical or confessional. Writing in the *Daily Worker* under the alias David Carpenter, David Vernon Zimmerman found it hard to believe that the same person who had written *The South in Progress* would publish *The Making of a Southerner*, which he characterized as a rambling, "unconscious apology" for slavery. In response, Myra Page mounted an insightful defense of her friend's memoir and, implicitly, of Katharine's left-wing political credentials. "Dr. Lumpkin has chosen the autobiographical method" to combat the process of miseducation that left white Southerners unprepared "to face current realities. . . . Having firmly established her kinship with her desired audience, she then takes them with her through experiences that step by step forced [her to recognize] racial inferiority to be a myth, useful to those who gain . . . wealth by keeping a whole people 'in their place,' and with them, the majority of laboring whites." To some, Page conceded, "the author's subtle handling verges on nostalgia," but this criticism was unwarranted. At worst, Lumpkin had "in a few instances . . . fallen victim to her method." Like a novelist writing in the first person, she had risked the possibility that her readers would identify the author with her protagonist and assume that Katharine as an adult still harbored the views she had held as a child.[103] Looking back, Katharine admitted that there had indeed been a "real risk in my method." "To my sorrow," she concluded, I "learned that when people read books, very often [they] read there what *they* wish to see, not what the author means at all. Read into it *their* feelings, *their* sentiments, *their* outlook—they kind of leave the poor author out in the cold."[104]

One reviewer in particular read Katharine's book through the lens of her own preoccupations in telling ways: Lillian Smith, the best-selling author of *Strange Fruit* (1944), a controversial novel about interracial sex and one of the white South's most outspoken opponents of segregation. Smith and Lumpkin were born ten days apart in 1897; each was initially inspired by liberal Christianity; each was preoccupied with how children were socialized in an oppressive society; each possessed a keen moral imagination; and, unusually for southern women, each dared to use her life story "to speak of, for, and to the South."[105] But they told about the region in very different ways.

In 1949, three years after Katharine's book appeared, Smith published *Killers of the Dream*, a mix of memoir, allegory, and social commentary. Linking racial phobias to sexual shame, she rooted the culture of segregation in white men's love for and then rejection of their black nannies, their sexual exploitation of black women, their infatuation with the notion of pure white southern womanhood, and their projection of their own conflicted desires onto the mythical black rapist. While Smith praised Katharine's "sincere and brave and genuinely moving book" for capturing experiences that many white Southerners shared, she faulted her for giving only "the surface facts of her life" and for failing to grapple with sin and sex.[106]

A model for what became a long series of "racial conversion narratives," *Killers of the Dream* anticipated the emergence in the 1950s and early 1960s of a brand of Cold War racial liberalism that relied on the argument that whites' treatment of African Americans undermined the United States' standing in the struggle against the Soviet Union and saw race relations primarily as an issue of morality, not as the class-inflected systemic problem that Popular Front intellectuals such as Katharine took it to be.[107] As the literary scholar Fred Hobson observes, "Racial discrimination and acute poverty were not social problems to Smith; they were 'evils'"—a word that was quite foreign to Lumpkin's sensibility—and the South was "a kind of hell," a twisted, grotesque, nightmare world. Like Lumpkin, Smith was repelled by the evangelical drama of public conversion, yet in her own way she took on the role of the evangelical preacher. Speaking in the register of sin and repentance, she called on white Southerners to break down racial and other barriers as much for their own spiritual and psychic benefit as to better the condition of blacks.[108]

SPEAKING TO NORTHERN audiences in the months after *The Making of a Southerner* appeared, Katharine sought to clarify the main themes of her book. She would never have put pen to paper, she said, had she believed that she was writing about herself as a singular individual. Using autobiography as a vehicle, she sought to show how she had rejected the culture of white supremacy precisely because she believed that other white Southerners were doing so as well, however small a minority they might be and however hostile the climate they faced.[109] Readers' responses seemed to vindicate that view. "The South is far from Solid . . . currents of change are truly moving down there!" she exclaimed. African Americans were at the forefront, but the battle was not between blacks and whites. Rather, on one side stood blacks and a dissenting minority of whites, all Southerners "born and bred," and on the other, a white majority determined to maintain the status quo.[110]

Katharine was also convinced—and said so pointedly each time she spoke—that the "doctrine and practice of 'white supremacy'" prevailed not just in the South but "all over America." "You do know, do you not, what I mean by the 'white supremacy system,'" she asked a class of Smith College students. "Of course, you *should* know . . . because . . . it is not merely a Southern phenomenon. It is . . . all around you in the North." She did not underestimate the system's power. But, buoyed by the accomplishments of the Second New Deal, the defeat of fascism, the militancy of blacks, and the gains of labor in the crucible of war, she looked forward to an era of postwar reconstruction and to new opportunities for writing and activism in an uncertain but exciting political world.[111]

WILDERNESS YEARS

ITHIN A YEAR AFTER *THE MAKING OF A SOUTHERNER*
appeared, Katharine was launching a challenging new project: a book
that would blend history and fiction to bring the story of a black Reconstruction era leader to life. In 1949, she applied for and won a coveted
Houghton Mifflin Literary Fellowship, a boon that, as Houghton Mifflin's editor-in-chief was quick to explain to the fifty-three-year-old
author, usually went to "younger writers."[1] Encouraged by this support,
Katharine began working furiously on an historical novel. The writing
has "gone along pretty swiftly for a slow writer like myself," she told the
publisher of her autobiography, Alfred A. Knopf.[2]

Then, a few weeks before she was scheduled to begin teaching her
usual classes, Dorothy Douglas opened the *Springfield Daily News* to
find herself featured in a front-page story headlined "Smith Educator
Is Listed As 'Red' Fund Contributor." Unbeknownst to her, J. B. Matthews, a Methodist minister who had recanted his left-wing views and
was now serving as the chief investigator for the House Committee on
Un-American Activities (HUAC), had gained access to her bank records
and was monitoring her donations. Drawing on information he leaked
to the press, the *Springfield Daily News* claimed that seven years earlier
(when the United States and the Soviet Union were allies), Dorothy had
given $3,500 to the tax-exempt American People's Fund to support orga-
nizations such as the National Council of American-Soviet Friendship,
an antifascist group that promoted cultural exchange with and knowl-

edge about the USSR.[3] The council had included Communists along with distinguished individuals from across the left-liberal political spectrum. But in the mid-1940s it found itself on the US attorney general's list of subversive organizations and under investigation by HUAC. In 1946 its executive director was convicted of contempt of Congress for refusing to turn over the group's records.[4] Besides associating Dorothy with this now suspect organization, the article sought to link her to the founder of the American People's Fund, Frederick Vanderbilt Field. Dubbed "America's Millionaire Communist," Field was a China expert under attack by Senator Joseph R. McCarthy, whose rise to power was being fueled by a search for scapegoats for the so-called "loss of China": the Communists' 1949 victory in the Chinese civil war.[5]

Within weeks of the "'Red' Fund" exposé, Dorothy's courses had been canceled or assigned to others and she had taken a "special leave."[6] Immediately after that, Katharine packed up her materials on Reconstruction, and the two women sailed for Oxford, England, where Dorothy's son John was a Rhodes Scholar. They planned to spend time in England and France and return to Northampton in time for the spring semester. Instead, Dorothy sent in her resignation, leaving the faculty position she had worked so hard to secure.[7]

The only acknowledgment of Dorothy's abrupt departure in the records of Smith College is a cryptic note in the minutes of the board of trustees accepting her resignation. For public consumption, she said then and repeated later that she left her job in order to stay in Europe and write. Still, the silence of the archives is telling. Dorothy was sixty-one, had not been planning to retire, and was soon searching for another teaching position. It seems clear that she left Smith so precipitously because of the exposé, whose impact was magnified by political and personal events that had profound consequences for Katharine as well.

BY 1950, WHEN the "'Red' Fund" article appeared, anticommunist hysteria was rapidly turning the left-liberal political ideas and associations of the 1930s and 1940s into "un-American activities" and transforming the fear of Soviet aggression into an obsession with internal subversion. The political climate had begun to change in the mid-1940s, as business hostility toward the New Deal exploded, the Republicans captured both houses of Congress, and the Soviet Union began expanding into Eastern

Europe. Harry Truman, who had been elevated to the presidency by the death of FDR in 1945, found himself under intense pressure to stave off Republicans' charge that Democrats were "soft on Communism" and subversives had infiltrated the federal government. Resolving to fight the "red menace" aggressively at home and abroad, he formalized a federal employee loyalty program that drove from public service a generation that shared Katharine's and Dorothy's social democratic commitment to an expansive welfare state.[8] Soon congressional investigating committees were spearheading a hunt for subversives that affected virtually every aspect of American life. At the center of that campaign stood J. Edgar Hoover's FBI, which drew few distinctions between CP members and liberals, saw homosexuals and civil rights activists as threats to national security, and resorted to illegal wiretaps, break-ins, and political sabotage to stamp out dissent.[9]

The attorney general's list of subversive organizations, authorized by Truman in 1947, gave the anticommunist crusade one of its most powerful weapons for discrediting groups and individuals. Granted "perhaps the most arbitrary and far-reaching power ever exercised by a single public official," the attorney general added organizations to the roster according to vague criteria, gave them no opportunity for appeal, and published the results. For most of these groups, merely being listed was "a kiss of death." Members and donors fled in droves, yet still found themselves blacklisted, under surveillance by the FBI, or called to testify before congressional investigating committees.[10]

Dorothy and Katharine had belonged to numerous organizations that appeared on the attorney general's list. Their names had also cropped up in several early HUAC hearings, where they appeared on lists of advocates for the Workers' Unemployment and Social Security Bill, signers of the "Open Letter to American Liberals" pleading for antifascist solidarity with the Soviet Union in the late 1930s, and members of various leftist organizations. They were singled out as supporters of social policies that had always been seen as "red" by the anticommunist, anti–New Deal right but that, until the late 1940s, had also been the signature issues of ascendant liberal reform. Although the FBI did not open a formal investigation of Dorothy until 1950, this attention had been enough to send its agents sleuthing around Northampton as early as 1943.[11]

Relying mainly on Smith College's registrar, its director of public relations, and a librarian, the FBI agents gathered detailed information on everything from Dorothy's political activities to her family background, her marriage, her house, and her relationship with Katharine. But they were especially interested in her *ideas*, which informants did their best to describe. Their speculations reflect the relative open-mindedness that prevailed in the early 1940s, even as they suggest how invasive the culture of surveillance and betrayal would become. According to the registrar, Dorothy "has always been interested in Communism from a theoretical standpoint" and was "regarded as mildly pink."[12] True, she had traveled to Russia and had asked the library to order numerous books about "Communistic philosophy," but both were perfectly "natural" since they served "the purpose of enabling her better to handle [these subjects] in her courses." She may have been "a believer in the Communistic form of government to a certain extent," but those beliefs had probably waned since she had come into a "substantial inheritance." After all, "the acquisition of any substantial amount of property tends to remove any Communistic sympathies. In any event . . . Mrs. Douglas is not dangerous insofar as foreign affairs are concerned and is not at present engaged in any subversive activities."[13]

Katharine came under scrutiny as well, mainly as what FBI agents called Dorothy's "roommate" and "a close personal friend" who was "in full sympathy with Dorothy W. Douglas concerning Labor agitation in educational institutions."[14] Local informants portrayed her as a bit of an outsider, but certainly not a danger to her country. As one put it, she "came to New England from one of the southern States and . . . has written many books reflecting the Negro situation as concerned with the South." She was also "a woman of great intellect" and there was no reason to doubt her "loyalty to the United States of America." She did not harbor "foreign sympathies," nor was she known as "one who advocated a different form of Government than now exists."[15] The bureau's sleuths added their own innuendos: they described Dorothy as small and attractive; Katharine, on the other hand, "usually wears sports clothes; [is] not attractive; [has] a rather mannish appearance."[16]

Interest in the "mildly pink" professor and her "roommate" intensified in the wake of the bitter presidential campaign of 1948. As fear of the Soviet Union spread and the struggle to expand the New Deal stalled, a critical new group had joined the anticommunist network: anticommunist liberals and disillusioned leftists who supported Truman's policy of aggressively containing the expansion of Communism abroad. Dorothy and Katharine, by contrast, opposed Truman's foreign policies and aligned themselves with the postwar movement for a "positive peace," which combined demands for an extension of New Deal reforms with efforts to halt the nuclear arms race, strengthen the United Nations, eliminate poverty and colonialism in the Third World, and pursue peaceful coexistence with the USSR.[17]

In support of these goals, they abandoned the Democratic Party, which nominated Truman for a second term, in favor of a third-party candidate: Henry A. Wallace, a Midwestern reformer who had served as Roosevelt's secretary of agriculture and vice president, and then as Truman's secretary of commerce. Forced to resign when, alone among Truman's cabinet members, he spoke out against the president's hard line against the Soviet Union, Wallace embraced the core ideas that animated the Southern Popular Front. "The problems of the Negro people," he proclaimed, "lie at the very heart of the problem of the South; and the problems of the South are basic to the critical problems of our entire nation. The cancerous disease of race hate, which bears so heavily upon Negro citizens, . . . at the same time drags the masses of southern white citizens into the common quagmire of poverty and ignorance and political servitude." Campaigning on the slogan "Jim Crow Has Got to Go," Wallace barnstormed through the South speaking at integrated meetings, a principled decision that added intense racial animus to the hostility his views on foreign policy aroused.[18]

The Wallace campaign, as the historian Robert Korstad points out, triggered "an ideological split that would have far-reaching reverberations." Many African Americans, left-wing unionists, and white southern left liberals—including women, to whom the Progressive Party offered unprecedented opportunities for political participation—were convinced that the Democrats had abandoned both the cause of world peace and efforts to restructure the South's economy and ensure black civil rights. By joining this third-party campaign, they hoped to stem the Democrats' rightward drift and rejuvenate the Southern Popular Front. The CIO executive committee and Democratic Party leaders, on the other hand, feared that Wallace would siphon off votes and ensure a Republican victory. The rift between these groups widened when the Progressive Party refused to exclude members of the Communist Party or reject the party's endorsement, leading to charges of Communist domination. In the end, even many of Wallace's most ardent supporters voted for Truman in the face of polls showing Republican candidate Thomas E. Dewey in the lead.[19]

In the wake of Truman's surprise victory and Wallace's crushing defeat, the peace movement Wallace stood for was branded as a Soviet plot. For Katharine and Dorothy, that shift was driven home in March 1949, when they signed on as sponsors of a Scientific and Cultural Conference for World Peace held at the Waldorf-Astoria Hotel in New York City.[20] The conference had been announced by a committee that emerged from a pro-Soviet peace conference in Poland, raising suspicions that it was directed by the Kremlin. Denying those allegations, the principal US organizers lined up an impressive list of peace advocates that encompassed Communists, pacifists, anti-imperialists, independent radicals, and left liberals, including a number of highly respected intellectuals. The plan was to meet with delegates from Western Europe and the USSR for an exchange of ideas about how to promote a more just international order and, as the playwright Arthur Miller put it, avoid "another war that might indeed destroy Russia but bring down our own democracy as well."[21]

Dorothy was instrumental in recruiting Smith president John Herbert Davis to chair a panel on education. But Davis and other prominent liberals withdrew just days before the conference in the face of a fierce counteroffensive spearheaded by Sidney Hook, the leader of a group dubbed by the CIA and the State Department the "Non-Communist Left," which was working feverishly to disrupt the conference, operating out of a bridal suite in the plush hotel.[22] In the streets, the American Legion and other rightwing groups led raucous demonstrations portraying the event as a platform for Soviet propaganda. Seldom had a meeting of writers and artists faced such public hostility. In April, the media mogul Henry Luce personally oversaw a double-page spread in *Life Magazine* featuring photographs of fifty sponsors, branding them as the Kremlin's dupes.[23] Although Katharine and Dorothy escaped mention in *Life*, their involvement made its way into their mushrooming FBI files and complicated their relationship with President Davis and the college.

The political career of Dorothy Douglas's ex-husband added an agonizing personal element to her increasingly precarious position. Like Katharine and Dorothy, Paul Douglas had stood well to the left of Roosevelt in 1932. But by 1936, he had thrown in his lot with the Democrats, warts and all. In 1939 he won a seat on the Chicago Board of Aldermen, where he cultivated an image as a "hard-boiled idealist," a pragmatic intellectual who could "tear up his classroom concept of the perfect society and join the ranks of politicians who . . . 'get things done.'"[24] While Katharine and Dorothy were supporting Henry Wallace and the Progressive Party in 1948, Paul was running for the Senate on the Democratic Party ticket. Winning an upset victory, he quickly emerged as one of Congress's leading anticommunist liberals and a contender for the Democratic presidential nomination. Although Paul combined support for civil rights, labor, and social welfare with a wholehearted endorsement of the Cold War, he was persistently red-baited by opponents who found ready fodder in his left-wing past, especially his 1927 trip to Russia and his earlier membership in "communist-front" organizations on the attorney general's list. Once in office, he walked a fine line between demonstrating his anticommunism and maintaining his reputation as a defender of civil liberties.[25]

As both international tensions and the domestic witch hunt intensified, that position became harder and harder to sustain. In the fall of 1950, Douglas and his fellow Senate liberals found themselves grappling with the McCarran Internal Security Act, which required the registration of members of the perfectly legal Communist Party and its allied groups and the incarceration of anyone advocating the violent overthrow of the government, a position that all Communists were presumed to hold. Douglas tried to sidetrack the legislation by introducing what critics called a "concentration camp" alternative authorizing the Attorney General to round up anyone believed to be engaged in subversive activities in case of a national emergency. That effort failed, and ten days after the "'Red' Fund" article appeared, he voted in favor of the McCarran Act, now containing both the original provisions and the concentration camp addition. That evening he found his and Dorothy's sons, John and Paul, "dispirited by what I had done. I somehow felt, despite my excuses, that I had failed morally. For the next two nights I could not sleep as I pictured . . . a new reign of terror settling over the country."[26]

A month later, the FBI added Dorothy's name to Hoover's Security Index, a vast collection of index cards on individuals who might be detained, marking her as a possible victim of the legislation Paul had supported.[27] Although unaware of that threat, she was quite conscious of the danger of coming under further scrutiny, all the more so because her ex-husband's enemies might use her political views to undermine his political career, dragging not just them but also their children into the Red Scare's glare. That anxiety may have contributed to her decision to resign from her job, and it was surely exacerbated by the knowledge that Paul had refused to speak out against the excesses of McCarthyism, which he privately deplored, and had helped to enact such draconian anticommunist legislation.[28]

The firing of leftist faculty at other colleges and universities also offered cause for heightened concern. In the first major academic freedom case of the Cold War, three tenured professors at the University of Washington were fired in January 1949, two on the grounds that they belonged to the Communist Party. At the time, Dorothy had reason to believe that Smith College would not succumb to this assault on free speech and academic freedom. Despite his withdrawal from the Waldorf conference, Smith's president John Herbert Davis remained a member of the National Council of American-Soviet Friendship and an advocate of engagement with socialist ideas. In the immediate aftermath of the University of Washington decision, he told the *Springfield Daily News* that he had found "no dangerous revolutionaries among either students or faculty" at Smith and argued that "no teacher can be discriminated against" simply on the grounds of membership in the Communist Party.[29] In the months that followed, he continued to uphold the position that professors should not be punished for political activities and beliefs that did not impair their teaching and research, a doctrine that was espoused in principle by the American Association of University Professors even as it was almost universally ignored by college administrators. But Davis retired at the end of the spring semester of 1949, and his replacement, Benjamin F. Wright, used his first public appearance to issue an ominous warning against Soviet aggression. Soon Wright was saying in no uncertain terms that "there is no place for a Communist on the Smith College Faculty."[30]

While college and university administrators and trustees throughout the country continued publicly to defend academic freedom, by the time Wright assumed office, they had redefined its meaning so as to exclude from protection anyone who refused to answer questions about his or her political affiliations and ideas, as well as known Communist Party members. Their rationale was twofold. First, all Communists were "slave[s] to immutable dogma" and thus too closed-minded to be capable of free inquiry. Second, professors had a duty publicly to reveal their past and present political beliefs and affiliations; failure to do so marked them as devious and dishonest. Whether faculty members' politics affected their teaching and research was irrelevant. Indeed, not one of the teachers dismissed during the Red Scare was ever accused of indoctrinating students or producing biased research.[31]

Whatever factors loomed largest in Dorothy's decision to leave her job, one thing seems clear, both from the silence surrounding the departure of such a well-regarded faculty member and from the evidence of later events: President Wright and the trustees were relieved to see her go. That relief was palpable when, a few months after her June 1951 resignation, a pamphlet on *Red-Ucators at Leading Women's Colleges* used the attorney general's list of subversive organizations to bring Smith College directly into the anticommunist line of fire. Published by a group devoted to ridding elite colleges and universities of "Socialistic, Un-American teaching and teachers," the pamphlet listed the "communist front" affiliations of twenty-three Smith faculty members, including Dorothy, the art historian and painter Oliver Larkin, and Hallie Flanagan Davis, the former head of the Federal Theater Project who was a dean and professor in the drama department.[32] At about the same time, Louis Budenz (an ex-Communist building his career as the best known of the professional witnesses who served as FBI informants and testified on the "evils of Communism" at hearings and trials) was naming Dorothy as a "concealed Communist" in secret reports to the FBI and using her as exhibit A for his contention that Smith College was "under the influence of subversives" in a course he was teaching at a Catholic church in New Jersey.[33]

To fend off these charges, the head of Smith's department of public relations offered up Dorothy, along with her friend Hulda McGarvey Flynn, an alumna who had taught in the psychology department and lived at the Manse until 1943, as the only faculty members who "were definitely charged with Communist leanings and . . . with having given leadership . . . to the most radical element among the student group." She hastened to add that the two women were long gone and had "no connection whatsoever with College."[34] According to FBI agents, another member of Smith's public relations staff, an actress and sculptor named

Frances Rich, drew an almost comically sinister portrait of Katharine and Dorothy that stood in contrast to the more anodyne descriptions previously offered by neighbors and friends. Katharine was "a Southerner who speaks Russian and has written several books on the negro situation from a Northerner's point of view." Dorothy also spoke Russian "and her home is known in Northampton as the 'Little Kremlin.'"[35] (This bit of gossip survived in local memory decades later when it was relayed to me by a man who remembered that, as a mischievous boy, he liked to throw rocks at the Manse on his way to school.)

As for the mood at the college, Smith officials reassured current and potential donors that it was "quite wholesome and free from radicalism," a disclaimer that, by the early 1950s, contained more than a kernel of truth. A *New York Times* reporter who interviewed students, faculty, and administrators at Smith and other institutions in 1951, a month before Dorothy sent in her resignation, found that "a subtle, creeping paralysis of freedom of thought and speech is attacking college campuses." To be sure, some individuals and organizations withstood that trend. Smith's "Interrace Group," an offshoot of the YWCA and other bastions of liberal Christianity, survived into the mid-1950s as other progressive student associations disbanded.[36] Despite being accused of exposing susceptible young women to "red" influences, "helping to promote the atheistic philosophy of Karl Marx," extolling "the alleged virtues of Godless Russia," and decrying "the so-called sins of the U.S.A," the YWCA's national leadership refused to impose loyalty oaths or purge members with Popular Front connections.[37] Standing its ground as "a Christian organization . . . compelled to be interested in the problems of society," it rejected the claims of critics such as Phyllis Schlafly, who later rose to fame as an antifeminist crusader, that "to speak of a 'better world' or 'a new society' [was] communistic."[38]

Still, despite such pockets of resistance, the *Times* reporter was right: throughout the country fear was stifling liberals and radicals alike. Faculty members were becoming increasingly guarded about their political opinions. Students were reluctant to express progressive, much less radical, views for fear of being labeled Communists, investigated by the government, and suffering damage to their future careers. Such caution "made many campuses barren of the free give and take of ideas" and encouraged a "passive acceptance of the status quo." The ostensibly wholesome but actually repressive atmosphere fostered by anticommunist hysteria, the *Times* concluded, struck a "body blow at the American educational process, one of democracy's most potent weapons."[39]

FOR KATHARINE AND DOROTHY, as for the country at large, that atmosphere darkened over the next few years. While they were in Europe, Grace Lumpkin had become an informant in the notorious trial of Alger Hiss. Hiss had been a rising star in the New Deal and, in 1945, had been involved in the Yalta peace conference, where the United States, Britain, and the Soviet Union made critical decisions regarding the shape of the postwar world. He had also helped to organize the United Nations and was then president of the Carnegie Endowment for International Peace. In the summer of 1948, Whittaker Chambers claimed under questioning by HUAC that Alger Hiss had been his best friend in the Communist Party in the late 1930s. Hiss sued Chambers for slander, setting off a long, drawn-out battle between the patrician insider and the brilliant, scruffy, overwrought outsider. At first Chambers denied under oath that he and Hiss had spied for the Soviet Union. But when the statute of limitations on espionage expired a few months later, he led investigators to a microfilm of State Department documents allegedly given to him by Hiss and concealed in what would become an infamous hollowed-out pumpkin on his Maryland farm.[40]

As the case dragged on, FBI agents ferreted out copious information regarding Chambers's sexuality and early life, as did investigators for Alger Hiss. Both took a keen interest in the relationships among Chambers, his future wife Esther Shemitz, and their friends Grace Lumpkin and Michael Intrator. The hundreds of pages of interviews generated by the investigation may not have shed much light on the Hiss–Chambers case, but they do tell us much of what we know about the foursome's early, East Village days, down to such unlikely details as the couples' decision to open a passageway between their apartments and the time Chambers "became rather lonesome for the country" and purchased a pair of rabbits, only to find both apartments overrun by bunnies.[41]

Michael Intrator, who was suffering from a serious cardiac condition related to having had rheumatic fever as a child, was initially "firm in his refusal to talk," although he later provided a few terse answers to the agents' persistent questions. In contrast, Grace was proud to play a role in the case. After Hiss's lawyer and a detective visited her during Christmas week in 1948, she claimed improbably that she had convinced them that "Hiss was lying and Whittaker Chambers was telling the truth." When the FBI arrived, she offered information eagerly, stressing charges against the Communist Party that she had leveled in "An Ex-Communist Speaks" and would often return to in later years.[42] Among these was one that became a particular obsession: that sexual promiscuity was practically a requirement for membership in the communist movement.

Asked whether Chambers had "some tendency toward homosexuality" as evidenced by what others referred to as his "peculiar" relationships with Intrator and other men, she demurred but suggested that anything was possible. Repeating an accusation that had been in circulation since the Russian Revolution, despite the party's deepening sexual conservatism both in the United States and in Soviet Russia, she explained that Communists "were taught that morals meant nothing to Party members and should in no way deter them from carrying out Party activities; that homosexuality had been legalized in Russia and that the only immorality recognized by the Communist Party was deviation from the Communist Party line." As for Alger Hiss, he may have started out as an idealist, but "subsequently in the Party he became a psychopath so that he had no moral sense." He should "come clean" so that he could serve as "an object lesson to youngsters in schools and colleges as well as adults who were being fooled into embracing Communism without knowing exactly what they were doing, just as she had been herself in the past."[43] Elaborating on her view of Hiss on another occasion, she chose words that, in the years that followed, she would habitually repeat. The Communist Party demands of members and fellow travelers "that they learn to lie cleverly. . . . This is why idealists like Hiss . . . become progressively corrupted so that in the end they cannot tell right from wrong." "They are to be deeply pitied," Grace concluded, but nonetheless they are a "thoroughly evil force."[44]

Looking back, Grace pointed to the Hiss case as a critical turning point in her political evolution. In her telling, when she began to distance herself from the Communist Party in the late 1930s and early 1940s, she still believed in the "Communist/Socialist philosophy of State power and social progress." For that reason, she "felt at home" in the New Deal wing of the Democratic Party.[45] But she had grown uneasy as the United States cemented its wartime alliance with Soviet Russia. Her unease intensified when, during the postwar peace talks in Yalta and Paris and then through the UN, we "lost the peace to the Communists." The country's leaders, she lamented, had been "fooled as badly as I had been when, as a youngster, I had believed in all the Communists promised." Nevertheless, she claimed to have been still voting a "straight Democratic ticket" when Chambers began his testimony in 1948 and initially assumed "that all the furor was merely a move by the 'conservative' Republicans to discredit the 'progressive' Democrats."[46]

Late in 1949, when Hiss was on trial, not for espionage but for perjury, Grace wrote to Eleanor Roosevelt explaining that Chambers was telling the truth. Roosevelt replied diplomatically: "I am returning your enclosures as I think we will have to leave this case to those involved." But a few days later, her "My Day" column included what Grace considered "a spiteful blast" against Chambers.[47] Convinced by Chambers's accusations, Grace was shocked and disillusioned when Democrats such as Roosevelt supported Hiss and disparaged her friend. As she recounted it, it was then, and only then, that her conversion was complete. She had already given her heart to God; now she gave her mind as well. To her that meant joining Chambers in the camp of anticommunists who believed that the road to communism was paved with liberal ideals.[48]

Riveted by a drama that put one of her closest friends at the symbolic center of the Red Scare and offered her the role of "friendly witness" in an ascendant anticommunist crusade, Grace came to see Chambers as a martyred hero and, like many conservatives, to view Hiss as standing for "all of the . . . subverters-from-within" who started the United States down the road toward socialism, allowed the Communists to take over China, and enabled the Soviet Union to overrun Eastern Europe and become the United States' only real rival in the postwar world.[49]

Still, despite her convictions and her efforts behind the scenes, Grace was reluctant to testify in public when Hiss and Chambers were facing off before HUAC or during Hiss's trial. "The publicity would hurt her family and friends and would cause her much difficulty," FBI agents reported.[50] Once Hiss was convicted in January 1950, however, she put those fears aside and began actively to pursue an informer's career. Reading about the charges against China experts in which Frederick Vanderbilt Field and, very indirectly, Dorothy Douglas were implicated, she wrote to Joe McCarthy, an obscure senator from Wisconsin who had rocketed to notoriety a few months earlier with a speech in Wheeling, Virginia, in which he claimed to be holding in his hand a list of Communist agents in the State Department. Thanking McCarthy for his courage, Grace said that she had met Field's first wife, Elizabeth, known as Betty, and offered to provide additional details. McCarthy wrote back immediately, asking her to convey all she knew.[51]

As the historian Richard Kluger observes, Betty was "a Bryn Mawr graduate with a serious and independent mind, who considered herself radical but was in no way politically doctrinaire." After a messy breakup with Field, she had married Joseph F. Barnes, a brilliant and equally independent-minded Moscow correspondent for the New York *Herald Tribune*. Betty lived in the Soviet Union in the late 1930s, where her Russian-speaking husband battled Soviet censorship to report on everything from Stalin's purges to ordinary Russians' lives. Replying to McCarthy, Grace painted a very different picture: Betty Barnes, whom she had met at the Southern Summer School for Women Workers, could be used to discredit Field because she was a member of the Communist Party and her second husband was a fellow traveler whom Whittaker Chambers had bribed with money from Moscow to write favorable stories about the Soviet Union.[52]

Warming to her subject, Grace went on to claim that Louise Leonard McLaren was also a Communist or a fellow traveler and her husband was an "ardent Communist."[53] Indeed, the Southern Summer School, which Grace had lauded at length in an article in *Social Work Today* when she accepted McLaren's invitation to teach there in 1938, had been wholly "captured" by the CP. Her chief example involved a secret class in Marxism to which only the most "advanced" students were recruited. Lois MacDonald, cofounder of the school and for many years its economics instructor, remembered that, during the 1938 session, Leo Huberman, a working-class Marxist who was teaching at the school for the first time, *did* hold small meetings at his house for the more radical students, and in 1939 she and others objected to inviting Huberman to return the following year. But there is no reason to think that the school ever strayed from its commitment to welcoming a wide range of left-leaning teachers without aligning itself with either the Socialist or the Communist Parties. Indeed, by 1940, economics was being taught by H. C. Nixon, a Vanderbilt Agrarian-turned-southern-liberal with a special interest in agriculture.[54]

Grace's digression on Betty Barnes and the Southern Summer School aroused no interest from McCarthy, and she heard no more from him. But on May 11, 1951, she was subpoenaed to appear before a closed session of the McCarran Committee, which sought to propagate the accusation that the Truman administration had lost China.[55] She was happy to help, she replied, reiterating her qualifications: she had been "very close" to the Communist Party for ten years and close to Whittaker Chambers before and after he "belonged to Soviet intelligence." The only problem was that, besides having met Frederick Vanderbilt Field's former wife, she knew next to nothing about the subject at hand. Nevertheless, a week later she traveled to Washington, where she reiterated what she had already told McCarthy, although with some differences in detail.[56]

Both McCarthy's office and the McCarran Committee furnished Grace's supposedly confidential allegations to the FBI, and the bureau sent agents to interview her, with strict instructions not to reveal that they knew about her involvement with the investigating committees. The FBI also contacted Whittaker Chambers, who denied ever passing money to Joseph Barnes or telling Grace Lumpkin that he had done so.[57] Chambers's denial, coupled with discrepancies between Grace's letter to McCarthy and her testimony before the McCarran Committee, raised questions in the investigators' minds. Was she a reliable informant? Had she truly broken with the Communist Party? If she had hoped to establish herself as one of the "informants of known reliability" on whom the red hunters relied, she had fallen short of her goal.[58]

Almost a quarter of a century later, I asked Grace about her involvement with the congressional investigating committees and received a startling reply. She remembered nothing about the Barneses. But there was one aspect of her testimony she could never forget:

> I had to tell on one of my sister's best friends, because she was really doing a lot of harm at Smith College. . . . She was handing out propaganda left and right. At that time, my sister was organizing for the Communist Party among the intellectuals in different colleges. . . . But I told a lie, I told the Senate committee that my sister had nothing to do with it, but that this woman was really doing a lot of harm. . . . And I knew that if I told about her, that would get my sister out of it and I wanted to get her out

of it. . . . She had gotten me into Communism, and I was trying
to get her out.

What impact did her efforts have? I asked. Dorothy "was dismissed
from Smith," she answered. Katharine "was very much hurt. . . . You
could understand how she could feel that way. . . . It sounds like a nasty
thing to . . . tell on my sister, or tell on this woman who was her friend.
But I did the right thing, just like Whittaker Chambers. A lot of people thought that it was nasty for him to come along and tell about Hiss
and tell about these other members of that spy ring, but he was trying to
right a wrong."[59]

Twenty-nine years after my conversation with Grace, the transcripts of her closed testimony before the McCarran Committee hearing
became available for the first time. I was taken aback to find no mention
of Katharine or Dorothy at all. Other documents in the committee's
files, however, were illuminating, as were the FBI reports I obtained
through repeated Freedom of Information Act requests and a civil suit
against the FBI. None suggested that Katharine had, in any sense, been
"organizing for the Communist Party among the intellectuals in different colleges." But they did reveal that, in early June 1951, a few weeks
after her closed testimony before the McCarren Committee, Grace
found herself on a train, enjoying a "good dinner" and a talk with a man
whom she later thanked for "the very quiet work you have (apparently)
been doing for years to help establish the right kind of peace in the
world." The man was Benjamin Mandel, a former teachers' union activist
and a Communist-turned-Lovestonite until he broke with the left and
joined J. B. Matthews and Louis Budenz as a key member of the professional anticommunist network. Having served on the staff of HUAC,
Mandel had just become the McCarran Committee's research director.[60]

In two sets of handwritten notes, Mandel passed along to the committee various new details that his train ride with Grace revealed, including her allegation that Dorothy Douglas, "ex-wife of the Senator," was
a Communist Party member and Katharine was "close to the party or
in it."[61] He seems also to have given this information to the FBI, which
interviewed Grace again a month or so later. This time she said that her
sister was "still a 'fellow traveler'" and "had told her at least 15 years ago
that Dorothy Douglas was a Communist Party member."[62] So in effect
Grace had, as she put it to me, "told on" Katharine and Dorothy, a chill-

ing phrase that suggests that even the rationale of saving her sister as Whittaker Chambers had saved her could barely shield her from feeling guilty about such an intimate act of betrayal.

TWO YEARS AFTER Grace's testimony before the McCarran committee, HUAC opened hearings on Communist infiltration of education, calling Smith College English professor Robert Gorham Davis as its first witness. Davis had written for leftist publications in the 1930s and, while teaching at Harvard from 1937 to 1939, had been a member of a tiny CP cell. He left the party after the Hitler–Stalin pact and began teaching at Smith in 1943. In 1949 he joined Sidney Hook in denouncing the Waldorf conference, and by 1953 he was well established as a contributor to conservative organizations and publications. Questioned at length in front of television cameras in a room packed with onlookers, Davis described the political milieu that had propelled him and others into the communist movement in the late 1930s: the "lively interest in Marxism" on college campuses, the yearning for solutions to the nation's economic miseries, the sense that Communists stood at the forefront of opposition to fascism, and that "the policy of the Soviet Union seemed consistent with American interests so far as the struggle against fascism and Hitler were concerned." The Communist faculty members he had known were "at heart democrats, liberals, progressives"; they had not used their classrooms to influence students or been under pressure to do so. Moreover, he observed, today "the influence of Communists is very slight . . . and among students at colleges like Smith . . . radicalism had disappeared entirely."[63]

Yet Davis also reassured the committee that it could in good conscience ignore critics who were complaining of "interference with academic freedom." He reinforced the presumption that Communist professors, "democrats, liberals, progressives" though they might be, were "necessarily . . . dishonest," and he welcomed the chance to ensure that teachers who were or had been Communists were exposed and removed. To that end, he readily named names. Asked by HUAC's general counsel whether he knew Katharine Lumpkin, Dorothy Douglas, and Hulda McGarvey Flynn, Davis recalled meeting them in Communist caucuses at American Federation of Teachers conventions, including the first "Battle of Buffalo" in 1939 when conservatives launched their takeover of the union. He also remembered having "struggled against" Lumpkin's and Douglas's leadership of the AFT local at Smith and resigning over the local's support for Henry Wallace in 1948.[64] A few months after his HUAC testimony, he told the FBI that although he had had no contact with Dorothy, he was certain that she "has [not] changed her political thinking today." Almost a year later, he was repeating that charge: he had not seen Dorothy in years, but he "feels she is as much of a Communist now as she was in the past."[65]

Of the twenty-one people whom Davis claimed to have known as "Reds" in the 1930s and 1940s, only a few were singled out by the *New York Times*. The most prominently targeted was Dorothy Douglas, "the first wife of Senator Douglas." Asked for a comment, the senator's office issued a claim that Paul Douglas would repeat over the years: he and Dorothy "were divorced nearly a quarter of a century ago and have had virtually no contact since."[66]

Fearing further accusations, Smith College president Benjamin Wright charged the Faculty Trustee Committee with deciding how the college should respond to investigating committees. As the trustees deliberated, faculty members engaged in an impassioned debate over whether they were obligated to name names when summoned before congressional inquisitors. Some argued in the affirmative. Others suggested that "some of the crucial advances in civilization . . . have been achieved by" those who "have felt compelled to set personal conscience above the law and to accept the legal results."[67]

By all accounts, Davis's testimony and the furor that followed sent Dorothy, Katharine, and Hulda into a spiral of uncertainty and anxiety. Eleanor Lincoln, a Smith alumna who lived at the Manse (and who described Robert Gorham Davis as a "rat"), remembered that Dorothy was devastated. She buried most of her library of Marxist-influenced books behind the barn at a friend's summer place.[68] She stayed on the move between an apartment at Bryn Mawr, where she was teaching temporarily, and one she and Katharine maintained in New York, quite possibly in order to avoid or at least delay a subpoena and gain time to plan before confronting whatever public questions and accusations she might face. Katharine, who was living at their permanent residence in Northampton, sought refuge at her old friend Myra Page's home in Yonkers, New York.[69]

As they feared, Davis's testimony provided HUAC with a pretext for summoning Dorothy Douglas and Hulda Flynn to testify before Congress. An exposé in which Flynn appeared as a manipulative communist operative made her especially vulnerable.[70] Ten years earlier, she had left her position in psychology at Smith (and her apartment in the Manse) to earn a PhD at Columbia University while also teaching at the Jefferson School of Social Science, a Marxist adult education institution associated with the Communist Party.[71] She moved to Boston in 1943, in part to be near John Patrick (Jack) Flynn, a fellow graduate student and former priest with whom she had fallen in love and whom she married in 1945. There she served as the assistant director of a similar adult education institution, the Samuel Adams School, which a soon-to-be-famous informer named Herbert A. Philbrick had infiltrated and to which Dorothy Douglas contributed. When Philbrick published *I Led Three Lives: Citizen, Communist, Counterspy* (1952), a sensational bestseller that went on to inspire one of the country's top-rated syndicated television series, Flynn found herself caricatured as a teacher who used the language of justice and democracy to disguise the school's real aim, which was to promote the destruction of capitalism through violent revolution.[72]

Testifying on February 27, 1953, Hulda Flynn claimed that she had given up "*all* political activity" when she married Jack Flynn in 1945, a fact which, she wrote, "everyone . . . knows full well." Asked to name friends and associates from the 1930s and early 1940s who had been in or close to the Communist Party, she planned to evoke her First Amendment rights to free speech and refuse to answer questions about her political beliefs and activities. That choice, however, carried the risk of being charged with contempt of Congress. Because she had just had her third child and did not want to go to jail, she finally took her lawyer's advice and instead pled the Fifth Amendment, which protects witnesses from being forced to incriminate themselves, a privilege that had been upheld by the courts but which, in the court of public opinion, was tantamount to admitting to membership in the Communist Party and thus to disloyalty and subversion. Flynn provided basic information about her education and employment up to 1943, when she completed her PhD, and then declined to answer all other questions on the grounds that "my answer might tend to incriminate me," adding immediately "that I use the word 'incriminate' strictly in the legal sense, not the moral sense."[73]

As Flynn was suffering through this interrogation, Dorothy Douglas's attorney, Ephraim S. London, fired off a letter to HUAC saying that his client was aware of Robert Gorham Davis's allegations and asking the committee to contact him if it wished to interrogate her. A few weeks later, the chair of HUAC telegraphed London asking him to arrange for Dorothy to appear for questioning on March 13, 1953.[74] She began her "brief but stormy" testimony by asking to read an introductory statement regarding not just herself but a member of the Senate, "as a matter of courtesy, for his protection." The chair of the committee refused her request, indicating that the committee would receive the statement after she had testified. He posed a few perfunctory questions before asking abruptly whether she had ever been a member of the Communist Party. She took the Fifth and then refused to answer the same question about Hulda Flynn and Katharine Lumpkin. Drawing on information secretly provided by the Bureau of Internal Revenue, the committee asked whether she had contributed $600 a month to the CP between 1936 and 1939. When she refused to answer that question as well, the chair drew the hearing to an end after just ten minutes. Despite his initial assurances and her repeated protests, he declined to allow Dorothy to read her prepared statement on the ground that she had not been a cooperative witness.[75]

Yet read the statement she did. Speaking to reporters on the steps of the Capitol, she made her stance clear. She had been prepared to answer all questions pertaining to her work at Smith College and to the years prior to 1930, when she and Paul Douglas were divorced, because she knew that refusing to do so would be misconstrued and used to the senator's disadvantage. But she would take the Fifth regarding her personal political beliefs or associations in later years. "The sole purpose of such inquiry would be to determine my political orthodoxy and that of my colleagues; to determine whether my political beliefs conform to those of this committee. Such inquisition can result only in the suppression of freedom of conscience and of the mind. Few would dare to maintain an unpopular opinion or support an unpopular cause, if that opinion or support can be the subject of public inquiry and subsequent penalty."[76]

Seizing a measure of control within a narrow range of options, Dorothy succeeded in getting her message out. Major newspapers from the *Los Angeles Times* to the *Chicago Daily Tribune* covered the story, focusing primarily on her prepared statement rather than her brief testimony. Asked to respond, Paul Douglas repeated his earlier disclaimer, but added: "This much I can say: During the years of our marriage she was

Dorothy Wolff Douglas on the steps of the Capitol brandishing a prepared statement she was denied permission to read during her appearance before HUAC in March 1953.

WAVES STATEMENT—Mrs. Dorothy W. Douglas, 63, onetime wife of Sen. Douglas of Illinois, waves a statement at House Un-American Activities Committee hearing, where she refused to say if she is a Red.
(P) Wirephoto

Two Professors Refuse to Tell if They're Reds

Physicist and Ex-Wife of Sen. Douglas Denounce Questioning by House Committee

certainly not a Communist. She was, on the contrary, deeply religious, generous and high-minded, with a strong sense of personal honor." He then hastened to add the required ideological mantra: "Needless to say, I believe the Communist Party is an organized conspiracy against the United States and the peace of the world and that we should use every effective means to combat it."[77]

A few weeks later, Senator Joe McCarthy summoned Grace Lumpkin for her turn on the public stage. With the election of Dwight D. Eisenhower in 1952, Republicans had taken control of both the presidency and Congress, raising hopes that they would lose interest in searching for Communists in government. Instead, McCarthy escalated his reckless campaign. Gaining his own platform as chair of the Permanent Investigating Subcommittee of the Government Operations Committee, he continued his attempt to expose subversives in the State Department, first charging that the Voice of America, the department's overseas broadcasting unit, was a font of Communist propaganda and then making the United States a laughingstock by forcing the department's overseas libraries to purge supposedly subversive books.[78] Included among those dangerous publications was Grace Lumpkin's 1935 novel, *A Sign for Cain*.

On April 2, 1953, Grace appeared before McCarthy's committee to answer questions about her work. Quizzed by Roy Cohn, McCarthy's shrewd, cold-blooded chief counsel, she readily admitted that she had written *A Sign for Cain* "under the influence and the discipline of the

Grace Lumpkin testifying before the Permanent Investigating Subcommittee of the Government Operations Committee, chaired by Joseph P. McCarthy, on April 2, 1953.

Communist movement." When the committee moved to dismiss her she asked—and, as an especially cooperative witness, received—permission to make this final statement: "If you are even remotely connected with the party, you get the corrupt influence that 'lies do not matter' [and] you have to give your inner consent to murder. . . . What is demanded, and given, by any member of the party as well as by anyone connected with the party . . . is complete loyalty to Moscow and contempt and hatred for everything that is basically and truly American. . . . From that demanded loyalty the step to active treacher[y] to one's own country is inconsequential."[79]

THROUGH THIS PERIOD of turmoil, Dorothy and Katharine found solace in work. Dorothy focused on writing evenhandedly about Eastern European Communist regimes. Katharine immersed herself in her historical novel on Reconstruction, an earlier era of great hopes and dashed promises. Living quietly in a community in which they had so recently played prominent public roles, they continued to express their ideals in engaged scholarship, as they had always done.

Dorothy, accompanied by Katharine, had traveled to Czechoslovakia, Poland, and the Soviet Union in 1948, gathering information from on-the-spot interviews and official documents about the rapid postwar take-off of economic development in Eastern Europe. In 1953 she published *Transitional Economic Systems: The Polish–Czech Example*, which traced the two countries' differing paths toward Soviet-style state socialism as well as the patterns they shared: a concentration on heavy industry, a substantial role for trade unions, a striking rise in female labor force participation, and the encouragement of equal wages for women's equal work. Dorothy could not foresee that the region's growth would prove unsustainable, nor was she aware of the increasing ferocity of political repression. But neither did she express any particular sympathy for Eastern Europe's Communist regimes. One friend characterized Dorothy's approach this way: "The thing that always distinguished [her was] her ability to free her intellect from the pressure of her sympathies, which were always on the side of the underdog and in favor of experiment, and to hunt down the facts, and having found the facts ask what they really mean. This way of looking at things has been called pro-communism on one side of the barrier and bourgeois objectivity on the other, but Dorothy was never influenced by labels." Nevertheless, because *Transitional Economic Systems* was published in the depths of the Cold War and did not dismiss state socialism out of hand, it sank like a stone, attracting almost no attention from scholars.[80]

Katharine's very different, but equally political project drew on the famous Ku Klux Klan hearings of 1871 in which she had first encountered the haunting stories that "stripped away from the Reconstruction period the overlay that so completely distorted it." She chose as her protagonist a York County, South Carolina, leader named Elias Hill, a former slave and self-educated preacher so crippled from a childhood illness that he could not walk.[81] In "Eli Hill," the novel she based on the life and times of this historical figure, she tried to do what she had not been able to do in *The Making of a Southerner*, and indeed, what no white historian had yet attempted. She tried to portray "the struggle . . . against white supremacy" as African Americans "knew it and felt about it." Indirectly, she grappled with her confusing childhood memories of her father's involvement in the Ku Klux Klan and the "sense of fear, of horror, or doom" that shadowed her current political moment. Echoing through the novel were issues that she herself was confronting: how best to exercise political courage, the nature and consequences of betrayal, the choice between secrecy and disclosure, and the relationship between speaking out and fleeing, either figuratively or literally, in the face of repression.[82]

On the one hand, Katharine surrounded her protagonist with black men, women, and children involved in densely layered relationships and reliant on varying strategies of resistance and survival. On the other, she pitted him against a former slave owner named John Temple who tries to convince him to depend on white benevolence and "interfere no more with politics." Resisting that pressure, Eli Hill is betrayed by his white neighbors and viciously beaten and interrogated by the Klan, which accuses him of holding secret meetings, preaching "political sermons," and inciting blacks to violence. He readily admits to his political activities but refuses to confess to "what I never said, done or thought of." In despair, he considers emigrating to Liberia, a solution that the real-life Elias Hill and 167 of the freedpeople he led actually chose. The fictional Eli decides to stay, risking his life by testifying at the Ku Klux Klan hearings of 1871, helping the army and the Department of Justice break the back of the secret society in South Carolina, and staving off the end of Reconstruction there for another five years.[83]

As he feared, Eli's testimony makes him a marked man. Within weeks he is shot and killed by two white assassins who go scot free. "Moses never saw the Land of Promise," says the elder standing beside Hill's grave. "The children of Israel were caught in the wilderness, a waste-howlin' place—did they quit a-movin'? No, Lord! They buried Moses. Then they girded up their loins and kept on their way."[84]

In March 1951 Katharine sent Houghton Mifflin what she thought was the final draft of "Eli Hill." But instead of seeing the book though production, she spent the next ten months responding to readers' critiques. One reader admitted that when she read Katharine's initial proposal, she had been "immediately prejudiced, as I thought: Here is one more of those southern ladies writing about the South," but she had found herself admiring Lumpkin's initial chapters, which focused on "the crippled little negro boy" and handled "what I suppose is a trite subject to many with . . . skill."[85] The later chapters, which followed Eli Hill into manhood and expanded the canvas to include the collective struggle of the black community, were another story. They reeked "of the girl writing on a history exam who doesn't know the answer and covers up with emotional prose." Above all, the editors thought Katharine was overly invested in her black characters. "In her prejudice on the racial question, Miss Lumpkin is unable to represent a truly good, baffled white southerner of the period."[86]

Speaking to Katharine for the press, managing editor Craig Wylie presented a critique that, in her view, revealed a fundamental misunderstanding of the ethical and political burden of her novel. She had begun "Eli Hill" in the spirit of the progressive literature and scholarship of the 1930s and 1940s, which took class and racial conflict as central themes and sought to overturn the white supremacist narrative of Reconstruction. As she wrote, however, both fiction and historical writing turned in new directions.[87] The Agrarians discarded regionalist polemics and took up an infinitely more influential role, that of detached men of letters. Foundations, government agencies, and other groups seeking to forge a cultural agenda for the Cold War were quick to embrace these "New Critics" and to grasp the political utility of their anticommunist animus, their disdain for protest literature, and their emphasis on the individual searching for meaning in the modern world. Making their way in an expanding academic marketplace and allying themselves with the "Non-Communist Left," which enjoyed similar support, the Agrarians-turned-New Critics ensconced themselves in leading universities, where they dominated literary scholarship in the decades after the war. Evaluating texts according to formal criteria and dismissing biographical, political, or historical interpretations, they relegated socially conscious books to the dustbin of "propaganda."[88]

At the same time, the Cold War ushered in "consensus history," a view of the American past that downplayed conflict and emphasized shared values. Pitting themselves against conservatives at home and Communists abroad, Cold War liberals drew on this history to enshrine the "vital center" as the American way. Over time, that stance would shift the Democratic Party to the right, as politicians claiming to represent the center increasingly sacrificed egalitarian principles for electoral success.[89]

In tune with these changes, Craig Wylie argued that Katharine should cut the "interesting irrelevancies" about the black community. She should concentrate on her two main characters, Eli Hill and the white paternalist, John Temple, and let her plot turn on the tragic failure of the "middle-of-the-road" position they represented. That story, if properly told, would appeal to contemporary readers "since certainly one of the greatest problems of our own day is . . . that of the intelligent moderate man trying to maintain his position."[90]

On the contrary, Katharine answered, the story is "not a parallel struggle of two . . . men of good will who seek . . . the same general end, a course of moderation in turbulent times," but "one of fundamental conflict of aim between the two men and their two peoples." During the Civil War African Americans had fought for freedom; during Reconstruction they tried to create a democratic biracial society. There was no "middle ground solution" to the struggle that ensued because from 1865 on white Southerners had "made known without any equivocation that 'White Supremacy' was . . . their solution to the two races living side by side." It was "idle to speculate" on what might have happened if moderates like John Temple had been willing to accept a different "solution" or "the black man had been more 'restrained,' and not taken advantage of his right to vote and hold public office."[91] African Americans would not give up "the drive to be free"; white Southerners would not give up their monopoly on power; and the white North did not have the will to intervene. Therein lay the national tragedy whose local and personal dimensions "Eli Hill" sought to explore. Yet, she concluded, Eli Hill "himself was not defeated. . . . He found himself. And having identified himself with his people he is likewise convinced that they will in time 'come out of the Wilderness' and not be denied the heritage of their common humanity."[92]

Although unwilling to distort her story's moral valence or abandon its basis in the historical record, Katharine did undertake two full cycles of revision. She eliminated many minor characters and tried to give "Eli Hill" a "stronger single story thread." But to no avail. In February 1952, Houghton Mifflin rejected the book. That year's blockbuster was *Witness*, Whittaker Chambers's massive anticommunist saga, with its drum-roll of alarm over the inevitable fall of a society in which liberals and Communists shared the same secular, materialistic faith.[93]

The sting of rejection must have been especially painful as Katharine watched her generation's battle for racial and economic justice threat-ened, as Eli Hill's was, by a wave of reaction and repression. Neverthe-less, she persisted. She contacted literary agents and began looking for potential publishers. Revising once more, she tried to make clear that her white protagonist's combination of paternalism and menace was not a sign of intelligent moderation. It was one of the barriers that Eli Hill had to overcome in order to forge the combination of solidarity and leader-ship the long freedom struggle required. But in the end, both the agents and the publishers definitively rejected "Eli Hill" on the grounds that, hewing too closely to the known past, it read like "fiction laid thinly over history."[94] In the fall of 1955 Katharine finally set the manuscript aside.[95]

WHEN, IN THE 1970S, young scholars and interviewers began to find their way to her door, Katharine refused to talk about the red-hunters who upended her life in the 1950s. Nor did she acknowledge the years she had devoted to writing "Eli Hill." She had always aspired to "academic study" and a professional career, she said; Grace was the one who had wanted to be a creative writer, which "usually makes much more of a stir in the world."[96] Privately, however, she revisited the manuscript into which she had poured the emotions that living through McCarthyism aroused.

In pages of scribbled notes, she listed her characters and identified her themes. She examined her own motives and choices, raising but rejecting the possibility that she had chosen her subject not only because he so poignantly symbolized the destructive effects of white supremacy on African Americans and the overwhelming obstacles they had to overcome but also because of some unexamined personal identification with a reluctant leader and a disabled and, finally, murdered man. Mapping out yet another set of revisions, she found herself writing and rewriting a set piece called "The Hearing" about Eli Hill's dramatic appearance before the congressional committee that came to his neighborhood in 1871 to gather information about the KKK.[97]

In her telling, "The Hearing" evokes the trauma that Katharine, Dorothy, and so many of their friends experienced during the "Great American inquisition."[98] At the actual hearings, which were held in a local hotel, the committee's questions were geared toward learning the truth about Elias Hill's experiences, and he responded with a riveting account of his life, political activities, and suffering at the hands of the Ku Klux Klan. Katharine, however, portrays the interrogators' questions as echoes of those of the KKK. With "the whole Court House to choose from," the committee picked a mean, ugly room, "stained, and windows on the alley, glass panes dust-smeared as though never washed, and mouldy smells seeping in from off the ground, and flies drifting round on the dank sultry air." As Hill sits facing an all-white crowd, one witness after another comes forward to suggest that he brought his suffering on himself by getting mixed up in politics rather than lining up "with the respectable white people." When Hill himself is finally allowed to speak, a hostile white southern Democrat offers this *j'accuse*:

> "By your secret meetings, [you] made white men insecure, arousing their suspicions that you stirred up hatred, race for race, incited your people."
>
> "Yes, I heard them [testify] here," Hill answers.
>
> "And you were urged to compromise, to use your influence against extremism, and for moderation."
>
> "I know what I did."
>
> "You've sown the wind, Hill, arousing the wild irresponsible white elements—you have reaped a whirlwind."
>
> "Am I the one who stands accused?"[99]

EXPATRIATES RETURN

———

"ONGRATULATIONS ON ONE MORE STEP TOWARD COMMU-nism or fascism in a godless era." I was astonished to hear that message from Grace Lumpkin read aloud by an actor on National Public Radio (NPR) in 2004. The occasion was the 50th anniversary of *Brown v. Board of Education*, and NPR was sampling the hundreds of letters received by President Dwight D. Eisenhower in the wake of the Supreme Court ruling. When she scribbled those angry words in May 1954, Grace was in limbo. Sam Shoemaker had moved his ministry to Pittsburgh, and she had lost her safe haven at Calvary Church. Living alone, she was eking out a living as a proofreader and nursing the obsessions to which she would give expression in her final novel, *Full Circle* (1962), a conversion narrative in which she remade herself in the image of a starkly conservative brand of Christian faith.[1]

Katharine, too, was beset by a "feeling almost of dread" in the weeks before the court's decision, but for quite different reasons. Little more than a year had passed since she and Dorothy had fled their home in anticipation of being called before HUAC, and they had seen few signs that the chill that event epitomized was about to disperse. Katharine feared that in this atmosphere the court would "evade or equivocate." When, instead, it declared racial segregation in the public schools unconstitutional, she felt "untold relief." In response to the long, arduous efforts of black parents and the NAACP, the nation's highest court had "alter[ed] drastically the potentials for change."[2]

The *Brown* decision "barely brushed the thoughts of a surprising number" of the nation's most prominent white writers and thinkers. When they commented at all, they came down on the side of a hands-off, go-slow approach rather than pressing for immediate and decisive governmental action.[3] Katharine, by contrast, wanted to participate in a revolution that she had predicted in the late 1940s but had not imagined she would live to see. Perhaps she could secure a position at a historically black educational institution and return to the South as it underwent a long-dreamed of transformation.

Katharine's mind turned in this direction for a number of reasons. Still living together in Northampton but searching for new academic positions, she and Dorothy faced discrimination against women and stiff competition from younger scholars, as well as a highly effective blacklist that prevented leftists from securing jobs in well-funded, predominantly white educational institutions. Financially strapped black colleges and universities, however, were sometimes willing to take a chance on controversial but highly qualified teachers.[4] For Katharine such institutions offered two other advantages. By living and working in an interracial but predominantly black community, she could minimize her complicity in segregation.[5] At the same time, she could "get the feel of things again" in her native region as she pursued an absorbing new research project with deep personal resonances: a book and a document collection on Angelina and Sarah Grimké, two sisters from South Carolina who, in the 1950s, were virtually unknown to the public, but who had been central figures "in the anti-slavery movement at the period of its greatest vigor and power, and . . . prime movers in the emerging cause of women's rights."[6]

SHE BEGAN BY WRITING to Horace Mann Bond, a distinguished black educator whose son Julian would soon become a founder of the Student Nonviolent Coordinating Committee (SNCC), asking for advice on finding a teaching position. She had sent Bond a copy of *The Making of a Southerner*, and he had replied with his own childhood memories of "growing up Jim Crow."[7] She also called on the interracial women's network with which she had worked in the YWCA. Juanita Jane Saddler, one of her African American counterparts in the Y's student division in the 1920s, had gone on to serve as dean of women at Fisk University in

Nashville; during the New Deal she had worked under Mary McLeod Bethune, director of Negro Affairs in the National Youth Administration and chair of FDR's informal "Black Cabinet." Saddler contacted Fisk's first black president, the eminent sociologist Charles S. Johnson, and vouched for Katharine as a "dear and trusted friend of mine," a person who "has a genuine interest in people, a readiness for listening to other points of view than her own, a gentle courtesy that makes it possible for her to put others at ease quickly." These qualities, "combined with a keen mind, make her a very useful person for getting the world's work done."[8] Charles Johnson had served on the advisory board of Katharine's and Dorothy's Institute of Labor Studies and written for its publications, so he was already familiar with her and her work. He invited her to meet him in Washington, D.C., and soon offered her a visiting position. She began planning her courses, but after a meeting of Fisk's board of trustees, Johnson wrote to "defer this plan until a later time." In explanation, he cited financial constraints.[9]

Katharine was not the first white leftist whom Fisk welcomed but then rejected. As head of a private college with a sizeable endowment and an interracial board, Charles Johnson had been able to recruit outstanding and outspoken scholars, both black and white. Still, he was a cautious leader who was convinced that the school's well-being depended on retaining at least some support from white conservatives. Four years earlier, he had dropped a young physicist who had taken the Fifth when he was called before HUAC during a futile search for Communist sympathizers who had allegedly leaked atomic secrets from the Berkeley Radiation Laboratory to the Soviet Union.[10]

In early 1955, when Saddler wrote in Katharine's behalf, Fisk was embroiled in a heated controversy over Lee Lorch, a white faculty member whom Johnson had brought in as chair of the mathematics department in 1950 after he lost two positions in northern colleges because of his civil rights activities. Lorch had continued the fight as vice president of the Tennessee NAACP. After the *Brown* decision, he and his wife tried to enroll their daughter in an all-black school. Their "one-girl attempt to desegregate the Nashville public schools" made them targets of red- and race-baiting by segregationists who sought to brand the civil rights movement as a Communist plot. Subpoenaed by HUAC in 1954, Lorch denied that he was a party member but, citing the First Amendment, refused to answer questions about his earlier political affiliations.

Johnson dismissed him, setting off protests among faculty, students, alumni, and black trustees. Within a week after the board voted to support Lorch's dismissal over the objections of most of its black members, Katharine learned that she would not be teaching at Fisk after all.[11]

Undeterred, she took an extended trip through the South, reaching out to scholars for advice on her Grimké sisters project, which she at one point called "Ordeal by Violence" and at another "Alien Daughters," a title she drew "from a phrase, 'My alien daughters,' often on the lips of the Grimkés' South Carolina slaveholding mother." She also visited "all of the Columbia family, young and older," noting at her parents' gravesides that the next year would mark one hundred years since Annette Lumpkin's birth.[12] Bryan, her only surviving brother, "was determined to try to have a reconciliation" despite his deep objections to her political views. At a memorable gathering at his house, she seems to have been embraced by her nephews and their children, whose attitude toward their unusual aunt, at least as they described it in retrospect, was not

From right to left, Katharine, Elizabeth, and Grace Lumpkin, at the home of their nephew William W. L. Glenn, New Haven, Connecticut, 1949.

marred by the sense of betrayal, incomprehension, or estrangement their parents had often felt. When I met them in the 1990s, those who had read *The Making of a Southerner* "thought she handled her criticism of the South very gently. And very deftly. . . . It was obvious she was fed up with the system," her nephew Alva Jr. remembered. But she "handled it in a sweet way, in a loving way."[13]

Meanwhile, another member of the southern women's network, Olive Matthews ("Polly") Stone, was doing everything she could think of to open doors. The granddaughter of slave owners, Stone—like Katharine and so many of their cohort—had been introduced to social justice issues through the YWCA and traveled to the Soviet Union in the 1930s. Studying with the famed reformers Edith Abbott and Sophonisba Breckinridge at the University of Chicago School of Social Services, she had written a master's thesis that fed into the efforts of leftists in the 1930s to recast Reconstruction as a battle for democracy rather than a dark day of federal overreach and "Negro rule." Returning home to teach at her alma mater, the Woman's College of Alabama (now Huntingdon College), Stone rose to the position of dean of women while making her home a way station for leftists coming south to support the Alabama Sharecroppers' Union. While studying for her PhD in sociology at UNC–Chapel Hill, she helped to found a civil rights group called the Southern Committee for People's Rights and extended her sophisticated and hard-hitting research on African American life.[14]

Now a professor in the School of Social Welfare at the University of California at Los Angeles, Stone wrote to Katharine Jocher, who, as she observed, shouldered much of the actual work of UNC's Institute for Research in Social Science, although Howard Odum "was the titular head." Research positions were reserved for Odum's prize students, but, in response to Stone's endorsement, Jocher arranged an appointment for Katharine as a visiting scholar.[15] She was looking forward to spending the spring in Chapel Hill, sitting in on courses and deepening her knowledge of recent research on the South, when, in part on the strength of a letter from Stone stressing her "first-rate mind" and "truly first-rate heart," she was offered a one-year position at Mills, a progressive and racially and ethnically diverse women's college in Oakland, California. Katharine took the salaried position; Dorothy went with her. While they were there, Katharine received another offer for which Stone had recommended her: a one-year post at the North Carolina College for Women in Greensboro.[16]

When this offer arrived in the spring of 1957, Katharine faced Eli Hill's dilemma in reverse. Should she remain at a critical distance in the North? Or could she find a productive place for herself in her native region? To her, that depended in large part on the prospects for progressive change. She had welcomed *Brown* as a powerful blow to the institutional under-pinnings of "white supremacy . . . as a social-economic-psychological complex." She had expected white resistance: "Given our history and upbringing, it was not surprising."[17] But like many observers—northern and southern, black and white—she was confident that the court's decisions would be accepted as the law of the land, the walls of segregation would begin to crumble, and the attitudes that were reinforced by seg-regation would change as well.[18] Her trip through the South two years earlier had strengthened that hopeful view.

By 1957, however, the scope and ferocity of white resistance had become abundantly clear. More than one hundred officeholders had signed the "Southern Manifesto" opposing compliance with the Supreme Court's ruling. In Virginia "massive resistance" had shut down the entire public school system in Prince Edwards County and sparked a statewide white flight to segregated academies. Her brother Bryan joined the resistance. Circulating a "Questionnaire to Editors and Preachers and Other White Citizens Who Favor the Integration of the Negroes with White Chil-dren in the Public Schools," he attempted to lead moderates to his own extreme conclusions, trotting out arguments—about black inferiority and immorality ("being at the most only 300 years from savagery and cannibalism") and the inviolability of states' rights—that Katharine and her activist YWCA cohort had refuted decades before. Throughout the South, segregationists were stirring racism, anticommunism, and sexual and gender conservatism into a homegrown witch's brew.[19] Although the Montgomery Bus Boycott of 1955–1956 had signaled the birth of a black-led direct action movement, civil rights activists had not yet attained critical mass. Confronted with this climate, Katharine hesitated. How-ever optimistic she might be about what the future would hold, the real-ities on the ground were daunting.

There was also Dorothy to consider. Like others in her situation, she had been advised by friends to "consider working in a Negro College." Colston Warne had also suggested that she contact Highlander Folk

School in Tennessee, which was reorienting itself from workers' education to civil rights. "It might be interesting, however, to join the Magnolia League," he added, referring to the single-sex colleges that still dominated white women's education in the South. Hollins College in Virginia, which was led by a dynamic young president fresh from serving as chair of the philosophy department at Columbia, seemed especially promising.[20]

Dorothy apparently followed up on some of Warne's suggestions. She also looked into Berea College in Kentucky, a tuition-free institution founded by abolitionists and aimed at educating Appalachian youth. She would not mind teaching in a "second string institution" as long as it "held some special interest," she said. At the same time, her assessment of the situation of her old friend Horace Bancroft Davis, who lost jobs in both the Midwest and the South for political reasons, could have been applied to herself: "His trouble, as I see it, is wholly as a citizen: he can't refrain from calling every spade a spade out loud, whatever the consequences."[21] For whatever reason—Dorothy's greater visibility and outspokenness as a leftist, her lack of Katharine's southern contacts and Protestant bona fides, the difficulty of picturing herself in the "Magnolia League"—nothing came of her efforts.

As for Katharine, she found herself pulled two ways. She was more intensely focused on the South than ever, and she was convinced that to deepen her understanding of the region she needed to spend time on home ground. Yet she was anxious about "adjusting once more to segregation." Looking back from a later vantage point, she elaborated: "If I couldn't live in the South and be able to feel free and at home in my whole relationship to friends and acquaintances in the Negro world, I knew I couldn't take it." In the end, she wrote a difficult letter to North Carolina's Woman's College turning down the offer. "Let me say that I love the South and the Southern people," it concluded. "If I had it [to] do over again, I think I would decide to make my life in the South. As it is, I am by no means sure that it would be the thing to do after so many years of being away."[22]

TWO MONTHS AFTER Katharine declined the position in North Carolina, temporary opportunities opened up for both her and Dorothy in the Northeast: a one-year visiting position in sociology for Katharine at Wells College in Aurora, New York, and a similar job in economics for Dorothy at Gettysburg College in Pennsylvania. "Aurora is a very

remote place, quite isolated, and the college smaller than I would pre-
fer," Katharine confided. Still, a year there "should help a good deal
toward whatever may come next."[23] In the meantime, she and Dorothy planned to maintain their home in Northampton, spending summers and Christmas vacations at the Manse and visiting back and forth
during the academic year.

As it turned out, Wells served not as a stepping stone but as Katharine's first and only secure professional position. Some faculty members
viewed her skeptically, in part because she had been hired without con-
sultation by an autocratic president and in part because she had so little
classroom teaching experience and had strayed so far from conventional
sociology. A few never warmed to her at all. Yet she soon became one of
Wells's most venerated faculty members.[24] In contrast to Northampton,
where memories of Dorothy remained sharp while Katharine's imprint
soon faded, Katharine's colleagues in Aurora remembered her as a striking presence: "a Southerner, a significant difference at the time," yet
also "a citizen of the world"; a gracious, genteel figure whose "radicalism came as a surprise"; "an egalitarian and an aristocrat"; and "a truly
loyal subject of a kingdom yet to be, one in which human beings live
in understanding, peaceful, faithful to justice and to one another's dignity."[25] "We don't always have giants in our faculty roster; I truly think
you are one," wrote one friend. Reappointed from year to year, Katharine
was promoted to full professor by the president and a campus-wide faculty committee in 1961.[26]

During her ten years at Wells, Katharine signed no petitions; she
published no articles on the issues of the day. She reportedly refused to
sign her colleagues' letters to the editor opposing the Vietnam War. Her
issues, she explained, were racial equality and women's rights. But her
brush with McCarthyism, which she "hated and deplored," had also had
an effect: the idea of going on record against the latest Cold War battle
against Communist aggression frightened her in ways that her younger
colleagues would have been hard put to understand.[27]

She would have been relieved to know that, on one front at least,
her strategy of reticence succeeded: the federal red-hunters soon lost
interest and closed her case. In 1959, when the FBI office in Albany,
New York, asked headquarters for permission to interview her to see
whether she had changed her political opinions, J. Edgar Hoover
denied the request: "Inasmuch as subject is a school teacher and has

not been active in ten years in a subversive organization, it appears the possibility of embarrassing the Bureau outweighs the worth of any information subject could apparently furnish if she were cooperative."[28] Hoover was right: Katharine would never talk about her own views to government inquisitors, let alone those of others. But neither would she join campaigns or organizations that seemed too closely related to the Popular Front and postwar peace movements that had been so fatally branded as Communist plots.

Given all this, it would be easy to see Katharine's time at Wells as a retreat, a period of silence and obscurity in which she withdrew from the political and intellectual fray. Located on the shores of Cayuga Lake in upstate New York, Wells was less than thirty miles from Cornell University, but it was light-years away both from centers of scholarly production and from the battles raging in the South. It had been established in 1868 by Henry Wells, the founder of Wells Fargo and American Express, as "a home in which . . . wealthy, young ladies may assemble to receive that education which may qualify them to fulfil their duties as women, daughters, wives or mothers," and its five hundred or so students were still all white and mostly well-to-do. Into the 1940s, the poorly paid single women who made up most of the faculty were assigned to dismal furnished rooms in one of two boarding houses, where they shared the bathrooms and ate communal meals. Katharine took up residence in one of these houses, which had been turned into apartments after the women rebelled against this "living-in system."[29] Tea was still served in the afternoon; students were required to attend chapel and not allowed to drive; and, as Katharine observed, during the long winters, students and faculty alike often found themselves "literally marooned" by the snow and buffeted by the winds that howled off the lake.[30] Yet her years in this small, self-contained community were filled with their own forms of political, intellectual, and romantic passion.

Teaching the college's course on "The Negro Minority in American Life," she delivered lectures on the civil rights movement that were "challenging, even for Northerners," explaining its twists and turns to students, faculty, and local citizens alike. Carefully preserving her notes and transcripts, she framed them with this annotation: the place of blacks "in American Life has been virtually a life-long interest for me. I believe these lecture notes, on the whole, are a reliable reflection of my personal outlook as it has developed from study and experience over the years. [They] also suggest my interpretation of the momentous events and changes" of the 1960s.[31]

We usually think of sit-ins and mass marches as the signature gestures of the civil rights movement. But Katharine and many other women contributed to what two scholars of oratory have called a "fascinating and moving rhetorical drama taking place across the nation," which was every bit as important. The great majority of their speeches "vanished upon utterance."[32] The fact that Katharine saved hers underscores the immense satisfaction with which she watched the movement unfold and suggests that she took pride in her own educational and intellectual participation.

These lectures made clear that as she provided her students with a real-time analysis of the movement, she revised and deepened her perspectives in response to its progression. She had hoped that court decisions, effectively enforced, could end segregation. But she soon recognized that the breakthroughs of the 1960s could not "come merely by court decisions or new laws by the Congress, though both were necessary." The principal instrument of change was a protest movement that "furnished incontrovertible evidence to any and all who had failed to comprehend, that black people were asserting that the time was now for an end to their burden of discrimination and segregation." "This knowledge remains etched in my memory," she reflected years later, "and I am bound to have a lift of spirit whenever it comes to mind."[33]

Katharine also used her research on the Grimké sisters and abolitionism to explore "the nature and careers of social movements" by placing the civil rights movement in a broad historical context. Unlike the vast majority of her white liberal peers, she was as keenly interested in Black Power as in the integrationist wing of the struggle. Comparing the debates over Black Power to the schisms in the ranks of abolitionists over issues of strategy and ideology, she attributed the tensions within both movements to the frustration born of their inability to achieve their goals in the face of "an ever-rising hostile opposition." She drew another parallel between the two movements as well: in both, middle-class leaders were far removed from "the host of the deprived."[34] Matching deeds to words, she continued to make donations to SNCC in its embattled Black Power phase, corresponding with its firebrand leader Stokely Carmichael at a time when southern liberals such as Lillian Smith were castigating black nationalists as "killers of the dream."[35]

LOOKING BACK, KATHARINE saw her time at Wells as "happy years." John M. Nesselhof, a friend in whom she confided, observed that she did seem contented. Yet he "could also catch a glimpse of suffering." Her handsome face could "look ravaged at times." She fell into "periods of black depression." He attributed that air of sorrow to having "come up out of a past that she repudiated," or perhaps to her single state or to some earlier private trauma.[36] What neither he nor any of her other colleagues realized, or at least openly acknowledged, was that Katharine was not "single." Moreover, the anguish that sometimes beset her was not rooted only in the past.

Sitting in the living room of one of Katharine's nephews in the late 1990s, I opened a first edition of *The Making of a Southerner*, one of a number of her books and letters he had kept. Inscribed in the book, I found the first words of endearment I had ever seen written in Katharine's hand: "For Elizabeth at Bread Loaf—1954, Katharine." I also found a card picturing Century House, the home in South Carolina that Katharine most vividly remembered. On it Katharine had written: "Elizabeth, all my blessings in all the days of this year, my dear love. Always—Katharine."[37] By the late 1950s, it turned out, Katharine's thirty-year relationship with Dorothy Douglas was collapsing, and she was falling in love with another woman.

Elizabeth Claydon Bennett taught English at Kingswood Cranbrook in Bloomfield Hills, Michigan, a boarding and day school for girls founded in 1931. It was part of an educational and arts-oriented complex that included the exclusive Cranbrook School for Boys, an elementary school for local children, and an Episcopal church—all situated on a campus built by the famous Finnish architect Eero Saarinen. Seven years Katharine's junior, Elizabeth had been born in New York, where her attorney father served in the state assembly and senate and stood for governor once and mayor of New York City four times on the Republican Party ticket, failing each time.[38] Following in the footsteps of her father, paternal grandparents, and other relatives, Elizabeth enrolled at Oberlin College in 1922, where her parents were living temporarily and her mother was teaching in the music conservatory. She served as president of the Women's Senate, which proudly extended its interests to "national and international affairs" and, only partly tongue-in-cheek, welcomed "revolutionary proposals" from "all young reformers, who protest against the existing order." At twenty, she spent a memorable summer teaching at the Pine Mountain School, a boarding school for poor elementary and middle-school children in the remote mountains of southeastern Kentucky. Graduating in 1926, she secured a job at Berea, citing her interest "in mountain people, and in teaching too."[39] After two years, she left to travel abroad and get a master's degree at Radcliffe, with the idea of eventually going to law school and into politics. Gradually abandoning her more unconventional aspirations, Bennett ended up studying the principles of progressive education at Columbia's Teachers College and following one of the few paths available to bright, well-educated women of her class and generation: teaching in a preparatory school for well-to-do girls.[40]

She began her career at Kingswood Cranbrook in 1936, but for almost fifteen years she lived catch-as-catch-can in rented rooms and the apartments of people who were away on leave. Until 1950 she was often on the lookout for a more attractive position, perhaps at a day rather than a boarding school or, better yet, at a junior college. But until her mother's death, family obligations limited her search to the Midwest; when opportunities arose later on, Bennett found that few institutions could match her Kingswood salary.[41] By the mid-1950s she had decided to stay put. Rising to the position of chair of the English department, she spent her summers traveling, taking on other teaching jobs, or continuing her education.

By that time, Elizabeth had abandoned both her father's political persuasion and her employers' denominational affiliation, switching her allegiance to the Democratic Party and the Unitarian Church which, in later years, Katharine also attended.[42] Elizabeth had also begun tutoring children in Detroit's inner city, an uncommon gesture for teachers at elite private schools in the 1950s. In the tense years after 1963, when aspiring black homeowners sought to breach the wall between Detroit and its all-white suburbs, she joined the Birmingham–Bloomfield Hills Human Relations Council, one of many such councils that sought to promote tolerance and, later, fair housing practices.[43]

Beyond these suggestive biographical details, the best descriptions we have of Elizabeth come from a "word portrait" created by Kingswood

students and teachers. Students, of course, never really *know* their teachers, and Bennett's both revered her and regarded her as something of
an enigma. She taught creative writing and advised the creative writing
club, the yearbook, and the literary magazine, imbuing students with her
"passion for precise and elegant . . . language." Guiding them through
the classics of English and American literature, she gave them analytical "tools . . . that sharpened our minds and converted our hearts."
She impressed them especially with her love for modern poetry. By all
accounts, she was a "master teacher!" Beyond that, students perceived
only those "aspects of her . . . elusive personality [that] she chose to
reveal." One remembered the "quiet self-mastery of her reserved, steely
gentleness." Others spoke of her "kindly acid wit," her shyness, the fact
that she "was not given to talking about herself." Still another remembered that she was "far from sentimental in her dealings with her students—'bracing' would be a better description of her personal style."[44]

A student who visited Elizabeth and Katharine in later years found
Elizabeth strikingly unchanged:

> sandy hair caught in a bun, a sphinx-like smile, yielding, nub-
> bly [*sic*] tweed skirts, a business-like moderately duck-footed
> stride. Miss Bennett's seeming disregard for fashion was counter-
> balanced by a fastidious attention to detail: often the severity of a
> blouse was challenged by a ruffled collar or hand-tucked bodice—
> perhaps a cameo at the neck.

A fellow teacher added depth to the students' memories of this "unfash-
ionable . . . private woman."

> One felt [her mind] always quietly asserting its control over mere
> impulse, prejudice, all the pressures of the moment. And it had,
> I suspect, a somewhat unruly kingdom to govern, for her feel-
> ings were warm and strong. She was capable, indeed, of passion:
> a passionate desire for excellence; a passionate anger at mean-
> ness, injustice, cruelty, or pettiness; a passionate affirmation of
> their opposites. In heart and head she combined to an altogether
> unusual degree maximum intensity and maximum control.[45]

Katharine met this woman of strong feeling and equally strong self-restraint at Middlebury College, home to the Bread Loaf Writers' Conference, in 1954. Katharine was at a low point in her struggle to finish "Eli Hill." She had "put this manuscript aside" after receiving devastating critiques and had gone to Middlebury in the hope that "it might get me unstuck and start me back on the novel, and it did."[46] Her six weeks in Vermont's Green Mountains made an indelible impression. They gave her the momentum to keep working on "Eli Hill." Most important, they introduced her to Elizabeth, and, little by little, their deepening friendship called her commitment to Dorothy Douglas into question.

What transpired between Katharine, Elizabeth, and Dorothy over the course of the late 1950s is impossible to ascertain. What was it in Elizabeth that captivated or comforted Katharine? What drew them together despite the distances that kept them apart? What were the fault lines in Katharine's relationship with Dorothy? Perhaps Dorothy's wealth, her past as a wife and mother, and her more conventionally feminine self-presentation separated her from the experience of closeted lesbianism that Katharine and Elizabeth shared. Her unflagging physical exuberance also set her apart. At sixty, she took a four-day horseback ride with Las Damas, the country's only all-woman trail-riding group; at seventy, she set out on a road trip with friends, "motoring from Germany all the way to India, then across to East Africa and back . . . camping and roughing it much of the time."[47] These were not late-life adventures that the more cautious, writerly, introspective Katharine had the temperament to share. More critically, I suspect, Katharine's desire to avoid the political spotlight clashed with the outspokenness of a partner who publicly opposed the Smith Act prosecutions of Communist Party leaders, which took place from 1949 to 1958; advocated for nuclear disarmament and protested against apartheid; organized campus events in support of the Congress of Racial Equality (CORE), which was best known for leading "freedom rides" into the Deep South, first in 1947 and then in 1961; protested against the Vietnam War; and steadily contributed money to liberal and leftist causes.[48]

Not surprisingly, while the FBI lost interest in Katharine, it renewed its attention to Dorothy, primarily because of "Operation SOLO," the code name for the bureau's most valued double agents, Jack and Morris Childs. Beginning in 1958, these Communist Party functionaries, who were on intimate terms with the top leaders of the Soviet Union and the People's Republic of China, began smuggling funds from the USSR into the United States while reporting on both foreign and internal CP affairs to their FBI handlers.[49] When the FBI initiated an investigation of "individuals who have been identified as past or present financial contributors to the communist party," Jack Childs reported that at one time Dorothy had been contributing as much as $30,000 a year, but that she was now giving half that amount. On the basis of this information, the bureau reopened her file, which had been closed in 1954, and put her back on its high-risk "security index." According to Childs, Dorothy's contributions continued from 1959 to 1964, though they dwindled to $500 a year.[50] Searching for independent verification of Childs's information in order to avoid inadvertently revealing his identity, the FBI rehashed all the old allegations regarding Dorothy's activities and contributions in the 1930s and early 1940s. Although it could find no evidence to verify that, beyond these reported contributions, she was "active in the Communist Party or communist fronts," Dorothy remained on the Security Index until she died in 1968.[51]

Neither Katharine nor Dorothy could have known about the Childs brothers; their identity was hidden even from the CIA and the president of the United States, to whom the FBI reported. But Katharine would have known or half-known about Dorothy's donations, including whatever contributions she made to the Communist Party, and she would have had every reason to fear that Dorothy was an ongoing object of the bureau's prying eyes. As Katharine devoted herself to teaching and writing, Elizabeth Bennett's less controversial politics, retiring personality, and love for the classroom and the written word may have offered an aura of safety and sustenance that life with the always audacious, peripatetic Dorothy did not.

In 1960 Elizabeth spent the summer with Katharine in Aurora and at a cottage near the Bread Loaf campus where they first met. In that same year, Katharine ceased to be listed in the Northampton city directory, and Dorothy left rural Gettysburg College, where she had never been particularly happy, to start "another chapter" at Hofstra College (Hofstra University after 1964) on Long Island, about six miles east of New York City.[52] She had been invited originally as a one-year replacement for Katharine's and Dorothy's old friend, Broadus Mitchell. Soon she was living during the academic year at Morningside Gardens, a cooperative apartment complex near Columbia on the Upper West Side, and endearing herself to—and out-walking—the young leftists with whom she taught. Staying on at Hofstra, Dorothy's interests turned increasingly to anticolonial struggles in Africa. In 1964–1965 she took a leave to teach at the University College in Nairobi, Kenya. She had fallen in love with the place when she traveled there in 1957 in the midst of the Mau Mau uprising against British rule; "now here it is with all the problems of a newly independent country," she observed.[53]

By July 1965, Katharine and Elizabeth had pooled their resources to buy a house in Charlottesville, Virginia.[54] In 1967, when Katharine turned seventy, she retired, and the two women moved south together. A year later, Dorothy died suddenly of a heart attack as she was striding across the Hofstra campus. Vigorous and vital as always, she was brimming with plans for visiting Cuba and teaching in Tanzania and with a passionate interest in what she called this "terrific and still-promising world."[55]

In late November 2000, long after all three women had passed away, I made reservations to fly to Annapolis, Maryland, to interview Hulda McGarvey Flynn, who had lived at the Manse in the 1940s, shared the trial by fire of the McCarthy inquisitions, and remained lifelong friends with Dorothy. She had agreed to see me and knew that I wanted to ask her about Katharine's and Dorothy's personal and political lives, but she had admired Katharine and loved Dorothy dearly and did not want "to betray either of them in any way." For her, as for Katharine and so many in their political generation, silence had become a badge of honor and a matter of faith. In a tearful conversation with her daughter Sarah before I arrived, Hulda said that when Katharine fell in love with Elizabeth Bennett, "it broke Dorothy's heart. But there was nothing she could do."[56] To my sorrow, Hulda died on the eve of my flight. At Sarah Flynn's invitation, I went to Annapolis anyway. In grief though she was, she welcomed me into her home and shared documents and memories. Among them was her mother's confirmation that whatever drove Katharine and Dorothy apart, and however much pain the separation caused Katharine, it was she who made the choice to spend the final years of her life with someone else.

One eloquent fact, however, suggests that, despite their separation, Katharine and Dorothy's loyalty to one another endured. Katharine was able to live in modest comfort and to count on an unusual degree of security in old age in part because Dorothy provided her with a nest egg managed by a fiduciary trust company in New York. Katharine husbanded her money with the utmost care, saving for contingencies and "building up a special fund which I do not touch, to cover such expenses [as] cremation and attorney's fees for settling my affairs." She spent only the interest on the money Dorothy gave her and, to their surprise, left the principal to Dorothy's children when she died.[57]

"I LOVE TEACHING," Katharine reflected after three years at Wells. But the demands of the classroom, coupled with her distance from the world of scholarly publication, slowed her research and writing to a crawl. Still, the materials on the Grimké sisters she had begun painstakingly to gather in 1953 remained constantly at her side, and she pushed the project forward whenever she could. The only biography of the sisters, written by a friend and contemporary in 1885, struck her as sentimental, misleading, and unlikely to convince readers that the Grimkés' stories were relevant to modern times.[58] She wanted to use these women's metamorphosis from slave owners' daughters to feminist abolitionists as she had used her own autobiography: as a discursive weapon, an exemplary tale. If women who were raised in the very heart of bondage could throw off the mental shackles that bound them and come to believe in "human equality regardless of race," all the more could contemporary white Southerners rise to the changes that had been long in the making but were "coming to a climactic point today."[59]

Angelina and her older sister Sarah, daughters of a prominent Charleston slave-owning family, left home in the 1820s to settle in Philadelphia as members of a Quaker community. In 1835 Angelina joined the vanguard of the antislavery movement and quickly emerged as one of the movement's most charismatic orators, holding so-called "promiscuous" audiences of men and women spellbound at a time when public speech was a marker of masculinity and central to male-dominated civic life. Sarah, who, at twelve, had insisted on becoming her newborn sister's godmother and taking over her care, objected to this daring course. Eventually, however, she overcame her doubts and joined Angelina for three dramatic years on the public stage. When fierce opposition forced them to defend their right to speak, they put themselves "in the forefront of an entirely new contest—a contest for the *rights of woman* as a moral, intelligent, & responsible being." The more they were attacked, the more unyielding in their principles they became. Sarah, who was an awkward public speaker but an original theorist and writer, published *Letters on the Equality of the Sexes and the Condition of Woman* (1837), the first major expression of feminist thought in the United States. Together with Angelina's lucid writings and compelling oratory, Sarah's book became "the standard for women's rights thinking" until an autonomous women's movement emerged in the 1850s.[60]

Katharine had launched her project by consulting the correspondence of the sisters and Angelina's husband Theodore Weld, which was published by the historians Gilbert H. Barnes and Dwight L. Dumond in the 1930s. Then, at Clement Library at the University of Michigan, where the original manuscripts resided, she discovered that, while Barnes and Dumond had included most of Theodore Weld's letters and made a case for him as abolitionism's most important organizer, they had omitted as much as two-thirds of Angelina's and Sarah's writings. Enthralled by this "vast . . . and marvelously rich" trove of personal documents, Katharine set out to restore these southern sisters to their rightful place in the history of their times.[61]

By 1955 she had already supplemented her research in the Clements Library with visits to archives around the country. She had also formulated the basic approach and purposes of her book. She would "go behind and beyond traditional (perhaps idealized) conceptions of 'the Grimké Sisters.'"[62] She would also try to resolve what she saw as one of the great mysteries of Angelina's life: Why, after her marriage, did both she and Sarah withdraw from public life, despite Angelina and Theodore's pledge not to let domesticity interfere with Angelina's career?

From the outset, Katharine saw Angelina as "the more brilliant and interesting of the two women," the one who "took the lead, set the pace."[63] But to write about Angelina, Katharine had to come to grips with her husband and her sister as well: "I want to try to explain all three" "insofar as one person can explain another." "I want to understand . . . how they came to do what they did and be what they became; explore what moved and changed them; and for Angelina and Sarah, see how they could come out of the background they did, yet take the course they came to take."[64] Perhaps most of all, she wanted to know what caused Angelina to fade from sight. "What were the frustrations, the curious play of circumstances, that interrupted what was so brilliantly begun?"

Ever thoughtful about the process of her own work, she asked herself, "Can such questions be answered? . . . Will the documents permit it? Do they penetrate deeply, reveal the inner life of Angelina and the others?"[65]

Within two years of her first visit to the archives, Katharine was seeking a contract from Alfred A. Knopf, who had published *The Making of a Southerner*: "I am ready to write," she told him. "I have had access to all of these [first-person materials] in the originals; my notebooks are bulging. . . . It is my intention to use this abundance with all the creativeness and imagination that I can command." Knopf sent back a tepid response. The work would have to be lively indeed "to lift it out of the general class of respectable biographies of minor figures."[66] In Katharine's long and ultimately futile search for a commercial publisher, this reluctance to see women as important historical actors, although usually unspoken, cropped up again and again. Equally daunting was the Cold War mentality that shaped scholars' assessments of the abolitionists just as it had editors' reactions to "Eli Hill." In the 1950s, most historians celebrated moderation and condemned radicalism. Those who noticed the Grimké sisters at all portrayed them and their allies not as scholars now see them—as activists who made black freedom thinkable to significant numbers of white people for the first time—but as reckless, uncompromising fanatics who pursued the perfectionist principle of "immediate emancipation" without regard to consequences.[67]

Beyond this discouraging context lay the writerly challenge. The decision to return to nonfiction—"a medium I feel at home in"—proved enormously liberating after the long and frustrating process of writing "Eli Hill."[68] Yet however riveting the sources, they did not speak for themselves. In biography as in autobiography and historical fiction, Katharine had to imagine her way into the inner lives of people who inhabited a world distant from her own and illuminate the sweep of history by making readers care about her characters' fate.

Although well aware of these difficulties, she was convinced that her strength as a biographer lay in the same combination of scholarly training and critical self-reflection that had made her autobiography such an affecting book. She continually reminded herself that Angelina's "beliefs, her religious experiences, her "*felt*-motivations" were "a reflection of her times" and "*quite* different from my own conceptions."[69] And she flinched at a question from me which seemed to imply that her interpretations were guided by her personal feelings about her characters. "I am sure you do not mean did I like them, dislike them? Admire them, not admire them, etc. and etc. and etc."[70] But she distinguished between allowing feelings of antipathy, admiration, or identification to distort her work and the value of quite intentionally and explicitly filtering her understanding of certain aspects of the sisters' lives through the prism of her own confrontation with the moral dilemmas inherent in a system of racial exploitation. Having grappled with the question of how consciousness changes by reflecting on her own life, she was, she believed, especially well prepared to elucidate the inner resources and external circumstances that allowed these earlier daughters of the plantation South to make their escape.

But Katharine did more than draw on her past experience as an interpretive lens. At a level more or less below conscious awareness, she also used the sisters' story to revisit the autobiographical self *The Making of a Southerner* had so skillfully constructed and to evoke the private feelings she hid so carefully behind a carapace of dignity and reserve. When I interviewed her in the summer of 1974, I was struck by the frequency and emotional intensity with which she referred to Angelina Grimké when asked about herself. *The Making of a Southerner*, she said, had not been "as personal as the publishers would have liked." The book "had a certain object to fulfill," and so she left out issues that "a full-fledged autobiography" might have included. "Have you ever thought of writing a full-fledged autobiography?" I asked. "No," she said. "Angelina Grimké satisfied me on that."[71] Indeed, throughout her notes and lectures and in the final book, we can hear her doing what the literary scholar Hermione Lee, writing about the novelist Alice Munro, characterizes as "asking questions of herself, returning to her own life as to an unresolved problem."[72]

Katharine's treatment of religion, memory, and violence illustrates her approach. When I used the terms "reformers" and "social critics" to describe her cohort of YWCA leaders in the early 1920s, she said that both were apt. But she took pains to remind me that "what we felt we were doing was also infused with something else." Social Christianity provided the "basic motivation and justification for our rebellion against the gross inhumanities we saw in ourselves and those around us. . . . We posed the way of Jesus against the contradictions we saw in the social order . . . and we hammered at the theme . . . of the need to be 'consistent' with what we believed in."[73] Likewise, she believed that the

conversion experience that led Angelina to leave her family's staid Episcopalianism was the beginning of her emancipation.

Yet Katharine also insisted that religion was not the only "motivating
force." As *The Making of a Southerner* had tried to show, "no young white
southerner who had lived her life surrounded by slavery—and the same
for segregation at a later time—was ever moved to turn against it on religious grounds *alone*. . . . Much more entered in from past experiences,
most of it probably unremembered, compounded of fears, revulsions,
aspirations, contradictions . . . *plus* the ungarnished ugly facts of daily
life." Why, both Katharine and Angelina asked themselves, had they not
been "totally hardened under the daily operation of this system?" Katharine's answer in both cases revolved around memories of violence in the
heart of the home.[74]

As a child Angelina enjoyed the "luxury and ease" made possible by the labor of slaves, yet she was "far from protected from sights,
sounds, and experiences that would come to haunt her life." Her "dread
of the work house," where slaves were sent to be whipped and tortured,
"reached back to early memory." But "what clung to her mind could
scarcely be termed knowledge; it was something so shadowy, so vaguely
remote." That knowledge coalesced when, at twelve, she fainted at the
sight of a boy who had been beaten so badly in the work house that he
could barely walk. Returning to South Carolina after her first sojourn
with Sarah among the Quakers of Philadelphia, Angelina found that
all the cruelty she had seen from "infancy . . . came back to [her] mind
as though it was only yesterday." Most painful of all was the memory of
being "awakened in the night by fearful sounds—the swish and thud of
the lash, her brother's angry curses, [a slave's] screams of pain." It was
only at that point, Katharine explained, that Angelina summoned the
will permanently to slip "the ties of home, with all their subtle pulls so
deeply rooted in her."[75]

Once she threw in her lot with the antislavery movement, Angelina
drew on her memories of violence to convey the evils of human bondage
and the sexual exploitation of enslaved women with an autobiographical authority that few white abolitionists could match. In *American
Slavery as It Is*, a hugely influential book written by the Grimké sisters
and Theodore Weld, Angelina testified against slavery by writing in
"grim and unrelieved" detail about the inhumanity of her own relatives and friends. Like Katharine, she found it impossible to identify

her loved ones by name, but she was determined to drive home what to her was a central point: slavery was not just a "curse to its victims"; "the exercise of arbitrary power works . . . fearful ruin upon the hearts of slaveholders" as well.[76]

KATHARINE ENDED HER autobiography when she was still in her twenties, implying that by then her remaking was complete and omitting the choices, achievements, and traumas of her later years. By contrast, she departed from most other writers, before and since, in devoting almost a third of *The Emancipation of Angelina Grimké* to the mystery of Angelina's retreat from the public stage. She acknowledged the pressures to which others pointed: the burdens of poverty, childcare, and poor health; the schisms among abolitionists that complicated Angelina's relationships with former friends.[77] But she discounted what she viewed as Theodore Weld's self-deceiving claim that Angelina's health problems "shattered her nervous system," making her "avoid exciting scenes and topics." She stressed instead how traditional gender relations and sisterly rivalries insinuated themselves into a household devoted to egalitarian ideals.[78]

Living together in the countryside, Angelina, Sarah, and Theodore seemed from the outside to be "a close-knit, loving three," Katharine observed. But theirs was a "home of hidden struggles." At issue was whether Angelina would return to her daring oratorical role, which for her had been profoundly fulfilling. In contrast, Weld had, "by sheer violence," suppressed in himself any satisfaction that fame and influence might have brought.[79] Having retreated into relative anonymity, he was "self-convinced" that both he and Angelina should wait for God to call them back to public life. He was equally certain that she would not be called until she had conquered what he termed "self-seeking and . . . she called ambition." Joining Weld "on the judgement seat," Sarah pointed out Angelina's faults and took over the care of "'Theodore's children,'" who "grew ever more dependent on her possessive love."[80]

Katharine did not doubt the earnestness of "the three's" struggle against the sin of pride. But she also pointed to "unconscious compulsions" and ingrained social patterns. In Weld's case, those included the ease with which, in a patriarchal society, he could move from the conviction that "his preferences were what he had learned from Christ" to the assumption that those preferences would become "dominant in the new household."[81] Sarah, the reserved, never married, older sister, buried her "intensely rivalrous nature" behind a "self-effacing spirit."[82] She had started out as Angelina's mentor and, in Katharine's view, had been a "catalytic agent at times of major crisis." Now she devolved into a "sadly baleful influence," more or less subliminally conspiring with Theodore Weld to bring an end to her younger sister's reform career.[83]

As for Angelina, she could not have done alone what she was able to achieve jointly with Sarah. She had benefited from having her older sister beside her during her unprecedented speaking tours, and she found caring for young children a trial. Complicit in her own undoing, she found it easier "to accept the humble Sarah, the unselfish older sister who lived to serve others," than to call into question the unique symbiosis that began when she was born. Most important, Angelina's immersion in an evangelical culture of sin and guilt made her vulnerable to Sarah's and Theodore's charges. Persuaded by the people she loved that her craving for "high duties and high attainments" in behalf of women and slaves came from worldly vanity, she lost what she needed most: the conviction that her public activism was authorized by God.[84]

"Perhaps no period of Angelina Grimké's life has more to say than these years of withdrawal," Katharine concluded. "In no respect is her life more a mirror of her age and of subsequent times, for that matter, than in the painful, unrelenting conflicts and frustrations that she could not escape because she was a woman. Yet "at no time was her drive for emancipation clearer," Katharine concluded. Little by little Angelina came to understand her own part in "the debacle of their lives, not . . . because her faults were 'sins' but because she had been vulnerable—weak, she now felt—in allowing the pronouncements of her loved ones to overcome her." She began "to think her own thoughts, assert her own strength." Moving with her family to a utopian community called the Raritan Bay Union, she devoted herself to what became her "absorbing vocation": teaching history to young people, including the sons and daughters of many of the family's abolitionist friends.[85]

Katharine ended her book with a climactic event that she pieced together partly from an extraordinary interview. Searching for the Grimkés' descendants, she found the sisters' grandniece and namesake, Angelina ("Nina") Weld Grimké, whose father was their brother's mixed-race son. Nina was now living "in quiet retirement in a New

York City apartment."[86] But she had been a prolific poet and the author of one of the earliest plays by an African American woman, and her work was later rescued from oblivion by black feminist scholars who sought to enlarge our understanding of the Harlem Renaissance by taking women's writing into account. Stressing the motifs of longing, loneliness, and suppression evident in her unpublished poems, they claimed her for the lesbian literary tradition as well.[87]

Drawing on her interview with this fascinating woman, along with a "priceless letter" that Nina allowed her to copy by hand, Katharine recounted the story of how, late in life, Angelina learned that her older brother Henry, whose vicious beatings of the family's slaves had tormented her youth, had had three children by Nancy Weston, an enslaved woman whom he had taken as a mistress after the death of his wife.[88] When Henry died, he left his black family to his white son "to be treated as members of the family." Instead, the son left the penniless Nancy Weston to fend for herself in Charleston's free black community, then seized and reenslaved her children. The family reunited after the Civil War, and Weston fought fiercely to give her children an education. When Angelina learned that two of the surviving sons, Archibald and Francis, were attending Lincoln University, she reached out to them and, with Sarah and Theodore, brought them into the family circle and encouraged and financed their careers.[89] "Any hint of color prejudice had long been absent from her nature and abhorrent to her when she saw it in others," Katharine said of Angelina, and her response to her mixed-race nephews was an acid test of the principles for which she stood.[90] It was also painful, for it was one thing to know that such things happened under slavery and another to face the dreadful fact that the perpetrators of sexual exploitation and cruelty were a dearly loved brother and his white son.

IT IS EASY to imagine that, at some level, Katharine found in Angelina's late-life emergence from the "ravaging years" validation of her own quiet modes of self-reinvention after the ruptures wrought by McCarthyism and her breakup with Dorothy.[91] Her treatment of the relationship between Angelina and Sarah is a more complicated matter. Was her determination to show that the Grimkés were temperamental oppo-

*Katharine Du Pre
Lumpkin at work on
biography of Angelina
Grimké, 1975,
Charlottesville, VA.*

sites, despite their similar roots and political commitments, linked to
her embroilment with Grace, whom she kept at arm's length but whose
needs and projections she could not escape?

Interviewing Katharine just a few months before *The Emancipation
of Angelina Grimké* appeared, I asked her, more insistently than I should
have, about the commonalities and differences in her and Grace's careers.
She deflected my curiosity, as she always did where Grace was concerned.
Then suddenly she took what she termed "a diverging route. . . . I go back
to Angelina Grimké's sister Sarah, who was 12 years her senior. To all
appearances for those who came after and looked superficially back on
their careers, their two careers were parallel, you see. They weren't in the
least. They were as different people as you can imagine." What brought
them into juxtaposition was Sarah's inability to dissuade Angelina from
plunging into the radical wing of the antislavery crusade and her decision, driven by personal unhappiness and a deep need for companionship, to accompany her younger sister onto the public stage. "And for a
brief period . . . when Angelina was this magnificent platform speaker
and Sarah was very dull and very uninteresting in her speaking but in
earnest. . . . they were known as the Grimké sisters and they remained

known as the Grimké sisters through the years."[92] The vehemence with which Katharine rejected an idealized view of sibling relations, her sensitivity to hidden rivalries, and the value she placed on taking responsibility for one's choices—all of these were heightened by her connection to a sister whose claims on her loyalty she could not avoid but whose temperament was so alien to her own.

AS KATHARINE LABORED over her Grimké book, her older sister Elizabeth was dedicating herself to becoming a writer in her own right, and Grace was writing and rewriting her "up from Communism" story. Elizabeth had always been "a hungry reader." After her husband's death, she began to think about drawing on her own experience and her view of the southern past to become an author of historical fiction. She enrolled in creative writing courses through the extension programs of the University of North Carolina and Columbia University. But before she could get far, "the Depression arrived . . . with banners flying," and she had to drop out. In 1944, when her children were grown, she rented a room in "Clio cottage," one of a number of guest houses scattered of the grounds of the Asheville resort where she had directed the Shakespeare pageant of 1916 in which the young Thomas Wolfe appeared, and settled in to write a novel about the Civil War and Reconstruction inspired by her parents' stories and the reminiscences of the Confederate veterans she had entertained over the years. She worked and worked, "but a book did not evolve." She sent the manuscript to editors at Houghton Mifflin, who "said many complimentary things about my material, but—'you have not a book.' . . . It was nerve-wracking and mind-shaking, not to be able to make a book."[93]

Finally, in the spring of 1960, at the age of seventy-nine, she applied to study creative writing at the University of Alabama. Needless to say, the administration saw her as an unusual student. Within days of the beginning of class in September, she still had not been admitted. She could not supply the usual transcripts, having studied so irregularly in such a less bureaucratic time. She did not feel that, at her age, she needed to receive all the vaccinations required of freshmen in the 1960s. Besides, she would be living with one of her sons, a doctor fifty-odd miles away in Birmingham who could care for her if she fell ill.[94] The administration relented, and she arrived at the university "with a mass of material"

Elizabeth at work on her never-published historical novel, 1961.

in hand. She stayed for four semesters, studying with Hudson Strode, known for his biography of her beloved Jefferson Davis, president of the Confederacy, and with Otha Hopper, who took her under his wing. Returning to Asheville, she finished "Bitterroot," the story of a disabled slave who is freed by his master, a saintly physician, but loyally stays on to work, only to be seduced and ruined by a mixed-race femme fatale.[95] Elizabeth's mentors were enthusiastic. They referred her to their literary agents and contacted publishers on her behalf. But before she could carry through on the revisions she knew she needed to make, she suffered the fate of so many elderly women: in 1963 she fell, broke her hip, and died within days.[96]

Grace, in the meantime, was working on what would prove to be her final novel: an effort to explain the evolution that had begun in earnest with "Remember Now," the play about the unraveling of her marriage she had drafted in 1951. The play evinced "my usual difficulty," she admitted to a critical reader. "I don't have enough plot and development of character coming out of it. Sometimes, though, I wonder why a struggle of ideas isn't dramatic."[97] Putting that work aside, she began writing a novel that used "a sort of fictionalized history of Grace Lumpkin" to do precisely what she wanted to do: dramatize "a struggle of ideas" between Communism and Christianity.[98] By 1960 she had completed a draft of *Full Circle*, her contribution to a literature of anticommunist confession that had by then run its course.

At the time, she was renting a nondescript one-room apartment in Mount Vernon, New York, to which she had moved to be near her job at the Golden Eagle Press and also because she could no longer afford to live in Manhattan. She saw *Full Circle* as a contribution to a cause in which she deeply believed, and, not least, as a way "to make some money." Most of all, she saw it as a way to redeem herself as a writer. Her work had not appeared in a literary venue since 1940, when a warm domestic tale entitled "The Treasure" was included in *O. Henry Prize Stories*, an annual collection of the year's twenty best short stories.[99] In 1948 an influential study of the literature of the Great Depression deemed Grace's previous work "almost unreadable." Some radical novels might be "salvaged from the . . . ruins" of the Depression decade, but not hers.[100]

Beginning in that same year, she had actively colluded in her own erasure. When her friend and former creative writing teacher, Lillian B. Gilkes, offered to reprint one of her short stories in a collection that included works by masters of the genre, Grace demurred. If she published the story at all, she wanted to date it and append a statement distinguishing between what she would later call her career's "two distinct . . . phases. . . first, the Communist Phase, and second, the Return to God." Gilkes rejected her conditions: "If you are not willing to stand by the story as a piece of writing with its own validity, then I don't want to give currency to something you now would disavow."[101]

Notwithstanding her repudiation of her own work, Grace continued to cherish her identity as a writer. "The Communist phase . . . was the more productive"—this she readily admitted.[102] But perhaps the critics who condemned her earlier work would embrace her recantation, as they had Whittaker Chambers's 1952 narrative of conversion to and disillusion with communism, which had solved his financial problems and made him one of the country's most famous writers.

Grace was an avid reader of William F. Buckley Jr.'s *National Review*, the voice of a new brand of conservatism that began gathering strength in the late 1950s and 1960s alongside the more visible insurgencies of civil rights activists and the New Left. Committed to driving centrists out of the Republican Party, its proponents fused Christian traditionalism with free-market individualism and made militant anticommunism at home and abroad "the operative element in [their movement's] self-definition."[103] Grace followed with special interest the contributions of Donald Davidson, a former Agrarian who was among the journal's go-to experts on the South. Contacting him in 1960, she praised his opposition to school desegregation and asked him to help her find a southern publisher for her novel. She had sent an initial draft to major New York presses and been devastated by their uniformly negative responses. Davidson assured her that she had written "a profoundly important book."[104] But no publisher materialized, southern or otherwise.

FULL CIRCLE TAKES THE FORM of a memoir in which a mother explains how she and her daughter were indoctrinated into Communism and how they returned to their Christian faith. These dual heroes represent aspects of how Grace saw and wanted to represent herself, but they are also modeled on two Alabama women she met in New York: Mary Martin Craik Speed and her daughter Jane Speed, descendants of an elite southern family who became involved in radical politics in the early 1930s. Aligning herself with the state's small Communist Party, Jane was arrested during a May Day demonstration in Birmingham while trying to address a largely black crowd. Refusing to pay the fine, she went to jail for nearly two months. Placed under police surveillance and ostracized by their friends, the Speeds became "exiles" in New York, where at some point they lived near Grace on the Lower East Side.[105] As they visited back and forth, Mary Craik Speed apparently told Grace enough about her daughter's love life to provide fodder for *Full Circle*'s lurid accounts of 1930s communist sexual culture. In truth, that radical milieu was anything but monolithic; it could nurture free spirits like Jane Speed even as it discouraged heterodox thinking about sex and marriage.[106] Grace also took from the Speeds the spine of her novel: the deep bond that kept Mary Craik Speed at her daughter's side.

Full Circle begins with the separation of Ann Braxton, the character based on Mary Speed, from her husband. When Ann's daughter Arnie joins the Scottsboro defense, Ann opens her house to the "Jewish intellectuals" (a type that appears in scare quotes throughout the novel) who stream into town to cover the case. Arnie is entranced by and has sex with them all. Ann resists what she sees as their abstract, deracinated intellectual discussions, but she can't stand being excluded. As she joins in their conversations, they ridicule and finally disabuse her of her "bourgeois moralities and hypocrisies."[107]

Eventually Ann decides that she wants to do her "part in bringing about . . . the 'Kingdom of God on earth.'" Following her daughter to New York, she transforms an apartment on the Lower East Side into a cozy bohemian "place for music and love as well as for discussion." Arnie quickly becomes a CP functionary and is promoted to undercover work. She also takes a black lover, a Harvard-educated, power-hungry cynic who reveals that his real goal is not "to make a better world" but to seize control of the one that Ann and Arnie left behind. "We won't be satisfied with the crumbs. We want it all," he says.[108]

Arnie's status as a party insider permits Grace to speak with authority about a world that she could have known only at second hand. Explaining Communist plots and tenets to her mother, Arnie also provides Grace with opportunities to insinuate her current political preoccupations into a story set twenty years before. Foremost among these was her belief that, influenced by Communists and liberal fellow travelers, the US Supreme Court was becoming an instrument of what Donald Davidson and the Agrarians had termed the "Leviathan" state, as witnessed by its imposition of school desegregation on the proverbial "prostrate South" and its effort to "abolish God from our Schools" by declaring that compulsory prayers and Bible readings in public schools violated the constitutional separation of church and state.[109]

In the end, Arnie is expelled from the party for her mother's "bourgeois deviations."[110] Bereft, she makes her way to a church and collapses on the steps. Ann takes her back to the South, where the two women eventually come "full circle," repudiating not only Communism but also the racial egalitarianism and Christian liberalism that brought them into the party's orbit in the first place. Although portrayed here and elsewhere as an "incredible return—to family, to country, to God," Grace's real-life return was not to the religion of her youth, as represented by Kirkman Finlay, the liberal rector of her childhood church, by the YWCA, whose transforming influence she and Katharine shared, or by *The World Tomorrow*, the voice of a Christian internationalism that adamantly rejected the notion of the United States as a Christian nation. It was not even a return to the political worldview of her parents, which, as Katharine explained, was itself riddled with contradictions and beset by change. Rather, the political worldview Grace began cobbling together in the late 1940s lay at the heart of the emerging "New Right." Its proponents were eager to exploit old southern shibboleths regarding "Negro rule" and the sanctity of states' rights. But it looked forward, not backward— toward the day when issues such as school prayer and abortion would cement the ties between white evangelicals and Republican politicians, and the party of Lincoln would become a haven for southern Democrats repelled by the civil rights movement's vision of racial equality and economic redistribution.[111]

"POLITICALLY I WAS ARNIE. Ideologically I was Arnie," Grace later explained. When I asked her about her novel's autobiographical dimensions, she came closer to the truth: "I was really both the mother and the daughter." Ann, the memoirist, was her older self, looking back from the perspective of "the Return to God" in order to redeem Arnie, her younger self.[112] Yet, unlike Katharine, Grace made no real effort to sustain the literary double-consciousness that would allow readers to enter into both her earlier and later points of view.

We learn little about the interior life of a young radical in the midst of the Great Depression. Like the heroines of nineteenth-century romantic novels who are seduced and abandoned and then pine away, Arnie remains a starry-eyed cipher who seems more sinned against than sinning. In her function as an alter ego, she allows Grace to claim that, while she did not commit Arnie's sins, she might as well have, for "giving an inner consent to Socialism/Communism . . . is . . . as corrupting as *doing* the things Arnie did."[113] In this often repeated formulation, Grace could have it both ways: she could do what she did before the McCarthy committee and elsewhere—condemn everyone associated with the communist movement as, in effect liars, murderers, and traitors—while absolving herself as a naïve, idealistic dupe.

Arnie's mother also serves an exculpatory purpose. Even when she too becomes a communist true believer, she constantly refutes her own beliefs by reminding the reader of her instinctive and virtuous reservations. This refusal to enter credibly into the mother's radical point of view allows Grace to recite a self-exonerating litany of what she saw as her own personal weaknesses to explain why the mother followed the daughter down the prodigal path. She was too anxious for acceptance. She was too indecisive.[114] She was "so sweet," so "gentle" and "loving," that she would do anything to avoid a quarrel. Above all, she gave "in to the loudest voice, the most authoritative ways."[115] One of *Full Circle*'s few reviewers put it bluntly: "Ann Braxton does not inspire the reader's confidence." Drifting with "the tide of Arnie's radical convictions" and then "just as easily drift[ing] back to religion," she lacks credibility in either her guilt or her redemption.[116]

After reading *Full Circle* and later unpublished writings in which Grace cycled back over the same ground, Lillian Gilkes posed a question to which Grace never attempted to reply: "One thing that puzzles me, and any other reader would probably ask the same question . . . : Why did you swallow whole everything you were told, or had drilled into you, while a member of the CP? . . . Did you never question anything until you were mortally hurt? This is something very hard to understand, how an active mind such as yours could have remained so long in a state of coma. Almost as though you were hypnotized."[117]

IN THE END, the only publisher interested in Grace's lurid tale was Western Islands Press, the organ of the far-right John Birch Society, whose founder conjectured in 1958 that President Dwight D. Eisenhower was "a dedicated, conscious agent of the Communist conspiracy." By the time *Full Circle* appeared under the society's imprint in December 1962, conservative intellectuals such as William Buckley were distancing themselves from such extremist groups, as well as from the anti-Semitism that pervaded Grace's text; the civil rights movement was in full swing; and the appetite for ex-communist confessionals had evaporated.[118] Weeping with disappointment over her novel's minuscule sales and failure to attract an iota of critical attention, Grace confided in the diary she had just begun to keep: "people have rejected *Full Circle* . . . something I put my heart's blood into. . . . It was born out of its time."[119]

Like many writers, Grace had always used her life as fodder for her work. But the folly of doing so in a novel that combined political didacticism with pulp fiction seems blindingly obvious. "The subject matter is of a kind unsuited to the novel form," Gilkes observed. "I think you should go straight to autobiography with *no* disguises . . .

and should take full responsibility for the correctness of facts, of your own statements and judgments." Fictionalized autobiography "lets the author off the hook and gives him an easy way out. He is relieved then of all responsibility to let the reader know when he is reporting fact, when resorting to make-believe or hearsay." These problems were compounded in Grace's case because she was not satisfied with traducing the ideas she had embraced in the 1920s and 1930s. She was also determined, as Gilkes put it, to throw her opinions on contemporary issues at the reader like "a fist in the face."[120]

ENDINGS

———

I N THE SUMMER OF 1963, SIX MONTHS AFTER *FULL CIRCLE*
appeared, Grace made up her mind to do what Whittaker Chambers
had long urged her to do: "go back South where she would be . . . with
people of her own kind." But the plan that possessed her did not involve
going back to Georgia, where she was born, or to Columbia, South Carolina, where she grew up. Instead, she wanted "a house and a garden" in
King and Queen Courthouse, Virginia, a county seat northeast of Richmond too small to be incorporated as a town.[1] Nearby, on the banks of
the Mattaponi River, a stone slab marked the grave of perhaps the first
Lumpkin to arrive in the New World: Jacob Lumpkin, who had settled
on land granted to him by the crown late in the seventeenth century.
Grace had grown up hearing stories about this putative ancestor, who
had refused to raise a toast to the monarchs who came to power after
Britain's Glorious Revolution. Bryan, the genealogist of the family, had
visited the site and done his best to document a family connection. Now
Grace wrote to the local postmistress, who put her in touch with a man
in King and Queen Courthouse who had a five-room house to rent, and
began planning a visit to the place.

The trouble was that Grace had no resources with which to finance
such a move and no money to live on once she arrived. To overcome
those obstacles, she looked to a critical new source of support: her grown
nephews and nieces. Bryan, the last of her brothers, had died two years
before. On February 15, 1963, Elizabeth passed away as well. At Eliza-

beth's funeral in Asheville, her son William Wallace Lumpkin Glenn, a renowned heart surgeon and medical innovator who had become chief of cardiovascular surgery at Yale two years later, offered to begin sending "Aunta Grace" a monthly check in the amount that he had been giving to his beloved mother. She declined that suggestion but accepted his offer to help her gradually pay off her considerable debts.[2]

By that point she had secured a clerical job at the National Council of Churches and was commuting from Mount Vernon to the council's headquarters on the Upper West Side. "The president of the Council is leaving . . . several months before his term is ended," she explained to William and his wife, Amory Potter Glenn, in one of the first of many letters in which she directly or indirectly sought their financial help. "The 1st vice-president is a Negro minister and he will automatically become president and therefore my 'boss.' . . . He is a rabid integrationist, and the rough, tough gangster type who keeps his cap on in the office to prove to me (and probably to himself) that he is just as good as I am." She hated where she lived for similar reasons: "The Negro population in Mount Vernon is growing by leaps and bounds," and "naturally the politicians . . . are catering" to them.[3] Previously a middle-class suburban enclave, the city had become a magnet both for "white flight" from the Bronx and Manhattan and for black migrants from the South who augmented a settled African American community. If the Glenns would pay off all her debts, not in increments but in one lump sum, Grace could quit her job, leave her matchbook apartment, and realize her King and Queen Courthouse dream. She was sure that, once ensconced in the Old Dominion among "sturdy, splendid citizens who know and acknowledge the Rock upon which our country was founded, and understand all that is meant by the nation 'Under God,'" she could live off her minuscule Social Security payments plus the income from her writing.[4]

At first the Glenns tried to discourage what they saw, with good reason, as an eminently impractical move. Grace could not live in such a rural area without a car, and, besides the fact that she could not afford one, she had no license and did not know how to drive. Her few pieces of furniture would not go far in a five-room house. It had been decades since she had earned a living with her pen. Grace thanked her nephew for "helping me to get right down to bedrock and face everything involved in such a move." But she secretly resented his response. And a few months later, when all of her nieces and nephews, including the Glenns, committed themselves to pooling their money and sending her $100 a month to "make it possible for you to continue to write or to realize other of your ambitions," she went back to planning her move.[5]

When Sam Shoemaker died on October 31, 1963, and friends paid Grace's way to Maryland to attend his funeral, she took the opportunity to visit Esther Chambers, who was now living alone at Pipe Creek Farm (Whittaker had died of a heart attack more than two years before). She then took a bus to King and Queen Courthouse and sent the Glenns a rapturous report. Although tiny, the village was charming, with its "old brick courthouse . . , a beautiful small Episcopal Church," two general stores and a few scattered homes. "Granpa" Jacob's gravesite two miles outside of town was all that she had imagined it would be and more. "One can see the foundation of the old manor house. . . . But the glory of the place, if one uses imagination, is the garden which slopes down . . . to the Mattaponi River in a series of terraces," with "an avenue of "boxwood, grown high as trees."[6] Here was a place with a "touch of romance. . . . Here is history."[7] As for the house she planned to rent, it was filthy and had only a wood stove for heat, but it had "solid lines," plenty of room for a garden, and furniture she could use.[8]

Beneath Grace's enthusiasm lay a deep vein of anxiety and self-doubt. She agonized over her own motivations: "Oh God—help me—help me to face myself," she wrote in her diary. "Have I been trying to run away from the . . . the disappointment that people have rejected *Full Circle?*" To stave off discouragement and maintain what for her was becoming the most necessary of fictions—that she was accepting funds from her relatives in order to write and "make enough money" to become self-supporting—she whipped herself forward. "You have been given the talent for writing—Then write. . . . The public has not accepted *Full Circle*—do not be discouraged about it. Work at it. Work. Work. Steadily day by day—hour by hour."[9]

Encouragement came from her sisters. Just before she died, Elizabeth wrote to say how much she liked *Full Circle* and to ask how she could help with publicity. More surprisingly, "Blessed Lump" (the pet name that Grace now took to using for the sister whom others in the family referred to as Katharine or "Kay") called to say that she thought King and Queen Courthouse was "a good idea."[10] In the months that followed, the two sisters kept in close touch, and when Grace reiterated the obvious—"that I cannot move down there without a car"—Katharine bought her one so that she could learn to drive. "Oh Lord, I thank you for this lovely thing that Lump has offered to do," Grace wrote in her diary. "I thank you for her. Show her thy way." Later, when the lease on the house Grace hoped to rent turned out to contain "preposterous" provisions, Katharine took the bus down from upstate New York to help Grace compose a reply. "So good to talk things over with her. We had a really loving family time—and she was such a great help. So sorry we are really enemies—about political things—she Communist/Socialist—me Christian/Conservative. But she is a dear and I love her." When the only other house Grace could find turned out to be in an isolated area on the outskirts of the village and she confided that she was "'scared to death' to live by myself down there," Katharine calmed her fears.[11]

In October 1964, Grace moved into her new home. Fourteen months later she was reporting to the Glenns that those months in Virginia had been "perhaps the happiest time of my life, and the most creative."[12] Her diary and other writings told a more complicated story. She was welcomed into the community, especially by Betty Taylor, the postmistress who had facilitated her move. In the political climate created by the ongoing effort to smear the civil rights movement as communist inspired, she even enjoyed a modicum of local renown. Speaking to church groups, women's clubs, PTAs, and, especially, to white students in Virginia's still almost completely segregated schools, Grace held forth "on the subject of Communism and Christianity. . . . There has been the most amazing response," she wrote to Sen. Harry Byrd, the state's preeminent segregationist leader. "In one high school 160 youngsters stood up when I finished speaking and clapped until I left the auditorium."[13]

She also reached out to James J. Kilpatrick, editor of the *Richmond News Leader*, columnist for the *National Review*, and influential proponent of massive resistance to school desegregation, praising his articles and trying in vain to interest him in publishing her short stories and reviewing *Full Circle*. She had better luck with another segregationist leader, Robert B. Crawford, who invited her to events in Richmond, the state capital. Crawford came to prominence as head of a group called the "Defenders of State Sovereignty and Individual Liberties," which had mobilized its supporters behind a plan to shut down the state's school system and use tax dollars to fund segregated schools for whites. The courts had declared that strategy unconstitutional in 1959, but Crawford had continued on as secretary-treasurer of the Defenders' fund-raising arm, which contributed many thousands of dollars to segregated private academies.[14] When Grace was not giving talks, participating in local church and club activities, or traveling to Richmond, she was drafting unpublished political diatribes on, among other things: the "unlawful demonstrations . . . pornography, perversions and other evils" that resulted from the decisions of the Supreme Court under Chief Justice Earl Warren; the Voting Rights Act, which she saw as a usurpation "by politicians in power" comparable to Reconstruction, "that era when Stevens, Sumner and Wade (called the Godless three) spitefully imposed an army of occupation on the South, took away voting privileges from white citizens and gave them to Negroes"; and Lyndon Johnson's "phony 'War on Poverty.'"[15] Most of all, she was sending a daily stream of letters to family and friends. What she was not doing was writing and selling fiction, which caused her no end of torment.

Grace had begun working on a film script based on *Full Circle* before she left New York, aided by the producer-director of an inspirational film narrated by Sam Shoemaker in which she had appeared in 1961. Then too there was the "whiz bang mystery" she was trying to write.[16] Although the producer-director got a job at Warner Brothers, neither project panned out, and once she was ensconced in Virginia with what she began to call a "trust check" from her nieces and nephews coming in, she found it harder and harder to make herself do what she felt she had to do. "How I hate myself—for not getting down to writing," she confided to her diary. "I must make more money. Discipline! Discipline! Oh Lord, help."[17]

She tried giving "up most neighborhood & county activity in order to concentrate on writing," but that made her feel increasingly isolated.[18] Worse, as the romance of small town life wore off, the vitriol that had long infected her politics began to consume her private life. The diary she had begun to keep shortly after her move had always contained at least small doses of disapproval and resentment along with endearments and pleas for God's help. Now her entries became increasingly bitter, sometimes in direct contrast to the public face she presented in letters and conversations. The postmistress, who seems to have been an endless font of companionship and good deeds, became a particular target. At the end of a day in which Betty Taylor had accompanied her to Richmond or taken her shopping or driven her somewhere in the snow, Grace might note without explanation that her friend was "stupid & immature" and so "smug & self-complacent [that] she thinks everyone adores her—and since she believes . . . that she never does anything wrong—she is encased in a sort of armor of self-satisfaction."[19]

After a visit from Esther Chambers, her oldest and closest friend, Grace's comments began with pleasure—she is like "a sister"; "we talked & talked . . . & it was like old times"—but soon descended into suspicion: Esther is "charming, but has no principles"; she is "still emotionally a child." Worst of all, Grace feared that Esther had become a baleful influence on her husband in his final years. Driven by her secular Jewish prejudices, she had lured him away from God and, after his death in 1961, had threatened to censor his posthumous publications to make sure they did not reflect his Christian faith.[20]

A visit from Katharine elicited a similarly ambivalent response. Coming down from upstate New York by bus to spend her spring vacation with Grace, Katharine met her sister's friends and visited her favorite sites. She also made herself useful. She repaired Grace's camera and record player: "What joy—Now I can have music & we had music all evening—Wonderful!!" She cooked a turkey and spent hours building a cold frame for seedlings and helping to prepare Grace's garden for planting in the spring: "Lump has a lovely way of going at a thing simply & not complicating it." Yet three days after Katharine's departure, Grace woke up "thinking of Lump my poor darling—So mistaken, and so arrogant—and insensitive—Like a Lady Bountiful condescendingly bestowing charity—and bossing . . . the recipients of her charity—But she is so good-looking—and in some ways kindly & generous & I love her."[21]

The holidays Grace spent with Katharine and Elizabeth Bennett after they retired to Charlottesville in 1967 were especially loaded. "I knew that Lump hates God, prayers, churches, everything that goes against her Socialistic conscience," Grace wrote after one ill-fated Christmas in which the sisters' delicate, probably unspoken, negotiations over which childhood rituals to enact went awry. Writing to the Glenns after an especially disturbing blowup, Katharine explained the pattern as she experienced it: a series of warm calls, long letters, or short notes acknowledging the monthly checks that Katharine had begun to send, punctuated by occasional visits that went reasonably well, at least as far as Katharine knew, and then, every few years, a sudden expression of rage that "was almost a relief." Getting "it out of her system, [Grace] was then able to feel better toward me."[22]

A "frightening accident" in 1970—a car wreck that sent her to the hospital—left Grace more isolated and dependent, and so more resentful than ever before. Convinced that it was too dangerous for their seventy-eight-year-old aunt to continue to drive, her nieces and nephews refused to buy her a new car. Although, behind the scenes, William Glenn tried to help by reimbursing Betty Taylor and others for the cost and time of taking Grace where she needed to go, he became a special object of her wrath. Earlier, she had trumpeted his accomplishments to her neighbors.[23] Now she realized that the nephew "whom I had thought was big & generous" was in fact arrogant, rotten, and cruel. As for his wife Amory: "such sweetness on top—and a lot of spite churning underneath." When Katharine agreed with the consensus and said no to her sister's request that she buy her a car, Grace was "cast into gloom." "I have no money & no family, no car." "I feel old & done for—finished."[24]

Still, she soldiered on. She complained that "small people look down on me for walking (this includes some Negroes, too, almost all Negroes in this county having one and even two cars of their own)." But she resumed her voluble correspondence, acknowledging her relatives' checks and gifts; sometimes expressing pleasure in seeing them or concern for their well-being; other times lashing out, usually in the privacy of her diary or in letters that she did not send, but occasionally in open confrontations. Praying fervently to God to "help me with the Book," she also buckled down to writing, reporting on her progress and holding out hope that she would soon have something to sell. By 1974, she had succeeded in drafting a manuscript entitled "God and a Garden" and sending it to a prominent literary agent in New York.[25]

A month later, she noted that "a Jacquelyn Hall [had written] from Chapel Hill, N.C., asking if I would let her come & interview me for a job she is doing on 'Southern Oral History' whatever that is." I arrived on August 6 and found my way to her ramshackle house, wondering what could have brought her to this out-of-the-way place. The paint was peeling, and the garden behind the house had gone to seed. A bright-eyed woman with wild yellow hair opened the ragged screen door when I knocked. Inside, the house seemed decrepit and lonely. Drab browns and faded greens, bric-a-brac everywhere, an atmosphere of mildew and must. On the living room wall hung a portrait of Jacob Lumpkin. On the coffee table lay an inscribed copy of *Witness*, which she read from after our interview began.[26]

Later, she took me to see Jacob Lumpkin's grave, a forlorn weedy mound that she saw as a *lieu de memoire*, the sacred site that drew her to live alone in this out-of-the-way place. She treasured Jacob "because he was very stubborn" and a "very original type." At the same time, he represented tradition. By contrast, Katharine hewed to the verifiable, omitting Jacob from the family tree entirely. When called upon to trace her genealogy, she did so through her mother's line.[27]

By the time I found my way to Grace's door, old age and poverty were on the verge of ending the dream that had sustained her for the past ten years—"a house & garden & a 2nd hand car" in a place where the Lumpkin name meant something and she could imagine that time had stood still. The agent to whom she had sent the manuscript of "God and a Garden" had torn it "to shreds." She had gone for years with no means of transportation, was again in debt, and was so poor that, by the time an anxiously awaited check from a relative finally arrived, she once had "exactly one dollar—& one cent left in my account."[28] Taking the initiative, her nieces and nephews, led by John Lumpkin Sr., a Harvard-educated lawyer who headed South Carolina's largest bank, joined forces to engineer what they knew was going to be a difficult transition. They pulled strings to get Grace into Finlay House, a retirement home in Columbia named after the rector of the church in which she had grown up. Sending her an application to review and sign, they told her "not to worry about money for moving."[29]

In the fall of 1974, Grace gave in and went along with the plan. But whatever she had pictured for herself in Columbia, it was not the efficiency apartment on an upper floor of Finlay House that her nephews were able to secure and that she could afford on her income of $4,029 a year ($2,169 of which came from Social Security, $1,200 from her nieces and nephews, and $660 from Katharine).[30] When Katharine stepped in to cover the costs of the move, she became the object of her sister's fury. "Do not discuss me with Katharine, No! no! no good comes of that," Grace admonished one of her nephews. As the move approached, she confided to her diary: "Much has happened—Katharine forcing me to go." Two months later, she told her former mentor Lillian Gilkes that Finlay House was "a chamber of horrors." Katharine had picked it out for her. "She is rich and could do so. I am the only poor one in the family." Repeating that charge later, she explained that she had allowed a

sister "who is very tough and has a lot more money than I have to persuade me to come down and live in this place."[31]

When the Glenns took the unusual step of calling to tell Katharine
about Grace's complaints, she was too shocked to reply at once. Writing
to them a few months later, she explained: "It took about 24 hours for
me to realize [the] full implications [of] what Grace is saying—that I
'wanted to get rid of her'"—but then "it suddenly struck me how invidious it is."[32] By then, however, Grace had finally written directly to Katharine, "verbalizing . . . her sense of outrage toward me about her move
to Columbia," and, to Katharine's relief, the tension had abated. ("Gra-
cie . . . is now feeling much better towards me, praised be.") From then
on Katharine was determined "to stay strictly away from doing anything
except write regularly, send monthly checks, keep as closely in touch as I
can, but without making suggestions."[33]

Little by little, Grace resigned herself to her situation. That adjustment was eased by the royal treatment she boasted of receiving from her
Columbia nephews, who, while they tended to see her as exasperatingly
volatile and irresponsible, also respected her intelligence and the interesting life she had lived.[34] Just as important were the two final triumphs
she enjoyed: the acquisition of her papers—or what she proudly called
"the Grace Lumpkin Literary Collection"—by the University of South
Carolina; and, in the spring of 1976, the publication of a new edition of
The Wedding in a "Lost American Fiction" series edited by University of
South Carolina English professor Matthew J. Bruccoli, with an admiring postscript by Lillian Gilkes.[35]

When Grace died in 1980 at the age of eighty-nine, her nephew Joe
Lumpkin, who assumed responsibility for his aunts' affairs in their final
years, consulted with Katharine about what to do with the papers that
Grace had not already given to the university. She advised him to destroy
Grace's diary, which she must have found painful to read. He ignored
her suggestion and, a decade or so later, chose to share with me one of
the very few intimate, revealing sources that either sister left behind.[36]

By republishing *The Wedding* and acquiring Grace's papers Matthew
Bruccoli, Lillian Gilkes, and University of South Carolina archivists
forwarded a project of recovery that, over the next twenty years, would
bring leftist and feminist writers in from the cold. Inspired by the social
movements of the 1960s, which Grace disdained, that project lifted her

reputation in ways she could not have hoped for or foreseen. Fifteen years after she passed away, *To Make My Bread* became the first book in an influential series on the "Radical Novel Reconsidered" published by the University of Illinois Press and edited by Alan Wald, a foremost scholar of the mid-twentieth century's socially conscious literature. Of the ten books issued under this imprimatur, the left feminist novels have attracted the most readers. Benefiting from the ongoing energy generated by the women's movement, the study of these writers remains generative to the present day.[37]

IN 1979, KATHARINE AND Elizabeth Bennett moved from Charlottesville, Virginia, to Chapel Hill, home of the University of North Carolina, whose reputation as a beacon of liberalism and a font of southern studies Katharine had long admired. Always meticulous planners and prudent to a fault, they had made their choice carefully, joining the first group of residents at Carol Woods, a not-for-profit, continuing-care retirement community established by local citizens who had been working toward that end for the previous ten years. Elizabeth fell ill with Alzheimer's disease not long after they arrived, leaving Katharine to manage her medical care and financial affairs and to bear the grief of her death in 1983. A year later, Katharine was diagnosed with the cancer to which she would succumb in 1988.[38] Yet she had nothing but positive things to say about those years at Carol Woods, which, by all accounts, were filled with interesting new friends; a full round of community activities that "are intrinsically interesting to me—along the lines of my one-time teaching interests"; and the attention of her nieces and nephews and their children, who, even more than their parents, looked up to her as a woman who had had "an astounding career for . . . her time."[39]

Katharine's contentment rested in part on the pride she took in having finally brought *The Emancipation of Angelina Grimké* to publication, although she had mixed feelings about its reception. By the time it appeared in 1974, the new field of women's history was exploding, creating a ready audience for stories of what had been considered "minor figures" when she was searching for a publisher for her *Grimké* book.[40] The timing, however, was not as auspicious as it might have been. When Katharine discovered the Grimkés' letters and diaries in the mid-1950s, she had hoped to produce the first modern study of two of the nineteenth century's most extraordinary female reformers and thinkers.[41] Instead, her book was scooped by Gerda Lerner, who published *The Grimké Sisters of South Carolina: Rebels against Slavery*, her Columbia University dissertation, in 1967. Once Lerner's book appeared in paperback in 1971 (with a new subtitle, "Pioneers for Woman's Rights and Abolition," which her editors had rejected five years before on the grounds that readers were not interested in women) and she launched her enormously influential career, it was perhaps inevitable that, despite being warmly received, Katharine's long-incubating biography would be upstaged by Lerner's account.[42]

When asked, Katharine admitted that the unexpected appearance of Gerda Lerner's book had been "a blow." But at the time she kept her counsel: she was too elderly, too far removed from the academic world, and too reserved to promote her own work.[43] In 1981, however, she got one more chance to have her say about the South. A few years earlier, a young feminist named Iris Tillman Hill had moved from Texas to Athens, Georgia, to become editor-in-chief of the University of Georgia Press. Casting about for an entrée into the unfamiliar world of the Deep South, she happened upon *The Making of a Southerner* and decided to reissue it as one of the "lost classics" that scholars across the country were avidly recovering. She also commissioned a new afterword, in which Katharine directed attention away from herself and toward the black protest movement that had toppled segregation. Louis Rubin, the dean of southern literary studies, wrote a revealing comment for the dust jacket of the book: "The South that Katharine Du Pre Lumpkin saw back in the 1940s was the South that many of us preferred not to see, and so we questioned both the veracity of her report—without offering much evidence to refute it—and her right to give it. . . . We need to have this book around again to remind us what it took to be what Katharine Lumpkin was in her time. Her book is no longer fond prophecy and faint hope; it is a record of the route we had to travel." Eloquent though they were, Rubin's reflections said less about the response to *The Making of a Southerner* in the late 1940s—which had been strikingly enthusiastic—than they did about the Agrarian-dominated literary establishment of the 1950s, which helped to ensure that books such as Katharine's lay moldering on the shelves.[44]

When, in 1991, another edition of *The Making of a Southerner* appeared, it was framed rather differently. In a foreword and later article, the black feminist historian Darlene Clark Hine opened with a comment on the parallels between Katharine Du Pre Lumpkin and Angelina Grimké and positioned Lumpkin perceptively and accurately, as a radical, a "southern white feminist scholar," and an "illuminating" autobiographer. "Hers is the poignant testimony of a woman steeped in traditions peculiar to her class and region, who through education and will removed the cataracts of racism, curing herself of the blindness that hid pervasive and unrelenting white poverty and the grinding exploitation of agricultural, factory, and mill workers."[45] Today, more than a quarter of a century after the revival of Katharine's and Grace's most important works, *The Making of a Southerner* and *To Make My Bread* are firmly established among students of women's and southern history as classics of autobiography and radical fiction. Likewise, the Grimké sisters and the movements they represented have inspired an outpouring of scholarship and fiction.[46] Rightly so, for all these lives and works speak, almost prophetically, to the issues of class, region, and racial subordination that continue to roil our nation.

Grace remained proud of her first novel, but she would have been nonplussed by the left-leaning scholars who saved it from oblivion and now view it as a window on an era of working-class insurgency and literary ferment in which women—both as workers and as writers—were "in the heart of the struggle."[47] Katharine graciously tolerated, or even welcomed, the young feminists who sought her out. She understood our desire to overcome the ruptures in historical memory created by political repression and literary neglect and to draw from her generation lessons for our own. But she was happiest talking about the black and white southern women with whom she had built an interracial student movement in the 1920s and did her best to deflect our interest in the decade of hope surrounding World War II, the years in which she came to maturity as an activist and a writer. I respected her reticence even as I became more and more committed to telling her, her sisters', and her cohort's story. She had lived through McCarthyism and immersed herself in the study of Reconstruction—she knew better than I did what it took to watch progress toward justice reversed and find the hope and courage to fight on nonetheless.

ACKNOWLEDGMENTS

THIS BOOK HAS BEEN WITH ME, AT SOME LEVEL OF CON-
sciousness, since I met Grace and Katharine in the early 1970s, at the
very beginning of my career. Given such a long entanglement, a true
accounting of the people who have walked with me on this journey
would be impossible to compile. So I'll start in 1994 when I began making public presentations and publishing articles on the Lumpkin sisters
and listeners and readers helped me find the story I wanted to tell. My
thanks go out to interlocutors in lecture halls and seminar rooms at the
California Institute of Technology, the Citadel, Duke University, Louisiana State University, the National Humanities Center, the Schlesinger
Library on the History of Women in America, Sidney Sussex College,
Smith College, Spelman College, the University of Cambridge, the
University of Georgia, the University of Mississippi, the University of
North Carolina at Chapel Hill, the University of the South, the University of Texas, and the University of Wisconsin, as well as at meetings
of the American Association of Universities, the Association for Theater
in Higher Education, the Berkshire Conference of Women Historians,
the Coordinating Council for Women in History, the Organization of
American Historians, the Southern Association of Women Historians,
and the Southern Historical Association. I am indebted as well to editors and referees at *American Quarterly*, *Feminist Studies*, the *Journal of
American History*, and the *Journal of Southern History*.

I was the lucky recipient of foundation support that allowed me
both to finish other projects and to lay the groundwork for this book.
Among these were fellowships from the Center for Advanced Study
in the Behavioral Sciences at Stanford, the John Simon Guggenheim

Jacquelyn Hall interviewing Katharine Du Pre Lumpkin at a retirement community in Chapel Hill, North Carolina, early 1980s.

Foundation, the National Humanities Center, the Radcliffe Institute for Advanced Study at Harvard, as well as a residency at the Rockefeller Foundation's Bellagio Study and Conference Center.

I had the good fortune to find my way to Alane Salierno Mason at W. W. Norton. Her patient, brilliant editing was a gift for which I will be ever grateful, as was the kindness and hard work of others at the press.

I also had Grey Osterud at my side. She signed on from early in her career as an independent scholar and editor, and she read every word of this book, often many times over, while at the same time shoring up many other writers and carrying forward her own impressive program of writing and research. A comrade as well as a consummate reader, Grey knows more about more things than anyone else I know. And who else would meet you at a conference and ride the subway with you to the airport in order to talk about a tangle in your work?

I have dedicated this book in part to my students. I framed some of my most memorable courses as writing workshops and invited them to read my messy first drafts. They rose to the occasion, critiquing the teacher and putting their own fragile efforts forward with perhaps more courage than before. Beyond that were the many, many scholars-in-the-making who not only helped me with the deep digs of research but also became fellow travelers in this work. A special shout-out to Bruce Baker and Blain Roberts, who stuck with me through a crucial time, thought alongside me, and are thinking alongside me still. Elizabeth McRae and Laura Moore did some sleuthing at the very outset that has guided me ever since. I cannot say enough about Elizabeth Brake, Will Goldsmith, Anna Krome-Lukens, and Michael Trotti, whose smarts and work ethics are second to none. Or about Kathryn Wall, who cut her research teeth working with me as a student and came back into my life as an independent photographer, teacher, and internet technology wizard as this project neared its end. Emma Parker and Francesca Prince, independent researchers, were absolutely indispensable in this final stage as well. I could go on in similar praise of others, including some whom I have never met but who helped me find invaluable material in far-flung archives, but will content myself with saying thank you so much to: Dave Anderson, Andy Arnold, Jessica Auer, Kirsten Delegard, Evan Faulkenbury, Bethany Keenan, Marla Miller, Kathryn Newfont, Katie Otis, Robin Payne, Susan Pearson, Linda Sellars, and Kerry Taylor. Finally, a salute to Salvatore Borriello, editorial manager of the Reading List, who stepped in to help corral the endnotes and bibliography as well as to Wojtek Wojdynski, for bringing new life to archival photographs.

I have profited more than I can say from two writing groups, both of which offered a rare combination of friendship, laughter, and astute, invested critique. Their memberships shifted over time, but in the end settled into Della Pollock, Joy Kasson, and Carol Mavor, in the first instance, and Laura Edwards, Lisa Levenstein, and Nancy MacLean in the other. Glenda Gilmore, Nancy Hewitt, Anastatia Sims, Susan Thorne, and Christine Stansell also read chapters and shared their peerless knowledge of women and/or the South. I am grateful as well to Christina L. Baker, Keith Bohannon, Dorothea Browder, Sarah Flynn, Joanne Marshall Mauldin, Jocelyn Olcott, Landon Storrs, and Kate Douglas Torrey, who gave me the benefit of their knowledge and research and, in Kate's and Sarah's case, their intimate acquaintance with the subjects of this book. And what would I have done without the steady comradeship of Natalie Fousekis, Jim Leloudis, Molly Rozum, and Jennifer Ritterhouse and my treasured walk-talks with Bryant Simon? Equally important: I would not have had the time or the heart to finish this book without my amazing colleagues, friends, and successors at the Southern Oral History Program and the Center for the Study of the American South, who stood with me through many hard and creative years and did so much to allow me to set that part of my life's work aside. Thanks to Brent Glass, Malinda Maynor Lowery, Beth Millwood, Rachel Seidman, Jessica Wilkerson, and, again, to Della, Natalie, and Jim.

I am deeply indebted to the members of the Lumpkin family who shared their memories and priceless documents and photographs with me, especially Katherine Glenn Kent, who salvaged the almost lost papers of Elizabeth Lumpkin Glenn and, at the last possible moment, made them available to me as well as to future students of women and the South. Thanks also to the descendants and friends of Grace's husband Michael Intrator, especially Roland Intrator, whom I met by chance when his family-owned business helped me move house in 1979 when my first marriage was ending and a new chapter of my life was about to begin.

Without archivists, no history! I am so grateful for what two of my favorite public radio producers, the Kitchen Sisters, call "the Keepers": Laura Hart and Biff Hollingsworth at the University of North Carolina's Southern Historical Collection; Henry Fulmer and Duncan Graham at the University of South Carolina's South Caroliniana Library; Maida Goodwin, Sherrill Redmon, and Nanci Young at the Sophia Smith Collection at Smith College; Deborah Thompson and her colleagues at Brenau University; Annadell Craig Lamb, historian of the Phi Mu Fraternity; and others at archives around the country. In my case, also: no Freedom of Information Act, no history. My thanks to James Hiram Lesar, attorney-at-law, a matchless champion of transparency and enemy of government secrets.

I lost my mother during the writing of this book. But I know how happy she would be to see how the loyalty and affection of my family have sustained me. Love always to my siblings, Jeanne Grimm, John Dowd, Jennifer Edmondson, and Jyl Dowd, and my nephews and nieces, Joshua Ormond, Jade Dowd-Vanderberg, Emily Dowd, and Nolan Edmondson.

Without the intellectual engagement, vigilant care, and unwavering confidence of my husband, Bob Korstad, I would never have set forth to write this book, let alone have been blessed with such a perfect room of my own (his old office!) and such a fulfilling life in and beyond what Patti Smith calls so simply and elegantly, "doing the work."

NOTES

SSC   Sophia Smith Collection, Smith College Special
         Collections, Northampton, MA
Tanenhaus Papers   Sam Tanenhaus Papers, Hoover Institution Library and
                   Archives, Stanford University, CA
van Kleeck Papers Mary van Kleeck Papers, Sophia Smith Collection,
                   Smith College Special Collections, Northampton, MA
Warne Papers   Colston E. Warne Papers, Consumers Union Archives,
               Yonkers, NY
YWCA Records   YWCA of the U.S.A. Records, Sophia Smith Collection,
               Smith College Special Collections, Northampton, MA

CHAPTER ONE: INTRODUCTION

Portions of this chapter are drawn from J. Hall, "Open Secrets," 110–24.

1. This photograph is on the cover of KDL, *Making* (1947; reprint, Athens: University of Georgia Press, 1981).
2. For this late 1960s, early 1970s context, see J. Hall and Nasstrom, "Case Study," 409–16.
3. KDL, "Lecture to a General Audience," 1947, 2 (quote), folder 64–65, KDL Papers.
4. KDL, *Making*, 112 (first quote), 128 (subsequent quotes).
5. Graham, "Expansion and Exclusion," 759–73.
6. KDL, *South in Progress*; Hobson, *But Now I See*, 18–19, 36–51. Unlike white Southerners, African Americans had a long antiracist autobiographical tradition. Two recent southern memoirs illustrate the durability of both of these traditions: Dew, *Making of a Racist*; Blow, *Fire Shut Up*.
7. Hobson, *Tell about the South* (first quote); Cash, *Mind of the South*, vii (second quote); KDL, "Lecture to Prof. Ralph Harlow's class—course in 'Christian Ethics,' Smith College, Spring 1947 (following publication of my book *The Making of a Southerner*)," 13 (third quote), folder 64–65, KDL Papers.
8. Tanenhaus, *Whittaker Chambers*, 65 (quote).
9. G. Lumpkin, *To Make My Bread*; Schachner, "Revolutionary Literature," 60 (first and second quotes); Gray, *Southern Aberrations*, 312 (third quote).
10. Kunitz and Haycraft, eds., *Twentieth Century Authors*, s.v. "Grace Lumpkin" (first and second quotes); L. Rubin, "Southern Literature," 98 (third quote). Five years before Grace died in 1980, *The Wedding* was reprinted in a series of Lost American Fiction. In 1995, *To Make My Bread* became the first book in the Radical Novel Reconsidered series published by the University of Illinois Press.
11. G. Lumpkin, "An Ex-Communist Speaks," *New Castle Tribune* (Chappaqua, NY), Sept. 20, 1946 (quote); G. Lumpkin interview, Aug. 6, 1974.
12. KDL interview, Apr. 24, 1985, 3 (quote); KDL, *Emancipation*.
13. Freedman, "The Burning of Letters," 181–200; Hellman, *Scoundrel Time*.
14. The metaphor of the biographer as burglar was suggested to me by Malcolm, *Silent Woman*, 8–9.
15. KDL interview, Aug. 4, 1974, 84–93 (quote on 88).

16. Foley, *Radical Representations*, 246 (quote); Korstad and N. Lichtenstein, "Opportunities Found and Lost."

17. Theoharis and J. Cox, *Boss*; Hall v. U.S. Department of Justice, Civil Action No. 96-2306 (D.D.C.).

18. Nelson, *Repression and Recovery*, 11 (quote).

CHAPTER TWO: "SOUTHERNERS OF MY PEOPLE'S KIND"

1. KDL, *Making*, 3–44, 102; Coleman and Gurr, *Dictionary of Georgia Biography*, s.v.v. "Joseph Henry Lumpkin," "Wilson Lumpkin"; B. Lumpkin and M. Lumpkin, *Lumpkin Family*, 9–14, 31–32; Huebner, "Joseph Henry Lumpkin," 123–25; Ragsdale, *Georgia Baptists*, 243.

2. "Colonel Lumpkin Died Yesterday," *Columbia (SC) State*, Mar. 14, 1910 (first quote) (hereafter "Colonel Lumpkin Died"); G. Lumpkin, "Southern Woman Bares Tricks of Higher-Ups to Shunt Lynch Blame," *Daily Worker*, Nov. 27, 1933 (second quote); KDL, *Emancipation*, 10 (third quote).

3. KDL, *Making*, 11 (quote); G. Lumpkin interview, Aug. 6, 1974; "Jacobitism in Virginia: Charges against Captain Jacob Lumpkin," *Virginia Magazine of History and Biography* 6, no. 4 (Apr. 1899): 389–96; B. Lumpkin and M. Lumpkin, *Lumpkin Family*, 5–8.

4. G. Lumpkin, *Wedding*, 14 (first quote); KDL, *Making*, 4, 7 (second quote), 9. The Lumpkin family can be traced through the following local records: Bryan H. Lumpkin, "Lumpkin," Dec. 1936, folders 101–6, KDL Papers; B. Lumpkin and M. Lumpkin, *Lumpkin Family*, 37–40; "William Lumpkin," in Fourth Census of the United States, 1820, Population Schedule, Lexington, Oglethorpe, GA, p. 188; "William Lumpkin," in Fifth Census of the United States, 1830, Population Schedule, Capt Lumpkins District, Oglethorpe, GA, roll 20, p. 87; "William Lumpkin," in Sixth Census of the United States, 1840, Population Schedule, District 228, Oglethorpe, GA, roll 48, p. 60; "Susan Lumpkin," in Seventh Census of the United States, 1850, Population Schedule, Division 66, Oglethorpe, GA, roll M432_80, p. 21B; "William Lumpkin," Feb. 8, 1847, Oglethorpe County Will Book, 1794–1903, Oglethorpe County Registrars Office, GA, in *Georgia, Wills and Probate Records, 1742–1992*, Ancestry.com; "Wm Lumpkin to Patsey Mickelborough," Nov. 29, 1803, *Georgia, Marriage Records from Select Counties, 1828–1978*, Ancestry.com; "William Lumpkin to Susannah Edwards," Jun. 6, 1815, *Georgia, Marriage Records from Select Counties, 1828–1978*, Ancestry.com.

5. KDL, *Making*, 8 (quotes); Bryant, *How Curious a Land*, 15.

6. W. W. Lumpkin, "An Old Time Georgia Christmas," *Columbia (SC) State*, Dec. 16, 1906 (quotes). See also "W. W. Lumpkin as Writer," *Columbia (SC) State*, Mar. 14, 1910, thanks to John H. Lumpkin Sr. for bringing this newsclip to my attention.

7. KDL, *Making*, 32 (first quote), 19 (second quote). For these legendary slaves, whom she refers to as "servants," see also Elizabeth Lumpkin Glenn, "Bitterroot," [1950], in J. Hall's possession, thanks to Amory and William W. L. Glenn (hereafter E. Glenn, "Bitterroot").

8. "W. W. Lumpkin as Writer," *Columbia (SC) State*, Mar. 14, 1910 (quote).

9. KDL, *Making*, 30 (first quote), 38–39 (second quote on 39, third quote on 38), 36. See also G. Lumpkin, *Sign for Cain*, 24–25.

10. KDL, *Making*, 44 (quotes).

11. KDL, *Making*, 47, 49, 50–51; "Lumpkin, A. J.," in Tenth Census of the United States, 1880, Population Schedule, District 141, Greene, GA, roll 149, ED 034, p. 221B, family 17, line 29.

12. KDL, *Making*, 51 (quote). Thanks to Keith Bohannon for sharing his expertise with me during a frustrating attempt to trace William Lumpkin's Civil War career. For family and United Confederate Veteran accounts of Lumpkin's service, see "Col. William Wallace Lumpkin," *Confederate Veteran*, May 1910, 245; "Colonel Lumpkin Died"; William Lumpkin, "Where and why I was a Kuklux," 1, box 76, folder 66, Civil War Collection, State Archives of North Carolina, Raleigh (hereafter W. Lumpkin, "Where and why"); "William Wallace Lumpkin," in Bryan H. Lumpkin, "Lumpkin," Dec. 1936, folders 101–6, KDL Papers (hereafter "William Wallace Lumpkin"); Elizabeth Lumpkin Glenn, "Notes in answer to a letter from Katharine Lumpkin," n.d., folder 34, KDL Papers (hereafter E. Glenn, "Notes in answer to a letter"); E. Glenn, "Bitterroot"; United Confederate Veterans, Camp Hampton No. 389, Columbia, Minutes, 1897–1923, 42, United Confederate Veterans, Confederate Survivors' Association, Richland County Records, SCL; KDL, *Making*, 51–52.

13. Rable, *Civil Wars*, 172 (first quote); KDL, *Making*, 72–73 (second and third quotes).

14. Bryan, *Confederate Georgia*, 171 (first quote); Bryant, *How Curious a Land*, 93 (second quote).

15. KDL, *Making*, 51 (quote), 22, 48–50; "[Adoniram] Judson Lumpkin," in Ninth Census of the United States, 1870, Agricultural Schedule, Greene County, GA, pp. 5–6; "A. J. Lumpkin," Greene County Tax Digests for the 141st Militia District, 1871, RGS: 34–61, Georgia Archives, Morrow.

16. W. Lumpkin, "Where and why," 1 (first and second quotes); KDL, *Making*, 13 (third quote).

17. W. Lumpkin, "Where and why," 1 (first quote); KDL, *Making*, 56 (second quote), 15. If William's memories are accurate, he was worse off than most planters. Freedom came late to Greene County. Most slaves stayed where they were after the Emancipation Proclamation, daring to declare their freedom only when federal troops arrived. Even then, they had nothing—no money, no land, no property—and most planters found ways to make them work under conditions that were not much different from slavery.

18. KDL, *Making*, 124 (first quote), 59–60; G. Lumpkin, "Memorial Day—1961" (second quote), folder 121, KDL Papers; G. Lumpkin, "Miserable Offender," 284 (third quote); G. Lumpkin, *Sign for Cain*, 172; G. Lumpkin, *Full Circle*, 171–72.

19. This discussion of the post–Civil War years draws on Blight, *Race and Reunion*; Bryant, *How Curious a Land*; Bryant, "We Have No Chance"; E. Foner, *Short History*; Hahn, *Nation under Our Feet*.

20. Pike quoted in Hahn, *Nation under Our Feet*, 218; Blight, *Race and Reunion*, 51; E. Foner, *Short History*, 156.

21. Hahn, *Nation under Our Feet*, 238 (first quote); Bryant, "We Have No Chance," 13–37 (second quote on 19); W. Lumpkin, "Where and why," 1 (third quote); Bryant, *How Curious a Land*, 102–28.

22. Trouillot, *Silencing the Past*, 73 (first quote); W. Lumpkin, "Where and why," 2–3 (second quote); KDL, *Making*, 58–60.

23. KDL, *Making*, 76, 90, 124; Ninth Census of the United States, 1870, Population Schedule, Militia District 161, Greene, GA, roll M593–153, p. 446B, lines 16–18; "A. J. Lumpkin," Greene County Tax Digests for the 141st Militia District, 1871, RGS: 34–61, Georgia Archives, Morrow; "William Wallace Lumpkin."

24. W. Lumpkin, "Where and why"; W. W. Lumpkin, "An Old Time Georgia Christmas," *Columbia (SC) State*, Dec. 16, 1906. Thanks to Amy Crow for discovering "Where and why" and sharing it with Bruce Baker, who shared it with me. Elizabeth Lumpkin Glenn had given a typed copy to the United Daughters of the Confederacy, likely keeping a handwritten one for herself. The corrections on the typed copy, which was deposited in the archives, are in Elizabeth's hand.

25. U.S. House, *Report of the Joint Select Committee to Inquire into the Condition of Affairs in the Late Insurrectionary States*, 42nd Cong., 2nd sess. (Washington, DC: Government Printing Office, 1872), 99 (quote).

26. Trelease, *White Terror*, 523–24.

27. T. Dixon, *Leopard's Spots*; T. Dixon, *Clansman*; Gilmore, "Meanest Books," 89 (first quote); Rice and C. W. Williams, *History of Greene County*, 423–24 (second and third quotes).

28. W. Lumpkin, "Where and why," 1 (quotes).

29. W. Lumpkin, "Where and why," 2 (quote), 4. The following account of Abram Colby draws on Bryant, *How Curious a Land*, 132–34; U.S. Congress, *Testimony Taken by the Joint Select Committee to Inquire into the Condition of Affairs in the Late Insurrectionary States*, Part 6: Georgia, vol. 2, 42nd Cong., 2nd sess. (Washington, DC: Government Printing Office, 1872), 695–707 (hereafter GA Klan Hearings). See also E. Foner, *Reconstruction*, 205, 359, 426, 432, 435.

30. Hahn, *Nation under Our Feet*, 222 (quote), 274.

31. GA Klan Hearings, 695–707 (quote on 702); Bryant, *How Curious a Land*, 132–34.

32. Bryant, *How Curious a Land*, 103–8 (first quote on 108), 132 (second quote), 122–25.

33. GA Klan Hearings, 696–97 (quotes on 697).

34. GA Klan Hearings, 698 (quote).

35. W. Lumpkin, "Where and why," 4 (quotes).

36. Hahn, *Nation under Our Feet*, 286–87.

37. W. Lumpkin, "Where and why," 4–5 (first and third quotes); Kantrowitz, *Ben Tillman*, 92 (second quote).

38. KDL, *Making*, 99 (quote).

39. Woodward, *Origins of the New South*, 1–22; Bryant, *How Curious a Land*, 9–11, 17–18, 50–54; Reidy, *From Slavery to Agrarian Capitalism*, 215–41; G. Wright, *Old South, New South*, 17–50.

40. KDL, *Making*, 76–77, 124; E. Glenn, "Notes in answer to a letter"; "William Wallace Lumpkin"; John H. Lumpkin Sr. interview, Aug. 17, 1990; "Family Donates Table to J. H. Lumpkin House," *Athens (GA) Banner Herald / Daily News*, n.d., newsclip in J. Hall's possession, thanks to Robert L. Lumpkin; Rice and C. W. Williams, *History of Greene County*, 359.

41. Crosse, *Patillo*, 163–65; KDL, "Katharine Du Pre Lumpkin," genealogical chart prepared for the Daughters of the American Revolution, folder 107, KDL Papers; Elizabeth Lumpkin Glenn, "A Personal Story, Aunt Sarah Frances Bryan," in J. Hall's possession, thanks to Thomas Bryan (hereafter E. Glenn, "A Personal Story"); "Henry Pattillo Married to Nancy Dupree," 1823, in Edmund West, comp., *Family Data Collection—Individual Records*, Ancestry.com.

42. KDL, *Making*, 52–53 (quote).

43. For Annette's memories, as well as family stories about and genealogical research on her, see KDL, *Making*, 51–55; McMaster, *Girls of the Sixties*, 103–5; G. Lumpkin, "Annette Caroline Morris," in Bryan H. Lumpkin, "Lumpkin," Dec. 1936, folders 101–6, KDL Papers (hereafter G. Lumpkin, "Annette Caroline Morris"); E. Glenn, "Bitterroot"; E. Glenn, "A Personal Story."

44. KDL, *Making*, 53–54 (first quote on 53); McMaster, *Girls of the Sixties*, 104 (second and third quotes).

45. "Henry Patillo," in Seventh Census of the United States, 1850, Population Schedule, 59 Division, Meriwether County, GA, 398, family 1317, line 30; "Henry Patillo," in Eighth Census of the United States, 1860, Agricultural Schedule, Meriwether County, GA, pp. 33–34; G. Lumpkin, "Annette Caroline Morris" (quote).

46. McMaster, *Girls of the Sixties*, 104; E. Glenn, "Bitterroot"; E. Glenn, "A Personal Story"; G. Lumpkin, "Annette Caroline Morris" (quote).

47. McMaster, *Girls of the Sixties*, 104–5 (quotes).

48. E. Glenn, "Bitterroot"; E. Glenn, "A Personal Story," 3–4; KDL, *Making*, 55; McMaster, *Girls of the Sixties*, 105; G. Lumpkin, "Annette Caroline Morris."

49. On the impact of the Civil War on white women, see Rable, *Civil Wars*; Faust, *Mothers of Invention*; Whites, *Crisis in Gender*; Censer, *White Southern Womanhood*.

50. G. Lumpkin, "Annette Caroline Morris" (quote); Cashin, *Story of Augusta*, 121, 125–26, 131; Martin V. Calvin, *Calvin's Augusta and Business Directory for 1865–'66* (Augusta, GA: Printed at the Constitutionalist Job Office, 1865), 3, 21; Arthur Ray Rowland, *Index to City Directories of Augusta, Georgia, 1841–1879* (Augusta, GA: Augusta Genealogical Society, 1995); Eighth Census of the United States, 1860, Population Schedule, Augusta Ward 1, Richmond County, GA, p. 749, family 364; Ninth Census of the United States, 1870, Population Schedule, Augusta Ward 1, Richmond County, GA, p. 45, family 818; Crosse, *Patillo*, 163–65; Annette Lumpkin obituary, *Columbia (SC) State*, Apr. 27, 1925; Eighth Census of the United States, 1860, Population Schedule, Augusta Ward 2, Richmond County, GA, p. 782, family 621; Ninth Census of the United States, 1870, Population Schedule, Augusta Ward 2, Richmond County, GA, p. 72, family 321; McMaster, *Girls of the Sixties*, 103; KDL, *Making*, 52.

51. G. Lumpkin, "Annette Caroline Morris" (quotes); E. Glenn, "Bitterroot"; G. Lumpkin interview, Aug. 6, 1974.

52. KDL to Mrs. Marvin B. Rosenberry, Mar. 12, 1947, folder 11, KDL Papers; Crosse, *Patillo*, 169; "Annette Carolina 'Annie' Morris Lumpkin," Find a Grave, added Aug. 7, 2010, https://www.findagrave.com/cgi-bin/fg.cgi?page=gr&GRid=56617320; Tenth Census of the United States, 1880, Mortality Schedule, ED 34, p. 1, Greene County, GA.

53. Tenth Census of the United States, 1880, Population Schedule, District 141, Greene, GA, roll 149, ED 034, p. 221B, family 17, lines 29–32; Greene County Tax Digests, vol. 2, Militia District 140, 1877, RGS: 34–61, Georgia Archives, Morrow.

54. G. Lumpkin, *Wedding*, 15 (first quote); Annette Lumpkin to Sister, Jan. 1893 (second quote), in J. Hall's possession, thanks to Joseph H. Lumpkin Sr.; G. Lumpkin, "Miserable Offender," 281–88.

55. G. Lumpkin, "Miserable Offender," 285 (quote).

56. "William Wallace Lumpkin" (quote); KDL, *Making*, 88, 99; "The J.B. Gordon Monument Association," *Confederate Veteran*, June 1905, 244–45; Annette Lumpkin to Sister, Jan. 1893; Old Capital Railway Company letterhead, W. W. Lumpkin listed as president, Oct. 10, 1894, both in J. Hall's possession, thanks to Joseph H. Lumpkin Sr.; W. W. Lumpkin, Georgia Property Tax Digests, 1887, Militia District 320, Georgia Archives, Morrow; "Colonel Lumpkin Died."

57. E. Glenn, "Bitterroot" (quote); "W.W. Lumpkin," *Union Recorder* (Milledgeville, GA), Apr. 10, 1894.

58. Annette to Brother and Sister, May 15, 1893 (quote), in J. Hall's possession, thanks to Joseph H. Lumpkin Sr.; KDL, *Making*, 100; *City Directory of Macon, Georgia, 1897* (Atlanta: Maloney Directory, 1987), 312.

59. "Colonel Lumpkin Died," (first quote); E. Glenn, "Bitterroot" (second quote).

60. KDL, *Making*, 107 (quote); *National Cyclopedia of American Biography*, s.v. "Lumpkin, Alva Moore"; Twelfth Census of the United States, 1900, Population Schedule, Columbia Ward 4, Richland, SC, ED 91, sheet 2A, family 30, lines 34–42.

CHAPTER THREE: "LEST WE FORGET"

Portions of this chapter are drawn from J. Hall, "You Must Remember This."

1. KDL, *Making*, 101 (quote).

2. J. Hall et al., *Like a Family*, 24–43; Ayers, *Promise of the New South*, 24–25.

3. G. Lumpkin, *Wedding*, 6–7 (first and second quotes); "Columbia to the Veterans," *Columbia (SC) State*, May 8, 1901 (third and fifth quotes); J. Moore, *Columbia and Richland County*, 276 (fourth quote).

4. G. Lumpkin, *Wedding*, 5 (quote).

5. This discussion of South Carolina politics draws on J. Moore, *Columbia and Richland County*, 274, 310, 371; Kousser, *Shaping of Southern Politics*, 145–52; Carlton, *Mill and Town*; B. Simon, "Appeal of Cole Blease"; B. Simon, *Fabric of Defeat*; Kantrowitz, *Ben Tillman*.

6. KDL, *Making*, 139–40 (quote). For the nexus between the rise of the New South

and the imposition of segregation, see also Woodward, *Origins of the New South*; Gaston, *New South Creed*; H. Rabinowitz, *First New South*.

7. *Walsh's Columbia South Carolina City Directory* (Charleston, SC: Walsh Directory), 1910, 1913–1917; J. Moore, *Columbia and Richland County*, 234–35; Warner, *Streetcar Suburbs*.

8. KDL, *Making*, 101 (first quote), 105 (second quote), 102 (third quote).

9. KDL, *Making*, 100, 105–8 (quote on 104); G. Lumpkin, *Wedding*, 7; Annette Lumpkin to Sister, Apr. 22, 1916, in J. Hall's possession, thanks to Joseph H. Lumpkin Sr.; *Walsh's Columbia South Carolina City Directory* (Charleston, SC: Walsh Directory), 1903, 1908–1910, 1913–1917, 1920; Writers' Program of the Work Projects Administration, *South Carolina*, 213.

10. KDL, *Making*, 107–8 (first and second quotes), 100 (third quote).

11. KDL, *Making*, 101–8 (first and third quotes); Annette Lumpkin to Sister, Oct. 23, 1900 (second quote), in J. Hall's possession; thanks to Joseph H. Lumpkin Sr.

12. KDL, *Making*, 106 (quotes). See also G. Lumpkin, *Wedding*, 86; Hunter, *To 'Joy My Freedom*, 56.

13. KDL, *Making*, 155 (first quote), 106; G. Lumpkin, "Debutante," 16 (second quote); Elizabeth Lumpkin Glenn, "Bitterroot," in J. Hall's possession, thanks to Amory and William W. L. Glenn (hereafter E. Glenn, "Bitterroot"); Twelfth Census of the United States, 1900, Population Schedule, Columbia Ward 4, Richland, SC, ED 91, sheet 2A, family 30, lines 34–42; G. Lumpkin, "Treasure," 171.

14. Annette Lumpkin to Sister, Apr. 22, 1916 (first quote), in J. Hall's possession; E. Glenn, "Bitterroot" (second and third quotes); W. W. Ball to Thomas R. Waring, Apr. 15, 1922 (fourth quote), box 12, W. W. Ball Papers, Duke University; G. Lumpkin, *Wedding*, 51–52; John H. Lumpkin Sr. interview, Aug. 17, 1990. For the suggestion that women of Annette's generation were more likely to do housework than their mothers had been, see Censer, "Changing World of Work."

15. KDL, *Making*, 102, 106, 114 (quotes); G. Lumpkin, *Wedding*, 61; Writers' Program of the Work Projects Administration, *South Carolina*, 40, 145; A. Thomas, *Historical Account*, 536–43; Graydon, "Trinity Church," 21–23.

16. KDL, *Making*, 106 (quotes); Phifer, *Kirkman George Finlay*, 17–19.

17. KDL, *Making*, 121 (first, second, and third quotes), 128 (fourth quote).

18. G. Lumpkin, *Wedding*, 15–16 (quote). See also G. Lumpkin, "Miserable Offender"; G. Lumpkin, *Sign for Cain*, 100.

19. This discussion of the Lost Cause relies on several waves of scholarship. The first, which appeared in the 1970s and '80s, includes Gaston, *New South Creed*; Osterweis, *Myth of the Lost Cause*; C. R. Wilson, *Baptized in Blood*; Foster, *Ghosts of the Confederacy*. More recent studies include Bailey, "Textbooks of the 'Lost Cause'"; Bishir, "Landmarks of Power"; Nina Silber, *Romance of Reunion*. Silber's work represents a critical turn to the question of how women and gender conventions figured in the construction of the Lost Cause and of the South's early twentieth-century historical awakening more generally. On this issue, I am especially indebted to Whites, *Crisis in Gender*; Faust, *Mothers of Invention*; Sims, *Power of Femininity*; Brundage, "White Women"; Montgomery, "Lost Cause Mythology"; K. Cox, *Dixie's Daughters*.

20. Faust, *Republic of Suffering*, 237–49; Gardner, *Blood and Irony*, 4–7.
21. Hobson, *But Now I See*, xiv (quote); KDL, *Making*, 111; Snead, *Address by Col. Claiborne Snead*.
22. KDL, *Making*, 113 (first quote), 112 (second quote); C. R. Wilson, *Baptized in Blood*, 30.
23. Nora, "Memory and History"; Gaston, *New South Creed*.
24. Woodward, *Origins of the New South*, 155 (first quote); KDL, *Making*, 15 (second quote).
25. KDL, *Making*, 127–30 (quote on 128).
26. KDL, *Making*, 126–27 (quote on 127); K. Cox, *Dixie's Daughters*; Faust, *Republic of Suffering*, 238–47.
27. FitzGerald, *America Revised*, 51–52. For the professionalization of southern history and the displacement of women by men, see Brundage, "White Women"; Brundage, *Southern Past*, 105–37; B. Johnson, "Regionalism, Race"; B. Johnson, "Southern Historical Association." See also B. Smith, "Gender and the Practices"; Des Jardins, *Historical Enterprise*.
28. Ayers, *Promise of the New South*, 334 (quote); Blight, *Race and Reunion*, 2–3.
29. Bishir, "Landmarks of Power," 7; Nina Silber, *Romance of Reunion*, 159–78.
30. UDC Minute Book 1901–1910, 265 (quote), UDC Minute Book June 1910–Nov. 1913, 85, Records of the United Daughters of the Confederacy, Wade Hampton Chapter (Columbia, SC), Confederate Relic Room, Columbia, SC; KDL, *Making*, 113.
31. Elizabeth Lumpkin Glenn, "At the home of William and Amory Glenn written on my seventy-fifth birthday, Nov 10, 1955," in J. Hall's possession, thanks to Katherine Glenn Kent (hereafter E. Glenn Letters).
32. *Columbia (SC) State*, Aug. 5, 1899 (quotes), newsclip in United Confederate Veterans, Minutes 1897–1923, Records of United Confederate Veterans, South Carolina Division, Camp Hampton (Columbia, SC), SCL.
33. "Hampton and Gordon, and a Young Woman Orator," *Columbia (SC) State*, May 9, 1901 (quotes).
34. Gopnik, *Philosophical Baby*; Greenberg, "What Babies Know."
35. KDL, *Making*, 114 (first and third quotes), 112 (second quote).
36. KDL, *Making*, 114–15 (first, second, and third quotes), 120 (fourth quote), 116. For this event, see also "Reunion Programme Given in Full," May 10, 1903; "Tomorrow Begins the Big Reunion," May 11, 1903; "Magnificent Floats and Carriages in Floral Parade," May 15, 1903, all in *Columbia (SC) State*.
37. KDL, *Making*, 116–19 (quotes); "Reception to the Sponsors Distinctively Gala Event," *Columbia (SC) State*, May 13, 1903.
38. "A Columbia Girl's Address to the Virginia Veterans," *Columbia (SC) State*, Nov. 1, 1905 (first quote) (hereafter "Columbia Girl's Address"); "Miss Lumpkin to Georgia Veterans," *Confederate Veteran*, Feb. 1904, 70 (second quote); "Columbia Girl Captured Grim Georgia Veterans," *Columbia (SC) State*, Sept. 25, 1904 (hereafter "Columbia Girl Captured Veterans").
39. "Hampton and Gordon, and a Young Woman Orator," *Columbia (SC) State*, May 9, 1901 (first and second quotes); "Miss Lumpkin to Georgia Veterans,"

Confederate Veteran, Feb. 1904, 69 (third quote). See also G. Lumpkin, *Wedding*, 31.

40. KDL, *Making*, 120 (quote); "Memorial to a Comrade," *Columbia (SC) State*, May 15, 1903.

41. William Lumpkin to Elizabeth Lumpkin, Nov. 4, Nov. 5, Nov. 12, Nov. 28, 1903; May 19, 1904, E. Glenn Letters.

42. "Columbia Girl Captured Veterans," (first quote); "Columbia Girl's Address," (second quote).

43. Foster, *Ghosts of the Confederacy*, 97 (quote), 136–37; Nina Silber, "Intemperate Men."

44. "Miss Lumpkin at Monteagle," *Columbia (SC) State*, Aug. 20, 1905 (quote); undated photocopy of letter fragment from Elizabeth Lumpkin Glenn, in J. Hall's possession, thanks to Amory and William W. L. Glenn; "Mrs. Eugene B. Glenn Dies," *Asheville (NC) Citizen*, Feb. 15, 1963.

45. "Columbia Girl Captured Veterans" (first quote); "Impassioned School Girl Stirred Veterans," n.p., Nov. 13, 1906 (subsequent quotes), newsclip in J. Hall's possession, thanks to Amory and William W. L. Glenn; "Miss Grace Lumpkin Charms Georgia Veterans," Nov. 14, 1906; "Hit of the Reunion," May 19, 1911; "Miss Lumpkin's Response," June 24, 1909, all in *Columbia (SC) State*; G. Lumpkin, *To Make My Bread*, 189.

46. G. Lumpkin, *To Make My Bread*, 188–89 (quotes).

47. W. Page, *Southerner*, 159–60 (quote on 160).

48. "Social Affairs in the Capital," *Columbia (SC) State*, Dec. 24, 1905 (quote) (hereafter "Social Affairs").

49. D. Gold and Hobbs, *New Southern Woman*, 4 (quote).

50. [Elizabeth Lumpkin], undated list of educational and employment experiences, E. Glenn Letters.

51. The most prestigious of the southern women's colleges were Sophie Newcombe in New Orleans, Agnes Scott in Decatur, Georgia, Goucher in Baltimore, Maryland, and Hollins and Randolph-Macon in Virginia. At the turn of the century only 2.3 percent of the country's population aged 18 to 24 was enrolled in college. Of that number, 36 percent were women. As late as 1940, only 5.9 percent of men and 4 percent of women in the United States had completed four years of college. For nonwhites, the figures were 1.4 percent and 1.2 percent: Snyder, *120 Years of American Education*, 76, 18–19.

52. C. H. Wilson, *Brenau University*, xix, 115–61, 133–41; *Brenau Bulletin* (1912), BUTL.

53. "Brenau College—Brenau Conservatory," *Atlanta Constitution*, Aug. 12, 1900; "Brenau's Summer Session," *Atlanta Constitution*, June 21, 1903; "Brenau Summer School of Music, Oratory, Languages, Literature, Etc.," *Atlanta Constitution*, May 12, 1907; F. M. [Florence Mae] Overton to Annabel Matthews, Feb. 11, 1930, folder 14, Annabel Matthews Papers, Schlesinger Library, Radcliffe Institute, Harvard University.

54. [Curry School of Expression] to Elizabeth Lumpkin, Mar. 1, 1930, E. Glenn Letters; KDL interview, Mar. 22, 1987, 11; D. Gold and Hobbs, *New Southern Woman*, 6, 56, 66, 68–72, 79, 80–81; "Mrs. Eugene B. Glenn Dies," *Asheville*

(NC) Citizen, Feb. 15, 1963; G. Lumpkin, *Wedding*, 18; Kalemaris, "No Longer Second-Class."

55. William Lumpkin to Elizabeth Lumpkin, 1901, Mar. 26, 1902, Nov. 22, 1904; Letter of recommendation from J. L. Corvin, Mt. Carmel Graded School, June 27, 1902; W. A. Clark to Elizabeth Lumpkin, July 16, 1902, all in E. Glenn Letters.

56. For Elizabeth's career at Winthrop, see Annual Departmental Reports, 1903–1905, box 2, Louise Pettus Archives and Special Collections, Winthrop University, Rock Hill, SC; KDL to My Dear Sister [Elizabeth Lumpkin], Jan. 3, 1904, KDL Papers; "Columbia Girl Captured Veterans."

57. "Columbia Girl's Address" (first and second quotes); "Miss Lumpkin to Georgia Veterans," *Confederate Veteran*, Feb. 1904, 70 (third quote); "Address by Miss Elizabeth Lumpkin," *Confederate Veteran*, July 1905, 298 (fourth quote).

58. "Columbia Girl's Address," (first and second quotes); "Address by Miss Elizabeth Lumpkin," *Confederate Veteran*, July 1905, 299 (third quote); "The Land of Our Desire," *Confederate Veteran*, Nov. 1906, 494–96.

59. KDL, *Making*, 124 (first quote), 125 (subsequent quotes).

60. KDL, *Making*, 137 (quotes).

61. KDL, Making, 127–28 (quote).

62. KDL, *Making*, 123 (first quote), 184–86 (subsequent quotes).

63. KDL interview, Mar. 22, 1987, 12 (first quote); KDL, *Making*, 123–24, 163, 185 (second quote); E. Glenn, "Bitterroot"; KDL, *Making*; G. Lumpkin, "Annette Caroline Morris," in Bryan H. Lumpkin, "Lumpkin," Dec. 1936, folders 101–6, KDL Papers (hereafter B. Lumpkin, "Lumpkin"). For the books read by children and taught in schools during Katharine's childhood, see Ritterhouse, *Growing Up Jim Crow.*

64. Annette Lumpkin to Elizabeth Lumpkin, Jan. 10, 1902; William Lumpkin to Elizabeth Lumpkin, Apr. 11, 1902; Hope Lumpkin to Elizabeth Lumpkin, July 31, 1904, E. Glenn Letters.

65. G. Lumpkin, *Wedding*, 9 (quotes), 18, 56, 269; *History of North Carolina*, s.v. "Eugene Byron Glenn, M.D."; D. Ward, *Heritage of Old Buncombe County*, s.v. "John Starnes"; "Marion S. Glenn Died at Local Hospital," Mar. 22, 1921; "Death Claims J. Frazier Glenn at Home Here," Apr. 22, 1949; "Funeral Rites of Dr. Eugene Glenn at Central Church," Mar. 31, 1924; "Beloved Surgeon to Sleep amid Hills He Loved," Mar. 31, 1924, all in *Asheville (NC) Citizen*; Stephens, *History of Medicine*, 67, 69; Mauldin, "Doctor and His Wife"; Elizabeth Lumpkin Glenn, "At the home of William and Amory Glenn written on my seventy-fifth birthday, Nov 10, 1955," E. Glenn Letters. Eugene Glenn was born on June 24, 1871. His parents were Ann Curtis Glenn and Marion Sevier Glenn, a Buncombe County commissioner.

66. "Social Affairs," 8 (first quote); G. Lumpkin, "Miserable Offender," 282 (second quote); G. Lumpkin, *Wedding*, 39; *Asheville (NC) Gazette-News*, Dec. 19, 1905; "Elizabeth Lumpkin, Daughter of the United Confederate Veterans, Married," Jan. 1906, 38 (hereafter "Elizabeth Lumpkin, Married"); O'Neil, "Tying the Knots."

67. William Lumpkin to Elizabeth Lumpkin, Apr. 28, 1905, Glenn Letters; "Social Affairs" (quotes).

68. *History of North Carolina*, s.v. "Eugene Byron Glenn, M.D." (quote); "Elizabeth Lumpkin, Married," 38; Graydon, "Trinity Church," 21–23; A. Thomas, *Historical Account*, 540; KDL, *Making*, 118; C. R. Wilson, *Baptized in Blood*, 55–61. See also *Asheville (NC) Gazette-News*, Dec. 22, 1905; G. Lumpkin, *Wedding*, 253.

69. "Elizabeth Lumpkin, Married," 38 (first and third quotes); G. Lumpkin, *Wedding*, 12 (second quote), 13 (fourth quote), 49 (sixth quote), 135 (seventh quote); T. Wolfe, *Look Homeward*, 142 (fifth quote).

70. "Elizabeth Lumpkin, Married," 38 (quotes).

71. UDC Minute Book 1901–1910, 265, 276, Records of the United Daughters of the Confederacy, Wade Hampton Chapter (Columbia, SC), South Carolina Confederate Relic Room and Military Museum, Columbia, SC; William Lumpkin to Elizabeth Lumpkin Glenn, Nov. 10, 1906, E. Glenn Letters (first quote); "Miss Lumpkin's Response," *Columbia (SC) State*, June 24, 1909 (second and third quote).

72. "Red Shirts Bands Pass in Review," *Columbia (SC) State*, Sept. 29, 1911 (quotes).

73. KDL, *Making*, 126 (quote).

74. KDL, *Making*, 130 (quote).

75. C. W. Mills, *Sociological Imagination*, 5. See also Maza, "Stories in History."

76. KDL, *Making*, 131–32 (quote).

77. KDL, *Making*, 121 (quotes), 132–33.

78. KDL, *Making*, 133. For the notion of a "magic circle" of belonging, see Durr, *Outside the Magic Circle*.

79. B. Fields and K. Fields, *Racecraft*, 93 (first quote); Brodhead, "Two Writers' Beginnings," 3, 11 (subsequent quotes).

80. KDL, *Making*, 133–35 (quotes).

81. This metaphor is drawn from Cheever, *Home before Dark*, 4.

82. KDL, *Making*, 137–47 (first quote on 142, second quote on 143).

83. L. Knight, *Reminiscences*, 351 (quote); "The State Campaign Opens at St. George," June 20, 1906; "Lyon Would Retire If Ragsdale Would," June 21, 1906; "Col. Lumpkin Ready to Debate," June 26, 1906; "Col. Lumpkin Has Withdrawn," July 6, 1906, all in *Columbia (SC) State*.

84. Simkins, *Pitchfork Ben Tillman*, 459; "Candidates for the Senate," *Columbia (SC) State*, June 17, 1908.

85. Kousser, *Shaping of Southern Politics*, 231–37; Walsh, "Horny-Handed Sons of Toil."

86. "Candidates for the Senate," June 17, 1908 (quotes); "Clarendon Voters Hear the Candidates," June 19, 1908, both in *Columbia (SC) State*; KDL, *Making*, 144.

87. KDL, *Making*, 121–22 (quotes).

88. "Feast of Oratory in Hill Country," July 22, 1908, 3 (first quote); "Campaign Party Visits Marion," June 25, 1908 (second quote); "Clarendon Voters Hear the Candidates," June 19, 1908 (third quote), all in *Columbia (SC) State*.

89. KDL, *Making*, 147 (quote); Kantrowitz, *Ben Tillman*, 296. See also "Candidates at Sumter for Opening Meeting," June 17, 1908; "Lumpkin Opens at Darling-

ton," June 28, 1908; "Spicy Meeting at Abbeville," July 18, 1908, all in *Columbia (SC) State.*

90. KDL, *Making,* 152 (quote); Letter from William Lumpkin to Annette Lumpkin, n.d., quoted in B. Lumpkin, "Lumpkin." On the Sand Hills, see J. Moore, *Columbia and Richland County,* 1–3; Kovacik and Winberry, *South Carolina.*

91. Hope Henry Lumpkin, Student Files, University of the South, Sewanee, TN.

92. "Hope Henry Lumpkin," in B. Lumpkin, "Lumpkin"; "Hope H. Lumpkin Made a Deacon," Sept. 9, 1907; "Hope H. Lumpkin Funeral Today," Oct. 13, 1932, both in *Columbia (SC) State*; State Historical Society of Wisconsin, *Dictionary of Wisconsin Biography,* s.v. "Hope Henry Lumpkin."

93. Alva M. Lumpkin Jr. interview, Aug. 4, 1995; Alva M. Lumpkin Jr. interview, Aug. 17, 1990; *National Cyclopedia of American Biography,* s.v. "Alva M. Lumpkin"; *Walsh's Columbia South Carolina City Directory* (Charleston, SC: Walsh Directory), 1910–1912; Thirteenth Census of the United States, 1910, Population Schedule, Center, Richland, S.C., Roll T624_1471, ED 0071, sheet 3B, family 65, lines 65–70.

94. "College for Women: What It Is and What It Does," Aug. 12, 1906; "Charity Workers Well Organized," Mar. 8, 1914, both in *Columbia (SC) State*; *Centennial History,* s.v. "McClintock, Ebenezer Pressley, D.D."; *Sixteenth Annual Program of the Woman's College of Baltimore* (Philadelphia: George H Buchanan, 1904), 32, https://books.google.com/books?id=haLOAAAAMAAJ; Summer, *Newberry County,* 152.

95. G. Lumpkin, "A Musical Courtship," *Palmetto,* Oct. 1908, 13–14; G. Lumpkin, "Christmas Greens," *Palmetto,* Feb. 1908, 66–71, both in SCL; G. Lumpkin interview, Sept. 25, 1971; G. Lumpkin interview, Aug. 4, 1974; G. Lumpkin Diary, 1963–1975, Nov. 13, 1967, in J. Hall's possession, thanks to Joseph H. Lumpkin Sr.

96. KDL, *Making,* 44 (quote), 153; Alva M. Lumpkin Jr. interview, Aug. 4, 1995; "W.W. Lumpkin Said to Be Dying," Mar. 11, 1910; "Colonel Lumpkin Died Yesterday," Mar. 14, 1910, both in *Columbia (SC) State*; Will of William Wallace Lumpkin, Mar. 9, 1911, *Wills, Vol. O–P, 1898–1913,* box 190, package 5950, Richland County Probate Judge's Office, Columbia, SC; KDL, *Making,* 153–57.

97. KDL, *Making,* 157–61 (quote on 160); Ogden, *Wil Lou Gray,* 36–39.

98. KDL, *Making,* 182–85 (quote on 183).

99. A. Thomas, *Historical Account,* 519 (quote); Registers, 1860–1925, Protestant Episcopal Church, Richland County, Trinity, Columbia, 295, SCL; KDL, *Making,* 161–62.

100. KDL, *Making,* 161–68 (quotes).

101. KDL, *Making,* 167–68 (quotes).

102. KDL, *Making,* 169 (quotes).

103. KDL, *Making,* 169–71 (quotes on 170).

104. KDL, *Making,* 167 (quote), 170–72.

105. KDL, *Making,* 172–73 (quotes).

106. KDL, *Making,* 173 (quote); G. Lumpkin Diary, 1963–1975, Nov. 13, 1967, in J. Hall's possession, thanks to Joseph H. Lumpkin Sr.; Adam K. George to

KDL, June 5, 1915, folder 1, KDL Papers; KDL interview, Apr. 24, 1985; Alva M. Lumpkin Jr. interview, Aug. 4, 1995.

107. KDL, *Making*, 155.

108. KDL, *Making*, 168, 183–84 (first quote on 183, third quote on 184); KDL to Leslie Blanchard, [Confidential—Very], Dec. 3, 1923 (second quote), KDL Papers.

109. KDL, *Making*, 182 (quote).

CHAPTER FOUR: "CONTRARY STREAMS OF INFLUENCE"

Portions of this chapter are drawn from J. Hall, "Widen the Reach."

1. KDL, *Making*, 177–200 (quote on 177).

2. *Bubbles*, 1918, 30 (quote), BUTL; KDL interview, Apr. 24, 1985; KDL, "Official Transcript of the Record of Katharine Lumpkin," 1915, folder 110, KDL Papers; Eva T. Pearce to Catherine [*sic*], July 7 [1915 or 1916], folder 1, KDL Papers.

3. KDL, *Making*, 177–78 (quotes).

4. KDL, *Making*, 180 (first quote); Connerton, *How Societies Remember*, 1–40 (second quote on 6). For a subtle exposition of the notion that "life consists of retellings," i.e., that we experience the present only by taking account of the past, see also Bruner, "Experience and Its Expressions," 3–30, esp. 12.

5. Founded by a local Baptist minister as the Georgia Baptist Female Seminary in 1878, the school was renamed Georgia Female Seminary when it passed into a new investor's hands in 1886. When it was purchased by Dr. Haywood Jefferson Pearce in 1900, it became Brenau College. It is now Brenau University.

6. H. Williams, *Self Taught*; J. Anderson, *Education of Blacks*; Ayers, *Promise of the New South*, 418.

7. Leloudis, *Schooling the New South*. The antebellum South had surpassed the rest of the nation in the founding of female colleges. Aimed at enhancing the status and marriageability of elite daughters by providing them with a classical education, these schools served only the privileged few, and many were swept away by the Civil War: Farnham, *Southern Belle*, 18.

8. Tolbert, "Commercial Blocks."

9. Censer, "Changing World"; Censer, *White Southern Womanhood*, 153–206; Mayo, *Southern Women*, xx–xxi.

10. Montgomery, *Politics of Education*, 23–61; P. Dean, *Women on the Hill*; Kalemaris, "No Longer Second-Class"; McCandless, *Past in the Present*, 86–87. In 1912, only seven southern universities admitted women: B. Solomon, *Company of Educated Women*, 53.

11. "Brenau College Conservatory," *Atlanta Constitution*, June 14, 1914 (quote); Eleanor Rigney, "Brenau College 1878–1978: Enriched by the Past, Challenged by the Future," 75–76 (hereafter Rigney, "Brenau College"); "Extracts from Second Annual Catalog of Georgia Baptist Female Seminary (Brenau, 1879–1880)," in *Bubbles*, 1918; *Brenau Bulletin*, 1912, 51, all in BUTL; C. H. Wilson, *Brenau University*, xix, 34–39, 66–72, 82, 84, 88–89, 106, 115, 120, 127, 170, 244, 285, 296, 355, 358, 396, 404–5, 467, 510; Orr, *History of Education*, 360; Federal Writers Project Georgia, *Georgia*, 288–92.

12. H. L. Horowitz, *Alma Mater*, 155–56; C. H. Wilson, *Brenau University*, xix, 188–215; Alexis M. Oliver, "A History of Blacks in Brenau University," unpublished paper, Brenau, 1998, in J. Hall's possession, thanks to Catherine M. Lewis.

13. KDL, *Making*, 134–35 (first quote on 134, second quote on 135).

14. Chirhart, "Gardens of Education," 833 (quote); Chirhart, *Torches of Light*; Reed, "Negro Women"; B. Oliver, *Rugged Pathway*.

15. Reed, "Negro Women," 8, 9, 12–13; Chirhart, *Torches of Light*, 35–37.

16. Cuthbert, *Juliette Derricotte*, 10 (first quote), 3 (second quote), 6 (subsequent quotes), 2; L. Anderson, "Nauseating Sentiment," 99, 108n76. According to Anderson, the census takers recorded her race as black but Derricotte told E. Franklin Frazier that her mother was white.

17. Du Bois, "Training of Black Men," 292 (quotes).

18. Cuthbert, *Juliette Derricotte*, 11 (quote); M. Jones and Richardson, *Talladega College*.

19. Brenau's records, although still sparse for the early years, are now available in the Archives Room, Brenau University Trustee Library, as well as in the Alumni Office.

20. Colton, *Southern Colleges for Women*; Colton, "Standards of Southern Colleges," 458–75; J. M. Johnson, "Standing Up."

21. For women's higher education generally, see B. Solomon, *Company of Educated Women*; H. L. Horowitz, *Alma Mater*; Palmieri, *Adamless Eden*. L. D. Gordon, *Gender and Higher Education*, includes an insightful chapter on two of the best southern women's colleges, Sophie Newcomb and Agnes Scott. For southern women's education in the postbellum period, see P. Dean, "Covert Curriculum"; Leloudis, *Schooling the New South*; McCandless, *Past in the Present*; Montgomery, *Politics of Education*.

22. *Brenau Bulletin*, 1912, 21 (quotes), BUTL.

23. *Aglaia of Phi Mu*, Jan. 1911, 76 (quote), Archives, Phi Mu National Headquarters, Peachtree City, GA (hereafter *Aglaia*).

24. *Gainesville (GA) News*, Apr. 21, 1915 (quote). For speakers, see also *The Brenau Girl*, 1912; *Brenau Bulletin*, 1912, 1913, 1916, all in BUTL; *Aglaia*, 1913.

25. *Brenau Bulletin*, 1916, 17, BUTL. I am indebted to Gavin James Campbell and his excellent book, *Music and the Making of a New South*, for helping me to place Brenau College in the context of this moment in the evolution of southern culture.

26. KDL, *Making*, 187 (quotes); Stansell, *American Moderns*, 55–57.

27. KDL, *Making*, 186–87; *Brenau Bulletin*, 1914, 33–34; *Bubbles*, 1901 and 1913, all in BUTL; S. G. Riley, "Princeton University General Biographical Catalogue 1746–1916" and "Memorials: Samuel Gayle Riley '96," box 241, folder "Riley, Samuel Gayle, 1896," Undergraduate Alumni Records, 19th Century, Seeley G. Mudd Manuscript Library, Princeton University; Ayers, *Promise of the New South*, 420–26; Harvey, *Redeeming the South*, 197–226.

28. KDL, *Making*, 186–87 (quote on 186).

29. *Bubbles*, 1915, 1916 (first, second, and third quotes); *Brenau Bulletin*, 1912, 16 (subsequent quotes), all in BUTL.

30. "Thesis returned by Adams Express May 17, 1907," box 241, folder "Riley, Samuel Gayle, 1896," Undergraduate Alumni Records, 19th Century, Seeley G. Mudd Manuscript Library, Princeton University; KDL, *Making*, 185 (first quote), 186 (second quote).

31. Pearce, *Philosophical Meditations*, 34–36 (quotes); "The Brenau Creed," *Bubbles*, 1914, BUTL.

32. *Brenau Bulletin* 1911, 22 (first quote), Apr. 1913 (subsequent quotes), all in BUTL; L. Shapiro, *Perfection Salad*; C. Goldstein, *Creating Consumers*.

33. *Brenau Bulletin*, 1912, 42 (quote), BUTL. I am indebted to H. L. Horowitz's *Alma Mater* for insights into "buildings and landscapes as historical texts" (xvi) and student culture. For Brenau's built environment, see "National Register of Historic Places Inventory—Nomination Form" [Brenau College District], https://npgallery.nps.gov/nrhp/AssetDetail?assetID=b4314a14-8268-4492-8835-4cdc65decf74; C. H. Wilson, *Brenau University*, 239–67; "Architecture," box 1, Brenau University Archived Webpages; Rigney, "Brenau College," 80–81; *Brenau Bulletin*, 1912, 42–43, all in BUTL; Ashley Bates, "Brenau University's Pearce Auditorium is home to legends, myths and great performances," *Gainesville (GA) Times*, July 1, 2008, http://www.gainesvilletimes.com/archives/6693/.

34. "Extracts from Second Annual Catalog of Georgia Baptist Female Seminary" (Brenau, 1879–1880), in *Bubbles*, 1918 (first and second quotes); *Brenau Bulletin*, 1912, 46 (third quote), both in BUTL.

35. *Bubbles*, 1911 (quote); *Bubbles*, 1915, both in BUTL.

36. *Brenau Bulletin*, 1912, 36 (quote), BUTL; Banta, *Imaging American Women*, xxvii–xl, 36–37, 68–69.

37. Henry James, paraphrased in Banta, *Imaging American Women*, 10 (quote).

38. *Bubbles*, 1914, 38–39, BUTL.

39. *Brenau Bulletin*, 1912, 38–39 (first and second quotes); Rigney, "Brenau College," 61–63 (subsequent quotes); "Change in Self-Governed System," *Brenau College Faculty Journal for Twelve Years*, 1910–1922, Sept. 25, 1912 (hereafter *Brenau Faculty Journal*), all in BUTL; C. H. Wilson, *Brenau University*, 312–17.

40. "A Friendly Invitation," *Bubbles*, 1901, 57 (quote). See also *Bubbles*, 1913 and 1914, both in BUTL.

41. Rigney, "Brenau College," 63; *Brenau Faculty Journal*, May 6, 1913, May 12, May 15, 1911, Feb. 6, 1912, Apr. 7 and Sept. 18, 1914, Feb. 2, 1915, Mar. 5, 1918, all in BUTL.

42. *Brenau Journal*, Oct. 1909 and Apr. 1911; *Brenau Faculty Journal*, Apr. 4, 1911; *Bubbles*, 1911; "Brenau College News," *Atlanta Constitution*, Nov. 22, 1914, 7, all in BUTL. For the importance of and conflicts over athletics at women's colleges, see H. L. Horowitz, *Alma Mater*, 159–62.

43. *Brenau Faculty Journal*, Mar. 26, 1914 (quotes); Rigney, "Brenau College," 61–62, both in BUTL.

44. *Brenau Faculty Journal*, Oct. 6, 1914 (quote), Jan. 5, 1915, Feb. 1, 1916, Mar. 2, 1926, May 23, 1916, Jan. 16, 1919, Feb. 9, 1920, Mar. 31, 1919, Mar. 1, 1921, Mar. 16, 1921, May 20, 1921, Dec. 12, 1922, May 27, 1935; Rigney, "Brenau College," 63, 80–83; G. Lumpkin, "The White Road," *Bubbles*, 1912, all in BUTL; *Aglaia*, Nov. 1914.

45. For "the life," see H. L. Horowitz, *Alma Mater*, 147–78.

46. *Bubbles*, 1914 (quote), BUTL.

47. "Mu Chapter, Brenau College, Gainesville, GA," *Aglaia*, Nov. 1910, 50–51; Lamb, *History of Phi Mu*, 273; Annadell C. Lamb to J. Hall, Sept. 1, 1998. Thanks to Annadell Craig Lamb for sharing with me a wealth of information on Phi Mu. For KDL's activities, see *Brenau Faculty Journal*, Mar. 27, 1914, BUTL; "Mu, Brenau College, Gainesville, GA," *Aglaia*, Jan. 1913, 223.

48. *Bubbles*, 1913 (quotes); Rigney, "Brenau College," 92–93, both in BUTL; KDL, *Making*, 202.

49. KDL, *Making*, 182 (quote).

50. Meyerowitz, *Women Adrift*, 46–55, 79–83.

51. For the Student Volunteer Movement, see R. White, *Liberty and Justice*, 187–207; Setran, *College "Y*,*"* 4, 7, 56, 77, 128, 222.

52. Cross, "Grace Hoadley Dodge"; G. Wilson, *Religious and Educational Philosophy*, 8–12; Bannan, "Management by Women."

53. Lasch-Quinn, *Black Neighbors*, 131–50; Setran, *College "Y*,*"* 1–4.

54. Eloise Smith, "Y.W.C.A.," *Brenau Journal*, Oct. 1909, 30 (quote); *Bubbles*, 1911; *Brenau Girl*, 1912, all in BUTL. For a similar trajectory, see P. Dean, "Covert Curriculum," 186–98. In 1911, the Brenau Y claimed 285 members at a time when there were probably fewer than 450 students.

55. *Brenau Bulletin*, 1912 (quote), BUTL.

56. H. L. Horowitz, *Alma Mater*, 150 (quotes).

57. *Aglaia*, Jan. 1917, 33 (quote).

58. "The Young Women's Christian Association," *Bubbles*, 1914, 111 (quotes), BUTL.

59. KDL, *Making*, 187 (quotes). For the Victorian struggle to reconcile religion and science, see Meyer, "American Intellectuals," 587–90. For the impact of these ideas on one of Katharine's friends and peers, see Myra Page interview, July 12, 1975.

60. Frances Davis, "Brenau College," *Aglaia*, Jan. 1917, 34 (quote).

61. KDL, *Making*, 177 (first quote), 187 (second quote), 192 (third quote), 188 (fourth quote).

62. Pearce, *Philosophical Meditations*, 34–36 (quote on 36). For the influence of the social gospel in the South's largest Protestant denomination, see Harvey, *Redeeming the South*, 197–226; Harvey, "Southern Baptists." Other studies that underscore the social gospel's importance to the South and to racial reform include J. McDowell, *Social Gospel*; Hobbie, "Walter L. Lingle"; Luker, *Social Gospel in Black and White*; R. White, *Liberty and Justice*.

63. M. King, "Beyond Vietnam," 158 (quote); V. Cook, "Martin Luther King, Jr."; Cline, *Reconciliation to Revolution*; S. Evans, *Journeys*; J. J. Farrell, *Spirit of the Sixties*; Izzo, *Liberal Christianity*; Rossinow, *Politics of Authenticity*.

64. Fox, "Liberal Protestant Progressivism"; Setran, *College "Y"*; Hollinger, *Cloven Tongues*; Hollinger, *Protestants Abroad*.

65. *Bubbles*, 1915 (first and second quotes), BUTL; Vicinus, *Independent Women*, 192 (third quote). For intense same-sex friendships among college women, see also Sahli, "Smashing"; Vicinus, "One Life"; Vicinus, "Distance and Desire."

66. *Brenau Bulletin*, 1912, 4, 41; *Bubbles*, 1913, both in BUTL; *Philomathean*, 1913; *Aglaia*, Nov. 1914, both in Archives, Phi Mu National Headquarters, Peachtree City, GA.

67. "'Salubrities' We Meet," *The Brenaurial Review*, June 1, 1915 (quote), BUTL.

68. For this shift in attitudes toward intimate partnerships, see Chauncey, "Sexual Inversion"; Bland and Doan, *Sexology in Culture*; Faderman, *Odd Girls*; Franzen, *Spinsters and Lesbians*; C. Hicks, *Talk with You Like a Woman*, 204–33; Simmons, "Companionate Marriage"; Simmons, *Making Marriage Modern*; Trimberger, "Feminism, Men, and Modern Love"; Smith-Rosenberg, *Disorderly Conduct*.

69. For continuities in the history of same-sex partnerships, see Vicinus, *Intimate Friends*, xxiii–xxiv; Rosenzweig, *Another Self*.

70. *Bubbles*, 1916, 180 (quote), 1915, BUTL.

71. "Sophomore-Senior Dance" and "Fit Number II," *Bubbles*, 1914 (quotes), BUTL.

72. "Why I Don't Like My Picture," *Bubbles*, 1914 (quotes), BUTL.

73. *The Brenaurial Review*, June 1, 1915 (quotes), BUTL.

74. Smith-Rosenberg, "Female World."

75. KDL, "The Game of 'Make Believe,'" *Bubbles*, 1917, 98 (quotes), BUTL. See also *Aglaia*, Jan. 1917.

76. G. Lumpkin, "The White Road," *Bubbles*, 1912 (quotes), BUTL.

77. "Class History and Prophecy," *Bubbles*, 1915 (quotes), BUTL.

78. Rich, *Compulsory Heterosexuality*.

79. KDL interview, Aug. 4, 1974, 77 (quote). See also Lauren Kientz Anderson, "Jumping Overboard: Interpreting Evidence about Same Sex Love: An Exploration of the Brief but Significant Life of Educator Juliette Derricotte," OutHistory, http://outhistory.org/exhibits/show/juliette-derricotte/derricotte -biography.

CHAPTER FIVE: "THE INNER MOTION OF CHANGE"

1. "Woman's News—the Social World," *Asheville (NC) Gazette-News*, May 27, 1915.

2. Eva T. Pearce to Catherine [*sic*], July 7, [1915 or 1916] (quotes); Adam K. George to KDL, June 5, 1915, both in folder 1, KDL Papers; KDL, "The Making of a Southerner: Description of the Subject of the Autobiography and Outline of the Program of Research and Method of Presentation," [May 29, 1944], folder 46, KDL Papers.

3. KDL, *Making*, 179–82 (quote on 180), 187; *Aglaia of Phi Mu*, Nov. 1914, 25, Archives, Phi Mu National Headquarters, Peachtree City, GA (hereafter *Aglaia*).

4. *Bubbles*, 1917, 157, BUTL; KDL, *Making*, 197.

5. J. Hall et al., *Like a Family*, 183–87; Orwell, *Coming Up*, 144 (quote); Cott, "Revisiting the Transatlantic 1920s," 50–52.

6. Myra Page interview, July 12, 1975, 29 (first quote), 50–51 (second and third quotes); Frederickson, "Myra Page," 10–12, 14–15.

7. *Aglaia*, Mar. 1918, 89; *Bubbles*, 1918, 143, 208; *Bubbles*, 1919, 51, 143, BUTL.

8. Burts, *Richard Irvine Manning*; Ogden, *Wil Lou Gray*; J. M. Johnson, *Southern*

Ladies. For this view of southern progressivism, see J. Hall, "Smith's Progressive Era," 166–98; Gilmore, *Gender and Jim Crow*, 147–228.

9. Phifer, *Kirkman George Finlay*, 1 (quote), 16–22; A. Thomas, *Historical Account*, 541.

10. Phifer, *Kirkman George Finlay*, 23–26, 41–48; J. M. Johnson, *Southern Ladies*, 78, 183–84, 186–87; A. Thomas, *Historical Account*. Finlay was also a constant presence at the legislature, advocating for social justice measures.

11. Sims, *Power of Femininity*, 144 (quote); Montgomery, "Lost Cause Mythology," 174–98; K. Cox, *Dixie's Daughters*.

12. Korstad, *Civil Rights Unionism*, 54–60.

13. Montgomery, "Lost Cause Mythology," 174–98; Sims, *Power of Femininity*, 135–37; McMaster, *Girls of the Sixties*, 105 (quote).

14. Parker, "Woman Power," 305–6 (first and third quotes); McMaster, *Girls of the Sixties*, 4 (second quote); Van Rensselaer, "National League for Woman's Service," 275–82.

15. "Girls of the Sixties," 1 (first and fifth quotes), 3–4 (second quote on 3), 2 (third and fourth quotes), folder 5, Girls of the Sixties Records, SCL.

16. "Girls of the Sixties," 4–5 (quotes); "Rich in Experience Young in Hope," *Columbia (SC) State*, Oct. 21, 1919, newsclip, both in folder 5, Girls of the Sixties Records, SCL.

17. "Mrs. Eugene B. Glenn Dies," *Asheville (NC) Citizen*, Feb. 15, 1963 (quote) (hereafter "Mrs. Eugene B. Glenn").

18. "The Land of Our Desire," *Confederate Veteran*, Nov. 1906, 494–96. For the ongoing history of this Chautauqua-related institution, see "Our History," Monteagle Sunday School Assembly, http://mssa1882.net/about/our-history.html.

19. William W. L. Glenn and Amory Potter Glenn interview, July 16, 1995; Katherine Glenn Kent interview, May 7, 2018.

20. A. Whisnant, *Super-Scenic Motorway*, 72–79.

21. "Beloved Surgeon to Sleep amid Hills He Loved," *Asheville (NC) Citizen*, Mar. 31, 1924; "Funeral Rites of Dr. Eugene Glenn at Central Church," *Asheville (NC) Times*, Mar. 31, 1924; Mauldin, "Doctor and His Wife," 38, 41; *History of North Carolina*, s.v. "Eugene Byron Glenn, M.D."; A. Whisnant, *Super-Scenic Motorway*, 17–21; "Mrs. Eugene B. Glenn."

22. Krome-Lukens, "Reform Imagination," 93 (quotes); Schoen, *Choice and Coercion*. Blacks initially escaped eugenicists' tender mercies just as they were excluded from other social welfare programs.

23. "Social Happenings," *Asheville (NC) Citizen*, Jan. 13, 1914 (quote); "Additional Social and Personal Notes," *Asheville (NC) Gazette-News*, Jan. 21, 1914, Feb. 4, 1914; Society and Personals, *Asheville (NC) Citizen*, Jan. 28, 1914.

24. Smialkowska, "Democratic Art," 1–13 (quote on 2); Society and Personals, *Asheville (NC) Citizen*, Apr. 29, 1916, May 6, 1916, May 16, 1916; "Society," *Asheville (NC) Times*, May 3, 1916; "Shakespeare Pageant Will Be Held Today," *Asheville (NC) Citizen*, May 15, 1916.

25. "The Land of Our Desire," *Confederate Veteran*, Nov. 1906, 494–96 (quote on 496); Mauldin, "Doctor and His Wife," 41; T. Wolfe, *Look Homeward*; T. Wolfe, *O Lost*; Thomas Wolfe, "The Death of Stoneman Gant," William B. Wisdom Col-

lection of Thomas Wolfe bMS Am 1883 (555), Houghton Library, Harvard University; "Tom Wolfe's Home Town," *Asheville (NC) Citizen-Times*, Jan. 26, 1969.

26. Society and Personals, *Asheville (NC) Citizen*, Mar. 13, 1917; "Notable Meeting of Asheville Red Cross," *Asheville (NC) Citizen*, Mar. 14, 1917; "Mrs. Eugene B. Glenn"; Gilmore, *Gender and Jim Crow*, 195–96. See also West, "Yours for Home and Country."

27. "Municipal History: A Public Library," n.p., May 1919 (quotes), Newspaper Clipping Files, Pack Memorial Library, Asheville, NC; "Western North Carolina District," *North Carolina Library Bulletin*, Dec. 1920; "Local Librarians Attend Conferences," *Sunday Citizen* (Asheville, NC), Mar. 21, 1920.

28. "Night Library Is in Operation Here," *Asheville (NC) Citizen*, Oct. 2, 1919 (quote).

29. Myrick, "Asheville Public Library," 21 (quote); "Western North Carolina District," *North Carolina Library Bulletin*, Dec. 1920.

30. Lenwood Davis, *Black Heritage*, 32–33 (quote on 33); Gilmore, *Gender and Jim Crow*, 221.

31. Theodore Harris, "Negro Library Depending upon Book Donations," *Asheville (NC) Citizen*, Dec. 12, 1926 (quote).

32. Theodore Harris, "Negro Library Depending upon Book Donations," *Asheville (NC) Citizen*, Dec. 12, 1926 (quotes).

33. "Negro Public Library Here Formally Opened," *Asheville (NC) Times*, Apr. 18, 1927 (quote); Knott, *Not Free*; Gilmore, *Gender and Jim Crow*, 195–96. For black leadership in this effort, see Lenwood Davis, *Black Heritage*, 33–34; "Asheville Library Desegregation," Heardtell: Pack Memorial Library's North Carolina Rooms, https://packlibraryncroom.wordpress.com/online-photo-exhibits/asheville -library-desegregation-2/.

34. Untitled packet of material on Asheville's playground movement, 1936, in J. Hall's possession, thanks to Katherine Glenn Kent.

35. For Grace's brief tenure at McMaster School, see Parkinson, *City Public Schools*, 92; *Thirtieth Annual Report of the Public Schools of Columbia, S.C., 1912–1913* (Columbia, SC: State Printing, 1913), 6; *Thirty-First Annual Report of the Public Schools of Columbia, S.C., 1913–1914* (Columbia, SC: R. L. Bryan, 1914), 7; *Walsh's Columbia South Carolina City Directory* (Charleston, SC: Walsh Directory), 1913; "Education Board Elects Teachers," *Columbia (SC) State*, May 15, 1913. According to this article, she may also have taught very briefly at Bolton College, a privately endowed agricultural and normal school in Brunswick, Tennessee, although her name does not appear in the extant records of the school.

36. M. Moore, "College for Women." For the College's financial woes, see W. W. Ball to Mrs. Jessie Massey, Feb. 4, 1922, box 12, W. W. Ball Papers, David M. Rubenstein Rare Book and Manuscript Library, Duke University; "For a University College for Women," *Columbia (SC) State*, Jan. 31, 1914.

37. "College Merger Plan Submitted," *Columbia (SC) State*, Jan. 15, 1914; "Committee Told Plan of Merger," *Columbia (SC) State*, Jan. 23, 1914. For other evidence of Alva Lumpkin's support for women's education, see "Diplomas Given Graduate Nurses," *Columbia (SC) State*, May 24, 1912.

38. M. Moore, "College for Women," 60 (quotes).
39. "College Merger Offer Indorsed," Jan. 25, 1914; "Columbia and Two Institutions," Jan. 28, 1914; "Opposed to Merger of Two Big Schools," Jan. 29, 1914; Mrs. W. L. Daniel, "Mrs. W. L. Daniel Calls Attention to Real Purpose of Proposed Merger," Jan. 29, 1914; "For a University College for Women," Jan. 31, 1914; "College Merger Bill Killed by Big Vote," Feb. 11, 1914, all in *Columbia (SC) State*.
40. Lois MacDonald interview, Aug. 25, 1977, 36 (quote). After traveling to Europe and studying sociology and economics at the University of Chicago, McClintock settled in Boston, where she taught at a school owned by her equally well-educated and independent sister and then founded and ran the Erskine School, a vocational and professional school for women: "Miss McClintock Goes to Chicago," *Columbia (SC) State*, June 4, 1915; "Miss McClintock To Be Buried Tuesday in SC," *Columbia (SC) State*, Mar. 9, 1953; "Euphemia M'Clintock," *New York Times*, Mar. 1, 1953; "McClintock Chair Established and Freshman Dorm Dedicated," *Columbia (SC) State*, Feb. 19, 1960; Betty Sadler, "They Recall Her As 'a Lady and a Scholar,'" *State and the Columbia (SC) Record*, Feb. 4, 1968; Tay Vaughan, "Mom: Erskine School: Her Boston Place," http://www.tayvaughan .com/people/family/mom/erskineSchool.html.
41. "Education Board Elects Teachers," *Columbia (SC) State*, May 15, 1913; "State Certificate, B.D.," certificate number 1519, in *Teachers Certification Record Book, 1907–1922*; "Holiday Party at Y. W. C. A.," *Columbia (SC) State*, Nov. 29, 1918; G. Lumpkin interview, Sept. 25, 1971; "All Art Propaganda Says Woman Author Who Confesses Her Novel Is Communistic," *Pittsburgh Press*, Feb. 3, 1933. For the poor condition of the community's schools and efforts to improve them, see D. Stokes, *History of Dillon County*, 299–314.
42. Clemson University Extension Service, *Annual Report on the Demonstration and Extension Work of 1914* (Clemson, SC: Clemson University Extension Service, 1915), 106 (quote).
43. Lamb, *History of Phi Mu*, 184; Annadell C. Lamb to J. Hall, Sept. 1, 1998; G. Lumpkin, "Report of Gamma Province President," *Philomathean*, Aug. 5–8, 1913, Archives, Phi Mu National Headquarters, Peachtree City, GA.
44. G. Lumpkin, "Report of Gamma Province President," *Philomathean*, Aug. 5–8, 1913, 15 (quote), Archives, Phi Mu National Headquarters, Peachtree City, GA.
45. KDL, "Phi Muism," *Aglaia*, Feb. 1914 (quotes).
46. Mary S. Du Pré, "Mu, Brenau College," *Aglaia*, Mar. 1916, 23 (quotes); Rebecca Goode, "The Creed of Phi Mu," *A Vibrant View: The Official Blog of Phi Mu Fraternity*, Aug. 15, 2015, http://phimublog.com/2015/08/31/the-foundation-of-phi-mu/; G. Lumpkin to Annadell Lamb, May 22, 1976, and July 29, 1976, in J. Hall's possession; Lamb, *History of Phi Mu*, 182–83.
47. *Aglaia*, Mar. 1917, 67–70 (quotes).
48. Lamb, *History of Phi Mu*, 65 (quote). The possibility of changing these requirements was first debated at the 1948 convention; they were removed in 1950. But throughout the 1960s and 1970s chapters resisted the efforts of college administrations to force them to sign agreements explicitly pledging not to discriminate in the selection of members.

49. Hammond, *Black and White*, 144 (quote). The sources for this conference are sketchy and almost entirely retrospective. For secondary accounts that differ somewhat among themselves, see A. L. Jones, "Struggle among the Saints," 166–67; N. Robertson, *Christian Sisterhood*, 21–44; Dossett, *Bridging Race Divides*, 70–71, 75–76.

50. "Brief History of Colored Work," n.d. (quotes), Young Women's Christian Association (Nashville, Tennessee) Papers, Tennessee State Library and Archives, Nashville (hereafter YWCA Nashville Papers), thanks to Carole Bucy for alerting me to these unusually rich local sources. See also J. Bell and Wilkins, *Interracial Practices*, 2–10.

51. Maclachlan, "Addie Waits Hunton," 596–97; Lutz, "Addie W. Hunton," 109–27; Carlton-LaNey, "Elizabeth Ross Haynes," 573–83; Bogin, "Elizabeth Ross Haynes," 324–25.

52. Karen Mittelman, "Spirit That Touches," 135; N. Robertson, *Christian Sisterhood*, 35, 38–44; A. L. Jones, "Struggle among the Saints," 165; A. L. Jones, "Eva del Vakia Bowles," 152–53; Hutson, "Eva del Vakia Bowles," 214–15. The original impetus for this conference came from Grace Dodge, who planned to hold the meeting at national headquarters. Dodge died before the meeting could take place, and Bowles decided to meet "on southern soil": "Brief History of Colored Work," n.d. (quote), YWCA Nashville Papers. Bowles became head of the subcommittee on colored work in 1913; in 1917 it became a full-fledged committee.

53. A. L. Jones, "Struggle among the Saints," 167–68; "Brief History of Colored Work," n.d.; "Conference in Louisville, Kentucky, Oct. 14 and 15, 1915," n.d.; "Suggestions from the Committee on Findings at the Conference on Colored Work, Louisville, KY, Oct. 14 and 15, 1915," n.d.; "Growth of Southern Work," n.d. [1916 or 1917], all in YWCA Nashville Papers. Note that the composition and labels for the fields changed over time. For simplicity's sake I will refer to the "southern field" throughout.

54. KDL, "The Making of a Southerner: Description of the Subject of the Autobiography and Outline of the Program of Research and Method of Presentation," [May 29, 1944], 9 (quote), folder 46, KDL Papers; KDL, *Making*, 189. The woman was likely Willa (Willie) R. Young, student secretary in the South Atlantic Field Committee: KDL interview, Apr. 24, 1985; Willa (Willie) R. Young, introduction to Ruffin, "Southern Colleges," 432.

55. KDL, *Making*, 189 (quote).

56. KDL, *Making*, 189–90 (quotes).

57. KDL, *Making*, 189–92 (first quote on 190, second quote on 191, third quote on 189, fourth quote on 192).

58. KDL, *Making*, 191 (quote), 192.

59. KDL, *Making*, 192 (quote). This incident, at least as Katharine later recounted it, followed the eloquent prototype provided by Mark Twain's *The Adventures of Huckleberry Finn* (1884). Huck Finn's sound heart (in opposition to his deformed social conscience) prompts him to treat Jim with common decency. For similar themes among white southern autobiographers, see Fred Hobson, *But Now I See*, 6–7, 11, 27–29, 49, 63, 66, 88, 123, 137–41.

60. KDL, *Making*, 193 (quotes).

61. Weatherford quoted in Canady, *Willis Duke Weatherford*, 76 (quote).

62. By the 1920s, upward of five thousand white Southerners were attending meetings at the assembly. For the assembly's funding sources and the range of groups that met there, see Canady, "Improving Race Relations," 414–17. For Ruffin's and Bowles's appearances, see Jane Olcott, *Work of Colored Women*, 127; *Aglaia*, Nov. 1918.

63. KDL, *Making*, 180 (first, second, and third quotes), 199 (subsequent quotes); *Bubbles*, 1916, 97, BUTL.

64. Myra Page interview, July 12, 1975, 28 (first quote); C. Baker, *Generous Spirit*, 31; KDL, *Making*, 199 (second quote).

65. KDL, *Making*, 199 (quote).

66. B. Simon, "Race Reactions," 244 (quote); Reed, *Negro Women*, 17, 46–47.

67. KDL, *Making*, 199–200 (quotes).

68. Benbow, "Birth of a Quotation."

69. "The Birth of a Nation," Apr. 26, 1916; "Generals Grant and Lee," May 17, 1916; "Be on Time at Birth of a Nation," May 24, 1917, all in *Gainesville (GA) News*.

70. KDL, *Making*, 200 (first quote); "The Birth of a Nation," *Gainesville (GA) News*, May 10, 1916 (second and third quotes).

71. "Brenau Auditorium," *Gainesville (GA) News*, May 17, 1916 (quotes).

72. Woodrow Wilson, quoted in M. Stokes, *"Most Controversial Motion Picture of All Time,"* 199.

73. KDL, *Making*, 200 (quotes).

74. *Bubbles*, 1915 (quote), BUTL.

75. KDL interview, Apr. 24, 1985, 23 (first quote), 24 (second and third quotes), 5 (fourth quote). For southern black women at Columbia's Teachers College, see Rosenberg, *Changing the Subject*, 141–47.

76. Zeiger, *Uncle Sam's Service*, 43 (quote), 45–47.

CHAPTER SIX: "FAR-THINKING . . . PROFESSIONAL-MINDED" WOMEN

1. "What Is America?" *Nation*, June 26, 1929, 755 (quote).

2. Salwen, *Upper West Side*, 89–90; Rosenberg, *Changing the Subject*, 136, 141.

3. Dewey and Tufts, *Ethics*, 4 (quote); Salwen, *Upper West Side*, 89.

4. Vera Shlakman interview, Apr. 12, 1986 (quote); Bender, *Intellect and Public Life*, 66–75; Butler, *Scholarship and Service*; *Current Biography*, s.v. "Nicholas Murray Butler"; McCaughey, *Stand, Columbia*, 245–55; Novick, *Noble Dream*, 64–68; Rosenberg, *Changing the Subject*, 130–33.

5. KDL, *Making*, 178 (first quote), 204, 202 (second quote), 201 (fourth quote); KDL interview, Aug. 4, 1974, 23 (third quote).

6. KDL, *Making*, 201, 202 (quote); Director of Admissions to KDL, June 5, 1919, folder III, KDL Papers. For accent as a marker of difference and a site of discrimination, see Matsuda, "Voices of America."

7. KDL, *Making*, 203 (first quote), 202 (second quote); 204–5 (third quote on 204).

8. Rogin, "Flashing Vision."

9. Preston, *Aliens and Dissenters*.

10. KDL, *Making*, 205 (first quote), 203 (subsequent quotes).

11. KDL, *Making*, 205 (quote). For other women who had similar experiences, see Rosenberg, *Changing the Subject*, 144.

12. Bannister, *Sociology and Scientism*, 76–78, 84–86; Engerman, *Modernization*, 133–35 (quote on 134); D. Ross, *American Social Science*, 130.

13. Hawkins, *European and American Thought*; Bellomy, "Social Darwinism"; Bellomy, "William Graham Sumner."

14. Newman, *White Women's Rights*, 52–55; Bederman, *Manliness and Civilization*.

15. Bannister, *Sociology and Scientism*, 83–84; Degler, *Human Nature*, 17–18; Fredrickson, *Black Image*, 311–17 (quote on 316); Rosenberg, *Beyond Separate Spheres*, 214.

16. KDL, *Making*, 203 (first quote); KDL interview, Aug. 4, 1974, 11 (second quote).

17. Sumner, *Folkways*, 28 (first quote); KDL, *Making*, 204 (subsequent quotes).

18. Myrdal, *American Dilemma*, 2:1027–64.

19. KDL, Transcript of Record, Columbia University, Feb. 23, 1926, folder III, KDL Papers; KDL, Curriculum Vita, Feb. 10, 1976, in J. Hall's possession; Columbia University, *Directory of Officers and Students, 1918–1919*, 91, University Archives, Rare Book and Manuscript Library, Columbia University Library; Rosenberg, *Changing the Subject*, 1–7, 28–32, 142–43.

20. KDL interview, Aug. 4, 1974, 23 (quote); KDL interview, Apr. 24, 1985, 24.

21. Bannan, "Management by Women," 105–50 (quotes on 108). The following account of John Dewey's thought relies especially on Westbrook, *John Dewey*; Westbrook, "John Dewey." For later feminist adaptations of pragmatism, see Seigfried, "Feminism and Pragmatism."

22. Hawkins, *European and American Thought*, 175–77.

23. Westbrook, *John Dewey*, 184 (quote).

24. Bannan, "Management by Women," 29–103, 338 (quote on 63); A. L. Jones, "Struggle among the Saints," 174.

25. Bannan, "Management by Women," 45–46, 89, 94, 261–314, 31; A. Scott, *Natural Allies*, 108 (quote). For "group work," which was also a staple of social work and the settlement house movement, see also Height, *Step by Step*; Lasch-Quinn, *Black Neighbors*, 142–49.

26. Bannan, "Management by Women," 1, 60 (quote).

27. KDL, Transcript of Record, Columbia University, Feb. 23, 1926, folder III; KDL, "Accomplishments," [1943 or 1944], folder 99, both in KDL Papers; Robinson, *New History*.

28. Edman, *Philosopher's Holiday*, 133–36.

29. Robinson, *New History*, 149 (quote).

30. Edman, *Philosopher's Holiday*, 135 (quote). For "monumental history," see Nietzsche, *Advantage and Disadvantage*, esp. 14–19. For differing views on the prevalence of this approach to the past on the part of southern writers, see R. King, *Southern Renaissance*, 7; Yaeger, *Dirt and Desire*, 44–60.

31. Hunt, "Forgetting and Remembering," esp. 1120–21, 1130, 1132–33, 1127 (first quote); Fink, *Progressive Intellectuals*, 244 (second quote). For the continuing relevance of Robinson's work, see also Fitzpatrick, *History's Memory*, 4–6, 239–52.

32. Edman, *Philosopher's Holiday*, 133 (quote).

33. Beineke, *There Were Giants*, 387–88 (quote on 388).

34. KDL, *Making*, 205–7 (quote on 204), 214–15; KDL interview, Apr. 24, 1985, 12–13; Rosenberg, *Changing the Subject*, 143–44, 341n49.

35. KDL, *Making*, 205 (first quote), 206 (second quote).

36. KDL, *Making*, 206 (first quote), 201 (subsequent quotes), 202–7.

37. KDL, *Making*, 206 (quote).

38. KDL, *Making*, 206 (quotes).

39. KDL interview, Aug. 4, 1974, 11 (quote).

40. KDL interview, Aug. 4, 1974, 74–75 (quote); KDL, "Social Interests of the Southern Woman" (master's thesis, Columbia University, 1919), folder 35, KDL Papers.

41. Hobson, *Tell about the South*.

42. KDL, "Social Interests," 1 (first quote), 4, 6 (second quote).

43. KDL, "Social Interests," 44 (first and second quote), 7 (third quote).

44. KDL, "Social Interests," 32 (first quote), 33 (second quote), 29 (third quote); Sumner, *Folkways*, 77 (fourth quote).

45. Albert Bushnell Hart, *The Southern South*, quoted in KDL, "Social Interests," 34.

46. KDL, "Social Interests," 34 (first and third quotes); 33 (second quote); Sumner, *Folkways* quoted in KDL, "Social Interests," 34 (fourth quote).

47. KDL, "Social Interests," 35 (first quote), 41 (second quote), 39 (third quote), 40 (fourth quote), 46 (fifth and sixth quotes). The term "cultural lag" was coined by sociologist William F. Ogburn in his 1922 work *Social Change with Respect to Culture and Original Nature*, esp. 200–13.

48. Kerber, *No Constitutional Right*. The following account of women and gender in World War I is indebted especially to Zeiger, *Uncle Sam's Service*, which the author kindly allowed me to read in manuscript form. See also Zeiger, "She Didn't Raise Her Boy," 29–30.

49. Zeiger, *Uncle Sam's Service*, 3–7; *Bubbles*, 1919, 51 (first quote), 143 (second quote), BUTL.

50. Bristow, *Making Men Moral*; Putney, "Muscular Christianity."

51. Zeiger, "She Didn't Raise Her Boy," 29–30; Zeiger, *Uncle Sam's Service*, 23–24, 53–60; N. Robertson, *Christian Sisterhood*, 45–51.

52. Browder, "Christian Solution," 90 (quote); Lasch-Quinn, *Black Neighbors*.

53. Browder, "Working Out."

54. Bannan, "Management by Women," 82 (first quote); Zeiger, *Uncle Sam's Service*, 45, 92–93 (second quote on 92); N. Robertson, *Christian Sisterhood*, 48; Gavin, *American Women*, 129–56; *American Y.W.C.A. in France*, 1, 4–5.

55. *American Y.W.C.A. in France*, 6; N. Robertson, *Christian Sisterhood*, 48; Susan Zeiger to J. Hall, July 13, 1999.

56. Zeiger, *Uncle Sam's Service*, 39–40, 52–53; I. Patterson, *History of Phi Mu Fraternity*, 541.

57. Zeiger, *Uncle Sam's Service*, 7–10, 48–50, 58–60, 154–63 (quote on 60); Gilbert, "Soldier's Heart."

58. *Aglaia of Phi Mu*, Nov. 1918 (quotes), Archives, Phi Mu National Headquarters, Peachtree City, GA (hereafter *Aglaia*).

59. Zeiger, *Uncle Sam's Service*, 53; *Aglaia*, Nov. 1918, 10 (first quote), 13 (second quote).

60. "Letters from Grace Lumpkin," *Aglaia*, May 1919, 16 (quotes); Gilbert, "Soldier's Heart."

61. C. Schneider and Dorothy Schneider, *Into the Breach*, 140; "Letters from Grace Lumpkin," *Aglaia*, May 1919, 16–21 (quote on 19); Lamb, *History of Phi Mu*, 183–85; I. Patterson, *History of Phi Mu Fraternity*, 541–46.

62. "Letters from Grace Lumpkin," *Aglaia*, May 1919, 16–21 (quotes on 19–20).

63. Zeiger, *Uncle Sam's Service*, 66–68.

64. G. Lumpkin, "A Musical Courtship," 13–14; "Programme, Second 'G Co. HOP,'" given by the Personnel of Co. G., First Provisional Regiment, May 10, 1919, Beune, Cote D'Or, France (quotes), G. Lumpkin Papers.

65. C. Schneider and Dorothy Schneider, *Into the Breach*, 139 (quote); *Aglaia*, May 1919, 20; Zeiger, *Uncle Sam's Service*, 52–74.

66. Zeiger, *Uncle Sam's Service*, 65–66; "Social Workers in France," *Atlanta Constitution*, Oct. 26, 1919; G. Lumpkin, "Our Worker in France," *Aglaia*, Nov. 1919; I. Patterson, *History of Phi Mu Fraternity*, 546.

67. Zeiger, *Uncle Sam's Service*, 143; Lentz-Smith, *Freedom Struggles*, 96–108; G. Lumpkin, "Our Worker in France," *Aglaia*, Nov. 1919, 62–64 (quote on 64).

68. G. Lumpkin, "Our Worker in France," *Aglaia*, Nov. 1919; "Programme, Soirée du 2 août 1919, 2ème Représentation de Chalassa" (quotes); Scrapbook, 1919–1923, G. Lumpkin Papers. She also served as recreation director at a YWCA near Lyons, where she "translated and directed the pageant 'Les Cities de France' . . . which was given on the grounds of a Chateau near Roanne": [G. Lumpkin], "Work in France" (quote), G. Lumpkin Papers.

69. Jacqueline to Ma chère amie, Jan. 10, 1923; Sonnet a Ma Chère Miss Grace Lumpkin by Jacqueline Lewis (Dancing girl of Opéra), n.d. (quotes), both in G. Lumpkin Papers; Susan Zeiger to J. Hall, July 13, 1999. See also Jacqueline to Ma chère amie, Jan. 10, 1923; Jacqueline to Bien Chère Miss Grace, n.d.; Yvonne Forest to Chère Miss Grace, June 6, 1923, all in G. Lumpkin Papers.

70. "News from Grace Lumpkin," *Aglaia*, Jan. 1920, 14–15 (quotes).

71. Gavin, *American Women*, 138–41; KDL, *Making*, 207–8 (quote).

72. Du Bois, "Documents of the War," 16–18 (quotes); Hunton and K. Johnson, *Two Colored Women*, 185–89; Weisenfeld, *African American Women*, 131–32; J. Johnson, *Black Manhattan*, 245; Barbeau and Henri, *Unknown Soldiers*, 114–15; Lentz-Smith, *Freedom Struggles*; C. L. Williams, *Torchbearers of Democracy*.

73. Hunton and K. Johnson, *Two Colored Women*, 23 (quotes).

74. Hunton and K. Johnson, *Two Colored Women*, 32 (first quote), 182 (second quote); Lentz-Smith, *Freedom Struggles*, 100–2, 138–39; C. L. Williams, *Torchbearers of Democracy*, 114–18.

75. Grace Lumpkin, S.S. *Lafayette*, List of U.S. Citizens Arriving at Port of New York, July 26, 1920, page 183, line 7, *New York, Passenger Lists, 1820–1957*, Ancestry.com; "Student Fellowship Drive at Florida State College Ends," *News-Press* (Fort Myers, FL), Nov. 13, 1923 (quote).

76. Grace recalled serving as a "home demonstration agent," but she was proba-

bly a "councilor" instead, since her name does not appear in the agency's files. Evidence of her activities during this period can be gleaned from G. Lumpkin, *Curriculum Vitae*, [ca. 1962], G. Lumpkin Papers; "All Art Propaganda Says Woman Author Who Confesses Her Novel Is Communistic," *Pittsburgh Press*, Feb. 3, 1933; G. Lumpkin interview, Aug. 6, 1974, 9; G. Lumpkin interview, Sept. 25, 1971; G. Lumpkin, "Mansion and Mill"; G. Lumpkin, "Treasure"; G. Lumpkin to Amory Potter Glenn, Feb. 25, 1974, in J. Hall's possession, thanks to Amory and William W. L. Glenn; Kunitz and Haycraft, *Twentieth Century Authors*, s.v. "Grace Lumpkin"; G. Lumpkin, "Where I Come From, It Is Bitter and Harsh: Why We Should Vote Communist"; G. Lumpkin, "Addenda," Oct. 12, 1932, both in box 3, folder 4, Mark Solomon and Robert Kaufman Research Files on African Americans and Communism, Tamiment Library and Robert F. Wagner Labor Archives, Elmer Holmes Bobst Library, New York University Library. This is a mimeographed document, marked "FOR IMMEDIATE RELEASE." Thanks to Glenda Gilmore for bringing it to my attention and to Mark Solomon for consulting with me about its possible origins. For the adult education movement in which Grace participated, see Ogden, *Wil Lou Gray*.

77. Pierce, *Iconic Mountain Community*, vii–x (first quote on ix), 48–52; D. Oliver, *Hazel Creek*, 85–86; Kephart, *Our Southern Highlanders*, 29 (second quote). Larimore, *Hazel Creek*, bases a character on Grace Lumpkin's summer in this iconic mountain town. He paints Grace as a spunky new schoolteacher whose candidacy is championed by Horace Kephart over the objections of a school board concerned about her communistic and feminist views (139–48). Thanks to Dan Pierce for consulting with me on this episode.

78. Hobson, *Serpent in Eden*, 3–32 (quote on 9); Mencken, "Sahara of the Bozart," 136–54; Ayers, *Promise of the New South*, 339–72.

79. L. Allen, *Bluestocking in Charleston*, 78 (quote); Tindall, *Emergence of the New South*, 292–93, 316.

80. Glasgow, *Barren Ground*; E. Kelley, *Weeds*; E. Roberts, *Time of Man*.

81. J. M. Johnson, *Southern Ladies*, 37, 46, 83; Du Bois, *Black Reconstruction*, 711–30.

82. *Daily Worker*, Nov. 19, 1932, 4 (first quote); Yaeger, *Dirt and Desire*, xv, 104 (second quote on both pages).

83. Stansell, *American Moderns*, 15–17 (Addams quoted on 15).

CHAPTER SEVEN: "A CLEAR SHOW-DOWN"

1. KDL interview, Aug. 4, 1974, 83; KDL interview, Apr. 24, 1985, 27–28; KDL interview, Mar. 22, 1987.

2. Bannan, "Management by Women," 108 (quote).

3. Ina Scherrebeck to Eva D. Bowles, Dec. 7, 1927 (first and second quotes); Cordelia A. Winn to Ina Scherrebeck, Dec. 13, 1927; Ada Starkweather to Mary Sims, Mar. 12, 1926 (third quote), YWCA Nashville Papers, Tennessee State Library and Archives; KDL interview, Apr. 24, 1985, 5 (fourth quote).

4. KDL, *Making*, 207 (first quote), 208 (second quote).

5. Hahamovitch, *Fruits of Their Labor*, 79–112; J. Hall et al., *Like a Family*, 183–236.

6. KDL, *Making*, 209 (quote); Gordon, *Second Coming*. Claiming six million members at its peak, the second KKK sent more than one hundred representatives to Congress.

7. Lentz-Smith, *Freedom Struggles*; C. L. Williams, *Torchbearers of Democracy*; Gilmore, *Defying Dixie*. For a different example of a growing historiography portraying the 1920s as an era of fierce struggle, see Cott, "Revisiting the Transatlantic 1920s."

8. J. Hall, *Revolt against Chivalry*; J. P. Holmes, "Youth Cannot Wait," 128–31 (quote on 129); Setran, *College "Y,"* 236–37; N. Robertson, *Christian Sisterhood*, 131; F. Taylor, "Edge of Tomorrow"; D. Gold and Hobbs, *New Southern Woman*, 112, 127–28. For the vitality of the Christian student movement in the 1920s, see Fox, *Reinhold Niebuhr*, 75; Fass, *Damned and the Beautiful*, 56.

9. For a sample of the literature on the Y's city division, see Mjagkij and Spratt, *Men and Women Adrift*. For an exemplary local study of an urban Y, see Weisenfeld, *African American Women*.

10. Browder, "Christian Solution," 86 (quote); Blanchard, *Student Movement of the Y. W. C. A.*, 5–6; "Industrial Council of Y.W.C.A. to Meet at Blue Ridge, August 3–13," *Blue Ridge Voice*, June 1920, 10, North Carolina Collection, Louis Round Wilson Special Collections Library, University of North Carolina at Chapel Hill; Simms, "Industrial Policies"; G. Wilson, *Religious and Educational Philosophy*, 72, 81–91, 117–28; Stewart, *Industrial Work*; Frederickson, "Citizens for Democracy"; Bannan, "Management by Women," 227–28.

11. Lasch-Quinn, *Black Neighbors*, 145 (quote). For the black women's demands, see "The Latest Farce from the Y.W.C.A.," *Cleveland Advocate*, Apr. 24, 1920; "Too Much Paternalism in 'Ys'," *Cleveland Advocate*, May 2, 1920; A. L. Jones, "Struggle among the Saints," 179–84.

12. F. Taylor, "Edge of Tomorrow," 1–7.

13. Eleanor Copenhaver, "Biennial Report for 1928 and 1929," Jan. 19, 1930, 8 (quote), YWCA Records. For a cogent expression of these women's approach, see G. Lumpkin and Kaiser, "Learning to Make History."

14. L. D. Gordon, *Gender and Higher Education*, 48–51, points out that, because most southern women's colleges were founded between 1880 and 1900, Southerners who attended college in the early twentieth century constituted the region's first generation of college-educated women. As such, they constituted a tiny but influential proportion of the population. By contrast, their counterparts in the Northeast were following in the footsteps of the pioneering generation of the 1830s and 1840s.

15. Cott, *Grounding of Modern Feminism*, 218–19; Graham, "Expansion and Exclusion"; Bannan, "Management by Women," 326–35; Cuthbert, "Negro Branch Executive"; Mittelman, "'Spirit That Touches,'" 155–62. According to Mittelman, a national YWCA survey conducted in 1933 found that only 10 percent of black Y leaders and 4 percent of their white counterparts were married (161). For black female social scientists' lack of professional opportunities and their

careers as activist-scholars "without portfolio," see F. Wilson, *Segregated Scholars*, 176 (quote).

16. Chauncey, "Christian Brotherhood"; Chauncey, *Gay New York*, 155–57; Vandenberg-Daves, "Manly Pursuit"; Lynn, *Progressive Women in Conservative Times*, 115–16; Bannan, "Management by Women," 31–104; Wrathall, "Taking the Young Stranger"; N. Robertson, *Christian Sisterhood*, 101–27.

17. Flexner, "Daisy Florence Simms"; Rosenzweig, *Another Self*, 138–40, 142, 145; Biographical Note, Winnifred Crane Wygal Papers, SSC; Lauren Kientz Anderson, "Jumping Overboard: Interpreting Evidence about Same Sex Love: An Exploration of the Brief but Significant Life of Educator Juliette Derricotte" (quote), OutHistory, http://outhistory.org/exhibits/show/juliette-derricotte/derricotte-biography; L. Anderson, "Nauseating Sentiment," 98; Juliette Derricotte to Jane [Juanita Saddler], 1924, Ken Oilschlager–Juliette Derricotte Collection, Archives and Special Collections, J. D. Williams Library, University of Mississippi.

18. Bannan, "Management by Women," 333–35. These women's relationships with their husbands were often quite unconventional. Industrial secretary Louise Leonard McLaren married late, had no children, and was the main wage earner in her family. Her successor, Eleanor Copenhaver, had an affair with the married writer Sherwood Anderson and was determined to maintain her career after they married. Both traveled extensively for their jobs. For Anderson, see M. Wolfe, "Eleanor Copenhaver Anderson"; M. Wolfe, "National Board YWCA"; M. Wolfe, "Sherwood Anderson." Katharine's successor, Betty Webb, married a man who fully shared her feminist ideals and kept her maiden name. For what a daring choice this was, see C. Baker, *Generous Spirit*, 74–75. For the unorthodox marriages of black YWCA activists, see Scanlon, *Until There Is Justice*, 170–71.

19. Freedman, "Burning of Letters"; J. M. Allen, *Passionate Commitments*, 7–10; Gurstein, *Repeal of Reticence*, 99.

20. G. Wilson, *Religious and Educational Philosophy*, 104–7; Cuthbert, *Juliette Derricotte*, 72–73; KDL interview, Aug. 4, 1974, 74–75 (quote); Scanlon, *Until There Is Justice*, 163–72.

21. Storrs, *Second Red*, 45 (quote).

22. Lynn, *Progressive Women in Conservative Times*, 149–56; Frederickson, "A Place to Speak Our Minds." For how religion—and in particular ecumenical women's organizations—shaped black women's social activism and their participation in the interracial movement, see Collier-Thomas's massive *Jesus, Jobs, and Justice*.

23. S. Evans, *Personal Politics*; F. Taylor, "Edge of Tomorrow," 216–18; Lynn, *Progressive Women in Conservative Times*, 141–56, 176–77; Rossinow, "Break-Through"; Rossinow, *Politics of Authenticity*; J. J. Farrell, *Spirit of the Sixties*; Spritzer and Bergmark, *Grace Towns Hamilton*; Curry et al., *Deep in Our Hearts*; S. Evans, *Journeys*; Braude, *Transforming the Faiths*; Ransby, *Ella Baker*, 58, 69, 70–71, 252, 253, 409n49, 260–61, 286; Scanlon, *Until There Is Justice*. For similar continuities regarding anti-imperialism and transnational activism, see Anne Queen interview, Apr. 30, 1976; Helgren, *American Girls*; Izzo, *Liberal Christianity*.

24. Niebuhr, "Glimpses of the Southland," 894 (quote).

25. KDL, "Katharine D. Lumpkin, Student Secretary, to the South Atlantic Field

Committee," Feb. 1922 (quote), folder 1, KDL Papers; KDL interview, Aug. 4, 1974, 60; F. Taylor, "Edge of Tomorrow," 7–8; Setran, *College "Y,"* 80–81.

26. KDL interview, Aug. 4, 1974, 60; Alice Spearman Wright interview, Feb. 28, 1976, 52 (quote); Frederickson, "Louise Leonard McLaren"; G. Wilson, *Religious and Educational Philosophy*, 100–101.

27. "Student Industrial Cooperation, Its History, Methods, Trends, Possibilities," Lucy P. Carner and Winnifred Wygal: Part III, "Possibilities—What Next," May 1926 (quotes), YWCA Records.

28. "Student Industrial Cooperation, Its History, Methods, Trends, Possibilities," KDL and Lois MacDonald: Part II, "Methods and Trends, B., Emphasis during the Summer Months," May 1926 (first quote); KDL and Louise Leonard, "Report of Student Industrial Research of Twelve College Students of Southern Region, July 6–Aug. 17, 1922," 20, both in YWCA Records; KDL interview, Aug. 4, 1974. Among these were seminal studies by Progressive era feminists and reformers, as well as such recent books as *The Acquisitive Society* (1920) by R. H. Tawney, a British socialist and economic historian who offered a powerful, ethical critique of capitalism and individualism.

29. KDL and Louise Leonard, "Report of Student Industrial Research of Twelve College Students of Southern Region, July 6–Aug. 17, 1922," 2 (first quote), 3, 16, 17 (second quote), YWCA Records.

30. KDL and Louise Leonard, "Report of Student Industrial Research of Twelve College Students of Southern Region, July 6–Aug. 17, 1922," 9 (first quote), 16 (second quote), YWCA Records.

31. Alice Spearman Wright interview, Aug. 8, 1976, 3 (quote). Published works on Alice Norwood Spearman Wright include: Daniel, *Lost Revolutions*, 229–36, 238–40, 244–45, 249–50, 284–85; Egerton, *Speak Now*, 407–9, 524–25; Synnott, "Civil Rights Apostle"; Synnott, "Civil Rights Activist"; Synnott, "Crusaders and Clubwomen."

32. Lois MacDonald interview, Aug. 25, 1977, 49 (quote); Lois MacDonald interview, June 24, 1975; Frederickson, "A Place to Speak Our Minds."

33. C. Baker, *Generous Spirit*, 48 (quote).

34. "Statement of Southern Division Council on Race Relations 1927–1928," [1928]; "Interracial Discussion of Southern Division of Council," [1928], both in YWCA Records; KDL, "Interracial Developments—Southern Division," Oct. 12, 1925, folder 2, KDL Papers (hereafter KDL, "Interracial Developments"). Black and white members would serve together as elected delegates to the National Student Council, a fully interracial national governing body. By contrast, there were no African American representatives on the Y's general governing body, the National Board.

35. F. Taylor, "Edge of Tomorrow," 31.

36. Frances Williams, "Memo to the Sub-committee on race of the National Student Council, Nov. 30, 1936" (first quote), Grace Towns Hamilton Papers, Atlanta History Center; KDL interview, Aug. 4, 1974, 46 (second quote). Williams speculated that at first Katharine did not like her, perhaps because she saw her one night in the white waiting room of an Atlanta train station and disap-

proved of Williams's presence there, then goes on to say, "We did not let our personal differences interfere with the work."

37. Ethel M. Caution to Juliette Derricotte, Nov. 9, 1924 (quote), folder 2, KDL Papers. For Caution, see M. Honey, *Shadowed Dreams*, 8, 213; Roses and Randolph, *Harlem's Glory*, 176, 200–2, 500; Caution, "Buyers of Dreams."

38. Juliette Derricotte quoted in L. Anderson, "Nauseating Sentiment," 98; Cuthbert, *Juliette Derricotte*, 4, 24, 27–30, 48–49.

39. Cuthbert, *Juliette Derricotte*, 22 (first quote); Ida Sloan Snyder, [Juanita Jane Saddler obituary], Bureau of Communications, National Board, YWCA, n.d. (second quote); Thirteenth Census of the United States, 1910, Guthrie Ward 3, Logan, OK, District 1026, sheet 11A, family 79, lines 8–10. For more on Saddler's career, see chapter 19.

40. Cuthbert, *Juliette Derricotte*, 18 (first quote), 24 (second quote).

41. Frances Williams interview, Nov. 14, 1981, tape 1, side A, 012-036 (quote); Frances H. Williams interview, Oct. 31–Nov. 1, 1977; N. Robertson, *Christian Sisterhood*, 224, 225n114, 233n123; Houck and D. Dixon, *Women and the Civil Rights Movement*, 61–71; Kindler, "Frances Harriet Williams." See also Mrs. David (Susie) Jones interview, 1978.

42. Frances Williams interview, Nov. 14, 1981, tape 1, side A, 012–037 (quote); "Biographical Sketch for Frances Williams," Dec. 19, 1972, Archives and Special Collections, Mount Holyoke College, MA; "Bureau of Colored Work," Oct. 28, 1921, YWCA Records.

43. Cuthbert, *Juliette Derricotte*, 24–25 (quote on 25).

44. Frances Williams interview, Nov. 14, 1981, tape 1, side A, 012–233, 252 (quote); Frances H. Williams interview, Oct. 31–Nov. 1, 1977.

45. Frances H. Williams interview, Oct. 31–Nov. 1, 1977.

46. Frances Williams interview, Nov. 14, 1981, tape 1, side A, 353–90; L. Anderson, "Nauseating Sentiment," 99. Derricotte was nominated by black and white women at the National Student Assembly to represent the Y at the World's Student Christian Federation in England in 1924.

47. Frances Williams to Walter White, June 21, 1934 (quotes), folder 001469-016-0602, National Association for the Advancement of Colored People Records, Manuscript Division, Library of Congress, Washington, DC (microfilm). Thanks to Kenneth Janken for alerting me to this letter.

48. KDL, "Interracial Developments (first quote); KDL to Constance Ball, June 26, 1924 (subsequent quotes), YWCA Records.

49. Frances Williams to Juliette Derricotte and Juanita Saddler, [Oct. 1924] (quotes), YWCA Records. Thanks to Nancy Robertson for sharing this letter with me. See also Frances Williams to KDL, Nov. 1, 1924, folder 2, KDL Papers.

50. Frances Williams to Juliette Derricotte and Juanita Saddler, [Oct. 1924] (quote), YWCA Records.

51. KDL to Frances Williams, Nov. 1, 1924 (quote), folder 2, KDL Papers.

52. Bannan, "Management by Women," 300 (quote).

53. KDL, "Interracial Developments" (first quote); Frances Williams, "Memo to

the Sub-committee on race of the National Student Council, Nov. 30, 1936" (second quote), Grace Towns Hamilton Papers, Atlanta History Center, GA.

54. Frances Williams to KDL, [Oct. 1924], folder 2, KDL Papers.

55. "Reports of Colored Student Work," Sept. 12, 1922; KDL, "Statement of My Work in Relation to Proposed Interracial Discussion Groups of White and Colored Students—1922–1923" (first quote), both in YWCA Records; KDL, "Report of Katharine D. Lumpkin, Student Secretary, to the Student Committee for March 1923, Confidential: An Account of the Visits Made with Derricotte to Hollins College and North Carolina College for Women," Mar. 1923 (second quote), folder 1, KDL Papers (hereafter KDL, "Report to the Student Committee").

56. KDL, "Interracial Developments" (quote); Ethel Caution to Emma [McAllister], "Re Interracial Education Committee," Jan. 14, 1924, YWCA Records.

57. "Special," 1931 [compendium of Council on Colored Work minutes, 1917–1931], Minutes for June 12, 1918 (quotes); "Reports of Colored Student Work," Sept. 12, 1922, both in YWCA Records; F. Taylor, "Edge of Tomorrow," 88–89. This reading material included works by Benjamin Griffith Brawley, the first dean of Atlanta's Morehouse College; Carter G. Woodson, the father of black history; George Edmund Haynes, cofounder of the Urban League and husband of Elizabeth Ross Haynes, the first African American woman appointed to the Y's National Board; and Alain Locke, editor of the pathbreaking anthology, *The New Negro: An Interpretation*, a manifesto of the Harlem Renaissance.

58. KDL, "Statement of My Work in Relation to Proposed Interracial Discussion Groups of White and Colored Students—1922–1923," YWCA Records; Frances Williams to the Student Department, "Report on Inter-Racial Study Group Held at Nashville, Tennessee, January–April, 1923," Sept. 17, 1923 (quote), folder 1, KDL Papers.

59. Frances Williams, "Report of Frances Williams to Student Department," n.d. (first quote), YWCA Records; R. Wright, "Ethics of Living Jim Crow"; KDL, *Making*, 211 (second quote). For the continuing importance of creating such respites and the constant threat of acts of discrimination and disrespect, see E. Anderson, *Cosmopolitan Canopy*.

60. Frances Williams to the Student Department, "Report on Inter-Racial Study Group Held at Nashville, Tennessee, January–April, 1923," Sept. 17, 1923 (quotes), folder 1, KDL Papers.

61. KDL, "Interracial Developments" (quote).

62. KDL, "Report to the Student Committee"; "Report of: Juliette Derricotte," Apr. 1, 1923 (quotes), both in folder 1, KDL Papers.

63. KDL, *Making*, 214 (quote).

64. Lois MacDonald interview, Aug. 25, 1977, 54–57 (quote on 56).

65. KDL, "Report to the Student Committee" (quotes).

66. "Report of: Juliette Derricotte," Apr. 1, 1923 (first, second, and third quotes); KDL, "Report to the Student Committee" (fourth quote), both in folder 1, KDL Papers.

67. "Interracial Education" ["Cannot trace origin, appeared on desk during 1925–26"] (quotes), YWCA Records.

68. KDL, "Report to the Student Committee"; KDL, *Making*, 199. For antimiscegenation laws as "the critical legal foundation" of Jim Crow and the persistence and explosiveness of "miscegenation anxiety," see Dailey, "Is Marriage a Civil Right?" 185 (quotes).

69. Lynn, *Progressive Women in Conservative Times*, 45. For the ideal of a frank, open conversational community, see Stansell, *American Moderns*, 83–84.

70. KDL, quoted in F. Taylor, "Edge of Tomorrow," 85 (first quote); Frances Williams, "Indianapolis Convention as an Interracial Experience: To the Council on Colored Work," Feb. 7. 1924 (second quote), YWCA Records (hereafter Williams, "Indianapolis Convention"). See also "Report of Katharine D. Lumpkin, National Student Secretary," Summer 1924, folder 2, KDL Papers.

71. KDL, "Interracial Developments" (quotes); KDL, "Confidential Notes on Some Colleges of Southern Division, Aug. 1925, both in folder 2, KDL Papers.

72. Thelma Stevens to Frances Anton Taylor, Feb. 6, 1982 (quotes), Southern Women, the Student YWCA, and Race (1920–1944) Collection, SSC. For Stevens's life and career, see Thelma Stevens interview, Feb. 13, 1972, 16 (quote); Stevens, *Legacy for the Future*; Knotts, "Methodist Women"; Knotts, "Thelma Stevens"; Knotts, *Fellowship of Love*; Lasch-Quinn, *Black Neighbors*, 127–31; S. Evans, *Journeys*, 27–29, 39; Harvey, *Freedom's Coming*, 85–86, 192; Cavazos, "Queen's Daughters," 2, 58–60, 73–74, 83–88, 126.

73. KDL, "Confidential Notes on Some Colleges of Southern Division," Aug. 1925, folder 2, KDL Papers; W. D. Weatherford to Mabel T. Everett, Apr. 16, 1926 (first quote), folder 182; C. O. Gray [President of Tusculum College in Greenville, TN] to W. D. Weatherford, Apr. 18, 1925 (second quote), folder 46, both in W. D. Weatherford Papers, SHC.

74. Grace Towns Hamilton interview, Apr. 29, 1974; Mullis, "Public Career of Grace Towns Hamilton"; Spritzer and Bergmark, *Grace Towns Hamilton*; Spritzer, "Grace Towns Hamilton."

75. Ethel Caution to Emma [McAllister], "Re Interracial Education Committee," Jan. 14, 1924, (quotes), YWCA Records.

76. Frances Williams, "Reports of Colored Student Work," Nov. 1922 (quotes), YWCA Records.

77. Jenness, *Twelve Negro Americans*, 165.

78. Frances Williams, "Report of Frances Williams to Student Department," n.d. (first and second quotes); "Interracial Discussion Groups: Report of Interracial Commission Meeting," Apr. 14, 1926 (third quote); Juliette Derricotte to Lucy Slowe, Feb. 15, 1926; "From Report of Maude Gwinn—June—Dec. 1927," all in YWCA Records.

79. "Turning a Y.W.C.A. Convention into a Scheme for Teaching Socialism," *Manufacturers Record*, June 24, 1920; "Danger of Socialistic Doctrines in Colleges and Christian Association Conventions," *Manufacturers Record*, Aug. 5, 1920. See also "Dr. MacCracken Not a Safe Adviser on Synonyms," July 31, 1924; "Anglo-Saxonism of North, South and West Must Combine for Good of All," July 31,

1924; "Is Socialism Spreading in Southern Colleges and in Other Institutions?" Aug. 14, 1924, all in *Manufacturers Record*.

80. Coolidge, "Are the 'Reds' Stalking" (quote on 4); Coolidge, "Trotsky versus Washington"; Coolidge, "They Must Be Resisted."

81. KDL interview, Apr. 24, 1985, 31–32; Mott, *Evangelization* (first quote); M. Thompson, *For God and Globe*, 1 (subsequent quotes); Setran, *College "Y,"* 56, 224. For the long-term impact of Christian internationalism, see Hollinger, *Protestants Abroad*; Izzo, *Liberal Christianity*.

82. "Leaders Endorse 'League of Youth,'" *New York Times*, Dec. 31, 1923 (quote); Williams, "Indianapolis Convention"; Forrest D. Brown, "Indianapolis Student Volunteer Convention," *Blue Ridge Voice*, Dec. 1923, North Carolina Collection, Louis Round Wilson Special Collections Library, University of North Carolina at Chapel Hill.

83. Williams, "Indianapolis Convention" (quotes).

84. KDL interview, Apr. 24, 1985, 31–32 (first quote on 32); "Leaders Endorse 'League of Youth,'" *New York Times*, Dec. 31, 1923 (second and third quotes).

85. Ethel Caution to Emma [McAllister], "Re Interracial Education Committee," Jan. 14, 1924 (first quote); KDL, "Brief notes on a conversation I had with Dr. Alexander of the Interracial Commission, Jan. 25th when talking with him about a place of meeting for the Curry Institute," n.d. (second quote); Williams, "Indianapolis Convention," all in YWCA Records; KDL, "Interracial Developments" (third and fourth quotes). For YMCA and YWCA activities in the wake of this conference, see J. W. Bergthold, "Interracial Discussion Groups: Student Interracial Work in the Ten States East of the Mississippi River (1925–26)," YWCA Records.

86. Lida B. Robertson to Editor, *Manufacturer Record*, July 24, 1925 (quote), newsclip in YWCA Records; "Claims that YWCA Camp at Blue Ridge Advocates Intermarriage of Negros and Whites," *Manufacturers Record*, Aug. 13, 1924; William Heyburn to W. I. McNair, Aug. 26, 1925; W. D. Weatherford to William Heyburn, Sept. 4, 1925, both in folder 148, W. D. Weatherford Papers, SHC.

87. W. I. McNair to Wiley B. Bryan, Aug. 26, 1925 (quotes), folder 148, W. D. Weatherford Papers, SHC.

88. "Council on Colored Work," Nov. 13, 1925 (quote); Emma Bailey Speer to Murrell Gray Ross, Dec. 3, 1925, both in YWCA Records.

89. KDL, "Confidential: Report of a recent situation in Columbia, S.C., resulting from reports made by some students on race relations discussions at Blue Ridge Student Conference," Nov. 14, 1924 (quotes), folder 2, KDL Papers; "Reminiscences of the Beginnings of Student Interracial Work in Atlanta 1922–1926 (unexpurgated)," YWCA Records.

90. Myra Page interview, July 12, 1975, 28; Lois MacDonald interview, Aug. 25, 1977, 30 (quote).

91. Thelma Stevens interview, Feb. 13, 1972, 16 (first quote); Alice Spearman Wright interview, Feb. 28, 1976, 53 (second quote).

92. N. Fraser, "Rethinking the Public Sphere," 67.

93. Logan, *What the Negro Wants* (first quote); Eva Bowles, "Negro Women and the Y. W. C. A. of the United States," n.d., 6 (second quote), YWCA Records.

94. Weatherford, *Negro Life*, 7 (quote). By 1915, this widely used text had gone through three printings. Weatherford estimated that by 1912 more than 10,000 college students had used it: Antone, "Willis Duke Weatherford," 53. In that year, he published a similar survey, Weatherford, *Present Forces in Negro Progress*. Weatherford was an exemplar of a conservative version of the social gospel that pervaded the YMCA between 1888 and 1915; it stressed manly character-building as a means of social change: Setran, *College "Y,"* 137–41.

95. Weatherford quoted in Canady, "Improving Race Relations," 416 (first quote), 432 (second quote).

96. Juliette Derricotte to Mrs. George E. Haynes, Oct. 30, 1924 (quote), YWCA Records. For a scathing account of this arrangement, see Niebuhr, "Glimpses of the Southland," 893–95.

97. KDL, *Making*, 212–13 (quotes on 213). Ruffin appears in an unflattering light in several studies of southern black women and the YWCA, but she was a substantial figure who had a remarkable, if troubled, career. Born in Norfolk, Virginia, in 1871, she was the daughter of Ottaway Francis Ruffin, a former slave who worked as a barber and post office clerk, and a grocer named Annie Elizabeth Langley, whose father had been freed in 1848. After receiving the equivalent of a high school education at Norfolk Mission College, Adela served as dean of women at Kittrell College in Western North Carolina, a coeducational school run by the African American Episcopal Church, and then as "Lady Principal" at the Slater Industrial Academy in Winston-Salem, North Carolina (now Winston-Salem State University). In 1915, she became one of the first black women to attend the Y's National Training School, then returned to the South to direct the Phyllis Wheatley branch of the Richmond, Virginia YWCA. When the federal government poured money into the YWCA's war work, she became a national war work secretary responsible for supervising black Ys throughout the South and was promoted to the position of Colored City Secretary for the region. She was forced out of that position when funds dried up after the war. In 1922, she was hired to direct the black branch of the Asheville Y, which she did with considerable success until 1938 when she was forced to resign by the leaders of the white central Y. See Brinson, "Helping Others," 90–93; Kent, *More Than Petticoats*, 93–104; Moseley-Edington, "Adela Ruffin," 93.

98. Lealtad, "Y.W.C.A. and the Negro"; Catherine D. Lealtad to Lugenia Hope, Mar. 5, 1920, both in Neighborhood Union Collection, Archives Research Center, Robert W. Woodruff Library, Atlanta University Center; N. Robertson, *Christian Sisterhood*, 94, 125.

99. Anna Arnold Hedgeman quoted in Lerner, *Black Women*, 489–97 (quote on 492).

100. Williams, "Indianapolis Convention" (quote); "Conventions and Regional Conferences," Council on Colored Work, [1920–1931], both in YWCA Records.

101. KDL, *Making*, 214–15 (quotes on 215).

102. For the persistence of such sites of racial injury, see E. Anderson, *Cosmopolitan Canopy*, 253.

103. "Blue Ridge 1923," YWCA Records.

104. KDL to Leslie Blanchard, Oct. 17, 1923 (quote), folder 1, KDL Papers.

105. KDL to Leslie Blanchard, [Confidential—Very], Dec. 3, 1923 (first and second quotes), folder 1, KDL Papers (hereafter KDL, Confidential—Very); "Interracial Discussion of Southern Division of Council," [1928] (third quote), YWCA Records.

106. KDL, Confidential—Very; "Interracial Discussion of Southern Division of Council," [1928], YWCA Records.

107. "Interracial Discussion of Southern Division of Council," [1928] (first quote), YWCA Records; KDL, "Report to the Student Committee." The concern that parents and college administrators would prevent white students from attending integrated conferences came up repeatedly in the 1930s and early 1940s, as the YWCA and YMCA struggled to move "in the direction of the elimination of segregation and the achievement of both equality and integration . . . within our own movement": Anne Queen, "A Study of the Development of the Interracial Conference in the South" (unpublished seminar paper, Yale Divinity School), n.d. [1948], 19 (quote), folder 357, Anne Queen Papers, SHC.

108. KDL, Confidential—Very (quote).

109. KDL, *Making*, 212–13 (quotes on 213).

110. KDL, Confidential—Very (quote).

111. KDL, Confidential—Very (quote).

112. KDL, *Making*, 192 (first quote); KDL, Confidential—Very (second quote); Newfield, *Prophetic Minority* (third quote); F. Taylor, "Edge of Tomorrow," 119–20.

113. KDL, Confidential—Very (quotes); KDL, *Making*, 199.

114. KDL, "Blue Ridge," Mar. 25, 1924, KDL Papers; Juliette Derricotte to Mrs. George E. Haynes, Oct. 30, 1924 (quote), YWCA Records.

115. W. D. Weatherford quoted in F. Taylor, "Edge of Tomorrow," 168–69 (quotes on 169).

116. Ruth Scandrett to W. D. Weatherford, May 10, 1926 (quote); W. D. Weatherford to Ruth Scandrett, May 20, 1926, both in box 1, Fred A. Perley Papers, North Carolina State Archives. The issue of separate restrooms provoked special conflict in workplaces and continued to do so into the 1970s. See Boris, "Racialized Bodies"; Cooper and Oldenziel, "Cherished Classifications"; Godfrey, "Bayonets, Brainwashing, and Bathrooms."

117. Until the founding of Koinonia farm in Georgia in 1942, even the most radical of the South's alternative educational institutions—including the Summer School for Women Workers, Commonwealth College in rural Arkansas, and Highlander Folk School in Tennessee—excluded blacks. Nearby Black Mountain College, arguably "the boldest progressive educational experiment in American history," refused to admit black artists out of fear of "arson and violence." In 1943 it even turned down a request to hold an integrated student YWCA/YMCA conference on its campus: Bathanti, "Mythic School" (first quote); Duberman, *Black Mountain*, 179 (second quote).

118. Anne Queen, "A Study of the Development of the Interracial Conference in the South" (unpublished seminar paper, Yale Divinity School), n.d. [1948], 19 (quote), folder 357, Anne Queen Papers, SHC.

119. Anne Queen, "A Study of the Development of the Interracial Conference in the South" (unpublished seminar paper, Yale Divinity School), n.d. [1948], 19, folder 357, Anne Queen Papers, SHC. After a stormy session in 1947, the YMCA followed suit.

120. "Black History Month Spotlight: Jean Fairfax," NAACP Legal Defense Fund, Feb. 13, 2014, http://www.naacpldf.org/press-release/black-history-month -spotlight-jean-fairfax (first quote); Jean Fairfax interview, Oct. 15, 1983; Egerton, *Speak Now*, 425–27 (second quote on 427). The white Y leader in the group was Rosalie Oakes, who, as head of the YWCA at the University of Texas in the 1960s, mentored white SNCC leader Casey Hayden and other student activists. Oakes herself was a "behind-the-scenes driving force" of the civil rights movement: Christine Milled Ford, "Quiet Champion for Civil Rights: Memorial Planned for Activist Rosalie Oakes," *Winchester Star*, Sept. 30, 2008 (quote); Rossinow, *Politics of Authenticity*, 90–91, 108.

121. Lynn, *Progressive Women in Conservative Times*, 46–49; Ida Sloan Snyder, [Juanita Jane Saddler obituary], Bureau of Communications, National Board, YWCA, n.d., YWCA Records; Laville, "If the Time Is Not Ripe." As Laville points out, the interracial charter put the Y well in advance of other liberal women's organizations and set it on course to become a strong ally of the direct action movement of the 1950s and 1960s.

122. KDL to Leslie Blanchard, Mar. 11, 1924 (quote), folder 2, KDL Papers.

123. "Report of Katharine D. Lumpkin, National Student Secretary," Summer 1924 (first quote), folder 2, KDL Papers; KDL, *Making*, 219–21 (second quote on 221).

124. KDL, *Making*, 189 (quote); J. Hall, *Revolt against Chivalry*, 100–1. For the equation of tilting the color line with "vertical segregation," see Kneebone, *Southern Liberal Journalists*, 74–96.

125. KDL, *Making*, 216 (quotes).

126. KDL, *Making*, 222 (quote).

127. KDL interview, Aug. 4, 1974, 80 (first quote); Sarah [?] to KDL, Jan. 14, 1948 (second quote), folder 13, KDL Papers.

128. Winnifred Wygal to KDL, Feb. 19, 1925 (quote), folder 2, KDL Papers.

129. KDL interview, Aug. 4, 1974, 45 (quotes).

130. KDL, "Democratic Ways," 29 (quotes).

131. KDL interview, Aug. 4, 1974, 70 (first quote); KDL, *Making*, 203 (second quote); Jane Saddler to Charles Johnson, Jan. 7, 1955 (third quote), folder 16, KDL Papers.

CHAPTER EIGHT: "GETTING THE WORLD'S WORK DONE"

1. C. McCarthy, *Wisconsin Idea*; P. Buhle, ed., *History and the New Left*, 1–13; Jane Saddler to Charles Johnson, Jan. 7, 1955 (first quote), folder 16, KDL Papers; KDL interview, Apr. 24, 1985, 37 (second quote).

2. Lampman, *Economists at Wisconsin*, xvii, xix–xx, 7.

3. KDL, "The Making of a Southerner: Description of the Subject of the Autobiography and Outline of the Program of Research and Method of Presentation," May 29, 1944, 12 (quote), folder 46, KDL Papers.

4. Katharine Lambert to KDL, May 29, 1923; KDL to Leslie Blanchard, Mar. 14 and 20, 1925; Leslie Blanchard to KDL, Mar. 18, 1925; KDL to Mrs. Marshall Monroe, Mar. 21, 1925, all in folder 2, KDL Papers; KDL interview, Aug. 4, 1974, 40.

5. KDL interview, Aug. 4, 1974, 70 (quote); G. Lumpkin, "Remember Now: A Play in Three Acts and Nine Scenes," 1951, 14, G. Lumpkin Papers.

6. H. Lumpkin, "Lady and the Moose," 73–76 (quote on 73); "Backward Glances," *Charleston News and Courier,* Mar. 5, 1970; State Historical Society of Wisconsin, *Dictionary of Wisconsin Biography,* s.v. "Hope H. Lumpkin"; Stuck, *Alaskan Missions,* 147–48; Robert L. Lumpkin interview, Aug. 5, 1995; John H. Lumpkin Sr. interview, July 29, 1995; John H. Lumpkin Sr. interview, Aug. 17, 1990.

7. Hope H. Lumpkin, Admission Records, Sept. 15, 1920, Archives and Records Management, University of Wisconsin–Madison Libraries; Hope H. Lumpkin to W. H. Kiekhofer, July 19, 1924 (quotes), box 12, William H. Kiekhofer Papers, Archives and Records Management, University of Wisconsin–Madison Libraries.

8. KDL interview, Aug. 4, 1974, 70 (quote); Robert L. Lumpkin interview, Aug. 5, 1995; John H. Lumpkin Sr. interview, July 29, 1995; "Hope Lumpkin's Death Regretted in Wisconsin," *Columbia (SC) State,* Oct. 16, 1932.

9. KDL interview, Aug. 4, 1974, 39 (first quote), 81 (subsequent quotes); Cott, *Grounding of Modern Feminism,* 215–39; Graham, "Expansion and Exclusion"; A. Scott, *Unheard Voices,* 6.

10. John H. Lumpkin Sr. interview, Aug. 17, 1990; John H. Lumpkin Sr. interview, July 29, 1995.

11. John H. Lumpkin Sr. interview, Aug. 17, 1990 (quote); John H. Lumpkin Sr. interview, July 29, 1995; Alva M. Lumpkin Jr. interview, Aug. 4, 1995; Alva M. Lumpkin Jr. interview, Aug. 17, 1990.

12. Thanks to John H. Lumpkin Sr. for sharing these photographs with me.

13. KDL interview, Aug. 4, 1974, 75 (quote).

14. John Nesselhof interview, Aug. 9, 1996 (first quote); C. Baker, *Generous Spirit,* 31 (second quote), 162. Like Markey, Nesselhof suspected that Katharine's suffering also had to do with her deep loyalty to a brother who had in some way abused her. "There may have been a sexual complication," he observed.

15. E. A. Ross to KDL, Nov. 8, 1927 (first and second quotes); Alva M. Lumpkin to KDL, Nov. 22, 1927 (third quote), both in folder 3, KDL Papers; KDL interview, Aug. 4, 1974, 65.

16. KDL, Official Transcript, Registrar's Office, University of Wisconsin–Madison, in J. Hall's possession; Commons, *Myself,* 2; "Deans Won't Protest Parade of U.W. Students at Kenosha Strike," *Capital Times* (Madison, WI), Mar. 23, 1928. For Gillin, see Curti and Carstensen, *University of Wisconsin,* 2:344.

17. KDL, "The Making of a Southerner: Description of the Subject of the Autobiography and Outline of the Program of Research and Method of Presentation," May 29, 1944, 12 (quotes), folder 46, KDL Papers.

18. John H. Lumpkin Sr. interview, Aug. 17, 1990; John H. Lumpkin Sr. interview, July 29, 1995.

19. E. Ross, *Seventy Years of It,* 180 (first quote), 223–26; D. Ross, *American Social Science,* 229–41 (second quote on 235).

20. KDL, "The Making of a Southerner: Description of the Subject of the Autobiography and Outline of the Program of Research and Method of Presentation," May 29, 1944, 12 (quote), folder 46, KDL Papers.

21. Bender, *Intellect and Public Life*, 62–66; Fink, "'Intellectuals' versus 'Workers,'" 395–421; Fink, *Progressive Intellectuals*, 52–79.

22. Lampman, *Economists at Wisconsin*, xx; Graham, "Expansion and Exclusion."

23. Cott, *Grounding of Modern Feminism*, 215–39 (first quote on 228); Lewontin, "Women versus the Biologists," 35 (second quote). For women and the ideology of professionalism see also Cookingham, "Social Economists and Reform"; Fitzpatrick, *Endless Crusade*; Furner, *Advocacy and Objectivity*; Reinharz, "Finding a Sociological Voice"; Rosenberg, *Beyond Separate Spheres*; D. Ross, *American Social Science*; Laslett, "Gender in/and Social Science"; L. Gordon, "Social Insurance"; Dzuback, "Women and Social Research"; B. Smith, "Gender and the Practices"; Folbre, "Sphere of Women"; Dzuback, "Berkeley Women Economists."

24. KDL, "Social Situations and Girl Delinquency"; KDL, "Factors in the Commitment"; KDL, "Parental Conditions."

25. L. Gordon, *Heroes*; Fitzpatrick, *Endless Crusade*, 183–98; Freedman, *Sisters' Keepers*, 109–25; Schlossman and S. Wallach, "Crime of Precocious Sexuality"; Lunbeck, "New Generation," 513–43; Odem and Schlossman, "Guardians of Virtue"; C. Hicks, *Talk with You Like a Woman*. The concept of a "culture of poverty" first appeared in O. Lewis, *Five Families*.

26. KDL, *Making*, 211 (first quote); KDL to Leslie Blanchard, [Confidential—Very], Dec. 3, 1923 (second quote), folder 1, KDL Papers.

27. L. H. Hubbard to KDL, May 12, 1928; Amy Hewes to KDL, Apr. 26, 1928, both in KDL Papers; Ann Baron to J. Hall, Sept. 10, 2003; Engerman, *Modernization*, 137–38; Rodgers, *Atlantic Crossings*, 376–79.

28. Glazer and Slater, *Unequal Colleagues*, 27–67.

29. Mount Holyoke College, *Report of the Department of Economics and Sociology*, 1928/29, 6, Department of Economics and Sociology Records, Archives and Special Collections, Mount Holyoke College; Elaine Trehub to Marla Miller, July 18, 1990, in J. Hall's possession. Katharine and Dorothy were drawn to one another by personal attraction and shared intellectual and political interests. Given the almost complete absence of letters, diaries, or other first-person evidence, we do not and cannot know whether or when they were sexually involved as well. For the pitfalls of, on the one hand, classifying women's partnerships on the basis of sexual activity alone and, on the other, of erasing lesbianism by refusing to acknowledge the presence of same-sex erotic passion in women's lives, see B. Cook, "Female Support Networks"; B. Cook, "Historical Denial"; J. Hall, "Open Secrets"; J. Bennett, "Lesbian-Like."

30. Birmingham, *"Our Crowd,"* 17–45 (quote on 17). Clara's mother was Sarah Seligman, the youngest daughter of David and Fanny Seligman. Her successful brothers brought her and the other younger siblings to the United States from Baersdorf, Germany (Bavaria), in 1842, when Sarah was two. She married Samuel Cohen, a merchant of old New York and the grand uncle of Robert Moses.

The family is buried in the Seligman mausoleum in the Salem Fields Cemetery of Temple Emanu-El, where Clara Wolff is also interred.

31. Phillips-Matz, *Many Lives*, 23; Birmingham, *"Our Crowd,"* 54; Collins, *Otto Kahn*, 9, 49.

32. S. Fraser, *Every Man*, 193–246. The term "malefactors of great wealth" was coined by Theodore Roosevelt.

33. Lewis S. Wolff, Will and Codicil, Jan. 20, 1904, Feb. 17, 1904, Surrogate's Court, Monmouth County, NY; Jacob Schiff quoted in Chernow, *Warburgs*, 101 (quote); "Wolff Estate $669,601," *New York Times*, June 13, 1913; Antler, *Journey Home*, 1–5, 40–72; Toll, "Quiet Revolution," 7–26; Muncy, *Female Dominion*.

34. "Mrs. Lewis S. Wolff," *New York Times*, Apr. 13, 1940; Birmingham, *"Our Crowd,"* 130–31; Frankel, *Bulletin of Jewish Charities*, 6; "Temple Emanuel Sisterhood, Celebration of 25th Anniversary at the Temple, Dec. 6 and 7," *New York Times*, Nov. 6, 1913; Clara F. Wolff, Last Will and Testament, Mar. 15, 1927, admitted to probate Apr. 23, 1940 (quote), Surrogate's Court, County of New York.

35. "Lewis S. Wolff," Passport Application, issued Sept. 2, 1892, in *U.S. Passport Applications, 1795–1925*, Ancestry.com; Lewis S. Wolff, Will and Codicil, Jan. 20, 1904, Feb. 17, 1904, Surrogate's Court, Monmouth County, NY; Chernow, *Warburgs*, 185; Birmingham, *"Our Crowd,"* 255, 342.

36. "Lewis Wolff," in Tenth Census of the United States, 1880, Population Schedule, New York, NY, ED 534, p. 448A; Kobler, *Otto, the Magnificent*, 20–22; Collins, *Otto Kahn*; Birmingham, *"Our Crowd,"* 198, 200–202; P. Douglas, *Fullness of Time*, 31 (quote); Birmingham, *"Our Crowd,"* 149, 342.

37. 1961 Bryn Mawr Alumnae Survey, Bryn Mawr College Library, Special Collections; *Scribner's Magazine*, Jun. 1913, 31 (quote); "Jessica Cosgrave, Educator, 78, Dies," *New York Times*, Nov. 1, 1949. Stanley married Helen Henderson at Trinity Church, a well-endowed Episcopal institution near the intersection of Wall Street and Broadway: "Wolff—Henderson," *New York Times*, Dec. 29, 1911.

38. H. Horowitz, *Power and Passion*, 155, 184, 422–23.

39. "Dorothy Sebel [*sic*] Wolff," Passport Application, Issued Jun. 11, 1915, in *U.S. Passport Applications, 1795–1925*, Ancestry.com; Dorothy S. Wolff, "Goodbye, 1912," *The Book of the Class of Nineteen-Twelve*; Louise Watson, "Mamie's 161st Chat with Her Friends; or, The Establishment of Dualism; or, The Last Class Meeting of 1912," *The Book of the Class of Nineteen-Twelve*, 125–28 (quotes), both in Bryn Mawr College Library, Special Collections. Dorothy continued to publish in the Bryn Mawr literary magazine after graduation, but as the years went by she became more critical of her alma mater. She did not participate in the array of alumni activities that engaged many of her classmates. Asked to summarize her life for an alumnae survey in 1961, she wrote "divorced" with a flourish across the section on "Marriage" and, under "General Interests and Activities," wrote, "I see you leave NO place for research!"

40. Sklar, *Florence Kelley*; Storrs, *Civilizing Capitalism*.

41. D. Douglas, "Instinct and Institution," *The Lantern* (Spring 1916), 25, Bryn Mawr College Library, Special Collections (first quote); P. Douglas, *Fullness*

of Time, 3–37 (second quote on 35); Dorothy S. Wolff, Transcript of Record, Columbia University, PhD, June 3, 1925; Amherst College News Bureau, Press release, June 3, 1966 (third quote), Archives and Special Collections, Robert Frost Library, Amherst College, MA; Rasmussen, introduction to *Pity Is Not Enough*, xi (fourth quote).

42. "Raquette Lake: Houses along the Shore Are Blossoming Out in Their Summer Attire," *New York Times*, June 26, 1910; "Wolff–Douglas," *New York Times*, Mar. 4, 1915; D. Douglas v. Paul H. Douglas, Findings of Fact and Conclusions of Law, Second Judicial Court of the State of Nevada, Washoe County, Sept. 3, 1930, Office of Clerk of the Court, Reno, Nevada; "Wolff Estate $669,601," *New York Times*, June 13, 1913; P. Douglas, *Fullness of Time*, 35–36 (quotes on 36).

43. D. Douglas to W. A. Neilson, Oct. 24, 1932, box 7, folder 43, Neilson Files.

44. P. Douglas, *Fullness of Time*, 35–36; Biles, *Crusading Liberal*, 8; "Biography—Dorothy W. Douglas," [1937], Faculty Biographical Files, D. Douglas, SCA; D. Douglas Resume attached to D. Douglas and KDL to Mary van Kleeck, May 29, 1931, van Kleeck Papers; D. Douglas, "Minimum Wage Laws." This article was reprinted as a pamphlet: D. Douglas, *American Minimum Wage Laws at Work*, Pamphlets in American History: Labor (New York: National Consumers' League, 1920). See also D. Douglas, "Cost of Living," 225–59.

45. D. Douglas to George W. Nasmyth, June 12, 1918 (first quote) in George Nasmyth and Florence Nasmyth Papers, Swarthmore College Peace Collection; Walton, *Women and Philanthropy in Education*, 1–6 (second quote on 4). Among the groups Dorothy funded was the research bureau of the leftist Intercollegiate Socialist Society (ISS). Renamed the League for Industrial Democracy in 1921, the ISS eventually gave birth to Students for a Democratic Society (SDS), a chief voice of student radicalism in the 1960s.

46. P. Douglas, *Fullness of Time*, 36–37; Keohane, "Paul Douglas," Dictionary of Unitarian and Universalist Biography, June 2003, http://uudb.org/articles/pauldouglas.html.

47. P. Douglas, *Fullness of Time*, 44 (quote), 45. Paul taught at the University of Illinois (1916–1917), Reed College (1917–1918), and the University of Washington (1919–1920). From 1918 to 1919 he served as a labor mediator for the Emergency Fleet Corporation.

48. P. Douglas, *Fullness of Time*, 35, 46 (quote), 614.

49. D. Douglas to W. A. Neilson, Oct. 24, 1932, box 7, folder 43, Neilson Files; "Biography—Dorothy W. Douglas," [1937], Faculty Biographical Files, D. Douglas, SCA; Douglas, *Fullness of Time*, 70; P. Douglas, D. Douglas, and Joslyn, *What Can a Man Afford?* Dorothy wrote sections of P. Douglas, *Worker in Modern Economic Society*. For the impact of nepotism rules, see Rossiter, *Women Scientists*, 198.

50. Adaline Pates Potter interview, May 26, 2000; Crowley, *Collected Scientific Papers*, 936 (quote).

51. Stansell, *American Moderns*, 224–72, esp. 258–62; P. Douglas, *Fullness of Time*, 70.

52. Biles, *Crusading Liberal*, 13; Renda, *Taking Haiti*, 191, 266–67 (quote on 267); P. Douglas, *Fullness of Time*, 48–50, 508; Engerman, "New Society, New Scholarship," 25–43.

53. D. Allen, *Adventurous Americans*, 179–91 (first and second quotes, 188–89); Engerman, "New Society, New Scholarship," 35 (third quote); American Trade Union Delegation to the Soviet Union, *Soviet Russia in the Second Decade*; Biles, *Crusading Liberal*, 218–19n30.

54. D. Douglas, *Guillaume de Greef*; D. Douglas, "Social Purpose," 433–54; D. Douglas, "Doctrines of Guillaume De Greef," 538–52; Smith Catalogue, 1924–25, 1925–27, and 1926–27, SCA. Paul Wolff Douglas was born on Sept. 12, 1926 in Springfield, MA. He died in 2011.

55. Photograph, D. Douglas, Faculty Biographical Files, SCA; P. Douglas, *Fullness of Time*, 70 (quote); John Keohane, "Emily Taft Douglas," July 19, 2002, Dictionary of Unitarian and Universalist Biography, http://uudb.org/articles/emilytaftdouglas.html; Ann T. Keene, "Emily Taft Douglas," American National Biography Online, https://doi.org/10.1093/anb/9780198606697.article.07007943; Adaline Pates Potter interview, May 26, 2000; Paul Douglas, Dorothy Douglas, Helen Douglas, John Douglas, Dorothea Douglas, Paul Douglas (Jr.), S.S. *Cedric*, List of U.S. Citizens Arriving at Port of New York, Sept. 17, 1928, p. 21, *New York, Passenger Lists, 1820–1957*, Ancestry.com.

56. Biles, *Crusading Liberal*, 13 (first quote); P. Douglas, "Why I Am for Thomas," 270; P. Douglas, "Lessons from the Last Decade," 29–57; P. Douglas, *Coming of a New Party*; P. Douglas, *Fullness of Time*, 29, 74; Rossinow, *Visions of Progress*, 103–42; "Busby Rips Douglas as Red Frontier," *Chicago Daily Tribune*, Sept. 14, 1948 (second quote).

57. D. Douglas to George W. Nasmyth, June 12, 1918 and July 7, 1918 (quotes), George Nasmyth and Florence Nasmyth Papers, Swarthmore College Peace Collection.

58. D. Douglas to W. A. Neilson, Oct. 24, 1932, box 7, folder 43, Neilson Files; Worcester, *Social Science Research Council*, 9–11; Kimball Young to KDL, May 9, 1929, folder 3, KDL Papers; KDL, "A Study of Social Situations as Related to Conduct of Problem Children in Dependent Families," Research Fellowships in the Social Sciences, [1929–30], box 254, folder 2465, Social Science Research Council records, Rockefeller Archive Center, Sleepy Hollow, NY; "Kathryn [*sic*] Lumpkin," in Fifteenth Census of the United States, 1930, Population Schedule, New York, NY, ED 0867, p. 6B; D. Douglas v. Paul H. Douglas, Findings of Fact and Conclusions of Law, (first quote), Second Judicial Court of the State of Nevada, Washoe County, Sept. 3, 1930, Office of Clerk of the Court, Reno, Nevada; Smith College Catalogue, 1930–31, SCA; P. Douglas, *Fullness of Time*, 35 (second quote), 76 (third quote).

CHAPTER NINE: WRITING AND NEW YORK

Portions of this chapter are drawn from J. Hall, "Women Writers."

1. "Report of Katharine D. Lumpkin, National Student Secretary," Summer 1924 (quote), folder 2, KDL Papers; G. Lumpkin interview, Aug. 6, 1974, 6.

2. G. Lumpkin interview, Sept. 25, 1971, 5 (first quote); G. Lumpkin interview, Aug. 6, 1974, 22–23 (second quote on 23); KDL interview, Mar. 22, 1987, 2 (third quote).

3. KDL, "Lecture to a general audience," 1947, 2 (quote), KDL Papers, folders 64–65, SHC; G. Lumpkin interview, Aug. 6, 1974, 8–11, 21–23; G. Lumpkin interview, Sept. 25, 1971, 6–10; G. Lumpkin to Amory Potter Glenn, Feb. 25, 1974, in J. Hall's possession, thanks to Amory and William W. L. Glenn (hereafter Glenn Letters).

4. The most reliable source for Grace Lumpkin's birth date is the Social Security Death Index, 075-18-8354, which indicates that she was born on March 3, 1891. This jibes with the Thirteenth Census of the United States, 1910, South Carolina, Richland County, E.D. 71, Sheet 3B, which says that she was nineteen at that time, and with KDL to Lillian Gilkes, Apr. 5, 1980, folder 32, KDL Papers, which says that Grace was eighty-eight when she died on March 23, 1980. Oddly, there is no birth date listed for Grace in the family Bible and no date given in the family genealogy her brother Bryan compiled: Bryan H. Lumpkin, "Lumpkin," Dec. 1936, typescript in KDL Papers. Most biographical accounts have followed her lead and offered the wrong birth date.

5. G. Lumpkin, "Kok-I House," unpublished short story, 1966, 1 (first quote), G. Lumpkin Papers (hereafter G. Lumpkin, "Kok-I House"); KDL interview, Mar. 22, 1987, 2 (second quote); G. Lumpkin interview, Aug. 6, 1974, 22; Dearborn, *Queen of Bohemia*.

6. Alva M. Lumpkin Jr. interview, Aug. 17, 1990 (first quote); G. Lumpkin to Kenneth Toombs, June 22, 1971 (second quote), G. Lumpkin Papers.

7. G. Lumpkin interview, Aug. 6, 1974, 6, 22; G. Lumpkin to Amory Potter Glenn, Feb. 25, 1974, Glenn Letters. For *The World Tomorrow*, see Barbara Addison, "Biography of Devere Allen, 1891–1955," unpublished ms in Devere Allen Papers, Swarthmore College Peace Collection, Swarthmore, PA (hereafter D. Allen Papers); M. Thompson, *For God and Globe*, 10–11, 19, 51–66; Chatfield, *For Peace and Justice*, 40, 111, 125, 138–42, 182, 197, 214, 223–25, 247–51. In 1927, the *World Tomorrow* editor Kirby Page brought in Grace Loucks, a staff member of the YWCA National Student Council, to write the magazine's signature discussion-group questions, a vivid example of the pedagogical goals the magazine shared with the Y.

8. "An Interpretation and Forecast," *World Tomorrow*, Jan. 1918, 4 (first quote); Blake, *Beloved Community* (second quote); Chatfield, *For Peace and Justice*, 32, 61; Stansell, *American Moderns*, 216–17. Bourne put forward the notion of the beloved community in a 1916 essay reprinted in Bourne, *Radical Will*, 248–64.

9. G. Lumpkin to Kenneth E. Toombs, June 22, 1971, 1 (quote), G. Lumpkin Papers; G. Lumpkin interview, Sept. 25, 1971, 7.

10. Anna Rochester to John Nevin Sayre, May 9, 1924; Anna Rochester to Alice Beal Parsons, May 26, 1923; Anna Rochester to Devere Allen, May 9, 1924; Grace Hutchins to Devere Allen, Christmas Day, [1924] (first and second quotes); [Devere Allen] to Ada Lichtenstein et al., Apr. 21, 1926 (fourth and fifth quotes), all in series C-4, box 2, D. Allen Papers; Ada Lichtenstein et al., "Experiment in Cooperation," 2 (third quote). For these tensions and organizational changes, see J. M. Allen, *Passionate Commitments*, 88–97, 300n4. After leaving her job at *The World Tomorrow*, Alice Beal Parsons wrote a book about professional equality for women.

11. Ada Lichtenstein et al., "Experiment in Cooperation," 2 (first quote); Devere Allen to Grace Hutchins, Mar. 27, 1927 (second quote); [Devere Allen] to Ada Lichtenstein et al., Apr. 21, 1926 (third quote); Anna Rochester to Nevin Sayre, May 9, 1924, all in series C-4, box 2, D. Allen Papers; M. Thompson, *For God and Globe*, 193–97.

12. Notes from interview with Mrs. Esther Chambers on Feb. 10, 1949, in FBI Report, New York, May 11, 1949, Jay David Whittaker Chambers, HQ-65-14920-335, 204–06; Memo on Levine-Shemitz Household of 280 Rochester Ave., Brooklyn, Jan. 8, 1953, in box 38, folder "Esther Shemitz Chambers," all in Tanenhaus Papers; Benjamin Shemitz, New Haven City Directory 1920, in *U.S. City Directories, 1822–1995*, Ancestry.com; "Benjamin Shemitz," in Fourteenth Census of the United States, 1920, Population Schedule, New Haven City Ward 5, CT, ED 335, family 19. Esther's parents, Benjamin and Rose, moved to New Haven in 1910. Benjamin had emmigrated from Russia in 1891, Rose in 1893. Both were naturalized citizens and spoke Russian and English. They owned a candy store at 858 Grand Street; he is listed as a confectioner by trade. From 1912 to 1919, the family lived at 866 Grand Street. Almost all of the families at this address were Russian or Hungarian and many spoke Yiddish. In 1919, Benjamin, Rose, Esther, and her three brothers moved to a rented house at 54 Olive Street. Esther, age 19, had been born in New York on June 25, 1900. In 1919–1920, she was attending school and working as a helper in a candy store. Thanks to Mary Reynolds for help in finding this information.

13. Elinor Ferry, Memo on Grace Hutchins interview, Oct. 20, [1951 or 1952], (first quote), box 45, folder "Grace Hutchins," Tanenhaus Papers; G. Lumpkin, "Kok-I House," 1 (second and fourth quotes); "Dr. Guthrie Seeks Peace in Jersey," *New York Times*, Dec. 15, 1923 (third quote).

14. Rosina A. Florio to Marchia Anne Durop, Nov. 19, 1991 (quote); Lawrence Campbell to Sam Tanenhaus, Feb. 10, 1992, Feb. 20, 1992, and Feb. 21, 1992, all in box 35, folder "Art Students League," Tanenhaus Papers; "Cross-Examination of Mrs. Chambers," box 38, folder "Esther Shemitz Chambers," Tanenhaus Papers; Tanenhaus, *Whittaker Chambers*, 64, 69, 537n54; Steiner, *Art Students League*.

15. Bertha Kosan interview, Nov. 22, 1989 (first and second quotes); Tanenhaus, *Whittaker Chambers*, 64, 65 (third quote); Chambers, *Witness*, 232, 265; Oct. 8, 1952, Memo on interview with A. B. Magil, box 49, folder "A. B. Magil," Tanenhaus Papers; Kunitz and Haycraft, *Twentieth Century Authors*, s.v. "Grace Lumpkin."

16. G. Lumpkin to Dorothy Gary Markey [Myra Page], July 1925, folder 1, Page Papers; C. Baker, *Generous Spirit*, 82; Annette Lumpkin to G. Lumpkin, Apr. 14, 1925, folder 121, KDL Papers; Annette Lumpkin to Sister, Sept. 24, 1924, in J. Hall's possession, thanks to Joseph H. Lumpkin Sr. (hereafter Annette Letters).

17. Rosenberg, *Changing the Subject*, 96; G. Lumpkin, "Novel as Propaganda."

18. Grace Lumpkin interview, Aug. 6, 1974, 9 (first quote); G. Lumpkin, "Kok-I House," 1 (second quote); Annette Lumpkin to G. Lumpkin, Apr. 14, 1925, folder 121, KDL Papers; G. Lumpkin and Shemitz, "Artist in a Hostile Environment"; D. Lewis, *When Harlem Was in Vogue*, 117–18.

19. Tate, "New Provincialism," 545 (quotes).

20. My observations have been influenced by revisionist critiques of the Agrarians' views and by feminist literary scholars such as Anne Goodwyn Jones, Susan Van Donaldson, and Patricia Yaeger who have challenged the gender biases of both the Agrarians and their revisionist critics: Gray, *Writing the South*; Gray, *Literature of Memory*; Hobson, *Tell about the South*; R. King, *Southern Renaissance*; O'Brien, *Idea of the American South*; O'Brien, "Heterodox Note"; Singal, *War Within*; Underwood, *Allen Tate*. I am also drawing on Denning, *Cultural Front*; Hutchinson, *Harlem Renaissance*; Maxwell, *New Negro*. A. Douglas, *Terrible Honesty*, stresses black/white interactions and influences in the 1920s but excludes the left-wing literary movement completely.

21. Annette Lumpkin to Sister, Apr. 17, 1924 (first and second quotes), Annette Letters; "Little Hope for Recovery of Dr. Eugene B. Glenn," *Asheville (NC) Times*, Mar. 30, 1924 (third quote); "No Change in Dr. Glenn's Condition," *Asheville (NC) Times*, Feb. 10, 1922, all in Newspaper Clipping Files, Pack Memorial Library, Asheville, NC; Standard Certificate of Death for Eugene Byron Glenn, North Carolina State Board of Health, Bureau of Vital Statistics, *North Carolina Death Certificates, 1909–1975*, Ancestry.com.

22. Donald, *Look Homeward*, 3, 468; Watkins, *Thomas Wolfe's Characters*, 56 (first and second quotes); Mauldin, "Doctor and His Wife," 35 (third quote); William W. L. Glenn and Amory Potter Glenn interview, July 16, 1995. According to William W. L. Glenn, Wolfe's portrait of his father was "pretty accurate."

23. T. Wolfe, *Of Time and the River*, 226; Thomas Wolfe, "The Death of Stoneman Gant," William B. Wisdom Collection of Thomas Wolfe, Houghton Library, Harvard University. By permission of Houghton Library, Harvard University and Eugene Winick, Administrator C.T.A. Estate of Thomas Wolfe, 17 (first quote), 6 (second quote), 3 (third quote), 7 (fourth quote), 9 (fifth quote). Mauldin, "Doctor and His Wife," 45. Wolfe's mistress was Aline Bernstein, a married woman eighteen years his senior and a well-known stage and costume designer.

24. "Personals," *Asheville (NC) Citizen*, Mar. 28, 1924; Annette Lumpkin to Sister, Apr. 17, 1924 (quotes), Annette Letters. For this well-known Richmond clinic, see the James King Hall Papers, SHC.

25. Elizabeth Lumpkin Glenn to William W. L. Glenn, n.d.; Elizabeth Lumpkin Glenn to William W. L. Glenn, 1930; Elizabeth Lumpkin Glenn to Treasurer of the University of South Carolina, Aug. 7, 1931; William W. L. Glenn to Elizabeth Lumpkin Glenn, July 30, 1934; Elizabeth Lumpkin Glenn to Alva Lumpkin, Aug. 17, 1937; Elizabeth Lumpkin Glenn to William W. L. Glenn, Dec. 6, 1937; note from Amory Glenn attached to Elizabeth Lumpkin Glenn to Ann Dudley Glenn, Eugene Byron Glenn, William Glenn, and Marion Sevier Glenn, May 19, 1939, all in Glenn Letters; "Mrs. Eugene B. Glenn Dies," *Asheville (NC) Citizen*, Feb. 15, 1963; "The Pack Memorial Library," *Asheville (NC) Times*, Apr. 15, 1926; "New Pack Library Superb, Visiting Experts Declare," *Asheville (NC) Citizen*, July 11, 1926; William W. L. Glenn and Amory Potter Glenn interview, July 16, 1995. For the settlement of E. B. Glenn's estate and Elizabeth's move to a new house and complex business dealings, see "In

the matter of the Administration of the Estate of E. B. Glenn," Aug. 30, 1930, Buncombe County Record of Administrator, Book 11, 126; Grantor Index to Deeds, Buncombe County, NC (Mar. 1, 1924–Dec. 31, 1966) Fl-Gn, 78, both in Buncombe County Courthouse; Elizabeth Lumpkin Glenn, "Application for Guardianship," Aug. 30, 1930, Buncombe County Court Records, State Archives of North Carolina, Raleigh, NC; Buncombe County Land Records Department, Asheville, NC.

26. *Who's Who in the South* (Mayflower Publishing, 1927), s.v. "Mrs. Elizabeth Elliott Lumpkin Glenn"; "Guild Play Attracts Crowd," *Asheville (NC) Citizen*, Nov. 30, 1943; "Three Asheville Women Licensed to Practice Law," *Asheville (NC) Citizen*, Jan. 29, 1932; William W. L. Glenn to Elizabeth Lumpkin Glenn, Jan. 27, 1932; Katharine Baird, "Author's Memories in Civil War Book," both in Glenn Letters; "Mrs. Eugene B. Glenn Dies," *Asheville (NC) Citizen*, Feb. 15, 1963; Colin and Roundtree, *Changing Face of Justice*, s.v. "Elizabeth Lumpkin Glenn." Elizabeth became a member of the Buncombe County and North Carolina Bar Associations, practiced in Federal District Court, and was admitted to the U.S. District Court Bar on June 25, 1941. She specialized in legal issues pertaining to women and children. But her practice left little trace.

27. Annette Lumpkin to Sister, Apr. 17, 1924 (quote); Annette Lumpkin to Sister, Sept. 24, 1924 (subsequent quotes), Annette Letters.

28. Annette Lumpkin to Sister, Sept. 24, 1924 (quote), Annette Letters.

29. Annette Lumpkin to G. Lumpkin and Esther Shemitz, Mar. 8, 1925 (first quote); Annette Lumpkin to G. Lumpkin, Apr. 14, 1925 (second, third, and fourth quotes); Annette Lumpkin to G. Lumpkin, Mar. 2, 1925 (fifth quote), all in folder 121, KDL Papers.

30. Annette Lumpkin to G. Lumpkin, Nov. 16, 1924; Annette Lumpkin to KDL, Good Friday, 1925 (first quote), both in folder 2, KDL Papers; Annette Lumpkin to Sister, Sept. 24, 1924 (second quote), Annette Letters; KDL interview, Apr. 24, 1985, 15 (third quote).

31. Annette Lumpkin to KDL, Apr. 2, 1925, folder 2, KDL Papers.

32. G. Lumpkin and Shemitz, "Artist in a Hostile Environment."

33. D. Lewis, *When Harlem Was in Vogue*, 48 (quote); Hutchinson, *Harlem Renaissance*, 7–13, 90–91.

34. Alice Walker quoted in Plant, *Zora Neale Hurston*, 60; D. Lewis, *When Harlem Was in Vogue*, 27, 53; Maxwell, "Proletarian as New Negro," 93, 98, 111.

35. Locke, *Harlem*, 631 (first quote); G. Lumpkin and Shemitz, "Artist in a Hostile Environment," 108–10 (subsequent quotes).

36. Locke, *Harlem*, 659 (first quote); G. Lumpkin and Shemitz, "Artist in a Hostile Environment," 108 (subsequent quotes).

37. Maxwell, *New Negro*, 22; G. Lumpkin and Shemitz, "Artist in a Hostile Environment," 108 (first quote), 109 (third quote), 110 (fourth quote); Hutchinson, *Harlem Renaissance*, 16–17 (second quote on 16). For these conflicts over musical forms, see P. Anderson, *Deep River*, 4–5, 8–9, 200.

38. D. Lewis, *When Harlem Was in Vogue*, 9, 17, 193–94; Henderson, "Portrait of Wallace Thurman," 15, 148–49, 160–61.

39. Devere Allen to Grace Hutchins, Mar. 27, 1927 (quote); Grace Hutchins to Kirby Page and Devere Allen, Mar. 11, 1927; Devere Allen to Grace Hutchins, Mar. 27, 1927; Grace Hutchins to Devere Allen, Apr. 11, 1927, all in series C-4, box 2, D. Allen Papers; D. Lewis, *When Harlem Was in Vogue*, 194; Henderson, "Portrait of Wallace Thurman," 153–54.

40. Ada Lichtenstein et al., "Experiment in Cooperation," 2 (first quote); Devere Allen to Grace Hutchins, Mar. 27, 1927 (second quote); Grace Hutchins to Kirby Page and Devere Allen, Mar. 11, 1927 (subsequent quotes); Grace Hutchins to Devere Allen, Apr. 11, 1927, all in series C-4, box 2, D. Allen Papers; J. Lee, *Comrades and Partners*, 121–48; Henderson, "Portrait of Wallace Thurman," 153–54.

41. Schuyler, "Negro-Art Hokum," 52 (first quote); Hughes, "Negro Artist," 27–30 (subsequent quotes on 28 and 29); Rampersad, *Life of Langston Hughes*, 130. Thanks to Douglas Flamming for sharing his insights into these debates.

42. Thurman, "Negro Artists," 37–39 (first quote on 37; second quote on 38); Thurman "Nephews of Uncle Remus."

43. A. Douglas, *Terrible Honesty*, 86.

44. G. Lumpkin and Shemitz, "Artist in a Hostile Environment," 109 (first and second quotes); "Who's Who in This Issue," *World Tomorrow*, Apr. 1926, 106 (third quote).

45. Garrison, *Mary Heaton Vorse*, 148.

46. The following account of the strike is based primarily on M. Siegel, "Passaic Strike."

47. M. Siegel, "Passaic Strike," 155–59, 234–36. See also Weisbord, *Radical Life*, 120.

48. Vorse, "Passaic Textile Strike," 24–25, 97–98; Garrison, *Mary Heaton Vorse*, 197–200; M. Siegel, "Passaic Strike," 180–90.

49. Chambers, *Witness*, 231–32 (first quote); U.S. District Court, Maryland, Civil No. 4176, Alger Hiss (Plaintiff) v. Whittaker Chambers (Defendant), deposition of Esther Chambers, Nov. 16, 1948, 470; "Cross-Examination of Mrs. Chambers," both in box 38, folder "Esther Shemitz Chambers," Tanenhaus Papers; Tanenhaus, *Whittaker Chambers*, 71 (second quote).

50. Vorse, "Passaic Textile Strike," 97–98 (quote on 98).

51. G. Lumpkin, "God Save the State!" 11 (quote).

52. Aaron, *Writers on the Left*, 100 (first quote), 111 (second quote); "Introducing an Epic," *New Masses*, June 1926, 8 (second quote).

53. G. Lumpkin, "God Save the State!" 11 (quotes). See also M. Tucker, "Read the Riot Act!"; M. Siegel, "Passaic Strike," 205–10.

54. M. Siegel, "Passaic Strike," 178; G. Lumpkin, "Kok-I House," 3; Garrison, *Mary Heaton Vorse*, 229.

55. Haessly, "Mill Mother's Lament," 146; M. Larkin, *Singing Cowboy*; Mary Heaton Vorse, "Strike Journal, Gastonia," 20 (quotes), box 155, Mary Heaton Vorse Papers, Walter P. Reuther Library, Wayne State University, Detroit, MI. For proletarian regionalism, see Botkin, "Regionalism and Culture."

56. Vorse, *Passaic Textile Strike*, 100 (first quote), 77 (second quote).

57. Dos Passos, "300 N.Y. Agitators"; N. Thomas, "Lessons of Passaic," 11 (quote).

58. Katharine Larkin quoted in Haessly, "Mill Mother's Lament," 147; G. Lumpkin, "God Save the State!" 11 (second quote).

CHAPTER TEN: "KOK-I HOUSE"

1. Sinclair, *Boston*, 632–33 (quote on 633).
2. "Committee Wants Radicals Here for Death Watch," *Boston Evening Transcript*, Aug. 8, 1927 (quotes); "100 Sympathizers on Way from New York," *Boston Evening Transcript*, Aug. 20, 1927.
3. Sacco was a shoeworker, which is quite different from a "shoemaker." Vanzetti was a fish peddler for less than a year, during a period in which he was trying to launch an anarchist journal: D'Attilio, "La Salute è in Voi," 77 (quote), 82–83, 87; Zinn, introduction to *Boston*, xii–xiii; D'Attilio, "Sacco-Vanzetti Case"; Avrich, "Italian Anarchism," 65.
4. D'Attilio, "La Salute è in Voi," 80; D'Attilio, "Sacco-Vanzetti Case," 667; Preston, *Aliens and Dissenters*.
5. D'Attilio, "Sacco-Vanzetti Case," 669 (first quote); International Labor Defense, *Labor Defense*, 10 (second quote); C. Martin, "International Labor Defense and Black America," 167–68. From 1921 until the middle of 1929, the Workers Party of America was the name of the legal political party organization. The underground Communist Party, with overlapping membership, conducted political agitation despite government repression. By 1923, the aboveground party was seeking to engage the Socialist Party of America in united front actions, but was rebuffed. At the group's 1925 convention, the Workers Party of America renamed itself the Workers (Communist) Party, and in 1929 the Communist Party, USA. For simplicity, I will use the terms Communist Party, the party, or CP throughout.
6. Joughin and E. Morgan, *Sacco and Vanzetti*, 241.
7. Zinn, introduction to *Boston*, xv–xvii; D'Attilio, "La Salute è in Voi," 80, 87–88.
8. Porter, *Never-Ending Wrong*, 24–28 (first quote on 24, second and third quotes on 28); "Police Take 156 of 'Death Watch,'" *Boston Globe*, Aug. 23, 1927; "Police Take 107 Pickets in State House 'Parade,'" *Boston Evening Transcript*, Aug. 22, 1927; Holladay, "I Paraded." For other evidence of Grace and Esther Shemitz's participation, see "Cross-Examination of Mrs. Chambers," both in box 38, folder "Esther Shemitz Chambers," Tanenhaus Papers; G. Lumpkin interview, Sept. 25, 1971, 13–14; G. Lumpkin, interview, Aug. 6, 1974, 9–10.
9. Porter, *Never-Ending Wrong*, 23–41 (quotes on 33).
10. Grace Lumpkin to Esther T. Shemitz, n.d., folder 2.12, series 2: Sacco and Vanzetti Case Correspondence, 1921–1930, Frances Russell Collection, 1921–1965, Brandeis University Archives.
11. Porter, *Never-Ending Wrong*, 45–46; Epstein, *What Lips My Lips Have Kissed*, 196–98.
12. Porter, *Never-Ending Wrong*, 42 (quote); "Prison Is Guarded by Veritable Army," *Boston Globe*, Aug. 23, 1927; Felix, *Protest*, 225, 228–29, 232.
13. Porter, *Never-Ending Wrong*, 43 (first quote), 44 (subsequent quotes).

14. Porter, *Never-Ending Wrong*, 48 (quotes); Felix, *Protest*, 235.

15. Sacco and Vanzetti to Dante Sacco, Aug. 21, 1927, in Frankfurter and Jackson, *Letters of Sacco and Vanzetti*, 325 (first quote); Joughin and E. Morgan, *Sacco and Vanzetti*, 511 (second quote); Porter, *Never-Ending Wrong*, 9 (third quote).

16. Edmund Wilson quoted in Denning, *Cultural Front*, 163.

17. Porter, *Never-Ending Wrong*; Edmund Wilson quoted in D'Attilio, "Sacco-Vanzetti Case," 670.

18. J. Lee, *Comrades and Partners*, 137–48; Rochester, "World Communism"; Felix, *Protest*, 203–5.

19. Hutchins, *Labor and Silk*; Hutchins, *Women Who Work*; J. Lee, *Comrades and Partners*, 167–76. For Grace Hutchins's importance as the "principal writer on wage-earning women for the CPUSA," see also R. Shaffer, "Women and the Communist Party," 81–93.

20. Notes from interview with Mrs. Esther Chambers on Feb. 10, 1949, in FBI Report, New York, May 11, 1949, Jay David Whittaker Chambers, HQ-65-14920-335, 206, G. Lumpkin FBI File; Kunitz and Haycraft, *Twentieth Century Authors*, s.v. "Grace Lumpkin" (quote).

21. G. Lumpkin, "Treasure," 168 (first quote); G. Lumpkin to Amory Potter Glenn, Dec. 6, 1967 (second quote), in J. Hall's possession, thanks to Amory Potter and William W. L. Glenn.

22. G. Lumpkin, "White Man"; Barry, *Rising Tide*, 285–86, 293–335, 416–17; Percy, *Lanterns on the Levee*, 269 (quote).

23. G. Lumpkin, "White Man," 7–8 (quotes on 7).

24. G. Lumpkin, "White Man," 8 (quote).

25. Spillers, "Mama's Baby," 67 (quote).

26. Yaeger, *Dirt and Desire*, 13–22 (first quote on 13, second quote on 15).

27. G. Lumpkin, "The White Road," *Bubbles*, 1912 (first quote), BUTL; Yaeger, *Dirt and Desire*, xv (second quote).

28. G. Lumpkin and Shemitz, "Artist in a Hostile Environment," 108 (quote).

29. Camacho, "Whites Playing in the Dark," 71–72.

30. Locke, *New Negro*, 3 (quote).

31. Printz, "Tracing the Fault Lines," 173.

32. Yaeger, *Dirt and Desire*, 31 (quote).

33. G. Lumpkin interview, Aug. 6, 1974, 9 (first quote); G. Lumpkin, "Kok-I House," 1966, 1 (second quote), G. Lumpkin Papers; G. Lumpkin, "Remember Now: A Play in Three Acts and Nine Scenes," 1951, iv, G. Lumpkin Papers (hereafter G. Lumpkin, "Remember Now"); Chambers, *Witness*, 265, 267.

34. Chambers, *Witness*, 265 (quotes); Bertha Kosan interview, Nov. 22, 1989.

35. G. Lumpkin, "Kok-I House," 1966, 1–3, 5 (quote on 3); G. Lumpkin, "Remember Now," iv, v, both in G. Lumpkin Papers; Buckley, *Odyssey of a Friend*, 180.

36. M. Josephson, *Infidel in the Temple*, 126 (quote); G. Lumpkin interview, Aug. 6, 1974, 10; G. Lumpkin interview, Sept. 25, 1971, 7.

37. G. Lumpkin to Toombs, June 22, 1971, G. Lumpkin Papers; G. Lumpkin interview, Aug. 6, 1974, 10 (first and third quotes); G. Lumpkin interview, Sept. 25, 1971, 7 (second quote).

38. U.S. District Court, Maryland, Civil No. 4176, Alger Hiss (Plaintiff) v. Whittaker Chambers (Defendant), deposition of Esther Chambers, Nov. 16, 1948, 470; "Cross-Examination of Mrs. Chambers," both in box 38, folder "Esther Shemitz Chambers," Tanenhaus Papers; FBI Report by SA Thomas G. Spencer, New York, May 11, 1949, "Jay David Whittaker Chambers," NY-65-14920-3357, 22, 206, G. Lumpkin FBI File; Tanenhaus, *Whittaker Chambers*, 65; Buckley, *Odyssey of a Friend*, 182.

39. Howard Zinn, "Sender Garlin," *HowardZinn.Org*, ZCommunications, Mar. 9, 2000, http://howardzinn.org/sender-garlin/. For Burck, see Burck, *Hunger and Revolt*; Hemingway, *Artists on the Left*, 31–34; G. Lumpkin interview, Aug. 6, 1974, 10–11; Nelson, *Repression and Recovery*, 319n256; Tanenhaus, *Whittaker Chambers*, 59. For O'Malley, see Halper, *Good-bye, Union Square*, 112, 114 (quote).

40. Tanenhaus, *Whittaker Chambers*, 63, 59 (quote).

41. Chambers, *Witness*, 229–30 (first quote); Buckley, *Odyssey of a Friend*, 180 (second quote); FBI Report by SA Robert F. X. O'Keefe, New York, Apr. 6, 1949, "Background and Personal History of Whittaker Chambers," NY-65-14920, 33, G. Lumpkin FBI File (hereafter FBI Report by SA Robert F. X. O'Keefe); G. Lumpkin interview, Aug. 6, 1974, 10–11.

42. G. Lumpkin interview, Aug. 6, 1974, 11.

43. For this ideal, see Stansell, *American Moderns*, 7, 253–54.

44. For the role of such gathering places and the social bonds they fostered, see K. Brown and Faue, "Social Bonds, Sexual Politics"; K. Brown and Faue, "Revolutionary Desire"; Langer, *Josephine Herbst*, 54.

45. Annette Lumpkin to G. Lumpkin and Esther Shemitz, Mar. 8, 1925 (first quote), folder 121; Annette Lumpkin to KDL, Good Friday, 1925 (second quote), folder 2, both in KDL Papers.

46. G. Lumpkin, "Kok-I House," 1966, 5 (quote); G. Lumpkin, "Remember Now," 1, 18, both in G. Lumpkin Papers. For other descriptions of Intrator, see Evelyn Scott to G. Lumpkin, [ca. 1940], G. Lumpkin Papers; G. Lumpkin interview, Aug. 6, 1974, 17, 19, 47–49; FBI Report by SA Robert F. X. O'Keefe, 40; Buckley, *Odyssey of a Friend*, 180–81; Chambers, *Witness*, 180–82, 229–30; Bertha Kosan interview, Nov. 22, 1989; Sophie Gerson interview, Aug. 30, 1996; Lil Intrator interview, Dec. 18, 1993; Roland Intrator interview, n.d. [early 1990s]; Carl Padover interview, Feb. 16, 2003.

47. Death Certificate for Michael Intrator, Feb. 25, 1954, file no. 3673, Florida Department of Health and Rehabilitative Services, Bureau of Vital Statistics, Jacksonville, FL (certified copy in J. Hall's possession); Certificate and Record of Marriage, Michael Intrator to G. Lumpkin, May 4, 1932, certificate no. 9313, Borough of Manhattan, City of New York, New York City Municipal Archives, Department of Records and Information Services, New York (copy in J. Hall's possession); "Nathan Intrater [*sic*]," in Fourteenth Census of the United States, 1920, Population Schedule, Borough of Manhattan, New York, 6th Assembly District, ED 463, p. 2A, family 27; "Nathan Intrator," State Population Census Schedules, 1925, Brooklyn, New York, Kings County, Election District 56, Assembly District 22, p. 47; "Nathan Intrator," in Fifteenth Census of the

United States, 1930, Population Schedule, Manhattan, New York, 6th Assembly District, ED 162, p. 1A, family 7; Schoenfeld, *Jewish Life in Galicia*. See also GENi.com, Michael Intrator and immediate family, updated Aug. 29, 2015, https://www.geni.com/people/Michael-Intrator/6000000015277607208. Intrator's mother's maiden name was Anna Freund, and his siblings included Sam, Benjamin, Jennie, Joseph, and Charles. Michael did not become a naturalized citizen until Dec. 11, 1939.

48. The following portrait of life in Brownsville is drawn from Kazin, *Walker in the City*, 8–17, 58–59, 67–70, 91, 99, 140–46 (quote on 12); Pritchett, *Brownsville, Brooklyn*, 2, 10, 15–16, 25, 35–36; Sorin, *Nurturing Neighborhood*.

49. This account of Michael's youth draws on Sophie Gerson interview, Aug. 30, 1996; Lil Intrator interview, Dec. 18, 1993; Carl Padover interview, Feb. 16, 2003; Carl Padover to J. Hall, n.d. [2000]; B. Wolfe, *Life in Two Centuries*, 404.

50. Howe, *World of Our Fathers*, 339 (quote).

51. Chambers, *Witness*, 229 (quote).

52. This account of the union's history is based on Bernstein, *Lean Years*, 139; Cochran, *Labor and Communism*, 41–42; P. Foner, *Fur and Leather Workers Union*; Georgakas, "Fur and Leather Workers"; David Schneider, *Workers' (Communist) Party*, 72–86.

53. Gettleman, "Workers Schools," 854; Gettleman, "Lost World"; The Workers School, Spring Program, 1925; Announcement of Courses, 1926–1927; Announcement of Courses, 1927–1928, all in box 66, folder "Bertram Wolfe," Tanenhaus Papers.

54. B. Wolfe, *Life in Two Centuries*, 403–4 (first quote on 404, second and third quotes on 403); Tanenhaus, *Whittaker Chambers*, 57–59, 234, 535n17; Chambers, *Witness*, 234–35; FBI Report by SA Robert F. X. O'Keefe. Accounts of this incident differ. Wolfe recalled that Intrator, Garlin, and Chambers asked together about where they could hone their writing skills and work for the party, but other records indicate that Chambers predated Intrator and Garlin at the *Daily Worker*; Chambers, *Witness*, 196–97, 217.

55. Garrison, *Mary Heaton Vorse*, 136 (quote), 183–84, 316–18.

56. Chambers, *Witness*, 217–31; "Memo on interview with A. B. Magil of Oct. 7," Oct. 8, 1952, box 49, folder "Magil," Tanenhaus Papers; G. Lumpkin interview, Aug. 6, 1974, 11; Masthead, *National Textile Worker*, Apr.–May 1929.

57. Barrett, *William Z. Foster*, 155–56, argues that this conflict involved issues that were not limited to the particular politics of the moment or to Jay Lovestone's position. See also Gilmore, *Defying Dixie*, 69–70, 78–79, 84–86; T. Morgan, *Covert Life*.

58. FBI Report by SA Robert F. X. O'Keefe, 40 (quote); "Our New National Council," *Revolutionary Age*, Nov. 1, 1929; "Fur Council Elects Officers," *Workers Age*, May 18, 1935; M. Intrator, "Furriers Fight," 5, 7. *Revolutionary Age* morphed into *Workers Age* in 1932. For two very different views of these tangled conflicts, see P. Foner, *Fur and Leather Workers Union*, 323, 343–44, 359, 371; Alexander, *Right Opposition*.

59. Chambers, *Witness*, 230, 265, 288; Tanenhaus, *Whittaker Chambers*, 67.

60. Halper, *Good-bye, Union Square*, 113; G. Lumpkin interview, Sept. 25, 1971.

61. Tanenhaus, *Whittaker Chambers*, 3, 5–7, 22 (quote), 23.

62. Tanenhaus, *Whittaker Chambers*, 57, 59.

63. Tanenhaus, *Whittaker Chambers*, 38–39, 45–46, 62–66, 536n43; G. Lumpkin interview, Aug. 6, 1974, 27.

64. G. Lumpkin, "Southern Cotton Mill Rhyme," 8.

65. Letter, New York to Director, FBI, Feb. 18, 1949, "Re: Jay David Whittaker Chambers," HQ-74-1333-2152, G. Lumpkin FBI File; Hutchins, *Labor and Silk*.

66. Chambers, *Witness*, 266–67; Oppenheimer, *Exit Right*, 47–48 (quote on 47); "Whittaker Chambers," Fifteenth Census of the United States, 1930, Population Schedule, Lynbrook, Nassau, New York, ED 58, p. 8B; Letter, New York to Director, FBI, Feb. 18, 1949, "Re: Jay David Whittaker Chambers," HQ-74-1333-2152, G. Lumpkin FBI File.

67. Tanenhaus, *Whittaker Chambers*, 61–66; FBI Report by SA Robert F. X. O'Keefe, 29–34 (quote); Letter, New York to Director, FBI, Feb. 18, 1949, "Re: Jay David Whittaker Chambers," HQ-74-1333-2152, G. Lumpkin FBI File.

68. G. Lumpkin interview, Aug. 6, 1974, 26 (quote), 27; G. Lumpkin, "Remember Now," 5; Letter, New York to Director, FBI, Feb. 18, 1949, "Re: Jay David Whittaker Chambers," HQ-74-1333-2152, G. Lumpkin FBI File.

69. Weinstein, *Perjury*, 110 (first quote); Oct. 8, 1952, Memo on interview with A. B. Magil (second and third quotes), box 49, folder "A. B. Magil"; "Memorandum of Conference with Sender Garlin," Feb. 8, 1949, box 42, folder "Sender Garlin," both in Tanenhaus Papers; Sender Garlin to J. Hall, Jan. 12, 1994; Carl Padover interview, Feb. 16, 2003.

70. Langer, *Josephine Herbst*, 213 (quote); Stansell, *American Moderns*, 273–308.

71. K. Brown and Faue, "Revolutionary Desire," 287–94; Chauncey, *Gay New York*, 227–44.

72. Tanenhaus, *Whittaker Chambers*, 342–45; G. Lumpkin to Myra Page, July 1925 (quote), Page Papers.

73. Edward C. McLean, "Interview with Grace Lumpkin on Jan. 5, 1949," 5 (first quote), box 48, folder "G. Lumpkin," Tanenhaus Papers; Interviews with G. Lumpkin, Mar. 16, 18, 23, 1949, summarized in FBI Report by Robert F. X. O'Keefe, Apr. 6, 1949, Jay David Whittaker Chambers, NY 65-14920-3130, 52 (second quote), G. Lumpkin FBI File; Tanenhaus, *Whittaker Chambers*, 342–43.

74. Chambers, *Witness*, 265 (first quote); Tanenhaus, *Whittaker Chambers*, 65 (second quote). For speculations regarding Intrator's unfaithfulness, see also Myra Page interview, Apr. 25, 1988; Myra Page interview, June 8, 1987.

75. Tanenhaus, *Whittaker Chambers*, 59 (quote).

76. John H. Lumpkin Sr. interview, Aug. 17, 1990, (quotes); John H. Lumpkin Sr. interview, July 29, 1995; *National Cyclopedia of American Biography*, s.v. "Alva Moore Lumpkin"; Alva M. Lumpkin Jr. interview, Aug. 4, 1995; Alva M. Lumpkin Jr. interview, Aug. 17, 1990; G. Lumpkin, "Remember Now," 14.

77. John H. Lumpkin Sr. interview, Aug. 17, 1990 (quotes); John H. Lumpkin Sr. interview, July 29, 1995.

78. G. Lumpkin, "Remember Now," 9–10 (quotes).

79. G. Lumpkin, "Remember Now," 3–4, 7–8, 10–11 (quotes on 4).
80. Evelyn Scott to G. Lumpkin, Nov. 24, 1940 (quotes), G. Lumpkin Papers.
81. KDL, *Making*, 236 (quote).
82. Du Pre, *Timid Woman.*
83. Du Pre, *Some Take a Lover*, 14 (quote), 22.
84. Du Pre, *Some Take a Lover*, 34, 30, 38 (first quote), 67 (second quote), 48 (third quote).
85. Du Pre, *Some Take a Lover*, 23–25 (quotes), 125.
86. Du Pre, *Some Take a Lover*, 25 (quote).
87. Du Pre, *Some Take a Lover*, 251–53 (quote on 253).
88. G. Lumpkin, "White Man," 8 (quote).
89. G. Lumpkin, "The Will," n.d. (early 1930s), G. Lumpkin Papers.
90. Du Pre, *Some Take a Lover*, 32 (quote).
91. Trimberger, "Feminism, Men, and Modern Love"; Stansell, *American Moderns.*
92. Mickenberg, "Suffragists and Soviets," 1024, 1045.
93. Mickenberg, "Suffragists and Soviets," 1044 (first and second quotes), 1049 (third quote); Delegard, *Battling Miss Bolsheviki*; Dilling, *Red Network*, 27–28; K. Brown and Faue, "Revolutionary Desire," 274; K. Brown and Faue, "Social Bonds, Sexual Politics," 34–35.
94. Trimberger, "Feminism, Men, and Modern Love."
95. "'Civilized' Marriage," *New York Times Book Review*, Mar. 5, 1933, 13 (first quote); "Some Take a Lover," *New York Herald Tribune Books*, Jan. 15, 1933, 8 (second quote).
96. Certificate and Record of Marriage of Michael Intrator and Grace Lumpkin, May 4, 1932, New York City Municipal Archives, Department of Records and Information Services, New York; G. Lumpkin interview, Sept. 25, 1971, 11; Personals, *Asheville (NC) Citizen*, Mar. 1, 1930, Nov. 15, 1933, July 11, 1937.
97. "Memo on Levine-Shemitz Household of 280 Rochester Ave., Brooklyn," Jan. 8, 1953 (quote), box 38, Tanenhaus Papers.

CHAPTER ELEVEN: "THE HEART OF THE STRUGGLE"

1. S. Cook, *Tobacco Road*, 86 (quote).
2. Louise Leonard, "A Worker's School and Organized Labor," reprint from *American Teacher*, [1929], 10–11 (first quote), Mary Cornelia Barker Papers, Stuart A. Rose Manuscript, Archives, and Rare Book Library, Emory University, Atlanta, GA; Louise Leonard to Robert Dunn, Aug. 8, 1929 (second quote), in American Fund for Public Service Records, Manuscript and Archives Division, New York Public Library, microfilm edition, roll 20, box 29, folder 6; Eleanor Copenhaver, "Biennial Report for 1928 and 1929," Jan. 19, 1930, YWCA Records.
3. M. Gold, "Go Left, Young Writers!" 3–4 (quotes). For an excellent survey of the "proletarian moment," which extends its influence both backward and forward, see Mullen, "Proletarian Literature."
4. G. Lumpkin, *To Make My Bread*; Burke, *Stone Came Rolling*; M. Page, *Gathering Storm.* This trio of Southerners was joined by three other writers who also found

the strike inspiring: the veteran labor journalist Mary Heaton Vorse; Sherwood Anderson, an expatriate Northerner who was drawn to writing about southern workers by Eleanor Copenhaver, head of the YWCA's industrial programs in the South, with whom he was having an affair and whom he would later marry; and William Rollins Jr., who transferred the action from Gastonia to a more familiar site of labor conflict, an immigrant community in a New England textile town.

5. Schachner, "Revolutionary Literature," 60 (quotes).

6. This description of the textile industry in the South is drawn from J. Hall et al., *Like a Family*.

7. Weller, *Yesterday's People* (first quote); E. Dawson, "Gastonia," 3 (second quote); S. Cook, *Tobacco Road*; J. Hall et al., *Like a Family*, 44–113; Inscoe, "Appalachian Otherness," 185–86; B. Roberts and N. Roberts, *Where Time Stood Still*; H. Shapiro, *Appalachia on Our Mind*; D. Whisnant, *All That Is Native and Fine*, 183–85, 250–52.

8. R. Flanagan, "Southern Peasantry," 561 (quote).

9. Gregory, *Southern Diaspora*, 43–65; "Diary of Mrs. T. M. Bryan While on a Trip with her Husband in 1890," 101 (quote). Thanks to Thomas Bryan, descendent of Sarah Frances Morris Bryan, for sharing this diary with me.

10. J. Hall et al., *Like a Family*, 212–36; Bernstein, *Lean Years*, 2–43.

11. Haessly, "Mill Mother's Lament"; Salmond, *Gastonia, 1929*, 51, 128. For similar forms of female consciousness, see T. Kaplan, *Crazy for Democracy*.

12. This discussion of Ella May is drawn from J. Hall et al., *Like a Family*, 226–29 (quote on 226–27).

13. Si Gerson, "Our Work in the South," *Daily Worker*, Jun. 10, 1930 (quote); R. Kelley, *Hammer and Hoe*, 38–52.

14. "Resolution of the Communist International on the Negro Question," Oct. 26, 1928, quoted in Sowinska, "Writing across the Color Line," 121–22; Gilmore, *Defying Dixie*, 29–66; M. Solomon, *Cry Was Unity*, 68–91.

15. J. Hall et al., *Like a Family*, 183–212, 219 (quote).

16. E. Dawson, "Gastonia," 3 (quote).

17. Mary Heaton Vorse, unpublished mss account of her first visit to Gastonia, 5, box 155, Mary Heaton Vorse Papers, Walter P. Reuther Library, Wayne State University, Detroit, MI; C. Baker, *Generous Spirit*, 119; Si Gerson, "Our Work in the South," *Daily Worker*, Jun. 10, 1930. This account of the strike is drawn primarily from E. Dawson, "Gastonia"; J. Hall et al., *Like a Family*, 214–15, 220, 221, 225, 226–29, 233, 235; Gilmore, *Defying Dixie*, 67–105; Salmond, *Gastonia 1929*.

18. Salmond, *Gastonia 1929*, 26 (quote).

19. Gilmore, *Defying Dixie*, 78–89, 93–95; Cora Harris quoted in Salmond, *Gastonia 1929*, 31.

20. Salmond, *Gastonia 1929*, 68; G. Lumpkin, *To Make My Bread*, 185–87.

21. Denning, *Cultural Front*, 13; Salmond, *Gastonia 1929*, 29.

22. Quoted in Gilmore, *Defying Dixie*, 94.

23. Salmond, *Gastonia 1929*, 165 (quotes); Gilmore, *Defying Dixie*, 103–4.

24. Woodward, "Southern Exposure," 31 (quote).

25. C. Baker, *Generous Spirit*, 161; M. Page, *Southern Cotton Mills.*

26. Jack Herling quoted in Frederickson, "A Place to Speak Our Minds," 100.

27. Eleanor Copenhaver, "Biennial Report for 1928 and 1929," Jan. 19, 1930, 1, 3–4 (quotes), YWCA Records; Eleanor Copenhaver Anderson interview, Nov. 5, 1974, 8.

28. Leonard, "School in the Old South," 22 (quote); Frederickson, "A Place to Speak Our Minds," 99–100.

29. Betty "can't be more than 20," Katharine exclaimed, and yet with her at the helm there was nothing the southern student council could not tackle: KDL to Leslie Blanchard, Oct. 17, 1923, KDL Papers; Betty Webb was "a remarkable person," Frances Williams recalled. She was "bright enough to teach herself; she didn't need any teacher": Frances Williams interview, Nov. 14, 1981, tape 1, side A, 012-037; Frances H. Williams interview, Oct. 31–Nov. 1, 1977.

30. Betty Webb quoted in Browder, "Uplift to Agitation," 177n342. For this convention, see "Students Halt Y. W. C. A. Harmony," *New York Times*, May 5, 1924; J. P. Holmes, "Youth Cannot Wait," 128–31.

31. Roy Veatch, "Enclosure C," June 1927 (quotes); Roy Veatch to Robert Brookings Graduate School, May 5, 1927, both in Students and Fellows Records 1924–1937, Brookings Institution Archives, Robert Brookings Graduate School, Washington, DC. See also Betty Webb, Application form and Enclosure C, Students and Fellows Records 1924–1937, Brookings Institution Archives, Robert Brookings Graduate School, Washington, DC.

32. Ruth to Mary Heaton Vorse, n.d. (quotes), Mary Heaton Vorse Papers, Walter P. Reuther Library, Wayne State University, Detroit, MI; Webb, "Textile Industry in North Carolina." Note that in 1927, the Institute of Economics and the graduate school merged to form the present-day Brookings Institution. Webb was hired by the ACLU at the suggestion of Mary Heaton Vorse, a labor journalist who spent a month in Gastonia, wrote about the strike for *Harper's Magazine*, and published *Strike!*, a novel inspired by the conflict: Garrison, *Mary Heaton Vorse*, ix–xi, 213–20.

33. Personals, *Asheville (NC) Citizen*, Mar. 1, 1930; G. Lumpkin, "Southern Cotton Mill Rhyme," 8; G. Lumpkin, "Cotton Mill Rhyme," 22; Agreement between G. Lumpkin and the Macaulay Company, Oct. 5, 1931, G. Lumpkin Papers; G. Lumpkin, "Why I as a White Southern Woman Will Vote Communist," *Daily Worker*, Aug. 12, 1932.

34. Aaron, *Writers on the Left*, 173.

35. Frost, *Contemporary Ancestors* (quote).

36. G. Lumpkin, "Southern Cotton Mill Rhyme," 8 (first quote); G. Lumpkin, "Cotton Mill Rhyme," 22; M. Larkin, "Ella May's Songs," 383 (second quote).

37. G. Lumpkin, "Southern Cotton Mill Rhyme," 8 (quote).

38. G. Lumpkin, "Cotton Mill Rhyme," 22 (quotes).

39. G. Lumpkin, "Cotton Mill Rhyme," 22 (quote).

40. A. Green, "Southern Cotton Mill Rhyme," 288 (first quote), 313 (second quote), 314 (third quote).

41. G. Lumpkin, "Southern Cotton Mill Rhyme," 8 (quotes). On Eva Davis, see

Bufwack and Oermann, *Finding Her Voice*, 73; G. Meade, Spottswood, and D. Meade, *Country Music Sources*, 63.

42. R. Reuss and J. Reuss, *American Folk Music*, 53.

43. Hans Eisler quoted in Cantwell, *When We Were Good*, 91–93 (quote on 93); R. Reuss and J. Reuss, *American Folk Music*, 268–70.

44. Garabedian, "Reds, Whites, and the Blues," 189 (quote).

45. Margaret Larkin quoted in R. Reuss and J. Reuss, *American Folk Music*, 70–72 (quotes on 71). Reuss and Reuss observe that "this was perhaps the boldest statement supporting folk song tradition in topical labor music to appear in an important communist cultural publication since Elizabeth Gurley Flynn wrote about Joe Hill's songs in *Solidarity* in 1915." See also Lieberman, *"My Song Is My Weapon,"* 30–39.

46. Garabedian, "Reds, Whites, and the Blues," 181 (quote); Lawrence Gellert's series, "Negro Songs of Protest," appeared in the *New Masses*, Nov. 1930, Jan. 1931, Apr. 1931, May 1932, and May 1933. See also Frank, "Negro Revolutionary Music"; Naison, *Communists in Harlem*, 211–13, 299–301.

47. P. Anderson, *Deep River*, 9 (quote).

48. R. Reuss and J. Reuss, *American Folk Music*, 105, 110; R. Kelley, *Hammer and Hoe*, 105, 149–51; McCallum, "Songs of Work."

49. S. Davis, "Ben Botkin's FBI File," 4 (quote).

50. Denning, *Cultural Front*, 259–72.

51. Kephart, *Our Southern Highlanders*; B. Roberts and N. Roberts, *Where Time Stood Still* (quote).

52. Abel, M. Hirsch, and Langland, *Voyage In* (quote).

53. Gray, *Southern Aberrations*, 312 (quotes).

54. Gray, *Southern Aberrations*, 313 (quote).

55. S. Cook, "Proletarian Novel," 687 (quote).

56. G. Lumpkin, "Novel as Propaganda," 1–2 (quote).

57. A. Whisnant, *Super-Scenic Motorway*, 54 (quote). The Glenn family, which went back generations in the mountains of North Carolina, made its fortune by investing in talc mines and real estate.

58. G. Lumpkin, *To Make My Bread*, 10 (quote).

59. G. Lumpkin, *To Make My Bread*, 140 (quote).

60. For recent work on the ethic of care, see Oksala, "Affective Labor"; N. Fraser, "Capital and Care"; Wilkerson, *Have to Fight*.

61. Z. Simon, *Double-Edged Sword*, 52 (quote).

62. G. Lumpkin, *To Make My Bread*, 219 (first quote), 212 (second and third quotes), 219 (fourth quote).

63. G. Lumpkin, *To Make My Bread*, 225 (quote).

64. G. Lumpkin, *To Make My Bread*, 73 (first quote), 157 (second quote).

65. Gray, *Southern Aberrations*, 312–19.

66. Gray, *Southern Aberrations*, 312 (quote).

67. G. Lumpkin, *To Make My Bread*, 276 (quote).

68. G. Lumpkin, *To Make My Bread*, 227 (first quote), 283 (second and third quotes), 319 (fourth quote).

69. Magil, "To Make My Bread," 20 (quote).
70. G. Lumpkin, *To Make My Bread*, 335 (first and second quotes), 343 (third quote).
71. Sowinska, "Writing across the Color Line."
72. G. Lumpkin, *To Make My Bread*, 350 (quote).
73. Sowinska, "Writing across the Color Line," 125, 133.
74. G. Lumpkin, *To Make My Bread*, 76 (quote); Chodorow, *Reproduction of Mothering*.
75. G. Lumpkin, *To Make My Bread*, 186 (first quote), 187 (second quote).
76. G. Lumpkin, *To Make My Bread*, 191 (quote).
77. G. Lumpkin, "To Make My Bread," Dec. 1933, Jan. 1934, Feb. 1934.
78. G. Lumpkin, "John Stevens."
79. Maxwell, *New Negro*, 129 (quote).
80. Key works in this recovery include Nekola and P. Rabinowitz, *Writing Red*; P. Rabinowitz, *Labor and Desire*; Coiner, *Better Red*. For such readings of *To Make My Bread*, see Foley, "Women and the Left," 155; Foley, *Radical Representations*, 229, 232–33. For the literary scholarship on Grace's novels more generally, see Sowinska, introduction to *To Make My Bread* by G. Lumpkin; Sowinska, "Writing across the Color Line"; Wells, "Anxiety and Orange Blossoms"; Mantooth, *"You Factory Folks"*; Lane, "Silenced Cry"; Miller, *Remembering Scottsboro*, 118–26; J. A. Williams, *Twentieth-Century Sentimentalism*.
81. "A Novel of the Southern Mills," *New York Times*, Sept. 25, 1932; Foley, *Radical Representations*, 10.
82. Gruening, "Vanishing Individual," 322 (first quote); Magil, "To Make My Bread," 19–20 (second quote); "A Novel of the Southern Mills," *New York Times*, Sept. 25, 1932 (third quote).
83. V. J. Jerome, "A Contribution to the American Proletarian Novel," *Daily Worker*, Jan. 3, 1933 (first and third quotes); Gray, *Southern Aberrations*, 313 (second quote). A prolific writer, Jerome became cultural commissar of the Communist Party in the mid–1930s. In the 1950s, he was prosecuted under the Smith Act on the grounds of having published a supposedly subversive pamphlet entitled "Grasp the Weapon of Culture" (1952).
84. For "proletarian regionalism," see Botkin, "Regionalism and Culture," 154.

CHAPTER TWELVE: CULTURE AND THE CRISIS

1. Contract for *A Timid Woman*, Mar. 24, 1932; Contract for *Swan Crossing*, Oct. 5, 1931; Advance payment for *Swan Crossing*, Nov. 11, 1932, all in G. Lumpkin Papers.
2. Elinor Ferry, Memo on Grace Hutchins interview, Oct. 20, [1951 or 1952], box 45, folder "Grace Hutchins," Tanenhaus Papers; J. M. Allen, *Passionate Commitments*, 140.
3. Elizabeth Ames to G. Lumpkin, Feb. 9, 1933 and June 23, 1933, both in Yaddo Records, Manuscript and Archives Division, New York Public Library; Marion Sheffield to Dr. Welker, Apr. 14, 1964 (quotes), Evelyn Scott Collection, Special Collections, University of Tennessee Libraries, Knoxville.

4. Elizabeth Ames to G. Lumpkin, June 23, 1933; G. Lumpkin to Elizabeth Ames, Feb. 18, 1933; G. Lumpkin to Elizabeth Ames, n.d., all in Yaddo Records, Manuscript and Archives Division, New York Public Library; "All Art Propaganda Says Woman Author Who Confesses Her Novel is Communistic," *Pittsburgh Press*, Feb. 3, 1933; G. Lumpkin to Leonardo Di Andrea, New York, Mar. 15, 1933 (quote), G. Lumpkin Papers.

5. League of Professional Groups for Foster and Ford, *Culture and the Crisis*, 14 (quote) (hereafter *Culture and the Crisis*).

6. Bird, "Invisible Scar"; Rossinow, *Visions of Progress*, 5–6.

7. D. Douglas to Friends, Dec. 1968, box 94, folder 7, Warne Papers.

8. Denning, *Cultural Front*, xiii–xx, 5–6; Rossinow, *Visions of Progress*, 143–94.

9. E. Wilson, "Appeal to Progressives," 77 (quote).

10. Barrett, *William Z. Foster*, 181; Norman Thomas quoted in A. Dunbar, *Against the Grain*, 34.

11. Carr, *Dos Passos*, 299 (quote).

12. Joseph Freeman quoted in Klehr, *Heyday of American Communism*, 75–76 (quote on 76).

13. G. Lumpkin, "Emancipation and Exploitation," 26–27 (quotes).

14. For this new attention to African Americans and to the South, where the vast majority still lived, see R. Kelley, *Hammer and Hoe*; M. Solomon, *Cry Was Unity*; Gilmore, *Defying Dixie*.

15. Gosse, "To Organize," 113 (quotes); Orleck, "That Mythical Thing."

16. Foley, *Radical Representations*, 246 (first quote), 245 (second quote).

17. "Georgia White Woman Says She Will Vote 'Red,'" Baltimore *Afro-American*, Aug. 6, 1932; G. Lumpkin, "Why I as a White Southern Woman Will Vote Communist," *Daily Worker*, Aug. 12, 1932, 4 (quote).

18. G. Lumpkin, "Why I as a White Southern Woman Will Vote Communist," *Daily Worker*, Aug. 12, 1932, 4 (quotes); Cardyn, "Sexualized Racism." See also G. Lumpkin, "Southern Woman Bares Tricks of Higher-Ups to Shunt Lynch Blame, Uses Civil War Method to Conceal Share in Crimes," *Daily Worker*, Nov. 27, 1933 (hereafter G. Lumpkin, "Southern Woman Bares Tricks").

19. G. Lumpkin, "Where I Come From, It Is Bitter and Harsh: Why We Should Vote Communist," and "Addenda," Oct. 12, 1932 (quotes), box 3, folder 4, Mark Solomon and Robert Kaufman Research Files on African Americans and Communism, Elmer Holmes Bobst Library, Tamiment Library and Robert F. Wagner Labor Archives, New York University Libraries.

20. "League of Professional Groups," in Mrs. Esther Corey's possession (quote), box 14, folder 13, Theodore Draper Papers, Stuart A. Rose Manuscripts, Archives, and Rare Book Library, Emory University.

21. *Culture and the Crisis*, 14 (quote). For this comparison to the Port Huron Statement, see Denning, *Cultural Front*, 112, 424. The ideas that animated *Culture and the Crisis* were carried forward in the 1940s and 1950s by the sociologist C. Wright Mills and reiterated in the founding document of Students for a Democratic Society. Student radicals in the 1960s, like left-wing intellectuals in the 1930s, believed that in advanced capitalist societies white collar workers were

not just workers' allies but "economically and functionally a part of the working class" and that the struggle for social justice must be waged not only in the workplace but on the cultural front: Denning, *Cultural Front*, 96–104, 112 (quote on 98); Geary, *Radical Ambition*, 179–82, 218–19.

22. *Culture and the Crisis*, 29 (first quote).

23. *Culture and the Crisis*, 29 (first and third quote), 10–11 (second quote).

24. *Culture and the Crisis*, 18 (quotes).

25. For the rank and file movement, see Ehrenreich, *Altruistic Imagination*, 102–21; L. Gordon, *Pitied but Not Entitled*, 219–23; Haynes, "Rank and File."

26. G. Lumpkin, "Why I as a White Southern Woman Will Vote Communist," *Daily Worker*, Aug. 12, 1932, 4 (quote).

27. "Scottsboro Unity Defense Committee," National Committee for the Defense of Political Prisoners, [1932] (quote), reel 4, frame 001; Acting National Secretary to G. Lumpkin, Jan. 28, 1936, reel 7, frame 048; "Memorandum to the Scottsboro Defense Committee," Dec. 1935, reel 4, frame 042, all in International Labor Defense, et al., Papers of the International Labor Defense (microfilm), Schomberg Center for Research in Black Culture, New York Public Library (hereafter ILD Papers); Naison, *Communists in Harlem*, 71–75. In 1936, when the CP, the ILD, the NAACP, and other groups provisionally overcame their fierce ideological differences and formed a united Scottsboro Defense Committee, the NAACP invited Grace to become a sponsor, along with her former pastor, the Rev. Kirkman G. Finlay, who was by then Bishop of the Protestant Episcopal Church for Mississippi, living in Jackson, MS: Acting National Secretary to G. Lumpkin, Jan. 28, 1936, reel 7, frame 048; "Memorandum to the Scottsboro Defense Committee," Dec. 1935, reel 4, frame 042, both in ILD Papers.

28. "Representative Harlem Citizens Rally to Scottsboro Defense," National Committee for the Defense of Political Prisoners, press release, Sept. 19, 1932 (first quote), reel 4, frame 002; "A Call to Men and Women of Good Will," Sept. 1932, reel 4, frame 032; both in ILD Papers; Naison, *Communists in Harlem*, 72.

29. "Representative Harlem Citizens Rally to Scottsboro Defense," National Committee for the Defense of Political Prisoners, press release, Sept. 19, 1932 (quote), reel 4, frame 002, ILD Papers.

30. Press release, International Labor Defense, Oct. 28, 1932, reel 9, frames 608–610, International Labor Defense et al., ILD Papers; FBI Report, Atlanta, Feb. 13, 1941, International Labor Defense, HQ-61-7347-1, 6 (quotes), KDL FBI File. The other lead signatories were Evelyn Scott, a critically acclaimed novelist from Tennessee whom Grace would soon befriend, and Anita Brenner, a Texan who became a discerning advocate for and interpreter of Mexican art.

31. J. Hall, *Revolt against Chivalry*, 197–201; Press release, International Labor Defense, Oct. 28, 1932, 2 (quote), reel 9, frames 608–10, ILD Papers.

32. Goodman, *Stories of Scottsboro*, 43–45, 172, 193 (quote on 43); J. Hall, *Revolt against Chivalry*, 201–6; R. Kelley, *Hammer and Hoe*, 84–85; Feimster, *Southern Horrors*; Maxwell, *New Negro*, 129–51. See D. Carter, *Tragedy of the American South*, 416–62, for a scholar wrestling with how to portray these women.

33. Goodman, *Stories of Scottsboro*, 189–90 (quotes).

34. Janken, *White*, 181–84, 235; Storrs, *Civilizing Capitalism*, 105.

35. For this campaign and the role played by white southern women's organizations within it, see J. Hall, *Revolt against Chivalry*, 237–53; Janken, *White*, 199–231; "Anti-Lynch Legislation Urged by Y. W. C. A. Convention," *New York Age*, May 19, 1934.

36. Janken, *White*, 205 (quote); Frances Williams to Walter White, Jan. 23, 24, and 30, 1934; Elizabeth S. Harrington to Walter White, Jan. 29, 1934, National Association for the Advancement of Colored People Records, Manuscript Division, Library of Congress, Washington, DC (microfilm).

37. Frances Williams to Henrietta Roelofs, Feb. 27, 1934 (first quote), YWCA Records; Janken, *White*, 203 (second quote), 204–5, 231.

38. For left feminism (also sometimes characterized as labor or Popular Front feminism) in the 1930s, 1940s, and 1950s, see Cobble, *Other Women's Movement*; E. DuBois, "Eleanor Flexner"; Gabin, *Feminism in the Labor Movement*; D. Horowitz, *Betty Friedan*, 50–152; Swerdlow, "Congress of American Women"; Lerner, *Fireweed*, 256–74; Storrs, *Second Red Scare*; Weigand, *Red Feminism*. For a distinctive black left feminist tradition, see Gore, J. Theoharis, and Woodard, *Want to Start a Revolution?*; Gore, *Radicalism at the Crossroads*; McDonald, *Feminism, the Left*; McDuffie, *Sojourning for Freedom*; McDuffie, "March of Young Southern Black Women"; Ransby, *Eslanda*; M. Washington, *Other Blacklist*.

39. [G. Lumpkin,] "Letter from the South," 31; G. Lumpkin, "Mayme Brown," 18–19; G. Lumpkin testimony, U.S. Senate, *Committee on Government Operations, State Department Information Program—Information Centers: Hearings before the Permanent Subcommittee on Investigations*, Part 2, Mar. 27, Apr. 1–2, 83rd Cong., 1st sess. (Washington, DC: Government Printing Office, 1953), 155–59; G. Lumpkin interview, Sept. 25, 1971, 14, 18–19; Lawson, "Dixieland," 6, 9–10; Folsom, *Days of Anger*, 91; R. Kelley, *Hammer and Hoe*, 22, 64, 71, 100, 102; C. Baker, *Generous Spirit*, 141–44.

40. Louis Colman, "Preparations to Lynching Scottsboro Boys," Nov. 1933 (first quote), reel 3, frames 549–53, ILD Papers; G. Lumpkin, "Southern Woman Bares Tricks," 3 (second quote); Raper, *Plight of Tuscaloosa*, 13–14, 17; Madison, "Shots in the Dark."

41. Feldman, *Politics, Society, and the Klan*, 9, 251–54; Goodman, *Stories of Scottsboro*, 204; Raper, *Plight of Tuscaloosa*, 22 (first quote), 31 (second quote).

42. For Raper, see Mazzari, *Southern Modernist*; Raper, *Tragedy of Lynching*; Arthur Franklin Raper interview, Jan. 18, 1971; Arthur Franklin Raper interview, Jan. 30, 1974.

43. Alfred H. Hirsch to George Fort Milton, Oct. 12, 1933, Arthur Franklin Raper Papers, SHC; "Delegation Leaves for Alabama to Investigate Lynching of Negroes," *Daily Worker*, Nov. 6, 1933.

44. Ransdall wrote one of the period's most penetrating accounts of the local forces moving beneath the surface of the case: Ransdall, *Scottsboro, Alabama, Case*. An independent journalist, Ransdall later joined the staff of the *CIO News*. Goodman, *Stories of Scottsboro*, 39–46, 184, 187–88, 263; Hollace Ransdall interview,

Nov. 6, 1974. For Kester, see R. Martin, *Howard Kester*; Kester, *Revolt among the Sharecroppers*; A. Dunbar, *Against the Grain*; Howard Kester interview, July 22, 1974; Howard Kester interview, Aug. 25, 1974; Nancy Alice Kester Neale interview, Aug. 6, 1983.

45. G. F. Milton to Alfred Hirsch, Oct. 17, 1933, Arthur Franklin Raper Papers, SHC.

46. Howard Kester to Alice Kester, Nov. 11, 1933 (quote), Howard Kester Papers, SHC.

47. Raper, *Plight of Tuscaloosa*, 22 (quotes).

48. G. Lumpkin, "Novel as Propaganda," 2 (quotes).

49. A. Dunbar, *Against the Grain*, 50 (first quote); Raper, *Plight of Tuscaloosa*, 38 (second quote).

50. G. Lumpkin, "Southern Woman Bares Tricks," 3 (first quote); Press release, International Labor Defense, Oct. 28, 1932, reel 9, frames 608–10, ILD Papers; FBI Report, Atlanta, Feb. 13, 1941, International Labor Defense, HQ-61-7347-1 (second quote), KDL FBI File.

51. G. Lumpkin, "Southern Woman Bares Tricks," 3 (quotes). See also KDL, *Making*, 90–91; G. Lumpkin, *To Make My Bread*, 192.

52. Elizabeth Lumpkin Glenn, "Notes in answer to a letter from Katharine Lumpkin," n.d. (quote), folder 34, KDL Papers.

53. Du Bois, *Black Reconstruction*.

54. "Grace Lumpkin, Plans for Work," n.d. [1938] (quotes), fellowship application summaries for Grace Lumpkin, John Simon Guggenheim Memorial Foundation, New York City; G. Lumpkin to Robert Cantwell, [1937] (quotes), Robert Cantwell Papers, Special Collections and University Archives, University of Oregon Libraries; Personals, *Asheville (NC) Citizen*, May 10 and May 20, 1939.

55. "Assignment," July 1935 [transferring contract from the Macaulay Co. to Lee Furman, Inc.]; Macaulay Co. to Maxim Lieber, Jan. 31, 1935, both in G. Lumpkin Papers; Book Notes, *New York Times*, Aug. 26, 1935 (quote).

56. At one point, Grace considered calling the book "The Gault Case," signaling her interest in the novel's white family from the start: The Macaulay Co. to Maxim Lieber, Jan. 31, 1935, G. Lumpkin Papers.

57. G. Lumpkin, *Sign for Cain*, 9, 156, 203–4 (first quote on both 9 and 156); KDL, *Making*, 121; G. Hicks, "Real South," 23 (second quote).

58. G. Lumpkin, *Sign for Cain*, 204 (first quote); G. Lumpkin, "Miserable Offender," 282 (second quote).

59. G. Lumpkin, *Sign for Cain*, 115–16 (quote on 115), 132–33.

60. G. Lumpkin, *Sign for Cain*, 177 (first quote), 147 (second quote), 170 (third quote), 148 (fourth quote), 175 (fifth quote), 169 (sixth quote).

61. G. Lumpkin, *Sign for Cain*, 369 (first quote), 374 (second quote).

62. Adams, "Two Novels," 7; Daniels, "Old Devil Cotton," 10. Other reviews included Edwin Grandberry, "Dramatic Novel of Class and Race Conflict: This Tragedy and Melodrama of the South Has Strength and Weakness of 'Proletarian' Writing," *New York Herald Tribune Books*, Oct. 27, 1935; Kronenberger, "Novel of the New South," 480; Warren, "Recent Books," 624–49; Don West, "Grace Lumpkin's Novel Great Story of the South," *Daily Worker*, n.d.,

newsclip in G. Lumpkin Papers. In addition, in September 1935, Grace entered into an agreement with dramatist Neil Brandt to produce a "first-class" play based on the novel: Maxim Lieber to Lee Furman, Sept. 30, 1935 (quote), G. Lumpkin Papers.

63. Miles, "Another Year," 44 (first quote), 45 (second quote), 47–48 (third quote). For this journal, see Perkins, "National Association of College Women." For Miles, see Isadore William Miles Papers, Walter P. Reuther Library, Wayne State University, Detroit, MI; "Died," *Jet*, Mar. 10, 1986, 18. Miles was a graduate of Howard University. She served as secretary of the American Federation of Teachers, Local 6, Teachers' Union, Washington, DC, 1949 to 1954. Beginning in 1952, she taught English at Spingarn High School. The "Isadore Williams Miles Award for the graduating senior majoring in sociology with highest cumulative grade-point average" is awarded annually by Paine College in Augusta, GA.

64. G. Lumpkin, *Sign for Cain*, 50–53 (quote on 53).

65. Miles, "Another Year," 47–48 (quote); Foley, *Radical Representations*, 386–88.

66. "Grace Lumpkin's Novel about Share-Croppers," *New York Post*, Oct. 14, 1935 (quote); Susan Sowinska observes that in *To Make My Bread*, Fielding Burke's *Call Home the Heart*, and Myra Page's *Gathering Storm*, "most of the 'Negro work' is, significantly, women's work": Sowinska, "Writing across the Color Line," 125 (quote). For the argument that, by contrast, most Communist Party–affiliated writers portray interracial brotherhood as the province of men, see Maxwell, *New Negro*, 125–51.

67. G. Lumpkin, "Emancipation and Exploitation," 26 (first quote), 27 (second quote).

68. G. Lumpkin, "Emancipation and Exploitation," 26 (quotes).

CHAPTER THIRTEEN: MISS LUMPKIN AND MRS. DOUGLAS

1. J. Edgar Park to KDL, Aug. 17, 1930, folder 3, KDL Papers; Horace B. Davis to Lynn Turgeon, Apr. 17, 1972 (first quote); Elizabeth Moos to Lynn Turgeon, Apr. 23, [1972] (second quote), both in J. Hall's possession, thanks to Lynn Turgeon; Werth, *Scarlet Professor*, 78–82.

2. P. Douglas, *Fullness of Time*, 70–71 (quote on 71); Christopher Densmore [Friends Historical Library of Swarthmore College], to J. Hall, July 31, 2003 and Aug. 1, 2003.

3. D. Douglas to W. A. Neilson, Oct. 4, 1932, box 7, folder 43, Neilson Files.

4. Adaline S. Pates (Potter) to Miss Voorhees, Nov. 7, 1931 (first quote); Adaline Pates (Potter) to Miss Voorhees, Dec. 1, 1931 (subsequent quotes); Helen Mac-Murtrie Voorhees to Adaline S. Pates (Potter), Dec. 9, 1931, all in Adaline S. Potter, Faculty Files, Archives and Special Collections, Mount Holyoke College. Known as Pates (pate eze), Adaline stayed with the family for four years, during which she finished an MA in English at Smith. She finally found a position in the English department at the Northfield School for Girls, but was forced to leave when she married Gordon E. Potter. After two years at Smith studying for a PhD in English, she began a freelance career teaching English

and editing the works of foreign refugee antifascist scholars in Northampton. After World War II, she returned to Mount Holyoke to teach composition and English as a foreign language.

5. D. Douglas to Miss Wiesman, Jan. 9, 193[4] (quote), Consumers' League of Massachusetts Papers, box 8, folder 121, Schlesinger Library, Radcliffe Institute, Harvard University.

6. For the labor historians of the 1970s and 1980s as the intellectual children of these progressive scholars, see Kessler-Harris, "Vera Shlakman," 195–200 (quote on 195).

7. Federal Writers Project, *Massachusetts*, 11; Van Vorhis, *Look of Paradise*.

8. Levenson and Natterstad, *Granville Hicks*, 26; Werth, *Scarlett Professor*, 23 (quote); Fuess, *Calvin Coolidge*, 77; Federal Writers Project, *Massachusetts*, 301; Fifteenth Census of the United States, 1930, Population, vol. 3, part 1, Reports by States, Alabama-Missouri; Shlakman, *Economic History of a Factory Town*, 234.

9. Heale, *McCarthy's Americans*, 154; Coolidge, "Are the 'Reds' Stalking," 4–5, 66–67; Coolidge, "Trotsky versus Washington," 10–11, 38–39; Coolidge, "They Must Be Resisted," 10–11, 42; Thorp, *Neilson of Smith*, 186–87.

10. Barton, *Man Nobody Knows*; Putney, "Muscular Christianity"; Vandenberg-Daves, "Manly Pursuit."

11. Werth, *Scarlet Professor*, 27 (quote); Donald Willard, "Smith College Head Finds Reds Lacking," *Daily Boston Globe*, Dec. 6, 1930.

12. H. Horowitz, *Alma Mater*, xxiv, 69–81, 179–97 (first quote on 80); "Esther Lowenthal" [unpublished memoir], 4 (second and third quotes), Faculty Biographical Files, Esther Lowenthal, SCA.

13. Rosenzweig, *Another Self*, 125–48; Werth, *Scarlet Professor*, 54.

14. Vera Shlakman interview, Apr. 12, 1986 (quote); Ellen Matteson Knox to Daniel Horowitz, May 27, 2000, in J. Hall's possession. Ellen Knox's mother was a classmate of Dorothy's at Bryn Mawr and a longtime friend. "As for any recognition of any lesbian relationship with Kay [KDL] there was utter denial in our household," Knox reflected. But years later, she crossed paths with one of Dorothy's grandsons at a funeral for an Act Up activist who had died of AIDS. "He rather delicately asked me whether I believed that Kay and his grandmother had had 'a Boston marriage'? I claimed no knowledge, but began then to think about the relationships . . . among my acquaintance that had sustained so many unmarried people. Times have changed."

15. Rosenberg, *Changing the Subject*, 167; Heale, *McCarthy's Americans*, 161 (first quote); Werth, *Scarlet Professor*, 193–251 (second quote on 201).

16. Adaline Pates Potter interview, May 26, 2000 (quote). In truth, there were probably no more lesbians in the women's colleges than in coeducational institutions, but with the rise of coeducation, the women's colleges came increasingly to be perceived as communities of lesbians, separatist feminists, and the like. For this point, see N. Davis and J. Scott, *Women's History*, 33–34.

17. Champagne, *Cauliflower Heart*, 28 (first quote); Levenson and Natterstad, *Granville Hicks*, 29 (second quote); Herring, *Neilson of Smith*, 14 (third quote); D. Horowitz, *Betty Friedan*, 33–38; Nicolson, "Neilson of Smith," 539–40, 546;

Morrow, "President Neilson of Smith," 43–50; Thorp, *Neilson of Smith*, 264–65; Neilson, *Intellectual Honesty*.

18. Herring, *Neilson of Smith*, 46–47 (quote on 46); Thorp, *Neilson of Smith*, 255; D. Horowitz, *Betty Friedan*, 37; H. Horowitz, *Alma Mater*, 154–56.

19. Newton Arvin to Granville Hicks, Jan. 21, 1929 (quote), Granville Hicks Papers, box 3, Special Collections Research Center, Syracuse University Libraries; Landrum, "More Firmly Based," 12; *Smith College Weekly*, Oct. 13 and Oct. 19, 1932, SCA (hereafter *SCW*).

20. Cohen, *Old Left Was Young*, xiv; *SCW*, Nov. 27, 1935; Landrum, "More Firmly Based," 13 (quotes).

21. *SCW*, Oct. 16, 1929 (first and second quotes) and Nov. 7, 1934 (third quote).

22. *SCW*, Jan. 13, 1932 and Apr. 15, 1936 (quotes).

23. *SCW*, Mar. 23, 1932 (quotes).

24. D. Douglas to Broadus Mitchell, Nov. 22, 1932 (first quote); D. Douglas to Broadus Mitchell, Dec. 1, 1932 (second quote), D. Douglas to Broadus Mitchell, Jan. 26, [1933] and Apr. 20, 1933, all in box 2, Broadus Mitchell Collection, Hofstra University Archives, Hempstead, New York (hereafter Mitchell Collection).

25. KDL to Colston Warne, Nov. 4, 1932 (first quote), box 9, folder 3, Warne Papers; D. Douglas, KDL, Colston Warne, and Others, "Cross-Currents of Reform: The Prospects for Working Class Security in the United States," [May 1933], (second quote), box 2, Mitchell Collection.

26. KDL to Colston Warne, Oct. 13, 1932, Nov. 4, 1932, Apr. 20, May 4, 1933, Warne Papers; Norman Silber, "Colston Estey Warne"; Glickman, "Strike in the Temple"; Warne, "Consumers on the March," pts. 1 and 2.

27. Singal, *War Within*, 58–82; J. Hall, "Broadus Mitchell"; [D. Douglas, KDL, Colston Warne, and Others], "Suggested Outline of Chapters for How America Met Unemployment, 1929–1932," [Nov. 1932]; D. Douglas to Broadus Mitchell, Nov. 22, 1932 (quotes), both in box 2, Mitchell Collection.

28. Russell A. Nixon to Lynn Turgeon, May 1, 1972 (first quote), in J. Hall's possession, thanks to Lynn Turgeon; "Smith Professor Speaks," *Daily Hampshire Gazette* (Northampton, MA), May 15, 1931; "Smith Faculty Members Elected to Office in Central Labor Union," Mar. 6, 1935; "Prof. Douglas Says Security Bill Will Pass," *Springfield (MA) Union*, May 5, 1936 (second quote), all news-clips in Faculty Biographical Files, Dorothy Wolff Douglas, SCA; *Daily Hampshire Gazette* (Northampton, MA), Dec. 6, 1932, Mar. 8, 1932, Mar. 21, 1932, May 25, 1932; File—"338 Seventh Region, Boyd, Edna (Miss)," Reel 32; File—"302 Reading Committee for a Federal[-]State Employment Service," Reel 32; File—"395 Women in Industry Comm (on) Douglas, Dorothy W. (Dr.)," Reel 34, Part III, "Series A, National Office Subject Files, 1920–1932," Papers of the League of Women Voters, Anne Firor Scott and William H. Chafe, eds., Research Collections in Women's Studies, Frederick, MD, University Publications of America, 1985. For other examples of Douglas's activism and advocacy, see D. Douglas to Margaret Wiesman, Nov. 16, 1931, box 8, folder 121, Consumers' League of Massachusetts Papers, Schlesinger Library, Harvard University; "Smith College Prober Flays Sweatshop Evil," *Boston American*, May 16, 1933;

Daily Hampshire Gazette (Northampton, MA), Dec. 6, 1932, both newsclips in Faculty Biographical Files, Dorothy Wolff Douglas, SCA; D. Douglas, "Wages and Hours Legislation and the Child Labor Problem," An address before the Annual Meeting of the National Consumers League on "Labor Standards Legislation: A Bulwark for Democracy," New York, NY, Dec. 8, 1939, Tamiment Library and Robert F. Wagner Labor Archive, New York University.

29. For succinct expressions of these ideas, see "Smith Professor Speaks," *Daily Hampshire Gazette* (Northampton, MA), May 15, 1931, newsclip; "Smith College Professor Speaks on Depression before Local Group," *Pittsfield (MA) Eagle*, May 14, 1932, newsclip, both in Faculty Biographical Files, Dorothy Wolff Douglas, SCA.

30. "Smith Professor Speaks," *Daily Hampshire Gazette* (Northampton, MA), May 15, 1931 (quotes), newsclip in Faculty Biographical Files, Dorothy Wolff Douglas, SCA.

31. D. Douglas to Edith Rockwood, Feb. 4, 1931, File—"#395 Women in Industry Comm (on) Douglas, Dorothy W. (Dr.)" (quotes), Reel 34, Part III, "Series A, National Office Subject Files, 1920–1932," Papers of the League of Women Voters, Anne Firor Scott and William H. Chafe, eds., Research Collections in Women's Studies, Frederick, MD, University Publications of America, 1985.

32. Margaret Wiesman to D. Douglas, Jan. 11, 1934 and Mar. 24, 1934; D. Douglas to Margret Wiesman, Jan. 14, 1935 (quote), and Nov. 16, 1931, folder 121, box 8, Consumers League of Massachusetts Papers, Arthur and Elizabeth Schlesinger Library; "Smith College Prober Flays Sweatshop Evil," *Boston American*, May 16, 1933, newsclip in Faculty Biographical Files, Dorothy Wolff Douglas, SCA.

33. Ann Seidman to Lynn Turgeon, Feb. 3, 1972 (quote), in J. Hall's possession, thanks to Lynn Turgeon. See also Hilda Lass to Lynn Turgeon, Apr. 21, 1972; Anna Aschenbach to J. Hall, Sept. 20, 1996, both in J. Hall's possession. Anna Aschenbach remembered especially Dorothy's skill at evoking the historical background of contemporary racial and economic struggles. It was Dorothy who taught her about the problems of workers, farmers, African Americans, and consumers. "I've seen myself," she concluded, "as a radical activist ever since." In order to share her memories with me, she took time out from lobbying for universal health care and other "tasks I might never have been involved in had it not been for the influence of Dorothy Wolff Douglas."

34. See for example, D. Douglas, "What Kind of Unemployment Insurance?" 3–6; D. Douglas, "Social Security Act," 18–19.

35. D. Douglas to Friends, Dec. 1968 (quote), box 94, folder 7, Warne Papers; D. Douglas to W. A. Neilson, Oct. 24, 1932, box 7, folder 43, Neilson Files.

36. KDL, *South in Progress*, 11 (first quote); KDL, "Factors in the Commitment"; D. Douglas and KDL to Mary van Kleeck, May 29, 1931, folder 16, van Kleeck Papers (second and third quotes); KDL, "Parental Conditions"; D. Douglas and KDL, "Communistic Settlements."

37. KDL, "Comparative Study of Work Life of Children in Massachusetts and Alabama" and "A study of the methods of prevention of child labor in urban and rural areas of the Soviet Union," Grant-in-Aid Minutes, 1932–1938, Social

Science Research records Accession 1, Rockefeller Archive Center, Sleepy Hollow, NY; "Katharine Du Pre Lumpkin," curriculum vitae enclosed in KDL to William Kiekhofer, May 6, 1932, box 18, William H. Kiekhofer Papers, Archives and Records Management, University of Wisconsin–Madison Libraries (hereafter Kiekhofer Papers); KDL and D. Douglas, *Child Workers in America*, ix, 293–95; KDL and D. Douglas, "Effect of Unemployment."

38. KDL, "A Study of Social Situations as Related to Conduct of Problem Children in Dependent Families," Research Fellowships in the Social Sciences, [1929–30] (first and second quotes), box 254, folder 2465; KDL, *Family*, v (third quote); KDL, "Final Report Katharine Du Pre Lumpkin, Fellow 1929–1930," enclosed in KDL to Donald Young, Oct. 10, 1933, box 387, folder 4734, both in Social Science Research Council Records, Rockefeller Archive Center, Sleepy Hollow, NY.

39. KDL to Assistant Director, University of North Carolina Press, Apr. 15, 1932; University of North Carolina Press to KDL, Apr. 18, 1932; W. T. Couch to KDL, Aug. 6, 1932; KDL to W. T. Couch, Aug. 8, 1932, all in folder 33, University of North Carolina Press Records, University Archives, Louis Round Wilson Special Collections Library, University of North Carolina at Chapel Hill.

40. KDL to W. T. Couch, Feb. 1933 and Mar. 23, 1933 (first quote), W. T. Couch to KDL, Mar. 4, 1933, both in folder 33, University of North Carolina Press Records, University Archives, Louis Round Wilson Special Collections Library, University of North Carolina, Chapel Hill; KDL, review of *The Family: Past and Present*, 405 (second quote); KDL, *Family*, xiii (third quote). Stern's Marxist survey included excerpts from both Grace's *To Make My Bread* and Katharine's *The Family*.

41. This tradition emerged in the Progressive era. Its evolution was epitomized by the career of Mirra Komarovsky (1905–1999), who began fieldwork on working-class families similar to Lumpkin's in the mid-1930s. She majored in economics and sociology at Barnard. When she told her mentor at Barnard College, William Ogburn, that she wanted to teach sociology, he responded: "Not a realistic plan. You are a woman, foreign born, and Jewish. I would recommend some other occupation": Komarovsky, "Women Then and Now," 7–10 (quote on 7). She went on to produce studies that became classics when the new field of gender studies emerged in the 1970s, became president of the American Sociological Association, and served as the first head of the Women's Studies Program at Barnard in 1977. See Rosenburg, *Changing the Subject*, 190–92; Tarrant, "Mirra Komarovsky's Feminism of the 1950s."

42. Friedrich Engels quoted in KDL, review of *The Family: Past and Present*, 405 (first quote); KDL, *Family*, 25 (second quote), 95 (subsequent quotes).

43. KDL, *Family*, 166 (quote).

44. KDL, *Family*, 42 (first quote), xii (second quote).

45. A. Clark, *Working Life of Women*; Pinchbeck, *Women Workers*; KDL, *Family*, xviii (quote).

46. Karl Marx quoted in KDL, review of *The Family: Past and Present*, 405.

47. KDL, review of *The Family: Past and Present*, 404 (first quote); Lumpkin, *Family*, 168 (second quote), 169; Kennedy, *Freedom from Fear*, 24–26.
48. D. Horowitz, *Betty Friedan*, 34; Pollard, *Women on College and University Faculties*, 29; Nicolson, "Neilson of Smith," 547.
49. Nicolson, "Neilson of Smith," 547 (quote); Worcester, *Social Science Research Council*, 20n22 (second quote).
50. W. H. Kiekhofer to Pres. W.A. Neilson, May 26, 1932 (first quote), box 18, Kiekhofer Papers; KDL, "Lecture to a general audience, 1947," 1 (subsequent quotes), KDL Papers; Nissenbaum, "New England." See P. Douglas, *Fullness of Time*, 28, for an anecdote about a "mild-mannered Southerner in my seminar whom we all thought slightly feeble-minded."
51. Worcester, *Social Science Research Council*; Worcester, *Fellows of the Social Science Research Council*.
52. [William H. Kiekhofer], "Recommendation of Katharine D. Lumpkin to Social Science Research Council," Jan. 3, 1929, box 18, Kiekhofer Papers.
53. Kimball Young to KDL, May 9, 1929 (first quote), folder 3; Handwritten note to Katharine at bottom of E. A. Ross to [?], [1949 or 1950], (second and third quotes); E. A. Ross to KDL, 1937, both in folder 4, KDL Papers; E. A. Ross to KDL, Aug. 11, 1931 (subsequent quotes), E. A. Ross to KDL, Mar. 11, 1933, both in folder 3, KDL Papers. See also [William H. Kiekhofer], "Recommendation of Katharine D. Lumpkin to Social Science Research Council," Jan. 3, 1929, box 18, Kiekhofer Papers; KDL to E. A. Ross, Feb. 20, 1930; E. A. Ross to KDL, Feb. 25, 1931; KDL to E. A. Ross, June 11, 1931 and Sept. 13, 1931; E. A. Ross to KDL, June 13, 1931, all in box 16, folder 4, Edward A. Ross Papers, Wisconsin Historical Society, Madison; W. H. Kiekhofer to KDL, May 17, 1932; KDL to Kiekhofer, May 26, 1932; Kiekhofer to KDL, May 31, 1932, all in folder 4, KDL Papers.
54. See A. Scott, *Unheard Voices*, for a poignant look at this system and how it disadvantaged women.
55. Jean Davis to KDL, Feb. 25, 1929 (quote); J. Edgar Park to KDL, Aug. 17, 1930, both in folder 3, KDL Papers; Zephorene L. Stickney to J. Hall, Sept. 8, 2003; C. Baker, *Generous Spirit*, 93, 101; M. Page, *Southern Cotton Mills*. See also Miriam West to KDL, May 22, 1934; Acting President, Pennsylvania College for Women to KDL, Feb. 12, 1935, both in folder 3, KDL Papers.
56. KDL to W. H. Kiekhofer, May 6, 1932 (quote), box 18, Kiekhofer Papers.
57. KDL, "Brief Resume of the Work of the Council of Industrial Studies, 1932–1938" (quote), (hereafter KDL, "Brief Resume"); KDL, "The Council of Industrial Studies," *Smith Alumnae Quarterly*, Nov. 1937, 31; KDL to W. A. Neilson, Feb. 20, 1939, all in box 31, folder 18, Neilson Files; Dzuback, "Women and Social Research"; Tindall, *Emergence of the New South*, 582–92; Singal, *War Within*, 115–52, 265–338.
58. KDL, "Report of the Director of Research of the Council of Industrial Studies," June 1933, *Report of the President of Smith College*, 1933, 51, SCA; Secretary to the President to KDL, Sept. 30, 1933, box 31, folder 17, Neilson Files; KDL, "Brief Resume."

59. P. Douglas, *Fullness of Time*, 36 (first quote); D. Douglas to W. A. Neilson, Sept. 16, 1932 (second quote), box 31, folder 17, Neilson Files.

60. Dzuback, "Creative Financing." At Smith in 1931, for example, faculty in the social sciences received no regular funding for travel or research, except for railroad fare to one major scholarly meeting. Only one department provided secretarial assistance: "Summary of the Conference on Research in the Social Sciences in Colleges," Dec. 12–13, 1931, 5, Marion Edwards Park Papers, Special Collections Department, Bryn Mawr College Library. The career of the anthropologist Elsie Crew Parsons exemplified these self-help efforts. Her patronage made possible the work of women anthropologists in the Southwest and had a major impact on the field.

61. KDL to Miss Annetta Clark [W. A. Neilson's secretary], Sept. 23, 1932 (quotes), box 31, folder 17, Neilson Files.

62. Landrum, "More Firmly Based," 12, 67; Vera Shlakman interview, Apr. 12, 1986; Alice Lazerowitz interview, Aug. 4, 1987.

63. KDL to W. A. Neilson, Apr. 18, 1939 (quote), box 31, folder 18, Neilson Files.

64. D. Douglas to W. A. Neilson, Apr. 29, 1939, box 31, folder 18, Neilson Files.

65. Vera Shlakman interview, Apr. 12, 1986, (first and third quotes); KDL and Combs, *Shutdowns in the Connecticut Valley*, 136 (second quote); Dzuback, "Creative Financing," 108–9.

66. Glazer and Slater, *Unequal Colleagues*, 197 (first quote); D. Douglas to W. A. Neilson, Nov. 22, 1936 (second quote), box 31, folder 17; KDL to W. A. Neilson, Feb. 20, 1939 and Sept. 18, 1939, box 31, folder 18, all in Neilson Files.

67. KDL, "Report of the Director of Research of the Council of Industrial Studies," *Report of the President of Smith College*, 1933, 51 (first quote), SCA; Jane Saddler to Charles Johnson, Jan. 7, 1955 (second quote), folder 16, KDL Papers.

68. KDL, "The Council of Industrial Studies," *Smith Alumnae Quarterly*, Nov. 1937, 32; KDL to Broadus Mitchell, Nov. 26, 1933, Mitchell Collection; Des Jardins, *Historical Enterprise*.

69. KDL, "Report of the Director of Research of the Council of Industrial Studies," June 1933, *Report of the President of Smith College*, 1933, 49, SCA; KDL, "Brief Resume"; Secretary to the President to KDL, July 18, 1933; KDL to Annette Clark, Feb. 27, 1937, both in box 31, folder 17, Neilson Files.

70. KDL and Combs, *Shutdowns in the Connecticut Valley*. The site of the study was Easthampton, MA, and the research was followed up by the Works Progress Administration National Research Projects with assistance from KDL and the Council. At her suggestion, the WPA also conducted a study of Holyoke: KDL, "Brief Resume."

71. J. Hall et al., *Like a Family*, 197; KDL, *South in Progress*, 2 (quote).

72. KDL to Broadus Mitchell, Nov. 6, 1933, box 2, Mitchell Collection. For a critical review, see N. Ware, review of *Shutdowns in the Connecticut Valley*.

73. KDL and Combs, *Shutdowns in the Connecticut Valley*, 252 (first quote); [D. Douglas, KDL, Colston Warne, and Others], "Suggested Outline of Chapters for How Americans Met Unemployment, 1929–1932," [Nov. 1932] (subsequent quotes), box 2, Mitchell Collection; KDL, "Acorns in the Storm," 27.

74. Vera Shlakman interview, Apr. 12, 1986 (quotes); KDL, "Report of the Director of Research to the Council of Industrial Studies," *Report of the President of Smith College*, 1935, 39; KDL, "Report of the Director of Research to the Council of Industrial Studies," *Report of the President of Smith College*, 1936, 40–41, both in SCA.

75. Shlakman, *Economic History of a Factory Town*. For Shlakman's significance, see Fitzpatrick, *History's Memory*, 141–42, 182–83, 186, 205–6, 221–22; Kessler-Harris, "Vera Shlakman"; Gutman and D. Bell, *New England Working Class*, ix–x; N. Davis and J. Scott, *Women's History*, 11.

76. Shlakman built on the work of an earlier left feminist scholar, Caroline F. Ware, whose pioneering study, *The Early New England Cotton Manufacture*, appeared in 1931. Hannah Josephson, author of *The Golden Threads: New England's Mill Girls and Magnates* (1949), carried Shlakman's—and the Council's—work forward. Josephson adopted both Shlakman's portrait of the Boston Associates and her commitment to putting women at the center of the action. It was Josephson who stamped the story of the New England mill girls in collective memory. Shlakman was a victim of the post–World War II Red Scare, which cut short her career.

77. Kessler-Harris, "Vera Shlakman," 196 (quote), 200; "The 'Shameful Era' Begins to End for Professors Dismissed by City U.," *New York Times*, Mar. 26, 1980; "10 Teachers Ousted in 50s Given Restitution from City," *New York Times*, Apr. 29, 1982; "Vera Shlakman, Professor Fired During Red Scare, Dies at 108," *New York Times*, Nov. 27, 2017.

78. Gutman quoted in Kessler-Harris, "Vera Shlakman," 200; Fink, *Progressive Intellectuals*, 52–79.

CHAPTER FOURTEEN: "HEARTBREAKING GAPS"

1. Kennedy, *Freedom from Fear*, 257, 260–61 (quote on 261).

2. Leuchtenburg, *Franklin D. Roosevelt*, 130–33.

3. KDL, "Acorns in the Storm," 27; D. Douglas, "What Kind of Unemployment Insurance?" 4 (first quote), 5 (third quote); D. Douglas to Miss Wiesman, Jan. 9, 1934 (second quote), Consumers' League of Massachusetts Papers, Schlesinger Library, Radcliffe Institute, Harvard University. The fullest accounts of the campaign for the Workers' Bill are Casebeer, "Unemployment Insurance"; Casebeer, "Workers' Unemployment." See also L. Gordon, *Pitied but Not Entitled*, 234–41.

4. Casebeer, "Unemployment Insurance," 274–75, 295–96. For the charge that the bill was a Communist plot aimed not at passing legislation but at recruiting members and whipping up revolutionary fervor, see Dies, *Trojan Horse*, 90–95; Klehr, *Heyday of American Communism*, 284–89. For van Kleeck, see L. Gordon, *Pitied but Not Entitled*, 209–10; E. Lewis, "Mary Abby van Kleeck"; Alchon, "Mary van Kleeck and Scientific Management"; Alchon, "Mary van Kleeck"; Oldenziel, "Gender and Scientific Management"; Nyland and Rix, "Mary van Kleeck"; Anthony, *Max Yergan*, 183–84, 193–96, 208–9.

5. D. Douglas, "Workers of America," 29–30 (first quote); "Prof. Douglas Says

Security Bill Will Pass," *Springfield (MA) Union*, May 5, 1936 (second quote), newsclip in Faculty Biographical File Collection, Dorothy Wolff Douglas, SCA.

6. Hahamovitch, *Fruits of Their Labor*, 140–50.

7. "Report of Fact-Finding and Co-operators' Committee appointed by Alumnae of the Bryn Mawr Summer School for Women Workers in Industry," May 5, 1935, box 34, van Kleeck Papers; "Bryn Mawr Scored on Barring School," *New York Times*, June 4, 1935; Dorothy Dunbar Bromley, "Shall Donors Control Collegiate Policies?" *New York World-Telegram*, June 5, 1935, newsclip in Faculty Biographical File Collection, Dorothy Wolff Douglas, SCA; F. Schneider, *Patterns of Workers' Education*, 72.

8. Ehrenreich, *Altruistic Imagination*, 113 (first quote); League of Professional Groups for Foster and Ford, *Culture and the Crisis*; Mary van Kleeck, "Inter-Professional Action for Social Insurance," *Monthly Review*, June 1934, 9–10 (second quote on 10), newsclip in box 35, van Kleeck Papers.

9. *IPA News Bulletin* 2, Jan. 1935, 1, box 35, van Kleeck Papers; D. Douglas, "Social Security Act," 18 (first quote); D. Douglas, "What Kind of Unemployment Insurance?" 3–6 (second and third quotes on 6); D. Douglas, "Workers of America," 29–30; van Kleeck, "Open Letter," 2. See Stott, *Documentary Expression*, for the authority enjoyed by social workers during the Great Depression.

10. D. Douglas, "What Kind of Unemployment Insurance?" 3–6; D. Douglas, "Unemployment Insurance," 34.

11. D. Douglas, "Social Security Act," 18–19 (quote); D. Douglas, "What Kind of Unemployment Insurance?" 6; D. Douglas, "Unemployment Insurance," 9; "Statement of Dr. Dorothy W. Douglas, Professor of Economics, Smith College," *Social Insurance: Hearings before the Committee on Education and Labor, United States Senate, Seventy-Fourth Congress, Second Session on S. 3475, A Bill to Provide for the Establishment of a Nation-Wide System of Social Insurance*, Apr. 14–17, 74th Cong., 2nd sess. (Washington, DC: Government Printing Office, 1936), 82–89; Kennedy, *Freedom from Fear*, 166.

12. In contrast, the national leaders of the American Federation of Labor opposed federal legislation altogether, relying instead on the ability of skilled craftsmen to bargain for benefits from individual employers: Casebeer, "Unemployment Insurance," 266; Poole, *Segregated Origins*, 22.

13. van Kleeck, "Security for Americans," 121–24 (quote on 124); Poole, *Segregated Origins*, 22. See P. Douglas, *Social Security*, 74–83, for a balanced and positive view of the bill.

14. Poole, *Segregated Origins*, 163; L. Gordon, *Pitied but Not Entitled*, 257–77. For another attempt on the part of a left feminist reformer to influence the social security debate, see Muncy, "Women, Gender, and Politics," 60–83, 204.

15. Storrs, *Second Red Scare*, 24 (quote). For the New Deal women's network, maternalism as viewpoint and strategy, and the ideal of the family wage, see S. Ware, *Beyond Suffrage*; S. Ware, *Partner and I*; Muncy, *Female Dominion*; L. Gordon, *Pitied but Not Entitled*; B. Cook, *Eleanor Roosevelt*; L. Gordon, *Women, the State and Welfare*; L. Gordon, "Social Insurance"; Ladd-Taylor, *Mother-Work*; Weiner,

"Maternalism as a Paradigm," 96–139; Mink, *Wages of Motherhood*; Kessler-Harris, *Pursuit of Equity*.

16. For this "entering wedge" strategy, see Storrs, *Civilizing Capitalism*, 41–59; Sklar, "Two Political Cultures."

17. Storrs, *Second Red Scare*.

18. Cohen, *Old Left Was Young*; Storrs, *Second Red Scare*, 16–50.

19. Frances H. Williams interview, Oct. 31–Nov. 1, 1977 (quote); Frances Williams interview, Nov. 14, 1981, tape 1, side B, 031–060, Southern Women, the Student YWCA, and Race (1920–1944) Collection, SSC. For the OPA and women's roles within it, see Korstad, *Civil Rights Unionism*, 163, 256–57; Storrs, *Second Red Scare*, 27, 51–53, 76–85; M. Jacobs, "How About Some Meat?"

20. Storrs, *Second Red Scare*, 27, 78–80; Bowles, *Promises to Keep*, 63–64; "Miss Frances H. Williams," Department of Public Relations, National Board, YWCA, Apr. 24, 1942 (quote), YWCA Records; F. Williams, "Minority Groups."

21. Frances H. Williams interview, Oct. 31–Nov. 1, 1977; Albin Krebs, "Chester Bowles Is Dead at 85; Served in 4 Administrations," *New York Times*, May 26, 1986.

22. Storrs, *Second Red Scare*, 49 (quote), 45.

23. "Prof. Douglas Says Security Bill Will Pass," *Springfield (MA) Union*, May 5, 1936 (first quote), newsclip in Faculty Biographical File Collection, Dorothy Wolff Douglas, SCA; Denning, *Cultural Front*, xiv (second quote), 21–37; U.S. House, *Unemployment Old Age and Social Insurance: Hearings before a Sub-Committee of the Committee on Labor on H.R. 2827, A Bill to Provide for the Establishment of Unemployment, Old Age and Social Insurance and for Other Purposes; H.R. 2859, A Bill to Provide for the Establishment of Unemployment and Social Insurance and for Other Purposes; H.R. 185, A Bill to Provide for the Establishment of a System of Unemployment Insurance and for Other Purposes; and H.R. 10, A Bill to Provide for the Establishment of Unemployment and Social Insurance and for Other Purposes*, Feb. 4–8, 11–15, 74th Cong., 1st sess. (Washington, DC: Government Printing Office, 1935), 652 (third quote); L. Gordon, *Pitied but Not Entitled*, 262, 304.

24. U.S. House, *Unemployment Old Age and Social Insurance: Hearings before a Sub-Committee of the Committee on Labor on H.R. 2827, A Bill to Provide for the Establishment of Unemployment, Old Age and Social Insurance and for Other Purposes; H.R. 2859, A Bill to Provide for the Establishment of Unemployment and Social Insurance and for Other Purposes; H.R. 185, A Bill to Provide for the Establishment of a System of Unemployment Insurance and for Other Purposes; and H.R. 10, A Bill to Provide for the Establishment of Unemployment and Social Insurance and for Other Purposes*, Feb. 4–8, 11–15, 74th Cong., 1st sess. (Washington, DC: Government Printing Office, 1935), 652 (first quote), 653 (second quote), 654 (third quote).

25. L. Gordon, *Pitied but Not Entitled*, 4; Kennedy, *Freedom from Fear*, 271.

26. Leuchtenburg, *Franklin D. Roosevelt*, 132 (quote); Kennedy, *Freedom from Fear*, 267. This discussion of the shortcomings of the Social Security Act and the two-tiered system it helped to create rests on a large body of scholarship. See,

in addition to the literature cited elsewhere in this chapter, M. Brown, *Race, Money*. For a different point of view, see DeWitt, "Decision to Exclude."

27. L. Gordon, *Pitied but Not Entitled*, 1.

28. Kennedy, *Freedom from Fear*, 169; D. Douglas, "What Kind of Unemployment Insurance?" 3–6 (quote on 3).

29. L. Gordon, *Pitied but Not Entitled*, 4; Storrs, *Second Red Scare*; Kennedy, *Freedom from Fear*, 270 (quote).

30. Katznelson, *Affirmative Action*.

31. *Booklist*, review of KDL and D. Douglas, *Child Workers in America*, June 1937, 298 (quotes); KDL and D. Douglas, *Child Workers in America*.

32. KDL and D. Douglas, *Child Workers in America*, 15 (quote); Stott, *Documentary Expression*.

33. See, for example, "Child Labor Problem," *Atlanta Constitution*, Oct. 3, 1937. For International Publishers, which brought out many of the era's left-wing books, see Lincove, "Radical Publishing." They issued two print runs of *Child Workers in America* at 2,000 copies each: Betty Smith to J. Hall, n.d. 1996.

34. KDL interview, Apr. 24, 1985, 42; "Katharine Du Pre Lumpkin," curriculum vitae enclosed in KDL to William Kiekhofer, May 6, 1932, Series 7/9/4, box 18, William H. Kiekhofer Papers, Archives and Records Management, University of Wisconsin–Madison Libraries; KDL, "Comparative Study of Work Life of Children in Massachusetts and Alabama" and "A study of the methods of prevention of child labor in urban and rural areas of the Soviet Union," Grant-in-Aid Minutes, 1932–1938, Social Science Research Council Accession 1, Rockefeller Archives Center, Sleepy Hollow, NY; KDL and D. Douglas, *Child Workers in America*, ix, 293–95.

35. KDL, *Making*, 155 (quote); R. M. B., "Child Labor Control," *Christian Science Monitor*, June 12, 1937, 18 (second quote). For the impact of these myths on child labor reform, see Effland, "Agrarianism."

36. KDL and D. Douglas, *Child Workers in America*, vi (first quote); Tomes, "From Useful to Useless," 50–54 (second quote on 50); Zelizer, *Priceless Child*, 58.

37. KDL, "Child Labor Provisions," 391 (quote); S. Ware, *Beyond Suffrage*, 19, 36, 80–84, 102–4. Also in 1933, Congress passed the National Industrial Recovery Act (NIRA), a temporary measure that sought to raise prices by allowing trade associations to ignore antitrust laws and reduce production through codes of fair competition, most of which limited child labor. Even the southern states, not one of which had ratified the amendment, returned decisive majorities in favor of its passage.

38. E. Matthews, review of *Child Workers in America*, 530 (quote); KDL and D. Douglas, *Child Workers in America*, 82–104; McWilliams, *Factories in the Field*.

39. Effland, "Agrarianism," 281–97; KDL and D. Douglas, *Child Workers in America*, 62 (quotes).

40. KDL and D. Douglas, *Child Workers in America*, 59 (quote).

41. KDL and D. Douglas, *Child Workers in America*, 86 (quote).

42. KDL and D. Douglas, *Child Workers in America*, 86 (quote), 62; Effland, "Agrarianism," 290.

43. D. Douglas, "Wages and Hours Legislation and the Child Labor Problem," an address before the Annual Meeting of the National Consumers League on "Labor Standards Legislation: A Bulwark for Democracy," New York, NY, Dec. 8, 1939, 4, Tamiment Library and Robert F. Wagner Labor Archive, New York University.

44. KDL and D. Douglas, *Child Workers in America*, 87 (first quote), 86 (second quote).

45. KDL and D. Douglas, *Child Workers in America*, 3–4 (first quote), 4 (second quote), 6 (third quote).

46. KDL and D. Douglas, *Child Workers in America*, 6 (quote).

47. Malcolm Cowley quoted in S. Ware, *Beyond Suffrage*, 152.

48. Stott, *Documentary Expression*, 92–95, 143–70. Examples include Raper, *Preface to Peasantry*; Raper, *Sharecroppers All*; Raper and Reid, *Tenants of the Almighty*; Dollard, *Caste and Class*; Hagood, *Mothers of the South*.

49. L. Gordon, "Social Insurance," 19–54; KDL and D. Douglas, *Child Workers in America*, 140 (first quote), 295 (second quote).

50. Rose C. Feld, "Child Labor in This Country," *New York Times*, June 13, 1937 (quote). Similar tensions marked other contemporary studies. John Dollard, author of *Caste and Class in a Southern Town*, feared that he might not be believed if he could not "hook his findings into the number system": Stott, *Documentary Expression*, 154 (quote). Arthur Raper followed his fact-filled *Preface to Peasantry* (1936), a brilliant study of the middle Georgia plantation belt where the Lumpkin sisters grew up, with *Sharecroppers All!* (1941), a jeremiad against industrial capitalism, and *Tenants of the Almighty* (1943), a documentary entwining pictures and words.

51. L. Gordon, *Dorothea Lange*, 193–300; D. Douglas, "Wages and Hours Legislation and the Child Labor Problem," an address before the Annual Meeting of the National Consumers League on "Labor Standards Legislation: A Bulwark for Democracy," New York, NY, Dec. 8, 1939, 1 (first quote), Tamiment Library and Robert F. Wagner Labor Archive, New York University; KDL and D. Douglas, *Child Workers in America*, 284 (second quote).

52. KDL and D. Douglas, *Child Workers in America*, 288 (first quote), 289 (second quote).

53. KDL, "Child Labor Provisions," 391.

54. Fuller, "Child Labor Today," 11–12 (first quote on 11); "Child Labor Problem in America Studied Exhaustively," *Springfield Republican*, May 18, 1937 (second and third quotes); John Selby, "Women Authors Severely Indict Child Labor," *Charlotte Observer*, May 9, 1937 (fourth quote).

55. Katznelson, Geiger, and Kryder, "Limiting Liberalism," 283–306; Korstad, *Civil Rights Unionism*, 132–33; J. Patterson, "Conservative Coalition."

56. KDL, "Child Labor Provisions," 403, 393 (quote).

57. D. Douglas, "Wages and Hours Legislation," 1 (first quote), 2 (second quote); KDL, review of *Child Labor Legislation*.

58. D. Douglas, "Social Security Act," 18–19 (first quote on 18); Storrs, *Civilizing Capitalism*, 198 (second quote); D. Douglas, "Wages and Hours Legislation, 5 (third quote); KDL, "Child Labor Provisions."

59. Having been ratified by a majority of the state governments but falling short of the requisite three-fourths majority demanded by the Constitution, the Child Labor Amendment remains pending to this day.

60. Daniel, *Breaking the Land*; Schulman, *Cotton Belt to Sunbelt*.

61. Gregory, "Second Great Migration"; Raper, *Preface to Peasantry*, 3.

62. K. Clark and W. Klein, *Humanity and Justice*, 30 (quote). Examples of studies of migrants and sharecroppers include McWilliams, *Factories in the Field*; Agee and W. Evans, *Let Us Now Praise*.

63. Effland, "Agrarianism," 293.

CHAPTER FIFTEEN: RADICAL DREAMS, FASCIST THREATS

1. KDL to Anna Rochester, May 16, 1936 (quote), Anna Rochester Papers, Special Collections and University Archives, University of Oregon Libraries.

2. Memo, SAC, WFO, to Director, FBI, 8/27/51, Dorothy Wolff Douglas, HQ-100-355436, D. Douglas FBI File; Dorothy Douglas, Dorothea Douglas, Paul Douglas, Katherine Lumpkin, S.S. *Empress of Britain*, Names of Alien Passengers, Cherbourg to Southampton, July 2, 1936, *UK, Incoming Passenger Lists, 1878–1960*, Ancestry.com; Walter Duranty, "Tourists Jamming Moscow's Hotels," *New York Times*, July 19, 1936. For Soviet institutions charged with managing tourism and presenting the country in the best possible light, see Engerman, *Modernization*, 155.

3. KDL, "Democratic Ways," 10–11, 29–30 (quote on 30).

4. Filene, *American Views of Soviet Russia*, xi (quote); Choi Chatterjee to J. Hall, Jan. 29, 2004; Chatterjee, "Odds and Ends"; D. Douglas and KDL, comment in *Soviet Russia Today*, Nov.–Dec. 1937, 78 (quote).

5. C. McKay and Jarrett, *Long Way from Home*, 5 (quote); Gilmore, *Defying Dixie*, 31–32, 49–50, 62, 167.

6. KDL, "Democratic Ways," 10–11, 29–30 (quotes on 10–11).

7. KDL, "Democratic Ways," 11 (first and third quotes), 29 (fourth through seventh quotes), 30 (eighth quote); KDL, *Making*, 215 (second quote).

8. D. Douglas, *Mexican Labor*, 24 (quote).

9. Sarah Flynn, "Hulda Rees Flynn, In Her Own Words," May 5, 2001 (quote). Thanks to Sarah Flynn for sharing this remembrance of her mother. *Smith College Weekly*, May 19, 1937; Oct. 20, 1937; Nov. 23, 1938; Feb. 1, 1939, all in SCA.

10. For these debates and their effect on leftist politics, see Engerman, *Modernization*, 237–43; Aaron, *Writers on the Left*; Klehr, *Heyday of American Communism*; Kutulas, *Long War*.

11. "An Open Letter to American Liberals," *Soviet Russian Today*, Mar. 1937, 14–15, reprinted in Filene, *American Views of Soviet Russia*, 117–21 (first quote on 119, second and third quotes on 117); Dewey Commission, *Not Guilty*.

12. Engerman, *Modernization*; Hollander, *Political Pilgrims*; "To All Active Supporters of Democracy and Peace," *Soviet Russia Today*, Sept. 1939, 24–25, 28.

13. This discussion of the Mexican Revolution and Cardenismo is drawn primarily from A. Knight, "Cardenismo"; Britton, *Revolution and Ideology*; Ashby, *Orga-*

nized Labor; Chasteen, *Born in Blood and Fire*; Sherman, *Mexican Right*; and Jocelyn Olcott, *Revolutionary Women*.

14. Secretary of State Cordell Hull quoted in Britton, *Revolution and Ideology*, 132. For the influence of the Communist Party in Mexico (the PCM) during the Popular Front period, see Jocelyn Olcott, *Revolutionary Women*, 106–22.

15. Britton, *Revolution and Ideology*, 129, 131–32, 140–42, 156, 158; Olsson, "Sharecroppers and *Campesinos*"; D. Douglas, *Mexican Labor*, 2 (quote).

16. D. Douglas, *Mexican Labor*, 21 (quote).

17. D. Douglas, *Mexican Labor*, 1 (first quote); D. Douglas, "Mexican Teachers' Union," 14 (second quote). For the *Southern Worker*, see https://www.marxists.org/history/usa/pubs/southernworker/.

18. C. Baker, *Generous Spirit*, 119–39; M. Page, *Moscow Yankee*; M. Page, "Mexico Speaks (plan of book)," folder 80, Page Papers.

19. KDL, "Democratic Ways," 30 (quote); C. Baker, *Generous Spirit*, 163.

20. Mary van Kleeck to D. Douglas, Aug. 4, 1938, van Kleeck Papers. For the International Industrial Relations Institute, see Oldenziel, "Gender and Scientific Management."

21. D. Douglas, *Mexican Labor*, 4 (quote); "Return of Mrs. Douglas from Sabbatical Leave of Absence," press release, Smith College, Feb. 3, 1939, Faculty Biographical Files, Dorothy Wolff Douglas, SCA; Ashby, *Organized Labor*.

22. Britton, *Revolution and Ideology*, 140 (quote), 158; C. Baker, *Generous Spirit*, 163.

23. Richard H. Thornton to To Whom It May Concern, Aug. 10, 1938, folder 2, Page Papers.

24. Vicente Lombardo Toledano to [?], Aug. 18, 1938, folder 2, Page Papers.

25. C. Baker, *Generous Spirit*, 163–64; M. Page, "Cárdenas Speaks for Mexico," 3–5; M. Page, "Mexico Speaks (plan of book)," 1 (first quote); M. Page, "Mexico— Behind the News" (second quote), both in folder 80, Page Papers. For Ana María Hernández, see Jocelyn Olcott, "Miracle Workers."

26. M. Page, "Mexico Speaks—outline," 2 (quote), folder 80, Page Papers; C. Baker, *Generous Spirit*, 163–64; M. Page, "Bordertown Girl," folder 81, Page Papers. For Briggs and the YWCA, which was the most successful of the US women's groups that sought to practice what they called "human internationalism"—a method of pursuing peace and cooperation through person-to-person contacts—in Mexico in the 1920s and 1930s, see Threlkeld, *Pan American Women*, 10, 22–24, 32–33, 39–42, 79–81, 97–99, 108–9, 178–83, 192.

27. M. Page, "Mexico Speaks: Highway of Nations," 9 (quote); M. Page, "Mexico Speaks—outline," 2, folder 80, both in Page Papers.

28. D. Douglas, *Mexican Labor*, 2 (first quote), 3 (second quote), 13 (third quote), 9 (fourth quote).

29. D. Douglas, "Land and Labor in Mexico," 128 (quote). For the La Laguna experiment, see Ashby, *Organized Labor*, 142–78; Jocelyn Olcott, *Revolutionary Women*, 123–58.

30. D. Douglas, *Mexican Labor*, 1 (first quote); D. Douglas, "Land and Labor in Mexico," 152 (second quote). The Southern Tenant Farmers Union had recently sent a delegation to Comarca Lagunera which reported back to its members on

"land and liberty for Mexican farmers": Bretton and H. Mitchell, *Land and Liberty for Mexican Farmers*.

31. D. Douglas, "Mexican Teachers' Union," 14–17, 15 (quotes). For rural teachers and the socialist educational experiment, see Jocelyn Olcott, *Revolutionary Women*, 96–101; A. Knight, "Cardenismo."

32. D. Douglas, *Mexican Labor*, 15–16 (quotes).

33. D. Douglas, "Land and Labor in Mexico," 145–46 (first quote); D. Douglas, *Mexican Labor*, 16 (second and fourth quote), 15 (third quote), 23 (fifth quote).

34. D. Douglas, *Mexican Labor*, 24 (quotes).

35. KDL to *New York Times*, Jan. 17, 1939 (first quote); KDL to Cordell Hull, Jan. 18, [1939], (second quote), both from FBI Report, Washington, DC, Jan. 15, 1954, Katherine D. Lumpkin, HQ 100–400110–10, 3–4, KDL FBI File.

36. Heale, *McCarthy's Americans*, 150–70 (first quote on 156); Delegard, *Battling Miss Bolsheviki*, 120 (second quote), 118 (third quote).

37. Schrecker, *No Ivory Tower*, 68–69; J. L. Holmes, "Politics of Anticommunism."

38. "Meeting of Smith Branch of University Professors Opposes Teacher's Oaths," *Smith College Weekly*, Nov. 27, 1935 (quotes), SCA; "Smith Professors Ask Teachers' Oath Repeal," *Boston Evening Globe*, Nov. 19, 1935.

39. Heale, *McCarthy's Americans*, 158 (quotes); Thorp, *Neilson of Smith*, 182–90.

40. "Innuendo of Moscow Connection Arouses Dr. Neilson's Mirth," *Springfield Daily Republican*, Mar. 6, 1936 (first, third, and fourth quotes); Thorp, *Neilson of Smith*, 182–90 (second quote); "State Educators Hold Hearing on Teachers Oath Bill in Boston," Smith College Weekly, Mar. 11, 1936, SCA; Herring, *Neilson of Smith*, 37 (fifth and sixth quotes); Dilling, *Red Network*, 310. See also Hadley, *Sinister Shadows*, a red-baiting novel in which Neilson appears as a villain.

41. R. Goldstein, *Little "Red Scares"*; "Justices Uphold a Teachers' Oath," *New York Times*, Jan. 22, 1967.

42. Mary van Kleeck, "Inter-Professional Action for Social Insurance," *Monthly Review*, June 1934, 10 (quote), van Kleeck Papers; M. Murphy, *Blackboard Unions*, 46–60, 90, 98–123, 150–74; C. Taylor, *Reds at the Blackboard*, 2–4, 11–75; Eaton, *American Federation of Teachers*, 18–37, 72; Frederickson, "Mary Cornelia Barker."

43. Brogan, "Education Deform and Social Justice Unionism" (quote); C. Taylor, *Reds at the Blackboard*, 2–4; M. Murphy, *Blackboard Unions*, 150–74; Robert Gorham Davis testimony, Feb. 25, 1953, in U.S. House, *Communist Methods of Infiltration (Education): Hearings before the Committee on Un-American Activities, House of Representatives*, 83rd Cong., 1st sess. (Washington, DC: Government Printing Office, 1953), 23, 25, 38; "Monthly Report," Nov. 1937, series 6, box 24, folder 230, American Federation of Teachers Records, Walter P. Reuther Library, Wayne State University, Detroit, MI; "Who Are the Teachers' Friends?"; "Mrs. Douglas to Address 3rd Annual Conference of AFT," Apr. 12, 1939, *Springfield Union*, Faculty Biographical File Collection, Dorothy Wolff Douglas, SCA; D. Douglas, "Democracy and Higher Education," 27–28.

44. M. Murphy, *Blackboard Unions*, 119–23, 150–74.

45. Eaton, *American Federation of Teachers*, 109–10; C. Taylor, *Reds at the Blackboard*,

29, 61–74; M. Murphy, *Blackboard Unions*, 150–74; Jerome Davis, "Address of President Jerome Davis to the Twenty-First Annual Convention of the American Federation of Teachers," series 3, box 3, folder "Jerome Davis," American Federation of Teachers Records, Walter P. Reuther Library, Wayne State University, Detroit, MI. For Counts, see Engerman, *Modernization*, 174–86.

46. Heale, *McCarthy's Americans*, 164–65, 168.

47. The following account of this play is drawn from Bein, *Let Freedom Ring*; A. Green, "Southern Cotton Mill Rhyme"; M. Goldstein, *Political Stage*, 130–31, 154, 218–19, 222–25, 233–34, 258; and contemporary newspapers. Will Geer, a Popular Front figure who played Granpap, went on to fame and fortune on *The Waltons*, an enormously popular television series that, in the wake of the civil rights revolution, took a backward glance at the bucolic (white) southern mountains.

48. G. Lumpkin to Lillian Gilkes, Dec. 20, 1974 (quotes), box 3, Gilkes Papers; G. Lumpkin Diary, 1963–1975, Nov. 13, 1967, in J. Hall's possession, thanks to Joseph H. Lumpkin Sr.; Harris, "Alone in the Dark," 97; Memorandum to Mr. McManus, n.d., G. Lumpkin Papers.

49. Worthington Minor, "Actors' Repertory Company," *New York Times*, Nov. 15, 1936 (quote). For examples of positive reviews from both leftist and mainstream critics, see Brooks Atkinson, "*Let Freedom Ring*, Being a Tragic Drama about the Fortunes of Labor in Cotton Mills," *New York Times*, Nov. 7, 1935; Dunne, "*Let Freedom Ring* Country," 26–27; J. T. Farrell, "Theater: *Let Freedom Ring*," 27–28; Clifford Odets to ed., *New York Times*, Nov. 17, 1935.

50. Albert Bein to ed., *New York Times*, Nov. 29, 1936; Mike Gold, "Change the World!" *Daily Worker*, Nov. 12, Dec. 10, and Dec. 11, 1935; M. Goldstein, *Political Stage*, 39–40, 130, 157, 218–19, 222–25, 233–34; A. Green, "Southern Cotton Mill Rhyme," 290; Himelstein, *Drama Was a Weapon*, 198; Margaret Larkin to ed., *New York Times*, Nov. 22, 1936; Worthington Minor, "Actors' Repertory Company," *New York Times*, Nov. 15, 1936; J. Williams, *Stage Left*, 186–87.

51. H. Flanagan, *History of the Federal Theatre*, 162–63; "Propaganda," *Newsweek*, July 25, 1936, 21; A. Green, "Southern Cotton Mill Rhyme," 289–92; Altenbaugh, "Proletarian Drama," 208; Sporn, *Against Itself*, 172, 178–79, 292 (quote on 179).

52. G. Lumpkin, "All South Meet for Union Civil Rights Called as Fight on Sedition Bill Grows," *Southern Worker*, Apr.–May 1935; G. Lumpkin, "Miserable Offender," 281–88; G. Lumpkin, "Let Us Speak," 4–5; G. Lumpkin, "Trial by Fire," 18–25; G. Lumpkin, "Pearl Necklace," 4–5; G. Lumpkin, "Mayme Brown," 18–19; G. Lumpkin, "Remember These Needy," 10; [G. Lumpkin,] "Letter from the South," 31; G. Lumpkin, "Debutante," 16–17, 28–30; G. Lumpkin, "Southern Women Salute Herndon!" 14; G. Lumpkin and Kaiser, "Learning to Make History," 17–21; G. Lumpkin, "Bridesmaids Carried Lilies," 345–70; G. Lumpkin, "Dory"; G. Lumpkin, "Treasure." "The Treasure" was reprinted in two prestigious anthologies: Hansen, *O. Henry Memorial Award*; Brooks and R. Warren, *Anthology of Stories*.

53. Folsom, *Days of Anger*, 332; "Grace Lumpkin, A.S.U. Speaker is Famed Proletarian Writer," May 4, 1936; "A.S.U. to Hear Grace Lumpkin," May 5, 1936;

"Grace Lumpkin Asks Assistance for Croppers," all in *Columbia (University) Daily Spectator*, May 6, 1936; "Phi Mu," *Brooklyn Daily Eagle*, Oct. 25, 1936.

54. Botkin, "Regionalism and Culture," 146–54 (quote on 154). Much of the following discussion of Botkin, proletarian regionalism, and the Agrarians is drawn from J. Hall, "Women Writers."

55. Denning, *Cultural Front*, 132–36; Wixson, *Worker-Writer in America*, 377 (first quote); Davidson, "Trend of Literature," 185, 199 (second quote), 204.

56. S. Davis, "Ben Botkin's FBI File," 16–17; Rourke, "Significance of Sections," 149, 151 (quotes); Denning, *Cultural Front*, 64–77. See also J. Rubin, *Constance Rourke*.

57. Botkin, "Regionalism and Culture," 152 (quote); Dorman, *Revolt of the Provinces*, 180–205.

58. Denning, *Cultural Front*, 134 (quote), 239. Rourke served as editor of the Federal Arts Project's *Index of American Design*; Botkin as national folklore editor of the Federal Writers' Project (FWP), chairman of the Works Progress Administration's Joint Committee on the Folk Arts, and head of the Library of Congress's Archive on American Folk Song; and Brown as national editor of Negro Affairs for the Federal Writers' Project, overseeing the research on African American culture for the state guidebook series as well as other major FWP publications. On the slave narratives, see Federal Writers' Project, *Lay My Burden Down*. Botkin saw the narratives not only as "history from the bottom up," but also as the voice of the disfranchised speaking in and to the present moment. "As the last of the ex-slaves speak, . . ." he wrote, "their words take on new meaning and relevance in the light of the present, with its new freedoms and new forms of slavery" (xiii).

59. Twelve Southerners, *I'll Take My Stand*. Sympathetic studies of the Agrarians' social views usually stress their critique of capitalism's assault on spiritual values. Few, however, have focused specifically on the Agrarians' political writings in the years after the publication of *I'll Take My Stand*. For a thorough examination of this period of conservative political activism, see Bingham and Underwood, *Southern Agrarians*; P. Murphy, *Rebuke of History*.

60. For critiques of the Agrarians by the African American writers of the time, see S. Brown, "Romantic Defense"; S. Brown, "Literary Scene," 20; and S. Brown, "Unhistoric History." Sterling Brown's highly acclaimed volume of poems, *Southern Road* (New York, 1932), could be seen as a powerful answer to the Agrarians as well. It drew on folk materials and idioms not to evoke a stable, organic past but to express the comedy and tragedy of contemporary black rural life. Zora Neale Hurston performed similar cultural work.

61. Underwood, *Allen Tate*, 106–7, 123–26 (quote on 107).

62. Tate, *Reactionary Essays*. *FIGHT* was the organ of the American League Against War and Fascism. For this incident see E. Shapiro, "American Conservative Intellectuals," 372 (quote); Underwood, *Allen Tate*, 239–42; M. J. Tucker, *They Loved Him*; A. Stone, "Seward Collins," 14–19; Brinkmeyer, *Fourth Ghost*.

63. G. Lumpkin, "I Want a King," 3 (first quote), 14 (second and third quotes). The editors of the *New Republic* featured excerpts from Grace's interview with Col-

lins and her subsequent exchange with Allen Tate in "Fascism and the Southern Agrarians," *New Republic*, May 27, 1936: 76 (subsequent quotes).

64. A. Stone, "Seward Collins," 14 (first quote); "Fascism and the Southern Agrarians," *New Republic*, May 27, 1936: 76 (subsequent quotes).

65. Allen Tate to Donald Davidson, Feb. 23, 1936, box 14, folder 1, Donald Davidson Papers, Special Collections and University Archives, Jean and Alexander Heard Library, Vanderbilt University, Nashville, TN (first quote); "Sunny Side of Fascism," 131–32 (second quote 132); A. Stone, "Seward Collins," 18–19; Underwood, *Allen Tate*, 242–44.

66. G. Lumpkin to Lillian Gilkes, n.d. [ca. 1939], (first quote), box 3, Gilkes Papers; G. Lumpkin to Robert Cantwell, [1937] (subsequent quotes), Robert Cantwell to G. Lumpkin, Aug. 26, 1937, both in box 2, folder 5, Robert Cantwell Papers, Special Collections and University Archives, University of Oregon Libraries; Fellowship application summary for Grace Lumpkin, 1938, John Simon Guggenheim Memorial Foundation, New York City.

67. G. Lumpkin and Kaiser, "Learning to Make History," 17–21; G. Lumpkin to Lillian Gilkes, [1938] (quote), box 3, Gilkes Papers.

68. Fellowship application summary for Grace Lumpkin, 1938–1939 (quote), John Simon Guggenheim Memorial Foundation, New York City.

69. G. Lumpkin, "Bridesmaids Carried Lilies," 345–70 (first quote on 349, second quote on 359, third quote on 358, fourth quote on 370). See also G. Lumpkin, "Debutante," 16–17, 28–30.

70. G. Lumpkin to Robert Cantwell, [1937] (quote), box 2, folder 5, Robert Cantwell Papers, Special Collections and University Archives, University of Oregon Libraries.

CHAPTER SIXTEEN: SISTERS AND STRANGERS

1. G. Lumpkin, *Wedding*, 286 (first and third quotes); Annette Lumpkin to Elizabeth Lumpkin Glenn, Dec. 18, [1906], in J. Hall's possession, thanks to Katherine Glenn Kent.

2. KDL, *South in Progress*.

3. G. Lumpkin, *Wedding*, 5–7, 137 (first quote); Gilkes, afterword to *Wedding*, 274 (subsequent quotes); Donaldson, "Gender and History," 3–14.

4. G. Lumpkin, *Wedding*, 18 (first quote), 64 (second and third quotes), 286, 178, 179 (fourth quote).

5. G. Lumpkin, *Wedding*, 234–35.

6. O'Neil, "Tying the Knots," 125–85.

7. G. Lumpkin, *Wedding*, 268–69, 72 (first quote); "Miss Lumpkin at Monteagle," *Columbia (SC) State*, Aug. 20, 1905 (second quote); "Mrs. Eugene B. Glenn Dies," *Asheville (NC) Citizen*, Feb. 15, 1963.

8. G. Lumpkin, *Wedding*, 266–68.

9. Lorrine Pruette, "New Regional Novels of the West and South," *New York Herald Tribune Books*, Mar. 5, 1939 (first quote); "Bride's Strike," *Time*, Feb. 27, 1939 (second, third, and fourth quotes); Armfield, "Cross Section"; Wallace, "Twenty-Four Hours"; Salomon, "South Carolina Town"; "The Wedding,"

Springfield (MA) Republican, Apr. 9, 1939; Charles Poore, "Books of the Times," *New York Times*, July 1, 1939.

10. Gilkes, afterword to *Wedding*, 273 (first quote), 281 (second quote); Printz, "Tracing the Fault Lines," 168 (third quote). For the dystopian elements in women's proletarian fiction, see also P. Rabinowitz, *Labor and Desire*. Examples of such works include Slesinger, *Unpossessed*; Herbst, *Rope of Gold*.

11. Printz, "Tracing the Fault Lines," 168, 182; Oppenheimer, *Exit Right*, 29 (quote).

12. Rosenfelt, "From the Thirties," 381 (quote).

13. My account of the shifting and contradictory stance of the CP on the woman question is especially indebted to Foley, *Radical Representations*, 213–46, 233n21, 344–45 (quote on 220); Foley, "Women and the Left"; R. Shaffer, "Women and the Communist Party"; Landes, "Marxism and the Woman Question"; Baxandall, "Question Seldom Asked"; Coiner, *Better Red*; Weigand, *Red Feminism*.

14. Gosse, "To Organize"; Orleck, "That Mythical Thing"; Baxandall, "Question Seldom Asked," 156; Weigand, *Red Feminism*, 23–24.

15. McDonald, *Feminism, the Left*.

16. Sargent, *Women and Revolution*.

17. On the politics of sex and gender in the CP and the Soviet Union, see G. Lumpkin, "Emancipation and Exploitation," 26–27; K. Brown and Faue, "Social Bonds, Sexual Politics"; K. Brown and Faue, "Revolutionary Desire"; Chauncey, *Gay New York*, 230–32; Mickenberg, "Suffragettes and Soviets," 1050; W. Goldman, *Women, the State*, 291–94, 331–43; Foley, *Radical Representations*, 245.

18. Harlick, "Life of the Party," 55 (quote). See also T. Morgan, *Covert Life*, 35–36.

19. M. Intrator, "Furriers Fight," 5, 7; B. Wolfe, *Life in Two Centuries*, 404 (quote).

20. [Benjamin Mandel], "Grace Lumpkin," n.d. [ca. June 7, 1951], RG 46: Senate Internal Security Subcommittee Records, Center for Legislative Archives, National Archives (quote).

21. C. Baker, *Generous Spirit*, 161–62 (quotes on 161); Myra Page interview, Apr. 25, 1988; Myra Page interview, June 8, 1987.

22. Eleanor Copenhaver, "Biennial Report for 1928 and 1929," Jan. 19, 1930, YWCA Records, 1 (first quote); Saunders, *Cultural Cold War*, 53 (second quote).

23. Oppenheimer, *Exit Right*, 11–68 (first quote on 25); Tanenhaus, *Whittaker Chambers*, 81 (second quote), 251–59.

24. Chambers, *Witness*, 63–64 (quote), 75–85; Tanenhaus, *Whittaker Chambers*, 75–85, 117–18, 123, 464–71. See also Hook, "Two Faiths"; M. Lee, *Creating Conservatism*; Diggins, *Up from Communism*, 423–24.

25. Tanenhaus, *Whittaker Chambers*, 75 (quote). For Chambers's portrayals of this first conversion experience, see also Herzog, *Spiritual-Industrial Complex*, 39; Chambers, *Witness*, 83.

26. Tanenhaus, *Whittaker Chambers*, 171 (quote), 464–71.

27. Chambers, *Witness*, 61 (first quote); Tanenhaus, *Whittaker Chambers*, 165 (second quote); Weinstein, *Perjury*, 347.

28. Tanenhaus, *Whittaker Chambers*, 164–65, 344–45; Chambers, *Witness*, 483.

29. "Re: Grace Hutchins, Reuben Shemitz," report of interview of Grace Hutchins by Special Agents Francis J. Gallant and Robert F. X. O'Keefe, Jan. 20, 1949,

folder "Grace Hutchins," Tanenhaus Papers; Grace Hutchins, "Not for Publication," Jan. 1949 (first quote), box 8, folder 12, Grace Hutchins Papers, Special Collections and Archives, University of Oregon Libraries; G. Lumpkin, "Law and the Spirit," 498 (second quote).

30. Evelyn Scott to G. Lumpkin, June 2, 1940 (first quote); Evelyn Scott to G. Lumpkin, Nov. 14, 1940 (subsequent quotes), both in G. Lumpkin Papers.

31. M. White, *Fighting the Current*, 205 (first and second quotes), 167 (third quote); Evelyn Scott to G. Lumpkin, June 2, 1940 (fourth quote); Evelyn Scott to G. Lumpkin, Nov. 24, 1940, both in G. Lumpkin Papers. See also Callard, *Pretty Good for a Woman*, 144–45.

32. Evelyn Scott to G. Lumpkin, [ca. 1940] (first and second quotes); Evelyn Scott to G. Lumpkin, Nov. 24, 1940 (subsequent quotes); G. Lumpkin, "Remember Now: A Play in Three Acts and Nine Scenes," 1951, 18 (hereafter G. Lumpkin, "Remember Now"), all in G. Lumpkin Papers.

33. G. Lumpkin interview, Aug. 6, 1974; G. Lumpkin interview, Sept. 25, 1971.

34. G. Lumpkin, "Remember Now," 60 (first quote), 100 (second quote), 3 (third, fifth, and sixth quotes), 102 (fourth quote).

35. G. Lumpkin, "Remember Now," 94 (first quote), 96 (second quote); Harris, "Alone in the Dark," 97 (third quote); *Track 13* (subsequent quotes), Archives of the Episcopal Church, Seminary of the Southwest, Austin, TX; G. Lumpkin interview, Sept. 25, 1971.

36. G. Lumpkin, "Remember Now," 104 (first quote); Harris, "Alone in the Dark," 97 (second quote).

37. G. Lumpkin, "Remember Now," 114 (quote). For a similar account, see Harris, "Alone in the Dark," 98.

38. *Track 13* (quotes), Archives of the Episcopal Church, Seminary of the Southwest, Austin, TX.

39. "Personals," *Asheville (NC) Citizen*, May 10, 1939; Elizabeth Lumpkin Glenn, "The Toombs of our Ancestors," 1939, in J. Hall's possession. Thanks to Thomas Bryan for sharing this manuscript with me. G. Lumpkin interview, Aug. 6, 1974, 48 (quotes).

40. Interviews with G. Lumpkin, Mar. 16, 18, 23, 1949, summarized in FBI Report by Robert F. X. O'Keefe, Apr. 6, 1949, Jay David Whittaker Chambers, NY 65-14920-3130, G. Lumpkin FBI File; Report of Divorce Granted Michael Intrator and Grace Lumpkin Intrator, Mar. 26, 1942, Dade County, State of Florida, Office of Vital Statistics; William W. L. Glenn to Elizabeth Lumpkin Glenn, Jan. 1, 1943, in J. Hall's possession, thanks to Amory Glenn and William W. L. Glenn; G. Lumpkin, "About Liberals," fragment of letter, [ca. 1966], G. Lumpkin Diary, 1963–1975, both in J. Hall's possession; Whittaker Chambers to William F. Buckley, May [19?], 1957, in Chambers, *Odyssey of a Friend*, 181 (first quote); Harris, "Alone in the Dark," 98 (second quote).

41. Elizabeth Lumpkin Glenn to William W. L. Glenn, Mar. 21, 1931 (first quote), in J. Hall's possession, thanks to Amory Glenn and William W. L. Glenn; Sack, *Moral Re-Armament*, 3–4 (second quote on 4), 53–54; Harris, "Alone in the Dark," 63–69. Founded by a former missionary named Frank Buchman,

Moral Re-Armament began as an attempt to convert college students on elite campuses after World War I, reinventing itself as a solution to international strife in the lead-up to World War II. Once war broke out, it devoted itself to maintaining harmony in labor relations, then turned to fighting communism in the 1950s. Buchman was a controversial figure throughout, in part because of his emphasis on sexual sin but especially because of his praise for Hitler as a bulwark against communism and his naïve effort to convert him to the cause. See "Men, Masters, and Messiahs," *Time Magazine*, Apr. 20, 1936.

42. J. S. Coleman Jr., "Unique Appeal of 'The Groups' Stirs Religious Life of Asheville," *Asheville (NC) Citizen-Times*, Mar. 29, 1931 (quote); Sack, *Moral Re-Armament*, 76–77.

43. By the time Grace met him, Shoemaker had broken with the group, in part because it had increasingly distanced itself from explicitly Christian language and the institutional church, but he continued to build his ministry around its message, techniques, and upper-class appeal: Sack, *Moral Re-Armament*, 22–25, 61–64, 116–17. For more on Shoemaker, see Hein and Shattuck, *Episcopalians*, 295–97; Shoemaker, *I Stand by the Door*; Sack, "Reaching the 'Up-and-Outers.'"

44. Sack, *Moral Re-Armament*, 4, 81–84, 192; Herzog, *Spiritual-Industrial Complex*; Kruse, *One Nation under God*; Norton-Taylor, "Businessmen on Their Knees"; "Religion: God and Steel in Pittsburgh," *Time*, Mar. 21, 1955.

45. Rossinow, *Politics of Authenticity*; Hollinger, *Protestants Abroad*; Cline, *Reconciliation to Revolution*. For groups that sustained the tradition of liberal Christianity and aligned themselves with the civil rights and women's movements of the 1960s, see Hartmann, *Other Feminists*, 92–131; Lynn, *Progressive Women in Conservative Times*.

46. Katherine Steward, "What 'Government School' Means," *New York Times*, July 31, 2017 (quote).

47. Harris, "Alone in the Dark," 63–69, 100.

48. G. Lumpkin interview, Aug. 6, 1974, 18–19 (quote), 26–27. See also G. Lumpkin interview, Sept. 25, 1971, 6–9; G. Lumpkin, "Remember Now," 94, 96; Report, New York, FBI, 1/26/54, Corless Lamont, HQ-61-5215-7, G. Lumpkin FBI File; G. Lumpkin, "How I Returned," 1; *Track 13*, Archives of the Episcopal Church, Seminary of the Southwest, Austin, TX.

49. G. Lumpkin interview, Aug. 6, 1974, 26–27 (quote). See also G. Lumpkin, "Remember Now," 38.

50. G. Lumpkin to [John] Gassner, Sept. 30, [1951] (quote), Recipient—Theatre Arts Collection, John Gassner Papers, Harry Ranson Center; G. Lumpkin interview, Sept. 25, 1971, 8. Gassner was a renowned theater critic, teacher, and anthologist: "Yale Drama Critic, John Gassner, Dies," *Norwalk (CT) Hour*, Apr. 3, 1967.

51. Whittaker Chambers to William F. Buckley, May [19?], 1957, in Chambers, *Odyssey of a Friend*, 180 (first and second quotes), 181 (third quote). See also FBI Memo by SA Francis X. Plant, New York, Feb. 15, 1949, "Re: Jay David Whittaker Chambers," NY-65-14920-2159, G. Lumpkin FBI File.

52. Whittaker Chambers to G. Lumpkin, July 24, 1941 (quote), G. Lumpkin Papers.

53. Whittaker Chambers to William F. Buckley, May [19?], 1957, in Chambers, *Odyssey of a Friend*, 181 (quote); G. Lumpkin, "Law and the Spirit"; G. Lumpkin, "How I Returned," 1, 4.

54. G. Lumpkin, "An Ex-Communist Speaks," *New Castle Tribune* (Chappaqua, NY), Sept. 20, 1946 (quotes); Hobson, *But Now I See*, 2–3. See also G. Lumpkin to Evelyn Scott, June 8, 1945; G. Lumpkin to Evelyn Scott, July 20, 1946, both in Evelyn Scott Collection, Special Collections, University of Tennessee Libraries, Knoxville.; "Lumpkin Takes Oath as New Senator from SC," *Columbia (SC) State*, July 23, 1941; "Senator Lumpkin Dies in National Capital," *Columbia (SC) State*, Aug. 2, 1941; "Senator Lumpkin of South Carolina," *New York Times*, Aug. 2, 1941; "Last Tribute Paid Senator Alva Lumpkin," *Columbia (SC) State*, Aug. 4, 1941.

55. KDL to Earl Browder, Mar. 11, 1946 (quote), Earl Browder Papers, Special Collections Research Center, Syracuse University Libraries.

56. Elizabeth Lumpkin Glenn to William W. L. Glenn, Jan. 2, 1957 in J. Hall's possession, thanks to Katherine Glenn Kent.

57. W. A. Neilson to D. Douglas, Nov. 25, 1936; W. A. Neilson to D. Douglas, Dec. 14, 1937; [?] to Harold U. Faulkner, Feb. 23, 1938; KDL to W. A. Neilson, Feb. 25, 1938; KDL to Neilson, Jan. 15, 1939, all in box 31, folder 17, Neilson Files.

58. [W. A. Neilson] to KDL, Feb. 20, 1939 (first quote); KDL to W. A. Neilson, Feb. 20, 1939 (subsequent quotes), both in box 31, folder 18, Neilson Files. See also "Report of a Preliminary Survey of the Economic Development of the Connecticut Valley of Massachusetts, with a View to Studies That Should be Projected by the Council of Industrial Studies," n.d., folders 44–45, KDL Papers.

59. KDL to Miss Lowenthal, Mar. 15, 1939; KDL to W. A. Neilson, Apr. 18, 1939 (quote); D. Douglas to W. A. Neilson, Apr. 23, 1939; Esther Lowenthal, "Memo on Miss Lumpkin's Letter," Mar. 16, 1939, all in box 31, folder 18, Neilson Files; Eleanor Lincoln interview, June 25, 1993.

60. W. A. Neilson to D. Douglas, Apr. 28, 1939 (first quote), box 31, folder 18, Neilson Files; D. Douglas, "Democracy and Higher Education," 27 (second quote).

61. W. A. Neilson to D. Douglas, Apr. 28, 1939; Esther Lowenthal to W. A. Neilson, Apr. 30, 1939 (quote), both in box 31, folder 18, Neilson Files.

62. KDL to Esther Lowenthal, Sept. 18, 1939 (first, second, third, and fifth quotes); KDL to W. A. Neilson, Feb. 20, 1939 (fourth quote); KDL to Mrs. Dwight W. Morrow, Sept. 18, 1939, all in box 31, folder 18, Neilson Files; Constance Green to Herbert Davis, Jan. 3, 1948, box 4, folder 16, Office of the President, Herbert John Davis Files, SCA. For Green as a pioneer in the field of urban history, see McKelvey, "Constance McLaughlin Green."

63. "Our Spirit's Home—A chronicle written by former RDC Manager Frank Perkins in April 1985" (quote), http://www.rdcsquam.com/about/history.html; KDL to W. A. Neilson, July 27, 1939, box 31, folder 18; W. A. Neilson to KDL, July 30, 1939, box 16, folder 36, both in Neilson Files; Ellen Matteson Knox to Dan Horowitz, May 27, 2000, in J. Hall's possession.

64. Dzuback, "Creative Financing"; Unsigned letter to Colston Warne, Apr. 17,

[1940]; D. Douglas to Colston Warne, n.d., both in box 4, folder 7, Warne Papers.

65. KDL to Broadus Mitchell, Dec. 9, 1940, Broadus Mitchell Collection, Special Collections Department, University Archives, Hofstra University.

66. KDL, "Memorandum on a Project for the Collection of Material on 'American Labor in War,'" Aug. 1942, 1 (quote), box 4, folder 7; KDL to Colston Warne, May 2, 1943; KDL to Colston E. Warne, May 14, 1953, both in box 9, folder 3, all in Warne Papers; Korstad, *Civil Rights Unionism*, 142–43, 202; Warne, *Yearbook of American Labor*; Warne, *Labor in Postwar America*.

67. Brandeis, review of *Yearbook of American Labor*, 434 (second quote).

68. *Daily Hampshire Gazette* (Northampton, MA), Sept. 21, 1940, newsclip in Faculty Biographical Files Collection, Dorothy Wolff Douglas, SCA.

69. Benjamin B. Hinkley Jr. to Phyllis E. Wilhelm, n.d. [1994]; Lynne Z. Bassett, "The Manse of Northampton, Massachusetts," both in J. Hall's possession; Alice H. Manning, "Venerable Manse in Northampton Boasts Interesting History," *Daily Hampshire Gazette* (Northampton, MA), Dec. 23, 1969; "Robert Raven Talks on Spanish Situation," *Smith College Weekly* (Northampton, MA), Apr. 13, 1938; "Meeting of Smith Branch of University Professors Opposes Teacher's Oath," *Smith College Weekly*, Nov. 27, 1935, both in SCA.

70. Alice Lazerowitz interview, Aug. 4, 1987; Benjamin B. Hinkley Jr. to Phyllis E. Wilhelm, n.d. [1994], in J. Hall's possession; "Author's Form A, Katharine Du Pre Lumpkin," received Oct. 31, 1944, 2, folder 1, box 1511, Knopf Records.

71. Adaline Pates Potter interview, May 26, 2000; Eleanor Lincoln interview, June 26, 1993; Edie Newman interview, Nov. 9, 2000; Sarah Flynn conversation with J. Hall, Annapolis, MD, Nov. 28, 2000; "Manse, Historic House, Sold to Prof. Douglas, Who Buys for Residence," *Daily Hampshire Gazette* (Northampton, MA), July 25, 1940.

72. Truettner and R. Stein, *Picturing Old New England*, xi–43, 171 (first quote), 173; Nissenbaum, "New England," 46 (second quote).

73. Landrum, "More Firmly Based," 75–76; A. Wallach, "Larkin's 'Art and Life'"; "Smith Professor to Speak against Fascism at Grace Church Forum," *Transcript Telegram*, Holyoke, MA, Feb. 2, 1935; "Peace Groups Hear Plan for Co-Ordination," *Springfield (MA) Union*, Feb. 27, 1937; "Prof. Larkin to Be Guest Speaker, Spanish Refugee Meeting Here Wednesday," *Springfield (MA) Union*, May 28, 1937; "Prof. Larkin States Stand of League for Peace and Democracy," *Daily Hampshire Gazette* (Northampton, MA), Oct. 15, 1938; "Art Group Plans Lecture Exhibit," *Springfield (MA) Republican*, Mar. 7, 1939; Larkin Will Speak on Refugee Relief," *Springfield (MA) Republican*, May 19, 1939, all in Faculty Biographical Files, Oliver Larkin, SCA.

74. Denning, *Cultural Front*, 77 (first quote); "Speaks on Art in a Changing Society," *Daily Hampshire Gazette* (Northampton, MA), Dec. 7, 1936 (second quote); O. Larkin, *Art and Life*, 478 (third quote).

75. "Manse, Historic House, Sold to Prof. Douglas, Who Buys for Residence," *Daily Hampshire Gazette* (Northampton, MA), July 25, 1940 (quote).

CHAPTER SEVENTEEN: "AT THE THRESHOLD OF GREAT PROMISE"

1. KDL, *South in Progress*, 12 (first quote); Stuart, "Our National Disgrace," 78 (second quote).
2. KDL to Alfred A. Knopf, [May 8, 1949] (quote), KDL Papers.
3. KDL, *South in Progress*, 12–13 (quote on 12).
4. Mencken, "Sahara of the Bozart"; L. Dunbar, "Changing Mind," 13 (first quote); Yaeger, *Dirt and Desire*, 250–51 (second quote on 250).
5. Franklin D. Roosevelt, Second Inaugural Address, Jan. 20, 1937, http://www .bartleby.com/124/pres50.html (first and second quotes); Martin Luther King quoted in MacLean, "New Deal History," 52 (third quote).
6. KDL, *South in Progress*, 40, 199–200 (quotes on 200); KDL, *Making*, 177–78. For the ubiquity and significance of this analogy, see Gilmore, *Defying Dixie*, 7, 157–200; Brinkmeyer, *Fourth Ghost*.
7. KDL, *South in Progress*, 200 (first quote); Schulman, *Cotton Belt to Sunbelt*, 3–8, 13–14, 47–51, 61 (second and third quotes on 3).
8. Gellman, *Death Blow*, 2 (quote), 3–4.
9. Key works on the Southern Popular Front include: A. Dunbar, *Against the Grain*; Egerton, *Speak Now*; Gilmore, *Defying Dixie*, 185–345; Korstad, *Civil Rights Unionism*, 5; Alex Lichtenstein, "Cold War," 186; Roll, *Spirit of Rebellion*; Sullivan, *Days of Hope*.
10. KDL, *South in Progress*, 234 (first, third, and fourth quotes), 116 (second quote).
11. KDL, *South in Progress*, 11 (first and second quote), 12–13 (third and fourth quote on 12).
12. KDL, "Lecture to Prof. Ralph Harlow's class—course in 'Christian Ethics,' Smith College, Spring 1947 (following publication of my book *The Making of a Southerner*)," 1 (quote), folder 64–65, KDL Papers (hereafter KDL, "Lecture to R. Harlow's class"). See also KDL, "Lecture to a general audience," 1947, 9, folders 64–65, KDL Papers (hereafter KDL, "Lecture to a general audience").
13. Ellison, *Shadow and Act*, 303–17 (quote on 306).
14. KDL, *South in Progress*, 13 (first quote), 2 (second quote).
15. KDL, *South in Progress*, 11 (quote).
16. KDL, *South in Progress*, v, 19, 17, 47 (quotes).
17. Woodward, *Thinking Back*, 21 (quote); Woodward, *Tom Watson: Agrarian Rebel*.
18. KDL, *South in Progress*, 205 (first and second quotes), 217 (third and fifth quotes), 207 (fourth quote).
19. For studies that emphasize collaboration and cross-fertilization across the left-liberal spectrum during this period, see Rossinow, *Visions of Progress*; Storrs, *Second Red Scare*, 9–10; Denning, *Cultural Front*.
20. KDL, *South in Progress*, 220–21 (quote on 221); Myra Page interview, June 8, 1987.
21. In "Another 'Great Migration,'" David L. Carlton and Peter A. Coclanis distinguish between what they called the "regionalist" southern liberals of the 1930s and 1940s and the "racial liberals" who substituted race for class concerns in the 1950s and 1960s. See also Ritterhouse, *Discovering the South*. Likewise,

accounts of New Deal liberalism often argue that it was "narrowly conceived" and embraced blacks, women, and members of ethnic groups "only when subsumed under economic categories": Gerstle, "Protean Character," 1044 (quotes). Attention to southern New Dealers such as Lumpkin reveals a broader political spectrum and a more complex southern liberal tradition.

22. Carlton and Coclanis, *Confronting Southern Poverty*, 6–7, 9–10, 16–17, 32–35; Persky, *Burden of Dependency*. For the era's most persuasive version of southern liberals' colonial critique, see Vance, *Human Geography*, 467–74.

23. D. Douglas, *Mexican Labor*, 2 (quote).

24. KDL, *South in Progress*, 91 (quote). The report's authors also added a section that brought the pamphlet in line with FDR's guiding principle: increasing the South's purchasing power would create a vast new market for manufactured goods, putting Americans across the country back to work and contributing mightily to economic recovery.

25. KDL, *South in Progress*, 169 (first quote), 92 (second quote).

26. Shorn of Katharine's link between a radically progressive income tax and special aid to the South's concentrated population of the black and white poor, the idea that the South was a national problem deserving special federal aid lay at the core of southern liberal strategies in Congress. In combination with pressure from the *Gaines* decision to equalize services to blacks, these efforts resulted in preferential funding for and marked improvement in southern health care, public education, and highways over the course of the 1940s and early 1950s: K. Thomas, *Deluxe Jim Crow*, 103–10; Schulman, *Cotton Belt to Sunbelt*, 3–8, 13–14, 47–51, 61.

27. Carlton and Coclanis, "Another 'Great Migration'"; Carlton and Coclanis, *Confronting Southern Poverty*, 25–26, 35–36; Kneebone, *Southern Liberal Journalists*; Ritterhouse, *Discovering the South*.

28. KDL, *South in Progress*, 56 (quote), 66.

29. Melamed, "Racial Capitalism"; KDL, *South in Progress*, 98–99 (first quote on 98), 60 (subsequent quotes).

30. KDL, *South in Progress*, 55 (first quote), 223 (subsequent quotes).

31. KDL, *South in Progress*, 100 (quotes).

32. KDL, "South's Unbalance in U.S. Pattern of Life," *Philadelphia Inquirer*, Apr. 27, 1947 (first quote); KDL, "Outlines of Lectures given in Ralph Harlow's class in his course at Smith College on religion and ethics" (second quote on 3), folders 64–65, KDL Papers.

33. KDL, *Making*, 252 (quote).

34. KDL, "Lecture to R. Harlow's class," 13 (quote).

35. Brinkmeyer, *Fourth Ghost*, 7–9; KDL, *South in Progress*, 115 (quote).

36. KDL, "The Making of a Southerner: Description of the Subject of the Autobiography and Outline of the Program of Research and Method of Presentation," [May 29, 1944], 4 (quote), folder 46, KDL Papers (hereafter KDL, "Description of the Subject"). *The South in Progress* met a mixed response. William M. Brewer, a fellow Georgian who served as editor of the *Journal of Negro History*, praised it as "the most enlightening study of the South which has

been completed in this generation" and called its author "a brilliant and emancipated southern scholar": Brewer, review of *South in Progress*, 100–3 (quotes). White reviewers were divided. Some faulted Katharine for being "more partisan and propagandistic than impartial, judicious, and scientific," although it says much about the times that none commented on her reliance on a Marxist publisher and Marxist approaches or saw her partisanship as anything other than support for the Second New Deal: T. Smith, review of *South in Progress*, 221 (quote). Others wanted fewer dry facts and more of "the rich human material of modern photography and case study": A. Davis, review of *South in Progress*, 566–67 (quote).

37. For the hopeful advances of the war years, see Cobble, *Other Women's Movement*; Dalfiume, "Forgotten Years"; Gerstle, "Crucial Decade"; Gilmore, *Defying Dixie*; Goluboff, *Lost Promise*; J. Hall, "Long Civil Rights Movement"; M. K. Honey, *Southern Labor*; W. Jones, *March on Washington*; Kellogg, "Civil Rights Consciousness"; Korstad, *Civil Rights Unionism*; Korstad and N. Lichtenstein, "Opportunities Found and Lost"; Krochmal, "Working-Class Vision"; Sitkoff, *New Deal for Blacks*; Sugrue, *Sweet Land of Liberty*; Sullivan, *Days of Hope*.

38. KDL, "Lecture to R. Harlow's class," 13 (quotes).

39. KDL, "Statement of the Need for the Projected Autobiography and a Bibliography of Related Works," [May 29, 1944], 1 (quotes), folder 46, KDL Papers. As Dorothy put it, she would be a "participant observer" of her own and her family's life: D. Douglas to Alfred A. Knopf, Inc., May 27, 1944, box 1232, folder 11, Knopf Records.

40. KDL, "Plans for Work," [May 29, 1944], 2 (quote), folder 46, KDL Papers.

41. KDL, "Lecture to a general audience," 2 (quote). For the "school of remembrance," see Hobson, *Tell about the South*, 1; Hobson, *But Now I See*, 15.

42. KDL to Groff Conklin, May 23, 1944; Alfred A. Knopf to KDL, July 3, 1945, both in folder 6, KDL Papers; Comments on Knopf fellowship application, Jun. 3, 1944, box 1232, folder 11, Knopf Records; Lumpkin to Alfred A. Knopf, July 8, 1945 (quote), folder 6, KDL Papers.

43. KDL, "Plans for Work," [May 29, 1944], 1 (quote), folder 46, KDL Papers. Among the books she mentions are Daniels, *Southerner Discovers the South*; Cash, *Mind of the South*; Percy, *Lanterns on the Levee*; B. Robertson, *Red Hills and Cotton*; Arnall, *Shore Dimly Seen*.

44. Benjamin Franklin's rags-to-riches tale of success through an act of willful self-invention was long seen by critics as setting the pattern for the American autobiographical tradition. For the history of white southern autobiography, see Berry, "Autobiographical Impulse"; Berry, introduction to *Located Lives*; Berry, "Southern Autobiographical Impulse"; Hobson, *But Now I See*; Hobson, *Tell about the South*; Inscoe, *Writing the South*; Nasstrom, "Between Memory and History," 334–35n30; Olney, "Autobiographical Traditions"; Ritterhouse, *Growing Up Jim Crow*; L. Simpson, "Autobiographical Impulse"; J. Wallach, "*Closer to the Truth.*"

45. S. Smith, *Poetics of Women's Autobiography*, 16, 44–62 (quotes on 52–53); S. Friedman, "Women's Autobiographical Selves"; Mason, "Other Voice."

46. Prenshaw, *Composing Selves*; Andrews, "Booker T. Washington."

47. E. Scott, *Escapade*; E. Scott, *Background in Tennessee*; Hobson, "Southern Women's Autobiography," 268–74 (quote on 268); P. Matthews, introduction to *Woman Within*; Brantley, *Feminine Sense*.

48. Faulkner, *Absalom, Absalom!*, 142 (quote); Hobson, *Tell about the South*, 11.

49. Cash, *Mind of the South*; Percy, *Lanterns on the Levee*.

50. Hobson, "Southern Women's Autobiography"; Hobson, *But Now I See*, 12–16.

51. William L. Andrews, "An Introduction to the Slave Narrative," Documenting the American South (quote), http://docsouth.unc.edu/neh/intro.html. Richard Wright's lacerating *Black Boy: A Record of Childhood and Youth* (1945) marked another turning point in this tradition.

52. Andrews, *Sisters of the Spirit*, 10–11 (quote); Braxton, *Black Women Writing*; Connor, *Conversions and Visions*; Fleischner, *Mastering Slavery*; H. Jacobs, *Life of a Slave Girl*; D. McDowell, "First Place"; N. McKay, "Narrative Self."

53. KDL, "Plans for Work," [May 29, 1944], 1 (first quote); KDL, "Description of the Subject," (second quote), both in folder 46, KDL Papers.

54. For various interpretations of how *The Making of a Southerner* deals with gender issues, see Fox-Genovese, "Individualism and Community," 29, 34; O'Dell, *Sites of Southern Memory*, 74–75; McPherson, *Reconstructing Dixie*, 240–43, 290n24; Prenshaw, *Composing Selves*, 318.

55. Bateson, *Composing a Life*; KDL, "Description of the Subject" (quote).

56. Hobson, *But Now I See*, 15; Nasstrom, "Between Memory and History."

57. Review of *The Making of a Southerner*, by KDL, *Harper's Magazine*, Feb. 1947 (first quote), newsclip in folder 51, KDL Papers; M. Page, reviews of *Making* and *Way of the South*, 276 (second quote).

58. KDL, "Lecture to R. Harlow's class," 7 (first quote); KDL, "Lecture to a General Audience," 2 (second and third quotes); KDL, *Making*, 235–36, 239. This paragraph is drawn in part from J. Hall, "You Must Remember This."

59. Becker, "Everyman His Own Historian," 221–36 (quote on 224); Woodward, review of *Making*; KDL, *Making*, 23 (quote).

60. KDL to Milton Rugoff, July 16, 1943, 1 (quote), folder 5, KDL Papers; KDL, "Description of the Subject."

61. Kemble, *Journal of a Residence*; KDL, "Plan of Work," [May 29, 1944], 2; KDL, "Statement of the Need for the Projected Autobiography and a Bibliography of Related Works," [May 29, 1944], 1, both in folder 46, KDL Papers.

62. KDL, "Description of the Subject," 5, 7 (quote); KDL, *Making*, 242. Katharine explicitly rejected the racial stereotypes that pervaded Phillips's work and drew on his meticulously edited volumes of original documents rather than his interpretive studies. For radical critiques of the literature on Reconstruction, see B. Baker, *What Reconstruction Meant*, 110–44.

63. Bryan H. Lumpkin, "Lumpkin," Dec. 1936, typescript in KDL Papers.

64. KDL, *Making*, 44 (quote); Fox-Genovese and Genovese, *Mind of the Master Class*.

65. KDL, *Making*, 22 (quotes), 44.

66. H. Carter, "Southern Heritage" (quote); Fox-Genovese, *Plantation Household*, 103–4; Fox-Genovese, "Individualism and Community," 28–34.

67. W. W. Lumpkin, "An Old Time Georgia Christmas," *Columbia (SC) State*, Dec. 16, 1906, 44; KDL, *Making*, 36 (first quote); Charles Poore, "Books of the Times," *New York Times*, Jan. 11, 1947 (second quote), newsclip in folder 51, KDL Papers.

68. KDL, *Making*, 40 (first quote), 37 (second quote), 51, 74 (third quote).

69. KDL, *Making*, 3–5, 29 (first quote), 28 (second quote). Plantation ledgers, which laid bare how ruthlessly slavery commodified its victims, also appear in Grace's fiction. In *A Sign for Cain*, Colonel Gault cum William Lumpkin does not shrink from this evidence of the "chattel principle, the property principle" (103–4). He is drawn to the numbers, lingers over them. For him they evoke, not the bottomless evils of slavery, but the bittersweet pull of the past: W. Johnson, *Chattel Principle*, iv (quote); G. Lumpkin, *Sign for Cain*, 103–4.

70. KDL, *Making*, 26–27, 44; Tawney, *Religion and the Rise of Capitalism*.

71. KDL, *Making*, 223 (first quote), 224 (second quote).

72. KDL, "Statement of the Need for the Projected Autobiography and a Bibliography of Related Works," [May 29, 1944], 1 (first quote), folder 46, KDL Papers; KDL, *Making*, 87 (subsequent quotes).

73. KDL, *Making*, 127–28 (quotes).

74. Ritterhouse, *Growing Up Jim Crow*; the hearings of the Joint Congressional Committee of 1871 are published as House Reports, 42d Cong., 2d sess., No. 22 (serial 1529-41) or as Senate Reports, 42d Cong., 2d sess., No. 41 (serial 1484-96).

75. William Lumpkin, "Where and why I was a Kuklux," 1, box 76, folder 66, Civil War Collection, State Archives of North Carolina State, Raleigh; Elizabeth Lumpkin Glenn, "Notes in answer to a letter from Katharine Lumpkin," n.d. (quotes), folder 34, KDL Papers. For how local histories repeated this myth as late as the 1970s, see F. Smith, *History of Oglethorpe County*, 218–19.

76. KDL, *Making*, 85 (first and third quotes), 84 (second quote).

77. KDL, *Making*, 90 (quotes).

78. KDL, *Making*, 10–11, 99–108; KDL, *Emancipation*, 10 (quote).

79. KDL, *Making*, 131–33 (quotes).

80. KDL, *Making*, 132 (quotes). For the charged meanings of "master" in the war of words between proslavery apologists and abolitionists, see J. Phillips, "Slave Narratives," 47.

81. KDL, *Making*, 133 (quotes).

82. KDL, undated, handwritten note left in her personal copy of *The Making of a Southerner*, thanks to Joseph H. Lumpkin Sr.

83. KDL, *Emancipation*, 3–5, 14–16; Weld, *American Slavery*, 52–57; KDL interview, Aug. 4, 1974, 7–8 (quote on 8).

84. KDL to Leslie Blanchard, Dec. 3, 1923 (first quote), folder 1, KDL Papers; KDL, *Making*, 191 (second quote).

85. KDL, *Making*, 173 (first quote), 182 (second and third quotes). On place as a palimpsest, see Jay Parini, "A Sense of Place Grounds History in Personal Discovery," *Chronicle of Higher Education*, Dec. 8, 2000.

86. KDL, *Making*, 182 (first quote), 222 (second quote), 217 (third and fourth quotes), 229 (fifth quote).

87. Du Bois, *Souls of Black Folk*, 1 (quote).

88. KDL, *Making*, 207, 192 (first quote), 215 (second quote).

89. Myrdal, *American Dilemma*, 1, xvii (quote).

90. KDL, *Making*, 235–36 (quotes), 239 (subsequent quotes). The much quoted dialogue between Shreve McCannon and Quentin Compson exemplified her dilemma: "'Now I want you to tell me just one thing more. Why do you hate the South?' 'I don't hate it,' Quentin said, quickly, at once, immediately; 'I don't hate it,' he said. I don't hate it he thought . . . : *I don't. I don't! I don't hate it! I don't hate it!*": Faulkner, *Absalom, Absalom!*, 303 (quote).

91. KDL, *Making*, 199 (quote).

92. For an earlier consideration of Katharine's reticence, see J. Hall, "Open Secrets." For similar strategies among other female authors, see Prenshaw, *Composing Selves*, 294.

93. Joseph H. Lumpkin Sr. interview, Aug. 1, 1995; Joseph H. Lumpkin Sr. and Joseph H. Lumpkin Jr. interview, Aug. 17, 1990; Alva M. Lumpkin Jr. interview, Aug. 4, 1995; Alva M. Lumpkin Jr. interview, Aug. 17, 1990.

94. [Elizabeth Lumpkin Glenn] to KDL, Jan. 9, 1947, folder 7, KDL Papers.

95. Elizabeth Lumpkin Glenn, untitled, undated letter fragment, in J. Hall's possession, thanks to Katherine Glenn Kent.

96. KDL interview, Aug. 4, 1974, 6–7 (quotes).

97. Grace to KDL, Jan. 25, 1947 (quote), folder 8, KDL Papers.

98. Adaleen [Mrs. John Elmer Sieber] to KDL, Feb. 2, 1947 (first quote), folder 9; Thomas Davis Jr. to KDL, Feb. 12, 1947 (second quote), folder 10, both in KDL Papers.

99. T. H. D., "Review of Current Books," *Columbia (SC) Record*, Jan. 16, 1947 (quote); Bessie Hart, "Looking at New Books," *Macon (GA) News*, Jan. 19, 1947, both newsclips in folder 51, KDL Papers.

100. John N. Ware, "Library Highlights," *Rome (GA) News-Tribune*, Apr. 15, 1947, 6 (first and second quotes); John L. Hill, review of *Making of a Southerner*, *Broadman Book Talk*, Aug. 1947 (third quote), both newsclips in folder 51, KDL Papers.

101. H. Carter, "Southern Heritage," 3, 32 (quotes).

102. Flowers, "The Courage of Her Conviction," 13 (first and second quotes); George Myers Stephens to Alfred A. Knopf, [Dec. 1949], 2 (third quote), folder 51, KDL Papers. For other warm reviews, see: Wilma Dykeman Stokely, "Member of Old Georgia Family Studies the South Objectively," *Chattanooga Times*, Jan. 26, 1947; Marian Sims, "Southern Ideals," *Atlanta Journal*, Feb. 9, 1947; M. J. T., review of *Making of a Southerner*, *Birmingham News*, Feb. 15, 1947, all newsclips in folder 51, KDL Papers.

103. David Carpenter, "The Unmaking of a Southerner," *Daily Worker*, Feb. 27, 1947 (first quote); M. Page, reviews of *Making* and *Way of the South*, 276–77 (subsequent quotes).

104. KDL, "Lecture to R. Harlow's class," 10 (first quote), np (second quote). Fred Hobson, the first modern literary scholar fully to appreciate Katharine's accomplishment, characterizes her success in portraying the antebellum past as her

family saw it and as she understood it as a child as a "triumph in point of view." Yet even he suggests that she "nearly fit into that post-bellum southern school of father-worship" by virtue of the attention she lavishes upon William Lumpkin in the early sections of her memoir: Hobson, *But Now I See*, 39 (first quote), 40 (second quote). In truth, Katharine simultaneously represents the father's powerful influence over the child and sends up his anachronistic pretensions. When, early on, she describes her father as "a 'Quaint reminder of long ago,'" a "teller of tales" in an old-fashioned "Prince Albert coat," it is hard to miss the disillusionment to come. Throughout, she calls attention to the constructed nature of family memories. "That is Father's story," "this is as Father told it," she reminds us at every turn, making clear that *The Making of a Southerner* is about the inherited stories that screen what we see and feel: KDL, *Making*, 120–21 (first, second, and third quotes), 7, 36 (fourth and fifth quotes). As Darlene O'Dell points out, she also uses quotation marks to distance herself from her father's interpretations and to warn the reader to question white supremacists' illusions. "The way free Negroes behaved, according to Father," she says pointedly, "merely showed they were even more 'ungrateful,' 'irresponsible,' 'childish,' than slave owners had thought": KDL, *Making*, 74 (quotes); O'Dell, *Sites of Southern Memory*, 13, 42–49, 57–69, 77, 80, 144–45. See also McPherson, *Reconstructing Dixie*, 289n21.

105. L. Smith, *Strange Fruit*; Hobson, *Tell about the South*, 36–38; Prenshaw, *Composing Selves*, 29, 291 (quote), 296.

106. L. Smith, *Killers of the Dream*; Lillian Smith, "The Crippling Effect of White Supremacy," *New York Herald Tribune Sunday Book Review*, Feb. 2, 1947 (quotes), newsclip in folder 51, KDL Papers. Although Smith called *Killers of the Dream* a personal memoir, she did not write revealingly about her personal life. Like Lumpkin, she lived for many years in a committed partnership with a woman. Also like Lumpkin, she could not and did not speak publicly about her own sexual desires and experiences. For her, as for Katharine, the taboo surrounding homosexuality was much more powerful than the barriers to frank discussions of race. See Hobson, *But Now I See*, 21; Gladney, "Personalizing the Political"; Inscoe, *Writing the South*, 201.

107. Hobson, *But Now I See*.

108. Hobson, *But Now I See*, 18–36 (quotes on 25).

109. KDL, "Lecture to R. Harlow's class," 7.

110. KDL, "Lecture to a general audience," 22 (first quote), 13 (second quote), 15, 18–19.

111. KDL, "Outlines of Lectures given in Ralph Harlow's class in his course at Smith College on religion and ethics," 2 (first quote), 3 (second quote), folders 64–65, KDL Papers.

CHAPTER EIGHTEEN: WILDERNESS YEARS

1. KDL, "Application for Literary Fellowship," [1949], folder 14; Paul Brooks to KDL, Mar. 14, 1950 (quote), folder 14; KDL to Groff Conklin, Jan. 15, 1948, folder 13; Groff Conklin to KDL, Jan. 19, 1948, folder 15, all in KDL Papers. See

also Paul Brooks, reader's report, Mar. 2, 1950, box 14, folder F-349-49, series F, Houghton Mifflin Literary Fellowship Applications, Boston office (MS Stor 197), Houghton Library, Harvard University (hereafter Houghton Mifflin Fellowship Applications).

2. KDL to Alfred A. Knopf, [May 8], 1949 (quote); KDL to Alfred A. Knopf, May 8, 1950, both in folder 14, KDL Papers.

3. "Smith Educator Is Listed as 'Red' Fund Contributor," *Springfield (MA) News*, Sept. 12, 1950 (quote); Frederick Woltman, "Dime Heir Gave Field Plenty for Red Fronts," *New York World-Telegram and Sun*, Sept. 8, 1950; [Unknown] to Robert E. Stripling, Apr. 22, 1943; and multiple reports, "American People's Fund, Inc.," n.d., box 43, folder 4, Vertical Files Series, J. B. Matthews Papers, David M. Rubenstein Rare Book and Manuscript Library, Duke University; N. Dawson, "Fellow Traveler to Anticommunist."

4. Caute, *Great Fear*, 175–76. For Dorothy's involvement with and service on the board of the National Council of American-Soviet Friendship, see Minutes of the meeting of the Board of Directors of the National Council of American-Soviet Friendship, Apr. 28, 1944, box 1, folder 29; Minutes of Board of Directors meeting of the National Council of American-Soviet Friendship, Nov. 8, 1945, box 1, folder 30; Agenda, Nov. 13, 1946, box 1, folder 31; Members of Board of Directors—N.C.A.S.F.—Resigned or withdrawn, n.d., box 5, folder 2; Meeting Minutes, Dec. 11, 1946, box 1, folder 31, National Council of American-Soviet Friendship Records, Tamiment Library and Robert F. Wagner Labor Archives, Elmer Holmes Bobst Library, New York University, New York.

5. Craig Thompson, "America's Millionaire Communist," *Saturday Evening Post*, Sept. 9, 1950; Field, *Right to Left*, 116–256; Levine, "Vanderbilt Scion."

6. *Smith College Courses of Study 1949–1950* (Northampton, MA: Smith College, Apr. 1949), 28–30; *Smith College Courses of Study 1950–1951* (Northampton, MA: Smith College, Apr. 1950), 28–30; "Courses of Study 1951–1952," a reprint from the *Smith College Catalogue* (Northampton, MA: Smith College, 1951), 63–66; "Smith College Bulletin: Courses of Study Number 1952–1953," a reprint from the *Smith College Catalogue* (Northampton, MA: Smith College, 1952), 66–68; "Smith College Bulletin: Courses of Study Number 1953–1954," a reprint from the *Smith College Catalogue* (Northampton, MA: Smith College, 1953), all in SCA; J. Hall conversation with Smith College archivists, Aug. 30, 2012.

7. FBI letter, SAC, Boston, to Director, FBI, Oct. 22, 1951, Dorothy Wolff Douglas, HQ-100-355436-17; FBI letter from John Edgar Hoover, Director, FBI, to Mr. Donald L. Michelson [?], Chief, Division of Security, Office of Consular Affairs, U.S. Department of State, Oct. 31, 1951, Polish Intelligence Activities in the U.S., HQ-100-350264-103; FBI letter, Director, FBI, to SAC, Boston, July 30, 1951, Dorothy Wolff Douglas, HQ-100-355436-11; FBI letter, Director, FBI, to SAC, Boston, Nov. 7, 1951, Dorothy Wolff Douglas, HQ-100-355436-17; FBI Memo, Director, FBI, to Legal Attache, London, May 20, 1952, Dorothy Wolff Douglas, HQ-100-355436-26; FBI letter, Director, FBI, to SAC, Boston, July 21, 1952, Dorothy Wolff Douglas, HQ-100-355436-28, all in D. Douglas FBI File.

8. Storrs, *Second Red Scare*.

9. Schrecker, *Age of McCarthyism*, especially 24, 41. These committees included the House Committee on Un-American Activities (HUAC); the Senate Permanent Investigating Subcommittee of the Government Operations Committee, headed after 1953 by the demagogic Joseph R. McCarthy (R.-Wisc., from whose name the catch-all label "McCarthyism" derived); and the more sober but quite powerful Senate Internal Security Subcommittee (known as the McCarran Committee). The committee's first chair was Patrick McCarran, D-Nev. Numerous state-level bodies carried out similar interrogations.

10. Barth, *Loyalty of Free Men*, 106 (first quote); Schrecker, *Age of McCarthyism*, 40 (second quote). For the loyalty-security program, see R. Goldstein, *American Blacklist*, xii–xiii, 43–147; Schrecker, *Age of McCarthyism*, 37–40, 167–72; Storrs, *Second Red Scare*.

11. "An Open Letter to American Liberals," *Soviet Russian Today* 6:1, Mar. 1937, 14–15, reprinted in Filene, *American Views of Soviet Russia*, 117–21. For the FBI's growing interest, first in Dorothy, and then in Katharine, see FBI Report by Hugh Anderson, Boston, Jan. 13, 1943, American Council on Soviet Relations, HQ-100-355436-1; FBI letter, Director, FBI, to SAC, Boston, July 19, 1950, Dorothy W. Douglas, HQ-100-355436-5; FBI Report, Boston, Sept. 20, 1950, Dorothy Wolff Douglas, HQ-100-355436-7; FBI letter, Director, FBI, to SAC, Boston, Aug. 15, 1951, Dorothy Wolff Douglas, HQ-100-355436-14 (hereafter Director, FBI, to SAC, Aug. 15, 1951); FBI letter, SAC, Boston, to Director, FBI, Mar. 13, 1953, Dorothy Wolff Douglas, HQ-100-355436-31, 1, all in D. Douglas FBI File; FBI letter, SAC, Boston, to Director, FBI, Mar. 19, 1953, Katherine Lumpkin, HQ-100-400110-1; FBI letter, Director, FBI, to SAC, Boston, May 14, 1953, Kathryn Lumpkin, HQ-100-400110-2, both in KDL FBI File.

12. FBI Report by Hugh Anderson, Boston, Jan. 13, 1943, American Council on Soviet Relations, HQ-100-355436-1, 1 (first quote), 2 (second quote), D. Douglas FBI File.

13. FBI Report by Hugh Anderson, Boston, Jan. 13, 1943, American Council on Soviet Relations, HQ-100-355436-1, 2 (first and second quotes), 1 (third quote), 3 (subsequent quotes), D. Douglas FBI File.

14. FBI letter, SAC, Boston, to Director, FBI, May 14, 1953, Kathryn Lumpkin, HQ-100-400110-2, 3 (first quote); FBI Report by Isaiah T. Woodbury, Boston, Oct. 22, 1953, Katherine D. Lumpkin, HQ-100-400110-7, 3 (second quote); FBI Memo, Director, FBI, to SAC, Boston, Mar. 19, 1953, Katherine Lumpkin, HQ-100-400110-1, 1 (third quote), citing FBI Report from DIO, First Naval District to Boston field office, Aug. 1949, "Subversive Activities of Smith College," HQ-100-355436, all in KDL FBI File. See also Director, FBI, to SAC, Aug. 15, 1951, 11.

15. FBI letter, SAC, Boston, to Director, FBI, Mar. 19, 1953, Katherine Lumpkin, HQ-100-400110-1, 3 (first, second, and third quotes), citing FBI Report by Isaiah T. Woodbury, Oct. 1947, BS-65-3153-262; FBI Report by Isaiah T. Woodbury, Boston, Oct. 22, 1953, Katherine D. Lumpkin, HQ-100-400110-7, 5; FBI Report by John B. Davidson, Boston, Apr. 16, 1947, Communist Infiltration of American Federation of Teachers, HQ-61-7546-380, 6 (fourth quote), 7 (fifth quote), all in KDL FBI File.

16. FBI Report, Boston, [Jan. 28,] 1954, HQ-100-400110-11, 4 (quote), KDL FBI File. For the role of gender and sexuality in the Red Scare of the 1950s, see May, *Homeward Bound*; Cuordileone, "Age of Anxiety"; Canaday, "Building a Straight State"; D. Johnson, *Lavender Scare*; Braukman, *Communists and Perverts*; A. Friedman, "Smearing of Joe McCarthy."

17. For the peace movement, see Castledine, *Cold War Progressives*, 7 (quote); Lieberman, *Strangest Dream*; Wittner, *Rebels against War*, 201–2, 213.

18. Henry A. Wallace, "Ten Extra Years," Address before the National Convention of the Alpha Phi Alpha Fraternity, Tulsa, Oklahoma, Dec. 28, 1947 (quote), Papers of Henry Wallace, Special Collections, University of Iowa; Korstad, *Civil Rights Unionism*, 265, 359–67.

19. Korstad, *Civil Rights Unionism*, 357–67 (quote on 357).

20. This account of the Waldorf Conference is drawn primarily from Saunders, *Cultural Cold War*, 45–57. On Katharine and Dorothy as sponsors, see California Senate, *Fifth Report of the Senate Fact-Finding Committee on Un-American Activities* (Sacramento, CA: The Senate, 1949), 480–81, http://archive.org/details/reportofsenatefa1949cali.

21. Arthur Miller quoted in Saunders, *Cultural Cold War*, 48.

22. On Dorothy's recruitment of Davis, see Director, FBI, to SAC, Aug. 15, 1951. On Davis's withdrawal, see Herbert Davis to Harlow Shapley, Mar. 15, 1949, box 7, folder 2, Office of the President, Herbert John Davis Files, SCA. For the "Non-Communist Left," see Saunders, *Cultural Cold War*, 59–66; Wald, *New York Intellectuals*.

23. "Red Visitors Cause Rumpus," *Life*, Apr. 4, 1949, 39–43; Saunders, *Cultural Cold War*, 59–66. Disenchanted with the Soviet system, Hook and his circle of New York intellectuals had been a beleaguered minority during the war. As the Cold War intensified, they rose to positions of tremendous cultural authority as exponents of an apocalyptic anticommunism and agents of the national security state. The Waldorf gathering was a catalytic event, both for them and for the Central Intelligence Agency (CIA), which enlisted Sidney Hook and other former leftists as its witting or unwitting representatives in a cultural cold war designed to counter Soviet propaganda by showcasing American arts and letters around the world.

24. "Idea Man for the Democrats," *Business Week*, Mar. 26, 1955, 128, 130–33 (quote on 130).

25. Biles, *Crusading Liberal*; Biles, "Senatorial Election of 1954"; P. Douglas, *Fullness of Time*; "Busbey Blasts Prof. Douglas as 'Deceiver,'" *Chicago Daily Tribune*, Sept. 19, 1948; "Busbey Queries Douglas about Red Charges," *Chicago Daily Tribune*, Sept. 21, 1948; Thomas Morrow, "Busbey Rips Douglas as Red Fronter," *Chicago Daily Tribune*, Sept. 14, 1948; "Douglas Aids Hit Red Front Charge as 'Smear Tactics,'" *Chicago Daily Tribune*, Sept. 14, 1948, 2; "Mr. Douglas' Contradictions," *Chicago Daily Tribune*, Oct. 3, 1948; Ray E. Rieke, "Finger on Douglas," *Chicago Daily Tribune*, Oct. 22, 1948; Thomas Morrow, "Visited Russia Only to Obtain Facts: Douglas," *Chicago Daily Tribune*, Sept. 23, 1948; Joseph Alsop, "Matter of Fact," *Washington Post*, Oct. 6, 1948; Drew Pearson, "Right and Left

Slap at Douglas," *Washington Post*, Oct. 27, 1948. Like other Cold War liberals, Douglas became the target of protests because of his support for the Vietnam War, a conflict that Dorothy vociferously opposed.

26. Biles, *Crusading Liberal*, 78–79, 227n41–42; Schrecker, *Age of McCarthyism*, 47–48, 192; P. Douglas, *Fullness of Time*, 304–9 (quote on 307). Schrecker calls this the "most important anti-Communist law passed during the Cold War" (192).

27. FBI letter, SAC, Boston, to Director, FBI, Nov. 3, 1950, Dorothy Wolff Douglas, HQ-100-355436-8; FBI letter, Director, FBI, to SAC, Boston, Nov. 30, 1950, Dorothy Wolff Douglas, HQ-100-355436-10; FBI letter, SAC, Boston, to Director, FBI, Nov. 28, 1950, Dorothy Wolff Douglas, HQ-100-355436-9; FBI letter, Director, FBI, to SAC, Boston, Dec. 21, 1950, Dorothy Wolff Douglas, HQ-100-355436-9, all in D. Douglas FBI File. For the security index, see Schrecker, *Many Are the Crimes*, 106–7, 208.

28. Biles, "Senatorial Election of 1954."

29. Schrecker, *No Ivory Tower*, 94–105; "Davis States Position of Smith on Communism," *Smith College Associated News*, Mar. 4, 1949 (quote). See also "New Englanders Defend Marsh, Dislike Textbook Inquiry," *New York Times*, June 19, 1949.

30. John H. Fenton, "Smith Installs Wright as President; He Asserts Changes Are Inevitable," *New York Times*, Oct. 20, 1949; Landrum, "More Firmly Based," 88–89 (quote).

31. R. Allen, "Communists Should Not Teach," 433–40 (quote on 434). This was an assumption that radicals could not have anticipated when they maintained a discreet silence about their CP membership. That secrecy cost them dearly in the court of public opinion, but the alternative carried a high risk of dismissal and blacklisting and of exposing others to the same fate: Schrecker, *No Ivory Tower*, 83–84, 109.

32. National Council for American Education, *Red-ucators at Leading Women's Colleges* (New York, NY), [Nov. 1, 1951] (quote), mimeographed copy in box 473, Office of the President, Benjamin Fletcher Wright Papers, SCA (hereafter Benjamin Fletcher Wright Papers). Among these faculty members were Ralph Harlow, Harold Faulkner, Newton Arvin, and Hallie Flanagan Davis, all named on the basis of guilt by association (they had at some point been associated with organizations that appeared on the attorney general's list of subversive organizations) or for taking positions that Communists also took. Such publications had been in constant circulation since the 1920s. Elizabeth Dilling's *Red Network*, for example, targeted Smith President William Allan and various Smith faculty in the mid-1930s, but at that point a man like Neilson could turn such accusations aside with a laugh.

33. Schrecker, *Age of McCarthyism*, 43 (first quote); FBI letter, Director, FBI, to SAC, Boston, July 19, 1950, Dorothy W. Douglas, HQ-100-355436-5 (second quote), D. Douglas FBI File; Clarice Goldstein (Mrs. Ralph) Rose to Mrs. Willson [Mrs. E. T. Willson], Dec. 18, 1952 (third quote), box 473, Benjamin Fletcher Wright Papers. Budenz, who was the former managing editor of the *Daily Worker*, left the party in 1945.

34. Mary Sheaffer to Mrs. E. T. Willson, Office of the Director of Public Relations, July 31, 1952; Mrs. E. T. Willson to Martha (Mrs. Jackson K.) Holloway, Sept. 19, 1952 (first quote); Mrs. E. T. Willson to Mrs. Ralph Rose, Dec. 29, 1952 (second quote), all in box 473, Benjamin Fletcher Wright Papers.

35. Director, FBI, to SAC, Aug. 15, 1951, 11 (first quote), 10 (second quote).

36. Mrs. E. T. Willson to Martha (Mrs. Jackson K.) Holloway, Sept. 19, 1952 (first quote), box 473, Benjamin Fletcher Wright Papers; Kalman Seigel, "College Freedoms Being Stifled by Students' Fear of Red Label," *New York Times*, May 10, 1951 (second quote); Landrum, "More Firmly Based,'" 26–29, 82–83, 90–91.

37. Kamp, *Lace Curtains of the YWCA*, 7 (quotes); Helgren, *American Girls*, 126–37; Izzo, *Liberal Christianity*. Kamp cited the Y's 1936 vote to support the Scottsboro defense as evidence of its communistic leanings and singled out Katharine's friend Winnifred Wygal as an example of leaders with Popular Front connections.

38. N. Robertson, *Christian Sisterhood*, 170–71 (first quote on 171); Helgren, *American Girls*, 136–37 (second quote). The Y paid a price for its defense of civil liberties. It struggled with declining donations and disaffiliating locals through the 1950s. But it continued to nurture a strand of student engagement that burst into action in the 1960s.

39. Kalman Seigel, "College Freedoms Being Stifled by Students' Fear of Red Label," *New York Times*, May 10, 1951 (quotes). See also Kalman Seigel, "Colleges Fighting Repressive Forces," *New York Times*, May 11, 1951, which offered a more positive view. Smith's curriculum narrowed as well. In addition to teaching the department's basic courses on labor issues in the United States, Dorothy had initiated wide-ranging comparative courses that introduced students to the economic principles underlying capitalism, fascism, and communism and to the contrasting social welfare systems of the United States, Great Britain, the Soviet Union, and Eastern Europe. Once she left, these courses disappeared from the Smith College Bulletins.

40. Tanenhaus, *Whittaker Chambers*, 214–29, 283. For an overview of the debate over the facts of the Hiss case, see Schrecker, "Soviet Espionage in America."

41. Letter, New York to Director, FBI, Feb. 18, 1949, "Re: Jay David Whittaker Chambers," HQ-74-1333-2152 (quote).

42. "Michael Intrator," Jan. 27, 1949, [Hiss Defense Interviews] (first quote), box 45, Tanenhaus Papers; G. Lumpkin, "Law and the Spirit," 498 (second quote); G. Lumpkin, "An Ex-Communist Speaks," *New Castle Tribune* (Chappaqua, NY), Sept. 20, 1946. See also "Grace Hutchins," Jan. 27, 1949, [Hiss Defense Interviews], box 45, Tanenhaus Papers.

43. Interview with Ida Dailes, Mar. 29, 1949, summarized in FBI Report by O'Keefe, Apr. 6, 1949, 32 (quotes); Interviews with G. Lumpkin, Mar. 16, 18, 23, 1949, summarized in FBI Report by O'Keefe, Apr. 6, 1949, 49 (quotes), both in G. Lumpkin FBI File. See also "Grace Hutchins," Jan. 27, 1949, [Hiss Defense Interviews], box 45, Tanenhaus Papers.

44. G. Lumpkin to Joseph McCarthy, Apr. 23, 1950 (quote), in RG 46: Senate Inter-

nal Security Subcommittee Records, Center for Legislative Archives, National Archives (hereafter SISS Records).

45. G. Lumpkin, "How I Returned," 1 (quotes).

46. G. Lumpkin, "Law and the Spirit," 499 (quotes).

47. Eleanor Roosevelt to G. Lumpkin, Jan. 9, 1950 (first quote); handwritten note by G. Lumpkin on the bottom of Eleanor Roosevelt to G. Lumpkin, Jan. 9, 1950 (second quote), both in G. Lumpkin Papers; G. Lumpkin, "Law and the Spirit," 499. "Whittaker Chambers," Roosevelt wrote, "has confessed to all the sins of which he accused Mr. Hiss, including perjury, but if you are a witness for the government, you are, of course, exempt from punishment. If you had a bad conscience and wanted to be sure you would be safe, this seems to me an eminently wise way to gain security and peace of mind for the future": Eleanor Roosevelt, "My Day, Jan. 25, 1950" (quote), *The Eleanor Roosevelt Papers Digital Edition*, https://erpapers.columbian.gwu.edu/browse-my-day-columns.

48. G. Lumpkin, "Law and the Spirit," 499; Herzog, *Spiritual-Industrial Complex*, 202.

49. Jacoby, *Alger Hiss*, 32 (quote).

50. FBI Memo by SA Francis X. Plant, New York, Feb. 15, 1949, "Re: Jay David Whittaker Chambers," NY-65-14920-2159; Interviews with G. Lumpkin, Mar. 16, 18, 23, 1949, in FBI Report by O'Keefe, Apr. 6, 1949, 55 (quote), G. Lumpkin FBI File. See also "Grace Hutchins," Jan. 27, 1949, [Hiss Defense Interviews], box 45, Tanenhaus Papers.

51. G. Lumpkin to Joseph McCarthy, Apr. 23, 1950; Joe McCarthy to G. Lumpkin, Apr. 25, 1950, SISS Records. Because of the statute of limitations, Hiss was convicted not of espionage but of perjury. He was sentenced to five years in a federal penitentiary.

52. Kluger, *Paper*, 297–99 (quote on 299); FBI letter, G. Lumpkin to [Sen. Joseph R. McCarthy], Apr. 26, 1950, NY-100-90777-71A, G. Lumpkin FBI File.

53. FBI Report by John L. Fagan, New York, Aug. 3, 1951, Joseph Fels Barnes, HQ-77-13677-187 (quote), G. Lumpkin FBI File.

54. G. Lumpkin and Kaiser, "Learning to Make History," 17–21 (quotes on p. 20); FBI letter, G. Lumpkin to [Sen. Joseph R. McCarthy], Apr. 26, 1950, NY-100-90777-71A (quotes); FBI Report by John L. Fagan, New York, Aug. 3, 1951, Joseph Fels Barnes, HQ-77-13677-187, both in G. Lumpkin FBI File; G. Lumpkin testimony, Senate Internal Security Subcommittee executive session, May 18, 1951, SISS Records; Lois MacDonald interview, Aug. 25, 1977, 111–16. For the Southern Summer School during this period, see Frederickson, "A Place to Speak Our Minds," 137–39, 152–55.

55. G. Lumpkin to Dorothy Baker, n.d., SISS Records. A copy of the May 11, 1951, subpoena was enclosed in this letter.

56. G. Lumpkin to Sen. McCarran, May 14, 1951 (quotes); G. Lumpkin testimony, Senate Internal Security Subcommittee executive session, May 18, 1951, both in SISS Records.

57. FBI letter, SAC, New York, to Director, FBI, June 16, 1951 (a), Joseph Fels

Barnes, HQ-77-13677-178; FBI letter, SAC, New York, to Director, FBI, July 10, 1950, Joseph Fels Barnes, NY-100-90777-77; FBI Memo, Mr. A. H. Belmont to Mr. C. E. Hennrich, June 16, 1951, Joseph Fels Barnes, HQ-77-13677-179, all in G. Lumpkin FBI File.

58. FBI Memo, Mr. A. H. Belmont to Mr. C. E. Hennrich, June 16, 1951, Joseph Fels Barnes, HQ-77-13677-179; FBI letter, SAC, New York, to Director, FBI, June 16, 1951, Joseph Fels Barnes, HQ-77-13677-178, both in G. Lumpkin FBI File.

59. G. Lumpkin interview, Aug. 6, 1974, 33–34 (quotes).

60. G. Lumpkin to Ben Mendel [Mandel], n.d. [ca. June 7, 1951] (quote); Benjamin Mandel to G. Lumpkin, June 7, 1951, both in SISS Records; Schrecker, *Many Are the Crimes*, 42–43. For the outsized role of Mandel and his friend J. B. Matthews in the loyalty investigations that drove so many left-leaning New Dealers out of public life, see Storrs, *Second Red Scare*.

61. [Benjamin Mandel], "Grace Lumpkin," n.d. [ca. June 7, 1951] (quotes), SISS Records.

62. FBI letter from John Edgar Hoover, Director, FBI, to Mr. Donald L. Michelson [?], Chief, Division of Security, Office of Consular Affairs, U.S. Department of State, Oct. 31, 1951, Polish Intelligence Activities in the U.S., HQ-100-350264-1035 (quotes), G. Lumpkin FBI File.

63. Robert Gorham Davis testimony, Feb. 25, 1953, in *Communist Methods of Infiltration (Education, Part 1): Hearings before the Committee on Un-American Activities*, House of Representatives, 83rd Cong., 1st sess. (Washington, DC: Government Printing Office, 1953), 28 (first quote), 26 (second quote), 16 (third quote), 13 (fourth quote). Davis went on to chair the American Committee for Cultural Freedom, one of the pillars of the non-Communist left.

64. Robert Gorham Davis testimony, Feb. 25, 1953, in *Communist Methods of Infiltration (Education, Part 1): Hearings before the Committee on Un-American Activities*, House of Representatives, 83rd Cong., 1st sess. (Washington, DC: Government Printing Office, 1953), 15 (first quote), 21, 23–25, 42 (second quote), 38 (third quote).

65. FBI Report, Boston, July 30, 1954, Dorothy Wolff Douglas, HQ-100-355436-45 (quotes), D. Douglas FBI File.

66. "Inquiry Curb Peril Seen by President," *New York Times*, Feb. 26, 1953 (quotes).

67. "Smith Plans to Weed Out Subversives," *Springfield (MA) Union*, Feb. 26, 1953; Landrum, "More Firmly Based," 54–64; Untitled Memo, Mar. 26, 1953, 1 (quote); "Statement on Congressional Investigations issued by Smith College Chapter, American Association of University Professors," Nov. 30, 1953, both in box 2, Benjamin Fletcher Wright Papers.

68. Eleanor Lincoln interview, June 25, 1993 (quote); Barbara Hadley Stein conversation with J. Hall, May 29, 1987; Margot Stein conversation with J. Hall, May 6, 1985; Sarah Flynn conversation with J. Hall, Nov. 27, 2000.

69. W. Jackson Jones to Louis J. Russell, Feb. 25, 1953, D. Douglas File, RG 233: Records of the House Un-American Activities Committee, Center for Legislative Archives, National Archives (hereafter HUAC Records); C. Baker, *Generous Spirit*, 183–86.

70. Harold H. Velde to James Andrews, Feb. 11, 1953, Hulda McGarvey Flynn File;

Louis J. Russell memo re: Dorothy Douglas, Feb. 10, 1953; James A. Andrews to Louis J. Russell, Feb. 12, 1953, all in HUAC Records.

71. For this school, see R. Goldstein, *American Blacklist*, 102–4; Gettleman, "No Varsity Teams."

72. FBI Correlation Summary, approved Oct. 11, 1963, Dorothy Wolff Douglas, HQ-100-355436-105, D. Douglas FBI File; Philbrick, *I Led 3 Lives*, 129–30, 150, 161–69, 223.

73. Hulda Rees Flynn to Otto [Klineberg], June 12, 1953, in J. Hall's possession, thanks to Sarah Flynn; Schrecker, *Age of McCarthyism*, 57–60; Hulda Rees Flynn testimony, HUAC executive session, Feb. 27, 1953, 4 (quote), Hulda Flynn HUAC Investigative File, HUAC Records.

74. Ephraim S. London to Bernard W. Kearney, Feb. 27, 1953; B. W. Kearney to Harold Velde, Mar. 3, 1953; Donald T. Appel to The File, Mar. 6, 1953, Dorothy W. Douglas HUAC Investigative File; Harold H. Velde to Ephraim S. London, Mar. 7, 1953, all in HUAC Records; Glenn Fowler, "Ephraim London, 78, a Lawyer Who Fought Censorship, Is Dead," *New York Times*, June 14, 1990.

75. Raymond J. Blair, "Sen. Douglas's Ex-Wife Defies Anti-Red Probe," Mar. 14, 1953 (first quote), box 473, Benjamin Fletcher Wright Papers; Dorothy W. Douglas testimony, Mar. 13, 1953, in *Communist Methods of Infiltration (Education— Part 2): Hearings before the Committee on Un-American Activities, House of Representatives*, 83rd Cong., 1st sess. (Washington, DC: Government Printing Office, 1953), 154–555 (second quote on 155); Donald T. Appel to The File, Mar. 6, 1953, Dorothy W. Douglas HUAC Investigative File, HUAC Records.

76. D. Douglas, "Statement of the Sub-Committee Investigating Unamerican Activities," n.d. (quote), Dorothy W. Douglas HUAC Investigative File, HUAC Records.

77. "2 Refuse Answers at School Inquiry, Senator Douglas' Ex-Wife and Professor Appear at House Hearing on Communism," *New York Times*, Mar. 14, 1953 (quotes); Raymond J. Blair, "Sen. Douglas's Ex-Wife Defies Anti-Red Probe," Mar. 14, 1953, box 473, Benjamin Fletcher Wright Papers; "2 Educators Balk at Quiz," *The Sun*, Mar. 14, 1953; "Two Professors Refuse to Tell if They're Reds," *Los Angeles Times*, Mar. 14, 1953; Willard Edwards, "Prof, Ex-Wife of Sen. Douglas Defy Red Probe," *Chicago Daily Tribune*, Mar. 14, 1953; C. Baker, *Generous Spirit*, 185.

78. Schrecker, *Many Are the Crimes*, 256–57.

79. G. Lumpkin testimony, U.S. Senate, *Committee on Government Operations, State Department Information Program—Information Centers: Hearings before the Permanent Subcommittee on Investigations*, Part 2, Mar. 27, Apr. 1–2, 83rd Cong., 1st sess. (Washington, DC: Government Printing Office, 1953), 158–59 (quote).

80. Hilda Lass to Lynn Turgeon, Apr. 21, 1972 (quote), in J. Hall's possession; D. Douglas, *Transitional Economic Systems*. See also D. Douglas, "Social Security in Czechoslovakia." Many years later, Dorothy's friend and colleague, the iconoclastic economist Lynn Turgeon, judged the book to be a pioneering work in what came to be called "comparative economic systems": Turgeon, "Transitional Economic Systems in Retrospect," vii. See also Gabriel, "Comparative Economic Systems," 441–50. Thanks to John Robertson for his expert help with this paragraph.

81. KDL to Groff Conklin, Jan. 15, 1948 (quote), folder 13, KDL Papers. For the real-life Elias Hill, see *Report of the Joint Select Committee to Inquire into the Condition of Affairs in the Late Insurrectionary States*, vol. 1: Report and Minority Views (Washington, DC: Government Printing Office, 1872), 44–47; *Testimony Taken by the Joint Select Committee to Inquire into the Condition of Affairs in the Late Insurrectionary States*, Part 5: South Carolina, vol. 3 (Washington, DC: Government Printing Office, 1872), 1406–15, 1462–79; Witt, "Elias Hill's Exodus."

82. KDL to Craig Wylie, June 10, 1951 [misdated; is in answer to his letter of June 15, 1951] (first and second quotes), folder 15, KDL Papers; KDL, "These on why I chose this crippled man," Dec. 2, 1976 (third quote), Eli Hill: Notes, folder 55, both in KDL Papers.

83. *Testimony Taken by the Joint Select Committee to Inquire into the Condition of Affairs in the Late Insurrectionary States*, Part 5: South Carolina, vol. 3 (Washington, DC: Government Printing Office, 1872), 1409 (first quote), 1407 (second quote), 1477 (third quote); Hahn, *Nation under Our Feet*, 337–42; Trelease, *White Terror*, 362–80; L. Williams, *Ku Klux Klan Trials*.

84. KDL, "Eli Hill," 337 (quote), folders 53–54, KDL Papers.

85. Rosalind W., reader's report, Jan. 26, 1950 (quotes), box 14, folder F-349-49, Series F, Houghton Mifflin Fellowship Applications.

86. Rosalind W., reader's report, Apr. 26, 1951 (first quote); Craig Wylie, reader's report, Nov. 30, 1951 (second quote), both in box 14, folder F-349-49, Series F, Houghton Mifflin Fellowship Applications.

87. B. Baker, *What Reconstruction Meant*, 110–62.

88. Gray, *Southern Aberrations*, 96–154; Bingham and Underwood, *Southern Agrarians*; P. Murphy, *Rebuke of History*. The CIA and the State Department sought simultaneously to censor and manipulate a wide range of musicians and writers: Von Eschen, *Satchmo Blows Up the World*; Whitney, *Finks*.

89. Higham, "Cult of the American Consensus"; Higham, "Changing Paradigms." For this slippage, as the Vietnam War torpedoed Lyndon Johnson's social democratic policies and Bill Clinton and other "New Democrats" wooed conservative voters, see Marcus, "Power Historian." See Fitzpatrick, *History's Memory*, 188–238, for the argument that historical scholarship during this period was more diverse than the label "consensus history" suggests.

90. Craig Wylie to KDL, June 15, 1951 (quotes), folder 15, KDL Papers. See also Craig Wylie, reader's report, June 11, 1951, box 14, folder F-349-49, Series F, Houghton Mifflin Fellowship Applications.

91. KDL to Craig Wylie, June 10, 1951 [misdated; in answer to his letter of June 15, 1951] (first and second quotes); "Notes on there being no truly 'moderate position' in the post–Civil War period," n.d. [early summer 1951] (subsequent quotes), both in folder 15, KDL Papers.

92. KDL, "These on why I chose this crippled man," Dec. 2, 1976 (first quote), folder 55; KDL to Craig Wylie, June 10, 1951 [misdated; in answer to his letter of June 15, 1951] (subsequent quotes), folder 15, both in KDL Papers.

93. Craig Wylie to KDL, June 15, 1951 (quote); Craig Wylie to KDL, Feb. 21, 1952;

Craig Wylie to KDL, Mar. 5, 1952, all in folder 15, KDL Papers; Hook, "Two Faiths."

94. KDL to Elizabeth McKee, July 5, 1952; KDL to Mavis McIntosh, Aug. 24, 1952; KDL to Mr. John S. Lamont [Rinehart and Co.], Sept. 3, 1952, all in box 15, KDL Papers; KDL to Naomi Burton [Curtis Brown, Ltd., literary agents], Jan. 28, 1955; Naomi Burton to KDL, Feb. 15, 1955; Mavis McIntosh to KDL, July 27, 1955 (quote); Paul Brooks to KDL, Oct. 19, 1955, all in folder 16, KDL Papers.

95. KDL to Jean Crawford, Jan. 26, 1956, folder 17, KDL Papers; KDL to C. Vann Woodward, Mar. 11, 1956, box 33, folder 396, C. Vann Woodward, Manuscripts and Archives, Yale University Library.

96. KDL interview, Mar. 22, 1987, 2–3, 13 (first quote), 15 (second quote); KDL interview, Aug. 4, 1974, 84, 86, 90.

97. KDL, "These on why I chose this crippled man," Dec. 2, 1976; KDL, "Re Eli Hill," [1976], both in Eli Hill: Notes, folder 55, KDL Papers. For two drafts of this vignette, see KDL, "The Hearing," folder 52; KDL, "The Hearing: A Tale I Never Heard," Eli Hill: Notes, folder 55, both in KDL Papers.

98. A. Theoharis and J. Cox, *J. Edgar Hoover and the Great American Inquisition* (quote).

99. KDL, "The Hearing" (quotes), folder 52, KDL Papers.

CHAPTER NINETEEN: EXPATRIATES RETURN

1. "'Brown v. Board': Letters to Eisenhower," All Things Considered, National Public Radio, May 17, 2004, http://www.npr.org/templates/story/story .php?storyId=1899657; G. Lumpkin, *Full Circle*.

2. KDL, *Making*, 243 (quotes).

3. Polsgrove, *Divided Minds*, xvii (quote).

4. Schrecker, *No Ivory Tower*, 273–80, 289–90; Williamson-Lott, "Battle over Power," 888.

5. KDL interview, Aug. 4, 1974, 71. For the experience of a white woman at a black college in Tennessee, see C. Kaplan, *Miss Anne in Harlem*.

6. KDL to Elizabeth Lumpkin Glenn, Jan. 29, n.d. [1956] (first quote), in J. Hall's possession, thanks to Amory and William W. L. Glenn (hereafter Glenn Letters); KDL, "Angelina Grimké: A Problem in Biography," paper given before Wells College Faculty Club, Feb. 1959, 3 (second quote), folder 67 (hereafter KDL, "A Problem in Biography"); KDL to Mavis McIntosh, Dec 8, 1954, folder 16; KDL to Naomi Burton [at Curtis Brown Ltd.], Jan. 28, 1955, folder 17; KDL to Jean Crawford, Jan. 26, 1956, folder 17; KDL to Bell Wiley, Mar. 24, 1956, folder 17, all in KDL Papers; KDL to Alfred A. Knopf, Oct. 22, 1955, box 172, [folder 14], Knopf Records.

7. Horace M. Bond to KDL, Jul. 21, 1953 and Dec. 13, 1954, folder 16, KDL Papers; Ritterhouse, *Growing Up Jim Crow* (quote).

8. Juanita Jane Saddler to Charles S. Johnson, Jan. 7, 1955 (quotes), folder 16, KDL Papers. For Saddler, see "Juanita Saddler, Led Struggle to Integrate YWCA in America," *New York Amsterdam News*, Jan. 24, 1970; "Miss J. J. Saddler, YWCA leader, 78," *Afro-American*, Jan. 24, 1970; "Juanita Saddler of YWCA Dies," *New*

York Times, Jan. 13, 1970; Robertson, *Christian Sisterhood*, 147, 232n108; Seay, "Saddler, Juanita Jane"; B. Ross, "Mary McLeod Bethune"; "NYA Official," *Chicago Daily Defender*, Mar. 14, 1936. In 1967, Saddler joined the Jeannette Rankin Brigade, representing the YWCA: Swerdlow, *Women Strike for Peace*, 136. In later life, she organized interracial and ecumenical activities among the churches of New York through Riverside Church and Church Women United. She was the first black woman to serve as a deacon at Christ Chapel at New York's Riverside Church.

9. Charles S. Johnson to KDL, Mar. 1, 1955; KDL to Charles S. Johnson, Apr. 21, 1955; Charles S. Johnson to KDL, May 4, 1955 (quote), all in folder 16, KDL Papers.

10. The faculty member was Giovanni Rossi Lomanitz, who took a job as an associate professor at Fisk in 1949: Williamson-Lott, "Battle over Power," 888–89; Schrecker, *No Ivory Tower*, 135–39, 146–47.

11. Schrecker, *No Ivory Tower*, 290–92 (quote on 290); Williamson-Lott, "Battle over Power," 888–89.

12. KDL to David Horne, Oct. 2, 1970 (first quote), folder 24; KDL to Peter H. Davison, Aug. 9, 1961 (second and third quotes), folder 20, both in KDL Papers; KDL to Elizabeth Lumpkin Glenn, Jan. 29, n.d. [1956] (fourth quote), Glenn Letters.

13. Joseph H. Lumpkin Sr. interview, Aug. 1, 1995 (quote); Joseph H. Lumpkin Sr. and Joseph H. Lumpkin Jr. interview, Aug. 17, 1990; Alva M. Lumpkin Jr. interview, Aug. 4, 1995; Alva M. Lumpkin Jr. interview, Aug. 17, 1990 (subsequent quotes).

14. Stone taught at Woman's College, a Methodist institution, from 1929 to 1934. She left this position in 1934 to raise money for and serve as executive of the Southern Committee for People's Rights while pursuing her research interests unfettered by academic pressures: Holden, *New Southern University*, 102; Olive Stone interviews, Mar.–Nov. 1975; O. Stone, "Agrarian Conflict in Alabama"; O. Stone, "Position of the Negro Farm Population"; Gilmore, *Defying Dixie*, 215–26.

15. Olive Stone interview, Aug. 13, 1975 (quote on 38); KDL to Katharine Jocher, Nov. 24, 1956; Katharine Jocher to KDL, Dec 5, 1956, both in folder 18, KDL Papers.

16. Olive Stone to George Hedley, Oct. 24, 1956 (quotes), folder 16; Olive Stone to Lyda Shivers, Feb. 26, 1957, folder 19, both in KDL Papers.

17. KDL, "Outlines of Lectures given in Ralph Harlow's class in his course at Smith College on religion and ethics," 3 (first quote), folders 64–65, KDL Papers; KDL, *Making*, 244 (second quote).

18. KDL, "Social Change." This is a reprint of KDL, "Social Change and the Southern Mind," lecture at Mills College, Oakland, California, Mar. 1957, folder 66, KDL Papers.

19. Bryan H. Lumpkin, [1961], "Questionnaire to Editors and Preachers and Other White Citizens Who Favor the Integration of the Negroes with White Children in the Public Schools," in J. Hall's possession, thanks to Katherine Glenn Kent; Woods, *Black Struggle, Red Scare*; Braukman, *Communists and Perverts*; Dailey, "Sex, Segregation."

20. Colston Warne to D. Douglas, Feb. 23, 1955 (quote), box 4, folder 7, Warne Papers. The president of Hollins was John ("Jack") Rutherford Everett: http://digitalcommons .hollins.edu/cgi/viewcontent.cgi?article=1001&context=archival_articles.

21. Colston Warne to D. Douglas, Feb. 23, 1955; D. Douglas to Colston Warne, Feb. 11, 1955 and Feb. 26, 1955; D. Douglas to Colston Warne, Mar. 23, 1961 (quotes), all in box 4, folder 7, Warne Papers; Schrecker, *No Ivory Tower*, 289. Davis was the father-in-law of the eminent historian Natalie Davis. He taught at Bennett and Shaw colleges in North Carolina after losing several other positions. His son, the mathematician Chandler Davis, who, like his father, was a member of the Communist Party, fled to Canada in order to find work.

22. KDL to Lyda Gordon Shivers, May 14, 1957 (quotes), folder 19, KDL Papers.

23. D. Douglas, "Dear 1912," 50th Reunion Booklet, Bryn Mawr College Class of 1912, 27, Bryn Mawr College Archives, Bryn Mawr, PA; KDL to Ted Newcomb, Aug. 14, 1957 (quotes), folder 19, KDL Papers.

24. John Nesselhof interview, Aug. 9, 1996; Jane Dieckmann interview, Aug. 8, 1996; "1868—The First Century Fund—1968," Wells College Archives, Louis Jefferson Long Library, Aurora, NY.

25. Chalmer McCormick and Arthur Bellinzoni interview, Aug. 9, 1996 (first, third, and fourth quotes); John Nesselhof interview, Aug. 9, 1996 (second quote); John M. Nesselhof, tribute at KDL memorial service, Chapel Hill, NC, May 12, 1988 (fifth quote); Mrs. Louis Jefferson Long to J. Hall, Sept. 7, 1996, both in J. Hall's possession. Katharine had retired by the late 1970s when the Texas state legislator and international human rights advocate Frances (Sissy) Farenthold became the first female president of the college and Wells was swept up in the feminist revolution, but her memory endured. To the young feminists who joined the faculty, she served as a model of feminist antiracism at a small women's college: Grey Osterud, conversation with J. Hall, 2016.

26. Jane A. Ayers, Executive Secretary, Wells College Alumnae Association, to Sarah H. McMillan, University of North Carolina Press, Nov. 12, 1974 (quote), in J. Hall's possession; John Nesselhof interview, Aug. 9, 1996; KDL file in Office of the Dean, Wells College, Aurora, NY.

27. John Nesselhof interview, Aug. 9, 1996 (quote).

28. FBI letter, SAC, Albany, to Director, FBI, July 31, 1959, Katherine D. Lumpkin, HQ 100-400110-23; FBI letter, Director, FBI, to SAC, Albany, Aug. 12, 1959, Katherine D. Lumpkin, HQ 100-400110-23 (quote); FBI letter, C. D. DeLoach to Mr. Tolson, Sept. 9, 1959, Katherine Du Pre Lumpkin, HQ 100-400110-25, all in KDL FBI File. The FBI closed her case on Aug. 19, 1959.

29. *Wells College Bulletin* 44, 1957–1958, 7 (quote); Jean S. Davis, "Facts and Folklore in Aurora," 99 (quote), 107–8, both in Wells College Archives, Louis Jefferson Long Library, Aurora, NY. For Wells College history, see Dieckmann, *Wells College*; Russ, "Higher Education for Women."

30. Chalmer McCormick and Arthur Bellinzoni interview, Aug. 9, 1996; KDL to Dorothy Markey (Myra Page), Feb. 27, [1958] (quote), Page Papers.

31. Chalmer McCormick and Arthur Bellinzoni interview, Aug. 9, 1996 (first quote); Lectures for Sociology 367 (second quote), folder 71, KDL Papers.

32. Houck and D. Dixon, *Women and the Civil Rights Movement*, xi (first quote), xviii (second quote).

33. KDL, afterword to *Making*, 250 (first quote), 252 (second quote).

34. KDL, "The Problem of Schisms in Movements for Civil Rights," a paper presented at the Southern Sociology Association, Atlanta, GA, Apr. 11, 1968, 6 (first and third quotes), folder 57, KDL Papers; KDL, *Emancipation*, ix (second quote). She relied for her understanding of black power especially on Carmichael and Hamilton, *Black Power*.

35. Hobson, *But Now I See*, 17, 35–36 (quote on 35).

36. KDL to Amory Potter Glenn and William W. L. Glenn, Jan. 10, 1974 (quote), Glenn Letters; John Nesselhof interview, Aug. 9, 1996 (subsequent quotes).

37. Thanks to Joseph H. Lumpkin Sr. for sharing this note and inscription with me. In another copy of the book, Katharine wrote, "1970—my dear love—good place to be as we enter the 1970s."

38. "W. M. Bennett Dies at 60 after Stroke," *New York Times*, Jan. 17, 1930.

39. *1927 Hi-O-Hi*, 128 (first quote); *1925 Hi-O-Hi*, 110 (second quote), both in Oberlin College Archives, Oberlin, OH; Elizabeth Bennett to President W. J. [Hutchins?], Feb. 22, 1926 (third quote), RG 9-A, Berea College Archives, Hutchins Library, Berea, KY.

40. Oberlin College Undergraduate Questionnaire, 1923 and 1935 Quinquennial Reports, Oberlin College Archives, Oberlin, OH; Elizabeth Bennett to President [Hutchins?], Apr. 10, 1926, RG 9-A, Berea College Archives, Hutchins Library, Berea, KY; "Personal data," Radcliffe [after 1936 "The Appointment Bureau of Radcliffe College"], Sept. 4, 1942, Radcliffe College Archives, Schlesinger Library, Radcliffe Institute, Harvard University; Carter Alexander to Margaret Augur, May 12, 1936, Kingswood Personnel Files, Cranbrook Archives, Cranbrook Educational Community, Bloomfield Hills, MI (hereafter Kingswood Personnel Files).

41. Elizabeth Bennett to Margaret Augur, Aug. 18, 1947; Elizabeth Bennett to Margaret Augur, June 12, [?], Kingswood Personnel Files; "Follow Up Information," Radcliffe's Appointment Bureau Files, [ca. 1951], "The Appointment Bureau of Radcliffe College," Sept. 4, 1942; "War Emergency Questionnaire: Radcliffe College Appointment Bureau," all in Radcliffe College Archives, Schlesinger Library, Radcliffe Institute, Harvard University.

42. For Bennett's political and religious affiliations, see Elizabeth Bennett to Marion Goodale, July 1, 1940, Kingswood Personnel Files; "Descriptive Blank for a Possible Worker in Berea College," 1926, RG 9-A, Berea College Archives, Hutchins Library, Berea, KY; "The Appointment Bureau of Radcliffe College," Sept. 4, 1942, Radcliffe College Archives, Schlesinger Library, Radcliffe Institute, Harvard University; Oberlin College Alumni Questionnaire, Dec. 6, 1975; "Oberlin College—125th Anniversary Alumni Catalogue—Report Blank," Oct. 30, 1958; both in Oberlin College Archives, Oberlin, OH.

43. *Elizabeth Bennett: A Word Portrait* (The Bennett Fund, Kingswood School Cranbrook, 1983), 14, Kingswood Personnel Files; "Alumni Reunion Class Question-

naire," Alumni Records Data, Jan. 31, 1966, Oberlin College Archives, Oberlin, OH; Darden et al., *Detroit*, 132.

44. *Elizabeth Bennett: A Word Portrait* (The Bennett Fund, Kingswood School Cranbrook, 1983) (quotes), Kingswood Personnel Files.

45. *Elizabeth Bennett: A Word Portrait* (The Bennett Fund, Kingswood School Cranbrook, 1983), 7 (first quote), 19 (second quote), Kigswood Personnel Files.

46. Una Harris to KDL, Sept. 19, 1954; KDL to Mavis McIntosh, Dec. 8, 1954 (quote), both in folder 16, KDL Papers. Both women were attending Middlebury's summer graduate program in English and American literature, not one of its more celebrated writers' conferences: Bain and M. Duffy, *Whose Woods These Are*. For Bread Loaf, see Cifelli, *John Ciardi*; Waldron, *Eudora*; and Lyons, "Bread Loaf Writers' School."

47. "Setting Off for 80-Mile Ride," May 10, 1955, n.p., n.d., newsclip in Faculty Biographical Files, Dorothy Wolff Douglas, SCA; Jean Eisler, tribute to Dorothy Douglas, [1972] (quote), in J. Hall's possession, thanks to Lynn Turgeon.

48. FBI Report, New York, Feb. 24, 1959, Dorothy Wolff Douglas, HQ-100-335436-51, D. Douglas FBI File; "73 Ask New View in Trials of Reds," *New York Times*, Aug. 8, 1955; "Eulogy by Lynn Turgeon given at Memorial Services for Dr. Dorothy W. Douglas held at Chapel of Peace, Community Church, 40 East 35th St., New York, Dec. 13, 1986," in J. Hall's possession, thanks to Lynn Turgeon. On campus, as Turgeon puts it, Dorothy always "made up the deficit" for the left. She also contributed to CORE, Carl and Anne Braden's Southern Conference Educational Fund (SCEF), the Communist Party, Eugene McCarthy's presidential campaigns, as well as to other individuals, groups, and causes.

49. Garrow, *"Solo" to Memphis*; Barron, *Operation SOLO*. See also the SOLO File on the National Security Archive website, which was declassified in 2011–2012, http://nsarchive.gwu.edu/NSAEBB/NSAEBB375/.

50. FBI letter, SAC, Boston, to Director, FBI, Mar. 14, 1958, Communist Party, USA—Funds, HQ 100-355436-NR (quote); FBI letter, SAC, Boston, to Director, FBI, Sept. 24, 1954, Dorothy Wolff Douglas, HQ 100-355436-47; FBI letter, [unknown] to Mr. A. H. Belmont, Jan. 15, 1959, Dorothy Wolf Douglas, HQ 100-355436-50; FBI Report, Philadelphia, July 31, 1961, Dorothy Wolff Douglas, HQ 100-355436-84; FBI Report, New York, Sept. 10, 1962, Dorothy Wolff Douglas, HQ 100-355436-97; FBI Report, New York, Jan. 27, 1965, Dorothy Wolff Douglas, HQ 100-355436-111, all in D. Douglas FBI File.

51. FBI letter, [unknown] to Mr. A. H. Belmont, Jan. 15, 1959, Dorothy Wolf Douglas, HQ 100-355436-50 (quote); FBI letter, SAC, Boston, to Director, FBI, Apr. 16, 1959, Dorothy Wolf Douglas, HQ 100-355436-53; and FBI letter, SAC, Washington, to Director, FBI, May 27, 1959, Dorothy Wolf Douglas, HQ 100-355436-55; 1968 FBI Report, New York, Jan. 26, 1968, Dorothy Wolff Douglas, HQ 100-355436-124, all in D. Douglas FBI File. For more on the FBI's monitoring of Dorothy Douglas, see FBI letter from Director, FBI, to SAC, Boston, July 30, 1951, Dorothy Wolff Douglas, HQ 100-355436-11; FBI letter, Director, FBI, to SAC,

Boston, July 21, 1952, Dorothy Wolff Douglas, HQ 100-355436-28; FBI letter, Director, FBI, to SAC, Boston, Aug. 20, 1954, Dorothy Wolf Douglas, HQ 100-355436-46; FBI letter, SAC, Boston, to Director, FBI, Dec. 31, 1958, Dorothy Wolf Douglas, HQ 100-355436-49; and FBI letter, Director, FBI, to SAC, Boston, Jan. 23, 1959, Dorothy Wolf Douglas, HQ 100-355436-49, all in D. Douglas FBI File.

52. Elizabeth Bennett to Miss [Marion] Goodale, Aug. 7, 1960, Kingswood Personnel Files; D. Douglas to Colston Warne, Jan. 26, [1961] (quote); Colston Warne to William J. L. Wallace, Jan. 30, 1961; D. Douglas to Colston Warne, Mar. 23, 1961, all in Warne Papers.

53. D. Douglas to Dear Friends, May 26, 1964 (quote), Page Papers.

54. KDL to G. Lumpkin, July 24, [1965], in G. Lumpkin Diary, 1963–1975, in J. Hall's possession, thanks to Joseph H. Lumpkin Sr. (hereafter G. Lumpkin Diary); "Alumni Reunion Class Questionnaire," Alumni Records Data, Jan. 31, 1966, Oberlin College Archives, Oberlin, OH; Elizabeth ("Benny") Bennett to Marion [Goodale], July 11, 1966, Kingswood Personnel Files.

55. Bryn Mawr College Class of 1912 50th Reunion Booklet, 27 (quote), Bryn Mawr College Archives, Bryn Mawr, PA; "Eulogy by Lynn Turgeon given at Memorial Services for Dr. Dorothy W. Douglas held at Chapel of Peace, Community Church, 40 East 35th St., New York, Dec. 13, 1986," in J. Hall's possession, thanks to Lynn Turgeon; Lynn Turgeon interview, Dec. 8, 1988; "Dorothy Douglas, Hofstra Professor," *New York Times*, Dec. 11, 1968.

56. Sarah Flynn, telephone conversations with J. Hall, Nov. 25 and Nov. 28, 2000; Sarah Flynn, email message to J. Hall, Oct. 23, 2000 (quote), Mar. 21, 2001.

57. KDL to Amory Potter Glenn, Mar. 18, [1975] (quote), Glenn Letters; "Last Will and Testament of D. Douglas," Sept. 2, 1960, Probate Court, Northampton, MA; "Last Will and Testament of Katharine D. Lumpkin," Apr. 21, 1986, Clerk of Court, Orange County, NC. Dorothy left no bequests to her children because she had "distributed the major part of my property among them during my lifetime" and because they were provided for by trusts established for them in her father's will. She did leave them her house in Northampton, her car, and her personal effects. She gave all the remainder of her real and personal property to John and Dorothy Markey (Myra Page), with full confidence that they would "administer such property as I should desire to see it used." If they predeceased her, the money would go to Hulda R. Flynn. The Markeys gave the money to the American Civil Liberties Union, the Marian Davis Scholarship Fund, Anne Braden, coal miners, and *Monthly Review Press* to reissue Dorothy's *Transitional Economic Systems*: C. Baker, *Generous Spirit*, 196–97. For the Marian Davis Scholarship Fund, founded by Horace Davis in honor of his wife and now called the Davis-Putter Scholarship Fund, see http://ousf.duke.edu/post-graduate-scholarships/search-all/2013/01/15/davis-putter-scholarship.

58. KDL to William S. Ewing (quote), Oct. 2, 1960, folder 20, KDL Papers; Birney, *Grimké Sisters*.

59. KDL, "Random notes on a projected biography of Angelina Grimké," June 26, 1955, 3 (first quote), folder 58, KDL Papers (hereafter KDL, "Random notes"); KDL, "Social Change," 52 (second quote).

60. Angelina Grimké quoted in Sklar, *Women's Rights*, 34 (quotes); KDL, "Author's Biographical Record and Publicity Questionnaire," Feb. 12, 1974, 3, University of North Carolina Press Records, University Archives, Louis Round Wilson Special Collections Library, University of North Carolina at Chapel Hill, NC; S. Grimké, *Equality of the Sexes.*

61. KDL, "A Problem in Biography," 2 (quote); KDL to Mavis McIntosh, Dec. 8, 1954, folder 16; KDL to Adrienne Koch, Sept. 10, 1960, folder 20, all in KDL Papers; Barnes and Dumond, *Letters of Theodore Dwight Weld*; KDL to J. Hall, July 1, 1985, in J. Hall's possession; KDL to Alfred A. Knopf, Oct. 22, 1955, box 172, [folder 14], Knopf Records.

62. KDL, "Author's Biographical Record and Publicity Questionnaire," Feb. 12, 1974, 3-A (quote), University of North Carolina Press Records, University Archives, Louis Round Wilson Special Collections Library, University of North Carolina at Chapel Hill.

63. KDL, "Random notes," 2 (quote). For the argument that, given the centrality of oratory in early nineteenth-century civic life, Angelina's eloquence made her a uniquely powerful agent of social change and that, in combination, her oratory and writings were likely more important than Sarah's denser Biblical exegesis in changing consciousness regarding women's rights, see Sklar, "Throne of My Heart," 222–25. In contrast, Lerner, *Feminist Thought*, argues that Sarah was the more original, and thus in the long run the more influential, feminist thinker.

64. KDL, "Random notes," 2 (first and third quotes); KDL, "A Problem in Biography," 11 (second quote), both in KDL Papers.

65. KDL, "Notes on a biography of Angelina Grimké (Now in progress)," [Oct. 22, 1955] (first quote), attached to KDL to Alfred A. Knopf, Oct. 22, 1955, box 172, [folder 14], Knopf Records; KDL, "A Problem in Biography," 11 (second quote).

66. KDL to Alfred A. Knopf, Oct. 22, 1955 (first quote); KDL, "Notes on a biography of Angelina Grimké (Now in Progress)," Oct. 2015 (second quote), attached to KDL to Alfred A. Knopf, Oct. 22, 1955; H. W. to Alfred A. Knopf, Oct. 25, 1955 (third quote), all in box 172, [folder 14], Knopf Records.

67. T. McCarthy and Stauffer, *Prophets of Protest*; Guasco, "War against Slavery," 60, 62. KDL had been at work on her book for almost six years when Louis Filler's *Crusade against Slavery, 1830–1860* (1960) appeared. Filler rejected the then still dominant view of the abolitionists as irresponsible fanatics, and his was the secondary work upon which she most strongly relied.

68. KDL to Jean Crawford, Jan. 26, 1956 (quote), folder 17, KDL Papers. See also KDL to Alfred A. Knopf, Oct. 22, 1955, box 172, [folder 14], Knopf Records.

69. KDL, "The Influence of Religion on the career of Angelina Grimké," n.d. [1974], 3 (quotes), folder 58, KDL Papers (hereafter KDL, "Influence of Religion"). See also KDL, "Notes on a biography of Angelina Grimké (Now in progress)," [Oct. 22, 1955], attached to KDL to Alfred A. Knopf, Oct. 22, 1955, box 172, [folder 14], Knopf Records.

70. J. Hall to KDL, May 6, 1985, copy in J. Hall's possession; KDL to J. Hall, July 1, 1985 (quote).

71. KDL interview, Aug. 4, 1974, 1, 12 (quotes), 65, 78, 86.

72. H. Lee, "Alice Munro's Magic," 30 (quote).

73. KDL to J. Hall, Sept. 9, 1975 (quote).

74. KDL, "Influence of Religion," 11 (first quote), 8–9 (second quote); Angelina Grimké quoted in Weld, *American Slavery*, 53 (third quote).

75. KDL, *Emancipation*, ii (first quote), 3 (second quote), 4 (third quote), 55 (fourth quote), 56 (fifth quote), 58 (sixth quote).

76. KDL, *Emancipation*, 171 (first quote), 172 (second and third quotes).

77. Scholars also point to the Welds' desire to prove that public activism had not made Angelina "spoiled for domestic life": Weld quoted in Abzug, *Passionate Liberator*, 204; Sklar, *Women's Rights*, 39, 43–45.

78. KDL, *Emancipation*, 166–67, 194 (quotes). Later studies that bolster Lumpkin's interpretation of the motivations behind the three reformers' withdrawal include Abzug, *Passionate Liberator*; Berkin, *Civil War Wives*, 3–100.

79. KDL, "Influence of Religion," 14 (first quote); KDL, *Emancipation*, xi (second quote), 122, 184 (third quote). While most Grimké scholars confirm Lumpkin's portrait of the tensions between the sisters, virtually none paint such a negative portrait of Sarah.

80. KDL, *Emancipation*, 185 (first quote), 191 (second and third quotes), 187 (fourth quote).

81. KDL, "Influence of Religion," 15 (first quote); KDL, *Emancipation*, 166–67 (third, fourth, and fifth quotes).

82. KDL, *Emancipation*.

83. KDL, *Emancipation*, 164 (first and second quotes), viii (third quote); KDL, "Random notes," 1 (fourth quote).

84. Sklar, *Women's Rights*, 30; KDL, *Emancipation*, 164 (first quote), 182 (second quote), 185–86.

85. KDL, *Emancipation*, xi (first and second quotes), 200 (third and fourth quotes), 205 (fifth quote).

86. Arna Bontemps quoted in K. Shaffer, "Angelina Weld Grimke," 151; KDL, "A few random notes on my three-hour talk with Miss Angelina Weld Grimké, n.d. [1957], folder 58, KDL Papers; KDL, *Emancipation*, xv, 219–27, 251–52.

87. Hull, *Color, Sex, and Poetry*; Christian, *Black Feminist Criticism*; Herron, *Selected Works*.

88. KDL, "A few random notes on my three-hour talk with Miss Angelina Weld Grimké, n.d. [1957] (quote on 3), folder 58, KDL Papers; KDL, *Emancipation*, xv, 219–27, 251–52.

89. Archibald H. Grimké quoted in Lerner, *Pioneers for Women's Rights*, 359.

90. KDL, *Emancipation*, 222 (quote).

91. KDL, *Emancipation*, 195 (quote).

92. KDL interview, Aug. 4, 1974, 84–93 (first quote on 87, second quote on 88).

93. Donald L. Clark to Elizabeth Lumpkin Glenn, Nov. 7, 1927; [Elizabeth Lumpkin Glenn], "Dr. Hudson Strode, Class in Fiction Writing," [1961], both in E. Glenn Letters (quotes).

94. Elizabeth Lumpkin Glenn to Dr. Scarfitt, Sept. 12, 1960, E. Glenn Letters.

95. [Elizabeth Lumpkin Glenn], "Dr. Hudson Strode, Class in Fiction Writing,"

[1961], E. Glenn Letters (quote); "Mrs. Eugene B. Glenn Dies," *Asheville (NC) Citizen*, Feb. 15, 1963; Katharine Baird, "Author's Memories in Civil War Book," n.d., n.p., newsclip; Elizabeth Lumpkin Glenn, "Bitterroot," both in J. Hall's possession, thanks to Amory and William W. L. Glenn.

96. Brentwood Manor, Convalescent Rehabilitation Center, Asheville, N.C., Feb. 4, 1963, E. Glenn Letters.

97. Diggins, *Up from Communism* (quote); G. Lumpkin to [John] Gassner, May 20, 1951; John Gassner to G. Lumpkin, Sept. 3, 1951; G. Lumpkin to John Gassner, Sept. 30, [1951] (quote), all in box 62, folder 6, John Gassner Papers, Harry Ransom Center, University of Texas at Austin; Mantooth, "You Factory Folks," 208n95.

98. G. Lumpkin to Lillian Gilkes, Sept. 11, 1974 (first quote), box 3, Gilkes Papers; G. Lumpkin to John Gassner, Sept. 30, [1951] (second quote), box 62, folder 6, John Gassner Papers, Harry Ransom Center, University of Texas at Austin; Lillian Gilkes to G. Lumpkin, Dec. 30, 1974, folder 121, KDL Papers.

99. G. Lumpkin interview, Aug. 6, 1974, 50–51 (quote); G. Lumpkin, "Treasure." This story was originally published in the *Southern Review*, an Agrarian magazine edited by Robert Penn Warren.

100. Wecter, *Age of the Great Depression*, 253 (first quote); Foley, *Radical Representations*, 21 (second quote). Foley notes how arbitrarily one author and not another has been labeled a "doctrinaire Communist."

101. Gilkes, *Short Story Craft*; G. Lumpkin interview, Sept. 25, 1971 (first quote); Lillian Gilkes to G. Lumpkin, May 11, [1948] (second quote), box 3, Gilkes Papers.

102. G. Lumpkin to Kenneth Toombs, June 22, 1971 (quote), G. Lumpkin Papers.

103. M. Lee, *Creating Conservatism*, 163–92 (quote on 165). See Lee for the galvanizing texts from which modern conservatives derived the "keystone expressions" (8) or "lingua franca" (7) through which they articulated their fusion of Christian moralism and free market individualism. Whittaker Chambers's *Witness* was one of these texts.

104. G. Lumpkin to Donald Davidson, Sept. 15, 1960, box 9, folder 10, Donald Davidson Papers, Special Collections and University Archives, Jean and Alexander Heard Library, Vanderbilt University, Nashville, TN; [Causy?] to G. Lumpkin, Dec. 22, 1962; G. Lumpkin, "About Liberals," fragment of letter to Florence [Murray?], [1966], both in G. Lumpkin Diary; Donald Davidson to G. Lumpkin, [ca. 1962 or 1963] (quote), G. Lumpkin Papers. For an example of the perspective Davidson offered *National Review* readers, see Davidson, "New South."

105. Fosl, "Life and Times," 51–52 (quote); U.S. Senate, *Violations of Free Speech and the Rights of Labor: Hearings before a Subcommittee of the Committee on Education and Labor*, Part 3, Jan. 14–15, 21–23, 75th Cong., 1st sess. (Washington, D.C.: Government Printing Office, 1937): 961–62.

106. Jane Speed had a number of lovers. Worse, in the eyes of her Alabama relatives, she married a man of color, a left-wing Puerto Rican labor leader: G. Lumpkin interview, Aug. 6, 1974, 13–14; Fosl, "Life and Times," 58–60.

107. G. Lumpkin, *Full Circle*, 31 (first quote), 126 (second quote). With Olive Stone

and other Montgomery, Alabama, liberals and leftists, the Speeds had also tried to help the Alabama Sharecroppers Union withstand a reign of terror that sent almost fifty alleged unionists to jail: Fosl, "Life and Times," 51–52.

108. G. Lumpkin, *Full Circle*, 2, 160 (first quote), 166–68 (second quote on 168), 187 (third quote), 188 (fourth quote).

109. Davidson, *Attack on Leviathan* (first quote); draft of letter from G. Lumpkin to Lillian Gilkes, [Jan. 1975] (second quote), folder 121, KDL Papers; G. Lumpkin, *Full Circle*, 194. See also G. Lumpkin to Senator Harry F. Byrd, Sept. 5, 1968, in G. Lumpkin Diary. For the period's roiling controversies regarding the place of religion in civic life, see Kruse, *One Nation under God*; Herzog, *Spiritual-Industrial Complex*.

110. G. Lumpkin, *Full Circle*, 179 (quote). "In a pique of anger Ann had said something to Arnie's black lover that she did not even know she thought: 'So far as I know your people have been on this earth just as long as my people have been. We have built our culture, the culture you so greedily covet. Where is yours?'": G. Lumpkin, *Full Circle*, 187 (quote).

111. G. Lumpkin, "How I Returned," 1 (quote). For the use of neo-Confederate shibboleths in a project of radical transformation, see MacLean, "Neo-Confederacy."

112. G. Lumpkin, "About Liberals," fragment of letter to Florence [Murray?], [1966] (first quote), in G. Lumpkin Diary; G. Lumpkin interview, Aug. 6, 1974, 13 (second quote); G. Lumpkin to Kenneth Toombs, June 22, 1971 (third quote), G. Lumpkin Papers. In "Between the Bookends," American Way Features, Inc., 133 (June 11, 1963), newsclip in G. Lumpkin Papers, she is quoted as saying, "The characters and incidents are composites created from life and experiences." The book is fiction, but "the truth is here for all those willing to open their hearts and minds to receive it."

113. G. Lumpkin, "About Liberals," fragment of letter to Florence [Murray?], [1966] (quote), in G. Lumpkin Diary.

114. G. Lumpkin, *Full Circle*, 166–68.

115. G. Lumpkin, *Full Circle*, 254 (first quote), 253 (second quote), 254 (third quote), 253 (fourth quote).

116. Free, review of *Full Circle*, 120 (quote).

117. Lillian Gilkes to G. Lumpkin, Dec. 30, 1974 (quote), folder 121, KDL Papers.

118. Whitfield, *Culture of the Cold War*, 41–42 (quote on 42); Perlstein, *Before the Storm*, 110–19, 153–57.

119. G. Lumpkin Diary, Nov. 21, 1963 (quote).

120. Lillian Gilkes to G. Lumpkin, Dec. 30, 1974 (quotes), folder 121, KDL Papers.

CHAPTER TWENTY: ENDINGS

1. Buckley, *Odyssey of a Friend*, 181 (first quote); G. Lumpkin to William W. L. Glenn and Amory Potter Glenn, Sept. 18, 1963 (second quote), in J. Hall's possession, thanks to Amory and William W. L. Glenn (hereafter Glenn Letters).

2. G. Lumpkin to William W. L. Glenn, May 23, 1963; G. Lumpkin to William W. L. Glenn and Amory Potter Glenn, [1967 or 1968], Glenn Letters.

3. G. Lumpkin to William W. L. Glenn, May 23, 1963 (quotes); G. Lumpkin to William W. L. Glenn and Amory Potter Glenn, June 24, n.d. [1963], Glenn Letters. The National Council of Churches (NCC) was founded in 1950 but traces its roots to the formation of the social gospel–oriented Federal Council of Churches in 1908. For the NCC's social stance, see Findlay, *Church People in Struggle*; Gill, *Embattled Ecumenism*.

4. G. Lumpkin to Beloved Nieces and Nephews, Aug. 5, 1965 (quote), G. Lumpkin Diary, 1963–1975, thanks to Joseph H. Lumpkin Sr. (hereafter G. Lumpkin Diary).

5. G. Lumpkin to William W. L. Glenn, n.d. [summer 1963] (first quote); G. Lumpkin to William W. L. Glenn and Amory Potter Glenn, Sept. 18, 1963 (second quote), both in Glenn Letters.

6. G. Lumpkin to Amory Potter Glenn and William W. L. Glenn, Nov. 12, 1963 (quotes), Glenn Letters.

7. G. Lumpkin to William W. L. Glenn, n.d. [summer 1963] (quotes), Glenn Letters.

8. G. Lumpkin to Amory Potter Glenn and William W. L. Glenn, Nov. 12, 1963 (quote), Glenn Letters.

9. G. Lumpkin Diary, Apr. 7, 1964 (first quote), Nov. 21, 1963 (subsequent quotes).

10. G. Lumpkin to William W. L. Glenn, Apr. 14, [n.d.], Glenn Letters; G. Lumpkin Diary, Apr. 5, 1964 (first quote), Nov. 19, 1963 (second quote).

11. G. Lumpkin Diary, Apr. 26, 1964 (first quote), Aug. 6, 1964 (second quote), Sept. 4, 1964 (subsequent quotes).

12. G. Lumpkin to Amory Potter Glenn and William W. L. Glenn, Dec. 9, 1965 (quote), Glenn Letters.

13. Mary Mowbray Branch to G. Lumpkin, May 6, 1965; Sherry Dixon to G. Lumpkin, July 27, 1965; Virginia Fox to G. Lumpkin, May 16, 1966; Shirley L. French to G. Lumpkin, May 24, 1966; Margaret C. Campbell to G. Lumpkin, Oct. 4, 1966; G. Lumpkin to Margaret C. Campbell, Oct. 4, 1966; G. Lumpkin to Hon. Harry Byrd, Sept. 5, 1968 (quotes), all in G. Lumpkin Diary.

14. G. Lumpkin to James J. Kilpatrick, Mar. 9, 1963, and Sept. 25, 1964; James J. Kilpatrick to G. Lumpkin, Sept. 30, 1964, all in James J. Kilpatrick Papers, Special Collections, University of Virginia Library, Charlottesville; James P. Lucier to G. Lumpkin, Apr. 21, 1965; Robert B. Crawford to G. Lumpkin, Mar. 3, 1965; C. G. Jones Jr. to G. Lumpkin, May 28, 1965, all in G. Lumpkin Papers; Allan Jones, "Gives Thousands to Private Schools," n.d., newsclip in G. Lumpkin Papers; Neff and *Dictionary of Virginia Biography*, "Robert B. Crawford." For the links between this resistance to school desegregation and today's efforts to privatize the public schools, see MacLean, *Democracy in Chains*.

15. G. Lumpkin, draft of letter to the editor, *Richmond News Leader*, Aug. 24, 1965 (first, second, and third quotes); G. Lumpkin to Florence [Murray?], n.d. [1966], postscript written at 6:00 a.m. (fourth quote), both in G. Lumpkin Diary.

16. G. Lumpkin to William W. L. Glenn, May 23, 1963 (quote); G. Lumpkin to William W. L. Glenn, n.d. [ca. summer 1963], both in Glenn Letters; G. Lumpkin Diary, Nov. 21, 1963, Jan. 27, 1964, Jan. 30, 1964, Apr. 8, 1964. Called "Track

13," the film was produced by the Episcopal Radio-TV Foundation, Inc., in Atlanta and first shown at the general convention of the Episcopal Church on Sept. 19, 1961. The title refers to a day coach in Grand Central Station where a black red cap who appears in the program held prayer meetings. It became the pilot in a series called "Each One Reach One" that was still showing on stations in thirty-five cities as late as 1968: Murray Illson, "Redcap Evangelist Stars in Film of His Grand Central Ministry," *New York Times*, Aug. 9, 1961; "The Word: Pop Preaching," *Time*, Mar. 1, 1968, 43.

17. G. Lumpkin Diary, Apr. 8, 1964, June 5, 1964, Oct. 7, 1969 (first quote), Dec. 11, 1963 (second quote), Feb. 8, 1965 (third quote).

18. G. Lumpkin Diary, Oct. 17, 1968 (quote).

19. G. Lumpkin Diary, Nov. 11, 1968 (quotes).

20. G. Lumpkin Diary, Aug. 22, 1967 (quotes), Sept. 25, 1964, Feb. 23, 1965; G. Lumpkin interview, Sept. 25, 1971, 38–39.

21. G. Lumpkin Diary, Mar. 21, 1965 (first and second quotes), Mar. 27, 1965 (third quote).

22. G. Lumpkin, draft of letter to Frances [Bryan Lumpkin's widow], 1972 (first quote); KDL to Amory Potter Glenn, Mar. 18, n.d. [1975] (subsequent quotes); KDL to Amory Potter Glenn and William W. L. Glenn, Dec. 24, 1974, all in Glenn Letters.

23. William W. L. Glenn to Mrs. John R. Taylor, Mar. 21, 1972 (quote), Glenn Letters.

24. G. Lumpkin Diary, Oct. 3, 1970 (first quote), Oct. 16, 1965 (second quote), Oct. 10, 1970 (third quote), Sept. 26, 1970 (subsequent quotes).

25. G. Lumpkin to Amory Potter Glenn and William W. L. Glenn, n.d. [summer 1971] (first quote), Glenn Letters; G. Lumpkin Diary, Mar. 14, 1974 (second quote), Jan. 25, 1973, Aug. 23, 1974; G. Lumpkin to Amory Potter Glenn and William W. L. Glenn, n.d. [Aug.–Sept. 1969]; G. Lumpkin to Amory Potter Glenn, Oct. 6, 1974, all in Glenn Letters; G. Lumpkin to Lillian Gilkes, [late Dec. 1974 or early Jan. 1975], box 3, Gilkes Papers. The agent was Scott Meredith, born Arthur Scott Feldman, founder of the Scott Meredith Literary Agency. She was also working on a manuscript entitled "Prototype Nineteen Fifty." "God and a Garden" does not seem to have survived.

26. G. Lumpkin Diary, July 19, 1974 (quote), Aug. 6, 1974.

27. G. Lumpkin interview, Aug. 6, 1974, 2–3 (quotes); "Katharine DuPre Lumpkin," genealogical chart prepared for the Daughters of the American Revolution, folder 107, KDL Papers.

28. G. Lumpkin Diary, Apr. 7, 1964 (first quote); G. Lumpkin to Lillian Gilkes, [late Dec. 1974 or early Jan. 1975] (second quote), box 3, Gilkes Papers; G. Lumpkin Diary, Dec. 20, 1969 (third quote).

29. John H. Lumpkin Sr. interview, Aug. 17, 1990; John H. Lumpkin Sr. interview, July 29, 1995; John H. Lumpkin Sr. to Eugene B. Glenn, Sept. 14, 1974 (quote), Glenn Letters.

30. Finlay House Evidence of Income form, n.d. [fall of 1974], Glenn Letters.

31. G. Lumpkin to Eugene B. Glenn, Sept. 14, 1974 (first quote), Glenn Letters; G.

Lumpkin Diary, Oct. 10, 1974 (second quote); G. Lumpkin to Lillian Gilkes, Dec. 4, 1974 (third quote), Aug. 2, 1975 (fourth quote), box 3, Gilkes Papers.

32. KDL to Amory Potter Glenn and William W. L. Glenn, Dec. 24, 1974 (quotes), Glenn Letters.

33. KDL to Amory Potter Glenn, Mar. 18, n.d. [1975] (quotes), Glenn Letters.

34. G. Lumpkin to Lillian Gilkes, Dec. 4, 1974, box 3, Gilkes Papers; Alva M. Lumpkin Jr. interview, Aug. 4, 1995; Alva M. Lumpkin Jr. interview, Aug. 17, 1990; Joseph H. Lumpkin Sr. interview, Aug. 1, 1995; Joseph H. Lumpkin Sr. and Joseph H. Lumpkin Jr. interview, Aug. 17, 1990.

35. G. Lumpkin to Amory Potter Glenn and William W. L. Glenn, n.d. [Summer 1971] (quote), Glenn Letters; G. Lumpkin Diary, May 5, 1971; G. Lumpkin, draft of letter to Frances Lumpkin, 1972, in G. Lumpkin Diary; G. Lumpkin, *Wedding*; Lillian Gilkes to G. Lumpkin, July 28, 1974; G. Lumpkin to Lillian Gilkes, Aug. 2, 1974; Lillian Gilkes to G. Lumpkin, Aug. 15, 1974; G. Lumpkin to Lillian Gilkes, Sept. 11, 1974, all in folder 121, KDL Papers; G. Lumpkin to Lillian Gilkes, Feb. 3, 1975; G. Lumpkin to Lillian Gilkes, July 26, 1975, both in box 3, Gilkes Papers.

36. Joseph H. Lumpkin Sr. interview, Aug. 1, 1995.

37. James C. Hall, "Rereading the Radical Novel in America: Defying Expecta-tions," Solidarity, https://solidarity-us.org/site/node/1848. See also "Alan Wald on 'The Radical Novel Reconsidered'—interviewed by Chris Faatz for *Reading the Left* 4 (Fall 1998)," The Literature and Culture of the 1950s, May 31, 2007, http://www.writing.upenn.edu/~afilreis/50s/wald-interview.html; Alan Wald, "End of a Series??" LBO-Talk (list), June 2, 2000, http://mailman.lbo-talk .org/2000/2000-June/011469.html; G. Lumpkin, *To Make My Bread. To Make My Bread* was reprinted in 1995 and included an introductory essay by Suzanne Sowinska that served as the first serious attempt to reconstruct Grace's life history.

38. KDL to Carolyn Wallace, Apr. 12, 1979, KDL Donor File, SHC; KDL to J. Hall, Aug. 6, 1979; Elizabeth Bennett obituary, *Durham (NC) Morning Herald*, May 6, 1988; Joseph H. Lumpkin Sr. and Joseph H. Lumpkin Jr. interview, Aug. 17, 1990; KDL to Amory Potter Glenn, Sept. 21, 1984; KDL to Amory Potter Glenn and William W. L. Glenn, Oct. 17, 1984, both in Glenn Letters.

39. KDL to Amory Potter Glenn and William W. L. Glenn, Nov. 12, n.d. [1971] (first quote); Amory Potter Glenn to Paul W. Douglas, June 2, 1988, both in Glenn Letters; Joseph H. Lumpkin Sr. and Joseph H. Lumpkin Jr. interview, Aug. 17, 1990 (second quote).

40. H. W. to Alfred A. Knopf, Oct. 25, 1955 (quote), box 172, [folder 14], Knopf Records; Tomas, "Women's History Movement."

41. She had also planned to bring out a collection of Angelina's unpublished letters: KDL to Jean Crawford, Jan. 26, 1956; KDL to Bell Wiley, Mar. 24, 1956, both in folder 17, KDL Papers. As late as 1979, she was still hoping to publish the cor-respondence between Angelina and her friend Jane Smith in the 1930s: KDL to Carolyn Wallace, June 4, 1979, KDL Donor File, SHC.

42. Lerner, *Rebels against Slavery*; Lerner, *Pioneers for Women's Rights*. According to

Lerner, the resistance to her original subtitle reflected "the contempt in which work on women in history was held in the 1960s": Lerner, *Feminist Thought*, xvii (quote). Like Lumpkin, Lerner was a woman of the left. Born in 1920, thirteen years after Lumpkin, she had been a member of the Communist Party, and she brought to her midlife career in women's history a race and class consciousness informed by the struggles of the 1930s and 1940s. The two women's books were in many ways quite similar as well, but Lerner's was a less intimate, more social movement–oriented study. For the response to Lumpkin's book, see "Freedom Fighter," *Times Literary Supplement*, June 13, 1975; K. Jeffrey, review of *Emancipation*; J. Pease, review of *Emancipation*; W. Pease, review of *Emancipation*; Perry, review of *Emancipation*; Rose, "Off the Plantation"; A. Ross, review of *Emancipation*.

43. KDL to J. Hall, July 1, 1985 (quote).

44. KDL, *Making* (quote on dust jacket).

45. Hine, foreword to *Making*, vi (first quote), xv (second and third quotes).

46. In addition to the studies of the Grimké sisters that followed the publication of Katharine Lumpkin's and Gerda Lerner's books, numerous scholars have underscored the importance of women to the antislavery movement and explored the emergence of an autonomous women's movement, ensuring that the Grimkés now occupy a secure place in the history of their times. See, for example, J. Jeffrey, *Great Silent Army*; Yellin and Van Horne, *Abolitionist Sisterhood*. Sue Monk Kidd's best-selling novel, *The Invention of Wings* (2014), has also made the Grimkés known to the general public.

47. Louise Leonard, "A Worker's School and Organized Labor," reprint from *American Teacher* (quote), Mary Cornelia Barker Papers, Stuart A. Rose Manuscript, Archives, and Rare Book Library, Emory University, Atlanta, GA.

BIBLIOGRAPHY
OF PRIMARY SOURCES
CONSULTED

Archival Collections

Amherst College, Amherst, MA
    Robert Frost Library
        Archives and Special Collections
Ancestry.com Operations Inc.
        Family Data Collection—Individual Records
        Georgia Marriages, 1699–1944
        Georgia, Marriage Records from Select Counties, 1828–1978
        Georgia, Wills and Probate Records, 1742–1992
        New York, Passenger Lists, 1820–1957
        UK, Incoming Passenger Lists, 1878–1960
        U.S. Passport Applications, 1795–1925
Atlanta History Center, Atlanta, GA
    Kenan Research Center
        Grace Towns Hamilton Papers
Atlanta University Center, Atlanta, GA
    Robert W. Woodruff Library, Archives Research Center
        Neighborhood Union Collection
Berea College, Berea, KY
    Hutchins Library, Berea College Archives
        Record Group 9-A
Brandeis University Archives, Waltham, MA
        Frances Russell Collection
Brenau University Trustee Library, Gainesville, GA
    Archives Room
        Alumni Files

Bryn Mawr College Library, Bryn Mawr, PA
    Special Collections
        College Archives
        Marion Edwards Park Papers
Columbia University Library, New York, NY
    Rare Book and Manuscript Library
        Robert Minor Papers
        University Archives
Consumers Union Archive, Yonkers, NY
        Colston E. Warne Papers
Cranbrook Educational Community, Bloomfield Hills, MI
    Cranbrook Archives
        Kingswood Personnel Files
Duke University, Durham, NC
    David M. Rubenstein Rare Book and Manuscript Library
        W. W. Ball Papers
        J. B. Matthews Papers
Emory University, Atlanta, GA
    Stuart A. Rose Manuscript, Archives, and Rare Book Library
        Mary Cornelia Barker Papers
        Theodore Draper Papers
Georgia Archives, Morrow, GA
        Tax Digests
Harvard University, Cambridge, MA
    Houghton Library
        Houghton Mifflin Literary Fellowship Applications
        William B. Wisdom Collection of Thomas Wolfe
    Schlesinger Library, Radcliffe Institute
        Annabel Matthews Papers
        Consumers' League of Massachusetts Papers
        Radcliffe College Archives
Hofstra University Archives, Hempstead, NY
        Broadus Mitchell Collection
John Simon Guggenheim Memorial Foundation, New York, NY
        Fellowship Application Summaries
Library of Congress, Washington, DC
    Manuscript Division
        National Association for the Advancement of Colored People Records,
        microfilm
Mount Holyoke College, South Hadley, MA
    Archives and Special Collections
        Alumnae Biographical Files
        Department of Economics and Sociology Records
        Faculty Files

National Archives, Washington, DC
    Center for Legislative Archives
        Record Group 46: Senate Internal Security Subcommittee Records
        Record Group 233: Records of the House Un-American Activities
        Committee
New York Public Library, New York, NY
    Manuscripts and Archives Division
        American Fund for Public Service Records
        Yaddo Records
    Schomburg Center for Research in Black Culture
        Papers of the International Labor Defense, microfilm
New York University, New York, NY
    Elmer Holmes Bobst Library, Tamiment Library and Robert F. Wagner
    Labor Archives
        Mark Solomon and Robert Kaufman Research Files on African
        Americans and Communism
        National Council of American-Soviet Friendship Records
Oberlin College Archives, Oberlin, OH
Pack Memorial Library, Asheville, NC
    Newspaper Clipping Files
Phi Mu National Headquarters, Peachtree City, GA
    Archives
Princeton University, NJ
    Seeley G. Mudd Manuscript Library
        Undergraduate Alumni Records, 19th Century
Robert Brookings Graduate School, Washington, DC
    Brookings Institution Archives
        Students and Fellows Records
Rockefeller Archive Center, Sleepy Hollow, NY
    Social Science Research Council Records
Seminary of the Southwest, Austin, TX
    Archives of the Episcopal Church
Smith College Special Collections, Northampton, MA
    Sophia Smith Collection
        Mary van Kleeck Papers
        Southern Women, the Student YWCA, and
        Race (1920–1944) Collection
        Winnifred Crane Wygal Papers
        Young Women's Christian Association of the U.S.A. Records
    Smith College Archives
        Faculty Biographical Files
        Office of the President, Benjamin Fletcher Wright Papers
        Office of the President / Board of Trustees Files, Faculty Cards
        Office of the President, Herbert John Davis Files
        Office of the President, William Allan Neilson Files

South Carolina Confederate Relic Room and Military Museum,
    Columbia, SC
        Records of the United Daughters of the Confederacy,
        Wade Hampton Chapter
Stanford University, CA
    Hoover Institution Library and Archives
        Sam Tanenhaus Papers
State Archives of North Carolina, Raleigh, NC
        Civil War Collection
        Fred A. Perley Papers
Swarthmore College Peace Collection, PA
        Devere Allen Papers
        George Nasmyth and Florence Nasmyth Papers
Syracuse University Libraries, Syracuse, NY
    Special Collections Research Center
        Earl Browder Papers
        Granville Hicks Papers
        Lillian B. Gilkes Papers
Tennessee State Library and Archives, Nashville, TN
        Young Women's Christian Association (Nashville, TN) Papers
University of Mississippi, Oxford, MS
    J. D. Williams Library, Archives and Special Collections
        Ken Oilschlager–Juliette Derricotte Collection
University of North Carolina at Chapel Hill, Chapel Hill, NC
    Louis Round Wilson Special Collections Library
        North Carolina Collection
        Southern Historical Collection
            Anne Queen Papers
            Arthur Franklin Raper Papers
            Howard Kester Papers
            Katharine Du Pre Lumpkin Papers
            Myra Page Papers
            W. D. Weatherford Papers
        University Archives
            University of North Carolina Press Records
University of Oregon Libraries, Eugene, OR
    Special Collections and University Archives
        Grace Hutchins Papers
        Anna Rochester Papers
        Robert Cantwell Papers
University of South Carolina, Columbia, SC
    South Caroliniana Library
        Girls of the Sixties Records
        Grace Lumpkin Papers
        Kenneth Toombs Oral History Collection

United Confederate Veterans, Confederate Survivors' Association,
Richland County Records
University of South Carolina Archives
University of the South, Sewanee, TN
University Archives and Special Collections
Student Files
University of Tennessee Libraries, Knoxville, TN
Special Collections
Evelyn Scott Collection
University of Texas at Austin, Austin, TX
Harry Ransom Center
Alfred A. Knopf, Inc. Records
John Gassner Papers
University of Virginia Library, Charlottesville, VA
Special Collections Department
James J. Kilpatrick Papers
University of Wisconsin–Madison Libraries, Madison, WI
Archives and Records Management
William H. Kiekhofer Papers
Vanderbilt University, Nashville, TN
Jean and Alexander Heard Library, Special Collections
and University Archives
Donald Davidson Papers
Wayne State University, Detroit, MI
Walter P. Reuther Library
American Federation of Teachers Records
Mary Heaton Vorse Papers
Wells College, Aurora, NY
Louis Jefferson Long Library
Wells College Archives
Office of the Dean
Winthrop University, Rock Hill, SC
Louise Pettus Archives and Special Collections
Wisconsin Historical Society, Madison, WI
Edward A. Ross Papers
Yale University Library, New Haven, CT
Manuscripts and Archives
C. Vann Woodward Papers

GOVERNMENT DOCUMENTS

CENSUSES CONSULTED

Fifteenth Census of the United States, 1930
Fourteenth Census of the United States, 1920

Thirteenth Census of the United States, 1910

Twelfth Census of the United States, 1900

Tenth Census of the United States, 1880

Ninth Census of the United States, 1870

Eighth Census of the United States, 1860

Seventh Census of the United States, 1850

Sixth Census of the United States, 1840

Fifth Census of the United States, 1830

Fourth Census of the United States, 1820

REPORTS, HEARINGS, ETC.

California State Senate. *Fifth Report of the Senate Fact-Finding Committee on Un-American Activities.* Sacramento, 1949.

U.S. Congress. *Report of the Joint Select Committee to Inquire into the Condition of Affairs in the Late Insurrectionary States.* 42nd Cong., 2nd sess. Washington, DC: Government Printing Office, 1872.

U.S. Congress. *Testimony Taken by the Joint Select Committee to Inquire into the Condition of Affairs in the Late Insurrectionary States.* Part 5: South Carolina. Vol. 3. 42nd Cong., 2nd sess. Washington, DC: Government Printing Office, 1872.

U.S. Congress. *Testimony Taken by the Joint Select Committee to Inquire into the Condition of Affairs in the Late Insurrectionary States.* Part 6: Georgia. Vol. 2. 42nd Cong., 2nd sess. Washington, DC: Government Printing Office, 1872.

U.S. House. *Communist Methods of Infiltration (Education): Hearings before the Committee on Un-American Activities, House of Representatives.* Part 1. Feb. 25–27. 83rd Cong., 1st sess. Washington, DC: Government Printing Office, 1953.

U.S. House. *Exposé of Communist Activities in the State of Massachusetts (Based on the Testimony of Herbert A. Philbrick), Hearings before the Committee on Un-American Activities.* July 23–24, Oct. 10–11. 82nd Cong., 1st sess. Washington, DC: Government Printing Office, 1951.

U.S. House. *Unemployment Old Age and Social Insurance: Hearings before a Sub-Committee of the Committee on Labor on H.R. 2827, A Bill to Provide for the Establishment of Unemployment, Old Age and Social Insurance and for Other Purposes; H.R. 2859, A Bill to Provide for the Establishment of Unemployment and Social Insurance and For Other Purposes; H.R. 185, A Bill to Provide for the Establishment of a System of Unemployment Insurance and for Other Purposes; and H.R. 10, A Bill to Provide for the Establishment of Unemployment and Social Insurance and for Other Purposes.* Feb. 4–8, 11–15. 74th Cong., 1st sess. Washington, DC: Government Printing Office, 1935.

U.S. Senate. *Social Insurance: Hearings before the Committee on Education and Labor on S. 3475, A Bill to Provide for the Establishment of a Nation-Wide System of Social Insurance.* Apr. 14–17. 74th Cong., 2nd sess. Washington, DC: Government Printing Office, 1936.

U.S. Senate. *State Department Information Program—Information Centers: Hearings before the Permanent Subcommittee on Investigations of the Committee on Govern-*

ment Operations Pursuant to S. Res. 40. Part 2. Mar. 27, Apr. 1–2. 83rd Cong., 1st sess. Washington, DC: Government Printing Office, 1953.

U.S. Senate. *Violations of Free Speech and the Rights of Labor: Hearings before a Subcommittee of the Committee on Education and Labor Pursuant to S. Res. 266.* Part 3. Jan 14–15, 21–23. 75th Cong., 1st sess. Washington, DC: Government Printing Office, 1937.

FEDERAL BUREAU OF INVESTIGATION FILES

Department of Justice, Washington, DC (by Freedom of Information Act and Hall v. U.S. Department of Justice, Civil Action No. 96–2306 (D.D.C. 2005) unless otherwise noted)
　　Chambers, Jay David Whittaker (FBI Vault)
　　Douglas, Dorothy Wolff
　　Flynn, Hulda Rees McGarvey
　　Lumpkin, Grace
　　Lumpkin, Katherine [sic] Du Pre

LOCAL GOVERNMENT ARCHIVES

　　Asheville, NC
　　　　Buncombe County Courthouse
　　　　Buncombe County Land Records Department
　　Columbia, SC
　　　　Board of Education
　　　　Richland County Probate Judge's Office
　　Dade County, FL
　　　　Office of Vital Statistics
　　Jacksonville, FL
　　　　Florida Department of Health and Rehabilitative Services, Bureau of Vital Statistics
　　Monmouth County, NY
　　　　Surrogate's Court
　　New York, NY
　　　　New York City Municipal Archives
　　Northampton, MA
　　　　Probate Court
　　Orange County, NC
　　　　Clerk of Court

ORAL HISTORY INTERVIEWS

Black Women Oral History Project, Schlesinger Library, Radcliffe Institute, Harvard University, Cambridge, MA.
　　Frances H. Williams. Interview by Merze Tate, Oct. 31–Nov. 1, 1977.

Kenneth Toombs Oral History Collection, South Caroliniana Library, University of South Carolina, Columbia.

Lumpkin, Grace. Interview by Kenneth E. Toombs, Sept. 25, 1971.

Southern Oral History Program Collection, Southern Historical Collection, Louis Round Wilson Special Collections Library, University of North Carolina at Chapel Hill.

Anderson, Eleanor Copenhaver. Interview by Mary Frederickson, Nov. 5, 1974.

Fairfax, Jean. Interview by Dallas A. Blanchard, Oct. 15, 1983.

Hamilton, Grace Towns. Interview by Jacquelyn Dowd Hall, Apr. 29, 1974.

Kester, Howard. Interview by Jacquelyn Dowd Hall and William R. Finger, July 22, 1974.

Kester, Howard. Interview by Mary Frederickson, Aug. 25, 1974.

Lumpkin, Grace. Interview by Jacquelyn Dowd Hall, VA, Aug. 6, 1974.

Lumpkin, Katharine Du Pre. Interview by Jacquelyn Dowd Hall, Aug. 4, 1974.

Lumpkin, Katharine Du Pre. Interview by Jacquelyn Dowd Hall, Apr. 24, 1985.

MacDonald, Lois. Interview by Marion Roydhouse, June 24, 1975.

MacDonald, Lois. Interview by Mary Frederickson, Aug. 25, 1977.

Neale, Nancy Alice Kester. Interview by Dallas A. Blanchard, Aug. 6, 1974.

Page, Myra. Interview by Mary Frederickson, July 12, 1975.

Queen, Anne. Interview by Joseph A. Herzenberg, Apr. 30, 1976.

Ransdall, Hollace. Interview by Mary Frederickson, Nov. 6, 1974.

Raper, Arthur Franklin. Interview by Daniel Singal, Jan. 18, 1971.

Raper, Arthur Franklin. Interview by Jacquelyn Dowd Hall, Jan. 30, 1974.

Stevens, Thelma. Interview by Jacquelyn Dowd Hall and Robert H. Hall, Feb. 13, 1972.

Stone, Olive. Interviews by Sherna Gluck, Mar.–Nov., 1975.

Wright, Alice Spearman. Interview by Jacquelyn Dowd Hall, Feb. 28, 1976.

Southern Women, the Student YWCA, and Race (1920–1944) Collection, Sophia Smith Collection, Smith College, Northampton, MA.

Williams, Frances. Interview by Frances Sanders Taylor Anton, Nov. 14, 1981.

William Henry Chafe Oral History Collection, David M. Rubenstein Rare Book & Manuscript Library, Duke University, Durham, NC.

Jones, Mrs. David (Susie). Interview by William H. Chafe, 1978.

In author's possession.

Dieckmann, Jane. Interview by Jacquelyn Dowd Hall, Aug. 8, 1996.

Gerson, Sophie. Telephone interview by Jacquelyn Dowd Hall, Aug. 30, 1996.

Glenn, William W. L., and Amory Potter Glenn. Telephone interview by Jacquelyn Dowd Hall, July 16, 1995.

Intrator, Lil. Telephone interview by Jacquelyn Dowd Hall, Dec. 18, 1993.

Intrator, Roland. Telephone interview by Jacquelyn Dowd Hall, n.d.

Kosan, Bertha. Telephone interview by Jacquelyn Dowd Hall, Nov. 22, 1989.

Lazerowitz, Alice. Telephone interview by Jacquelyn Dowd Hall, Aug. 4, 1987.

Lincoln, Eleanor. Interview by Jacquelyn Dowd Hall, June 25, 1993.

Lumpkin, Alva M., Jr. Interview by Jacquelyn Dowd Hall, Aug. 4, 1995.

Lumpkin, Alva M., Jr. Interview by Marla Miller, Aug. 17, 1990.

Lumpkin, John H., Sr. Interview by Marla Miller, Columbia, SC, Aug. 17, 1990.

Lumpkin, John H., Sr. Telephone interview by Jacquelyn Dowd Hall, July 29, 1995.

Lumpkin, Joseph H., Sr., and Joseph H. Lumpkin Jr. Interview by Marla Miller, Aug. 17, 1990.

Lumpkin, Joseph H., Sr. Interview by Jacquelyn Dowd Hall, Aug. 1, 1995.

Lumpkin, Katharine Du Pre. Interview by Christina L. Baker, Mar. 22, 1987.

Lumpkin, Robert L. Interview by Jacquelyn Dowd Hall, Aug. 5, 1995.

McCormick, Chalmer, and Arthur Bellinzoni. Interview by Jacquelyn Dowd Hall, Aug. 9, 1996.

Nesselhof, John. Interview by Jacquelyn Dowd Hall, Aug. 9, 1996.

Newman, Edie. Telephone interview by Jacquelyn Dowd Hall, Nov. 9, 2000.

Padover, Carl. Telephone interview by Jacquelyn Dowd Hall, Feb. 16, 2003.

Page, Myra. Interview by Christina Baker, June 8, 1987.

Page, Myra. Interview by Jacquelyn Dowd Hall, Apr. 25, 1988.

Potter, Adaline Pates. Telephone interview by Jacquelyn Dowd Hall, May 26, 2000.

Shlakman, Vera. Interview by Jacquelyn Dowd Hall, Apr. 12, 1986.

Torrey, Kate. Interview by Jacquelyn Dowd Hall, June 18, 1993.

Turgeon, Lynn. Telephone interview by Jacquelyn Dowd Hall, Dec. 8, 1988.

Theses and Dissertations

Antone, George Peter. "Willis Duke Weatherford: An Interpretation of His Work in Race Relations, 1906–1946." PhD diss., Vanderbilt University, 1969.

Bannan, Regina. "Management by Women: The First Twenty-Five Years of the YWCA National Board, 1906–1931." PhD diss., University of Pennsylvania, 1994.

Brinson, Betsy. "'Helping Others to Help Themselves': Social Advocacy and Wage-Earning Women in Richmond, Virginia, 1910–1932." PhD diss., Union Graduate School, 1984.

Browder, Dorothea. "From Uplift to Agitation: Working Women, Race, and Coalition in the Young Women's Christian Association." PhD diss., University of Wisconsin–Madison, 2008.

Cavazos, Mary K. "Queen's Daughters: African American Women, Christian Mission, and Racial Change, 1940–1960." PhD diss., Drew University, 2007.

Dean, Pamela Evelyn. "Covert Curriculum: Class, Gender, and Student Culture at a New South Woman's College, 1892–1910." PhD diss., University of North Carolina at Chapel Hill, 1995.

Frederickson, Mary E. "'A Place to Speak Our Minds': The Southern School for Women Workers." PhD diss., University of North Carolina at Chapel Hill, 1981.

Haessly, Lynn. "'Mill Mother's Lament': Ella May, Working Women's Militancy, and the 1929 Gastonia Strikes." Master's thesis, University of North Carolina at Chapel Hill, 1987.

Holmes, Judith Larrabee. "The Politics of Anticommunism in Massachusetts, 1930–1960." PhD diss., University of Massachusetts Amherst, 1996.

Johnson, Bethany Leigh. "Regionalism, Race, and the Meaning of the Southern Past: Professional History in the American South, 1896–1961." PhD diss., Rice University, 2001.

Kalemaris, Victoria Terhecte. "No Longer Second-Class Students: Women's Struggle for Recognition and Equity at the University of South Carolina, 1914–1935." Master's thesis, University of South Carolina, 1998.

Krome-Lukens, Anna. "The Reform Imagination: Gender, Eugenics, and the Welfare State in North Carolina, 1900–1940." PhD diss., University of North Carolina at Chapel Hill, 2014.

Landrum, Renee (Shane). "'More Firmly Based Today': Anti-Communism, Academic Freedom, and Smith College, 1947–1956." Honors Thesis, Smith College, 1998.

Lane, Janet E. "The Silenced Cry from the Factory Floor: Gastonia's Female Strikers and Their Proletarian Authors." PhD diss., Indiana University of Pennsylvania, 2007.

Lumpkin, Katharine Du Pre. "Social Interests of the Southern Woman." Master's thesis, Columbia University, 1919.

Lumpkin, Katharine Du Pre. "Social Situations and Girl Delinquency: A Study of Commitments to the Wisconsin Industrial School." PhD diss., University of Wisconsin–Madison, 1928.

Madison, Mary Jo. "Shots in the Dark: Lynching in Tuscaloosa, Alabama, 1933." Master's thesis, Auburn University, 1991.

Mittelman, Karen Sue. "'A Spirit That Touches the Problems of Today': Women and Social Reform in the Philadelphia Young Women's Christian Association, 1920–1945." PhD diss., University of Pennsylvania, 1987.

Moore, Maude. "History of the College for Women, Columbia, South Carolina." Master's thesis, University of South Carolina, 1932.

Mullis, Sharon Mitchell. "The Public Career of Grace Towns Hamilton: A Citizen Too Busy to Hate." PhD diss., Emory University, 1976.

Myrick, James Robert. "The History of the Asheville Public Library." Master's thesis, University of North Carolina at Chapel Hill, 1977.

O'Neil, Patrick W. "Tying the Knots: The Nationalization of Wedding Rituals in Antebellum America." PhD diss., University of North Carolina at Chapel Hill, 2009.

Putney, Clifford Wallace. "Muscular Christianity: The Strenuous Mood in American Protestantism, 1880–1920." PhD diss., Brandeis University, 1995.

Russ, Anne J. "Higher Education for Women: Intent, Reality and Outcomes, Wells College, 1868–1913." PhD diss., Cornell University, 1979.

Siegel, Morton. "The Passaic Strike of 1926." PhD diss., Columbia University, 1953.

Stone, Olive M. "Agrarian Conflict in Alabama: Sections, Races, and Classes in a Rural State from 1800 to 1938." PhD diss., University of North Carolina at Chapel Hill, 1939.

Taylor, Frances Sanders. "'On the Edge of Tomorrow': Southern Women, the Student YWCA, and Race, 1920–1944." PhD diss., Stanford University, 1984.

Tomas, Jennifer Ellen. "The Women's History Movement in the United States: Professional and Political Roots of the Field, 1922–1987." PhD diss., State University of New York at Binghamton, 2012.

Webb, Elizabeth Yates. "The Development of the Textile Industry in North Carolina." Master's thesis, Brookings Institution, 1929.

Wells, Ida Maxwell. "Anxiety and Orange Blossoms: Sexual Economics in Wedding Texts by Grace Lumpkin, Eudora Welty, and Alice Childress." PhD diss., Louisiana State University Agricultural and Mechanical College, 2000.

Bibliography of Published Sources

Aaron, Daniel. *Writers on the Left*. New York: Avon Books, 1961.

Abel, Elizabeth, Marianne Hirsch, and Elizabeth Langland, eds. *The Voyage In: Fictions of Female Development*. Hanover, NH: Published for Dartmouth College by University Press of New England, 1983.

Abzug, Robert. *Passionate Liberator: Theodore Dwight Weld and the Dilemma of Reform*. New York: Oxford University Press, 1980.

Adams, Donald J. "Two Novels about Industrial Unrest." *New York Times Book Review*, Dec. 15, 1935.

Agee, James, and Walker Evans. *Let Us Now Praise Famous Men*. Boston: Houghton Mifflin, 1941.

Alchon, Guy. "Mary van Kleeck and Scientific Management." In *A Mental Revolution: Scientific Management since Taylor*, edited by Daniel Nelson, 102–29. Columbus: Ohio State University Press, 1992.

———. "Mary van Kleeck of the Russell Sage Foundation: Religion, Social Science, and the Ironies of Parasitic Modernity." In *Philanthropic Foundations: New Scholarship, New Possibilities*, edited by Ellen Condliffe Lagemann, 151–66. Bloomington: Indiana University Press, 1999.

Alexander, Robert J. *The Right Opposition: The Lovestoneites and the International Communist Opposition of the 1930s*. Westport, CT: Greenwood Press, 1981.

Allen, Devere. *Adventurous Americans*. New York: Farrar and Rinehart, 1932.

Allen, Julia M. *Passionate Commitments: The Lives of Anna Rochester and Grace Hutchins*. Albany: State University of New York Press, 2013.

Allen, Louise Anderson. *A Bluestocking in Charleston: The Life and Career of Laura Bragg*. Columbia: University of South Carolina Press, 2001.

Allen, Raymond B. "Communists Should Not Teach in American Colleges." *Educational Forum* 13, no. 4 (May 1949): 433–40.

Altenbaugh, Richard J. "Proletarian Drama: An Educational Tool of the American Labor College Movement." *Theatre Journal* 34, no. 2 (May 1982): 197–210.

American Trade Union Delegation to the Soviet Union. *Soviet Russia in the Second Decade: A Joint Survey by the Technical Staff of the First American Trade Union Delegation*. New York: John Day, 1928.

American Y.W.C.A. in France. Paris: G. Gorce, Photographer and Printer, n.d.

Anderson, Elijah. *The Cosmopolitan Canopy: Race and Civility in Everyday Life*. New York: W. W. Norton, 2011.

Anderson, James D. *The Education of Blacks in the South, 1860–1935.* Chapel Hill: University of North Carolina Press, 1988.

Anderson, Lauren Kientz. "A Nauseating Sentiment, a Magical Device, or a Real Insight?: Interracialism at Fisk University in 1930." In *Higher Education for African Americans before the Civil Rights Era, 1900–1964,* edited by Marybeth Gasman and Roger L. Geiger, 75–112. New Brunswick, NJ: Transaction, 2012.

Anderson, Paul Allen. *Deep River: Music and Memory in Harlem Renaissance Thought.* Durham, NC: Duke University Press, 2001.

Andrews, William L. "Booker T. Washington, Belle Kearney, and the Southern Patriarchy." In *Home Ground: Southern Autobiography,* edited by J. Bill Berry, 85–97. Columbia: University of Missouri Press, 1991.

———. ed. *Sisters of the Spirit: Three Black Women's Autobiographies of the Nineteenth Century.* Bloomington: Indiana University Press, 1986.

Anthony, David Henry, III. *Max Yergan: Race Man, Internationalist, Cold Warrior.* New York: New York University Press, 2006.

Antler, Joyce. *The Journey Home: Jewish Women and the American Century.* New York: Free Press, 1997.

Armfield, Eugene. "A Cross Section of a Southern Town." *Saturday Review of Literature,* Feb. 25, 1939.

Arnall, Ellis Gibbs. *The Shore Dimly Seen.* Philadelphia: J. B. Lippincott, 1946.

Ashby, Joe. *Organized Labor and the Mexican Revolution under Lázaro Cárdenas.* Chapel Hill: University of North Carolina Press, 1967.

Avrich, Paul. "Italian Anarchism in America: An Historical Background to the Sacco-Vanzetti Case." In *Sacco-Vanzetti: Developments and Reconsiderations, 1979,* edited by Robert D'Attilio and Jane Manthorn, 61–67. Boston: Boston Public Library, 1979.

Ayers, Edward L. *The Promise of the New South: Life after Reconstruction.* New York: Oxford University Press, 1992.

Bailey, Fred Arthur. "The Textbooks of the 'Lost Cause': Censorship and the Creation of Southern State Histories." *Georgia Historical Quarterly* 75, no. 3 (Fall 1991): 507–33.

Bain, David Haward, and Mary Smyth Duffy, eds. *Whose Woods These Are: A History of the Bread Loaf Writers' Conference, 1926–1992.* Hopewell, NJ: Ecco, 1993.

Baker, Bruce. *What Reconstruction Meant: Historical Memory in the American South.* Charlottesville: University of Virginia Press, 2007.

Baker, Christina L. *In a Generous Spirit: A First-Person Biography of Myra Page.* Urbana: University of Illinois Press, 1996.

Bannister, Robert. *Sociology and Scientism: The American Quest for Objectivity, 1880–1940.* Chapel Hill: University of North Carolina Press, 1987.

Banta, Martha. *Imaging American Women: Idea and Ideals in Cultural History.* New York: Columbia University Press, 1987.

Barbeau, Arthur, and Florette Henri. *The Unknown Soldiers: Black American Troops in World War I.* Philadelphia: Temple University Press, 1974.

Barrett, James. *William Z. Foster and the Tragedy of American Radicalism.* Urbana: University of Illinois Press, 1999.

Barron, John. *Operation SOLO: The FBI's Man in the Kremlin*. Washington, DC: Regnery, 1996.

Barry, John. *Rising Tide: The Great Mississippi Flood of 1927 and How It Changed America*. New York: Simon and Schuster, 1997.

Barth, Alan. *The Loyalty of Free Men*. New York: Viking Press, 1951.

Barton, Bruce. *The Man Nobody Knows: A Discovery of Jesus*. Indianapolis: Bobbs-Merrill, 1925.

Bateson, Mary Catherine. *Composing a Life*. New York: Plume, 1990.

Bathanti, Joseph. "The Mythic School of the Mountain: Black Mountain College." *Our State*, Apr. 2, 2014.

Baxandall, Rosalyn. "The Question Seldom Asked: Women and the CPUSA." In *New Studies in the Politics and Culture of U.S. Communism*, edited by Michael E. Brown, Randy Martin, Frank Rosengarten, and George Snedeker, 141–61. New York: Monthly Review Press, 1993.

Becker, Carl. "Everyman His Own Historian." *American Historical Review* 37, no. 2 (1932): 221–36.

Bederman, Gail. *Manliness and Civilization: A Cultural History of Gender and Race in the United States, 1880–1917*. Chicago: University of Chicago Press, 1995.

Bein, Albert. *Let Freedom Ring: A Play in Three Acts*. New York: Samuel French, 1936.

Beineke, John A. *And There Were Giants in the Land: The Life of William Heard Kilpatrick*. New York: P. Lang, 1998.

Bell, Juliet O., and Helen J. Wilkins. *Interracial Practices in Community Y.W.C.A.'s*. New York: Woman's Press, 1944.

Bellomy, Donald. "Social Darwinism." In *A Companion to American Thought*, edited by Richard Wightman Fox and James T. Kloppenberg, 631–32. Oxford: Blackwell, 1995.

———. "William Graham Sumner." In *A Companion to American Thought*, edited by Richard Wightman Fox and James T. Kloppenberg, 661–63. Oxford: Blackwell, 1995.

Bender, Thomas. *Intellect and Public Life: Essays on the Social History of Academic Intellectuals in the United States*. Baltimore: Johns Hopkins University Press, 1993.

Bennett, Judith M. "'Lesbian-Like' and the Social History of Lesbianisms." *Journal of the History of Sexuality* 9, no. 1/2 (2000): 1–24.

Berkin, Carol. *Civil War Wives: The Lives and Times of Angelina Grimké Weld, Varina Howell Davis, and Julia Dent Grant*. New York: Alfred A. Knopf, 2009.

Bernstein, Irving. *The Lean Years: A History of the American Worker, 1920–1933*. Baltimore: Penguin Books, 1966.

Berry, J. Bill. "Autobiographical Impulse." In *Companion to Southern Literature: Themes, Genres, Places, People, Movements, and Motifs*, edited by Joseph M. Flora and Lucinda H. MacKethan, 77–82. Baton Rouge: Louisiana State University Press, 2002.

———. Introduction to *Located Lives: Place and Idea in Southern Autobiography*, ix–xvii. Athens: University of Georgia Press, 1990.

———. "The Southern Autobiographical Impulse." *Southern Cultures* 6, no. 1 (Spring 2000): 7–22.

Biles, Roger. *Crusading Liberal: Paul H. Douglas of Illinois*. DeKalb: Northern Illinois University Press, 2002.

———. "Paul H. Douglas, McCarthyism, and the Senatorial Election of 1954." *Journal of the Illinois State Historical Society* 5, no. 1 (Spring 2002): 52–67.

Bingham, Emily, and Thomas A. Underwood, eds. *The Southern Agrarians and the New Deal: Essays after "I'll Take My Stand."* Charlottesville: Published for the Southern Texts Society by the University Press of Virginia, 2001.

Bird, Caroline. "The Invisible Scar." *Challenge* 14, no. 6 (1966): 36–43.

Birmingham, Stephen. *"Our Crowd": The Great Jewish Families of New York.* New York: Harper and Row, 1967.

Birney, Catherine H. *The Grimké Sisters: Sarah and Angelina Grimké, the First American Women Advocates of Abolition and Woman's Rights.* Boston: C. T. Dillingham, 1885 [electronic resource].

Bishir, Catherine W. "Landmarks of Power: Building a Southern Past, 1885–1915." *Southern Cultures* 1, no. 1 (1993): 5–43.

Blake, Casey Nelson. *Beloved Community: The Cultural Criticism of Randolph Bourne, Van Wyck Brooks, Waldo Frank, and Lewis Mumford.* Chapel Hill: University of North Carolina Press, 1990.

Blanchard, Leslie. *The Student Movement of the Y.W.C.A.* New York: Woman's Press, 1928.

Bland, Lucy, and Laura L. Doan. *Sexology in Culture: Labelling Bodies and Desires.* Chicago: University of Chicago Press, 1998.

Blight, David W. *Race and Reunion: The Civil War in American Memory.* Cambridge, MA: Belknap Press of Harvard University Press, 2001.

Blow, Charles M. *Fire Shut Up in My Bones: A Memoir.* Boston: Houghton Mifflin Harcourt, 2014.

Bogin, Ruth. "Elizabeth Ross Haynes." Edited by Barbara Sicherman and Carol Hurd Green. In *Notable American Women: The Modern Period, A Biographical Dictionary.* Cambridge, MA: Belknap Press of Harvard University Press, 1980.

Boris, Eileen. "'You Wouldn't Want One of 'Em Dancing with Your Wife': Racialized Bodies on the Job in World War II." *American Quarterly* 50, no. 1 (1998): 77–108.

Botkin, B. A. "Regionalism and Culture." In *The Writer in a Changing World*, edited by Henry Hart, 140–57. New York: American Writers' Congress, 1937.

Bourne, Randolph. *Radical Will: Selected Writings, 1911–1918.* Edited by Olaf Hansen. New York: Urizen Books, 1977.

Bowles, Chester. *Promises to Keep: My Years in Public Life, 1941–1969.* New York: Harper and Row, 1971.

Brandeis, Elizabeth. Review of *Yearbook of American Labor.* Vol. 1: *War Labor Policies*, by Colstane Warne et al. *Social Service Review* 19, no. 3 (Sept. 1945): 434.

Brantley, Will. *Feminine Sense in Southern Memoir: Smith, Glasgow, Welty, Hellman, Porter, and Hurston.* Jackson: University Press of Mississippi, 1993.

Braude, Ann. *Transforming the Faiths of Our Fathers: Women Who Changed American Religion.* New York: Palgrave Macmillan, 2004.

Braukman, Stacy Lorraine. *Communists and Perverts under the Palms: The Johns Committee in Florida, 1956–1965.* Gainesville: University Press of Florida, 2012.

Braxton, Joanne M. *Black Women Writing Autobiography: A Tradition within a Tradition.* Philadelphia: Temple University Press, 1989.

Bretton, F. R., and H. L. Mitchell. *Land and Liberty for Mexican Farmers: Report of the S.T.F.U. Delegation to Laguna Conference, Torreón, Coahuila, Mexico.* N.p.: Southern Tenant Farmers' Union, 1939.

Brewer, William M. Review of *The South in Progress,* by Katherine Du Pre Lumpkin. *Journal of Negro History* 28 (1943): 100–103.

Brilliant, Mark. *The Color of America Has Changed: How Racial Diversity Shaped Civil Rights Reform in California, 1941–1978.* New York: Oxford University Press, 2010.

Brinkmeyer, Robert H., Jr. *The Fourth Ghost: White Southern Writers and European Fascism, 1930–1950.* Baton Rouge: Louisiana State University Press, 2009.

Bristow, Nancy K. *Making Men Moral: Social Engineering during the Great War.* New York: New York University Press, 1996.

Britton, John. *Revolution and Ideology: Images of the Mexican Revolution in the United States.* Lexington: University Press of Kentucky, 1995.

Brodhead, Richard H. "Two Writers' Beginnings: Eudora Welty in the Neighborhood of Richard Wright." *Yale Review* 84, no. 2 (Apr. 1996): 1–21.

Brogan, Peter. "Education Deform and Social Justice Unionism." *Labour/Le Travail* 77 (Spring 2016): 225–41.

Brooks, Cleanth, and Robert Penn Warren, eds. *An Anthology of Stories from the Southern Review.* Baton Rouge: Louisiana State University Press, 1953.

Browder, Dorothea. "A 'Christian Solution of the Labor Situation': How Working-women Reshaped the YWCA's Religious Mission and Politics." *Journal of Women's History* 19, no. 2 (Summer 2007): 85–110.

———. "Working Out Their Economic Problems Together: World War I, Working Women, and Civil Rights in the YWCA." *Journal of the Gilded Age and Progressive Era* 14, no. 2 (Apr. 2015): 243–65.

Brown, Kathleen A., and Elizabeth Faue. "Revolutionary Desire: Redefining the Politics of Sexuality of American Radicals, 1919–1945." In *Sexual Borderlands: Constructing an American Sexual Past,* edited by Kathleen Kennedy and Sharon Ullman, 273–302. Columbus: Ohio State University Press, 2003.

———. "Social Bonds, Sexual Politics, and Political Community on the U.S. Left, 1920s–1940s." *Left History* 7, no. 1 (2000): 9–45.

Brown, Michael K. *Race, Money, and the American Welfare State.* Ithaca, NY: Cornell University Press, 1999.

Brown, Sterling A. "The Literary Scene: Chronicle and Comment." *Opportunity,* Jan. 1931.

———. "A Romantic Defense." In *A Son's Return: Selected Essays of Sterling A. Brown,* edited by Mark A. Sanders, 281–83. Boston: Northeastern University Press, 1996.

———. *Southern Road: Poems.* New York: Harcourt, Brace, 1932.

———. "Unhistoric History." *Journal of Negro History* 15 (Apr. 1930): 134–61.

Brundage, W. Fitzhugh. *The Southern Past: A Clash of Race and Memory.* Cambridge, MA: Belknap Press of Harvard University Press, 2005.

———. "White Women and the Politics of Historical Memory, 1880–1920." In *Jumpin' Jim Crow: Southern Politics from Civil War to Civil Rights,* edited by Jane Elizabeth Dailey, Glenda Elizabeth Gilmore, and Bryant Simon, 115–39. Princeton, NJ: Princeton University Press, 2000.

Bruner, Edward M. "Experience and Its Expressions." In *The Anthropology of Experience*, edited by Victor W. Turner and Edward M. Bruner, 3–30. Urbana: University of Illinois Press, 1986.

Bryan, Thomas Conn. *Confederate Georgia*. Athens: University of Georgia Press, 1953.

Bryant, Jonathan M. *How Curious a Land: Conflict and Change in Greene County, Georgia, 1850–1885*. Chapel Hill: University of North Carolina Press, 1996.

———. "'We Have No Chance of Justice before the Courts': The Freedmen's Struggle for Power in Greene County, Georgia, 1865–1874." In *Georgia in Black and White: Explorations in the Race Relations of a Southern State, 1865–1950*, edited by John C. Inscoe, 13–37. Athens: University of Georgia Press, 1994.

Bucy, Carole Stanford. *Women Helping Women: The YWCA of Nashville 1898–1998*. Nashville, TN: J. S. Sanders, 1998.

Bufwack, Mary A., and Robert K. Oermann. *Finding Her Voice: The Illustrated History of Women in Country Music*. New York: H. Holt, 1995.

Buhle, Mari Jo, Paul Buhle, and Dan Georgakas. *Encyclopedia of the American Left*. Urbana: University of Illinois Press, 1992.

Buhle, Paul, ed. *History and the New Left: Madison, Wisconsin, 1950–1970*. Philadelphia: Temple University Press, 1990.

Burck, Jacob. *Hunger and Revolt: Cartoons*. New York: Daily Worker, 1935.

Burke, Fielding. *Call Home the Heart*. New York: Longmans, Green, 1932.

———. *A Stone Came Rolling*. New York: Longmans, Green, 1935.

Burts, Richard Milton. *Richard Irvine Manning and the Progressive Movement in South Carolina*. Columbia: University of South Carolina Press, 1974.

Butler, Nicholas. *Scholarship and Service: The Policies and Ideals of a National University in a Modern Democracy*. New York: Charles Scribner's Sons, 1921.

Callard, D. A. *Pretty Good for a Woman: The Enigmas of Evelyn Scott*. London: J. Cape, 1985.

Camacho, Roseanne V. "Whites Playing in the Dark: Southern Conversation in Willa Cather's *Sapphira and the Slave Girl*." In *Willa Cather's Southern Connections: New Essays on Cather and the South*, edited by Ann Romines, 65–74. Charlottesville: University of Virginia Press, 2000.

Campbell, Gavin James. *Music and the Making of a New South*. Chapel Hill: University of North Carolina Press, 2004.

Canaday, Margot. "Building a Straight State: Sexuality and Social Citizenship under the 1944 G.I. Bill." *Journal of American History* 90, no. 3 (Dec. 2003): 935–57.

Canady, Andrew McNeill. "The Limits to Improving Race Relations in the South: The YMCA Blue Ridge Assembly in Black Mountain, North Carolina, 1906–1930." *North Carolina Historical Review* 86 (Oct. 2009): 404–36.

———. *Willis Duke Weatherford: Race, Religion, and Reform in the American South*. Lexington: University Press of Kentucky, 2016.

Cantwell, Robert. *When We Were Good: The Folk Revival*. Cambridge, MA: Harvard University Press, 1996.

Cardyn, Lisa. "Sexualized Racism / Gendered Violence: Outraging the Body Politic in the Reconstruction South." *Michigan Law Review* 100, no. 4 (2002): 675–896.

Carlton, David L. *Mill and Town in South Carolina, 1880–1920*. Baton Rouge: Louisiana State University Press, 1982.

Carlton, David L., and Peter A. Coclanis. "Another 'Great Migration': From Region to Race in Southern Liberalism, 1938–1945." *Southern Cultures* 3, no. 4 (1997): 37–62.

———. *Confronting Southern Poverty in the Great Depression: The Report on Economic Conditions of the South with Related Documents*. Boston: Bedford/St. Martin's, 1996.

Carlton-LaNey, Iris. "Elizabeth Ross Haynes: An African American Reformer of Womanist Consciousness, 1908–1940." *Social Work* 42, no. 6 (1997): 573–83.

Carmichael, Stokely, and Charles V. Hamilton. *Black Power: The Politics of Liberation in America*. New York: Random House, 1967.

Carr, Virginia Spencer. *Dos Passos: A Life*. Garden City, NY: Doubleday, 1984.

Carter, Dan T. *Scottsboro: A Tragedy of the American South*. Rev. ed. Baton Rouge: Louisiana State University Press, 2007.

Carter, Hodding. "Southern Heritage." *New York Times Book Review*, Jan. 12, 1947.

Casebeer, Kenneth M. "Unemployment Insurance: American Social Wage Labor Organization and Legal Ideology." *Boston College Law Review* 35, no. 259 (1994): 259–348.

———. "The Workers' Unemployment Insurance Bill: American Social Wage, Labor Organization, and Legal Ideology." In *Labor Law in America: Historical and Critical Essays*, edited by Christopher L. Tomlins and Andrew J. King, 231–59. Baltimore: Johns Hopkins University Press, 1992.

Cash, W. J. *The Mind of the South*. New York: Alfred A. Knopf, 1941.

Cashin, Edward J. *The Story of Augusta*. Augusta, GA: Richmond County Board of Education, 1980.

Castledine, Jacqueline L. *Cold War Progressives: Women's Interracial Organizing for Peace and Freedom*. Urbana: University of Illinois Press, 2012.

Caute, David. *The Great Fear: The Anti-Communist Purge under Truman and Eisenhower*. New York: Simon and Schuster, 1978.

Caution, Ethel. "Buyers of Dreams." In *African American Classics: Graphic Classics*, edited by Tom Pomplun and Lance Tooks, 22:76–80. Mount Horeb, WI: Eureka, 2011.

Censer, Jane Turner. "A Changing World of Work: North Carolina Elite Women, 1865–1895." *North Carolina Historical Review* 73, no. 1 (Jan. 1996): 28–55.

———. *The Reconstruction of White Southern Womanhood, 1865–1895*. Baton Rouge: Lousiana State University Press, 2003.

The Centennial History of the Associate Reformed Presbyterian Church, 1803–1903. Charleston, SC: Walker, Evans and Cogswell, 1905.

Chambers, Whittaker. *Odyssey of a Friend: Whittaker Chambers' Letters to William F. Buckley, Jr., 1954–1961*. Edited by William F. Buckley Jr. New York: Putnam, 1970.

———. *Witness*. New York: Random House, 1952.

Champagne, Marian G. *The Cauliflower Heart*. New York: Dial Press, 1944.

Chasteen, John. *Born in Blood and Fire: A Concise History of Latin America*. New York: W. W. Norton, 2001.

Chatfield, Charles. *For Peace and Justice: Pacifism in America, 1914–1941*. Knoxville: University of Tennessee Press, 1971.

Chatterjee, Choi. "'Odds and Ends of the Russian Revolution,' 1917–1920: Gender and American Travel Narratives." *Journal of Women's History* 20, no. 4 (Dec. 2008): 10–33.

Chauncey, George, Jr. "Christian Brotherhood or Sexual Perversion?: Homosexual Identities and the Construction of Sexual Boundaries in the World War One Era." *Journal of Social History* 19, no. 2 (Winter 1985): 189–211.

———. "From Sexual Inversion to Homosexuality: Medicine and the Changing Conceptualization of Female Deviance." *Salmagundi*, Fall–Winter 1982–1983, 114–46.

———. *Gay New York: Gender, Urban Culture, and the Makings of the Gay Male World, 1890–1940.* New York: Basic Books, 1994.

Cheever, Susan. *Home before Dark: A Biographical Memoir of John Cheever by His Daughter.* New York: Washington Square Press, 2015.

Chernow, Ron. *The Warburgs: The Twentieth-Century Odyssey of a Remarkable Jewish Family.* New York: Random House, 1993.

Chirhart, Ann Short. "'Gardens of Education': Beulah Rucker Oliver and African-American Culture in the Twentieth-Century Georgia Upcountry." *Georgia Historical Quarterly* 82, no. 4 (Winter 1988): 829–47.

———. *Torches of Light: Georgia Teachers and the Coming of the Modern South.* Athens: University of Georgia Press, 2005.

Chodorow, Nancy. *The Reproduction of Mothering: Psychoanalysis and the Sociology of Gender.* Berkeley: University of California Press, 1978.

Christian, Barbara. *Black Feminist Criticism: Perspectives on Black Women Writers.* New York: Pergamon Press, 1985.

Clark, Alice. *Working Life of Women in the Seventeenth Century.* With a new introduction by Amy Louise Erickson. 1919. Reprint, London: Routledge and Kegan Paul, 1982.

Clark, Kenneth Bancroft, and Woody Klein. *Toward Humanity and Justice: The Writings of Kenneth B. Clark, Scholar of the 1954 "Brown v. Board of Education" Decision.* Westport, CT: Praeger, 2004.

Cline, David P. *From Reconciliation to Revolution: The Student Interracial Ministry, Liberal Christianity, and the Civil Rights Movement.* Chapel Hill: University of North Carolina Press, 2016.

Cobble, Dorothy Sue. *The Other Women's Movement: Workplace Justice and Social Rights in Modern America.* Princeton, NJ: Princeton University Press, 2004.

Cochran, Bert, and Columbia University Research Institute on International Change. *Labor and Communism: The Conflict That Shaped American Unions.* Princeton, NJ: Princeton University Press, 1977.

Cohen, Robert. *When the Old Left Was Young: Student Radicals and America's First Mass Student Movement, 1929–1941.* New York: Oxford University Press, 1993.

Coiner, Constance. *Better Red: The Writing and Resistance of Tillie Olsen and Meridel Le Sueur.* New York: Oxford University Press, 1995.

Coleman, Kenneth, and Charles Stephen Gurr, eds. *Dictionary of Georgia Biography.* Vol. 2. Athens: University of Georgia Press, 1983.

Colin, Emily, and Lynn P. Roundtree, eds. *The Changing Face of Justice: A Look at the First 100 Women Attorneys in North Carolina.* Cary: North Carolina Bar Association, 2004.

Collier-Thomas, Bettye. *Jesus, Jobs, and Justice: African American Women and Religion.* New York: Alfred A. Knopf, 2010.

Collins, Theresa. *Otto Kahn: Art, Money, and Modern Time.* Chapel Hill: University of North Carolina Press, 2002.

Colton, Elizabeth Avery. "Standards of Southern Colleges for Women." *School Review* 20 (Sept. 1912): 458–78.

———. *The Various Types of Southern Colleges for Women.* Raleigh, NC: Edwards and Broughton, 1916.

Commons, John R. *Myself.* New York: Macmillan, 1934.

Connerton, Paul. *How Societies Remember.* New York: Cambridge University Press, 1989.

Connor, Kimberly Rae. *Conversions and Visions in the Writings of African-American Women.* Knoxville: University of Tennessee Press, 1994.

Cook, Blanche Wiesen. *Eleanor Roosevelt: The Defining Years, 1933–1938.* Vol. 2. New York: Penguin Books, 2000.

———. "Female Support Networks and Political Activism: Lillian Wald, Crystal Eastman, Emma Goldman." *Chrysalis,* no. 3 (Autumn 1977): 43–61.

———. "The Historical Denial of Lesbianism: A Review Essay." *Radical History Review,* no. 20 (Spring/Summer 1979): 60–65.

Cook, Sylvia. *From Tobacco Road to Route 66: The Southern Poor White in Fiction.* Chapel Hill: University of North Carolina Press, 1976.

———. "Proletarian Novel." In *The Companion to Southern Literature: Themes, Genres, Places, People, Movements, and Motifs,* edited by Joseph Flora and Lucinda MacKethan, 684–87. Baton Rouge: Louisiana State University Press, 2002.

Cook, Vanessa. "Martin Luther King, Jr., and the Long Social Gospel Movement." *Religion and American Culture: A Journal of Interpretation* 26, no. 1 (Winter 2016): 74–100.

Cookingham, Mary E. "Social Economists and Reform: Berkeley, 1906–1961." *History of Political Economy* 19, no. 1 (Mar. 1, 1987): 47–65.

Coolidge, Calvin. "Enemies of the Republic: Are the 'Reds' Stalking Our College Women?" *Delineator,* June 1921.

———. "Enemies of the Republic: They Must Be Resisted." *Delineator,* Aug. 1921.

———. "Enemies of the Republic: Trotsky versus Washington." *Delineator,* July 1921.

Cooper, Patricia, and Ruth Oldenziel. "Cherished Classifications: Bathrooms and the Construction of Gender/Race on the Pennsylvania Railroad during World War II." *Feminist Studies* 25, no. 1 (Spring 1999): 7–41.

Cott, Nancy F. *The Grounding of Modern Feminism.* New Haven, CT: Yale University Press, 1987.

———. "Revisiting the Transatlantic 1920s: Vincent Sheean vs. Malcolm Cowley." *American Historical Review* 118, no. 1 (Feb. 2013): 46–75.

Cox, Karen L. *Dixie's Daughters: The United Daughters of the Confederacy and the Preservation of Confederate Culture.* Gainesville: University Press of Florida, 2003.

Cross, Robert D. "Grace Hoadley Dodge." In *Notable American Women, 1607–1950: A Biographical Dictionary,* edited by Edward T. James. Cambridge, MA: Belknap Press of Harvard University Press, 1971.

Crosse, Melba C. *Patillo, Pattillo, Pattullo, and Pittillo Families*. Fort Worth, TX: American Reference, 1972.

Crowley, Kate, ed. *The Collected Scientific Papers of Paul A. Samuelson*. Vol. 5. Cambridge, MA: MIT Press, 1986.

Cuordileone, K. A. "'Politics in an Age of Anxiety': Cold War Political Culture and the Crisis in American Masculinity, 1949–1960." *Journal of American History* 87, no. 2 (Sept. 2000): 515–45.

Current Biography: Who's News and Why. New York: H. W. Wilson, 1940.

Curry, Constance, et al. *Deep in Our Hearts: Nine White Women in the Freedom Movement*. Athens: University of Georgia Press, 2000.

Curti, Merle, and Vernon Rosco Carstensen. *The University of Wisconsin: A History*. Vol. 2. Madison: University of Wisconsin Press, 1949.

Cuthbert, Marion. *Juliette Derricotte*. New York: Woman's Press, 1933.

———. "The Negro Branch Executive." *Woman's Press*, Apr. 1933, 190–91.

Dailey, Jane. "Is Marriage a Civil Right? The Politics of Intimacy in the Jim Crow Era." In *The Folly of Jim Crow: Rethinking the Segregated South*, edited by Stephanie Cole and Natalie J. Ring, 176–208. College Station: Texas A&M University Press, 2012.

———. "Sex, Segregation, and the Sacred after *Brown*." *Journal of American History* 91, no. 1 (June 1, 2004): 119–44.

Dalfiume, Richard M. "The 'Forgotten Years' of the Negro Revolution." *Journal of American History* 55, no. 1 (June 1968): 90–106.

Daniel, Pete. *Breaking the Land: The Transformation of Cotton, Tobacco, and Rice Cultures since 1880*. Urbana: University of Illinois Press, 1985.

———. *Lost Revolutions: The South in the 1950s*. Chapel Hill: University of North Carolina Press for Smithsonian National Museum of American History, Washington, DC, 2000.

Daniels, Jonathan. "Old Devil Cotton." *Saturday Review of Literature*, Nov. 9, 1935.

———. *A Southerner Discovers the South*. New York: Macmillan, 1938.

Darden, Joe T., Richard Child Hill, June Thomas, and Richard Thomas. *Detroit: Race and Uneven Development*. Philadelphia: Temple University Press, 1987.

D'Attilio, Robert. "Sacco-Vanzetti Case." In *Encyclopedia of the American Left*, edited by Mari Jo Buhle, Paul Buhle, and Dan Georgakas, 667–70. Urbana: University of Illinois Press, 1992.

———. "La Salute è in Voi: The Anarchist Dimension." In *Sacco-Vanzetti: Developments and Reconsiderations, 1979*, edited by Robert D'Attilio and Jane Manthorn, 75–89. Boston: Boston Public Library, 1979.

Davidson, Donald. *The Attack on Leviathan: Regionalism and Nationalism in the United States*. Chapel Hill: University of North Carolina Press, 1938.

———. "The New South and the Conservative Tradition." *National Review*, Sept. 10, 1960.

———. "The Trend of Literature: A Partisan View." In *Culture in the South*, edited by W. T. Couch, 183–210. Chapel Hill: University of North Carolina Press, 1935.

Davis, Alice. Review of *South in Progress*, by Katharine Du Pre Lumpkin. *Social Forces* 19, no. 4 (May 1941): 566–67.

Davis, Lenwood. *The Black Heritage of Western North Carolina*. Asheville: University Graphics, University of North Carolina at Asheville, 1983.

Davis, Natalie Zemon, and Joan Wallach Scott. *Women's History as Women's Education: Essays by Natalie Zemon Davis and Joan Wallach Scott*. Northampton, MA: Sophia Smith Collection and Smith College Archives, 1985.

Davis, Susan G. "Ben Botkin's FBI File." *Journal of American Folklore* 122 (Winter 2010): 3–30.

Dawson, Ellen. "Gastonia." *Revolutionary Age* 1, no. 1 (Nov. 1, 1929): 3–4.

Dawson, Nelson L. "From Fellow Traveler to Anticommunist: The Odyssey of J. B. Matthews." *Register of the Kentucky Historical Society* 84, no. 3 (1986): 280–306.

Dean, Pamela E. *Women on the Hill: A History of Women at the University of North Carolina*. Chapel Hill: Division of Student Affairs, University of North Carolina at Chapel Hill, 1987.

Dearborn, Mary. *Queen of Bohemia: The Life of Louise Bryant*. Boston: Houghton Mifflin, 1996.

Degler, Carl. *In Search of Human Nature: The Decline and Revival of Darwinism in American Social Thought*. New York: Oxford University Press, 1991.

Delegard, Kirsten. *Battling Miss Bolsheviki: The Origins of Female Conservatism in the United States*. Philadelphia: University of Pennsylvania Press, 2012.

Denning, Michael. *The Cultural Front: The Laboring of American Culture in the Twentieth Century*. London: Verso, 1996.

Des Jardins, Julie. *Women and the Historical Enterprise in America: Gender, Race, and the Politics of Memory, 1880–1945*. Chapel Hill: University of North Carolina Press, 2003.

Dew, Charles B. *The Making of a Racist: A Southerner Reflects on Family, History, and the Slave Trade*. Charlottesville: University of Virginia Press, 2016.

Dewey, John, and James H. Tufts. *Ethics*. New York: Henry Holt, 1908.

Dewey Commission. *Not Guilty; Report of the Commission of Inquiry into the Charges Made against Leon Trotsky in the Moscow Trials, John Dewey, Chairman*. New York: Harper and Brothers, 1938.

DeWitt, Larry. "The Decision to Exclude Agricultural and Domestic Workers from the 1935 Social Security Act." *Social Security Bulletin* 70, no. 4 (2010): 49–68.

Dieckmann, Jane. *Wells College: A History*. Aurora, NY: Wells College Press, 1995.

Dies, Martin. *The Trojan Horse in America*. New York: Dodd, Mead, 1940.

Diggins, John P. *Up from Communism: Conservative Odysseys in American Intellectual History*. New York: Harper and Row, 1975.

Dilling, Elizabeth. *The Red Network: A Who's Who and Handbook of Radicalism for Patriots*. Kenilworth, IL: Self-published, 1934.

Dixon, Thomas. *The Clansman: An Historical Romance of the Ku Klux Klan*. 1905. Reprint, Ridgewood, NJ: Gregg Press, 1967.

———. *The Leopard's Spots: A Romance of the White Man's Burden, 1865–1900*. 1902. Reprint, Ridgewood, NJ: Gregg Press, 1967.

Dollard, John. *Caste and Class in a Southern Town*. Garden City, NY: Doubleday, 1937.

Donald, David Herbert. *Look Homeward: A Life of Thomas Wolfe.* Boston: Little, Brown, 1987.

Donaldson, Susan Van. "Gender and History in Eudora Welty's *Delta Wedding.*" *Southern Central Review* 14, no. 2 (Summer 1994): 3–14.

Dorman, Robert L. *Revolt of the Provinces: The Regionalist Movement in America, 1920–1945.* Chapel Hill: University of North Carolina Press, 1993.

Dos Passos, John. "300 N.Y. Agitators Reach Passaic." *New Masses,* June 1926.

Dossett, Kate. *Bridging Race Divides: Black Nationalism, Feminism, and Integration in the United States, 1896–1935.* Gainesville: University of Florida Press, 2008.

Douglas, Ann. *Terrible Honesty: Mongrel Manhattan in the 1920s.* New York: Farrar, Straus and Giroux, 1995.

Douglas, Dorothy Wolff. "American Minimum Wage Laws at Work." *American Economic Review* 9, no. 4 (1919): 701–38.

———. "Books in Review: To the Workers of America." *Social Work Today,* June 1936.

———. "The Cost of Living for Working Women: A Criticism of Current Theories." *Quarterly Journal of Economics* 34, no. 2 (Feb.1920): 225–59.

———. "Democracy and Higher Education." *American Teacher,* Feb. 1940.

———. "The Doctrines of Guillaume de Greef: Syndicalism and Social Reform in the Guise of a Classificatory Sociology." In *An Introduction to the History of Sociology,* edited by Harry Elmer Barnes, 538–52. Chicago: University of Chicago Press, 1948.

———. "Guillaume de Greef: The Social Theory of an Early Syndicalist." PhD diss., Columbia University, New York, 1925.

———. "Land and Labor in Mexico." *Science and Society* 4, no. 2 (Spring 1940): 127–52.

———. *Mexican Labor: A Bulwark of Democracy.* New York: American League for Peace and Democracy, 1939.

———. "The Mexican Teachers' Union." *American Teacher,* May 1939.

———. "The Social Purpose in the Sociology of de Greef." *American Journal of Sociology* 31, no. 4 (Jan. 1926): 433–54.

———. "The Social Security Act and the Unemployed." *American Teacher,* June 1937.

———. "Social Security in Czechoslovakia." *Social Service Review* 24, no. 3 (Sept. 1950): 310–18.

———. *Transitional Economic Systems: The Polish-Czech Example.* New York: Monthly Review Press, 1972. First published 1953 by Routledge and Kegan Paul (London).

———. "Unemployment Insurance—For Whom?" *Social Work Today,* Feb. 1935.

———. "What Kind of Unemployment Insurance?" *Social Work Today,* June 1934.

Douglas, Dorothy Wolff, and Katharine Du Pre Lumpkin. "Communistic Settlements." In *Encyclopedia of the Social Sciences.* Vol. 4, edited by Edwin R. A. Seligman, 95–102. New York: Macmillan, 1931.

Douglas, Paul H. *The Coming of a New Party.* New York: Whittlesey House, 1932.

———. *In the Fullness of Time: The Memoirs of Paul H. Douglas.* New York: Harcourt Brace Jovanovich, 1972.

———. "Lessons from the Last Decade." In *The Socialism of Our Time,* edited by Harry W. Laidler, 29–57. New York: Vanguard, 1929.

———. *Social Security in the United States: An Analysis and Appraisal of the Federal Social Security Act.* New York: Whittlesey House, 1936.

———. "Why I Am for Thomas." *New Republic* 56, no. 725 (Oct. 24, 1928): 268–70.

———. *The Worker in Modern Economic Society.* Chicago: University of Chicago Press, 1923.

Douglas, Paul H., Dorothy Wolff Douglas, and Carl S. Joslyn. "What Can a Man Afford?: Two Essays Awarded the Karelsen Prize by the American Economic Association." Supplement no. 2 of *American Economic Review* 11, no. 4 (Dec. 1921): 1–118.

Duberman, Martin B. *Black Mountain: An Exploration in Community.* New York: Dutton, 1972.

DuBois, Ellen. "Eleanor Flexner and the History of American Feminism." *Gender and History* 3 (Spring 1991): 81–90.

Du Bois, W. E. B. *Black Reconstruction: An Essay toward a History of the Part Which Black Folk Played in the Attempt to Reconstruct Democracy in America, 1860–1880.* New York: Harcourt, Brace, 1935.

———. "Documents of the War." *Crisis,* May 1919.

———. "Of the Training of Black Men." *Atlantic Monthly,* Sept. 1902.

———. *The Souls of Black Folk: Essays and Sketches.* 2nd ed. Chicago: A. C. McClurg, 1903.

Dunbar, Anthony P. *Against the Grain: Southern Radicals and Prophets, 1929–1959.* Charlottesville: University Press of Virginia, 1981.

Dunbar, Leslie W. "The Changing Mind of the South: The Exposed Nerve." *Journal of Politics* 26, no. 1 (Feb. 1, 1964): 3–21.

Dunne, William F. "In the 'Let Freedom Ring' Country." *New Masses,* Nov. 26, 1935.

Du Pre, Ann. *Some Take a Lover.* New York: Macaulay, 1933.

———. *Timid Woman.* New York: Macaulay, 1933.

Durr, Virginia Foster. *Outside the Magic Circle: The Autobiography of Virginia Foster Durr.* Edited by Hollinger F. Barnard and Fred Hobson. University: University of Alabama Press, 1985.

Dzuback, Mary Ann. "Berkeley Women Economists, Public Policy, and Civic Sensibility." In *Civic and Moral Learning in America,* edited by Donald R. Warren and John Patrick, 153–71. New York: Palgrave Macmillan, 2006.

———. "Creative Financing in Social Science: Women Scholars and Early Research." In *Women and Philanthropy in Education,* edited by Andrea Walton, 105–26. Bloomington: Indiana University Press, 2005.

———. "Women and Social Research at Bryn Mawr College, 1915–40." *History of Education Quarterly* 33, no. 4 (Winter 1993): 579–608.

Eaton, William. *The American Federation of Teachers, 1916–1961: A History of the Movement.* Carbondale: Southern Illinois University Press, 1975.

Edman, Irwin. *Philosopher's Holiday.* New York: Viking Press, 1938.

Effland, Anne B. W. "Agrarianism and Child Labor Policy for Agriculture." *Agricultural History Society* 79, no. 3 (Summer 2005): 281–97.

Egerton, John. *Speak Now against the Day: The Generation before the Civil Rights Movement in the South.* New York: Alfred A. Knopf, 1994.

Ehrenreich, John. *The Altruistic Imagination: A History of Social Work and Social Policy in the United States.* Ithaca, NY: Cornell University Press, 1985.

Ehrmann, Herbert. *The Case That Will Not Die: Commonwealth vs. Sacco and Vanzetti.* Boston: Little, Brown, 1969.

Ellison, Ralph. *Shadow and Act.* New York: Random House, 1964.

Engerman, David C. *Modernization from the Other Shore: American Intellectuals and the Romance of Russian Development.* Cambridge, MA: Harvard University Press, 2003.

———. "New Society, New Scholarship: Soviet Studies Programmes in Interwar America." *Minerva* 37, no. 1 (1999): 25–43.

Epstein, Daniel Mark. *What Lips My Lips Have Kissed: The Loves and Love Poems of Edna St. Vincent Millay.* New York: Henry Holt, 2001.

Evans, Sara M., ed. *Journeys That Opened Up the World: Women, Student Christian Movements, and Social Justice, 1955–1975.* New Brunswick, NJ: Rutgers University Press, 2003.

———. *Personal Politics: The Roots of Women's Liberation in the Civil Rights Movement and the New Left.* New York: Vintage Books, 1980.

Faderman, Lillian. *Odd Girls and Twilight Lovers: A History of Lesbian Life in Twentieth-Century America.* New York: Penguin, 1991.

Farnham, Christie Anne. *The Education of the Southern Belle: Higher Education and Student Socialization in the Antebellum South.* New York: New York University Press, 1994.

Farrell, James J. *The Spirit of the Sixties: Making Postwar Radicalism.* New York: Routledge, 1997.

Farrell, James T. "The Theater: *Let Freedom Ring.*" *New Masses,* Nov. 19, 1935.

Fass, Paula. *The Damned and the Beautiful: American Youth in the 1920's.* New York: Oxford University Press, 1977.

Faulkner, William. *Absalom, Absalom!* New York: Random House, 1936.

Faust, Drew Gilpin. *Mothers of Invention: Women of the Slaveholding South in the American Civil War.* Chapel Hill: University of North Carolina Press, 1996.

———. *This Republic of Suffering: Death and the American Civil War.* New York: Alfred A. Knopf, 2008.

Federal Writers' Project. *Lay My Burden Down: A Folk History of Slavery.* Edited by B. A. Botkin. Chicago: University of Chicago Press, 1945.

Federal Writers Project Georgia. *Georgia: A Guide to Its Towns and Countryside.* Atlanta, GA: Tupper and Love, 1940.

Federal Writers' Project of the Works Progress Administration of Massachusetts. *Massachusetts: A Guide to Its Places and People.* Boston: Houghton Mifflin, 1937.

Feimster, Crystal Nicole. *Southern Horrors: Women and the Politics of Rape and Lynching.* Cambridge, MA: Harvard University Press, 2009.

Feldman, Glenn. *Politics, Society, and the Klan in Alabama, 1915–1949.* Tuscaloosa: University of Alabama Press, 1999.

Felix, David. *Protest: Sacco-Vanzetti and the Intellectuals.* Bloomington: Indiana University Press, 1965.

Field, Frederick. *From Right to Left: An Autobiography.* Westport, CT: L. Hill, 1983.

Fields, Karen E., and Barbara J. Fields. *Racecraft: The Soul of Inequality in American Life.* New York: Verso, 2012.

Filene, Peter G., ed. *American Views of Soviet Russia, 1917–1965.* Homewood, IL: Dorsey, 1968.

Filler, Louis. *The Crusade against Slavery, 1830–1860.* New York: Harper and Row, 1960.

Findlay, James F. *Church People in the Struggle: The National Council of Churches and the Black Freedom Movement, 1950–1970.* New York: Oxford University Press, 1993.

Fink, Leon. "'Intellectuals' versus 'Workers': Academic Requirements and the Creation of Labor History." *American Historical Review* 96, no. 2 (Apr. 1991): 395–421.

———. *Progressive Intellectuals and the Dilemmas of Democratic Commitment.* Cambridge, MA: Harvard University Press, 1997.

FitzGerald, Frances. *America Revised: History Schoolbooks in the Twentieth Century.* Boston: Little, Brown, 1979.

Fitzpatrick, Ellen F. *Endless Crusade: Women Social Scientists and Progressive Reform.* New York: Oxford University Press, 1990.

———. *History's Memory: Writing America's Past, 1880–1980.* Cambridge, MA: Harvard University Press, 2002.

Flanagan, Hallie. *Arena: The History of the Federal Theatre.* 1940. Reprint, New York: B. Blom, 1965.

Flanagan, Roy. "Southern Peasantry." *Survey,* Nov. 1, 1932, 560–62.

Fleischner, Jennifer. *Mastering Slavery: Memory, Family, and Identity in Women's Slave Narratives.* New York: New York University Press, 1996.

Flexner, Eleanor. "Daisy Florence Simms." In *Notable American Women, 1607–1950: A Biographical Dictionary,* edited by Edward T. James, 3:291–93. Cambridge, MA: Belknap Press of Harvard University Press, 1971.

Flowers, Paul. "The Courage of Her Conviction." Review of *The Making of a Southerner,* by Katharine Du Pre Lumpkin. *Saturday Review of Literature,* Mar. 29, 1947.

Folbre, Nancy. "The 'Sphere of Women' in Early Twentieth-Century Economics." In *Gender and American Social Science: The Formative Years,* edited by Helene Silverberg, 35–60. Princeton, NJ: Princeton University Press, 1998.

Foley, Barbara. *Radical Representations: Politics and Form in U.S. Proletarian Fiction, 1929–1941.* Durham, NC: Duke University Press, 1993.

———. "Women and the Left in the 1930s." *American Literary History* 2, no. 1 (Spring 1990): 150–68.

Folsom, Franklin. *Days of Anger, Days of Hope: A Memoir of the League of American Writers, 1937–1942.* Niwot: University Press of Colorado, 1994.

Foner, Eric. *A Short History of Reconstruction, 1863–1877.* New York: Harper and Row, 1990.

———. *Reconstruction: America's Unfinished Revolution, 1863–1877.* New York: Harper and Row, 1988.

Foner, Philip. *The Fur and Leather Workers Union: A Story of Dramatic Struggles and Achievements.* Newark, NJ: Nordon Press, 1950.

Fosl, Catherine. "Life and Times of a Rebel Girl: Jane Speed and the Alabama Communist Party." *Southern Historian: A Journal of Southern History* 18 (Spring 1997): 45–65.

Foster, Gaines M. *Ghosts of the Confederacy: Defeat, the Lost Cause, and the Emergence of the New South, 1865 to 1913*. New York: Oxford University Press, 1987.

Fox, Richard Wightman. "The Culture of Liberal Protestant Progressivism, 1875–1925." *Journal of Interdisciplinary History* 23, no. 3 (Winter 1993): 639–60.

———. *Reinhold Niebuhr: A Biography*. San Francisco: Harper and Row, 1985.

Fox-Genovese, Elizabeth. "Between Individualism and Community: Autobiographies of Southern Women." In *Located Lives: Place and Idea in Southern Autobiography*, edited by J. Bill Berry, 20–38. Athens: University of Georgia Press, 1990.

———. *Within the Plantation Household: Black and White Women of the Old South*. Chapel Hill: University of North Carolina Press, 1988.

Fox-Genovese, Elizabeth, and Eugene D. Genovese. *The Mind of the Master Class: History and Faith in the Southern Slaveholders' Worldview*. Cambridge: Cambridge University Press, 2005.

Frank, Richard. "Negro Revolutionary Music." *New Masses*, May 15, 1934.

Frankel, Lee F., ed. *Bulletin of the National Conference of Jewish Charities, 1913–1914*. Vol. 4. Baltimore: n.p., 1914.

Frankfurter, Marion Denman, and Gardner Jackson, eds. *The Letters of Sacco and Vanzetti*. New York: Viking, 1928.

Franzen, Trisha. *Spinsters and Lesbians: Independent Womanhood in the United States*. New York: New York University Press, 1996.

Fraser, Nancy. "Contradictions of Capital and Care." *New Left Review* 100 (Aug. 2016): 99–117.

———. "Rethinking the Public Sphere: A Contribution to the Critique of Actually Existing Democracy." *Social Text* 25/26 (1990): 56–80.

Fraser, Steve. *Every Man a Speculator: A History of Wall Street in American Life*. New York: HarperCollins, 2005.

Frederickson, Mary E. "Citizens for Democracy: The Industrial Programs of the YWCA." In *Sisterhood and Solidarity: Workers' Education for Women, 1914–1984*, edited by Joyce L. Kornbluh and Mary E. Frederickson, 76–106. Philadelphia: Temple University Press, 1984.

———. "Louise Leonard McLaren." In *Notable American Women: The Modern Period; A Biographical Dictionary*, edited by Barbara Sicherman and Carol Hurd Green, 252–54. Cambridge, MA: Belknap Press of Harvard University Press, 1980.

———. "Mary Cornelia Baker." In *Notable American Women: The Modern Period; A Biographical Dictionary*, edited by Barbara Sicherman and Carol Hurd Green, 50–52. Cambridge, MA: Belknap Press of Harvard University Press, 1980.

———. "Myra Page: Daughter of the South, Worker for Change." *Southern Changes: The Journal of the Southern Regional Council* 5, no. 1 (1983): 10–12, 14–15.

Fredrickson, George. *The Black Image in the White Mind: The Debate on Afro-American Character and Destiny, 1817–1914*. New York: Harper and Row, 1971.

Free, William. Review of *Full Circle*. *Georgia Review*, Spring 1964.

Freedman, Estelle B. "'The Burning of Letters Continues': Elusive Identities and the Historical Construction of Sexuality." *Journal of Women's History* 9, no. 4 (Winter 1998): 181–200.

————. *Their Sisters' Keepers: Women's Prison Reform in America, 1830–1930.* Ann Arbor: University of Michigan Press, 1981.

Friedman, Andrea. "The Smearing of Joe McCarthy: The Lavender Scare, Gossip, and Cold War Politics." *American Quarterly* 57, no. 4 (Dec. 2005): 1105–29.

Friedman, Susan Stanford. "Women's Autobiographical Selves: Theory and Practice." In *The Private Self: Theory and Practice of Women's Autobiographical Writings*, edited by Shari Benstock, 34–62. Chapel Hill: University of North Carolina Press, 1988.

Frost, William Goodell. *Our Contemporary Ancestors in the Southern Mountains.* Boston: Atlantic Monthly, 1899.

Fuess, Claude M. *Calvin Coolidge: The Man from Vermont.* Boston: Little, Brown, 1940.

Fuller, Raymond G. "Child Labor Today." *Saturday Review of Literature*, June 19, 1937.

Furner, Mary O. *Advocacy and Objectivity: A Crisis in the Professionalization of American Social Science, 1865–1905.* Lexington: University Press of Kentucky, 1975.

Gabin, Nancy. *Feminism in the Labor Movement: Women and the United Auto Workers, 1935–1975.* Ithaca, NY: Cornell University Press, 1990.

Gabriel, Satyanda J. "Comparative Economic Systems." In *21st Century Economics: A Reference Handbook*, edited by Rhona C. Free, 1:441–50. Los Angeles: Sage, 2010.

Garabedian, Steven. "Reds, Whites, and the Blues: Lawrence Gellert, 'Negro Songs of Protest,' and the Left-Wing Folk-Song Revival of the 1930s and 1940s." *American Quarterly* 57, no. 1 (Mar. 2005): 179–206.

Gardner, Sarah E. *Blood and Irony: Southern White Women's Narratives of the Civil War, 1861–1937.* Chapel Hill: University of North Carolina Press, 2004.

Garrison, Dee. *Mary Heaton Vorse: The Life of an American Insurgent.* Philadelphia: Temple University Press, 1989.

Garrow, David J. *The FBI and Martin Luther King, Jr.: From "Solo" to Memphis.* New York: W. W. Norton, 1981.

Gaston, Paul M. *The New South Creed: A Study in Southern Mythmaking.* New York: Alfred A. Knopf, 1970.

Gavin, Lettie. *American Women in World War I: They Also Served.* Niwot: University Press of Colorado, 1997.

Geary, Daniel. *Radical Ambition: C. Wright Mills, the Left, and American Social Thought.* Berkeley: University of California Press, 2009.

Gellert, Lawrence. "Negro Songs of Protest." *New Masses*, Nov. 1930.

————. "Negro Songs of Protest." *New Masses*, Jan. 1931.

————. "Negro Songs of Protest." *New Masses*, Apr. 1931.

————. "Negro Songs of Protest." *New Masses*, May 1932.

————. "Negro Songs of Protest." *New Masses*, May 1933.

Gellman, Erik S. *Death Blow to Jim Crow: The National Negro Congress and the Rise of Militant Civil Rights.* Chapel Hill: University of North Carolina Press, 2014.

Georgakas, Dan. "Fur and Leather Workers." In *Encyclopedia of the American Left*, edited by Mari Jo Buhle, Paul Buhle, and Dan Georgakas, 249–50. Urbana: University of Illinois Press, 1992.

Gerstle, Gary. "The Crucial Decade: The 1940s and Beyond." *Journal of American History* 92, no. 4 (Mar. 1, 2006): 1292–99.

———. "The Protean Character of American Liberalism." *American Historical Review* 99, no. 4 (Oct. 1994): 1043–73.

Gettleman, Marvin. "The Lost World of United States Labor Education: Curricula at East and West Coast Schools." In *American Labor and the Cold War: Grassroots Politics and Postwar Political Culture*, edited by Robert W. Cherny, William Issel, and Kieran Walsh Taylor, 205–15. New Brunswick, NJ: Rutgers University Press, 2004.

———. "'No Varsity Teams': New York's Jefferson School of Social Science, 1943–1965." *Science and Society* 66, no. 3 (2002): 336–59.

———. "Workers Schools." In *Encyclopedia of the American Left*, edited by Mari Jo Buhle, Paul Buhle, and Dan Georgakas, 853–55. Urbana: University of Illinois Press, 1992.

Gilbert, Sandra M. "Soldier's Heart: Literary Men, Literary Women, and the Great War." In *Behind the Lines: Gender and the Two World Wars*, edited by Margaret Randolph Higonnet, Jane Jenson, Sonya Michel, and Margaret Collins Weitz, 197–226. New Haven, CT: Yale University Press, 1987.

Gilkes, Lillian Barnard. *Short Story Craft*. New York: Macmillan, 1949.

———. Afterword to *The Wedding*, by Grace Lumpkin, 273–86. New York: Popular Library, 1977. First published 1939 by Lee Furman (New York) and reprinted 1976 by Southern Illinois University Press (Carbondale). Page references are to the 1977 edition.

Gill, Jill K. *Embattled Ecumenism: The National Council of Churches, the Vietnam War, and the Trials of the Protestant Left*. DeKalb: Northern Illinois University Press, 2011.

Gilmore, Glenda Elizabeth. *Defying Dixie: The Radical Roots of Civil Rights, 1919–1950*. New York: W. W. Norton, 2008.

———. *Gender and Jim Crow: Women and the Politics of White Supremacy in North Carolina, 1896–1920*. Chapel Hill: University of North Carolina Press, 1996.

———. "'One of the Meanest Books': Thomas Dixon and *The Leopard's Spots*." *North Carolina Literary Review* 2, no. 1 (Spring 1994): 87–101.

Gladney, Margaret Rose. "Personalizing the Political, Politicizing the Personal: Reflections on Editing the Letters of Lillian Smith." In *Carryin' On in the Lesbian and Gay South*, edited by John Howard, 93–103. New York: New York University Press, 1997.

Glasgow, Ellen Anderson Gholson. *Barren Ground*. Garden City, NY: Doubleday, Page, 1925.

Glazer, Penina, and Miriam Slater. *Unequal Colleagues: The Entrance of Women into the Professions, 1890–1940*. New Brunswick, NJ: Rutgers University Press, 1987.

Glickman, Lawrence B. "The Strike in the Temple of Consumption: Consumer Activism and Twentieth-Century American Political Culture." *Journal of American History* 88, no. 1 (June 2001): 99–112.

Godfrey, Phoebe. "Bayonets, Brainwashing, and Bathrooms: The Discourse of Race, Gender, and Sexuality in the Desegregation of Little Rock's Central High." *Arkansas Historical Quarterly* 62, no. 1 (Spring 2003): 42–67.

Gold, David, and Catherine L. Hobbs. *Educating the New Southern Woman: Speech,*

Writing, and Race at the Public Women's Colleges, 1884–1945. Carbondale: Southern Illinois University Press, 2014.

Gold, Michael. "Go Left, Young Writers!" *New Masses*, Jan. 1929.

Goldman, Wendy Z. *Women, the State, and Revolution: Soviet Family Policy and Social Life, 1917–1936.* Cambridge: Cambridge University Press, 1993.

Goldstein, Carolyn M. *Creating Consumers: Home Economists in Twentieth-Century America.* Chapel Hill: University of North Carolina Press, 2012.

Goldstein, Malcolm. *The Political Stage: American Drama and Theater of the Great Depression.* New York: Oxford University Press, 1974.

Goldstein, Robert Justin. *American Blacklist: The Attorney General's List of Subversive Organizations.* Lawrence: University Press of Kansas, 2008.

———. ed. *Little "Red Scares": Anti-Communism and Political Repression in the United States, 1921–1946.* Surrey: Ashgate, 2014.

Goluboff, Risa Lauren. *The Lost Promise of Civil Rights.* Cambridge, MA: Harvard University Press, 2007.

Goodman, James. *Stories of Scottsboro.* New York: Pantheon Books, 1994.

Gopnik, Alison. *The Philosophical Baby: What Children's Minds Tell Us about Truth, Love, and the Meaning of Life.* New York: Farrar, Straus and Giroux, 2009.

Gordon, Linda. *Dorothea Lange: A Life Beyond Limits.* New York: W. W. Norton, 2009.

———. *Heroes of Their Own Lives: The Politics and History of Family Violence: Boston, 1880–1960.* New York: Viking, 1988.

———. *Pitied but Not Entitled: Single Mothers and the History of Welfare, 1890–1935.* New York: Free Press, 1994.

———. *The Second Coming of the KKK: The Ku Klux Klan of the 1920s and the American Political Tradition.* New York: Liveright, 2017.

———. "Social Insurance and Public Assistance: The Influence of Gender in Welfare Thought in the United States, 1890–1935." *American Historical Review* 97, no. 1 (Feb. 1992): 19–54.

———. ed. *Women, the State and Welfare.* Madison: University of Wisconsin Press, 1990.

Gordon, Lynn D. *Gender and Higher Education in the Progressive Era.* New Haven, CT: Yale University Press, 1990.

Gore, Dayo F. *Radicalism at the Crossroads: African American Women Activists in the Cold War.* New York: New York University Press, 2011.

Gore, Dayo F., Jeanne Theoharis, and Komozi Woodard, eds. *Want to Start a Revolution? Radical Women in the Black Freedom Struggle.* New York: New York University Press, 2009.

Gosse, Van. "'To Organize in Every Neighborhood, in Every Home': The Gender Politics of American Communists between the Wars." *Radical History Review*, no. 50 (Spring 1991): 109–41.

Graham, Patricia Albjerg. "Expansion and Exclusion: A History of Women in American Higher Education." *Signs: Journal of Women in Culture and Society* 3, no. 4 (Summer 1978): 759–73.

Gray, Richard. *The Literature of Memory: Modern Writers of the American South.* Baltimore: Johns Hopkins University Press, 1977.

———. *Southern Aberrations: Writers of the American South and the Problem of Regionalism*. Baton Rouge: Louisiana State University Press, 2000.

———. *Writing the South: Ideas of an American Region*. Cambridge: Cambridge University Press, 1986.

Graydon, Augustus T. "Trinity Church." *Sandlapper* 3, no. 1 (Jan. 1970): 20–23.

Green, Archie. "A Southern Cotton Mill Rhyme." In *Wobblies, Pile Butts, and Other Heroes*, by Archie Green, 275–319. Urbana: University of Illinois Press, 1993.

Green, Constance McLaughlin. *Holyoke, Massachusetts: A Case History of the Industrial Revolution in America*. New Haven, CT: Yale University Press, 1939.

———. *Washington*. Princeton, NJ: Princeton University Press, 1962.

Greenberg, Michael. "What Babies Know and We Don't." *New York Review of Books*, Mar. 11, 2010.

Gregory, James N. "The Second Great Migration: A Historical Overview." In *African American Urban History since World War II*, edited by Kenneth L. Kusmer and Joe W. Trotter, 19–38. Chicago: University of Chicago Press, 2009.

———. *The Southern Diaspora: How the Great Migrations of Black and White Southerners Transformed America*. Chapel Hill: University of North Carolina Press, 2005.

Grimké, Angelina Emily. *Appeal to the Christian Women of the South*. New York: American Anti-Slavery Society, 1836. http://catalog.hathitrust.org/Record/006539541.

———. *Letters to Catherine E. Beecher: In Reply to an Essay on Slavery and Abolitionism, Addressed to* A. E. *Grimké*. Boston: printed by Isaac Knapp, 1838. http://catalog.hathitrust.org/Record/000410460.

Grimké, Sarah Moore. *Letters of Theodore Dwight Weld, Angelina Grimké Weld and Sarah Grimké, 1822–1844*. Edited by Gilbert H. Barnes and Dwight L. Dumond. New York: D. Appleton-Century, 1934.

———. *Letters on the Equality of the Sexes, and Other Essays*. Edited by Elizabeth Ann Bartlett. New Haven, CT: Yale University Press, 1988.

Gruening, Martha. "The Vanishing Individual." *Hound and Horn*, Mar. 1934.

Guasco, Suzanne Cooper. "The War against Slavery, Reconsidered and Reframed." *Reviews in American History* 43, no. 1 (2015): 60–69.

Gurstein, Rochelle. *The Repeal of Reticence: A History of America's Cultural and Legal Struggles over Free Speech, Obscenity, Sexual Liberation, and Modern Art*. New York: Hill and Wang, 1996.

Gutman, Herbert G., and Donald H. Bell, eds. *The New England Working Class and the New Labor History*. Urbana: University of Illinois Press, 1987.

Hadley, Edwin Marshall. *Sinister Shadows*. Chicago: Tower, 1929.

Hagood, Margaret Jarman. *Mothers of the South: Portraiture of the White Tenant Farm Woman*. Chapel Hill: University of North Carolina Press, 1939.

Hahamovitch, Cindy. *The Fruits of Their Labor: Atlantic Coast Farmworkers and the Making of Immigrant Poverty, 1870–1945*. Chapel Hill: University of North Carolina Press, 1997.

Hahn, Steven. *A Nation under Our Feet: Black Political Struggles in the Rural South, from Slavery to the Great Migration*. Cambridge, MA: Belknap Press of Harvard University Press, 2003.

Hall, Jacquelyn Dowd. "Broadus Mitchell." *Radical History Review* 45 (Fall 1989): 31–38.

———. "The Long Civil Rights Movement and the Political Uses of the Past." *Journal of American History* 91, no. 4 (2005): 1233–63.

———. "O. Delight Smith's Progressive Era: Labor, Feminism and Reform in the Urban South." In *Visible Women: New Essays on American Activism*, edited by Nancy Hewitt and Suzanne Lebsock, 166–98. Urbana: University of Illinois Press, 1993.

———. "Open Secrets: Memory, Imagination, and the Refashioning of Southern Identity." *American Quarterly* 50, no. 1 (Mar. 1998): 109–24.

———. *Revolt against Chivalry: Jessie Daniel Ames and the Women's Campaign against Lynching*. 2nd ed. New York: Columbia University Press, 1993.

———. "'To Widen the Reach of Our Love': Autobiography, History, and Desire." *Feminist Studies* 26, no. 1 (Spring 2000): 230–47.

———. "Women Writers, the 'Southern Front,' and the Dialectical Imagination." *Journal of Southern History* 69, no. 1 (Feb. 2003): 3–38.

———. "'You Must Remember This': Autobiography as Social Critique." *Journal of American History* 85, no. 2 (Sept. 1998): 439–65.

Hall, Jacquelyn Dowd, James L. Leloudis, Robert R. Korstad, Mary Murphy, Lu Ann Jones, and Christopher B. Daly. *Like a Family: The Making of a Southern Cotton Mill World*. 2nd ed. With a new afterword by the authors and a foreword by Michael Frisch. Chapel Hill: University of North Carolina Press, 2000.

Hall, Jacquelyn Dowd, and Kathryn L. Nasstrom. "Case Study: The Southern Oral History Program." In *The Oxford Handbook of Oral History*, edited by Donald A. Ritchie, 409–16. New York: Oxford University Press, 2010.

Halper, Albert. *Good-Bye, Union Square: A Writer's Memoir of the Thirties*. Chicago: Quadrangle Books, 1970.

Hammond, Lily Hardy. *In Black and White: An Interpretation of the South*. Edited by Elna C. Green. Athens: University of Georgia Press, 2010.

Hansen, Harry, ed. *O. Henry Memorial Award Prize Stories of 1940*. New York: Doubleday, Doran, 1940.

Harlick, Jeanene. "Life of the Party." *Stanford Magazine*, Feb. 2002.

Harris, Irving. "Alone in the Dark—Communist Turns Christian." In *The Breeze of the Spirit: Sam Shoemaker and the Story of Faith at Work*, 95–106. New York: Seabury, 1978.

Hartmann, Susan M. *The Other Feminists: Activists in the Liberal Establishment*. New Haven, CT: Yale University Press, 1998.

Harvey, Paul. *Freedom's Coming: Religious Culture and the Shaping of the South from the Civil War through the Civil Rights Era*. Chapel Hill: University of North Carolina Press, 2005.

———. *Redeeming the South: Religious Cultures and Racial Identities among Southern Baptists, 1865–1925*. Chapel Hill: University of North Carolina Press, 1997.

———. "Southern Baptists and the Social Gospel: White Religious Progressivism in the South, 1900–1925." *Fides et Historia* 27, no. 2 (1995): 59–77.

Hawkins, Mike. *Social Darwinism in European and American Thought, 1860–1945:*

Nature as Model and Nature as Threat. Cambridge: Cambridge University Press, 1997.

Haynes, John Earle. "The 'Rank and File Movement' in Private Social Work." *Labor History* 16, no. 1 (Winter 1975): 78–98.

Heale, M. J. *McCarthy's Americans: Red Scare Politics in State and Nation, 1935–1965.* Athens: University of Georgia Press, 1998.

Height, Dorothy I. *Step by Step with Interracial Groups.* New York: Woman's Press, 1946.

Hein, David, and Gardiner H. Shattuck Jr. *The Episcopalians.* Westport, CT: Praeger, 2004.

Helgren, Jennifer. *American Girls and Global Responsibility: A New Relation to the World during the Early Cold War.* New Brunswick, NJ: Rutgers University Press, 2017.

Hellman, Lillian. *Scoundrel Time.* Boston: Little, Brown, 1976.

Hemingway, Andrew. *Artists on the Left: American Artists and the Communist Movement, 1926–1956.* New Haven, CT: Yale University Press, 2002.

Henderson, Mae Gwendolyn. "Portrait of Wallace Thurman." In *The Harlem Renaissance Remembered: Essays Edited with a Memoir,* edited by Arna Bontemps, 147–70. New York: Dodd, Mead, 1972.

Herbst, Josephine. *Rope of Gold.* New York: Harcourt Brace, 1939.

Herring, Hubert. *Neilson of Smith.* Brattleboro, VT: Stephen Daye, 1939.

Herron, Carolivia, ed. *Selected Works of Angelina Weld Grimké.* New York: Oxford University Press, 1991.

Herzog, Jonathan. *The Spiritual-Industrial Complex: America's Religious Battle against Communism in the Early Cold War.* New York: Oxford University Press, 2011.

Hicks, Cheryl. *Talk with You Like a Woman: African American Women, Justice, and Reform in New York, 1890–1935.* Chapel Hill: University of North Carolina Press, 2010.

Hicks, Granville. "Review and Comment: The Real South." *New Masses,* Nov. 12, 1935.

Higham, John. "Changing Paradigms: The Collapse of Consensus History." *Journal of American History* 76, no. 2 (Sept. 1989): 460–66.

———. "The Cult of the American Consensus: Homogenizing Our History." *Commentary* 27, no. 2 (1959): 93–100.

Himelstein, Morgan Y. *Drama Was a Weapon: The Left-Wing Theatre in New York, 1929–1941.* New Brunswick, NJ: Rutgers University Press, 1963.

Hirschman, Albert. *Exit, Voice, and Loyalty: Responses to Decline in Firms, Organizations, and States.* Cambridge, MA: Harvard University Press, 1970.

History of North Carolina. Vol. 5. Chicago: Lewis, 1919.

Hobbie, Peter H. "Walter L. Lingle, Presbyterians, and the Enigma of the Social Gospel in the South." *American Presbyterians: Journal of Presbyterian History* 69, no. 3 (1991): 191–202.

Hobson, Fred C., Jr. *But Now I See: The White Southern Racial Conversion Narrative.* Baton Rouge: Louisiana State University Press, 1999.

———. *Serpent in Eden: H. L. Mencken and the South.* Chapel Hill: University of North Carolina Press, 1974.

———. "Southern Women's Autobiography." In *The History of Southern Women's Lit-*

erature, edited by Carolyn Perry and Mary Louise Weaks, 268–74. Baton Rouge: Louisiana State University Press, 2002.

———. *Tell about the South: The Southern Rage to Explain*. Baton Rouge: Louisiana State University Press, 1983.

Holden, Charles. *The New Southern University: Academic Freedom and Liberalism at UNC*. Lexington: University Press of Kentucky, 2012.

Holladay, Paula. "I Paraded." *New Republic*, Oct. 19, 1927.

Hollander, Paul. *Political Pilgrims: Travels of Intellectuals to the Soviet Union, China, and Cuba*. New York: Oxford University Press, 1981.

Hollinger, David A. *After Cloven Tongues of Fire: Protestant Liberalism in Modern American History*. Princeton, NJ: Princeton University Press, 2013.

———. *Protestants Abroad: How Missionaries Tried to Change the World but Changed America*. Princeton, NJ: Princeton University Press, 2017.

Holmes, Josephine Pinyon. "Youth Cannot Wait." *Crisis* 28 (July 1924): 128–31.

Honey, Maureen, ed. *Shadowed Dreams: Women's Poetry of the Harlem Renaissance*. New Brunswick, NJ: Rutgers University Press, 1989.

Honey, Michael K. *Southern Labor and Black Civil Rights: Organizing Memphis Workers*. Urbana: University of Illinois Press, 1993.

Hook, Sidney. "The Two Faiths of Whittaker Chambers." *New York Times Book Review*, May 25, 1952.

Horowitz, Daniel. *Betty Friedan and the Making of "The Feminine Mystique": The American Left, the Cold War, and Modern Feminism*. Amherst: University of Massachusetts Press, 1998.

Horowitz, Helen Lefkowitz. *Alma Mater: Design and Experience in the Women's Colleges from Their Nineteenth-Century Beginnings to the 1930s*. 2nd ed. Amherst: University of Massachusetts Press, 1993.

———. *The Power and Passion of M. Carey Thomas*. New York: Alfred A. Knopf, 1994.

Horton, Carol A. *Race and the Making of American Liberalism*. Oxford: Oxford University Press, 2005.

Houck, Davis W., and David E. Dixon, eds. *Women and the Civil Rights Movement, 1954–1965*. Jackson: University Press of Mississippi, 2009.

Howe, Irving. *World of Our Fathers*. New York: Harcourt Brace Jovanovich, 1976.

Huebner, Timothy S. "Joseph Henry Lumpkin." In *American National Biography*, edited by Mark C. Carnes and John A. Garraty, 14:123–25. New York: Oxford University Press, 1999.

Hughes, Langston. "The Negro Artist and the Racial Mountain." In *African American Literary Theory: A Reader*, edited by Winston Napier, 27–30. New York: New York University Press, 2000.

Hull, Gloria T. *Color, Sex, and Poetry: Three Women Writers of the Harlem Renaissance*. Bloomington: Indiana University Press, 1987.

Hunt, Lynn. "Forgetting and Remembering: The French Revolution Then and Now." *American Historical Review* 100, no. 4 (Oct. 1995): 1119–35.

Hunter, Tera W. *To 'Joy My Freedom: Southern Black Women's Lives and Labors after the Civil War*. Cambridge, MA: Harvard University Press, 1997.

Hunton, Addie, and Kathryn M. Johnson. *Two Colored Women with the American*

Expeditionary Forces and William Alphaeus Hunton: A Pioneer Prophet of Young Men. New York: G. K. Hall, 1996.

Hutchins, Grace. *Labor and Silk*. New York: International Publishers, 1929.

———. *Women Who Work*. New York: International Publishers, 1934.

Hutchinson, George. *The Harlem Renaissance in Black and White*. Cambridge, MA: Belknap Press of Harvard University Press, 1995.

Hutson, Jean Blackwell. "Eva Del Vakia Bowles." In *Notable American Women, 1607–1950: A Biographical Dictionary*. Vol. 1, edited by Edward T. James, 214–15. Cambridge, MA: Belknap Press of Harvard University Press, 1971.

Inscoe, John C. "Appalachian Otherness, Real and Perceived." In *The New Georgia Guide*, 185–86. Athens: University of Georgia Press, 1996.

———. *Writing the South through the Self: Explorations in Southern Autobiography*. Athens: University of Georgia Press, 2011.

International Labor Defense. *Labor Defense: Manifesto, Resolutions, Constitution Adopted by the First National Conference, Held in Ashland Auditorium, Chicago, June 28, 1925*. Chicago: International Labor Defense, 1925.

Intrator, Michael. "The Furriers Fight for a Union." *Workers Age*, Apr. 15, 1934.

Izzo, Amanda. *Liberal Christianity and Women's Global Activism: The Young Women's Christian Association of the USA and the Maryknoll Sisters*. New Brunswick, NJ: Rutgers University Press, 2018.

Jacobs, Harriet A. *Incidents in the Life of a Slave Girl: Written by Herself*. Edited by Lydia Maria Child and Jean Fagan Yellin. 3rd ed. Cambridge, MA: Harvard University Press, 1987.

Jacobs, Meg. "'How About Some Meat?': The Office of Price Administration, Consumption Politics, and State Building from the Bottom Up, 1941–1946." *Journal of American History* 84, no. 3 (Dec. 1997): 910–41.

Jacoby, Susan. *Alger Hiss and the Battle for History*. New Haven, CT: Yale University Press, 2009.

Janken, Kenneth. *White: The Biography of Walter White, Mr. NAACP*. New York: W. W. Norton, 2003.

Jeffrey, Julie Roy. *The Great Silent Army of Abolitionism: Ordinary Women in the Antislavery Movement*. Chapel Hill: University of North Carolina Press, 1998.

Jeffrey, Kirk. Review of *The Emancipation of Angelina Grimké*, by Katharine Du Pre Lumpkin. *New York Historical Society Quarterly* 59, no. 3 (July 1975): 288–90.

Jenness, Mary. *Twelve Negro Americans*. New York: Friendship Press, 1936.

Johnson, Bethany Leigh. "The Southern Historical Association: Seventy-Five Years of History 'in the South' and 'of the South.'" *Journal of Southern History* 76, no. 3 (2010): 655–82.

Johnson, David K. *The Lavender Scare: The Cold War Persecution of Gays and Lesbians in the Federal Government*. Chicago: University of Chicago Press, 2004.

Johnson, James. *Black Manhattan*. New York: Da Capo Press, 1991.

Johnson, Joan Marie. *Southern Ladies, New Women: Race, Region, and Clubwomen in South Carolina, 1890–1930*. Gainesville: University of Florida Press, 2004.

———. "'Standing Up for High Standards': The Southern Association of College Women." In *The Educational Work of Women's Associations, 1890–1960*, edited by

Anne Meis Knupfer and Christine Woyshner, 17–37. New York: Palgrave Macmillan, 2008.

Johnson, Walter. *The Chattel Principle: Internal Slave Trades in the Americas*. New Haven, CT: Yale University Press, 2004.

Jones, Adrienne Lash. "Eva Del Vakia Bowles (1875–1943)." In *Black Women in America: An Historical Encyclopedia*, edited by Darlene Clark Hine, 152–53. Brooklyn, NY: Carlson, 1993.

———. "Struggle among the Saints: African American Women and the YWCA, 1870–1920." In *Men and Women Adrift: The YMCA and the YWCA in the City*, edited by Nina Mjagkij and Margaret Spratt, 160–87. New York: New York University Press, 1997.

Jones, Maxine D., and Joe M. Richardson. *Talladega College: The First Century*. Tuscaloosa: University of Alabama Press, 1990.

Jones, William P. *The March on Washington: Jobs, Freedom and the Forgotten History of Civil Rights*. New York: W. W. Norton, 2013.

Josephson, Hannah. *The Golden Threads: New England's Mill Girls and Magnates*. New York: Duell, Sloan and Pearce, 1949.

Josephson, Matthew. *Infidel in the Temple: A Memoir of the Nineteen-Thirties*. New York: Alfred A. Knopf, 1967.

Joughin, Louis G., and Edmund M. Morgan. *The Legacy of Sacco and Vanzetti*. New York: Harcourt, Brace, 1948.

Kamp, Joseph P. *Behind the Lace Curtains of the YWCA: A Report on the Extent and Nature of Infiltration by Communist, Socialist and Other Left Wing Elements, and the Resultant Red Complexion of Propaganda Disseminated in, by and through the Young Woman's [!] Christian Association*. New York: Constitutional Educational League, 1948. https://babel.hathitrust.org/cgi/ssd?id=osu.32435017562752.

Kantrowitz, Stephen. *Ben Tillman and the Reconstruction of White Supremacy*. Chapel Hill: University of North Carolina Press, 2000.

Kaplan, Carla. *Miss Anne in Harlem: The White Women of the Black Renaissance*. New York: Harper, 2013.

Kaplan, Temma. *Crazy for Democracy: Women in Grassroots Movements*. New York: Routledge, 1997.

Katznelson, Ira. *When Affirmative Action Was White: An Untold History of Racial Inequality in Twentieth-Century America*. New York: W. W. Norton, 2005.

Katznelson, Ira, Kim Geiger, and Daniel Kryder. "Limiting Liberalism: The Southern Veto in Congress, 1933–1950." *Political Science Quarterly* 108, no. 2 (Summer 1993): 283–306.

Kazin, Alfred. *A Walker in the City*. New York: Harcourt, Brace, 1951.

Kelley, Edith Summers. *Weeds*. New York: Harcourt, Brace, 1923.

Kelley, Robin D. G. *Hammer and Hoe: Alabama Communists during the Great Depression*. Chapel Hill: University of North Carolina Press, 1990.

Kellogg, Peter J. "Civil Rights Consciousness in the 1940s." *Historian* 42, no. 1 (1979): 18–41.

Kemble, Frances Anne. *Journal of a Residence on a Georgian Plantation in 1838–1839*. London: Longman, Roberts and Green, 1863.

Kennedy, David M. *Freedom from Fear: The American People in Depression and War, 1929–1945.* New York: Oxford University Press, 1999.

Kent, Scotti. *More Than Petticoats: Remarkable North Carolina Women.* Helena, MT: TwoDot, 2000.

Kephart, Horace. *Our Southern Highlanders.* New York: Outing Publishing Company, 1913.

Kerber, Linda K. *No Constitutional Right to Be Ladies: Women and the Obligations of Citizenship.* New York: Hill and Wang, 1998.

Kessler-Harris, Alice. *In Pursuit of Equity: Women, Men, and the Quest for Economic Citizenship in 20th-Century America.* Oxford: Oxford University Press, 2001.

———. "Vera Shlakman, *Economic History of a Factory Town: A Study of Chicopee, Massachusetts* (1935)." *International Labor and Working-Class History,* no. 69 (Spring 2006): 195–200.

Kester, Howard. *Revolt among the Sharecroppers.* With an introduction by Alex Lichtenstein. Knoxville: University of Tennessee Press, 1997.

Kidd, Sue Monk. *The Invention of Wings.* New York: Viking, 2014.

Kindler, Christine. "Frances Harriet Williams." In *The Kentucky African American Encyclopedia,* edited by Gerald L. Smith, Karen Cotton McDaniel, and John Hardin. Lexington: University Press of Kentucky, 2015.

King, Martin Luther, Jr. "Beyond Vietnam, April 4, 1967." In *A Call to Conscience: The Landmark Speeches of Dr. Martin Luther King, Jr.,* edited by Clayborne Carson and Kris Shepard, 133–64. New York: Intellectual Properties Management, in association with Warner Books, 2001.

King, Richard H. *A Southern Renaissance: The Cultural Awakening of the American South, 1930–1955.* New York: Oxford University Press, 1980.

Kleeck, Mary van. "An Open Letter from Mary van Kleeck." *Social Work Today,* Mar. 1934.

———. "Security for Americans, IV: The Workers' Bill for Unemployment and Social Insurance." *New Republic,* Dec. 1934.

Klehr, Harvey. *The Heyday of American Communism: The Depression Decade.* New York: Basic Books, 1984.

Kluger, Richard. *The Paper: The Life and Death of the "New York Herald Tribune."* New York: Alfred A. Knopf, 1986.

Kneebone, John T. *Southern Liberal Journalists and the Issue of Race, 1920–1944.* Chapel Hill: University of North Carolina Press, 1985.

Knight, Alan. "Cardenismo: Juggernaut or Jalopy?" *Journal of Latin American Studies* 26, no. 1 (Feb. 1994): 73–107.

Knight, Lucian Lamar. *Reminiscences of Famous Georgians: Embracing Episodes and Incidents in the Lives of the Great Men of the State.* Atlanta: Franklin-Turner, 1907.

Knott, Cheryl. *Not Free, Not for All: Public Libraries in the Age of Jim Crow.* Amherst: University of Massachusetts Press, 2015.

Knotts, Alice G. *Fellowship of Love: Methodist Women Changing American Racial Attitudes 1920–1968.* Nashville, TN: Abingdon, 1996.

———. "Methodist Women Integrate Schools and Housing, 1952–1959." In *Women in the Civil Rights Movement: Trailblazers and Torchbearers, 1941–1965,* edited by

Vicki L. Crawford, Jacqueline Anne Rouse, and Barbara Woods, 251–58. Brooklyn, NY: Carlson, 1990.

———. "Thelma Stevens: Crusader for Racial Justice." In *Spirituality and Social Responsibility: Vocational Vision of Women in the United Methodist Tradition*, edited by Rosemary Skinner Keller, 231–47. Nashville, TN: Abingdon Press, 1993.

Kobler, John. *Otto, the Magnificent: The Life of Otto Kahn*. New York: Scribner Book Co., 1988.

Korstad, Robert R. *Civil Rights Unionism: Tobacco Workers and the Struggle for Democracy in the Mid-Twentieth-Century South*. Chapel Hill: University of North Carolina Press, 2003.

Korstad, Robert R., and Nelson Lichtenstein. "Opportunities Found and Lost: Labor, Radicals, and the Early Civil Rights Movement." *Journal of American History* 75, no. 3 (Dec. 1, 1988): 786–811.

Kousser, J. Morgan. *The Shaping of Southern Politics: Suffrage Restriction and the Establishment of the One-Party South, 1880–1910*. New Haven, CT: Yale University Press, 1974.

Kovacik, Charles F., and John J. Winberry. *South Carolina: A Geography*. Boulder, CO: Westview Press, 1987.

Krochmal, Max. "An Unmistakably Working-Class Vision: Birmingham's Foot Soldiers and Their Civil Rights Movement." *Journal of Southern History* 76, no. 4 (2010): 923–60.

Kronenberger, Louis. "A Novel of the New South." *Nation*, Oct. 23, 1935.

Kruse, Kevin. *One Nation under God: How Corporate America Invented Christian America*. New York: Basic Books, 2015.

Kunitz, Stanley L., and Howard Haycraft, eds. *Twentieth Century Authors: A Biographical Dictionary of Modern Literature*. New York: H. W. Wilson, 1942.

Kutulas, Judy. *The Long War: The Intellectual People's Front and Anti-Stalinism, 1930–1940*. Durham, NC: Duke University Press, 1995.

Ladd-Taylor, Molly. *Mother-Work: Women, Child Welfare, and the State, 1890–1930*. Urbana: University of Illinois Press, 1994.

Lamb, Annadell Craig. *The History of Phi Mu: The First 130 Years*. Atlanta: Phi Mu Fraternity, 1982.

Lampman, Robert J., ed. *Economists at Wisconsin, 1892–1992*. Madison: University of Wisconsin System, 1993.

Landes, Joan B. "Marxism and the Woman Question." In *Promissory Notes: Women in the Transition to Socialism*, edited by Sonia Kruks, Rayna Rapp, and Marilyn B. Young, 15–28. New York: Monthly Review Press, 1989.

Langer, Elinor. *Josephine Herbst*. Boston: Little, Brown, 1984.

Larimore, Walt. *Hazel Creek*. New York: Howard, 2012.

Larkin, Margaret. "Ella May's Songs." *Nation*, Oct. 9, 1929.

———. *Singing Cowboy: A Book of Western Songs*. New York: Alfred A. Knopf, 1931.

Larkin, Oliver. *Art and Life in America*. Rev. ed. New York: Rinehart and Winston, 1960.

Lasch-Quinn, Elisabeth. *Black Neighbors: Race and the Limits of Reform in the Amer-*

ican Settlement House Movement, 1890–1945. Chapel Hill: University of North Carolina Press, 1993.

Laslett, Barbara. "Gender in/and Social Science History." *Social Science History* 16, no. 2 (Summer 1992): 177–95.

Laville, Helen. "'If the Time Is Not Ripe, Then It Is Your Job to Ripen the Time!': The Transformation of the YWCA in the USA from Segregated Association to Interracial Organization, 1930–1965." *Women's History Review* 15, no. 3 (July 2006): 359–83.

Lawson, John Howard. "In Dixieland We Take Our Stand." *New Masses*, May 29, 1934.

League of Professional Groups for Foster and Ford. *Culture and the Crisis: An Open Letter to the Writers, Artists, Teachers, Physicians, Engineers, Scientists and Other Professional Workers of America.* New York: Workers Library, 1932.

Lealtad, Catharine D. "The National Y.W.C.A. and the Negro." *Crisis* 19 (Apr. 1920): 317–18.

Lee, Hermione. "Alice Munro's Magic." *New York Review of Books*, Feb. 5, 2015.

Lee, Janet. *Comrades and Partners: The Shared Lives of Grace Hutchins and Anna Rochester.* Lanham, MD: Rowman and Littlefield, 2000.

Lee, Michael J., and Charlie Sharp. *Creating Conservatism: Postwar Words That Made an American Movement.* East Lansing: Michigan State University Press, 2014.

Leloudis, James L. *Schooling the New South: Pedagogy, Self, and Society in North Carolina, 1880–1920.* Chapel Hill: University of North Carolina Press, 1996.

Lentz-Smith, Adriane. *Freedom Struggles: African Americans and World War I.* Cambridge, MA: Harvard University Press, 2009.

Leonard, Louise. "A School in the Old South: Women Workers Study Industrial Problems." *Labor Age* 17, no. 12 (Dec. 1928): 22–23.

Lerner, Gerda. *Black Women in White America: A Documentary History.* New York: Pantheon Books, 1972.

———. *The Feminist Thought of Sarah Grimké.* New York: Oxford University Press, 1998.

———. *Fireweed: A Political Autobiography.* Philadelphia: Temple University Press, 2002.

———. *The Grimké Sisters from South Carolina: Pioneers for Women's Rights and Abolition.* Rev. ed. Chapel Hill: University of North Carolina Press, 2004.

———. *The Grimké Sisters from South Carolina: Rebels against Slavery.* Boston: Houghton Mifflin, 1967.

Leuchtenburg, William E. *Franklin D. Roosevelt and the New Deal, 1932–1940.* New York: Harper and Row, 1963.

Levenson, Leah, and Jerry Natterstad. *Granville Hicks: The Intellectual in Mass Society.* Philadelphia: Temple University Press, 1993.

Levine, Harold. "How a Vanderbilt Scion Became a Kremlin Tool." *Newsweek*, May 15, 1950.

Lewis, David Levering. *When Harlem Was in Vogue.* New York: Vintage Books, 1982.

Lewis, Eleanor Midman. "Mary Abby van Kleeck." In *Notable American Women: The Modern Period; A Biographical Dictionary*, edited by Barbara Sicherman and Carol Hurd Green, 707–9. Cambridge, MA: Harvard University Press, 1980.

Lewis, Oscar. *Five Families: Mexican Case Studies in the Culture of Poverty*. New York: Basic Books, 1959.

Lewontin, Richard C. "Women versus the Biologists: An Exchange." *New York Review of Books* 41, no. 13 (July 14, 1994).

Lichtenstein, Ada, et al. "An Experiment in Cooperation." *World Tomorrow*, May 15, 1926.

Lichtenstein, Alex. "The Cold War and the 'Negro Question.'" *Radical History Review* 72 (Fall 1998): 185–93.

Lieberman, Robbie. *"My Song Is My Weapon": People's Songs, American Communism, and the Politics of Culture, 1930–1950*. Urbana: University of Illinois Press, 1989.

———. *The Strangest Dream: Communism, Anticommunism, and the U.S. Peace Movement, 1945–1963*. New York: Syracuse University Press, 2000.

Lincove, David A. "Radical Publishing to 'Reach the Million Masses': Alexander L. Trachtenberg and International Publishers, 1906–1966." *Left History* 10, no. 1 (Fall/Winter 2004): 85–124.

Locke, Alain, ed. *Harlem: Mecca of the New Negro*. Baltimore: Black Classic Press, 1925.

———. ed. *The New Negro: An Interpretation*. New York: A. and C. Boni, 1925.

Logan, Rayford Wittingham. *What the Negro Wants*. Chapel Hill: University of North Carolina Press, 1944.

Luker, Ralph E. *The Social Gospel in Black and White: American Racial Reform, 1885–1912*. Chapel Hill: University of North Carolina Press, 1991.

Lumpkin, Ben Gray, and Martha Neville Lumpkin, comps. and eds. *The Lumpkin Family of Virginia, Georgia, and Mississippi*. Clarksville, TN: n.p., 1973.

[Lumpkin, Grace.] "A Letter from the South to Grace Lumpkin." *Woman Today*, Jan. 1937.

Lumpkin, Grace. "The Bridesmaids Carried Lilies." *North American Review*, Summer 1937.

———. "The Cotton Mill Rhyme (Letter to the Editor)." *New Masses*, June 1930.

———. "The Debutante." *Woman Today*, Feb. 1937.

———. "The Dory." *Signatures: Work in Progress* 1, no. 3 (Winter 1937–38): 255–59.

———. "Emancipation and Exploitation, review of Grace Hutchins, *Women Who Work*." *New Masses*, May 15, 1934.

———. "The Foreman and the Proofreader." *Guideposts*, Nov. 1950.

———. *Full Circle*. Boston: Western Islands, 1962.

———. "God Save the State!" *New Masses*, June 1926.

———. "How I Returned to the Christian Faith." *Christian Economics*, June 23, 1964.

———. "'I Want a King.'" *FIGHT against War and Fascism*, Feb. 1936.

———. "John Stevens." In *Proletarian Literature in the United States: An Anthology*, edited by Granville Hicks, 110–15. New York: International Publishers, 1935.

———. "The Law and the Spirit." *National Review*, May 25, 1957.

———. "Mansion and Mill." *New Masses*, May 28, 1935.

———. "Mayme Brown, Editor." *Woman Today*, June 1936.

———. "A Miserable Offender." *Virginia Quarterly Review*, Apr. 1935.

———. "The Novel as Propaganda." *MS.: A Magazine for Writers*, Mar. 1934.

———. "The Pearl Necklace." *Woman Today*, Apr. 1936.

————. "Remember These Needy." *Social Work Today*, Jan. 1937.

————. *A Sign for Cain*. New York: Lee Furman, 1935.

————. "A Southern Cotton Mill Rhyme." *New Masses*, May 1930.

————. "Southern Women Salute Herndon!" *Southern Worker*, May 1937.

————. "To Make My Bread." *Working Woman*, Dec. 1933; Jan. 1934; Feb. 1934.

————. *To Make My Bread*. Edited by Suzanne Sowinska. Urbana: University of Illinois Press, 1995. First published 1932 by Macaulay (New York).

————. "The Treasure." In *O. Henry Memorial Award: Prize Stories of 1940*, edited by Harry Hansen, 167–77. New York: Doubleday, Doran, 1940.

————. "The Treasure." *Southern Review* 5, no. 4 (1939–1940): 677–83.

————. "Trial by Fire." *Partisan Review*, Nov. 1935.

————. *The Wedding*. New York: Popular Library, 1977. First published 1939 by Lee Furman (New York) and reprinted 1976 by Southern Illinois University Press (Carbondale). Page references are to the 1977 edition unless otherwise noted.

————. "White Man—A Story." *New Masses*, Sept. 1927.

————. "Will You Let Us Speak, O Men of America: The Story of May Day's Traditions." *Labor Defender* 11, no. 5 (May 1935).

Lumpkin, Grace, and Clara A. Kaiser. "Learning to Make History." *Social Work Today*, May 1938.

Lumpkin, Grace, and Esther Shemitz. "The Artist in a Hostile Environment." *World Tomorrow*, Apr. 1926.

Lumpkin, Henry. "The Lady and the Moose." *Sandlapper*, Dec. 1973.

Lumpkin, Katharine Du Pre. "Acorns in the Storm." *Social Work Today*, Oct. 1934.

————. "The Child Labor Provisions of the Fair Labor Standards Act." *Law and Contemporary Problems* 6, no. 3 (Summer 1939): 391–405.

————. "The Council of Industrial Studies." *Smith Alumnae Quarterly* (Nov. 1937): 31–32.

————. "Democratic Ways in the USSR." *Soviet Russia Today*, Apr. 1937.

————. *The Emancipation of Angelina Grimké*. Chapel Hill: University of North Carolina Press, 1974.

————. "Factors in the Commitment of Correctional School Girls in Wisconsin." *American Journal of Sociology* 37, no. 2 (Sept. 1931): 222–30.

————. *The Family: A Study of Member Roles*. Chapel Hill: University of North Carolina Press, 1933.

————. *The Making of a Southerner*. With a foreword by Darlene Clark Hine. Athens: University of Georgia Press, 1991. First published 1946 by Alfred A. Knopf (New York).

————. "Parental Conditions of Wisconsin Girl Delinquents." *American Journal of Sociology* 38, no. 2 (Sept. 1932): 232–39.

————. Review of *Child Labor Legislation in the Southern Textiles States*, by Elizabeth H. Davidson. *Science & Society* 3 (Fall 1939): 553.

————. Review of *The Family: Past and Present*, by Bernard J. Stern. *Science & Society* 2, no. 3 (Summer 1938): 404–6.

————. "Social Change and the Southern Mind." In *Women and the Civil Rights*

Movement, 1954–1965, edited by Davis W. Houck and David E. Dixon, 50–60. Jackson: University Press of Mississippi, 2009.

———. *The South in Progress.* New York: International, 1940.

Lumpkin, Katharine Du Pre, and Mable Van Able Combs. *Shutdowns in the Connecticut Valley: A Study of Worker Displacement in the Small Industrial Community.* Vols. 3–4. Smith College Studies in History 19. Northampton, MA: Department of History, Smith College, 1934.

Lumpkin, Katharine Du Pre, and Dorothy W. Douglas. *Child Workers in America.* New York: Robert McBride and Company, 1937.

Lumpkin, Katharine Du Pre, and Dorothy Wolff Douglas. "The Effect of Unemployment and Short-Time during 1931 in the Families of 200 Alabama Child Workers." *Social Forces* 11, no. 4 (May 1933): 548–59.

Lunbeck, Elizabeth. "'A New Generation of Women': Progressive Psychiatrists and the Hypersexual Female." *Feminist Studies* 13, no. 3 (Autumn 1987): 513–43.

Lutz, Christine. "Addie W. Hunton: Crusader for Pan-Africanism and Peace." In *Portraits of African American Life Since 1865*, edited by Nina Mjagkij, 109–27. Wilmington, DE: Scholarly Resources, 2003.

Lynn, Susan. *Progressive Women in Conservative Times: Racial Justice, Peace, and Feminism, 1945 to the 1960s.* New Brunswick, NJ: Rutgers University Press, 1992.

Mack, Kenneth W. "Law and Mass Politics in the Making of the Civil Rights Lawyer, 1931–1941." *Journal of American History* 93, no. 1 (June 2006): 37–62.

Maclachlan, Gretchen E. "Addie Waits Hunton (1866–1943)." In *Black Women in America: An Historical Encyclopedia*, edited by Darlene Clark Hine, 596–97. Brooklyn, NY: Carlson, 1993.

MacLean, Nancy. *Democracy in Chains: The Deep History of the Radical Right's Stealth Plan for America.* New York: Viking, 2017.

———. "Getting New Deal History Wrong." *International Labor and Working-Class History* 74, no. 1 (Fall 2008): 49–55.

———. "Neo-Confederacy versus the New Deal: The Regional Utopia of the Modern American Right." In *The Myth of Southern Exceptionalism*, edited by Matthew D. Lassiter and Joseph Crespino, 308–29. Oxford: Oxford University Press, 2010.

Magil, A. B. "To Make My Bread." *New Masses*, Feb. 1933.

Malcolm, Janet. *The Silent Woman: Sylvia Plath & Ted Hughes.* New York: Alfred A. Knopf, 1994.

Mantooth, Wes. *"You Factory Folks Who Sing This Rhyme Will Surely Understand": Culture, Ideology, and Action in the Gastonia Novels of Myra Page, Grace Lumpkin, and Olive Dargan.* New York: Routledge, 2006.

Marcus, David. "The Power Historian: What Was Arthur Schlesinger's 'Vital Center'?" *Nation*, Oct. 30, 2017.

Martin, Charles H. "The International Labor Defense and Black America." *Labor History* 26, no. 2 (Spring 1985): 165–94.

Martin, Robert F. *Howard Kester and the Struggle for Social Justice in the South, 1904–1977.* Charlottesville: University Press of Virginia, 1991.

Mason, Mary G. "The Other Voice: Autobiographies of Women Writers." In *Women, Autobiography, Theory: A Reader*, edited by Sidonie Smith and Julia Watson, 321–24. Madison: University of Wisconsin Press, 1998.

Matsuda, Mari J. "Voices of America: Accent, Antidiscrimination Law, and a Jurisprudence for the Last Reconstruction." *Yale Law Journal* 100, no. 5 (Mar. 1991): 1329–1407.

Matthews, Ellen Nathalie. Review of *Child Workers in America*, by Katharine DuPre Lumpkin and Dorothy Wolff Douglas. *Social Service Review* 11, no. 3 (1937): 529–31.

Matthews, Pamela R. Introduction to *The Woman Within: An Autobiography*, by Ellen Glasgow, vii–xxxi. Charlottesville: University Press of Virginia, 1994.

Mauldin, Joanne Marshall. "The Doctor and His Wife: Might There Have Been a Kinder, Gentler Wolfe?" *Thomas Wolfe Review* 34, no. 1–2 (2010): 35–53.

Maxwell, William J. *New Negro, Old Left: African-American Writing and Communism between the Wars*. New York: Columbia University Press, 1999.

———. "The Proletarian as New Negro: Mike Gold's Harlem Renaissance." In *Radical Revisions: Rereading 1930s Culture*, edited by Bill Mullen and Sherry Lee Linkon, 91–119. Urbana: University of Illinois Press, 1996.

May, Elaine Tyler. *Homeward Bound: American Families in the Cold War Era*. Fully rev. and updated 20th anniversary ed. with a new post 9/11 epilogue. New York: Basic Books, 2008.

Mayo, A. D. *Southern Women in the Recent Educational Movement in the South*. Edited by Dan T. Carter and Amy Friedlander. Baton Rouge: Louisiana State University Press, 1978.

Maza, Sarah. "Stories in History: Cultural Narratives in Recent Works in European History." *American Historical Review* 101, no. 5 (Dec. 1996): 1493–1515.

Mazzari, Louis. *Southern Modernist: Arthur Raper from the New Deal to the Cold War*. Baton Rouge: Louisiana State University Press, 2006.

McCallum, Brenda. "Songs of Work and Songs of Worship: Sanctifying Black Unionism in the Southern City of Steel." *New York Folklore* 14, no. 1–2 (1988): 9–33.

McCandless, Amy. *The Past in the Present: Women's Higher Education in the Twentieth-Century American South*. Tuscaloosa: University of Alabama Press, 1999.

McCarthy, Charles. *The Wisconsin Idea*. New York: Macmillan, 1912.

McCarthy, Timothy Patrick, and John Stauffer, eds. *Prophets of Protest: Reconsidering the History of American Abolitionism*. New York: New Press, 2006.

McCaughey, Robert. *Stand, Columbia: A History of Columbia University in the City of New York, 1754–2004*. New York: Columbia University Press, 2003.

McDonald, Kathlene. *Feminism, the Left, and Postwar Literary Culture*. Jackson: University Press of Mississippi, 2012.

McDowell, Deborah E. "In the First Place: Making Frederick Douglass and the African-American Narrative Tradition." In *Critical Essays on Frederick Douglass*, edited by William Andrews, 192–214. Boston: G. K. Hall, 1991.

McDowell, John Patrick. *The Social Gospel in the South: The Woman's Home Mission Movement in the Methodist Episcopal Church, South, 1886–1939*. Baton Rouge: Louisiana State University Press, 1982.

McDuffie, Erik S. "The March of Young Southern Black Women: Esther Cooper Jackson, Black Left Feminism, and the Personal and Political Costs of Cold War Repression." In *Anticommunism and the African American Freedom Movement: "Another Side of the Story,"* edited by Robbie Lieberman and Clarence Lang, 81–114. New York: Palgrave Macmillan, 2009.

———. *Sojourning for Freedom: Black Women, American Communism, and the Making of Black Left Feminism.* Durham, NC: Duke University Press, 2011.

McKay, Claude. *A Long Way from Home.* Edited and with a new introduction by Gene Andrew Jarrett. New Brunswick, NJ: Rutgers University Press, 2007.

McKay, Nellie Y. "The Narrative Self: Race, Politics and Culture in Black American Women's Autobiography." In *Women, Autobiography, Theory: A Reader,* edited by Sidonie Smith and Julia Watson, 96–107. Madison: University of Wisconsin Press, 1998.

McKelvey, Blake. "Constance McLaughlin Green." In *Notable American Women: A Biographical Dictionary Completing the Twentieth Century,* edited by Susan Ware, 291–92. Cambridge, MA: Belknap Press of Harvard University Press, 2004.

McMaster, Elizabeth Waring. *The Girls of the Sixties.* Columbia, SC: The State, 1937.

McPherson, Tara. *Reconstructing Dixie: Race, Gender, and Nostalgia in the Imagined South.* Durham, NC: Duke University Press, 2003.

McWilliams, Carey. *Factories in the Field: The Story of Migratory Farm Labor in California.* Boston: Little, Brown, 1939.

Meade, Guthrie T., Jr., Richard K. Spottswood, and Douglas S. Meade. *Country Music Sources: A Biblio-Discography of Commercially Recorded Traditional Music.* Chapel Hill: University of North Carolina Press, 2002.

Melamed, Jodi. "Racial Capitalism." *Critical Ethnic Studies* 1, no. 1 (2015): 76–85.

Mencken, H. L. "The Sahara of the Bozart." In *Prejudices: Second Series,* by H. L. Mencken, 136–54. New York: Alfred A. Knopf, 1920.

Meyer, D. H. "American Intellectuals and the Victorian Crisis of Faith." *American Quarterly* 27, no. 5 (Dec. 1975): 585–603.

Meyerowitz, Joanne J. *Women Adrift: Independent Wage Earners in Chicago, 1880–1930.* Chicago: University of Chicago Press, 1988.

Mickenberg, Julia, L. "Suffragists and Soviets: American Feminists and the Specter of Revolutionary Russia." *Journal of American History* 100, no. 4 (Mar. 2014): 1021–51.

Miles, Isadore William. "Another Year of Negro Literature." *Journal of the National Association of College Women* 13 (1936): 44–48.

Miller, James A. *Remembering Scottsboro: The Legacy of an Infamous Trial.* Princeton, NJ: Princeton University Press, 2009.

Mills, C. Wright. *The Sociological Imagination.* New York: Oxford University Press, 1959.

Mink, Gwendolyn. *The Wages of Motherhood: Inequality in the Welfare State, 1917–1942.* Ithaca, NY: Cornell University Press, 1995.

Mjagkij, Nina, and Margaret Spratt. *Men and Women Adrift: The YMCA and the YWCA in the City.* New York: New York University Press, 1997.

Montgomery, Rebecca S. "Lost Cause Mythology in New South Reform: Gender, Class, Race, and the Politics of Patriotic Citizenship in Georgia, 1890–1925." In *Negotiating Boundaries of Southern Womanhood: Dealing with the Powers That Be*, edited by Janet L. Coryell, Thomas H. Appleton Jr., Anastatia Sims, and Sandra Gioia Treadway, 158–73. Columbia: University of Missouri Press, 2000.

———. *The Politics of Education in the New South*. Baton Rouge: Louisiana State University Press, 2005.

Moore, John Hammond. *Columbia and Richland County: A South Carolina Community, 1740–1990*. Columbia: University of South Carolina Press, 1993.

Morgan, Ted. *A Covert Life, Jay Lovestone: Communist, Anti-Communist, and Spymaster*. New York: Random House, 1999.

Morrow, Mrs. Dwight Whitney. "President Neilson of Smith." *Atlantic Monthly*, Nov. 1946.

Moseley-Edington, Helen. "Miss Adela Ruffin." In *Angels Unaware: Asheville Women of Color*, by Helen Moseley-Edington, 93. Asheville, NC: Home Press, 1996.

Mott, John Raleigh. *The Evangelization of the World in This Generation*. New York: Student Volunteer Movement for Foreign Missions, 1900.

Mullen, Bill. "Proletarian Literature Reconsidered." *Oxford Research Encyclopedias*. Oxford: Oxford University Press, June 2017. http://literature.oxfordre.com/view/10.1093/acrefore/9780190201098.001.0001/acrefore-9780190201098-e-236.

Muncy, Robyn. *Creating a Female Dominion in American Reform, 1890–1935*. New York: Oxford University Press, 1991.

———. "Women, Gender, and Politics in the New Deal Government: Josephine Roche and the Federal Security Agency." *Journal of Women's History* 21, no. 3 (Fall 2009): 60–83, 204.

Murphy, Marjorie. *Blackboard Unions: The AFT and the NEA, 1900–1980*. Ithaca, NY: Cornell University Press, 1990.

Murphy, Paul V. *The Rebuke of History: The Southern Agrarians and American Conservative Thought*. Chapel Hill: University of North Carolina Press, 2001.

Musmanno, Michael A. "Was Sacco Guilty?" *New Republic*, Mar. 2, 1963.

Myrdal, Gunnar. *An American Dilemma: The Negro Problem and Modern Democracy*. 2 vols. New York: Harper and Row, 1962. First published 1944 by Harper and Brothers (New York).

Naison, Mark. *Communists in Harlem during the Depression*. Urbana: University of Illinois Press, 1983.

Nasstrom, Kathryn L. "Between Memory and History: Autobiographies of the Civil Rights Movement and the Writing of Civil Rights History." *Journal of Southern History* 74, no. 2 (2008): 325–64.

National Cyclopedia of American Biography. Vol. 35. New York: James T. White, 1949.

Neff, David Pembroke, and the *Dictionary of Virginia Biography*. "Robert B. Crawford (1895–1973)." *Encyclopedia Virginia*. Virginia Foundation for the Humanities, Jan. 24, 2014. https://www.encyclopediavirginia.org/Crawford_Robert_Baxter_1895–1973.

Neilson, William Allan. *Intellectual Honesty, and Other Addresses, Being Mainly Chapel Talks at Smith College*. Litchfield, CT: Prospect, 1940.

Nekola, Charlotte, and Paula Rabinowitz, eds. *Writing Red: An Anthology of American Women Writers, 1930–1940*. New York: Feminist, 1987.

Nelson, Cary. *Repression and Recovery: Modern American Poetry and the Politics of Cultural Memory, 1910–1945*. Madison: University of Wisconsin Press, 1989.

Newfield, Jack. *A Prophetic Minority*. New York: New American Library, 1970.

Newman, Louise. *White Women's Rights: The Racial Origins of Feminism in the United States*. New York: Oxford University Press, 1999.

Nicolson, Marjorie Hope. "Neilson of Smith." *American Scholar* 15, no. 4 (Autumn 1946): 539–49.

Niebuhr, Reinhold. "Glimpses of the Southland." *Christian Century Magazine*, July 16, 1930.

Nietzsche, Friedrich. *On the Advantage and Disadvantage of History for Life*. Indianapolis: Hackett, 1980.

Nissenbaum, Stephen. "New England as Region and Nation." In *All Over the Map: Rethinking American Regions*, edited by Edward Ayers, Patricia Nelson Limerick, Stephen Nissenbaum, and Peter S. Onuf, 38–61. Baltimore: Johns Hopkins University Press, 1996.

Nora, Pierre. "Between Memory and History: Les Lieux de Mémoire." *Memory and Counter-Memory. Special Issue of Representations* 26 (Spring 1989): 7–24.

Norton-Taylor, Duncan. "Businessmen on Their Knees." *Fortune*, Oct. 1953.

Novick, Peter. *That Noble Dream: The "Objectivity Question" and the American Historical Profession*. Cambridge: Cambridge University Press, 1988.

Nyland, Chris, and Mark Rix. "Mary van Kleeck, Lillian Gilbreth and the Women's Bureau Study of Gendered Labor Law." *Journal of Management History* 6, no. 7 (2000): 306–22.

O'Brien, Michael. "A Heterodox Note of the Southern Renaissance." In *Rethinking the South: Essays in Intellectual History*, by Michael O'Brien, 157–78. Baltimore: Johns Hopkins University Press, 1988.

———. *The Idea of the American South, 1920–1941*. Baltimore: Johns Hopkins University Press, 1979.

O'Dell, Darlene. *Sites of Southern Memory: The Autobiographies of Katharine Du Pre Lumpkin, Lillian Smith, and Pauli Murray*. Charlottesville: University Press of Virginia, 2001.

Odem, Mary E., and Steven L. Schlossman. "Guardians of Virtue: The Juvenile Court and Female Delinquency in Early 20th-Century Los Angeles." *Journal of Research in Crime and Delinquency* 37, no. 2 (Apr. 1, 1991): 186–203.

Ogden, Mary Macdonald. *Wil Lou Gray: The Making of a Southern Progressive from New South to New Deal*. Columbia: University of South Carolina Press, 2016.

Oksala, Johanna. "Affective Labor and Feminist Politics." *Signs: Journal of Women in Culture and Society* 41, no. 2 (2016): 281–303.

Olcott, Jane. *The Work of Colored Women*. New York: Colored Work Committee, War Work Council, National Board, Young Women's Christian Association, 1919.

Olcott, Jocelyn. "Miracle Workers: Gender and State Mediation among Textile and Garment Workers in Mexico's Transition to Industrial Development." *International Labor and Working-Class History* 63 (Spring 2003): 45–62.

———. *Revolutionary Women in Postrevolutionary Mexico.* Durham, NC: Duke University Press, 2005.

Oldenziel, Ruth. "Gender and Scientific Management: Women and the History of the International Institute for Industrial Relations, 1922–1946." *Journal of Management History* 6, no. 7 (2000): 323–42.

Oliver, Beulah Rucker. *The Rugged Pathway.* N.p., 1953.

Oliver, Duane. *Hazel Creek from Then till Now.* Hazelwood, NC: Duane Oliver, 1989.

Olmsted, Frederick Law. *A Journey in the Seaboard Slave States, with Remarks on Their Economy.* New York: Dix and Edward, 1856.

Olney, James. "Autobiographical Traditions in Black and White." In *Located Lives: Places and Idea in Southern Autobiography,* edited by J. Bill Berry, 66–77. Athens: University of Georgia Press, 1990.

Olsson, Tore C. "Sharecroppers and *Campesinos*: The American South, Mexico, and the Transnational Politics of Land Reform in the Radical 1930s." *Journal of Southern History* 81, no. 13 (Aug. 2015): 607–46.

Oppenheimer, Daniel. *Exit Right: The People Who Left the Left and Reshaped the American Century.* New York: Simon and Schuster, 2016.

Orleck, Annelise. "'We Are That Mythical Thing Called the Public': Militant Housewives during the Great Depression." *Feminist Studies* 19, no. 1 (Spring 1993): 147–72.

Orwell, George. *Coming Up for Air.* New York: Harcourt Brace, 1950.

Osterweis, Rollin G. *The Myth of the Lost Cause, 1865–1900.* Hamden, CT: Archon Books, 1973.

Page, Myra. "Cárdenas Speaks for Mexico: An Interview with Mexico's Progressive Leader." *New Masses,* Aug. 30, 1938.

———. *Gathering Storm: A Story of the Black Belt.* New York: International, 1932.

———. *Moscow Yankee.* Urbana: University of Illinois Press, 1995. First published 1935 by G. P. Putnam's Sons (New York).

———. Review of *The Making of a Southerner,* by Katharine Du Pre Lumpkin, and *The Way of the South,* by Howard Odum." *Science and Society* 12, no. 2 (Spring 1948): 276–78.

———. *Southern Cotton Mills and Labor.* New York: Workers Library, 1929.

Page, Walter Hines. *The Southerner, a Novel: Being the Auto-Biography of Nicholas Worth.* New York: Doubleday, Page, 1909.

Palmieri, Patricia Ann. *In Adamless Eden: The Community of Women Faculty at Wellesley.* New Haven, CT: Yale University Press, 1995.

Parker, Grace. "Woman Power of the Nation." *Independent,* Feb. 19, 1917.

Parkinson, B. L. *A History of the Administration of the City Public Schools of Columbia, South Carolina.* Columbia: University of South Carolina, Extension Division, 1925.

Patterson, Isabel Garrard, comp. *History of Phi Mu Fraternity (1852–1927).* Edited by Louise Monning Elliott. Columbus, GA: Standard Printing, 1927.

Patterson, James T. "A Conservative Coalition Forms in Congress, 1933–1939." *Journal of American History* 52, no. 4 (Mar. 1966): 757–72.

Pearce, Haywood J. *Philosophical Meditations: Talks to College Girls.* Boston: Stratford, 1917.

Pease, Jane H. Review of *The Emancipation of Angelina Grimké*, by Katharine Du Pre Lumpkin. *Journal of Southern History* 41, no. 2 (May 1, 1975): 259–60.

Pease, William H. Review of *The Emancipation of Angelina Grimké*, by Katharine Du Pre Lumpkin. *Journal of American History* 62, no. 4 (Mar. 1, 1976): 992–93.

Percy, William Alexander. *Lanterns on the Levee: Recollections of a Planter's Son*. New York: Alfred A. Knopf, 1941.

Perkins, Linda M. "The National Association of College Women: Vanguard of Black Women's Leadership in Education, 1923–1954." *Journal of Education* 172, no. 3 (1990): 66–75.

Perlstein, Rick. *Before the Storm: Barry Goldwater and the Unmaking of the American Consensus*. New York: Hill and Wang, 2001.

Perry, Lewis. Review of *The Emancipation of Angelina Grimké*, by Katharine Du Pre Lumpkin. *Civil War History* 21, no. 2 (1975): 175–76.

Persky, Joseph J. *The Burden of Dependency: Colonial Themes in Southern Economic Thought*. Baltimore: Johns Hopkins University Press, 1992.

Phifer, Mary Hardy. *Kirkman George Finlay, 1877–1938, Bishop of Upper South Carolina, 1922–1938*. Chicago: Manz, 1949.

Philbrick, Herbert A. *I Led 3 Lives: Citizen, "Communist," Counterspy*. 2nd ed. Washington, DC: Capitol Hill Press, 1972.

Phillips, Jerry. "Slave Narratives." In *A Companion to the Literature and Culture of the American South*, edited by Richard J. Gray and Owen Robinson, 43–56. Malden, MA: Blackwell, 2004.

Phillips-Matz, Mary Jane. *The Many Lives of Otto Kahn*. New York: Macmillan, 1963.

Pierce, Daniel S. *The Life and Death of an Iconic Mountain Community*. Gatlinburg, TN: Great Smoky Mountains Association, 2017.

Pinchbeck, Ivy. *Women Workers and the Industrial Revolution: 1750–1850*. With a new introduction by Kerry Hamilton. 3rd ed. London: Virago Press, 1981. First published 1930 by Frank Cass (New York).

Plant, Deborah G. *Zora Neale Hurston: A Biography of the Spirit*. Westport, CT: Praeger, 2007.

Pollard, Lucille A. *Women on College and University Faculties: A Historical Survey and a Study of Their Present Academic Status*. New York: Arno Press, 1977.

Polsgrove, Carol. *Divided Minds: Intellectuals and the Civil Rights Movement*. New York: W. W. Norton, 2001.

Poole, Mary. *The Segregated Origins of Social Security: African Americans and the Welfare State*. Chapel Hill: University of North Carolina Press, 2006.

Porter, Katherine. *The Never-Ending Wrong*. Boston: Little, Brown, 1977.

Prenshaw, Peggy Whitman. *Composing Selves: Southern Women and Autobiography*. Baton Rouge: Louisiana State University Press, 2011.

Preston, William, Jr. *Aliens and Dissenters: Federal Suppression of Radicals, 1903–1933*. Cambridge, MA: Harvard University Press, 1963.

Printz, Jessica Kimball. "Tracing the Fault Lines of the Radical Female Subject: Grace Lumpkin's *The Wedding*." In *Radical Revisions: Rereading 1930s Culture*, edited by Bill Mullen and Sherry Lee Linkon, 167–86. Urbana: University of Illinois Press, 1996.

Pritchett, Wendell. *Brownsville, Brooklyn: Blacks, Jews, and the Changing Face of the Ghetto*. Chicago: University of Chicago Press, 2002.

Rabinowitz, Howard. *The First New South, 1865–1920*. Arlington Heights, IL: Harlan Davidson, 1992.

Rabinowitz, Paula. *Labor and Desire: Women's Revolutionary Fiction in Depression America*. Chapel Hill: University of North Carolina Press, 1991.

Rable, George C. *Civil Wars: Women and the Crisis of Southern Nationalism*. Urbana: University of Illinois Press, 1989.

Ragsdale, B. G. *Story of Georgia Baptists*. Vol. 1. Atlanta: Foote and Davies, 1932.

Rampersad, Arnold. *The Life of Langston Hughes, 1902–1941: I, Too, Sing America*. New York: Oxford University Press, 1986.

Ransby, Barbara. *Ella Baker and the Black Freedom Movement: A Radical Democratic Vision*. Chapel Hill: University of North Carolina Press, 2005.

———. *Eslanda: The Large and Unconventional Life of Mrs. Paul Robeson*. New Haven, CT: Yale University Press, 2013.

Ransdall, Hollace. *Report on the Scottsboro, Alabama, Case*. New York: American Civil Liberties Union, 1931. http://www.famous-trials.com/scottsboroboys/2344-firsttrial-2.

Raper, Arthur Franklin. *The Plight of Tuscaloosa*. Atlanta: Southern Commission on the Study of Lynching, 1933.

———. *Preface to Peasantry: A Tale of Two Black Belt Counties*. Chapel Hill: University of North Carolina Press, 1936.

———. *The Tragedy of Lynching*. Chapel Hill: University of North Carolina Press, 1933.

Raper, Arthur Franklin, and Ira De Augustine Reid. *Sharecroppers All*. Chapel Hill: University of North Carolina Press, 1941.

———. *Tenants of the Almighty*. New York: Macmillan, 1943.

Rasmussen, Mary Ann. Introduction to *Pity Is Not Enough*, by Josephine Herbst, x–xxxix. Urbana: University of Illinois Press, 1998.

Reed, Ruth. *The Negro Women of Gainesville, Georgia*. Bulletin of the University of Georgia. Vol. 22, no. 1; Phelps-Stokes Fellowship Studies, no. 6. Gainesville: [University of Georgia], 1921.

Reidy, Joseph P. *From Slavery to Agrarian Capitalism in the Cotton Plantation South: Central Georgia, 1800–1880*. Chapel Hill: University of North Carolina Press, 1992.

Reinharz, Shulamit. "Finding a Sociological Voice: The Work of Mirra Komarovsky." *Sociological Inquiry* 59, no. 4 (Fall 1989): 374–95.

Renda, Mary. *Taking Haiti: Military Occupation and the Culture of U.S. Imperialism, 1915–1940*. Chapel Hill: University of North Carolina Press, 2001.

Reuss, Richard, and JoAnne C. Reuss. *American Folk Music and Left-Wing Politics, 1927–1957*. Lanham, MD: Scarecrow Press, 2000.

Rice, Thaddeus Brockett, and Carolyn White Williams. *History of Greene County, Georgia, 1786–1886*. Macon, GA: J. W. Burke, 1961.

Rich, Adrienne. *Compulsory Heterosexuality and Lesbian Existence*. London: Onlywomen Press, 1981.

Ritterhouse, Jennifer Lynn. *Discovering the South: One Man's Travels through a Changing America in the 1930s*. Chapel Hill: University of North Carolina Press, 2017.

———. *Growing Up Jim Crow: How Black and White Southern Children Learned Race*. Chapel Hill: University of North Carolina Press, 2006.

Roberts, Bruce, and Nancy Roberts. *Where Time Stood Still: A Portrait of Appalachia*. New York: Crowell-Collier, 1970.

Roberts, Elizabeth Madox. *The Time of Man*. New York: Viking, 1926.

Robertson, Ben. *Red Hills and Cotton: An Upcountry Memory*. New York: Alfred A. Knopf, 1942.

Robertson, Nancy Marie. *Christian Sisterhood, Race Relations, and the YWCA, 1906–1946*. Urbana: University of Illinois Press, 2007.

Robinson, James. *The New History: Essays Illustrating the Modern Historical Outlook*. New York: Macmillan, 1912.

Rochester, Anna. "Communism: A World Movement." *World Tomorrow*, Jan. 1930.

Rodgers, Daniel. *Atlantic Crossings: Social Politics in a Progressive Age*. Cambridge, MA: Belknap Press of Harvard University Press, 1998.

Rogin, Michael P. "'The Sword Became a Flashing Vision': D. W. Griffith's *The Birth of a Nation*." *Representations*, no. 9 (Winter 1985): 150–95.

Roll, Jared. *Spirit of Rebellion: Labor and Religion in the New Cotton South*. Chicago: University of Chicago Press, 2010.

Rose, Willie Lee. "Off the Plantation." *New York Review of Books*, Sept. 18, 1975.

Rosenberg, Rosalind. *Beyond Separate Spheres: The Intellectual Roots of Modern Feminism*. New Haven, CT: Yale University Press, 1982.

———. *Changing the Subject: How the Women of Columbia Shaped the Way We Think about Sex and Politics*. New York: Columbia University Press, 2004.

Rosenfelt, Deborah. "From the Thirties: Tillie Olsen and the Radical Tradition." *Feminist Studies* 7, no. 3 (Autumn 1981): 371–406.

Rosenzweig, Linda. *Another Self: Middle-Class American Women and Their Friends in the Twentieth Century*. New York: New York University Press, 1999.

Roses, Lorraine Elena, and Ruth Elizabeth Randolph. *Harlem's Glory: Black Women Writing, 1900–1950*. Cambridge, MA: Harvard University Press, 1996.

Ross, Aileen D. Review of *The Emancipation of Angelina Grimké*, by Katharine Du Pre Lumpkin. *Annals of the American Academy of Political and Social Science* 423 (Jan. 1, 1976): 187–88.

Ross, B. Joyce. "Mary McLeod Bethune and the National Youth Administration: A Case Study of Power Relationships in the Black Cabinet of Franklin D. Roosevelt." In *Black Leaders of the Twentieth Century*, edited by John Hope Franklin and August Meier, 191–219. Urbana: University of Illinois Press, 1982.

Ross, Dorothy. *The Origins of American Social Science*. Cambridge: Cambridge University Press, 1991.

Ross, Edward Alsworth. *Seventy Years of It: An Autobiography of Edward Alsworth Ross*. New York: D. Appleton-Century, 1936.

Rossinow, Douglas C. "'The Break-Through to New Life': Christianity and the Emergence of the New Left in Austin, Texas, 1956–1964." *American Quarterly* 46, no. 3 (Sept. 1994): 309–40.

————. *The Politics of Authenticity: Liberalism, Christianity, and the New Left in America*. New York: Columbia University Press, 1998.

————. *Visions of Progress: The Left-Liberal Tradition in America*. Philadelphia: University of Pennsylvania Press, 2008.

Rossiter, Margaret. *Women Scientists in America: Struggles and Strategies to 1940*. Baltimore: Johns Hopkins University Press, 1982.

Rourke, Constance. "The Significance of Sections." *New Republic*, Sept. 20, 1933.

Rubin, Joan Shelley. *Constance Rourke and American Culture*. Chapel Hill: University of North Carolina Press, 2001.

Rubin, Louis D., Jr. "Trouble on the Land: Southern Literature and the Great Depression." In *Literature at the Barricades: The American Writer in the 1930s*, edited by Ralph F. Bogardus and Fred Hobson, 96–113. Tuscaloosa: University of Alabama Press, 1982.

Ruffin, Adela F. "In the Southern Colleges." *Southern Workman*, Sept. 1920.

Russell, Francis. *Tragedy in Dedham: The Story of the Sacco-Vanzetti Case*. New York: McGraw-Hill, 1962.

Sack, Daniel. *Moral Re-Armament: The Reinventions of an American Religious Movement*. New York: Palgrave Macmillan, 2009.

————. "Reaching the 'Up-and-Outers': Sam Shoemaker and Modern Evangelicalism." *Anglican and Episcopal History* 61, no. 1 (1995): 37–57.

Sahli, Nancy. "Smashing: Women's Relationships before the Fall." *Chrysalis* 8 (Summer 1979): 17–27.

Salmond, John. *Gastonia, 1929: The Story of the Loray Mill Strike*. Chapel Hill: University of North Carolina Press, 1995.

Salomon, Louis B. "South Carolina Town." *Nation*, Mar. 11, 1939.

Salwen, Peter. *Upper West Side Story: A History and Guide*. New York: Abbeville Press, 1989.

Sargent, Lydia, ed. *Women and Revolution: A Discussion of the Unhappy Marriage of Marxism and Feminism*. Boston: South End, 1981.

Saunders, Frances Stonor. *The Cultural Cold War: The CIA and the World of Arts and Letters*. New York: New Press, 2000.

Scanlon, Jennifer. *Until There Is Justice: The Life of Anna Arnold Hedgeman*. New York: Oxford University Press, 2016.

Schachner, E. A. "Revolutionary Literature in the United States Today." *Windsor Quarterly Journal* 2 (1934): 27–64.

Schlossman, Steven L., and Stephanie Wallach. "The Crime of Precocious Sexuality: Female Juvenile Delinquency in the Progressive Era." *Harvard Educational Review* 48, no. 1 (1978): 65–94.

Schneider, Carl J., and Dorothy Schneider. *Into the Breach: American Women Overseas in World War I*. New York: Viking, 1991.

Schneider, David. *The Workers' (Communist) Party and American Trade Unions*. Vol. 2. Johns Hopkins University Studies in Historical and Political Science 46. Baltimore: Johns Hopkins Press, 1928.

Schneider, Florence Hemley. *Patterns of Workers' Education: The Story of the Bryn Mawr Summer School*. Washington, DC: American Council on Public Affairs, 1941.

Schoen, Johanna. *Choice and Coercion: Birth Control, Sterilization, and Abortion in Public Health and Welfare*. Chapel Hill: University of North Carolina Press, 2005.

Schoenfeld, Joachim. *Jewish Life in Galicia under the Austro-Hungarian Empire and in the Reborn Poland, 1898–1939*. Hoboken, NJ: Ktav Pub. House, 1985.

Schrecker, Ellen W. *The Age of McCarthyism: A Brief History with Documents*. Boston: Bedford/St. Martin's, 1994.

———. *Many Are the Crimes: McCarthyism in America*. Boston: Little, Brown, 1998.

———. *No Ivory Tower: McCarthyism and the Universities*. New York: Oxford University Press, 1986.

———. "Soviet Espionage in America: An Oft-Told Tale." *Reviews in American History* 38, no. 2 (June 2010): 355–61.

Schulman, Bruce J. *From Cotton Belt to Sunbelt: Federal Policy, Economic Development, and the Transformation of the South, 1938–1980*. New York: Oxford University Press, 1991.

Schuyler, George S. "The Negro-Art Hokum." In *Within the Circle: An Anthology of African American Literary Criticism from the Harlem Renaissance to the Present*, edited by Angelyn Mitchell, 51–54. Durham, NC: Duke University Press, 1994.

Scott, Anne Firor. *Natural Allies: Women's Associations in American History*. Urbana: University of Illinois Press, 1991.

———. *Unheard Voices: The First Historians of Southern Women*. Charlottesville: University of Virginia Press, 1993.

Scott, Evelyn. *Background in Tennessee*. New York: R. M. McBride, 1937.

———. *Escapade*. New York: Thomas Seltzer, 1923.

Seay, Scott D. "Saddler, Juanita Jane (1872–1970)." In *The Westminster Handbook to Women in American Religious History*, edited by Susan Hill Lindley and Eleanor J. Stebner, 190. Louisville, KY: Westminster John Knox, 2008.

Seigfried, Charlene Haddock, ed. "Feminism and Pragmatism." *Special Issue of Hypatia* 8, no. 2 (Spring 1993).

Setran, David P. *The College "Y": Student Religion in the Era of Secularization*. New York: Palgrave Macmillan, 2007.

Shaffer, Kerri. "Angelina Weld Grimke." In *Dictionary of Literary Biography: African-American Writers before the Harlem Renaissance*, edited by Trudier Harris, 151. Detroit: Gale, 1986.

Shaffer, Robert. "Women and the Communist Party, USA, 1930–1940." *Socialist Review* 9, no. 3 (June 1979): 73–119.

Shapiro, Edward S. "American Conservative Intellectuals, the 1930s, and the Crisis of Ideology." *Modern Age* 23, no. 4 (Fall 1979): 370–80.

Shapiro, Henry D. *Appalachia on Our Mind: The Southern Mountains and Mountaineers in the American Consciousness*. Chapel Hill: University of North Carolina Press, 1978.

Shapiro, Laura. *Perfection Salad: Women and Cooking at the Turn of the Century*. Berkeley: University of California Press, 2009.

Sherman, John. *The Mexican Right: The End of Revolutionary Reform, 1929–1940*. Westport, CT: Praeger, 1997.

Shlakman, Vera. *Economic History of a Factory Town: A Study of Chicopee, Massachusetts*. Northampton, MA: Department of History of Smith College, 1935.

Shoemaker, Helen Smith. *I Stand by the Door: The Life of Sam Shoemaker.* New York: Harper and Row, 1967.

Silber, Nina. "Intemperate Men, Spiteful Women, and Jefferson Davis." In *Divided Houses: Gender and the Civil War,* edited by Catherine Clinton and Nina Silber, 283–305. New York: Oxford University Press, 1992.

———. *The Romance of Reunion: Northerners and the South, 1865–1900.* Chapel Hill: University of North Carolina Press, 1993.

Silber, Norman. "Colston Estey Warne." In *American National Biography,* edited by John A. Garraty and Mark C. Carnes, 22:683–84. New York: Oxford University Press, 1999.

Simkins, Francis Butler. *Pitchfork Ben Tillman, South Carolinian.* Baton Rouge: Louisiana State University Press, 1944.

Simmons, Christina. "Companionate Marriage and the Lesbian Threat." *Frontiers: A Journal of Women Studies* 4, no. 3 (Fall 1979): 54–59.

———. *Making Marriage Modern: Women's Sexuality from the Progressive Era to World War II.* New York: Oxford University Press, 2009.

Simms, Florence. "The Industrial Policies of the Young Women's Christian Association." *Annals of the American Academy of Political and Social Science* 103, no. 1 (Sept. 1922): 138–40.

Simon, Bryant. "The Appeal of Cole Blease of South Carolina: Race, Class and Sex in the New South." *Journal of Southern History* 62, no. 1 (Feb. 1996): 57–86.

———. *A Fabric of Defeat: The Politics of South Carolina Millhands, 1910–1948.* Chapel Hill: University of North Carolina Press, 2000.

———. "Race Reactions: African American Organizing, Liberalism, and White Working-Class Politics in Postwar South Carolina." In *Jumpin' Jim Crow: Southern Politics from Civil War to Civil Rights,* edited by Jane Elizabeth Dailey, Glenda Gilmore, and Bryant Simon, 239–59. Princeton, NJ: Princeton University Press, 2000.

Simon, Zoltán. *The Double-Edged Sword: The Technological Sublime in American Novels between 1900 and 1940.* Budapest: Akadémiai Kiadó, 2003.

Simpson, Lewis P. "The Autobiographical Impulse in the South." In *Home Ground: Southern Autobiography,* edited by J. Bill Berry, 63–84. Columbia: University of Missouri Press, 1991.

Sims, Anastatia. *The Power of Femininity in the New South: Women's Organizations and Politics in North Carolina, 1880–1930.* Columbia: University of South Carolina Press, 1997.

Sinclair, Upton. *Boston: A Documentary Novel of the Sacco-Vanzetti Case.* 1928. Reprint, Cambridge, MA: R. Bentley, 1978.

Singal, Daniel. *The War Within: From Victorian to Modernist Thought in the South, 1919–1945.* Chapel Hill: University of North Carolina Press, 1982.

Sitkoff, Harvard. *A New Deal for Blacks: The Emergence of Civil Rights as a National Issue.* New York: Oxford University Press, 1978.

Sklar, Kathryn Kish. *Florence Kelley and the Nation's Work: The Rise of Women's Political Culture, 1830–1900.* New Haven, CT: Yale University Press, 1997.

———. "'The Throne of My Heart': Religion, Oratory, and Transatlantic Community in Angelina Grimké's Launching of Women's Rights, 1828–1838." In *Women's Rights and Transatlantic Anti-Slavery in the Era of Emancipation*, edited by Kathryn Kish Sklar and James Brewer Stewart, 211–41. New Haven, CT: Yale University Press, 2007.

———. "Two Political Cultures in the Progressive Era: The National Consumers' League and the American Association for Labor Legislation." In *U.S. History as Women's History: New Feminist Essays*, edited by Linda K. Kerber, Alice Kessler-Harris, and Kathryn Kish Sklar, 36–62. Chapel Hill: University of North Carolina Press, 1995.

———. *Women's Rights Emerges within the Anti-Slavery Movement, 1830–1870: A Brief History with Documents*. Boston: Bedford/St. Martin's, 2000.

Slesinger, Tess. *The Unpossessed: A Novel of the Thirties*. New York: Simon and Schuster, 1934. Reprinted with a new introduction by Alice Kessler-Harris and Paul Lauter and an afterword by Janet Sharistanian. Feminist Press at City University of New York, 1984.

Smialkowska, Monika. "'A Democratic Art at a Democratic Price': The American Celebrations of the Shakespeare Tercentenary, 1916." *Transatlantica* 1 (2010): 1–13.

Smith, Bonnie G. "Gender and the Practices of Scientific History: The Seminar and Archival Research in the Nineteenth Century." *American Historical Review* 100, no. 4 (Oct. 1995): 1150–76.

Smith, Florrie Carter. *The History of Oglethorpe County, Georgia*. Washington, GA: Wilkes, 1970.

Smith, Lillian Eugenia. *Killers of the Dream*. Rev. ed. Garden City, NY: Doubleday, 1963.

———. *Strange Fruit*. New York: Reynal and Hitchcock, 1944.

Smith, Sidonie. *A Poetics of Women's Autobiography: Marginality and the Fictions of Self-Representation*. Bloomington: Indiana University Press, 1987.

Smith, T. Lynn. Review of *The South in Progress*, by Katharine Du Pre Lumpkin. *Annals of the American Academy of Political and Social Sciences* 215 (1941): 221.

Smith-Rosenberg, Carroll. *Disorderly Conduct: Visions of Gender in Victorian America*. New York: Oxford University Press, 1986.

———. "Female World of Love and Ritual: Relations between Women in Nineteenth-Century America." *Signs* 1, no. 1 (Autumn 1975): 1–29.

Snead, Claiborne. *Address by Col. Claiborne Snead at the Reunion of the Third Georgia Regiment, at Union Point, on the 31st July, 1874: History of the Third Georgia Regiment, and the Career of Its First Commander, Gen. Ambrose R. Wright*. Augusta: Chronicle and Sentinel, 1874.

Snyder, Thomas D., ed. *120 Years of American Education: A Statistical Portrait*. Washington, DC: U.S. Department of Education, Office of Educational Research and Improvement, 1993. https://nces.ed.gov/pubs93/93442.pdf.

Solomon, Barbara Miller. *In the Company of Educated Women: A History of Women and Higher Education in America*. New Haven, CT: Yale University Press, 1985.

Solomon, Mark. *The Cry Was Unity: Communists and African Americans, 1917–1936*. Jackson: University Press of Mississippi, 1998.

Sorin, Gerald. *The Nurturing Neighborhood: The Brownsville Boys Club and Jew-

ish Community in Urban America, 1940–1990. New York: New York University Press, 1990.

Sowinska, Suzanne. Introduction to *To Make My Bread*, by Grace Lumpkin, vii–xxxix. Urbana: University of Illinois Press, 1932.

———. "Writing across the Color Line: White Women Writers and the 'Negro Question' in the Gastonia Novels." In *Radical Revisions: Rereading 1930s Culture*, edited by Bill Mullen and Sherry Lee Linkon, 120–43. Urbana: University of Illinois Press, 1996.

Spillers, Hortense J. "Mama's Baby, Papa's Maybe: An American Grammar Book." *Diacritics* 17, no. 2 (1987): 65–81.

Sporn, Paul. *Against Itself: The Federal Theater and Writers' Projects in the Midwest.* Detroit: Wayne State University Press, 1996.

Spritzer, Lorraine Nelson. "Grace Towns Hamilton." In *Notable American Women, A Biographical Dictionary, Completing the Twentieth Century*, edited by Susan Ware, 270–71. Cambridge, MA: Belknap Press of Harvard University Press, 2004.

Spritzer, Lorraine Nelson, and Jean B. Bergmark. *Grace Towns Hamilton and the Politics of Southern Change.* Athens: University of Georgia Press, 1997.

Stansell, Christine. *American Moderns: Bohemian New York and the Creation of a New Century.* New York: Metropolitan Books, 2000.

State Historical Society of Wisconsin, ed. *Dictionary of Wisconsin Biography.* Madison: State Historical Society of Wisconsin, 1960.

Steiner, Raymond J. *The Art Students League of New York: A History.* New York: CSS Publications, 1999.

Stephens, Freeman Irby. *The History of Medicine in Asheville.* Asheville, NC: Grateful Steps, 2013.

Stevens, Thelma. *Legacy for the Future: The History of Christian Social Relations in the Woman's Division of Christian Service, 1940–1968.* Cincinnati, OH: Women's Division, Board of Global Ministries, United Methodist Church, 1978.

Stewart, Annabel M. *The Industrial Work of the Y.W.C.A.: Report of a Study Made for the Laboratory Division of the National Board of the Young Women's Christian Association.* New York: Woman's Press, 1937.

Stokes, Durward T. *The History of Dillon County, South Carolina.* Columbia: University of South Carolina Press, 1978.

Stokes, Melvyn. D. W. *Griffith's "The Birth of a Nation": A History of "the Most Controversial Motion Picture of All Time."* New York: Oxford University Press, 2007.

Stone, Albert E., Jr. "Seward Collins and the *American Review:* Experiment in Pro-Fascism, 1933–37." *American Quarterly* 12, no. 1 (Spring 1960): 3–19.

Stone, Olive M. "The Present Position of the Negro Farm Population: The Bottom Rung of the Farm Ladder." *Journal of Negro Education* 5, no. 1 (1936): 20–31.

Storrs, Landon R. Y. *Civilizing Capitalism: The National Consumers' League, Women's Activism, and Labor Standards in the New Deal Era.* Chapel Hill: University of North Carolina Press, 2000.

———. *The Second Red Scare and the Unmaking of the New Deal Left.* Princeton, NJ: Princeton University Press, 2013.

Stott, William. *Documentary Expression and Thirties America*. New York: Oxford University Press, 1973.

Stuart, Maxwell S. "Our National Disgrace." *Nation*, July 17, 1937.

Stuck, Hudson. *The Alaskan Missions of the Episcopal Church: A Brief Sketch, Historical and Descriptive*. New York: Domestic and Foreign Missionary Society, 1920.

Sugrue, Thomas J. *Sweet Land of Liberty: The Forgotten Struggle for Civil Rights in the North*. New York: Random House, 2008.

Sullivan, Patricia. *Days of Hope: Race and Democracy in the New Deal Era*. Chapel Hill: University of North Carolina Press, 1996.

Summer, George Leland. *Newberry County, South Carolina: Historical and Genealogical Annals*. Baltimore: Clearfield, 1985. First published 1950 by George Leland Summer (Newberry, SC).

Sumner, William Graham. *Folkways: A Study of the Sociological Importance of Usages, Manners, Customs, Mores, and Morals*. Boston: Ginn, 1907.

Swerdlow, Amy. "The Congress of American Women: Left-Feminist Peace Politics in the Cold War." In *U.S. History as Women's History: New Feminist Essays*, edited by Linda K. Kerber, Alice Kessler-Harris, and Kathryn Kish Sklar, 296–312. Chapel Hill: University of North Carolina Press, 1995.

———. *Women Strike for Peace: Traditional Motherhood and Radical Politics in the 1960s*. Chicago: University of Chicago Press, 1993.

Synnott, Marcia G. "Alice Buck Norwood Spearman Wright: A Civil Rights Activist." In *South Carolina Women: Their Lives and Times*, edited by Marjorie Julian Spruill, Joan Johnson, and Valinda W. Littlefield, 3:200–220. Athens: University of Georgia Press, 2012.

———. "Alice Norwood Spearman Wright: Civil Rights Apostle to South Carolinians." In *Beyond Image and Convention: Explorations in Southern Women's History*, edited by Janet L. Coryell, Martha H. Swain, Sandra Gioia Treadway, and Elizabeth Hayes Turner, 184–207. Columbia: University of Missouri Press, 1998.

———. "Crusaders and Clubwomen: Alice Norwood Spearman Wright and Her Women's Network." In *Throwing Off the Cloak of Privilege: White Southern Women Activists in the Civil Rights Era*, edited by Gail S. Murray, 49–76. Gainesville: University Press of Florida, 2004.

Tanenhaus, Sam. *Whittaker Chambers: A Biography*. New York: Random House, 1997.

Tarrant, Shira. "When Sex Became Gender: Mirra Komarovsky's Feminism of the 1950s." *Women's Studies Quarterly* 33, no. 3/4 (Fall–Winter 2005): 334–55.

Tate, Allen. "The New Provincialism (1945)." In *Essays of Four Decades*, by Allen Tate, 535–46. Chicago: Swallow, 1968.

———. *Reactionary Essays on Poetry and Ideas*. New York: C. Scribner's Sons, 1936.

Tawney, R. H. *Religion and the Rise of Capitalism, a Historical Study*. Gloucester, MA: P. Smith, 1962.

Taylor, Clarence. *Reds at the Blackboard: Communism, Civil Rights, and the New York City Teachers Union*. New York: Columbia University Press, 2011.

Theoharis, Athan G., and John Stuart Cox. *The Boss: J. Edgar Hoover and the Great American Inquisition*. Philadelphia: Temple University Press, 1988.

Thomas, Albert Sidney. *A Historical Account of the Protestant Episcopal Church in South Carolina, 1820–1957; Being a Continuation of Dalcho's Account, 1670–1820.* Columbia, SC: R. L. Bryan, 1957.

Thomas, Karen Kruse. *Deluxe Jim Crow: Civil Rights and American Health Policy, 1935–1954.* Athens: University of Georgia Press, 2011.

Thomas, Norman. "Lessons of Passaic." *New Masses,* June 1926.

Thompson, Michael G. *For God and Globe: Christian Internationalism in the United States between the Great War and the Cold War.* Ithaca, NY: Cornell University Press, 2015.

Thorp, Margaret Ferrand. *Neilson of Smith.* New York: Oxford University Press, 1956.

Threlkeld, Megan. *Pan American Women: U.S. Internationalists and Revolutionary Mexico.* Philadelphia: University of Pennsylvania Press, 2014.

Thurman, Wallace. "Negro Artists and the Negro." *New Republic,* Aug. 31, 1927.

———. "Nephews of Uncle Remus." *Independent,* Sept. 24, 1927.

Tindall, George. *The Emergence of the New South, 1913–1945.* Baton Rouge: Louisiana State University Press, 1967.

Tolbert, Lisa. "Commercial Blocks and Female Colleges: The Small-Town Business of Educating Ladies." In *Shaping Communities: Perspectives in Vernacular Architecture,* edited by Carter L. Hudgins and Elizabeth Collins Cromley, 6: 204–15. Knoxville, TN: Vernacular Architecture Forum, 1997.

Toll, William. "A Quiet Revolution: Jewish Women's Clubs and the Widening Female Sphere, 1870–1920." *American Jewish Archives* 61, no. 1 (Spring/Summer 1989): 7–26.

Tomes, Nancy. "From Useful to Useless: The Changing Social Value of Children; Review of *Pricing the Priceless Child: The Changing Social Value of Children,* by Viviana A. Zelizer." *Reviews in American History* 14, no. 1 (Mar. 1, 1986): 50–54.

Trelease, Allen W. *White Terror: The Ku Klux Klan Conspiracy and Southern Reconstruction.* Baton Rouge: Louisiana State University Press, 1995.

Trimberger, Ellen Kay. "Feminism, Men, and Modern Love: Greenwich Village, 1900–1925." In *Powers of Desire: The Politics of Sexuality,* edited by Ann Snitow, Christine Stansell, and Sharon Thompson, 131–52. New York: Monthly Review Press, 1983.

Trouillot, Michel-Rolph. *Silencing the Past: Power and the Production of History.* Boston: Beacon Press, 1995.

Truettner, William H., and Roger B. Stein, eds. *Picturing Old New England: Image and Memory.* Washington, DC: National Museum of American Art, Smithsonian Institution, 1999.

Tucker, Marguerite. "Read the Riot Act!" *New Masses,* June 1926.

Tucker, Michael Jay. *And Then They Loved Him: Seward Collins and the Chimera of an American Fascism.* New York: Peter Lang, 2006.

Turgeon, Lynn. "Transitional Economic Systems in Retrospect." In *Transitional Economic Systems: The Polish-Czech Example,* by Dorothy W. Douglas, vii. New York: Monthly Review Press, 1972.

Twelve Southerners. *I'll Take My Stand: The South and the Agrarian Tradition.* New York: Harper and Brothers, 1930.

Underwood, Thomas A. *Allen Tate: Orphan of the South*. Princeton, NJ: Princeton University Press, 2000.

Vance, Rupert B. *The Human Geography of the South: A Study in Regional Resources and Human Adequacy*. Chapel Hill: University of North Carolina Press, 1932.

Vandenberg-Daves, Jodi. "The Manly Pursuit of a Partnership between the Sexes: The Debate over Women and Girls in the YMCA, 1914–1933." *Journal of American History* 78, no. 4 (Mar. 1992): 1324–46.

Van Rensselaer, Mrs. Coffin. "The National League for Woman's Service." *Annals of the American Academy of Political and Social Science* 79 (Sept. 1918): 275–82.

Van Vorhis, Jacqueline. *The Look of Paradise: A Pictorial History of Northampton, Massachusetts, 1654–1984*. Northampton, MA: Northampton Historical Society, 1984.

Vicinus, Martha. "Distance and Desire: English Boarding-School Friendships." *Signs* 9, no. 4 (1984): 600–622.

———. *Independent Women: Work and Community for Single Women, 1850–1920*. Chicago: University of Chicago Press, 1988.

———. *Intimate Friends: Women Who Loved Women, 1778–1928*. Chicago: University of Chicago Press, 2004.

———. "'One Life to Stand beside Me': Emotional Conflicts in First Generation College Women in England." *Feminist Studies* 8, no. 3 (1982): 603–28.

Von Eschen, Penny M. *Satchmo Blows Up the World: Jazz Ambassadors Play the Cold War*. Cambridge, MA: Harvard University Press, 2004.

Vorse, Mary Heaton. *The Passaic Textile Strike, 1926–1927*. Passaic, NJ: General Relief Committee of the Textile Strikers, 1927.

———. *Strike!* New York: H. Liveright, 1930.

Wald, Alan M. *The New York Intellectuals: The Rise and Decline of the Anti-Stalinist Left from the 1930s to the 1980s*. Chapel Hill: University of North Carolina Press, 1987.

Wallace, Margaret. "Twenty-Four Hours." *New York Times Book Review*, Feb. 25, 1939.

Wallach, Alan. "Oliver Larkin's 'Art and Life in America': Between the Popular Front and the Cold War." *American Art* 15, no. 3 (Autumn 2001): 80–89.

Wallach, Jennifer Jensen. *"Closer to the Truth Than Any Fact": Memoir, Memory, and Jim Crow*. Athens: University of Georgia Press, 2008.

Walsh, Julia. "'Horny-Handed Sons of Toil': Mill Workers, Populists and the Press in Augusta, 1886–1894." *The Georgia Historical Quarterly* 81, no. 2 (Summer 1997): 311–44.

Walton, Andrea, ed. *Women and Philanthropy in Education*. Bloomington: Indiana University Press, 2005.

Ward, Doris Cline, ed. *The Heritage of Old Buncombe County*. Vol. 1. Asheville, NC: Old Buncombe County Genealogical Society, 1981.

Ware, Caroline F. *The Early New England Cotton Manufacture: A Study in Industrial Beginnings*. New York: Houghton Mifflin, 1931.

Ware, Norman J. Review of *Shutdowns in the Connecticut Valley: A Study of Worker Displacement in the Small Industrial Community*, by Katharine Du Pre Lumpkin and Mable Van Able Combs. *Journal of Political Economy* 45, no. 2 (Apr. 1937): 276–77.

Ware, Susan. *Beyond Suffrage: Women in the New Deal*. Cambridge, MA: Harvard University Press, 1981.

———. *Partner and I: Molly Dewson, Feminism, and New Deal Politics*. New Haven, CT: Yale University Press, 1987.

Warne, Colston E., ed. *Labor in Postwar America*. Brooklyn, NY: Remsen Press, 1949.

———. "Consumers on the March." Pts. 1 and 2. *Nation*, June 5, 1937; June 12, 1937.

———. ed. *Yearbook of American Labor*. Vol. 1, *War Labor Policies*. New York: Philosophical Library, 1945.

Warner, Sam Bass. *Streetcar Suburbs: The Process of Growth in Boston, 1870–1900*. Cambridge, MA: Harvard University Press, 1962.

Warren, Robert Penn. "Some Recent Novels." *Southern Review* (Winter 1936): 624.

Washington, Mary Helen. *The Other Blacklist: The African American Literary and Cultural Left of the 1950s*. New York: Columbia University Press, 2014.

Watkins, Floyd C. *Thomas Wolfe's Characters: Portraits from Life*. Norman: University of Oklahoma Press, 1957.

Watson, Bruce. *Sacco and Vanzetti: The Men, the Murders, and the Judgment of Mankind*. New York: Viking, 2007.

Weatherford, Willis D. *Negro Life in the South: Present Conditions and Needs*. New York: Young Men's Christian Association Press, 1910.

———. *Present Forces in Negro Progress*. New York: Association, 1912.

Wecter, Dixon. *The Age of the Great Depression, 1929–1941*. New York: Macmillan, 1948.

Weigand, Kate. *Red Feminism: American Communism and the Making of Women's Liberation*. Baltimore: Johns Hopkins University Press, 2001.

Weiner, Lynn Y. "Maternalism as a Paradigm: Defining the Issues." *Journal of Women's History* 5, no. 2 (Fall 1993): 95–139.

Weinstein, Allen. *Perjury: The Hiss-Chambers Case*. 3rd ed. Stanford, CA: Hoover Institution Press, Stanford University, 2013.

Weisbord, Vera Buch. *A Radical Life*. Bloomington: Indiana University Press, 1977.

Weisenfeld, Judith. *African American Women and Christian Activism: New York's Black YWCA, 1905–1945*. Cambridge, MA: Harvard University Press, 1997.

Weld, Theodore Dwight. *American Slavery as It Is: Testimony of a Thousand Witnesses*. New York: Arno, 1969.

Weller, Jack E. *Yesterday's People: Life in Contemporary Appalachia*. Lexington: University of Kentucky Press, 1965.

Werth, Barry. *The Scarlet Professor: Newton Arvin, a Literary Life Shattered by Scandal*. New York: Anchor Books, 2002.

West, Elizabeth Cassidy. "'Yours for Home and Country': The War Work of the South Carolina Woman's Committee." In *Proceedings of the South Carolina Historical Association*, by South Carolina Historical Association, 59–68. Columbia: South Carolina Historical Association, 2001.

Westbrook, Robert B. "John Dewey." In *A Companion to American Thought*, edited by Richard Wightman Fox and James T. Kloppenberg, 177–79. Oxford: Blackwell, 1995.

———. *John Dewey and American Democracy*. Ithaca, NY: Cornell University Press, 1991.

Whisnant, Anne Mitchell. *Super-Scenic Motorway: A Blue Ridge Parkway History*. Chapel Hill: University of North Carolina Press, 2006.

Whisnant, David E. *All That Is Native and Fine: The Politics of Culture in an American Region*. Chapel Hill: University of North Carolina Press, 1983.

White, Mary Wheeling. *Fighting the Current: The Life and Work of Evelyn Scott*. Baton Rouge: Louisiana State University Press, 1998.

White, Ronald C., Jr. *Liberty and Justice for All: Racial Reform and the Social Gospel (1877–1925)*. Louisville, KY: Westminster John Knox, 2002.

Whites, LeeAnn. *The Civil War as a Crisis in Gender: Augusta, Georgia, 1860–1890*. Athens: University of Georgia Press, 1995.

Whitfield, Stephen J. *The Culture of the Cold War*. Baltimore: Johns Hopkins University Press, 1991.

Whitney, Joel. *Finks: How the CIA Tricked the World's Best Writers*. New York: OR Books, 2016.

Who's Who in the South: A Business, Professional and Social Record of Men and Women of Achievement in the Southern States. Washington, DC: Mayflower, 1927.

Wilkerson, Jessica. *To Live Here, You Have to Fight: How Women Led Appalachian Movements for Social Justice*. Urbana: University of Illinois Press, 2019.

Williams, Chad L. *Torchbearers of Democracy: African American Soldiers in the World War I Era*. Chapel Hill: University of North Carolina Press, 2013.

Williams, Frances. "Minority Groups and the OPA." *Public Administration Review* 2 (Apr. 1947): 123–28.

Williams, Heather Andrea. *Self-Taught: African American Education in Slavery and Freedom*. Chapel Hill: University of North Carolina Press, 2005.

Williams, Jay. *Stage Left*. New York: Scribner, 1974.

Williams, Jennifer Ann. *Twentieth-Century Sentimentalism: Narrative Appropriation in American Literature*. New Brunswick, NJ: Rutgers University Press, 2014.

Williams, Lou Falkner. *The Great South Carolina Ku Klux Klan Trials, 1871–1872*. Athens: University of Georgia Press, 1996.

Williamson-Lott, Joy Ann. "The Battle over Power, Control, and Academic Freedom at Southern Institutions of Higher Education, 1955–1965." *Journal of Southern History* 79, no. 4 (Nov. 2013): 879–920.

Wilson, Charles H. "Trey," III. *History of Brenau University, 1878–2012: A Study of Student, Faculty, and Staff Negotiation to Shape the Collegiate Experience*. Amherst, NY: Teneo Press, 2014.

Wilson, Charles Reagan. *Baptized in Blood: The Religion of the Lost Cause, 1865–1920*. Athens: University of Georgia Press, 1980.

Wilson, Edmund. "An Appeal to Progressives." In *American Views of Soviet Russia, 1917–1965*, edited by Peter G. Filene, 72–78. Homewood, IL: Dorsey Press, 1968.

Wilson, Francille Rusan. *The Segregated Scholars: Black Social Scientists and the Creation of Black Labor Studies, 1890–1950*. Charlottesville: University of Virginia Press, 2006.

Wilson, Grace H. *The Religious and Educational Philosophy of the Young Women's Christian Association*. New York: Teachers College, Columbia University, 1933.

Witt, John Fabian. "Elias Hill's Exodus: Exit and Voice in the Reconstruction Nation." In *Patriots and Cosmopolitans: Hidden Histories of American Law*, by John Fabian Witt, 85–154. Cambridge, MA: Harvard University Press, 2007.

Wittner, Lawrence S. *Rebels against War: The American Peace Movement, 1941–1960*. New York: Columbia University Press, 1969.

Wixson, Douglas. *Worker-Writer in America: Jack Conroy and the Tradition of Midwestern Literary Radicalism, 1898–1990*. Urbana: University of Illinois Press, 1994.

Wolfe, Bertram D. *A Life in Two Centuries: An Autobiography*. New York: Stein and Day, 1981.

Wolfe, Margaret Ripley. "Eleanor Copenhaver Anderson and the Industrial Department of the National Board YWCA: Toward a New Social Order in Dixie." In *The Human Tradition in the New South*, edited by James C. Klotter, 111–28. Lanham, MD: Rowman and Littlefield, 2005.

———. "Eleanor Copenhaver Anderson of the National Board YWCA." *Iris* 41 (2000): 36–39.

———. "Sherwood Anderson and the Southern Highlands: A Sense of Place and the Sustenance of Women." *Southern Studies* 3 (1992): 253–75.

Wolfe, Thomas. *Look Homeward, Angel: A Story of the Buried Life*. New York: Scribner, 1995.

———. *Of Time and the River: A Legend of Man's Hunger in His Youth*. New York: Charles Scribner's Sons, 1935.

———. *O Lost: A Story of the Buried Life*. Edited by Arlyn Bruccoli and Matthew J. Bruccoli. Columbia: University of South Carolina Press, 2000.

Woods, Jeff R. *Black Struggle, Red Scare: Segregation and Anti-Communism in the South, 1948–1968*. Baton Rouge: Louisiana State University Press, 2004.

Woodward, C. Vann. *Origins of the New South, 1877–1913*. Baton Rouge: Louisiana State University Press, 1951.

———. Review of *The Making of a Southerner*, by Katharine Du Pre Lumpkin. *Mississippi Valley Historical Review* 34, no. 1 (June 1947): 141–42.

———. "Southern Exposure." *New York Review of Books*, Mar. 3, 1983.

———. *Thinking Back: The Perils of Writing History*. Baton Rouge: Louisiana State University Press, 1986.

———. *Tom Watson: Agrarian Rebel*. New York: Rinehart, 1938.

Worcester, Kenton W. *Fellows of the Social Science Research Council, 1925–1951*. New York: Social Science Research Council, 1951.

———. *Social Science Research Council, 1923–1988*. New York: Social Science Research Council, 2001. https://www.ssrc.org/publications/view/1F20C6E1-565F-DE11-BD80-001CC477EC70/.

Wrathall, John D. "Taking the Young Stranger by the Hand: Homosexual Cruising at the YMCA, 1890–1980." In *Men and Women Adrift: The YMCA and the YWCA in the City*, edited by Nina Mjagkij and Margaret Spratt, 250–70. New York: New York University Press, 1977.

Wright, Gavin. *Old South, New South: Revolutions in the Southern Economy since the Civil War.* Baton Rouge: Louisiana State University Press, 1996.

Wright, Richard. *Black Boy: A Record of Childhood and Youth.* New York: Harper and Brothers, 1945.

———. "The Ethics of Living Jim Crow: An Autobiographical Sketch." In *Uncle Tom's Children*, 3–15. New York: Harper and Row, 1938.

Writers' Program of the Work Projects Administration in the State of South Carolina. *South Carolina: A Guide to the Palmetto State.* New York: Oxford University Press, 1941.

Yaeger, Patricia. *Dirt and Desire: Reconstructing Southern Women's Writing, 1930–1990.* Chicago: University of Chicago Press, 2000.

Yellin, Jean Fagan, and John C. Van Horne, eds. *The Abolitionist Sisterhood: Women's Political Culture in Antebellum America.* Ithaca, NY: Cornell University Press, 1994.

Zeiger, Susan. *In Uncle Sam's Service: Women Workers with the American Expeditionary Force, 1917–1919.* Ithaca, NY: Cornell University Press, 1999.

———. "She Didn't Raise Her Boy to Be a Slacker: Motherhood, Conscription, and the Culture of the First World War." *Feminist Studies* 22, no. 1 (Spring 1996): 7–39.

Zelizer, Viviana A. Rotman. *Pricing the Priceless Child: The Changing Social Value of Children.* Princeton, NJ: Princeton University Press, 1985.

Zinn, Howard. Introduction to *Boston: A Documentary Novel of the Sacco-Vanzetti Case*, by Upton Sinclair, xi–xxx. Cambridge, MA: R. Bentley, 1978.

ILLUSTRATION CREDITS

187   Courtesy of John H. Lumpkin Sr.

198   Courtesy of Kate Douglas Torrey.

237   Courtesy of the South Caroliniana Library, University of South Carolina, Columbia, South Carolina.

252   Courtesy of the South Caroliniana Library, University of South Carolina, Columbia, South Carolina.

262   Courtesy of the Millican Pictorial History Museum.

349   Courtesy of May Kanfer.

384   Courtesy of Kate Douglas Torrey.

412   Courtesy of the Southern Historical Collection, the Wilson Library, University of North Carolina at Chapel Hill.

436   *Los Angeles Times*, Mar. 14, 1953.

437   AP Photo/Henry Griffin.

447   Courtesy of the Southern Historical Collection, the Wilson Library, University of North Carolina at Chapel Hill.

468   Courtesy of the Southern Historical Collection, the Wilson Library, University of North Carolina at Chapel Hill.

470   Courtesy of William W. L. and Amory Potter Glenn.

490   Courtesy of Jacquelyn Dowd Hall.

INDEX

NOTE: Page numbers in *italics* indicate photographs.